110⁰⁰/82⁰⁰
RF

D0204643

The Cambridge History of the English Language is the first multi-volume work to provide a full account of the history of English. Its authoritative coverage extends from areas of central linguistic interest and concern to more specialised topics such as personal names and place names. The volumes dealing with earlier periods are chronologically based, whilst those dealing with more recent periods are geographically based, thus reflecting the spread of English over the last 300 years.

Volume V looks at the dialects of England since 1776, the historical development of English in the former Celtic-speaking countries of Scotland, Wales and Ireland, and at varieties of English in Australia, New Zealand, South Africa, the Caribbean and South Asia. This unique volume will be welcomed by all those interested in the spread of English around the world.

THE CAMBRIDGE HISTORY
OF THE ENGLISH LANGUAGE

GENERAL EDITOR Richard M. Hogg

VOLUME V English in Britain and Overseas: Origins and Development

THE CAMBRIDGE HISTORY OF THE ENGLISH LANGUAGE

VOLUME V *English in Britain and Overseas: Origins and Development*

EDITED BY

ROBERT BURCHFIELD

Emeritus Fellow in English Language and Literature, St Peter's College, University of Oxford

CAMBRIDGE
UNIVERSITY PRESS

Published by the Press Syndicate of the University of Cambridge
The Pitt Building, Trumpington Street, Cambridge CB2 1RP
40 West 20th Street, New York, NY 10011-4211, USA
10 Stamford Road, Oakleigh, Melbourne 3166, Australia

First published 1994

Printed in Great Britain at the University Press, Cambridge

A catalogue record for this book is available from the British Library

Library of Congress cataloguing in publication data

The Cambridge history of the English language.
Vol. 1 edited by Richard M. Hogg.
Vol. 2 edited by Norman Blake.
Vol. 5 edited by Robert Burchfield.
Includes bibliographical references and index.
Contents: v. 1. The beginning to 1066 – v. 2. 1066–
1476 – v. 5. English in Britain and Overseas:
origins and development.
1. English language – History.   I. Hogg, Richard M.
II. Blake, N. F. (Norman Francis)   III. Burchfield,
R. W. (Robert William)
PE1072.C36 1992   420'.9   91-13881
ISBN 0 521 26474 X (v. 1)
ISBN 0 521 26475 8 (v. 2)
ISBN 0 521 26478 2 (v. 5)

ISBN 0 521 26478 2 hardback

CONTENTS

Contents

Contents

ILLUSTRATIONS

TABLES

CONTRIBUTORS

LAURIE BAUER *Reader in Linguistics, Victoria University of Wellington*

WILLIAM BRANFORD *Emeritus Professor of Linguistics and English Language, Rhodes University*

ROBERT BURCHFIELD *Emeritus Fellow in English Language and Literature, St Peter's College, University of Oxford*

JOHN A. HOLM *Professor of English and Linguistics, Hunter College and the Graduate Center of the City University of New York*

†OSSI IHALAINEN *Professor of English Philology, University of Helsinki*

BRAJ B. KACHRU *Center for Advanced Study Professor of Linguistics, and Jubilee Professor of Liberal Arts and Sciences, University of Illinois at Urbana–Champaign, Urbana*

JEFFREY L. KALLEN *Senior Lecturer in Linguistics and Phonetics, Trinity College Dublin*

J. DERRICK McCLURE *Senior Lecturer, Department of English, University of Aberdeen*

ALAN R. THOMAS *Research Professor in Linguistics, University of Wales, Bangor*

GEORGE W. TURNER *Honorary Research Associate, English Department, University of Adelaide*

This volume is dedicated to the memory of Professor Ossi Ihalainen, who died on 15 September 1993 from injuries sustained in a road accident in Finland. At the time of his death his chapter had been completed and the volume was on the point of going to press.

GENERAL EDITOR'S PREFACE

Although it is a topic of continuing debate, there can be little doubt that English is the most widely spoken language in the world, with significant numbers of native speakers in almost every major region – only South America falling largely outside the net. In such a situation an understanding of the nature of English can be claimed unambiguously to be of world-wide importance.

Growing consciousness of such a role for English is one of the motivations behind this History. There are other motivations too. Specialist students have many major and detailed works of scholarship to which they can refer, for example Bruce Mitchell's *Old English Syntax*, or, from an earlier age, Karl Luick's *Historische Grammatik der englischen Sprache*. Similarly, those who come new to the subject have both one-volume histories such as Barbara Strang's *History of English* and introductory textbooks to a single period, for example Bruce Mitchell and Fred Robinson's *A Guide to Old English*. But what is lacking is the intermediate work which can provide a solid discussion of the full range of the history of English both to the Anglicist who does not specialise in the particular area to hand and to the general linguist who has no specialised knowledge of the history of English. This work attempts to remedy that lack. We hope that it will be of use to others too, whether they are interested in the history of English for its own sake, or for some specific purpose such as local history or the effects of colonisation.

Under the influence of the Swiss linguist, Ferdinand de Saussure, there has been, during this century, a persistent tendency to view the study of language as having two discrete parts: (i) synchronic, where a language is studied from the point of view of one moment in time; (ii) diachronic, where a language is studied from a historical perspective. It might therefore be supposed that this present work is purely diachronic.

But this is not so. One crucial principle which guides *The Cambridge History of the English Language* is that synchrony and diachrony are intertwined, and that a satisfactory understanding of English (or any other language) cannot be achieved on the basis of one of these alone.

Consider, for example, the (synchronic) fact that English, when compared with other languages, has some rather infrequent or unusual characteristics. Thus, in the area of vocabulary, English has an exceptionally high number of words borrowed from other languages (French, the Scandinavian languages, American Indian languages, Italian, the languages of northern India and so on); in syntax a common construction is the use of *do* in forming questions (e.g. *Do you like cheese?*), a type of construction not often found in other languages; in morphology English has relatively few inflexions, at least compared with the majority of other European languages; in phonology the number of diphthongs as against the number of vowels in English English is notably high. In other words, synchronically, English can be seen to be in some respects rather unusual. But in order to understand such facts we need to look at the history of the language; it is often only there that an explanation can be found. And that is what this work attempts to do.

This raises another issue. A quasi-Darwinian approach to English might attempt to account for its widespread use by claiming that somehow English is more suited, better adapted, to use as an international language than others. But that is nonsense. English is no more fit than, say, Spanish or Chinese. The reasons for the spread of English are political, cultural and economic rather than linguistic. So too are the reasons for such linguistic elements within English as the high number of borrowed words. This History, therefore, is based as much upon political, cultural and economic factors as linguistic ones, and it will be noted that the major historical divisions between volumes are based upon the former type of events (the Norman Conquest, the spread of printing, the declaration of independence by the USA), rather than the latter type.

As a rough generalisation, one can say that up to about the seventeenth century the development of English tended to be centripetal, whereas since then the development has tended to be centrifugal. The settlement by the Anglo-Saxons resulted in a spread of dialect variation over the country, but by the tenth century a variety of forces were combining to promote the emergence of a standard form of the language. Such an evolution was disrupted by the Norman

Conquest, but with the development of printing together with other more centralising tendencies, the emergence of a standard form became once more, from the fifteenth century on, a major characteristic of the language. But processes of emigration and colonisation then gave rise to new regional varieties overseas, many of which have now achieved a high degree of linguistic independence, and one of which, namely American English, may even have a dominating influence on British English. The structure of this work is designed to reflect these different types of development. Whilst the first four volumes offer a reasonably straightforward chronological account, the later volumes are geographically based. This arrangement, we hope, allows scope for the proper treatment of diverse types of evolution and development. Even within the chronologically oriented volumes there are variations of structure, which are designed to reflect the changing relative importance of various linguistic features. Although all the chronological volumes have substantial chapters devoted to the central topics of semantics and vocabulary, syntax, and phonology and morphology, for other topics the space allotted in a particular volume is one which is appropriate to the importance of that topic during the relevant period, rather than some pre-defined calculation of relative importance. And within the geographically based volumes all these topics are potentially included within each geographical section, even if sometimes in a less formal way. Such a flexible and changing structure seems essential for any full treatment of the history of English.

One question that came up as this project began was the extent to which it might be possible or desirable to work within a single theoretical linguistic framework. It could well be argued that only a consensus within the linguistic community about preferred linguistic theories would enable a work such as this to be written. Certainly, it was immediately obvious when work for this History began, that it would be impossible to lay down a 'party line' on linguistic theory, and indeed, that such an approach would be undesirably restrictive. The solution reached was, I believe, more fruitful. Contributors have been chosen purely on the grounds of expertise and knowledge, and have been encouraged to write their contributions in the way they see most fitting, whilst at the same time taking full account of developments in linguistic theory. This has, of course, led to problems, notably with contrasting views of the same topic (and also because of the need to distinguish the ephemeral flight of theoretical fancy from genuine new insights into linguistic theory), but even in a work which is concerned to provide a unified approach (so that, for example, in most cases every contributor to a volume has read all the other contributions to that volume), such contrasts, and even contradictions, are stimulating and fruitful. Whilst this work aims to be authoritative, it is not prescriptive, and the final goal must be to stimulate interest in a subject in which much work remains to be done, both theoretically and empirically.

The task of editing this History has been, and still remains, a long and complex one. As General Editor I owe a great debt to many friends and colleagues who have devoted much time and thought to how best this work might be approached and completed. Firstly, I should thank my fellow-editors: John Algeo, Norman Blake, Bob Burchfield, Roger Lass and Suzanne Romaine. They have been concerned as much with the History as a whole as with their individual volumes. Secondly, there are those fellow linguists, some contributors, some not, who have so generously given of their time and made many valuable suggestions: John Anderson, Cecily Clark, Frans van Coetsem, Fran Colman, David Denison, Ed Finegan, Olga Fischer, Jacek Fisiak, Malcolm Godden, Angus McIntosh, Lesley Milroy, Donka Minkova, Matti Rissanen, Michael Samuels, Bob Stockwell, Tom Toon, Elizabeth Traugott, Peter Trudgill, Nigel Vincent, Anthony Warner, Simone Wyss. One occasion stands out especially: the organisers of the Fourth International Conference on English Historical Linguistics, held at Amsterdam in 1985, kindly allowed us to hold a seminar on the project as it was just beginning. For their generosity, which allowed us to hear a great many views and exchange opinions with colleagues one rarely meets face-to-face, I must thank Roger Eaton, Olga Fischer, Willem Koopman and Frederike van der Leek.

With a work so complex as this, an editor is faced with a wide variety of problems and difficulties. It has been, therefore, a continual comfort and solace to know that Penny Carter of Cambridge University Press has always been there to provide advice and solutions on every occasion. Without her knowledge and experience, encouragement and good humour, this work would have been both poorer and later. After the work for Volume I was virtually complete, Marion Smith took over as publishing editor, and I am grateful to her too, not merely for ensuring such a smooth change-over, but for her bravery when faced with the mountain of paper from which this series has emerged.

Richard M. Hogg

VOLUME EDITOR'S PREFACE

As was to be expected, a volume of this complexity has taken a long while to prepare. The procedures followed were the same as those that worked well in other volumes. As the first drafts of chapters arrived they were circulated for comment to the volume editors and to the writers of other chapters in this volume. The results, though time-consuming and sometimes challenging, were always beneficial, and I would like to record my thanks to all those who helped in this way.

It should be emphasised that contributors to this volume were not required to follow strict guidelines in the way in which they presented their findings. Any such attempt would have been doomed to failure, since the subject matter is so diverse and the scholarly evidence available in each area so markedly unequal.

It comes as no surprise that one work above all was found by the contributors to be a central point of comparison and a landmark for all future scholarly research into the pronunciation of present-day varieties of English: this seminal work is J. C. Wells' *Accents of English* (Cambridge University Press, 3 vols., 1982).

For their invaluable comments on the glossary of linguistic terms I am grateful to John Algeo, Laurie Bauer, John Holm, Jeffrey Kallen and Derrick McClure. Some other scholars gave welcome advice on particular entries.

I should also like to place on record my special thanks to two Cambridge University Press editors: to Penny Carter, who drew me into the project and governed its fortunes with exemplary enthusiasm and efficiency until she moved to another department in the Press; and to Judith Ayling, who gave me excellent advice and unfailing guidance during the later stages of the editorial process. I am also indebted to Jenny Potts, who brought her considerable copy-editing skills to bear on the complex typescripts of the contributors to this volume.

Robert Burchfield

ACKNOWLEDGEMENTS

The contributors to this volume are grateful for the help and advice they have received from friends and colleagues, as well as from their fellow contributors and the editors of and contributors to other volumes. We wish especially to thank the following:

Winifred Bauer, Ciarán Brady, Jean Branford, David Gough, John Harris, Niël Hauptfleisch, Janet Holmes, Jonathan Hope, Daniel Huws, M. A. James, Yamuna Kachru, Juhani Klemola, Merja Kytö, L. W. Lanham, Roger Lass, William Liston, Daryl McLean, Margaret Mannion, Jim Milroy, Lesley Milroy, Michael Montgomery, Cecil L. Nelson, Harry Orsman, Elizabeth Pearce, Michael Pye, Tomos Roberts, Graham Shorrocks, Penny Silva, Peter Trudgill, Wolfgang Viereck.

The index was compiled by Fiona Barr. Juhani Klemola, University of Joensuu, deserves special mention for his reading of the proofs of chapter 5 after the death of Ossi Ihalainen.

ABBREVIATIONS

AES	*Atlas of English Sounds* (ed. E. Kolb *et al.* Berne: Francke, 1979)
Afrik.	Afrikaans
AL	Aitken's Law
AmerE	American English
AND	*Australian National Dictionary* (see p. 327)
AUMLA	*Journal of the Australasian Universities Language and Literature Association*
AustE	Australian English
aux	auxiliary
C	consonant
CCDE	*Corpus of Contemporary Dialects of England* (see p. 589)
CE	Creole English
CV	consonant followed by vowel
DOST	*Dictionary of the Older Scottish Tongue* (see p. 92)
DSAE: Hist.	Dictionary of South African English on Historical Principles (In preparation. See pp. 443; 616: Silva 1990)
Du.	Dutch
EDD	*English Dialect Dictionary* (ed. J. Wright, London: Oxford University Press. 6 vols. 1898–1905)
EDG	*English Dialect Grammar*
EDS	*English Dialect Society*
EFL	English as a foreign language
ESc.	Early Scots
ESL	English as a second language
GenAm.	General American

GIE	General Indian English
GVS	Great Vowel Shift
HRT	high rising tone
IE	Indian English
Ir.	Irish
Kh.	Khoisan
LAE	*Linguistic Atlas of England* (ed. H. Orton *et al.* London: Croom Helm, 1978)
LAS	*Linguistic Atlas of Scotland* (see p. 92)
L1	first language
L2	second language
MCC	Miskito Coast Creole
ME	Middle English
ModE	Modern English
ModSc.	Modern Scots
MSc.	Middle Scots
Ng.	Nguni
NLW	National Library of Wales
NZE	New Zealand English
OE	Old English
OED	*Oxford English Dictionary*
ON	Old Norse
OSc.	Older Scots
P	Portuguese
PDE	Present-Day English
RP	Received Pronunciation
SAE	South Asian English
SAEP	South African English Pronunciation
SAfrDu.	South African Dutch
SAfrE	South African English
SED	*Survey of English Dialects* (ed. H. Orton *et al.* Leeds: Arnold, 1962–71)
SND	*Scottish National Dictionary* (see p. 92)
So.	Sotho
SSE	Scottish standard English

ST	Sotho-Tswana
StE	standard English
SVO	subject + verb + object
TMA	tense, modality and aspect
Ts.	Tswana
VP	verb phrase
VSO	verb + subject + object
WE	Welsh English
Xh.	Xhosa
Zu.	Zulu

1 INTRODUCTION

Robert Burchfield

1.1 Variety and diversity

1.1.1 Varieties of English: some introductory remarks

The essays in this volume give an account of the history and development of a number of distinct and highly diversified varieties of English – varieties that, in varying degrees, are recognisably different from one another and from standard British and standard American English. Most people would have little difficulty in identifying the English-speaking region in which the following sentences might be heard:

> Ye'll be duin wi't afore I win hame, will ye no?
> There's tall you are!
> I'm after missing the bus ('I have just missed the bus')
> The ooms and oupas of the platteland

without having to turn to the Scottish, Welsh, Irish and South African English chapters that follow. But few people could describe in any systematic way how the separate constituents of these sequences of words came to be emblematic of the varieties they represent.

It should be borne in mind that speakers of local forms of English are often unaware that others regard their speech as in any way unusual. Martyn Wakelin, in his book *The Archaeology of English* (1988), for example, cites a conversation between Lady Constance Chatterley and her husband's gamekeeper Mellors, who, although having been a lieutenant in the Indian Army, used 'broad Derbyshire' when it suited him:

> ''Appen yer'd better 'ave this key, an' Ah mun fend for t'bods some other road.' (*Perhaps you had better have this key, and I must make provision*

for the birds in some other way.) ... She looked at him, getting his meaning through the fog of the dialect. 'Why don't you speak ordinary English?' she said coldly. 'Me! Ah thowt it wor ordinary.'

According to Defoe 1724–6 (see Bibliography, ch. 5), local speakers have a tendency to render standard English into the manner of speaking to which they are accustomed. He quoted a specific example. On a visit to a school in Martock, Somerset, he listened to 'one of the lowest Scholars' reading his lesson to the Usher:

> [H]is Lesson was in the Cant. [Song of Solomon] 5.3. of which the Words are these, 'I have put off my Coat, how shall I put it on, I have wash'd my Feet, how shall I Defile them?' The Boy read thus, with his Eyes, as I say full on the text. 'Chav a Doffed my Cooat, how shall I Don't, Chav a wash'd my Veet, how shall I Moil 'em?' (p. 198)

1.1.2   *Varieties of English studied in this volume*

The volume spans five main areas:

1   dialects of England since 1776;
2   English in the originally Celtic-speaking lands, Scotland, Wales and Ireland;
3   the 'settler' Englishes of Australia, New Zealand and South Africa;
4   creole Englishes of the Caribbean;
5   the Englishes (largely non-native) of South Asia (i.e. the subcontinent that was all once called India).

For convenience the chapters are divided into two parts: those dealing with the language as it is found within weather-forecasting reach of London; and those further afield, dealing in alphabetical order with English in Australia, the Caribbean, New Zealand, South Africa and South Asia.

1.1.3   *Diversity of speech and regions*

The following opening remarks from chapters 2 and 7 give some indication of the diversity of subject matter and of the different time-frames represented in the chapters of this volume:

> Insular West Germanic speech was first established in what is now Scotland in the sixth century. (p. 23)

> After that period [*sc.* the early seventeenth century] the massive importation of slaves from Africa brought about a restructuring of English...that resulted in Creole, a distinct system with words derived from English but with phonology, semantics and morphosyntax influenced by African languages and other forces.   (p. 328)

On the one hand, innumerable dialects have survived in England (while changing on their own axes) unaffected by the *Schriftsprache* or written standard of Æthelwold in the monastery in Winchester in the late Old English period, by the arrival of printed books in the late fifteenth century and by the gradual establishment of a recognisable standard. Meanwhile English-speakers moved into Wales, Scotland and Ireland in increasing numbers, and, as the centuries passed, caused the local vernaculars to become minority languages. From the seventeenth century onwards soldiers, settlers and convicts took the language abroad to distant lands, and it began to take on new shapes around the world.

These new shapes were governed by a number of factors. The vast majority of the invading troops, civic officials and colonising settlers were not speakers of any recognised standard form of English. For every major-general, district commissioner or land-purchaser there were innumerable 'other ranks' who spoke in a different manner from their leaders and employers. The settlers in Australia, New Zealand and South Africa, for example, included emigrants from a great many of the complex dialectal areas shown in A. J. Ellis' dialect map of England and Wales, 1887, 'English dialect districts' (p. 236), as well as from other parts of the British Isles and from Ireland.

Detailed accounts of the development of the English language in England from the time of the earliest written records in the eighth century down to the present day, and also of the establishment and development of the language in North America, are provided in other volumes of *The Cambridge History of the English Language*. The present volume contains historical accounts of the way in which the language reached its present shape in each of the areas specified in section 1.1.2 above.

1.1.4   *Excluded varieties*

At an early stage in the planning of the volume, round about 1984, it was decided, after much discussion, that the forms of English spoken and written in numerous other overseas regions had received too little attention from linguistic scholars to form a satisfactory part of this volume. It was the notable lack of professional scholarship at the time on the English of African countries such as Kenya, Nigeria, Tanzania and so on, and of small countries such as Bermuda, Fiji, Western Samoa and others, that led to the exclusion of these varieties. Their turn will come one day: research projects are in hand in these regions, and learned articles bearing titles like 'Nigerian Englishes in Nigerian English literature' and 'Discourse particles in Singaporean English' are now appearing with great regularity. It is to be noted that scores of such books, articles and theses are listed in Görlach 1992.

1.2 A general survey of the varieties

1.2.1 *The advance of English and the retreat of Celtic languages in Scotland, Wales and Ireland*

In Scotland, Wales and Ireland the process has been broadly the same but with local historical differences and within different time-frames. The various stages are classically shown in Scotland. McClure (ch. 2) describes how Insular West Germanic made two inroads in Scotland, first partly displacing Gaelic with what became Scots, then partly displacing both Scots and what was left of Gaelic with what became Scottish standard English. After the establishment of burghs – trading townships – in the south and east of Scotland by kings intent on reorganising the country's administration according to Anglo-Norman practices,

> Gaelic-speakers from the hinterland coming to trade in the markets or to litigate in the courts found it advantageous to acquire a working knowledge of English, and individual bilingualism must have become frequent. (p. 28)

As time went on, the outlook changed but Gaelic was still unchallenged at least in a major part of the kingdom:

> It should be borne in mind that until the end of the thirteenth century, when the extinction of the old Gaelic royal house began a new phase in the national history, Scotland was essentially a Gaelic-speaking country: the Celtic tongue was spoken as a first or only language by at least half the population and over more than half the land area. (p. 29)

The centuries that followed witnessed first the rise of Scots to the position of official language of the kingdom, and then its gradual decline, along with that of Gaelic in the Highlands. The introduction of printing in Scotland in 1508 played its part: it became normal to assimilate the language of Scots texts to English models of spelling and grammar (p. 33). John Knox, apparently, did not even '[recognise] the preservation of the Scots language as an issue' (p. 34); and 'the integrity of written Scots in the Reformation period ... went by default' (p. 34). At the present time Gaelic survives by the skin of its teeth:

> a truly astonishing degree of energy, enthusiasm and optimism is currently visible among workers in the Gaelic field. Whether this will be sufficient to preserve the language in active life remains to be seen. (p. 45)

The position of Scots is less easy to determine, but it too is far from having been totally eclipsed by English.

In Wales and Ireland the retreat of the mother-tongue Celtic languages has been less dramatic but has followed the same general pattern. In each case an originally monolingual community, for social and political reasons, gradually acquired a second language, namely English, for commercial, administrative and other business. The proportion of people speaking only the original Celtic language grew smaller. In due course the retreat of Welsh and Irish reached a point where the number of bilingual speakers in each country exceeded the number of those who spoke only Welsh or only Irish. Then the stage was reached where the number of monolingual English speakers exceeded the number of bilingual speakers. In the present century vigorous efforts have been made to preserve both Welsh and Irish. Both survive as living languages but their long-term prospects are uncertain. Thomas (ch. 3) and Kallen (ch. 4) respectively describe the latest state of affairs in the two countries. Perhaps the most significant factor is that in all three countries the entire population can read English and the vast majority can speak it, in locally differentiated forms; though the number of speakers still having a command of Scots or a Celtic language is not negligible.

1.2.2 *The transported Englishes of three of the former British colonies*

The transported Englishes of three of the former British colonies, namely South Africa, Australia and New Zealand, were, to begin with, those of 'emigrant communities speaking several different dialects' (p. 430). The dialect mix of each emigrant community, in so far as its nature can be determined, was not the same. Moreover each group of settlers encountered already established inhabitants speaking other tongues – in South Africa the Cape Dutch and the Black and Khoisan peoples, in Australia the Aborigines, and in New Zealand the Maoris. These contact languages greatly influenced the forms of English brought from the homeland, especially in vocabulary. The contributions of these contact languages, together with the usual sociolinguistic factors, ensured that three clearly distinguishable forms of English (South African, Australian and New Zealand English) would emerge, each with its own spectrum of standardness. Details of the history and present state of these transported forms of English are provided by Branford, Turner and Bauer respectively in chapters 9, 6 and 8 below.

1.2.3 Three special cases

Chapters 5 (the dialects of England), 7 (the Caribbean) and 10 (South Asia) stand apart from the others in that the mechanisms involved are less easy to chronicle. Unsettled linguistic boundaries are characteristic of English dialects and the evidence available at any given period is often woefully inadequate; the creoles of the Caribbean stand at the farthest remove from standard British English of all varieties treated in this volume; and the types of English used as lingua francas in the vast subcontinent of South Asia vary in a complex manner from city to city and from province to province as millions of South Asians struggle to learn the language from standard English textbooks, dictionaries, grammars and recordings.

Ihalainen (ch. 5) provides a richly detailed account of the history of investigations into the nature and types of dialects in England since 1776: the substantial work done by A. J. Ellis, Joseph Wright, Orton, Trudgill and many others is duly reported, as is the distribution of individual dialects and their future prospects. What remains uncaptured and elusive, however, is perhaps just as important as what has been collected and analysed. We lack an up-to-date dialect dictionary to augment, and possibly to replace, that of Joseph Wright, completed nearly a century ago. Furthermore

> We...know far more about the distribution of *byre/shippon/ mistall/cow-stable/cow-shed/neat-house/beast-house* for 'cow-shed' [i.e. the terminology of rural areas] than we do about urban synonyms for pedestrian crossings, lollipop men, machines used to wash cars, forecourts of petrol stations, bollards, sleeping policemen, pay-out desks, supermarket trolleys, traffic wardens, telephone booths, and hundreds of other items found in every city in the United Kingdom.
>
> (Burchfield 1985: 128)

In chapter 7 the story is of the emergence of Caribbean Creole English, 'a distinct language system with words derived from English but with phonology, semantics and morphosyntax influenced by African languages and other forces' (p. 328). In a systematic way Holm sets down an account of the main linguistic features, from the basilectal to the acrolectal, in broad chronological bands of all the main basically English-speaking Caribbean islands (the Leeward Islands, Barbados, Jamaica, the Bahamas and so on) and other territories (Guyana, Suriname and elsewhere). As in the other chapters, complex linguistic facts have been most effectively joined to the time-frame involved.

In chapter 10 Kachru describes the way in which English has prospered as a lingua franca in South Asia. The contact languages are very numerous – Bengali, Tamil, Hindi, Urdu, Sinhala and so on – and their influence on the forms of English used in the subcontinent has been substantial. Kachru catalogues the decisions taken at government level about the role of English in the communities concerned, especially in the educational system. All this is important and needed saying. But he has run into controversy in a way that no one foresaw.

One of the important (and unresolved) linguistic debates of the present time concerns the nature and standard of the forms of English used by non-native speakers of English, especially in countries of what Kachru calls the 'Outer Circle', for example South Asia, West Africa and Southeast Asia. He does not believe that adherence to a standard British model is an attainable target ('the exocentric "monomodel" position is less favoured, and the "functional polymodel" approach has proved more insightful') (p. 551). The *locus classicus* for the opposing view is that of Sir Randolph Quirk (1988). In this paper Quirk insists that 'because there is still no grammar, dictionary, or phonological description of non-native norms [in Indian English] that is, or could hope to become, recognized as authoritative in India', the only conclusion to be drawn is that teachers of English in India (and by implication elsewhere in Outer Circle countries) must aim to follow native norms, that is, in practice, British English (with a normal ration of local differences). Elsewhere, in a typology of language variation, Quirk (1990) uses the term 'liberation linguistics' to designate the (to him unacceptable) view that imperfectly learned English should be treated as a 'variety' of English on a par with Australian English or Canadian English. The debate, which has far-reaching implications, continues.

The arguments are evenly balanced, and sides are being taken. Graeme Kennedy, commenting in the same volume (Quirk & Widdowson 1985) on Quirk's 1985 paper, asked: 'Although standards of English may be adopted or encouraged [in EFL and ESL countries], can they influence significantly the directions English moves in and the use of English in a global context?' His question implied that he believed that they cannot. In the same volume (p. 34) the Swedish scholar Jan Svartvik, by contrast, stressed that 'for non-native speakers the acquisition of English is an investment worth the effort and the money only as long as the language functions as a means of international communication for a range of purposes'. He questioned the need for 'a variety of norms even for institutionalized outer circle fellowships, considering the likely long-term negative consequences for global English'.

1.3   Distinctive and shared features

1.3.1   Some distinctive features

In the chapters that follow an account of the development of English in each of nine designated areas is systematically set down. Each chapter draws attention to the permanence of certain characteristics, for example, the continuing significance of the Humber–Lune–Ribble boundary in England as a divider of northern types of regional English from southern types (p. 251). In some cases emphasis is placed upon the number of people who are bilingual in a given country: for example, it is worthy of note that, to judge from the census returns of 1980, nearly 80 per cent of Whites in South Africa reported themselves able to read and write both English and Afrikaans (p. 438); and of those South Africans claiming English as their mother tongue, about one in three were English by descent. By contrast only a small proportion of Maoris can speak, read or write Maori, and only a minute proportion of white New Zealanders and Pacific Islanders have even a rudimentary knowledge of the Maori language. But all people resident in New Zealand can speak, read and write English.

Apart from describing the sociological and political developments in each area – for example, the complex politicisation of South African vocabulary during the period of apartheid – each writer is at pains to identify linguistic features that seem to be particular to his region. It would be impracticable to gather all such features up here but a list of some of the more interesting and distinctive of them follows. They are listed in the order in which they appear in this volume, not in any imagined order of importance.

Scotland

1 The survival of a number distinction in the second-person pronoun (*thou* distinguished from *ye*) in parts of Scotland (p. 69). (But the feature is not quite restricted to parts of Scotland. 'It is also true that Irish English shows a distinction between the second person plural and singular – *you* in the singular and *ye* in the plural (most often in the west and possibly other rural areas) or *yiz, yous*, etc. (the form in Dublin and Belfast, at least)' (J. L. Kallen, private communication).)

2 *Can* in periphrastic constructions with other modals, that is, double modals, as they are usually called (e.g. *He'll **can get** it feenisht by the week-enn*), in Scots (p. 72).

3 Cliticised forms of the negative (*canna, isna*, etc.) in Scots (p. 73).

4 The survival in Scots of some of the older weak plurals, e.g. /in/ 'eyes', /ʃin/, /ʃɪn/ and /ʃøn/ 'shoes'.

5 The prevalence of /u/ in words like *down, house, town* (sometimes written as ⟨doon⟩, ⟨hoose⟩, ⟨toon⟩), because the Great Vowel Shift failed to apply in respect of ME /uː/ in Scotland (p. 49).

Wales

1 The use of expletive *there* (e.g. ***There's** tall you are!* reflecting Welsh *Dyna dal wyt ti!*) (p. 138).

2 Intervocalic graphic double consonants in medial position (e.g. *dinner, supper*) pronounced as double consonants by contrast with RP (p. 125).

3 A use of the tag *isn't it?* (e.g. *You're going home now, **isn't it?***) (p. 141).

4 The fronting of sentence constituents (e.g. ***Coal** they're getting out mostly*) under the influence of Welsh (p. 137). (Irish English also shows a good deal of the same phenomenon, as Kallen shows on pp. 179–80, e.g. *Cold as ever it were; Aye, in the middle of the night they'd probably arrive.*)

Ireland

1 The use of *after* as a marker of tense/aspect (e.g. *I'm **after missing** the bus* 'I have missed the bus') (p. 173).

2 Habitual use of inflected *do + be* (e.g. *Those pancakes* **do be** *gorgeous*) (p. 181).

3 An 'extended present' perfect (e.g. *We're living here seventeen years*) (p. 182).

4 The Irish diminutive suffix *-ín* is sometimes attached to words of English origin (e.g. *girleen, maneen*) (p. 183).

Dialects of England

The use of the suspended *t'* ('the') (see the Glossary) in several northern counties of England (p. 220).

Australia

The Australian and New Zealand 'interview tune' or 'high rising tone' in declarative sentences, 'used to seek confirmation that one's interlocutor is following' (pp. 297 and 396).

Caribbean

1 The presence of African-derived vocabulary and calques in Caribbean creoles (ch. 7 *passim*).

2 The emergence in basilectal Caribbean creoles of a distinction between *you* 'you, your' (singular) and *unu* 'you, your' (plural) (derived from an African language; cf. Ibo *unu*) because standard English lacked distinctive singular and plural forms by the late seventeenth century (p. 379).

New Zealand

The swift intake of further Maori words into New Zealand English in recent times, and the attempt to persuade white monolingual New Zealanders to pronounce Maori place-names in a Maori manner (in order 'to show solidarity with Maori ideals in the use of the Maori language') (p. 398).

South Africa

1 The substantial input of Afrikaans words and constructions in South African English: for example, the use of *busy* in *We're* **busy** *waiting for him now* (reflecting Afrikaans *besig om te*) (p. 490); and possibly the 'informal propredicate' *Is it?* (e.g. *He has to leave town. –* **Is it?**), reflecting Afrikaans *Is dit?* (p. 491).

2 The use of the 'loan consonant' /x/ (from Afrikaans), for example, the first consonant in *gom* 'lout'; and (for some speakers) of an African-derived click in the initial sound of *Xhosa* (p. 484).

South Asia
The effect on the rhythm and stressing of South Asian English
sentences arising from the fact that South Asian languages are
syllable-timed as opposed to English, which is a stress-timed
language (p. 516).

1.3.2   Some shared features

Cross-border influence, as that between Wales and England and between
Scotland and England, leads to the presence of the same linguistic
features in borderland areas. Thus in Radnor (now in Powys) dialects in
Wales it has been noted that negative auxiliaries such as *inna* 'isn't', *anna*
'hasn't' and *shanna* 'shan't' occur just as they do in parts of the West
Midlands. Similarly, the objective/possessive pronouns *his self* (*He hit his
self*) and *their selves* (*They hit their selves*) are likely to be heard in many
dialects of England as well as in Wales. But this phenomenon is not
restricted to geographically contiguous counties and countries. Several
contributors to this volume underline the non-exclusiveness of linguistic
features in the English-speaking communities they have dealt with.
Migrants take their speech and their writing conventions with them,
and, as a consequence, many features that are non-standard or are in
restricted use in the United Kingdom form part of the standard language
in the former British colonies. Because of the many cross-Tasman links
between Australia and New Zealand, Australian and New Zealand
English share many features (though they are far from being in-
distinguishable varieties of English: see ch. 6 and 8 below).

Sometimes it is not clear how widespread a tendency is. Thus, for
example, McClure reports (p. 71) that

> In educated speech and writing [in Scotland], prescriptions regarding
> *may* to indicate possibility often lead to the hypercorrection of using it
> with a past reference, as in the sub-headline of a newspaper article
> 'Accident may have been avoided, say police', referring to an accident
> which was not avoided.

But this widely condemned use is found in educated use elsewhere in
Britain and in America. Dwight Bolinger cites American examples from
1968 onwards in *English Today* January 1988: and non-Scottish UK
examples are given in Burchfield 1992, such as 'A mentally ill man may
not have committed suicide had he been kept in hospital, rather than
been discharged to be cared for in the community' (*Guardian*, 4 May
1990). This counterfactual use probably came into being because in

certain other circumstances *may* and *might* are interchangeable with only slight change of focus or emphasis. Its currency in other English-speaking areas awaits further research, but it seems likely that it occurs in educated speech and writing in all areas.

Numerous other shared features are dealt with in this volume. Some of the more important ones are as follows:

1   *l*-vocalisation (see the Glossary) is found in many English-speaking countries.

2   Double or multiple negation is likely to be encountered in non-standard speech in all English-speaking countries, and so are examples of non-standard grammatical concord (e.g. *They was here yesterday*). These features are described in several of the chapters in this volume, and are subject to complex linguistic assumptions and constraints within each language variety.

3   The use of epenthetic /ə/ between a final liquid and a nasal in some types of speech in Ireland and South Africa (e.g. *film* /'fɪləm/, *harm* /'harəm/) (pp. 175, 485). G. W. Turner (private communication) reports that this is 'a pronunciation also heard in Sydney'; and J. D. McClure (private communication) commented, 'This is common in Scottish usage too, the epenthetic vowel often being /ʌ/. When very conspicuous, it is associated with western urban working-class speech.'

4   Ulster Scots has much in common with the Scots of Scotland, e.g. enclitic forms like *cannae*, *dinnae*, etc. (p. 183).

5   Numerous UK dialect words have become part of the standard (or colloquial) language of Australia and New Zealand, e.g. *cobber*, *dunny* 'lavatory', *fossick* (verb) 'search around', *larrikin* 'hooligan'.

6   Although clearly distinguishable in vocabulary (largely because of the Aboriginal/Maori input) Australian and New Zealand English sound very much alike. One distinction is that in words like *dance* and *chance* many Australian speakers favour /dæns/ and /tʃæns/ whereas most New Zealand speakers favour /dɑːns/ and /tʃɑːns/ (pp. 293, 394).

7   Many speakers of Australian and New Zealand English insert an epenthetic /ə/ in words of the type *grown*, *thrown*, thus making them disyllabic, i.e. *grow/ə/n, throw/ə/n* (pp. 288, 391). 'This is also common in Scotland' (J. D. McClure, private communication).

8   In words ending in -ey, -y (e.g. *money*, *party*) Australian, New Zealand and South African English-speakers tend to favour /i/ of varying length instead of /ɪ/. This may reflect a similar tendency in RP, where final unstressed /i/ is found increasingly alongside /ɪ/. In such circumstances /i/ is also found in many varieties of Irish English (J. L. Kallen, private communication).

However irrecoverable all the facts about distinctive features and shared features are, it must always be borne in mind that varieties of English, spoken at whatever distance, or however close up, are not discrete entities. When Branford says (p. 493) that 'South African English reflects a complex symbiosis of cultures and languages *without sacrificing its basic Englishness*' (my italics), he is speaking for all the Englishes described in this volume. The similarities greatly exceed the differences.

1.4   Some general verdicts, comments and predictions

In so far as any broad pattern emerges in the chapters that follow it is that the introduction of English in different physical and cultural environments has everywhere produced a similar set of results: markedly distinguishable speech patterns in each of the regions, considerable diversity of local vocabulary (the new elements being chiefly drawn from the languages of the indigenous inhabitants) and the essential sameness (with only limited exceptions) of the accidence and syntax. In those countries where languages other than English were spoken before the English arrived as conquerors or colonists these indigenous languages are almost everywhere in retreat despite attempts to preserve them.

Each of the chapters that follow provides a detailed account of the fortunes of the English language in the areas concerned. It may be useful if at this point I set down side by side some of the central statements, conclusions and predictions of the essayists themselves.

Scotland

Gaelic and traditional Scots are spoken only by relatively small numbers, and most of the population conducts its daily business (or such of it as is shown to incomers) in what is in principle of a piece with the speech heard in England, Canada or New Zealand: the international English language with some local colouring in pronunciation. More intimate acquaintance reveals how pervasive has been the influence not only of the Scots tongue – which, even where apparently 'dead', haunts the scene with unshakable persistence – but of the enormous edifice of religious, legislative, scholarly and literary achievement which developed during Scotland's centuries of existence as an independent state. (p. 92)

Wales

Welsh English will increasingly come to be characterised as a distinct accent, rather than as a dialect, though its vocabulary and idiomatic usage will no doubt continue to be significantly distinguished from other varieties of English in Britain – at least in speech. (p. 146)

Ireland

The only possibility for a national future as a distinct or distinctive people that Ireland can have lies in conserving, strengthening, renewing the Irish Gaelic tradition ... The monoglot English-speaking Irishman is dominated by the manner of England either immediately or ultimately ... An Irishman speaking English is not in the same category as an Englishman. The language has only been rented out to him. (p. 186, quoting P. L. Henry 1974)

Dialects of England

There are ... reasons to expect that London and its environs, the south-east, will continue to be a source of linguistic innovations. More and more southern English is likely to end up as 'Received English'. However ... it is also likely that certain regionalisms will ... resist a specific prestige feature, but cultural, social and economic differences may turn out to be an even more efficient wall against southern influence. (p. 263)

Australia

It seems that the outlines of Australian English pronunciation were established by the end of the first century of European settlement.
(p. 285)

It is a reminder that even monolinguals might preserve within themselves, in Australia as elsewhere, a complex of linguistic variation.
(p. 327)

Caribbean

Understanding the history and nature of English in the West Indies requires an understanding of Creole. The literary language of the Commonwealth Caribbean is much the same as that of Britain except for a relatively limited amount of lexicon; but the folk speech of most territories is a mixture of English and Creole, and it is the latter that is not well known outside the West Indies. (p. 380)

today basilectal Jamaican is farther from standard English than is basilectal Bahamian, but it seems likely that a century ago both were farther yet from the standard. (p. 332)

New Zealand

I do not believe that the arguments are cut and dried, but it does seem to me that, in the current state of our knowledge, the hypothesis that New Zealand English is derived from Australian English is the one which explains most about the linguistic situation in New Zealand.

(p. 428)

South Africa

English … has a significant role in a future South Africa, but exactly what that role is to be is a matter both for explicit language planning and for the actual dynamics of a society which has yet to come into being. (p. 495)

South Asia

In recent years it has been shown that the 'deficit' and 'deviational' approaches to South Asian English are not very meaningful, since these two discount the contextual and pragmatic variables. (p. 551)

Each of the chapters in its own way underlines the fact that at present the various forms of English described in this volume are holding together, though each variety is separated by innumerable intricate details of vocabulary, idiom, syntax and, especially, pronunciation. What the future holds cannot be known, but it is likely, I believe, to be marked by further local diversification, by divergence rather than convergence, as the centuries go by, in the spoken word, though with only limited changes to the written word.

1.5   Standard English: local or international?

As a postscript it should perhaps be emphasised that there has not been any agreed definition of the term *standard* (or *Standard*) *English* among linguistic scholars in the twentieth century. Henry Sweet (1908: 7) defined it in terms of Great Britain only:

> Standard English itself was originally that mixture of the Midland and Southern dialects which was spoken in London during the Middle Ages, just as Standard French is the dialect of that district of which Paris is the centre.

> Standard English, like Standard French, is now a class-dialect more than a local dialect: it is the language of the educated all over Great Britain... The best speakers of Standard English are those whose pronunciation, and language generally, least betray their locality.

So did Burchfield (1985: 124–5):

> Within the British Isles, now as in the past, the English language exists and persists in an uncountable number of forms. Only one form – that taught to foreigners – is 'standard'. This broadly rationalized prestigious form of English is a lineal descendant of a dialect that began to acquire its potency in the fourteenth and fifteenth centuries... Standard English is the variety considered most suitable for use on the spoken channels of our broadcasting systems emanating from London... It is seen as unequivocally 'English' by people in Beijing, Kaliningrad, and Tokyo, who learn it as they might learn the lines in a gigantic play.

Both these descriptions fail to account for the various kinds of standard English used abroad. American scholars quite properly include the usage of educated people in North America. Strevens (1985: 6) takes the matter further:

> Standard English dialect (remember, we are referring to patterns of grammar and vocabulary, but not to pronunciation) has no local base. On the contrary, it is acceptable throughout the English-using world. And it is spoken with any accent. Consequently Standard English is the only dialect which is neither localised in its currency nor paired solely with its local accent.

> How does this state of affairs arise? The answer, at least in the past century or so, seems to be that Standard English has become the only acceptable model or target for normal educational use. Teachers everywhere learn, and then teach, the same grammar and the same core vocabulary. There really are remarkably few variations in grammar in Standard English, whether the writer or speaker comes from Britain or Ghana or Canada or Hong Kong or India or the United States.

In *The Oxford Companion to the English Language* (1992) McArthur qualified Strevens' view and particularly his statement that standard

English 'applies to grammar, vocabulary, writing, and print, but not to accent'. McArthur continued:

> although it is widespread among contemporary 'liberal' linguists, [Strevens'] view is relatively recent and is not universal... The question of whether *standard English* does, can, or ought to include norms of speech remains the most controversial of the many difficulties associated with the term.

McArthur provides 'a general definition' of the term:

> In everyday usage, *standard English* is taken to be the variety most widely accepted and understood within an English-speaking country or throughout the English-speaking world. It is more or less free of regional, class, and other shibboleths, although the issue of a 'standard accent' often causes trouble and tension. It is sometimes presented as the 'common core' (what is left when all regional and other distinctions are stripped away), a view that remains controversial because of the difficulty of deciding where core ends and peripheries begin. Linguists generally agree on three things: (1) The standard is most easily identified in print, whose conventions are more or less uniform throughout the world, and some use the term *print standard* for that medium. (2) Standard forms are used by most presenters of news on most English-language radio and television networks, but with regional and other variations, particularly in accent. (3) Use of standard English relates to social class and level of education, often considered (explicitly or implicitly) to match the average level of attainment of students who have finished secondary-level schooling.

The difficulty in determining the nature of standard English is further emphasised by Greenbaum 1990. In this essay he described the possessiveness of the English in England towards their language. In a rousing speech in April 1988 to the Royal Society of St George, for example, the former Member of Parliament Enoch Powell affirmed the permanent claim of the English to English:

> Others may speak and read English – more or less – but it is our language not theirs. It was made in England by the English and it remains our distinctive property, however widely it is learnt or used.
>
> (cited from the *Independent*, 23 April 1988)

'His possessive attitude towards the English language', Greenbaum says, 'is probably shared by most English people, and indeed by the other ethnic groups that are native to the British Isles.' By the same token it is not surprising that it is not shared by the vast majority of English-speakers in the former British colonies.

FURTHER READING

Indispensable reference works include the *Oxford English Dictionary* (2nd edition, 20 vols., 1989); J. C. Wells *Accents of English* (3 vols., Cambridge University Press, 1982); O. Jespersen *A Modern English Grammar on Historical Principles* (7 vols., Munksgaard, Copenhagen, 1909–49); F. T. Visser *An Historical Syntax of the English Language* (4 vols., Brill, Leiden, 1963–73); R. Quirk, S. Greenbaum, G. Leech & J. Svartvik *A Comprehensive Grammar of the English Language* (Longman, 1985); and *The Oxford Companion to the English Language*, ed. Tom McArthur (Oxford University Press, 1992).

For works dealing with the terms of phonetic classification see the headnote to the Glossary of linguistic terms, p. 554.

The following books and journals contain many articles that are relevant to matters discussed in the Introduction and elsewhere in this volume.

Journals

Dictionaries: Journal of the Dictionary Society of North America, Cleveland State University, 1979–   ; at present one issue a year.

English Today, Cambridge University Press, 1985–   ; at present four issues a year.

English World-wide: a Journal of Varieties of English. John Benjamins, Amsterdam, 1980–   ; at present two issues a year.

World Englishes, Pergamon Press, Oxford, 1981–92; Basil Blackwell, Oxford, 1993–   ; at present three issues a year.

Other sources

Bailey, R. W. & M. Görlach (eds.) (1982). *English as a World Language*. Ann Arbor: The University of Michigan Press.

Burchfield, R. (1985). *The English Language*. Oxford: Oxford University Press. (1992). *Points of View*. Oxford: Oxford University Press.

Görlach, M. (1992). Englishes. A selective bibliography 1984–1991 (excluding Britain, Ireland and USA/Canada). *English World-wide* 13, 1: 59–109.

Greenbaum, S. (ed.) (1985). *The English Language Today*. Oxford: Pergamon Press.
(1990). Whose English? In Ricks & Michaels (eds.), 15–23.

Hausmann, F. J., O. Reichmann, H. E. Wiegand and L. Zgusta, (eds.) (1989–91). *Wörterbücher, Dictionaries, Dictionnaires*. 3 vols. Berlin: Walter de Gruyter.

Holm, J. (1988–9). *Pidgins and Creoles*. Cambridge: Cambridge University Press.

Kachru, B. B. (1983). Models for non-native Englishes. In B. B. Kachru (ed.), *The Other Tongue, English across Cultures*. Oxford: Pergamon Press, 31–57.
(1991). Liberation linguistics and the Quirk concern. *English Today* 25: 3–13.

Michaels, L. & C. Ricks, (eds.) (1980). *The State of the Language*. Berkeley and Los Angeles: University of California Press.

Platt, J., H. Weber and M. L. Ho (1984). *The New Englishes*. London: Routledge and Kegan Paul.

Quirk, R. (1985). The English language in a global context. In Quirk & Widdowson (eds.), 1–6.

(1988). The question of standards in the international use of English. In P. H. Lowenburg (ed.), *Language Spread and Language Policy*. Washington, DC: Georgetown University Press, 229–41.

(1990). Language varieties and standard language. *English Today* 21: 3–10.

Quirk, R. & G. Stein (1990). *English in Use*. Harlow: Longman.

Quirk, R. & H. G. Widdowson (eds.) (1985). *English in the World*. Cambridge: Cambridge University Press.

Ricks, C. & L. Michaels (eds.) (1990). *The State of the Language*. Berkeley and Los Angeles: University of California Press.

Romaine, S. (ed.) (1992). *Language in Australia*. Cambridge: Cambridge University Press.

Schmied, J. (1991). *English in Africa: an Introduction*. Harlow: Longman.

Strevens, P. (1985). Standards and the standard language. *English Today* 2: 6.

Sweet, H. (1908). *The Sounds of English*. Oxford: Clarendon Press.

Trudgill, P. (ed.) (1984). *Language in the British Isles*. Cambridge: Cambridge University Press.

Wakelin, H. (1988). *The Archaeology of English*. London: B. T. Batsford.

Zgusta, L. (1988). *Lexicography Today. An Annotated Bibliography of the Theory of Lexicography*. Tübingen: Niemeyer.

PART I

REGIONAL VARIETIES OF ENGLISH IN GREAT BRITAIN AND IRELAND

2 ENGLISH IN SCOTLAND

J. Derrick McClure

2.1 Introduction

Insular West Germanic speech was first established in what is now Scotland in the sixth century. Two phases are clearly identifiable in its history: the first includes the emergence of a distinctively Scottish form, developing independently of the Northern dialect of England though like it derived from Northumbrian Old English, and its attainment to the rank of official language in an autonomous nation–state; and the second, the gradual adoption in Scotland of a written, and subsequently also a spoken, form approximating to those of the English metropolis, with consequent loss of status of the previously existing Scottish tongue. In the course of the linguistic history of Scotland, that is, first one and then two speech forms, both descended from Old English, have been used within the national boundaries. For convenience we will choose to designate the first *Scots* and the second *Scottish English*. This situation has no exact parallel in the English-speaking world.

Uniquely among Old English-derived speech forms other than standard literary English, Scots has a claim to be regarded as a distinct language rather than a dialect, or latterly a group of dialects, of English. This claim has been, and continues to be, the subject of serious, reasoned and at times heated debate, at both popular and scholarly level (see Aitken 1981a and McClure 1988: 17–31 for contributions from opposing viewpoints): a debate which embraces historical, political, social and literary as well as linguistic issues and has important implications in the field of education. However, it is beyond the scope of the present chapter, for the purposes of which it is sufficient to note that Scots, being descended from Old English and sharing in the general history of West Germanic speech in the British Isles, is appropriately considered as part of 'English' in the purely linguistic sense of the term. That Scottish English, as opposed to Scots, is a form of English is of course non-controversial. The distinction between Scots and Scottish English, which though not always clear in practice is soundly based on historical facts, should be borne in mind throughout the chapter.

2.2   History of the speech community

2.2.1   *Establishment and spread of Old English in Scotland: 547–1067*

The Venerable Bede and the northern texts of the *Chronicle* give the year 547 for the founding of the kingdom of Bernicia, and a permanent foothold for Germanic speech north of the Tweed must have been established not long after that. The turbulent history of the next few decades reveals heavy defeats suffered by the native peoples at the hands of the encroaching Angles: the kingdom of Rheged, with its power-base in the area of Carlisle, fell to Anglian domination after the death of its King Urien ca 590, the Scots of Dal Riada were vanquished at Degsastan – possibly Dawston in Liddesdale – in 604, and around the same time the Gododdin of Lothian were wiped out as a fighting force at Catraeth: a site generally identified with Catterick, but according to a recent theory (McDiarmid 1983) somewhere in the west Borders or Galloway. It was the Picts, by the victorious battle of Nechtansmere (Dunnichen) in 685, who halted the Anglian advance.

Germanic speech was thus established in what had been an area of Celtic language and culture. The scarcely Romanised Britons of the intervalline territory had of course retained their Brythonic tongue, and the Scots of Dal Riada, whose settlements had begun in the fourth century, spoke a language identical, then and until much later, to that heard in their Irish homeland. The language of the Picts poses more of a historical problem. Brythonic place-names, or names which (like the well-known *Pit-* group) are hybrids of Brythonic and Goidelic, predominate in their homeland; and of the attested tribal and individual names few can be shown definitely *not* to be Celtic and many certainly are (e.g. those of the chieftains Calgacus 'swordsman' and Argentocoxus 'silver leg' mentioned respectively by Tacitus and Dio Cassius). Confusingly, however, there is also evidence of two kinds for a non-Celtic language spoken in Pictland: a group of undeciphered inscriptions in stone, two using the Latin and the remainder the Ogam alphabet (Jackson 1955; Padel 1972; Price 1984: ch. 2); and some clearly non-

Celtic place-names. The stone inscriptions, it must be acknowledged, are too scanty, fragmentary and in some cases indistinct to prove anything. Valiant efforts have been made to identify known Pictish names and words such as Gaelic *mac* and Latin *et*, and to find evidence regarding the nature of Pictish grammar and vocabulary from the residue (one scholar (Guiter 1968) has put a serious case for relating the language of the stones to Basque); but in the end it has proved impossible either to identify the inscriptions conclusively with any known language or even to show that they are linguistic at all: the suggestion has been made that they are random jumbles carved by artisans who knew the *figurae* of the letters but not their *potestates* (Anderson 1948). Much more firmly based is the evidence of river-names such as *Ness, Naver, Nevis, Sheil* and *Shin*, which have been shown (Nicolaisen 1976; ch. 9) to belong to a pre-Celtic but Indo-European (and therefore of course not Basque) language formerly widely distributed over western Europe. This seems to be conclusive proof that a non-Celtic language was once spoken in Pictland: *when* it was spoken, however, is another matter. Place-names, and especially names of water-courses, can be extremely tenacious: the Scottish map shows several that have survived one, two or even three changes of language in their area. An example is the river-name Ayr, itself evidently pre-Celtic and established in a region where the language in historical times has been successively Brythonic, Gaelic and Scots. To argue from the certain existence of non-Celtic toponymic elements in Pictland to the conclusion that the Picts whom the Romans and Angles knew were anything other than a Celtic people is clearly unwarranted.

An uneasy balance of power between Picts and Northumbrians was the prevailing situation in the later eighth and ninth centuries. Anglian speech must by then have been dominant in the Lothians and eastern Borders, and was probably to be heard in some measure even in the South-West, where an Anglian bishopric had been established at Whithorn ca 720. It was the achievement of what had been a lesser power in northern Britain, the Scots of Dal Riada, to extend their rule over parts of the former kingdom of Northumbria, with results far more momentous than could have been foreseen at the time. The catalytic force in this process was the Scandinavian attacks and settlements. The Viking conquest of the Western Isles and parts of the Atlantic seaboard of Scotland caused an eastward shifting of the power base of Dal Riada, formerly centred on Iona, and a weakening of contact with the Irish culture area of which Dal Riada was an extension. The destruction of Northumbrian power, and establishment of a formidable Viking axis lying athwart Britain from York to Dublin, at first seemed to end the Northumbrian threat to Pictland but soon replaced it with a still greater menace. The response in Scotland was, evidently, a period of close military and dynastic interaction between Picts and Scots. Relations between these two peoples are not easy to decipher, but it is clear that the royal lines were closely interconnected by marriage some time before the union of the two kingdoms in the person of Kenneth Mac Alpin (ca 843 – ca 858), traditionally regarded as the first king of a state identifiable with the Scotland of later times. It is also clear that the Gaelic church, with its attributes of Latin and vernacular literacy, high artistic and intellectual achievement and missionary fervour, had strongly influenced the Picts well before the close union of the peoples: despite the merit and the distinctiveness of Pictish art, the Scots were the dominant force culturally as well as militarily in the new kingdom. The Scottish national mythos of a later age held that the Picts were totally exterminated: in fact, their weakening by Viking attacks was one factor which led to their absorption into the Scottish state, in which they rapidly lost their distinctive identity.

The rulers of the Scoto-Pictish kingdom, called in Latin *Scotia* and in Gaelic (then and now) *Alba*, showed skill and enterprise in dealing with the Viking power blocs, and with the Saxons beyond the Norse-held areas as the House of Wessex proceeded with the reconquest of England. The Battle of Brunanburh, celebrated in the eponymous Old English poem, was one incident in the lengthy struggle of Celts, Saxons, Vikings in Ireland and Vikings in England for control over the middle parts of the island: the Scots king Constantine II, the *har hilderinc* ('white-haired warrior') of the poem, had during a long and – until then – strikingly successful reign effectively held the balance of power among Dublin Vikings, York Vikings and Saxons, and increased Scots influence in Galloway. Constantine even held a *de facto* overlordship in Bernicia, protecting that precariously independent state against Viking aggression from York; and his successors' attempts to progress from overlordship to annexation came to fruition in the reign of Malcolm II, who in 1018 by his victory over the Angles at Carham brought his frontier to the Tweed. Though English speech had long been established north of the present-day border, that is, it was in the early eleventh century that 'Scotland' officially expanded to incorporate English-speaking territory.

Of the precise form of Scottish Anglo-Saxon in this period we have virtually no direct evidence. One of the earliest texts in any form of Old

English, the fragments of *The Dream of the Rood* carved on the Ruthwell Cross (see Swanton 1970: 9–38) is in the Northumbrian dialect and emanates from what is now part of Scotland, but no more than the *Gododdin* (see Jackson 1969) can this be credibly claimed as a Scottish poem. Place-names come to our aid in determining the distribution of early Anglian settlement: the south-east of Scotland differs strikingly from the rest of the country in the predominantly Anglian character of its village- and town-names (though the names of natural features, here as elsewhere in Scotland, are principally Celtic). Scotland's only authentic early names of the *inga-ham* 'homestead of the followers of' form, Whittinghame, Tynninghame and Coldingham, are found in East Lothian and Berwickshire; and the few (fewer than a dozen) genuine *inga-tun* names appear in the same area: *Eddington, Edrington, Thirlington, Haddington, Upsettlington.* The element *worþ* 'enclosure', notably common in Northumberland, gives three early Scottish names: Polwarth, and the original forms *Gedwearde* and *Cesseworth* for the villages now known as Jedburgh (still locally pronounced Jeddart) and Cessford. The settlement nomenclature makes it clear that this part of Scotland was linguistically a virtual extension of Northumbria. Notably absent are names containing references to pagan deities or to elements of pre-Christian practices such as cremation, comparable to those found in southern regions of England, suggesting that Anglian settlement in Scotland post-dates the conversion to Christianity: also lacking are names in *-ing* or *-ingas*, in England found principally in the south and south-east and dating from early in the settlement period (Nicolaisen 1976: ch. 5).

The oldest forms of these and other names in Scotland are attested in charters, acts and similar documents (Craigie 1924). The institution of the charter is of course associated with Anglo-Norman feudalism; and it was events in Scotland consequent on the Norman Conquest of England that fundamentally altered the status of the Anglo-Saxon language in the northern kingdom, besides initiating a new and much more productive phase in its recorded history.

2.2.2 *Growing social importance of the language: 1067–1286*

Following on the victory of William the Conqueror, the dispossessed Saxon royal house, consisting of Edgar the Atheling and his sisters Margaret and Christina, fled with a group of English loyalists to Scotland. The reigning King Malcolm III (the Malcolm of Shakespeare's

Macbeth) not only gave them refuge but took the elder sister Margaret as his queen: a marriage with far-reaching results. By providing the Saxon house with a powerful and bellicose ally it precipitated armed confrontation between Malcolm and William; and though Malcolm's fighting strength proved no match for the Norman forces, his adventurous fishing in troubled waters won him the lordship of some northern English manors (though it did nothing for the cause of his brother-in-law). And since Malcolm had learned English while exiled in England during the reign of Macbeth, and his queen knew no Gaelic, the Saxon tongue became, if not yet the medium of government, at least the private language of the royal family. The learned and saintly Margaret seems to have made it her personal mission to bring the organisation and observances of the Celtic church into line with the prescribed usages of Rome; and to further this cause she invited English bishops into Scotland and established a Benedictine priory, staffed by monks from Canterbury, at Dunfermline. Much more important than the personal influence of the queen, however, was the transformation of Scottish government and society brought about by Malcolm, and the three of his sons by Margaret who successively occupied the throne, in imitation of the feudal government of Norman England. In this 'peaceful Norman Conquest' (Dickinson & Duncan 1977: 77) of Scotland, not only was the native aristocracy merged with (rather than displaced by) a new ruling class of feudal landowners from Norman territories, but burghs – trading townships with rights and privileges defined by charter – were established all over Scotland, though predominantly in the south and east. The burgh was an Anglo-Norman institution, and the Scottish burghs were from the first centres of English speech. Many of the earliest were founded in the English-speaking parts of the kingdom, and as the non-Celtic population of Scotland increased with the influx of refugees from the oppressions of William I and II and the anarchy of Stephen's reign, and of the Saxon households of the new Norman landowners, these incomers gravitated to the newly established burghs. The increased trading and commercial opportunities in a Scotland which was, and was seen to be, developing new and attractive economic links with Europe resulted in immigration: of English, and of Flemings and Scandinavians both directly from those countries and from communities settled in England. Those latter, speaking Germanic languages closely related to Old English, would naturally adopt that in preference to Gaelic. As the burghs grew, Gaelic-speakers from the hinterland coming to trade in the markets or to litigate in the courts found it advantageous to acquire a working knowledge of English, and individual bilingualism must have become frequent.

The fundamental importance of the burghs as centres of English speech is demonstrated by the fact that almost the entire vocabulary associated with the institution is Old English in origin. The word *burgh* itself is an obvious example, and others are *toft* (homestead and land), *croft* (smallholding), *ruid* (a piece of land belonging to a burgh rented for building or farming), *guild* (a trading association) and *gildry*, *alderman* (chief officer of a guild), *bow* (an arched gateway), *wynd* (lane), *raw* (row of houses), *sac*, *soc* and *them* (certain rights of jurisdiction).

The growing complexity of the Scottish linguistic situation, with French and English emerging as functioning languages of the kingdom, can be deduced from official documents of the eleventh, twelfth and thirteenth centuries. Personal names of French and English origin began to appear alongside names in Gaelic, Brythonic and – a short-lived element – Scandinavian; and the new names grew more fashionable as the years passed: families bearing Gaelic names gave Saxon names to their children, but the reverse was much less frequent (Murison 1974). The royal family itself appears to have set the fashion, the names of Malcolm's eight children by Margaret all being biblical, classical or Saxon, and none Gaelic: after a troubled period of Celtic reaction following his death, his throne was held successively by three sons called Edgar, Alexander and David. (It is fair, however, to observe that Malcolm had sons by a previous marriage who would have been expected to take precedence over Margaret's children on the Scottish throne – one did reign briefly as Duncan II – whereas his sons by Margaret, Edgar the Atheling being childless, had at least a theoretical claim to the crown of England.) New township-names given in the thirteenth century, even in the Gaelic heartland north of the Forth, were generally in English: *Reidfurde*, *Staneycroft*, *Stobstane*, *Byermoss* and *Bradwell*, for example. It should be borne in mind that until the end of the thirteenth century, when the extinction of the old Gaelic royal house began a new phase in the national history, Scotland was essentially a Gaelic-speaking country: the Celtic tongue was spoken as a first or only language by at least half the population and over more than half the land area; and the last king of the Gaelic line, Alexander III, a ruler of European stature whom even England's formidable Edward Long-shanks (Edward I) treated with respect, was inaugurated in accordance with ancient Gaelic rites. Yet the development of Scotland to a European nation–state is intimately linked with a steady increase in the demographic and cultural importance of English speech. A formula used more than once by the kings in addressing the people of the realm in the twelfth century is 'Franci, Angli, Scoti et Gallovidiani', and the order of precedence is significant: the French-speaking aristocrats of continental or Anglo-Norman origin are mentioned first, next the English-speakers of the south-east and the burghs, only then the native Gaelic-speakers, and last of all the men of Galloway, an area populated by a mixed race of Scandinavian, Brythonic and Gaelic blood (though probably Gaelic-speaking by this time), relatively recently annexed by the Scottish crown and troublesome for many years after its acquisition. The advent of Anglo-Norman feudalism, in fact, in the long run confirmed and deepened the cultural dichotomy, a fundamental and tragic feature of Scottish history in later times, between the English-speakers of the south and east and the Gaelic-speakers of the central hinterland and the west: in common parlance, between Lowlands and Highlands. In the thirteenth century this was not yet obvious. The steady social, juridical and economic development of the country under the strong and skilful rule of Alexander II and III extended to all areas; and it is permissible to imagine that had this progress continued unchecked, a peaceful and total integration of Gaelic, Saxon and Norman culture might eventually have taken place. Though English at this period was clearly the dominant language of commerce and the law it was not the language of the court (French) nor of the majority of the population (Gaelic); and *might* ultimately have been displaced by Gaelic as French was by English in the southern kingdom. 'Bot uþir wayis all ȝheid þe gle' ('But different far the run of play').

2.2.3   Emergence of 'Scottis': 1286–1560

The deaths of Alexander III and his grand-daughter and heir brought the line of Dunkeld to an end, and the efforts of Edward Longshanks to take advantage of the ensuing contest for the succession initiated the Three Hundred Years' War between Scotland and England, of which folk memories are still very much alive. The concern of this essay is not with the memorable historical events of the late thirteenth and early fourteenth centuries, but with the effects of the political situation on the linguistic history of Scotland. The last kings of the old royal line, though affecting French as a court language, were Gaelic by blood and sympathy; but now the throne passed successively to three Lowland families, the Balliols, Bruces and Stewarts, who identified themselves to an increasing extent with the English-speaking parts of the kingdom. The Lord of the Isles, the most powerful Gaelic-speaking magnate, became in the fourteenth century virtually an independent sovereign; sometimes an ally but more often an avowed enemy, and certainly not a vassal, of the King of Scots. The royal capital was shifted from Perth to Edinburgh, in the heart of the English-speaking territory. With the return of James I from English captivity in 1411 the Lowland tongue replaced Latin as the language in which the Acts of Parliament were recorded. Already it had proved its worth as a literary medium: the first important piece of literature to survive in the Saxon speech of Scotland, John Barbour's epic of King Robert Bruce and his part in the War of Independence, dates from 1377.

As the fifteenth century progressed and the vigorous rule of the Stewart kings restored Scotland's status as a European power, weakened during the previous strife-torn century, the flourishing cultural life of the small but confident kingdom and its diplomatic, military and commercial links with other countries were reflected in an exuberant development of Scots, as we may now call the West Germanic speech of Scotland, in its written form. A peculiar strength of the language as a poetic medium, the extreme contrast in phonæsthetic quality between the polysyllabic Latin- and French-derived vocabulary of learning and the shorter words and more consonantal phonology of the native word-stock, was exploited by the poets with outstanding skill (Aitken 1983). On a more utilitarian level, distinctive registers of Scots arose for Acts of Parliament, treasurers' accounts, burgh records and letters of various degrees of formality: two of the first extant specimens of Scots prose are letters written by Scottish magnates to the English King Henry IV. Narrative and expository prose was late in emerging and has always been a register in which literary Scots has been weak: the vernacular appears to have taken longer than in other countries to assert its claims as a language of scholarship against the unquestioned supremacy of Latin: but in 1490 John Ireland's theological writings, showing in their syntax the pervasive influence of the learned tongue, initiated the development of Scots scholarly prose.

Gavin Douglas in the Prologue to his *Eneados* (Coldwell edn 1951–6) stated explicitly the attitude of a major poet who was also a scholar and a member of the Scottish ruling class to his language and its resources. As compared to Virgil's Latin, Scots is a 'bad harsk spech and lewit barbour tung...[a] rurall vulgar gross'; and later he repeats 'Besyde Latyn our langage is imperfite', and demonstrates this in a manner familiar to

medieval humanism by citing some Latin words which have no vernacular equivalent. To make Scots a fit vehicle for conveying something
of the 'scharp sugurate sang Virgiliane', therefore, he will augment it
with 'sum bastart latyne, frensche or inglis' – just as Latin had adopted
loanwords from Greek. But though his language may require to be
reinforced for the enormous task he has set himself, it is 'the langage of
Scottis natioun', and he will write 'kepand na sudron bot our awyn
langage'. Here is clearly manifest a realistic awareness of both the
necessity and the rightfulness and desirability of expanding the Scots
tongue by borrowing and other forms of linguistic experimentation,
coupled with a patriotic pride in what was now identified as Scotland's
own language. Significantly, though the original Scots were Gaelic-
speakers, it was the Lowland tongue that was now laying claim to the
national adjective.

This is the period in which the claim of Scots to be a distinct language
was most surely established. Its development as the vehicle for an
extensive and diverse national literature, in quality far excelling that of
England in the fifteenth and early sixteenth centuries; its status as the
language of government and administration; its individual features of
phonology, grammar and vocabulary: these are sufficient to qualify it as
a fully developed language by any objective criterion. However, the
growth of a sense of distinctive linguistic identity in Lowland Scotland
was curiously late and hesitant. The first recorded use of *Scottis* as a name
for the tongue is in 1494, and the first major writer to make a point of
insisting on the independent status of 'Scottis' as compared to 'Inglis'
was Gavin Douglas in 1513. Hitherto the term *Inglis* had been used,
naturally and unreflectingly, to refer to Anglo-Saxon in either of its
national forms: the mutual hostility of the Scottish and English
monarchies and peoples, an invariable feature of European politics from
the late thirteenth century, appears to have had no influence – for a long
time, at least – on Scottish attitudes to the language. The clearest
illustration of this is the mid-fifteenth-century epic poem *Wallace*, by an
author known only as Blind Harry (McDiarmid 1968–9): a brilliant
embodiment of Scottish national feeling in a (much distorted) life
history of the greatest of patriotic heroes, which, despite its passionately
anti-English tone, freely uses *Inglis* as the name for the poet's language.
Even after Gavin Douglas had established the practice of designating
the language *Scottis* in contradistinction to *Inglis*, this was by no means
universally followed: some writers adopted it while others simply
continued using *Inglis* to include the two national forms. Actual

references to the language, too, suggest an absence of any strong or widespread awareness that Scots was, or could or should be regarded as, a distinct language and a focus for patriotic pride. Expressions of belief and assumptions regarding the Lowland tongue suggest something of the same mixture of attitudes as is visible even today: the views that the speech of the Scottish and of the English kingdoms were essentially the same, essentially different, or even different dialects of the same language, can all be found expressed in sixteenth-century texts. And, naturally, the status of Scots was sometimes a card to be played in political or social argument (McClure 1981a).

2.2.4 Increase of Southern English influence: 1560–1700

It was when a perception of Scots as a distinct national language was at best only incipient that the tongue was faced with the first of the series of sociohistorical developments that were to challenge its status; and the absence of a clear sense of linguistic identity and language loyalty proved crucial. This challenge was the Reformation; and it is indeed a historical oddity that a movement which in its central issues had no possible relevance to the importance of the Scots tongue should have had such profound effects on it.

The conventional view is that the Reformation brought about an Anglicisation of the Scots language: or more accurately, that it introduced English (as opposed to Scots) to a position of high social and cultural prominence in Scotland, with the result that Scots became displaced from certain areas of its use and subject to adulteration by English in those which remained. This, however, is an oversimplification. In the first place, it should be noted that even when the language was at its peak of independent development, it was never so remote from the literary English of London as to be immune to influence from this; and Scottish writers apparently never regarded such influence as particularly undesirable. Well before the Reformation, too, the introduction of printing to Scotland in 1508, seen in the first instance as a means of strengthening national awareness and national pride by publishing Scottish Acts of Parliament, laws and historical chronicles as well as literary and devotional works, had ironically paved the way for the dilution of Scots as a written language: the mutual intelligibility of Scots and English in their written forms led the printers, some of whom were Englishmen or foreigners accustomed to printing English texts, to assimilate the language of Scots texts to English models of spelling and grammar. This practice became common in the late sixteenth century and virtually universal in the seventeenth (Bald 1926).

It is also possible that the fascinating but highly idiosyncratic personality and career of the reformer John Knox has shaped our impression of the linguistic, as well as of the doctrinal, social and political, aspects of the Reformation to an unwarranted extent; and certainly it is a tenable historical view that his personal influence on the progress of the Reformation has been exaggerated in popular thought. The periods in Knox's life spent as chaplain to Edward VI of England and as minister to congregations of English Protestant exiles in Frankfurt and Geneva, and the fact that his earlier writings are in English, his *magnum opus* the *History of the Reformation* in a wholly erratic mixture of English and Scots, and only a few personal letters in anything approaching unmixed Scots (Sprotte 1906), has been taken to suggest that he and his co-religionists deliberately imposed a policy of linguistic and cultural Anglicisation on Scotland.

The truth, however, appears to be that neither Knox nor the Reforming party as a whole had any language policy whatever: there is no evidence that they even recognised the preservation of the Scots tongue as an issue. Early printed texts of the Scots Confession of 1560 show a seemingly random mixture of Scots and English forms: the authors of the document and its printers were simply not concerned for linguistic consistency at all (Robinson 1983). The Geneva Bible and the prayer books of English Protestant reformers were introduced into Scotland, as they were, to disseminate not the English language but – a far more important matter – Protestant doctrine; and since their language in its written form was readily intelligible to Scotsmen there was no need to provide texts in distinctively Scottish forms. A small but interesting piece of evidence that not all Scots found English Bible translations wholly satisfactory exists in the form of a Scots adaptation of the Wycliffite New Testament made ca 1520 by one Murdoch Nisbet, and retained in his family for several generations (Low 1901–5); but the wholesale importation of the Geneva Bible later in the century was accomplished with no widespread protests regarding its language. It is probable that Scots readers, at least initially, simply associated the English orthographic forms of the sacred texts with Scots pronunciations.

The integrity of written Scots in the Reformation period, that is, went by default. The absence of any strong or widespread feeling for the distinctiveness of Scots and its status as a national language – and such a feeling would have had to be very forcefully held and expressed for the issue to make any headway among the impassioned religious and political controversies of the Reformation – ensured that written forms of English permeated Scottish linguistic awareness almost unchallenged. Such challenges as *did* emerge, too, appeared as minor debating points in the context of attacks on the theology and politics of the Reformers by Catholic spokesmen; which ensured that, to the extent that the cause of preserving Scots was noticed at all, it was associated with the losing side. Political changes supported the linguistic development: the Reformers had expected and received help from England; and the triumph of the Protestant party led to a sundering of Scotland's traditional alliance with France – already sorely tried by the disastrous military defeats at English hands which had ended the reigns of the pro-French James IV and James V – and the establishment of intimate contact with England, or at any rate with its church. Queen Mary in her brief personal reign was too intent on obtaining Elizabeth Tudor's recognition as her heir to pursue a Counter-Reformation or pro-French policy with any vigour; and her far abler son, though admiring of French culture and deliberately encouraging its influence on the literary productions of his court, was a moderate Protestant with no intention of committing Scotland to alliance with a Catholic power.

The personal reign of James VI saw a temporary lull in Scotland's religious strife, and with it a revival, with the king as its self-appointed head and director, of literature and the arts. The great tradition of poetry in Scots, which had suffered a serious decline in the third quarter of the century, enjoyed a short-lived recovery; and if the linguistic inventiveness of James' court poets did not match that of their greatest predecessors, their efforts were sufficient to prove that Scots could still show vitality as a poetic language. The status of the Scots tongue became again at least a passing issue: James in his *Reulis and Cautelis*, a short but creditable treatise on the art of poetic composition, comments on the need for such a work for the use of Scots poets: 'For albeid sindrie hes written of it [*sc.* versification] in English quhilk is lykest to our language, ȝit we differ from thame in sindrie reulis of Poesie.' James' own poetic language, ironically in view of this observation, is more Anglicised than that of several of his court poets; but by contrast the language of his prose (a medium for which he had decidedly greater talent) is unmistakeably Scots.

The departure of James in 1603, however, put an abrupt and definitive end to this period in the cultural history of the Scots tongue.

Most of his court poets travelled south with him and began adapting the language and style of their verse to the tastes of the English market: James likewise adjusted the language of his prose treatises, and his *magnum opus* the *Basilikon Doron*, written in 1598 (Craigie 1944–50), was published in an edited version showing Anglicisation on a massive scale. The loss of the court left a cultural vacuum in Scotland which was not to be filled for over a century: only one major poet, William Drummond of Hawthornden, remained in the homeland, and he used as his medium a language which on the printed page is virtually indistinguishable from English. And as the advance of the seventeenth century embroiled Scotland in steadily worsening scenes of factionalism and civil and national war, the tradition of poetry in Scots disappeared almost completely, succumbing not only to linguistic Anglicisation but to a religious and intellectual climate in which all poetic endeavour was blighted.

The sudden and total eclipse of Scots as a literary language, like that of Old English after the Norman Conquest, is one of the most important transitional events in the history of English. Yet it is essential to understand clearly what was, and what was not, lost in this period. The sequence of poetry in Scots, which in the 200 years from John Barbour to the Castalian Band of James VI had produced one of the great vernacular literatures of Europe, was at an end: the re-emergence of Scots poetry in the eighteenth century was a new development rather than a genuine revival. The case of prose is different. The growth of this, as already observed, had been late in Scotland, resulting in a striking asymmetry – present in all subsequent periods – in the literary de- velopment of the language. It was the mid-sixteenth century before original vernacular prose appeared in any considerable quantity (though there had been a few notable translations, such as those from Livy and from Hector Boece's Latin history of Scotland by John Bellenden (Chambers *et al.* 1938–41), before then); and one of the first large-scale works in vernacular prose by a Scot was the Anglicised *History of the Reformation* by John Knox. Other original works of contemporary or slightly earlier date do little more than demonstrate what might have been: the outstanding example is the *Complaynt of Scotland* (Stewart 1979), attributed plausibly though not certainly to John Wedderburn, with its impassioned rhetoric and the florid aureation of its vocabulary. The wide circulation of theological and polemical prose works emanating from England in the Reformation period, when the practice of writing prose in Scots was barely established, in effect stifled the development of Scots as a vehicle for narrative or expository prose. It also forestalled the growth of a set of canonical rules for spelling and grammar in written Scots: as such a set emerged for English, with the codification by usage of the London-based Chancery standard, Scottish writers simply accommodated their language to the increasingly prescriptive canons of English. Whereas in poetry a fully established tradition was extinguished, that is, literary prose scarcely had a chance to develop at all.

Official prose, by contrast, had a secure position, and succumbed to Anglicisation much more slowly. The Acts of Parliament, the treasurers' accounts, the records of the burghs and latterly of the Kirk Sessions, form a substantial corpus of prose in Scots; and the language of its register was self-perpetuating, as notaries and official scribes were trained by the study of their predecessors' writings. The distinctive vocabulary of Scots law, which to some extent survives even today, remained unaffected by Anglicisation for the simple reason that exact equivalents in English were in many cases not to be found; and even at the turn of the seventeenth and eighteenth centuries, by which time the spelling and grammar of Scottish official documents had become pervasively Anglicised, free use was still made of traditional Scots legal terms. Those texts were not written with a wide reading public in mind; and though a slow, inconsistent but inexorable Anglicisation is visible throughout the seventeenth century, the contrast with the catastrophic decline of Scots in poetry is noteworthy.

Most importantly, there is no evidence that the *spoken* language of the mass of the populace was affected to any extent. The mother tongue of non-Gaelic Scotland was, and remained, Scots: English was becoming familiar as a written language, but there is no reason to believe that the ordinary citizens at the time of the Union of the Crowns were any less Scots in their speech than they had ever been. Some members of the ruling class had acquired a knowledge of English in anticipation of James' accession to the English throne (it should be borne in mind that his court contained men of high intellectual distinction and wide experience of European culture, already familiar with several languages, for whom the mastery of English would present little difficulty), but this was restricted to courtly circles (Bald 1927). There is also evidence, incidentally, that Elizabeth Tudor included Scots among the foreign languages in which she was fluent. With the departure of king and court, many Scots went south in search of advancement; and in the course of the seventeenth century (particularly after the Restoration) it became customary for members of the Scottish aristocracy to spend much of their time in London, many of them marrying English heiresses: this led to their adoption of English as an alternative spoken language. At home, however, and among the common people, Scots simply continued as the native tongue.

One major influence in, if not as yet undermining, at least restricting the status of spoken Scots was that of the Church. The common statement that English was the language of the prayers, preaching and Bible reading heard during regular worship must not be interpreted too narrowly. Of course the translation of the Bible used in the Scottish Kirk in the seventeenth century was the Authorised Version; but readings would be given (as still, naturally, today) in the ministers' native accents, and it is likely that the English spellings would where possible be interpreted with reference to Scots phonology. Sermons, which occupied a central place in Scottish Presbyterian worship, would no doubt vary according to the preference of individual ministers in the extent to which Scots vocabulary was used: published collections from the period, besides demonstrating some well-defined stylistic tendencies (such as a high degree of skill in imitating the rhetorical cadences of the Authorised Version, especially the Prophetic Books of the Old Testament, and a remarkable combination of biblical imagery with homely and unexalted metaphors and similes) suggest that some ministers were by no means averse to Scots words (see e.g. Rutherford 1885). The density of the Scots could vary with the tenor of the discourse: a minister might deliver a theological exposition in an Anglicised register and resume the full force of Scots to castigate the sins of the congregation. All being said, however, it remains clear that the enormous influence of the Authorised Version resulted in a de-Scotticising of the language of the Church; and confirmed the association, begun in the Reformation period, of English as opposed to Scots with services of worship and with the exposition and discussion of theological topics.

2.2.5   *Partial retrenchment of written and decline of spoken Scots:*
1700–1900

The eighteenth century in Scotland forms an extraordinary contrast to the seventeenth. By 1700, chronic feuding in Church and state, combined with a succession of bad harvests and the economic catastrophe of the Darien Scheme, had reduced the country to an impoverished wasteland; yet a remarkable regeneration which began in the 1720s not only improved the quality of life beyond recognition but gave rise to the outburst of intellectual activity in all fields which earned for Edinburgh the nickname 'the Athens of the north'. The status of Scots, as a spoken and a literary language, was profoundly affected by these developments.

The first sign of a literary recovery took the form of a renewed awareness of the great Scots poetry of the past. James Watson's *Choice Collection of Comic and Serious Scottish Poems* was published in three parts in 1706, 1709 and 1711 (Wood 1977), and was shortly followed by editions of Gavin Douglas' *Eneados* by Thomas Ruddiman in 1710 (which contained a glossary of Scots words) and Blind Harry's *Wallace* by William Hamilton in 1722, and by Allan Ramsay's *The Ever Green* in 1724, an anthology which included many poems of the Stewart period. Collections of songs and proverbs in Scots also became popular. The revival of interest in the Scots poetic tradition of the past quickly led to the production of new poetry, drawing for its inspiration not only on the art poetry of earlier periods but on the flourishing tradition of folk song and folk poetry which had never (despite the efforts of the Church) been eclipsed among the Scottish populace. One of the few memorable Scots poems of the mid-seventeenth century, Robert Sempill's mock-elegy *The Life and Death of Habbie Simpson, the Piper of Kilbarchan* (Wood 1977: 32ff.), became the fountain-head of a whole genre: comic or satiric poetry in broad vernacular Scots couched in the distinctive six-line stanza form. The most important figure in the poetic revival was Allan Ramsay, who confirmed the recovery of Scots as a poetic medium with his prolific and highly entertaining corpus of (principally) comic, satirical and pastoral poems in the language.

Ramsay's poetic practice, however, demonstrates the conflicting attitudes to Scots which had come to prevail by the early eighteenth century. In some cases, his energetic championship of the vernacular, taking the form of strongly worded arguments in its favour as well as his deliberately conspicuous use of it in his poetry, represents a reaction away from the steady Anglicisation of polite taste in Scotland, which had led to a growing disdain among the educated classes for Scots as a spoken tongue as well as its virtual disappearance in written form. Ramsay saw the Scots tongue as a symbol of, and a means of expressing, the Scottish national identity which was now under threat following the abolition of Scotland's parliament in 1707: his use of Scots in some poems has the same motivation as his expressions of praise for Edinburgh or for

Scottish scenes, and of confidence in the nation's future prosperity, in others. Conversely, he was unable altogether to escape the prevailing assumptions regarding the lower status of Scots as compared to standard literary English: in his work as editor he was responsible for Anglicising the language of some of the medieval poems in his anthologies, and – though this is certainly due rather to his individual poetic taste and talent than to any consciously held theory of linguistic propriety – the language of his serious poems is as a rule more Anglicised than that of his comic ones (McClure 1987).

It is something of a paradox that the outstanding literary and intellectual achievements of eighteenth-century Scotland should so clearly manifest an almost pathological confusion, which has never been resolved, in the matter of language, arising from a still deeper confusion regarding the national identity. While Ramsay was vigorously up-holding, by precept and example, the viability of Scots, other major literary figures – the philosopher David Hume is the outstanding example – were making determined efforts to purge their language totally of Scottish features. Motivated not only by the desire to make themselves understood when in England, but by a feeling that in the new 'British' era things recalling Scotland's unhappy past, including the Scots tongue, were better forgotten, many of the Enlightenment scholars elevated the almost negligent linguistic Anglicisation of the previous century to a guiding principle: a feature of Edinburgh's literary scene in this period was the popularity of debating societies founded to give members the opportunity to practise their English, and of lectures on elocution given by, among others, the Irish actor Thomas Sheridan. Conscientious explorations of the principles of literary taste led to strange aberrations, such as the preference among the literati for poetry by such now-forgotten figures as James Wilkie and Hugh Blacklock, in what reads like a parody of Augustan English, over the splendidly vivid and realistic Scots poems of Robert Fergusson (for a full discussion see Simpson 1988). The poetic efforts of Ramsay, and later of Fergusson, Burns and their many lesser contemporaries, were de-liberately and defiantly aimed at countering this Anglicisation of taste: in Burns' case at least, the Scots of his poetry was a sign not only of his cultural patriotism but of his notorious social radicalism and iconoclasm. The individual in whom the national confusion is most startlingly manifest is probably James Beattie, the professor of moral philosophy at Aberdeen University, who argued in print for the adoption of not only the grammar and vocabulary but even the accent of metropolitan

English, and yet wrote a poem in Scots expressing hearty admiration for the north-east dialect writings of Alexander Ross (Hewitt 1987).

This period in the history of Scottish letters is known as the Vernacular Revival, but the term is not entirely accurate. The implied contrast in the word *vernacular* is presumably with standard literary English, but the fact is that literature in either tongue represented a revival of artistic and intellectual activity in Scotland after the bleak seventeenth century. And it was in this period that Scots as a spoken language, far from undergoing any kind of revival, came to be subjected to unremitting social pressure. By the beginning of the eighteenth century, an ability to speak English, as well as to read and write it, was fairly widespread among all classes: Robert Burns' father, a north-east-born farmer of little formal education, was locally renowned for the excellence of his spoken English. It does not appear, however, that Scots speech was regarded with actual hostility: a stable bilingualism was probably the sociolinguistic norm. By the 1750s this had changed: Scots was being described as a language only fit for rustics and the urban mob, educated men expressed their dislike of it in unequivocal terms, and predictions of its imminent demise were regularly made – as they are still, incidentally. It is characteristic of the period that the poetry of Robert Burns, in which the full expressive resources of Scots – its picturesque vocabulary, its wealth of proverbial and aphoristic phrases, its aptitude for sharp witty epigrams and for powerful rhetoric – reach their greatest literary development, should have been hailed with enormous enthusiasm while the poet, in reality a man of considerable learning, found it necessary to adopt the wholly spurious pose of an untaught peasant in order to excuse his preference for writing in Scots.

Burns in his own lifetime remarked on a decline in the quality of Scots poetry; and for decades after his death no poet of remotely comparable stature wrote in the language. Unlike the seventeenth century there was no diminution in quantity of Scots poetry: only a woeful decline in quality. The literary development of the language continued in a different direction, however, in the fictional dialogue of the Waverley Novels. Walter Scott was not the first author to make Scottish characters speak in a literary rendition of their native vernacular, but he was the first to apply serious artistry to the technique; and also the first to emancipate it from the assumption that Scots speech from a fictional character automatically branded him as funny, disreputable or both (see McClure 1983b; Letley 1988). Yet even in Scott's work the declining social status of Scots is shown by the fact that in most cases (though not all) his Scots-speaking characters belong to the lower social orders – servants, peasants, vagrants – or represent a historic age which is passing or dead.

As the Enlightenment period had differed from the previous century in waging a much more conscious and determined campaign against Scots, the following century showed, at first, something of a relaxation of attitudes. Burns and Scott, the greatest among an imposing company of writers in the language, had given it a literary prestige which could hardly be challenged, and the scholar John Jamieson in 1808 published in Edinburgh, to wide acclaim, a monumental *Etymological Dictionary of the Scottish Language*, which enhanced its academic prestige. The assumption – a self-fulfilling prophecy – that Scots speech was a social and educational disadvantage was not overthrown, but a new phase in its cultural history was marked by a growing academic and antiquarian interest, fuelled to some extent by a realisation that traditional words and idioms were indeed beginning to disappear from the speech of the common people. Remarks on the erosion of Scots continued to be made through the nineteenth century; but whereas in the Enlightenment period the supersession of Scots by English was almost universally seen as desirable, the expressed attitude now changed to one of regret. Historical societies (such as the Woodrow and Spalding Clubs) began programmes of research into and publication of earlier Scots texts, increasing the respectability of the language as a field of study. The inveterate confusion of attitudes towards Scots began to take a different form: the Scots of earlier periods was held to be respectable in an academic sense, but the habit of speaking the language was not to be encouraged: the spoken Scots of contemporary life was somehow perceived as different from and less worthy than the written language (and presumably also the spoken language from which it was derived) of the past. In the schools, a promotion of English to a position of comparable importance to Latin as a teaching subject, and a new approach to the teaching of it by the use of formal grammars and pronunciation manuals, led to a widespread emphasis on instilling 'correct' English in pupils: the Scots tongue, which had hitherto been the normal medium for teachers and pupils alike (except for actual reading aloud of texts and reciting of memorised ones) came to be regarded as unsatisfactory. The abolition of parish schools and establishment of a uniform state system by governmental fiat in 1872 elevated this principle to a national policy; and though the decline of spoken Scots had been frequently remarked on before then, the

Education Act and its consequences certainly speeded up the process (Williamson 1982, 1983).

A scholarly work on Scots literature, published in 1898, ends with the following statement: 'His [Burns'] death was really the setting of the sun; the twilight deepened very quickly; and such twinkling lights as from time to time appear serve only to disclose the darkness of the all encompassing night' (Henderson 1898: 458). This was unaltered for revised editions in 1900 and 1910. The excellent Scots poetry of R. L. Stevenson, at least, might have been rated as more than a twinkling light; but the author could have been forgiven such defeatism at the dawn of the twentieth century. Certainly he could not have predicted that Scots, by now visibly declining as a spoken tongue as well as virtually exhausted, to all appearances, as a literary medium, would undergo a poetic revival more remarkable than that of the eighteenth century within a few years of his book; nor that this new literary activity would play a central part in an increasingly urgent debate on the desirability or otherwise of preserving Scots as a spoken tongue besides extending the range of uses of the written form. The sociolinguistic developments of the present century will be examined in a later section. (As some readers will have noted, the historical relations between Scots and English can be paralleled, to some extent, in other European speech communities. For a comparison of Scots with the analogous case of Low German, see Görlach (1985).)

2.2.6   *Spread of English in the Gaidhealtachd and the Northern Isles*

As the conflict between Scots and English proceeded in the Lowlands, a different and more brutal conflict gathered momentum in the Highlands. The progress of English speech in Scotland in the early Middle Ages had, as already noted, been at the expense of Gaelic; but one result of the identification of the monarchy and government with the language of the Lowlands had been to confirm and stabilise the separation of the kingdom into two well-defined parts, between which the language difference was only one sign of an almost total contrast in culture. References to the Highlands in Lowland literature of the later Stewart period show an unattractive mixture of contempt and fear, manifest at levels ranging from an anonymous doggerel squib entitled

> How the First Helandman off God was maid
> Of ane Horss Turd in Argyle, as is said

(see Hughes & Ramson 1982: 313–14)

through Dunbar's virtuoso taunts at his rival Kennedy's Gaelic speech (see Kinsley 1979: 80), to the historian John Major's scholarly examination of the differences between the 'wild' (Highland) and the 'domestic' (Lowland) Scots. (For discussion see Williamson (1979: ch. 5).) The relatively unchanging balance between the two sections of the kingdom was upset, however, by the Reformation, when the greater part of the Highlands (the most important exception being the powerful Clan Campbell in Argyll) remained faithful to the Catholic Church. This led to active intervention by the central government; and James VI, whose actions evince a peculiarly virulent distaste for his Highland subjects, in 1609 passed the Statutes of Iona, forcing the clan chiefs not only to establish Protestant churches among their people but to withdraw their patronage from the bards – highly trained hereditary guardians of traditional Gaelic culture – and to send their sons to Lowland schools. This was followed in 1616 by an Act establishing parish schools in the Highlands, with the avowed aim of extirpating the Gaelic tongue 'whilk is one of the cheif and principall causis of the continewance of barbaritie and incivilitie amangis the inhabitantis of the Ilis and Heylandis'. This anti-Gaelic policy on the part of the government and the established Church remained constant for the next two centuries and beyond; and though the process was far more gradual and more painful than had presumably been hoped at first, the effect was the steady undermining of Gaelic in Scotland. Governmental hostility to the Highlands was intensified by the increasingly active involvement of the clans in the political and military disturbances of the seventeenth and eighteenth centuries, most notably the Montrose Wars and the Jacobite uprisings of 1715 and 1745. With the vicious repression of the Highlands after the defeat of the Young Pretender's rebellion, efforts to destroy Gaelic culture reached a pitch which can be described in objective seriousness as genocidal.

The story of the decline of Gaelic is extremely complex, and the story of the advance of English in the Highlands is not, despite what might be assumed, related to it in any clear fashion (Withers 1984). Familiar in textbooks is a series of census-based maps plotting the changing proportion of Gaelic-speakers in the Highland counties, which shows the language over the last hundred years in a rapid retreat westwards: this, however, represents a misleading oversimplification, since the maps do not take account of changing demographic patterns (but see Withers 1984: 225–34), much less of the status of bilingual or diglossic speakers or of the sometimes extremely subtle sociolinguistic conventions governing the use of Gaelic. The distinction made in this essay between Scots and Scottish English, furthermore, is not customarily made either by the Gaels themselves or by commentators on the Gaelic language situation – understandably, since not only are the languages similar from a Gaelic perspective but there has been little to choose from between their speakers as regards historical attitudes to the Gaels and their culture – so that it is often quite impossible to determine whether what is referred to as 'English' (or in Gaelic *Beurla*), and stated to be replacing Gaelic in a given time and place, is literary English, vernacular Scots or both.

Nevertheless, it is fairly clear that an isolated pocket of Gaelic speech in the south-west survived until the late seventeenth century, thereafter giving place to Scots; and that the really catastrophic phase in the decline of the language began in the late nineteenth century and continued unchecked until the 1970s. Of late there has been evidence that the decline has 'bottomed out', and signs of a recovery, not only in the Isles but among exiled Gaels in the cities, have been detected (McKinnon 1990): indeed, a truly astonishing degree of energy, enthusiasm and optimism is currently visible among workers in the Gaelic field. Whether this will be sufficient to preserve the language in active life remains to be seen.

An ironic result of the progressive attrition of the Gaelic mode of life was the emergence of a colourful, stirring and highly romanticised impression of it in Lowland literature. This was widely diffused by the pseudo-Ossianic poems of James MacPherson, and developed to some extent by Walter Scott – though his portrayals of Highlanders are at least more credible than those in MacPherson's epics.

While the Gaelic of the Highlands was being forcibly suppressed, the final stages were taking place in a similar, if less heavy-handed, displacement of the native language in the Northern Isles. The Earldom of Orkney, which included Shetland, though a dependency of the Danish crown, was held by Scottish magnates from the later fourteenth century, resulting in the introduction of Scots alongside Norn as a language of administration. In 1467 the islands were pawned to James III of Scots by Christian I of Denmark as surety for the future payment of the dowry for the Scots king's bride, a Danish princess; and as this was never paid, the islands passed permanently under Scottish control. In Orkney and Shetland this event is regarded as a disaster in the history of the islands, initiating their decline from a virtually independent earldom to an appanage of a distant and unsympathetic monarchy which immediately attempted to replace their distinctive Norn language and culture by Scots; but although the Norn tongue thereafter lost ground and finally disappeared, in Orkney in the eighteenth century and in Shetland as late as the nineteenth, it left an indelible influence on the form taken by Scots in the islands. The dialects are permeated with Scandinavian-derived words; and the traditional independence of the islanders is manifest not only in their determined refusal to regard themselves as Scots, but in a confident pride in their Scandinavian linguistic and cultural heritage. In Orkney, and to an even greater extent in Shetland, the traditional dialects are vigorously maintained (the contrast with the apathy and defeatism often expressed towards Gaelic, at least by older speakers, in the Western Isles is striking), and local newspapers and periodicals, most notably the *New Shetlander*, support a flourishing dialect literature in both verse and prose. It is reported of Shetland (Melchers 1985) that the children of English-speaking, including ethnic English, incomers in the local schools rapidly adopt the dialect, with encouragement from their teachers as well as their compeers: a situation which must be unique in the British Isles.

2.3 History of the language

The periods in the history of Scots may be tabulated as follows (Robinson 1985):

Old English	to 1100
Older Scots	to 1700
Pre-literary Scots	to 1375
Early Scots	to 1450
Middle Scots	1450–1700
Early Middle Scots	1450–1550
Late Middle Scots	1550–1700
Modern Scots	1700 onwards

Scots shares with northern English a common ancestor in Northumbrian Old English. In the period between 1100 (the conventional date for the end of the Old English period) and 1375 (the date of the first considerable extant literary text in Scots) evidence regarding the nature of the language, though not negligible in quantity, is somewhat restricted in kind (Craigie 1924); thereafter, documentary evidence for the development of Scots is continuous to the present day.

2.3.1 Older Scots

The two manuscripts of Barbour's *Brus*, which though dating from ca 1489 preserve features of the language as it was at the time of the poem's composition, suggest that the phonology and grammar of Scots were still substantially the same as those of northern English; but the vocabulary was already becoming distinctive, and a set of characteristic spelling conventions make the language of Barbour *look* strikingly unlike that of, say, Richard Rolle. Whereas all dialects of England other than that of the metropolitan area show in the course of the fifteenth century a progressive assimilation towards London norms, the history of Older Scots until the end of the Early Middle Scots period is of steady independent development; both internally, with the emergence of a variety of styles and registers, and in the direction of increasing divergence from the southern English form. Evidence of geographical diversification – the formation of regional dialects – is sparse in the early period; but this too can to some extent be demonstrated. In the Late Middle Scots period, texts produced in Scotland show a rapidly increasing influence of southern English at all levels; and by the end of the period distinctively Scots linguistic features are extremely rare in written texts and virtually restricted to certain well-defined registers.

Phonology

The vowel system of Early Scots contained the following items:

Long vowels	/iː eː ɛː aː oː uː øː/
Short vowels	/i e a o u/
i-diphthongs	/ei ai oi ui/
u-diphthongs	/iu eu au ou/

The most important difference between this system and that of southern English is the presence of a front rounded vowel, the reflex of OE /oː/. The phonetic quality of this vowel may have been higher than the symbol ø suggests: the /y(ː)/ of French loanwords uniformly merged with it: but the fact that its various reflexes in the modern dialects (see pp. 66–8) are more commonly high-mid than high vowels is evidence that it was not fully high. The distribution of /aː/ and /oː/ was also notably different from that of the corresponding items in the southern system: /oː/ (phonetically probably low-mid rather than high-mid in Early Scots) in words of native origin was invariably the result of open-syllable lengthening of OE /o/ and never a reflex of OE /aː/, which did not undergo the characteristic southern rounding in Scots but survived with its distribution unaltered, but for augmentation from open-syllable lengthening of /a/, until the Great Vowel Shift.

A change occurring early in the attested history of Scots was the merger of /ei/ with /eː/. Words such as ⟨dey⟩ 'die', ⟨drey⟩ 'endure', ⟨ley⟩ 'tell lies', ⟨wey⟩ 'a small amount' thus came to rhyme with ⟨he⟩, ⟨tre⟩ 'tree', or (the material) 'wood', etc. The digraph spelling, however, was not only retained but generalised, so that words with original /ei/ and original /eː/ were frequently, though not invariably, written with ⟨ei⟩ or ⟨ey⟩. Rhyme evidence suggests that this change had become general by the end of the fourteenth century. By the same period, /eu/ had also merged with /iu/.

Shortly afterwards (in the first quarter of the fifteenth century) occurred a characteristic Scots change known as *l*-vocalisation: the development of /l/ following /a/, /o/ and (inconsistently) /u/ to /u/, causing words with /al, ol, ul/ to merge with those containing /au, ou, uː/. This change too had notable effects on the orthography. ⟨al⟩, ⟨cal⟩, ⟨fal⟩ (the favoured Early Scots spellings for the words written with ⟨ll⟩ in Present-Day English), ⟨gold⟩, ⟨folk⟩, ⟨colt⟩, etc., were now pronounced with the same diphthongs as ⟨aw⟩ 'to owe or own', ⟨grow⟩ etc.; and the result was a widespread use of the digraphs ⟨al, ol⟩ and ⟨au/aw, ou/ow⟩ as free variations, in words both with and without the historical /l/. The development of /ul/ to /uː/ was less regular (/puː/ and /pʌl/, /fuː/ and /fʌl/, are both found in Modern Scots as cognates of *pull* and *full*); but its effects are similarly observable in unetymological back-spellings such as ⟨ulk⟩ *ouk* (i.e. 'week') and ⟨puldir⟩ 'powder'. This change, incidentally, is the explanation for the not infrequent appearance on the Scottish toponymic map of names in which an orthographic ⟨l⟩ corresponds to nothing in the pronunciation – *Kirkcaldy, Culross, Tillicoultry* – giving natives the opportunity to correct the invariable mispronunciations of outsiders.

l-vocalisation was prevented by one factor: the presence of the cluster in the sequence /ald/. Here breaking of the vowel to /au/ occurred, but not loss of the /l/. This change was sometimes, but not always, reflected in the spelling, thus ⟨ald/auld⟩, ⟨bald/bauld⟩, ⟨cald/cauld⟩, etc. Intervocalically, too, /l/ was always preserved.

Prior to the Great Vowel Shift, that is, two elements, /eu/ and /ei/, had disappeared from the system; and the distribution of /au/, /ou/ and /uː/ had been considerably widened.

The Great Vowel Shift occurred north of the Tweed as in other regions of the island; but an important factor in the history of Scots is that the shift was only partial compared to what took place in southern dialects. Most strikingly, /uː/ remained unaffected. To this day one of the most widely known stereotypical features of Scots is the pronunciation represented by such spellings (etymologically misspellings, incidentally, and for that reason now avoided by serious writers) as *hoose*, *toon*, *doon*, etc. The Shift had the effect of raising /oː/ from [ɔː] to [oː], but this involved no systemic change. /øː/ was also unaffected: there are considerable differences among the reflexes of this vowel in the modern dialects (see pp. 66–8), but these are due to later changes. The front monophthongs were uniformly affected by the Great Vowel Shift; /iː eː ɛː aː/ became /əi iː eː ɛː/. In southern and south-eastern Scotland the raising of /aː/ was not, as in English dialects, prevented by a preceding labial continuant. As in southern dialects, the subsequent history of the front vowels shows developments not predictable from the Great Vowel Shift. The /aː/ of Early Scots, raised to /ɛː/, is never represented by a vowel of this quality in modern dialects but always by one in the high-mid range. /eː/ resulting from earlier /ɛː/ underwent a split, some words retaining the new high-mid vowel and others pursuing an upward course to become fully high. The latter group is much more sparsely represented in Scots than in southern English, however: *beast*, *heap*, *heal*, *meat*, for example, are now pronounced in Scots with an [e]-like rather than an [i]-like vowel.

/au/, whether original or resulting from *l*-vocalisation, was monophthongised to a low back vowel: in the first instance presumably [ɒː]-like, though modern dialects are divided into a group which retains a vowel of this quality and one in which it has an unrounded [a(ː)]-like reflex. The history of /ai/ is more complex. In word-final position it frequently remained diphthongal, instead of being monophthongised as in English. There are exceptions, however, in such words as *day*, *pay*, *pray*, *say*, where a monophthongisation did occur (in most modern dialects those words have /eː/, contrasting with *ay* (always), *clay*, *hay*, *May*, *Tay*, which have /ʌi/). This is explained by Kohler (1967) as resulting from a 'smoothing' of the diphthong before the syllabic ⟨is⟩ of inflectional endings: /paiɪz/ → /paːz/. This monophthongisation preceded the Great Vowel Shift: when non-final /ai/ was monophthongised by the latter change, the result (still visible in some, though not all, modern dialects) was a phonetically lower vowel than that resulting from the effect of the Shift on /aː/. Before /r/ a full merger of /ai/ and /aː/ occurred prior to the Great Vowel Shift. Other diphthongs remained unaffected by it, and their modern reflexes show phonetic rather than systemic changes from the medieval forms.

The partial merger of /ai/ and /aː/, like the complete merger of /ei/ and /eː/, contributed to the practice of using the digraph ⟨ai⟩ or ⟨ay⟩ to represent a long monophthong whether or not it had resulted from an original diphthong: the reflex of /aː/ and the monophthongal reflex of /ai/, that is, by the end of the early Middle Scots period were both regularly written ⟨ai/ay⟩ (with ⟨aCe⟩ as an alternative). Other factors contributed to this orthographic development, such as the existence of Scandinavian- and Old English-derived cognates of certain words (e.g. *hale* (OE *hal*) and *haill* (ON *heill*)), alternative spellings for French and Gaelic loanwords containing [ʎ] and [ɲ] (e.g. *balyhe–bailʒe, taylʒe–talye*), and the ambiguity of ⟨ai⟩ in Old French (see Kohler 1967; Kniesza 1986, 1990.) The use of ⟨i⟩ to indicate a long vowel even if not derived from a historical diphthong was extended to /øː/ and even /oː/, giving such characteristic Middle Scots spellings as *rois, throit, befoir, guid, muin, suir*; ⟨yi⟩ was also adopted, though less generally, as a spelling for the diphthong resulting from Early Scots /iː/.

An important development in the vowel system, which began somewhat prior to the Great Vowel Shift, reached its most characteristic phase shortly after it, and has apparently continued to some extent in the modern period, with results which vary in the different dialects, is the Scottish Vowel-Length Rule or Aitken's Law (for the most comprehensive exposition see Aitken 1981b). This series of changes may be characterised as a movement towards the obliteration of length as a phonologically relevant factor in the vowel system (see Lass 1974 for an argument relating it to earlier quantitative changes in the history of Germanic speech); and its essential feature may be summarised as follows: originally long vowels are generally shortened except in stressed open syllables and when preceding a voiced fricative or /r/; and originally short vowels show a tendency to lengthening in the same environments. In Modern Scots dialects, and in Scottish standard English, this results in a very different system of vowel-length variations from that which prevails in other forms of English: instead of a set of 'long' and a set of 'short' vowels, the members of each of which show a more or less continuous range of allophonic length variations, we find that most vowels have a set of long and a set of short allophones with a definite break between them.

Unlike the changes so far discussed, the effects of Aitken's Law are not attested to any extent in Middle Scots orthography, and it is accordingly difficult to establish its precise chronology. Its manifestations in the Modern Scots dialects and in Scottish English will be examined in later sections (see pp. 67–9 and 80–2). However, the universality of the effects of the change in the otherwise highly divergent phonological systems of the modern dialects suggests a relatively early date for its inception. A more specific piece of evidence for this is that in the dialects of Shetland, where /ð/ in all positions had merged with /d/ by the eighteenth century, words with final /d/ < /ð/ show lengthening of the vowel by Aitken's Law whereas words with final *original* /d/ do not: e.g. *need* [nidd̪] but *meed* 'landmark' [miːd̪] (Aitken 1981b: 141). That it was not completed before the Great Vowel Shift, conversely, is shown by the specific development of ESc. /iː/. In the environments where Aitken's Law would predict a long vowel, the modern reflex of this is a long open diphthong, phonetically [aˑe] or [ɑˑe]; elsewhere it is a shorter, closer diphthong varying with locality from [ʌi] to [ëi]. This suggests that the diphthongisation of /iː/ by the Great Vowel Shift had begun before the operation of Aitken's Law, but was arrested in words where the Law resulted in shortening and carried to completion only in those where the vowel remained long. The same short diphthong is the reflex of ESc. /ai/ in words where this has remained diphthongal; thus in Modern Scots dialects *May* [mʌi] does not rhyme with *cry* [kraˑe]; and also of ESc. /ui/, thus [dʒʌin], [pʌint] (*join, point*), [pʌizn̩] (*poison*) with a different diphthong from that of [raˑezn̩] (*rising*): this suggests that the two diphthongs must be regarded as representing distinct /ʌi/ and /ae/ phonemes.

Some less important changes affecting Scots in the Middle Scots period are the loss of /v/ in medial and final position, giving *deil* 'devil', *ein* 'even', *ser* 'serve'; and the simplification of certain consonant clusters: *ack* 'act', *colleck* 'collect', *sen* 'send', *han* 'hand'.

The following transcriptions are of texts dating from 1405, 1531 and 1599. They represent reconstructions of the pronunciation used in the Edinburgh and Lothian area, in an upper-class pronunciation and formal delivery appropriate to the status of the writers and content of the texts.

(1)   He Excellent and rycht mychty prynce likit to ȝour henes to wyte me
        haff resavit ȝour honorabile l[ette]ris to me send be a Rev[er]end Fadir
        þe abbot of Calkow contenand þat it is well knawin þat trewis war
        tane & sworn o late betwix þe rewmis of ingland & scotland & forþi
        yhu mervalis gretly þ[a]t my men be my wille & assent has byrnde þe

toun of berwicke & in oþ[i]r c[er]tayne places wythin þe rewme of inglande.

heː ɛksələnt ən rɪxt mɪxtiː prɪns liːkɪt tø juːr heːnɛs tø wiːt meː haf resaːvɪt juːr ɔnɔrabl̩ lɛtɪrz tø meː sɛnd be a rɛvərɛnd faːdɪr ðɪ abət əv kalkuː kɔnteːnən ðat ɪt ɪz weːl knawɪn ðat treuɪs war taːn ən swøːrɪn əv laːt betwɪks ðɪ reumɪs əv ɪŋgland ən skɔtland ən fɔrði juː mɛrvaʎɪs greːtli ðat miː mɛn be miː wɪl ən asɛnt haz bɪrnɪt ðɪ tuːn əv bɛrwɪk ən ɪn øːðɪr sɛrtaːn plaːsɪs wɪθɪn ðɪ reum əv ɪŋgland

(Part of a letter from James Douglas, Warden of the Marches, to Henry IV of England (*Facsimiles of National Manuscripts of Scotland* vol. II, no. LIV. HM General Register House, Edinburgh, 1870), p. 44)

(2)   Incontinent be sound of trumpett baith þe armyis ionytt in maist fury, and faucht lang with vncertane victory, quhill at last þai war severitt be þe nycht, and returnit to þair campis to fecht with þe licht of þe mone, eftir quhais rysing þe batellis ionytt *with* mair fury þan afoir. And quhen þe forbront of Scottis war slayn, þe Inglismen began to put þe Scottis abak; and but doute þai had wo*m*nyn þe ansenȝeis of þe Douglas and put his army to disconnfitoure, war no*ch*t Patrik Hepburn *with* his son and vther þair frendis had cu*m*in haistlye to his support, be quhais grete manhede þe batall was renewitt.

ɪnkɔntɪnɛnt bi suːn ə trumpɛt bɛːθ ðɪ armeiz dʒɔinɪt ɪn mɛːst føːri ən faːxt laŋ wɪθ unsɛrteːn vɪktori xweil ət last ðei war sɛvɪrɪt bi ðɪ nɪxt ən rɪtuːrnɪt tø ðeir kampɪs tø fɛxt wɪθ ðɪ lɪxt ə ðɪ møːn eftɪr xwaːz reiziŋ ðɪ bateilɪz dʒɔinɪt wɪθ mɛːr føːri ðan afoːr ən xwɛn ðɪ foːrbrunt ə skɔtɪz war slein ðɪ ɪŋɪlzmɛn bigan tø pɪt ðɪ skɔtɪz abak ən bɔt duːt ðei həd wunɪn ðɪ asɛŋiz ə ðɪ duglas ən pɪt hɪz armei tø dɪskumfɪtuːr war nɔxt patrɪk hɛburn wɪθ hɪz sun ən øðɪr ðeir friːnɪz had kumɪn heːstli tø hɪz supoːrt bi xwaːz greːt manhiːd ðɪ bateil waz riniuɪt

(From *The Chronicles of Scotland* by Hector Boece, tr. John Bellenden, 1531, vol. II, ed. C. Batho and H. W. Husbands, Scottish Text Society, Third Series 15, Edinburgh, 1941, p. 349)

(3)   … & after usurping the libertie of the tyme in my lang minoritie setled thame selfis sa fast upon that imagined democratie, as thaye fedd thame selfis uith that hoape to becume tribuni plebis, & sa in a populaire gouuernement be leading the people be the nose to beare the suey of all the reule, & for this cause thaire neuir raise faction in the tyme of my minoritie nor truble sensyne but thay uaire euer upon the urang ende of it.

… ən eftɪr øsørpɪn ðɪ lɪbɪrti ə ðɪ tɛim ɪn mɛi laŋ mɪnorɪti setl̩t ðɛmselz seː fast ɵpon ðat ɪmadʒɪnd dɛmokrəsi az ðɛː fɛd ðɛmsɛlz wɪθ ðat hop tø bikɵm trɪbøni plɛbɪs an sɛː ɪn ə popələːr gɵvɪrnmɛnt bi lidɪn ðɪ pɪpl bi ðɪ noːz tø bɛːr ðɪ swɛː ə ɒː ðɪ røl ən for ðɪs kɒːz ðɛr nɛvɪr rɛːz faksjun ɪn ðɪ tɛim ə mɛi mɪnorɪti nor trɵbl sɪnsɛin bɵt ðɛː war ɛːr ɵpon ðɪ vraŋ ɛn ə ɪt

(From *The Basilicon Doron of King James VI*, vol. I, ed. J. Craigie, Scottish Text Society, Third Series 16, Edinburgh, 1944, pp. 75–6)

Morphology and syntax

By comparison with the very considerable differences in phonology between Scots and southern English, the inflexional system of Older Scots is much less distinctive; though certain characteristics, notably in the verb system, serve to differentiate it from the English metropolitan form, and in some cases survive to the present day.

The most widespread class of nouns has *-is* as the ending for both plural and possessive, thus *housis*, *knichtis*, etc. The *-n* plural of the Old English weak declension survives in *ene* 'eyes', *schuin* 'shoes'; *childir* (with variant spellings) is found alongside *childrin*, *childerene* and similar forms, and another word which characteristically retains an *-r* plural is *cair* /kaːr/ 'calves'; a few mutation plurals, additional to those which survive in all forms of English, are found, such as *kye* 'cows' (also *kyne*), *bredir* or *brethir* 'brothers'.

A characteristic of Middle Scots, at least in certain registers (official and legal documents, such as Acts of Parliament, accounts of legal proceedings and burgh records) is the use of a plural ending for certain adjectives: *utheris*, *principallis*, *the saidis*, *thir presentis*. It is uncertain to what extent, if at all, this occurred in common speech: there is no trace of it in the modern spoken dialects.

The personal pronouns scarcely differ in form or usage from southern English of the late Middle English period except that the third person singular feminine is regularly written *scho*, objective and possessive *hir*. In the neuter, a distinction is sometimes, though not consistently, made between a nominative/objective form *hit* and a possessive *it*; though the possessive, in written texts at least, is more commonly expressed by *thairof* or *of the samin*. Demonstratives show an invariable tripartite distinction between *this*, pl. *thir*, *that*, pl. *thai*, and *yon*, unmarked for number: the assimilated form *thon*, familiar in modern dialects, is not attested in Older Scots. *This* and *that* may be used in the plural, as in present-day north-eastern dialect speech.

Of much greater interest is the system of verb inflexions. At no time have the endings *-st* (2 sg.), *-th* (3 sg.) and *-n* (pl.) been characteristic of Scots (though they were optional in written Middle Scots for the most formal styles of poetry). The personal endings of the present tense were as follows: 1 sg. ø or -*e*, 2 sg. -*is*, 3 sg. -*is*, pl. ø or -*e*, or *is*. The -*is* ending in the plural is so common in Older Scots that the paradigm could virtually be characterised as a uniform use of -*is* except in the first person singular. Infinitives end in ø or -*e*, not in -*n*. The present participle in -*and* is distinguished from the verbal noun in -*ing*. The past tense and past participle ending of weak verbs is -*it*; the prefix *y*- is very rarely used in Older Scots and only in certain stylistic registers.

A feature of the Older Scots verbal morphology is that the universal English tendency to loss of distinctiveness in the strong verb system, both by reducing the number of different forms in individual verbs and allowing formerly strong verbs to adopt weak inflexions, began earlier and proceeded both more rapidly and more systematically than in southern English. Even by the late fourteenth century the past-tense plural of strong verbs was distinguished from the singular neither by an -*n* ending nor by a change of stem vowel: a form derived from the Old English singular was used without distinction of person or number. Strong verbs of Old English classes 2 and 3b uniformly become weak: *chesit*, *lesit* (or later, as an alternative, *losit*), *helpit*, *warpit*. Striking evidence of an early date for at least incipient operation of Aitken's Law is provided by the fact that vowel quantities in the past-tense forms are not always predictable from their Old English originals but rather from the lengthening or shortening processes predicted by the Law: thus *fell* and *held* (long in Old English and southern Middle English), *bair* and *gave* (short in Old English and southern Middle English). (For full discussion see Gburek 1986.)

The relative-pronoun system of Older Scots shows some individual features. The commonest relative in the Early Scots period is *that* or an apocopated form *at* (possibly influenced by the Norse borrowing *at* of northern Middle English: Caldwell (1974: 31), whom see further for extended discussion of the material presented in this section). *That/at* is found with personal, non-personal and indefinite subjects, in restrictive and non-restrictive clauses, as subject and as direct object of the relative clause. Governing prepositions, when they occur, are usually placed after the verb: the exceptions are restricted to verse and are constructions of the form *thir war paganes that I of tald*. The commonest method of indicating a possessive is to associate *that/at* with a possessive pronoun: *mony vtheris that I knaw nocht thair names*. An alternative is (*the*) *quhilk*, a form which to some extent competes with *that/at* throughout the Older Scots period. It appears – at first always with the article – in prose (very seldom in verse) in the earliest Scots texts, but is rare until the mid-fifteenth century, and even after that point is much more common in prose than in poetry. A regularly occurring plural (*the*) *quhilkis* is a feature seemingly peculiar to Scots. As with the inflected adjectives already mentioned, this was probably never part of the spoken language; and indeed, (*the*) *quhilk* itself was apparently a written rather than a spoken feature: Romaine (1981a) provides evidence that in written texts (her examples are from the sixteenth century) suggestive of a colloquial style all wh-relatives are extremely rare compared to *that/at*.

A form which established itself much later as a relative in Scots is *quha*. Though in regular use as an interrogative and an indefinite pronoun (meaning 'whoever' or 'anyone who') from the beginning of the Early Scots period, its strictly relative use is not attested until the sixteenth century. *Quham* (also *quhom* and other variant spellings) occurs as a relative earlier and more frequently than the nominative form, and more commonly after a preposition than as a direct object: a fact prompting the speculation that this personal relative was introduced specifically to provide for the most complex of relative constructions, and gradually extended its use into simpler functions where the use of *that/at* and (*the*) *quhilk* was already established (Romaine 1980a). This conclusion is supported by the fact that it is in stylistically elaborate texts – legal prose as compared to narrative prose, for example – that the *quha* forms first appear with any degree of frequency. The possessive *quhais/quhois* is rare before the sixteenth century except in legal documents, where it is often preceded by a preposition: again the implication is that this usage was at first reserved for a specific register of the written language and gradually diffused into other registers. The first regular use of *quha* is in a formula used as a valediction in letters: *god, quha haue ʒou in his keping.* This is true of all forms of English, but the practice is attested later in Scotland than in England.

The commonest forms of the auxiliary verbs in Older Scots are as follows (for full lists of variants see the *DOST*):

> *Be*; *am*, *is* (in second and third persons singular: *art* is a rare Anglicism), *ar/is* (pl.); often *beis* in subordinate clauses; *wes/was, war/wer*; *beand, being, bene*.
> *Haif/haue* (infin. and 1 sg.), *hais* (2 and 3 sg. and pl.); *had/haid* (p.t. and p.p.); *hav(e)and, hav(e)ing*.
> *Do*; *dois*; *did*; *doand, doing*; *done/doin*.
> *Can*; *cuth/culd*.
> *Sal*; *suld*.

Wil; *wald*.
May; *micht*/*might*/(rarely) *mith*; *mocht*/*moght*, *moucht*/*mought*.
Man/*mon*.
Mot; *most*.

Usages differ little from those of northern Middle English or in many cases English in general; but certain distinctively Scottish practices are observable. *Do* as a tense marker with the infinitive, in a usage virtually restricted to late fifteenth- and sixteenth-century poetry, can be used not only in the present and past tenses but in the present participle (*doing all sable fro the hevynnis chace*) and even in periphrastic constructions (*he has done petously devour…, that will nocht do the word of God embrace*). Older Scots shares with northern Middle English the use of *gan*, an apocopated form of *began* but weakened in sense, as a past-tense marker and the conflation with this of the form *can*: more peculiarly Scots is the erroneous adoption of the past-tense *cuth* for the same purpose (*the tane couth to the tother complene*). This use of *gan*/*can*/*cuth* is principally a feature of narrative poetry, and it is observable that *cuth* increases in frequency until the mid-fifteenth century, by then being preferred to some extent over *gan*/*can*, but that both forms thereafter are fairly rapidly displaced by *did*. *Most* is rare and before the mid-sixteenth century restricted to poetry: the sense of necessity or obligation is expressed in Scots by *man*/*mon*. The most frequent use of *mot* is to express a wish or request (*thair sawlis till Paradys mot pas*): it is also used, though rarely, to imply necessity. The past-tense forms of *may* are not entirely interchangeable: when the main verb is elided and understood from a preceding clause, *mocht* is decidedly more frequent than *micht*.

Lexis

The core vocabulary of Scots at all periods in its history is, naturally, Germanic; though the actual selection of Old English-derived words in Scots includes several which were superseded in the southern dialects. The pattern of foreign borrowings in the medieval period is also broadly similar (except for the presence of a small but pervasive Gaelic element) but different in detail from that shown by metropolitan English: in particular, French influence, partly because of the long-lasting Franco-Scottish political and military alliance, remained active for rather longer in Scots than in English; and the imaginative use of Latin derivations in certain registers gave Middle Scots literature much of its individual character.

Barbour's *Brus*, with a total word-count of 3,506 (Bitterling 1970), shows a fair number of words almost or completely unique to Scots: considering only words of Old English origin we find, for example *anerly* 'alone', *berynes* 'grave', *clenge* 'cleanse', *halfindall* 'a half part', *heirschip* 'predatory raid', *scathful* 'harmful', *sturting* 'contention', *thyrllage* 'bondage', *umbeset* 'surround'. A more individual feature of Barbour's language, necessitated by his subject matter, is an abundance of French-derived terms relating to weapons and warfare: *assaile, baner, fortras, harnes; arsoun* 'saddle-bow', *assenye* 'war-cry', *eschell* 'battalion', *bassynet* 'helmet', *hawbrek* 'coat of mail', *qwyrbolle* 'hardened leather', *tropell* 'troop', *vaward* 'vanguard', *vyre* 'crossbow bolt'. French also gave numerous less specialised words to the Older Scots vocabulary, most of which survive to the modern period: *cummer* 'godmother, or a female gossip', *disjune* 'breakfast', *dour* 'stern, resolute, grim', *fasch* 'annoy', *grosser*, later *grosset* 'gooseberry', *ladroun* 'rascal', *moyen* 'means', *murdris* 'murder', *plenissing*, later *plenishing* 'furniture', *vevaris* 'provisions'. A few words never fully naturalised in Middle English, such as *esperance* and *verite*, appear to have attained far wider currency in Scots. Despite the abundance of French words established in the basic vocabulary, the proportion of Gallicisms increases somewhat in elevated literary styles: Dunbar has the distinctively Scots forms *fassoun* 'fashion', *gamaldis* 'gambols', *jevellour* 'jailor' and the unique word *lucerne* 'lantern'; Gavin Douglas is the first writer of any form of English to adopt *minion*. An extreme degree of Gallicisation is shown in *The Complaynt of Scotland* (see Murray 1872b: civ–cvi), which introduces to the English word-stock *amplitude* and *machine*, and contains such rare or unique forms as *afflige* 'afflict', *dedie* 'dedicate', *gazophile* 'treasury', *pasvolan* 'a type of small cannon', *rammasche* 'fierce, wild', *salutiffere* 'healthful' and *temerare* 'rash'.

In the language as spoken by the ordinary populace, the most important foreign influences were not French but the Netherlandic dialects and Scandinavian: the latter coming principally from the Anglo-Danish dialects of northern England, the former being brought in the first instance by Flemish settlers and augmented over many centuries by a long and close trading relationship between Scotland and the Low Countries. The Scandinavian influence is responsible for some characteristic features of Scots (and northern English) phonology, attested from early times: well known are the absence of the southern palatalisation in such words as *kirk, birk, kist, breeks, meikle, rig, brig*, and the retention of Germanic *au* in *loup* 'jump', *coup* 'buy and sell' and *nowt* 'cattle': cf. *leap*, *cheap* and archaic *neat*. It also gives the demonstrative *thae* (those), the prepositions *fra* 'from' and *til* 'to', the relative *at*, and the auxiliary verbs *man/mon* later spelt *maun* 'must' and *gar* 'make, cause'. Contributions to the vocabulary include *big* 'build', *bak*, later often *baukie* 'bat', *bla*, later *blae* 'blue in colour or livid', *bra*, later *brae* 'hill', *ithand*, later *eident* 'industrious', *ferlie* 'marvel (n. and vb)', *flit* 'remove', *gowk* 'cuckoo', *harns* 'brains', *lowe* 'flame', *lug* 'ear', *neive* 'fist', *sark* 'shirt', *spae* 'prophesy', *tinsell* 'loss', *wicht* 'valiant', *will* 'lost, confused'. Dutch gives to Scots a large number of words indicative of the practical, homely nature of the relationship between the countries: a selection, some attested in Scots from as early as the fourteenth century, is *bonspeil* (a sporting contest, in recent usage specifically a curling match), *bucht* (originally a sheep pen, later also a boxed-in pew, now the back seat of a car), *cavie* 'hen-coop', *crame* 'a stall or booth', *fleerish* (shaped piece of steel for striking flint), *forehammer* 'sledge-hammer', *forpack* 'repack', *grotken* 'a gross', *howff* 'public house', *kesart* 'cheese vat', *kit* 'small tub', *kylie* 'game of ninepins', *lunt* 'match', *mutch* 'a woman's hood or cap', *mutchkin* (a measure of capacity, often specifically for spirits), *plack*, *steke* and *doit* (various coins of little value), *scaff* 'scrounge' (hence the modern *scaffie*, street sweeper), *skaillie* 'slate pencil', *wapenschaw* (practice muster of local militia, now used in some localities for a rifle-shooting match), *wissel* 'exchange of money' (Murison 1971).

The influence of the other language of the kingdom is not easy to ascertain. A considerable number of Gaelic-derived topographical terms have been established in Scots from its earliest recorded period: some survive to the present as common nouns, others only as place-name elements. Examples are *ben* 'mountain', *bog*, *cairn* (pile of stones set up as a landmark), *corrie* 'hollow in a mountainside', *craig* 'rock', *drum* 'ridge', *glen*, *inch* (small island, or stretch of low-lying land beside a river), *knock* 'hill', *loch*, *mounth* (area of high ground) and *strath* 'river valley'. Early legal documents in Scots, and still earlier ones in Latin, provide evidence that some Gaelic terms relating to the Celtic legal system had been at least temporarily adopted into the language of Scots-speaking scribes (Bannerman 1990): *kenkynolle* (*cenn cineoil* 'head of the kindred'), *clan* (*clann*), *toschachdor* and *toschachdorschip* (terms derived from *toiseach*, a royal official), *duniwassal* (*duin-uasal*, a nobleman), *couthal* (*comhdhail*, a court of justice), *cane* (*cain*, tribute paid in kind), *mair* (*maer*, collector of taxes), *breive* (*brithem*, a judge), *davach* (*dabhach*, literally a tub but used in both languages to refer to a measure of land). Of a puzzling trio of terms in an early thirteenth-century Act of Parliament, *Le cro et le galnys et le enach unius cuiusque hominis sunt pares* – all appear to be fines or compensation for injury or death inflicted on a man – the first and last are Gaelic and the second Brythonic. Apart from those special groups, however, and a relatively few terms reflecting Gaelic cultural influence on Lowland Scotland such as *bard* (poet) and *clarschach* (harp), the number of Gaelic borrowings in the early history of the language appears to have been relatively small: Barbour's only Gaelic-derived word other than topographical terms is *lauchtane* 'homespun cloth'. However, a small but definite number of common words, some appearing in early texts, are of Gaelic origin: examples are *bladdoch* 'buttermilk', *brat* (a rag, or a garment – in Modern Scots, often an apron), *brock* 'badger', *caur* 'left', *clachan* 'village' (or later 'alehouse') *cranreuch* 'frost', *fail* 'turf', *ingle* 'hearth', *kelpie* 'a water sprite', *messan* 'small dog or cur', *quaich* 'a wooden drinking bowl', and *tocher* 'dowry'. Much later, in the eighteenth and nineteenth centuries, many Gaelic words referring to items of Highland culture appeared in Lowland speech: some examples will be given later (p. 87). But despite the paucity of early borrowings, a subtle, but pervasive, Gaelic presence in Scots of recent times, witnessed by a surprising number of words which crop up unobtrusively in unexpected literary contexts, suggests that the influence of Gaelic on everyday Scots speech may have been more extensive than the literary records suggest (McClure 1986).

Learned Latinisms of vocabulary abound in religious and courtly poetry: some examples are *arbitrement, benignite, celsitude, delectatioun, dissimulance, infelicitie, mellefluate, similitude, transformate, venerabill.* Dunbar in a single poem, 'Ane ballat of Our Ladye', uses a dozen Latinate words with no earlier recorded attestation, of which some (e.g. *hodiern, regyne, genetryce, salvatrice, palestrall*) are apparently unique to this poem (Ellenberger 1977).

As elegant Latinisms and Gallicisms adorned the most learned register of Scots and practical loans augmented its utilitarian vocabulary, the native word-stock at its most forceful was allowed to emerge in a definite literary context: poets showed fully as much linguistic virtuosity in satire and flytings (poetic insult competitions), and in passages of vulgar slapstick, as in more refined styles; and the most earthy and even obscene reaches of vernacular Scots were deployed as ammunition. The most outstanding example is Dunbar's flyting with Walter Kennedy, in which the names these two great poets call each other include *brybour* 'beggar', *crawdoun* 'coward', *dowbart* 'dullard', *fowmart* 'polecat', *larbour* 'impotent', *mymmerkin* 'dwarf', *nagus* 'miser', *skamelar* 'sponger', *walidrag* 'sloven', *yadswivar* 'bestial sodomite' and *luschbald*, *carrybald*, *heiggirbald* and *chittirlilling*, for which no definition has even been guessed.

Dialect variation

Systematic investigation of regional variants in Middle Scots is as yet incomplete: on the ongoing Middle Scots Dialect Atlas project see McIntosh 1978. However, it is clear that the Scottish form of English, having attained to the status of an official national language, was by the Early Middle Scots period at any rate as close as metropolitan English to developing a standard written form (Agutter 1988a); and though Middle Scots texts show extreme linguistic diversity among contrasting literary styles and registers (see Aitken 1983 for the most comprehensive account) and considerable individual variations in orthographic practices (Aitken 1971), scribal evidence for regional dialect variations is much less than might have been expected. Some certain instances are found, however; local texts, such as burgh records, occasionally show spellings suggesting a regional pronunciation; and the works of major literary figures whose place of birth or domicile is known (e.g. Richard Holland (Orkney), David Lyndsay (Fife), John Knox (West Lothian)) sometimes provide lexical or rhyme evidence of local usages. The north-eastern replacement of /xw/ ⟨quh⟩, corresponding to English ⟨wh⟩, by /f/, still one of the best-known shibboleths of the dialect, is first attested in 1539 by a spelling ⟨for⟩, instead of the same scribe's normal use of the standard ⟨quhar⟩, for *where*. Sporadically in sixteenth-century Aberdeenshire texts, spellings such as ⟨neyn⟩ /nin/ *none*; ⟨reif⟩ /rif/ *roof*, ⟨sein⟩ /sin/ *soon*; ⟨quyne⟩ /kwəin/ *quean*, show, respectively, the raising of the post-GVS reflex of /aː/ to /i/ before /n/, /i(ː)/ as a reflex of earlier /øː/, and the diphthongisation in certain specific words of post-GVS /i(ː)/ to /əi/ (Aitken 1971: 195; and see further Macafee 1990). A Wigtown scribe in the early sixteenth century consistently writes ⟨t⟩ instead of ⟨th⟩: ⟨towsand, tyrd, tryis⟩: suggesting the dialect feature referred to in a 1684 document of replacing /θ/ by /t/. Besides phonological features, lexical items with regionally restricted distribution are found: examples are *cloggand* 'pasture-land', *hafe-wrack* 'wreckage washed ashore', from the Northern Isles; *daker* 'ransack a house for stolen goods' and *leit* 'a stack of peats' from the north-east; *clat* 'scrape clean' and *lime-craig* 'limestone quarry' from the south-west.

The disappearance of written Middle Scots

The Late Middle Scots period is characterised by progressive assimilation of the written language to southern English norms (MacQueen 1957; Devitt 1989). The dates of the following illustrative extracts from the records of the Burgh of Stirling (Renwick 1887–9) are 21 September 1629, 19 June 1665, 19 July 1708 and 18 April 1743. As will be easily recognised, the language of the first is almost wholly Scots. The only exceptions are the following: English *-es* has replaced Scots *-is* in noun and verb endings, the present participle in *-ing* is an Anglicism in grammar, and *demoleische* (as contrasted with *demoliss*) might be regarded as one in phonology, though the ⟨sch⟩ spelling is Scots. *Foirstair* is an external stair on the front of a house, *umquhile* is 'the late', *foirland* is a tenement facing the street, the *Procurator Fiscal* is the public prosecutor, the *Dene of Gild* is the head of the merchant company of a burgh. The second extract shows almost a balance of Scots and English features (where the national forms differ): we see *quhair, thairon, thairannent, twa shilling* (though it could have been *schilling*), *utheris burghs, payes* (but not *payis*) with a plural subject; on the other hand, we also see *getting, goe, who, such* (instead of *sic*), and *bridge* (instead of *brig*). *Nominat* is shortly followed by *commisionated*. Forty years later, Scots forms appear to be greatly diminished. The spelling *conveiner*, the pronunciations suggested by *doune* and *standart*, the indefinite article *ane*, the idioms *conform to* and *cause make*, and the words *tuck* 'sound of drum' and *furth* 'beyond', impart only a slight Scots flavour to a language which on the whole looks very like English. Yet even by the mid-century, Scots forms have not gone entirely: *the saids, toun, haill, bailliary* (district under the jurisdiction of a baillie), *dispone* 'assign by law', *ay, fials* 'payment for services', *the samen*.

1   Findis that Alexander Cunynghame, merchand, hes contravenit the acttis and ordinances of this burgh and gildrie thairof, in bigging and building with timber under the foirstair of umquhile James Stevinsones foirland foiranent the mercat croce of this burgh, quhairof baith the procurator fischall and his nychtbouris hes complenit to the dene of gild and his bretherine and to the counsall ... Ordanes the said Alexander Cunynghame to demoleische and take doun his said timber wark and mak all again in als guid estait as it wes of befoir within xlviij houris eftir this present hour, under the pane of xl li.

2   Duncan Nairn, provest, and utheris nominat to advyse the best way for getting intelligence weeklie of publict newes, made report that

they had commisionated James Norie, clerke, to goe to Edinburgh and doe the same, who has settled with Robert Mean, postmaster, thairannent, for twa shilling sterling weeklie, as Glasgow and utheris burghs payes, and this weeke beginns the same; which was approvin.

The councill nominatis the provest and dean of gild to meet with such of the justices of peace of this shire and magistratis of the burgh of Glasgow as are appoynted to be at Carron foord to visite the place quhair a new bridge is to be built upon the said water in stead of the last new bridge built thairon, now demolished with the impetuousnes of the water, and to confer with them thairanent.

3   The councill appoints intimation to be made by tuck of drum, in obedience to ane act of the general convention of burrows of 15th current, that noe weights nor measures are to be used within this burgh furth and after the first of November next, except such as shall be conforme to the standarts latelie sent doune from Engleand.

The small seall belonging to the burgh of Sterling delivered at the council table to John Archbald, conveiner, in ordor to the causeing of workmen make ane litle stamp conforme theirto for marking of the setts of the severall liquid measurs conforme to the standarts sent here from Engleand.

4   Thereafter the saids magistrats and toun council having proceeded to chuse a clerk for this burgh in room and in place of the said deceast David Nicoll, they did unanimously nominate and elect, and hereby do nominate and elect, Thomas Christie, commissar clerk of Stirling, to be clerk of this burgh and haill bounds and territories thereof, and to the bailliary of the water of Forth, sherriffship, royalty, and other jurisdictions, courts and proviledges whatsoever, any ways pertaining and belonging thereto, and that till Michaelmas next to come; and the saids magistrats and councill hereby give, grant, and dispone to the said Thomas Christie ay and till the said time the said places and offices, profites, fials, emoluments, and casualities of the samen, to be uplifted, used, and disponed upon by him.

2.3.2   Modern Scots

Whereas in the Older Scots period, until its last stage, the Scottish form of English shows the characteristics of an autonomous language, an essential factor affecting the development of Scots in the modern period is the absence of any officially recognised standard or sociolinguistic norm – that place being held by Scottish standard English. This has led to extensive diversification of the spoken dialects; and on the written level, to a sporadic and unbalanced literary development, and to a variability and inconsistency in its written representation reflecting not only the presence of different dialects but the lack of any agreed spelling conventions even for any individual dialect. None the less, an essential unity still exists among the Scots dialects; and the deliberate promotion and development of Scots as a literary vehicle has certainly contributed, along with local and national pride, to their preservation in much greater strength than, say, the non-standard dialects of England.

Phonology

It is in their sound systems that the dialects of Modern Scots are most highly diversified; but since all systems are derived from that of Early and Middle Scots already discussed, it is possible to trace the historical development of each dialect's phonology and to devise a descriptive pattern relating the variation forms to a single general system.

COMMON FEATURES

In the most general terms, the reflexes of the Older Scots vowel phonemes are as shown in the following chart (based on Aitken 1977: 3, but with omission of some details and a slightly different choice of symbols). Symbols are phonemic throughout: the presence of a larger number, implying a narrower range of phonetic implication for each, in the Modern Scots section, is explained by the fact that after the operation of Aitken's Law quantity largely ceased to operate as a distinguishing factor in Scots phonology, necessitating a symbol inventory which indicates all relevant quality distinctions. Commas separate alternative reflexes with regional distribution; 'and' implies that both reflexes are present under different phonologically or lexically conditioned circumstances in a given dialect. Length distinctions due to Aitken's Law are not indicated unless a quality distinction is also present.

	Early Scots	Middle Scots	Modern Scots
Long vowels	iː	əi	ʌi and aˑe
	eː	iː	i
	ɛː	eː and iː	e and i
	aː	eː	e
	oː	oː	o
	uː	uː	u
	øː	øː	ɪ and eː, (w)i, e, ø
Short vowels	i	i	ɪ
	e	e	ɛ

	a	a	a
	o	o	o
	u	u	ʌ
i-diphthongs	ei	iː	i
	ai	ai and ɛː	ʌi and e
	oi	oi	oi
	ui	ui	ʌi
u-diphthongs	iu	iu	ju
	eu	iu	ju
	au	ɔː	ɑ, ɔ, o
	ou	ou	ʌu

Except for the regionally distributed reflexes of OSc. /øː/, none of which can be said to be typical of Scots as a whole, the system thus developed can be seen as that with reference to which the numerous dialect variations can be described. Certain combinative changes affecting individual vowels, however, are sufficiently widespread to be characteristic of Scots in general rather than of any individual dialect. OE /oː/ when followed by a velar fricative was not fronted but raised and shortened, and developed a palatal on-glide. Middle Scots spellings such as ⟨beuch, eneuch, leuch (OE *hlōh*, p.t. of *hlāhian*), pleuch⟩ suggest /bjux/ etc., and the commonest modern reflexes are /ux/ (east and north-east), /ʌx/ (west and south-west). /l/ in a cluster preceding original /oːx/ was later elided: *plough* is in some regional dialects /pjʌx/, and a common word in modern vernacular speech is *sheuch* /ʃʌx/ 'a gutter' (cognate with English *slough*). A following velar plosive had the same effect on original /oː/, but less consistently: in Middle Scots ⟨buik⟩ and ⟨beuk⟩, ⟨huik⟩ and ⟨heuk⟩, ⟨luik⟩ and ⟨leuk⟩, suggesting /bøːk/ /bjuk/ etc., are all found, and the modern reflexes /bjuk, ljuk/ are largely restricted to the north-east (though /hjʌk/ was the author's familiar name in his Ayrshire boyhood for a tool with a convex blade used for edging a lawn).

The short vowels of Older Scots have all undergone changes in the modern period. Original /e/ before /r/ has not been lowered, as in English, but raised or left unchanged: /hert/, /sterv/, /ʃerp/, /ferm/, /herst/ (harvest); also /hɛrt/ etc. /a/ shows an important combinative change: before /s/, /ʃ/ and sometimes other voiceless fricatives its modern reflex is /ɛ/: /glɛs/, /grɛs/, /ɛʃ/ (tree), /ɛftɪr/, /pɛθ/. Unpredictably *apple* is /epl/. A preceding /w/ has not had a rounding effect on /a/: /watɪr/, /waʃ/, /warm/, /wasp/. /o/ – phonetically [o] rather than [ɔ] in most forms of Scots – has given /a/ when in contact with a labial consonant: /tap/, /drap/, /rab/ (the familiar Scots form of the name *Robert*), /af/, /saft/. This change is occasionally seen in other phonetic contexts too: /saŋ/ 'song', /tam/ (Scots form of *Tom*). /u/ in all Scots dialects, as in southern (but not northern) English, is lowered to /ʌ/: a Scots characteristic, however, is that this vowel, especially when preceding or following a nasal, is often fronted to /ɪ/: /sɪmɪr/, /hɪne/ 'honey', /nɪt/, /wɪnɪr/ 'wonder'. /i/ gives a vowel characteristically somewhat lower and more central than the corresponding vowel in English, and when preceded by a /w/ or /ʍ/ (the modern reflex, except in north-east dialects, of OSc. /xw/) it becomes /ʌ/: /wʌl/, /wʌt/, /wʌtʃ/, /ʍʌn/, /ʍʌp/. For some reason, this change appears to be one of the more socially stigmatised features of Scots; and though the others have accepted representations in Scots writing — ⟨stairve, fairm, gress, efter, watter, tap, aff, simmer, hinney⟩ etc. — spellings such as ⟨wull, whup⟩ are rarer and often used for a definite literary effect.

Of the general features which distinguish the Scots consonant system the most important is the retention of /x/: /brɪxt/ 'bright', /rox/ 'rough', /doxtɪr/ 'daughter', etc. Other consonant features which endured until well into the modern period, but are now virtually obsolete except in peripheral dialects or in a few specific words, are the retention of the initial clusters /kn/, /gn/ and /wr/. It has been observed that in the dialects spoken from Aberdeenshire southwards to the River Tay, original /kn/ is heard as, successively, [kn], [tn], [n̥n] and [n]. /wr/ has given /vr/ in north-eastern dialects, a pronunciation still heard from elderly speakers.

The loss of a plosive following its homorganic nasal is not selective, as in English, but general: /lan/ 'land', /sun/ 'sound', /nʌmɪr/ 'number', /kanl/ 'candle', /fɪŋɪr/ 'finger'. The antiquity of this development is demonstrated by the absence of lengthening in words where such a cluster has caused it in English: /fɪn/ 'find', /blɪn/ 'blind', /fʌn/ 'found', /grʌn/ 'ground'. Where in English a nasal–plosive cluster has developed inorganically or been preserved for phonotactic reasons, no such tendency is observable in Scots: /braml/ 'bramble', /θʌnɪr/ 'thunder', /laŋɪr/ 'longer'.

DIALECT *DIFFERENTIAE*

There is no possibility, in the space available, of providing a full description of each dialect's sound system: what is offered is merely an account of a few of the most salient features of three of the most distinctive dialects. For the most comprehensive description of the various dialects see Mather & Speitel (1986), hereafter referred to as *LAS*.

The North-East (see Dieth 1932; Wölck 1965)

Besides the developments already noted (p. 60) as attested from the Middle Scots period, the following are characteristics of north-east dialects. /i/ resulting from ESc. /ø:/, when preceded by a velar plosive, has developed a labial on-glide: /skwil/ 'school', /gwid/ 'good': this feature distinguishes the north-east dialects from those of Easter Ross, where the conservative pronunciation is /gid/, /skil/. ESc. /aː/ has in some words not participated in the Great Vowel Shift, remaining unchanged except for the development of a palatal on-glide and (possibly) the loss of phonemic length: /bjak/ 'bake', /kjak/ 'cake', /snjav/ 'snow', /bjav/ 'blow'. The Gaelic loanwords *ceard* 'tinker' and *carn* 'pile of stones' give not /kerd/, /kern/ as in other dialects, but /kjard/, /kjarn/. Original diphthongs have certain developments peculiar to this dialect. ESc. /iu/ gives /jʌu/, and the same diphthong is also audible in loanwords: /fjʌu/ 'few', /njʌu/ 'new', /bjʌute/ 'beauty'. /ʌi/ arises, with lexeme-specificity, from ESc. /eː/, /ɛː/ and /aː/: /kwʌin/ *quean* (this is the regular north-east word for 'girl'), /wʌiv/ (cognate with *weave* but generally means 'knit'), /sʌivn/ 'seven'; /swʌit/ 'sweat', /fʌit/ 'wheat', /wʌim/ (cognate with *womb* but means 'stomach'). The same diphthong appears in /kwʌit/ (coat, often used in the specific sense of a fisherman's oilskin jacket) and /kwʌil/ 'coal' (used only of glowing embers): there is evidence (Macafee 1990) that this arises from a Middle Scots dialect variation. The consonant system shows some distinctive features: /f/ from earlier /xw/ is general in the northern area of the dialect: /fʌit/ 'white', /fʌn/ 'whin', /fʌil/ 'while'; but in the southern restricted to pronouns and adverbs: /fa/ 'who', /fit/ or /fat/ 'what', /far/ 'where'. Medial /ð/ is replaced by /d/: /fadɪr/ 'father', /bridɪr/ 'brother', /hɛdɪr/ 'heather', /wɪdɪr/ 'weather'. /xt/ is assimilated to /θ/: /miθ/ 'might', /doθɪr/ 'daughter'.

The Borders

(See Zai 1942: also Taylor 1974, though both her data and the force of her argument are questionable.) This dialect is characteristic of the Border area except where the River Tweed forms the political boundary. Its main distinguishing feature is the diphthongisation of /i/ and /u/ in stressed open syllables: the pronunciation 'yow and mey' is held to be typical of this area. /ʌi/ (phonetically [ëi]) is represented not only in words with MSc. /ai/: *way, clay, hay*; but with MSc. /iː/: *die, three, tree*. MSc. /əi/ gives in open syllables /ae/, phonetically [ɑe] or even [ɔe]. Similarly /ʌu/ arises not only from MSc. /ou/ but from MSc. /uː/: *cow, now, pull, full*. Elsewhere than in stressed open syllables, former /uː/ has not been diphthongised: *about, town, down, house*, etc. have /u/ as in other Scots dialects. Murray (1872a) recorded diphthongs of quality [ɪə] and [ʊə] arising from ESc. /aː/ and /oː/ (i.e. where vowels of [e]-like and [o]-like quality would be expected): [bɪəθ], [brɪəd], [fɪəs]; [kʊət], [nʊəz], [kʊəl]. When in syllable-initial position these diphthongs became vowels with on-glides: [jɪts] (oats), [wʌpən] (open); a preceding /h/ made the glide voiceless: [çɪl] (whole), [ʍʌl] (hole). Zai reports these pronunciations as obsolete; and the only such form regularly attested in the *LAS* is /hjɪm/ [çëm], [çɛm] 'home'.

Shetland (see Graham 1979)

The dialects of this island group show considerable variations; but some of the most common characteristics are as follows: /θ/ and /ð/ are represented by /t/ and /d/ in all positions except when final and not in a cluster: /taŋk/, /tɪŋ/, /ert/ 'earth', /dɪs/, /du/ 'thou' (the contrastive use of *du* and *ye* is still active in this dialect); but /muθ/ 'mouth'. Initial /kw/ gives /xw/; initial /tʃ/ is reduced to /ʃ/. /kn/, /gn/ and /wr/ are retained, at least in conservative speech. The vowel system is highly distinctive, and (like other features of this dialect, and of the closely related ones of Orkney and Caithness) shows extensive Scandinavian influence. ESc. /øː/ is kept distinct systemically and represented by a rounded vowel, phonetically varying from [y(ː)] to [ø(ː)]. /ʌ/ is often phonetically a vowel in the [ɔ] range, the reflexes of ESc. /o/ and /oː/ being merged as a fully low back rounded vowel: data from Fetlar in *LAS* show that *cot, rod, hop, coat, road* and *hope* have [ɒ]. [a]-like and [æ]-like vowels are both found, distributed according to principles which simply cannot be deduced from historical factors (a situation by no means unusual in Scots dialects): in the Fetlar dialect words containing [æ] include *bad, fraud, apple, milk, shell* and *bound*.

Aitken's Law as a dialect differentia

The operation of Aitken's Law is visible in all dialects. However, some modifications to the general statement made on pages 50–1 require to be specified. Firstly, ESc. short /i/ and /u/, ModSc. /ɪ/ and /ʌ/, are not subject to the lengthening process predicted by the Law: these vowels have no long allophones, remaining short even before voiced fricatives and /r/ (they do not occur in stressed open syllables). ModSc. /i/ and /u/ show length variations considerably more marked than other vowels: when short they are *very* short, and the difference in auditory impression between their long and their short allophones (e.g. *peace–breeze*; *house–bruise*) is striking. In dialects where the reflex of ESc. /ø:/ remains a distinct phoneme and is not merged with /i/ or /e/, or split between /ɪ/ (short) and /e/ (long) (as in Central and Western dialects, where *good* is /gɪd/ and *poor* /per/ [peːr]), the same is true of this vowel: an example is the dialect of Kirriemuir (in Angus), where the modern reflex is an [ø]-like vowel; another is that of Coldstream (Berwickshire), where despite a loss of rounding the vowel remains distinct, *boot* [bët] contrasting with *bait* [bet] and *bit* [bɪt], and *poor* [pëːr] with *pair* [peːr]. In the dialect of Morebattle as described by Zai (1942) a quality as well as a duration difference is audible between the long and the short allophones of this phoneme: [œː] and [ɵ].

The reflex of ESc. /au/ is invariably monophthongal, rounded or not according to dialect; and in many dialects provides a counterexample to Aitken's Law by always remaining long. /sat/ (*sat*) contrasts with /saːt/ (*salt*) in northern and north-eastern dialects. In other areas, however, the reflexes of ESc. /a/ and /au/ are contrasted not quantitatively but qualitatively; and in some both a quality and a duration difference are present: one of several consistent pronunciation features distinguishing the dialects of Cupar and Auchtermuchty, towns 10 miles apart in Fife, is that in the former *fat*, *sat* contrast with *fault*, *salt* in that the first group has [ä] and the other [ɔˑ] (words like *cot*, *knot* have a much higher vowel), whereas in the latter a very similar quality difference is accompanied by no duration difference at all. There appears to be no dialect in which ESc. /au/ is realised, in any environment, as a short [a]-like vowel.

The effects of Aitken's Law on the reflexes of ESc. /iː/ show an interesting distributional pattern of variants. As already noted, the combined effect of Aitken's Law and the Great Vowel Shift on this vowel has been a phonemic split into /ae/ and an /ʌi/ which merges with the reflex in word-final position of ESc. /ai/. However, it is not invariably true that former /iː/ gives /ae/ in 'long' environments of Aitken's Law and /ʌi/ in 'short'. A characteristic of north-eastern dialects is that the shorter and closer diphthong is used before /r/: /fʌir/ [fɜiᵊr], [fëiᵊr], not /faer/. Southern dialects show a still further restriction: /ae/ appears only in word-final position (or syllables closed by an inflectional /d/ or /z/), and /ʌi/ elsewhere: /ʍae/ 'why' but /rʌiz/ [rɛiz], [rëiz] 'rise'. (*LAS* data suggest that many speakers in this area make an unpredictable distinction between *five*, *size* with /ae/ and *drive*, *rise* with /ʌi/.) Conversely, the sequence /aeθ/ appears among many speakers in *scythe*, *tithe* and the proper names *Kilsyth*, *Rosyth*, *Forsyth*: the geographical distribution of this has not been investigated, and it is possible that a social as well as a regional factor is involved. The different extents to which Aitken's Law has resulted in /ae/ as contrasted with /ʌi/ in 'long' environments suggests a greater degree of conservatism in north-eastern dialects, and still greater in the southern, than in the central area.

Morphology and syntax

Several of the grammatical features of Older Scots listed on pp. 53–6 have survived in the Scots of the modern period.

The old weak plurals /in/ (*eyes*), /ʃɪn/ or its dialect variants /ʃin/, /ʃøn/ (*shoes*), survive in many areas. It is interesting to note (Glauser 1970) that the domains of these forms have demonstrably receded northwards to the political border, or almost, in the last hundred years; and that speakers from Northumberland and Cumberland now regard them as 'Scottish', though they were to be heard in northern England almost within living memory.

The first-person possessive absolute pronoun is often *mines*, a usage attested from the eighteenth century. A more important feature in which the personal-pronoun system differs from that of standard English is in having retained, or redeveloped, a number distinction in the second person. *Thou* (/ðu/, in the west /tu/, in the Northern Isles /du/) used as a familiar singular survived in all dialects until the nineteenth century, to at least the beginning of the twentieth in the west, and in peripheral dialects is still to be heard. It is in Shetland that the usage is best maintained, though Graham (1979) reports that the *du/ye* distinction is no longer consistently observed by young speakers; but the dialects of Orkney and the northern mainland also preserve it, and in those of the western Borders it was attested as being in regular use in 1962. In the plural, a consistent distinction between nominative *ye* and objective *you* survived into the modern period: the evidence of one literary text (see McClure 1981b) suggests that it was known in the Ayrshire dialect in the nineteenth century. *Ye*, however, is now general; though when emphatic even traditional speakers are often heard to substitute *you*. A recent development is a plural form pronounced /jɪz/, when stressed /juz/ (written ⟨yiz⟩, ⟨yese⟩, ⟨yous⟩, etc.): this is first attested in the early twentieth century and is now very common in the dialects of the west and the central belt, where it is held to be characteristic of urban working-class speech. (See Macafee 1983 for a full discussion.) The form *hit*, possessive *hits*, survives as the third person neuter singular in most dialects. When unstressed the pronunciation is /ɪt/ or /t/ (a cliticised /d/, known to have existed in the Older Scots period from occasional spellings such as ⟨dude⟩ (do it), can still be heard in eastern dialects), but this is probably a parallel to the similar loss of initial /h/ in unemphatic *he, his, him, her*.

Most of the dialects which preserve *thou* use it with a verb having the same form as the third person: *thou is, thou has, thou will, thou comes*, etc. The dialect of Orkney, exceptionally, prefers *thou are, thou have*. This is an instance of the general preference, surviving from Older Scots, for -*s* endings in both numbers and in all persons except the first singular. An aspect of the verb distinct from the simple present tense, in which -*s* is invariable for all forms including the first person singular, is in common use. Its most characteristic application is with past reference, for continuous narrative: *Sae I says tae'm weel awa an dae't*. It also appears in statements of general or universal truth: a distinction is thus visible between *When I tell him…* (simple present with future reference), *When I telt him…* (past) and *When I tells him…* (generalising).

A feature of the verb system retained from Older Scots, but only in peripheral dialects, is the distinction between the present participle and the verbal noun: the endings are pronounced respectively /ɪn/ and /in/. In some recent literature, particularly from the mid-century, this distinction has been punctiliously observed, writers employing the spellings ⟨an⟩ (participle) and ⟨in⟩ (verbal noun).

The auxiliary-verb system in contemporary usage differs from those of both Older Scots and modern standard English. In the following account, the practice will be to use spellings customarily employed in written representations of Scots of the east central area (the dialect which is the basis for the most widely used literary form of Scots): this differs from the practice of Brown & Millar (1980) and Miller & Brown (1982), where the most comprehensive account of the auxiliary-verb system of any form of Scots is to be found. The spellings suggest the pronunciation in accordance with normal orthographic rules, but it should be understood that other spoken forms may be heard in Scotland: for instance, the Scots cognate of *do* is written ⟨dae⟩, representing /de/, the most widespread form; but in the north-east and the Northern Isles, where the local pronunciations are respectively /di/ and /dø/, spellings ⟨dee⟩ and ⟨dü⟩ are regular in regional literature. It should also be noted that Scots writers show a wide range of variation in individual orthographic practice, and that the form selected for this section of the present chapter is not necessarily the only one in use even for a given regional pronunciation: for example, the commonest spoken form of the Scots cognate of *has*, when stressed, is /hɪz/, written ⟨his⟩, ⟨hiz⟩, ⟨hez⟩, ⟨haes⟩ or quite regularly ⟨has⟩, as well as the form ⟨hes⟩ selected here.

The following auxiliaries are in regular use in traditional Scots: *be, am, are* (the spelling ⟨ur(r)⟩ is not infrequent, especially in literary representations of urban demotic speech), *is*; *wis, were*; *bein*; *been. Hae* or a frequent emphatic form *hiv, hes*; *hed* /hɪd/, *haein*; a weak past participle *haen* survives in northern and north-eastern dialects. *Dae* (an emphatic *div*, by analogy with *hiv*, is first attested in the early nineteenth century), *daes* or *dis* /dɪz/, *did, daein, duin* /dɪn/. *Can, cud*; *will, wad* or *wid*; *sud*; *micht*; *maun*.

The loss of *sall* from contemporary speech is fairly recent. Literary attestations of both the full form and the reduced *'se* /z/, used with personal pronouns, are common until the beginning of the present century; the reduced form may still be heard in conservative speech. Evidence for its loss as a productive form is found in such occasional spellings, occurring in reputable literature, as ⟨I sepad⟩ (for *I'se uphaud*) or ⟨aswarn⟩ (for *I'se warran*): spellings which suggest that the writers were ignorant of the historical identity of the form and therefore, presumably, unfamiliar with *'se* as an auxiliary in active use. In most forms of contemporary Scots both simple futurity and necessity or obligation are expressed by *will* – this in spite of the fact that until very recently the practice in schools has been to insist on the canonical standard English usage of the two verbs. Pedagogic prescription has also been notably unsuccessful in preserving *may*. Permission is generally expressed by *can* or by a distinctive use of *get* with either the *to*-infinitive or the present participle: *He'll get tae gang/get gaun the morn*; and possibility by *micht* or an adverbial use of *maybe* (/mɪbe/, often written ⟨mebbe⟩). In educated speech and writing, prescriptions regarding *may* to indicate possibility often lead to the hypercorrection of using it with a past reference, as in the sub-headline of a newspaper article 'Accident may have been avoided, say police', referring to an accident which was not avoided.

Wilson (1926:91) states 'The past of *maun* or *mun* is *bid*, e.g. *it bid tay be* ('It had to be') – *A bid tay gang* ('I had to go').' This form, generally written ⟨bude⟩, is in fact the Scots cognate of *behoved*, found in Middle Scots as *behuifit* and successively reduced to *behuit* and *buit*. Originally an impersonal verb, the possibility of using it with a personal subject arose in Middle Scots and had virtually superseded the impersonal usage by the end of the sixteenth century. Though etymologically a past-tense form, it is not (as Wilson appears to suggest) used exclusively with past reference. Its range of meaning – logical, moral or physical necessity or obligation – is virtually identical to *maun*. In the north-east, the local pronunciation /bit/ has led, with assimilation of the final /t/ to that of the *to* which follows, to conflation of the form of the verb with that of *be*: *Ye jist be tae tire an faa tee again* 'You just have to tire and fall to [set to work] again' (J. M. Caie, 1878–1949). (See *SND* s.v. *Bude* for further discussion of this form.)

A feature of Scots as of other forms of English in the modern period has been the reduction or disappearance of non-periphrastic negative and interrogative constructions (*Comes he?* – *He comes not*) and their replacement by constructions with the *do*-auxiliary. In Scots, literary evidence suggests a much greater degree of conservatism than in southern English, non-periphrastic constructions appearing in written texts suggestive of colloquial usage (e.g. dialogue in novels and stories) until well into the nineteenth century: for instance, *Hoo mak ye that oot?* (George MacDonald, 1824–1905), *I ken na weel what it was* (George Douglas Brown, 1869–1902). With the possible exception of a few stock phrases such as *Say ye sae?*, however, contemporary Scots follows general English usage. In the north-east dialect *div*, generally emphatic, can be used as an alternative to *dee* as an unstressed interrogation marker.

The modal verb *can* has the property of forming periphrastic constructions with other modals: *I'll no can come*, *The teacher'll can tell ye*, *He'll can get it feenisht by the week-enn*. There is evidence (Miller & Brown 1982) that the construction is commoner in negative than in affirmative phrases, but both are regularly found. In the past tense *cud* can likewise follow another auxiliary: *He uist tae cud dae't*, *Ye micht cud hae gaen*, *I widnae cud get it wantin the siller*. In the Shetland dialect even *cud can*, followed by the *to*-infinitive, is possible. Murray (1872a) records *Thay haena cuid geate eane* ('They haven't been able to get one'), but it is doubtful whether constructions with *cud* and a primary auxiliary are still to be heard. (See Scur 1968 for full discussion and citations from the *EDD* of comparable forms from northern English dialects.) The *will can* construction was certainly in being early in the modern period: Miller & Brown (1982) cite extensive evidence that other double modal constructions too have now become regular in Edinburgh dialect, their examples including *Do they need to can do it?*, *He used to would drink black coffee late at night*, *He might should have claimed his expenses*, *They might no would like to come with us.*

Various possibilities are available for the formation of verbal negatives. The non-clitic form is *no* /no/ in dialects south of the Tay, *nae* /ne/ north of it: the latter is the result of an assimilation of the verbal negative to the negative quantifier, which is *nae* in all dialects. The clitic is *-na* or *-nae* /nʌ, ne/, with a regional distribution which has evidently altered in recent decades: *-nae* was formerly restricted to the east midland dialect, but is now prevalent also in the western conurbation and the south-west. With auxiliary verbs the clitic gives characteristic forms: *isna*, *disna*, *hinna* ('haven't'), *canna*, *willna* or *winna*, *maunna*; or *isnae*, etc. For the first person singular negative of *be* a peculiar form /ʌ mʌrne/ is heard in Glasgow dialect: this is variously written ⟨I murnae⟩ and ⟨I'm urnae⟩, suggesting a quite understandable difficulty on the part of the authors as to how it should be interpreted (Macafee 1983: 50). Negative interrogatives do not as a rule begin with verb plus clitic, but are formed by placing the full negative between the subject and the infinitive: *Dinna ye hear it?*, though not impossible, is now recessive compared to *Dae ye no hear it?* The decided preference for the latter construction, confirmed by Brown & Millar (1980), again appears to be recent, interrogatives of the *dinna ye ...* form being regularly attested in literature until the present century. Regional north-east dialect texts suggest its survival in this locality, sometimes with a local form of the clitic *-nin*, until the period of the Second World War: 'Cannin ye be sairious?' (from *Cried on Sunday* by D. Bruce 1936). The same is true of tag questions: *Ye'll be duin wi't afore I win hame, will ye no?* – not *winna ye?* A distinctive development reported by Millar & Brown (1979) for Edinburgh dialect, and certainly to be heard also in western speech, is the use of a double negative tag of the form *isn't it no?* The clitic seems invariably to be not Scots *-na/-nae* but English *-n't*: certain evidence for the late emergence of the construction. It occurs only with negative sentences, and its function appears to be to seek confirmation of the negative: *She didnae like him, didn't she no?* This usage is related to a possibility in Scots of using two negatives in a sentence independently, implicitly cancelling or contradicting each other (a construction distinct from the simple double negative *I hinna got nane*, which is of regular occurrence in Scots as in most English dialects other than the standard): *He isnae still no workin* (i.e. now he is), *It isnae that I've been no gaun out wi her, I juist hinnae been out wi her!* (examples from Brown & Millar 1980, respelt).

The differences between the relative pronoun systems of Older and Modern Scots are intriguing. Romaine (1980a, 1981a, and 1981b) suggests that though the use of *quh-* (later *wh-*) forms was adopted in Middle Scots for more complex relative constructions and gradually diffused down the stylistic scale, the forms never came to be firmly established in the spoken tongue. Romaine appears not to have examined the evidence of dialogue passages in nineteenth-century prose fiction; and though it is certainly true that though *wha, whase* and (most particularly) *wham* as relatives are rarely, if ever, heard in modern spoken Scots, the frequency of the nominative and possessive forms in literature, including dialogue, makes it necessary to acknowledge the possibility that they were formerly more common, and had perhaps passed for a time from the written into at least the more formal registers of the spoken language (e.g. 'There's Ane abune whase commands I maun obey before your leddyship's', from Walter Scott's *Old Mortality*). Murray (1872a), however, makes what must (given contemporary attitudes) have been the uncomfortable observation that Robert Burns' celebrated lines

> Scots! wha hae wi Wallace bled!
> Scots! wham Bruce has aften led!

are not authentic Scots but a quasi-Scotticisation of a standard English usage, the genuine Scots idiom being *Scots at haes...*

The only relatives now in common use are *that/at* and zero, (*the*) *whilk* surviving into the present century only in legal language and not attested in the *SND* after 1928. *That/at* is used as in Middle Scots: a recent development, however, is of possessive *that's* (*the wumman that's sister mairriet the postie*) originating in a re-interpretation of reduced *his* (*the man at's* (i.e. 'that his') *wife's deid*) as the possessive ending. Alternatively to this, the practice of combining *that* with a possessive pronoun is common (*The crew at their boat was vrackit*). When the antecedent is not the subject of the relative clause, a construction of the form *the wumman at ye ken her son* (not *at's son ye ken*) is used. A zero relative can be employed not only as a direct object or governed by a preposition (*the gless ye drappit, the man ye spak til*) but also as a subject (*Wha was the leddy gaed doun the road afore ye?*).

Lexis

The recorded vocabulary of Scots – that is, the stock of words not forming part of the standard literary English vocabulary which are attested as having been used in recent times within Scotland – is extraordinarily large and diverse. The *Scottish National Dictionary* (Grant & Murison 1931–76), in intention a comprehensive record of all distinctively Scots words and Scots usages of common English words confirmed since 1700, is a ten-volume work containing 70,000 entries. Word-lists for individual regional dialects (e.g. *The Dialect of Banffshire*, Gregor 1866; *The Roxburghshire Wordbook*, Watson 1923; 'A selection of Caithness dialect words', Ross, in Omand 1972; *The Shetland Dictionary*, Graham 1979; *Orkney Wordbook*, Lamb 1988; *A Galloway Glossary*, Riach 1988) run to many hundreds of words: not all the items listed by any given scholar are in fact unique to his stated locality, but many are. The two lexical volumes of the *Linguistic Atlas of Scotland* (Mather & Speitel 1975, 1977) likewise testify to the remarkable number of words in use at least until within living memory in the various local dialects of Scotland. A small selection of regional words follows:

> *Shetland: blogga* 'marsh marigold', *cockalorie* 'daisy', *smora* 'clover', *lorin* 'cormorant', *swaabie* 'great black-backed gull', *shalder* 'oyster-catcher', *aandoo* row against the tide to keep the boat stationary, *brimtud* sound of waves crashing on the shore, *mareel* 'phosphorescent plankton', *roost* 'strong tidal current', *shürmal* 'foreshore', *vaddle* 'tidal pool'.
>
> *Orkney: alamotti* 'storm petrel', *arvo* 'chickweed', *arroo* 'pullet', *brooser* 'red face', *chiggo* 'thick-set girl', *fortam* 'fishing-line', *lathowy* 'insipid', *muggro-fue* 'mist, drizzle', *reevligo* 'rash, hurried', *vandit* 'striped, of cattle'.
>
> *The North-East: spurgie* 'sparrow', *rooser* 'watering can', *sharger* weakest animal in a litter, or youngest child in a family, *futtle* thick-bladed knife for gutting fish, *mineer* 'uproar', *bailie* 'cattleman on a farm', *hallach* 'scatterbrained', *habber* 'stutter', *brodmal* 'brood of chickens', *thraaheuk* instrument for twisting straw ropes.
>
> *Galloway: banter* 'exchange', *bask* 'cold dry east wind', *caddilack* 'sea lamprey', *carrunt* 'outing', *essert* 'stubborn, awkward', *feugie* 'left-handed', *grooblie* 'louse', *lummin* 'raining heavily', *pillock* 'porpoise', *shelpie* 'missel-thrush'.

> *South-East and Borders: bobquaw* 'waterlogged turf', *crackie* 'three-legged stool', *daidlie* 'apron', *elshin* 'bradawl', *gump* 'catch trout by groping', *huller* 'cold mist', *rind* 'hoar-frost', *scotchibell* 'earwig', *trivage* partition between stalls in a byre, *yorlin* 'yellow-hammer'.

It is not only in the variety of regional dialect words that the remarkable size of the Scots vocabulary is shown. Many trades and vocations preserve their traditional esoteric vocabularies, words from which many survive in folk memory long after the practicalities of the work have altered out of recognition. The dialect literature of the north-east, for example, its literary interest apart, is a monument to the system of large-scale arable farming which developed in the area and a repository of not only the vocabulary but the entire folk culture associated with it. The production in the near future of a series of specialised word-lists is a project of the Scottish National Dictionary Association; but see the *Scots Thesaurus* (Macleod 1990), and among earlier studies Mather 1966, 1969 (on fishing), MacPhee 1983 (on mining), Pride 1987 (on architecture) and Fenton 1987 (on farming). Illustrative lists again follow:

> *Farming: brecham* 'horse-collar', *cavie* 'hen-coop', *dinmont* a wether between its first and second shearing, *cailleach* or *clyack* 'last sheaf', *feer* plough the first guiding furrow, *hapshackle* 'hobble (a horse)', *quey* 'heifer', *nickie-tams* strings or straps tied below the knees, *ruskie* basket for seed corn, *stilts* 'plough shafts'.
> *Fishing: clip* 'long-handled gaff', *cran* 'barrel of fresh herring', *gansey* 'thick jersey', *gavel* or *gale* 'side-rope of a net', *iron man* 'a hand winch', *rouse* cure fish by sprinkling them with salt, *scauder* 'jellyfish', *spelder* split fish for drying, *spoucher* 'long-handled scoop', *three-leggit mask* 'broken mesh in a net'.
> *Coal mining: blin-heidin* 'blind passage', *gauton* 'watercourse', *gum* shovel out loose coal from an undercut, *hawk* 'pick-ended hammer', *jawk* hard stone within a coal seam, *lye* 'the main level', *nog* 'wooden wedge', *pat-erse* bulge in the roof of a coal seam, *rance* 'wooden prop', *tumphy* 'coaly fireclay'.

The sheer size of the distinctive Scots word-stock, and its diversity of registers, is easy to demonstrate, and is on any showing one of the unique features of this branch of the English language. However, though there is no question that many characteristically Scots words still exist in current usage, the task of assessing the extent to which the vocabulary of the dictionaries, the word-lists and the literature survive in contemporary speech is not easy.

The reasons for the difficulty are various. Firstly, to what assumed earlier state of the language are we to compare the present situation? The vocabularies of the various regions throughout the English-speaking parts of the island of Britain have always overlapped considerably; and it would be absurd to assume that there was ever a time when the Lowland Scottish populace uniformly had at its disposal the entire word-stock of the *SND* and invariably used these words to the exclusion of words familiar in, say, London. A considerable number of words in the *SND* have only a tiny number of attestations, a single one in many cases. An evident assumption that the active vocabulary of Scots once was, and still should be, more strongly differentiated from that of standard literary English than was probably ever the case appears to underlie much popular thought on the 'decline' of Scots (see Aitken 1981a), and some characteristic practices of recent and contemporary Scots poets (see Macafee 1981).

The widespread assumption that the traditional Scots vocabulary is suffering rapid attrition certainly has some support in observable fact. As one example, Hettinga (1981) reports a quite drastic loss on all levels, but especially lexis, of local dialect features among young speakers, as contrasted with the generations of their parents and grandparents, in a particular area of Fife. Hettinga, however, is describing a small, long-established and relatively static community, dependent for most of its history on fishing and trade; and his observations are countered in a most interesting way by Pollner (1985), who demonstrates that in the *a priori* unlikely environment of a new town with an almost entirely immigrant and predominantly young population, at least a representative selection of traditional Scots words are still in active use.

It is of course true that much of the attrition of the Scots vocabulary has occurred for the simple reason that the language of rural and pre-industrial communities was bound inescapably to be affected by the large-scale social changes of urbanisation and industrialisation which began in Scotland in the last century and have continued until recent times. Agutter & Cowan (1981), however, provide convincing evidence that while words reflecting rural occupations and pursuits are certainly disappearing, contemporary urban Scottish communities have evolved a local dialect vocabulary which is in itself wholly distinctive. This too raises a difficulty, at least in popular thought: there is no question that speakers of Glasgow or Edinburgh working-class demotic employ a lexis as individual, probably, as any form of spoken Scots ever was, though the word-stock of pre-industrial communities and the literature associated with those is almost wholly unknown to them; but the right of such words as *bevvy* 'alcoholic drink', *clenny* Glasgow Corporation Cleansing Department, *didgy* 'dustbin', *flyman* 'a wide boy', *ginger* any carbonated soft drink, *hee-haw* 'nothing', *lumber* 'one's companion on a date', *manky* 'dirty', *riddy* 'source of embarrassment', *steamboats* 'drunk (adj.)' to be classed as Scots is not always recognised. (Examples from Munro 1985: for a comprehensive account of the sociolinguistic situation in Glasgow, including its individual and highly innovative vocabulary, see Macafee 1983.)

A further complicating factor is that the enduring popularity of at least a selection from the corpus of Scottish literature (most importantly, of course, the poetry of Robert Burns) has ensured that numerous words which would otherwise have gone out of use remain in at any rate the passive competence of many speakers. Aitken (1979) points out the fact, of which this literary knowledge is the plausible explanation, that some traditional Scots words are somewhat better known to middle-class than to working-class speakers; and this is confirmed by MacAulay (1977: 55–6) and Pollner (1985). Readers of more experimental poetry of the present century have become familiar with a considerable number of rare, archaic, markedly regional or even invented words – often used to excellent literary effect – which collectively could never have formed part of any individual's speech habits but are now accepted currency among the small, but enthusiastic and vociferous, circle of writers, readers and critics of modern Scots literature. Examples of such words are *bluidwyte* 'bloodshed fine', *dronach* 'punishment', *fantice* 'vision', *granderie* 'pride', *keethanlie* 'apparently', *musardrie* 'pensiveness', *ramskeerie* 'restless', *scelartrie* 'infamy', *shilpiskate* 'nonentity', *skrymmorie* 'terrifying'. (See further McClure 1981c.) That is, there are many speakers who show a wide discrepancy between passive knowledge and active use of Scots vocabulary, and also many whose experiences of Scots as a literary and as a spoken language are very dissimilar.

An attempt to fit this complex situation into a schematised framework was made by Görlach (1987), who proposed that individual Scots words in the competence of living speakers could be categorised as 'unknown', 'known as probably obsolete', 'known exclusively from literature', 'not common in speech but regular in literature', 'common in Scots', 'can be used in Scottish English', and in a different dimension as 'not used except when forced by context, such as rhyme', 'used only in writing', 'used in speech only as a conscious Scotticism', and 'used regularly in speech'. This has not been used as the basis of any large-scale investigation: it would seem to require informants of a considerable degree of literary and linguistic sophistication, though these are by no means rare in Scotland. However, there is no doubt that the situation which it presupposes, of an enormous number of words in indeterminate states between full familiarity and total oblivion, is very characteristic of the sociolinguistic circumstances of Scots.

The dialect vocabulary of Scots is a subject of widespread interest, as is witnessed by the 'best-seller' status not only of the frequently appearing popular works on the subject but also of scholarly studies like the *Concise Scots Dictionary* and the *Scots Thesaurus*. It is safe to say that this popular interest will be sufficient to preserve not only a fair selection of the words themselves, but the theoretical issue of their survival, in active life for the foreseeable future.

2.3.3 Scottish English

Scottish standard English, as already noted, originated as a compromise between London standard English and Scots: a compromise resulting partly from the natural interference of a native on a learned language and partly from a conscious belief among most of the eighteenth-century literati that a total Anglicisation of their speech, leaving no Scottish features whatever, was not a desirable aim. It is now an autonomous speech form, having the status of one among the many national forms of the international English language, and is recognised as an established national standard, thoughout the English-speaking world: less so in European countries, where the misconception of Daniel Jones' RP as an international norm is proving very difficult to eradicate. Like other national forms of English, it is characterised to some extent by grammar, vocabulary and idiom, but most obviously by pronunciation. Regional, social and in lesser degree age and sex variations exist, principally on the phonetic level and very noticeably in intonation; but a common phonological system, differing in several conspicuous ways from those of other accents of English, is shared by most forms of SSE and is close to being a defining feature of it. Within Scotland it is widely spoken in all regions (including the Gaidhealtachd, where 'Highland English' is a highly distinctive variant of the model rather than one with a separate identity), and is the characteristic speech of the professional class and the accepted norm in schools. Speakers who choose to excise strongly marked regional and/or social features from their idiolects endeavour to assimilate them to the SSE model. The English accent known as RP is not a native form in Scotland, nor is it generally regarded as a social desideratum. (Romaine (1980b) provides experimental evidence that Scottish accents are more favourably regarded than RP in Scotland, and that the use of RP by ethnic Scots evokes negative social reactions.) RP speakers in Scotland, if not actual English nationals, have generally acquired their accent through direct English influence, such as education in England or in a quasi-English private school, and their speech is customarily described as 'English' or 'Anglicised'. Some Scots adopt RP-like accents for special purposes such as singing, acting or reciting: one is not infrequently confronted with the ludicrous spectacle of amateur and professional singers, particularly women, rendering Burns songs in accents more Anglicised than their normal speech; but apart from this restricted use RP is not associated with Scottish nationality. The fact that it is uniformly the accent of the titled landowning class is widely seen as confirming the alienation of this class from the mass of the Scottish populace. The clear awareness of a Scottish as contrasted with an English national identity is manifested in language attitudes as elsewhere: it is a noteworthy fact that Scots with Anglicised or wholly English accents often show some sensitivity when the fact is mentioned, sometimes being heard to deny that their accents are English on the grounds that they themselves are Scots.

Phonology (see Wells 1982: 2)

Several of the individual pronunciation features of SSE are due to the underlying influence of Aitken's Law. A detailed comparison of the effects of the Law on SSE and on Scots has yet to be made: an intriguing study by Agutter (1988b), citing instrumental measurements of vowel duration in SSE and arguing that the distinctively Scottish nature of the Law has been overstated, appears to neglect the consideration that when a language (English) having one system of vowel-length distinctions comes under the influence of another (Scots) having a very different system, the operation of a principle native to the original language will not necessarily be identical in the language which it has affected. It is certainly true that SSE shares with Scots a tendency for most vowels to have markedly longer realisation in stressed open syllables, before voiced fricatives (but not voiced plosives) and before /r/ than in other positions. Exceptional are /ɪ/ and /ʌ/, which show no significant length variations whatever: as between *hiss* and *his*, or *bus* and *buzz*, the duration of the vowels is unchanged. The vowels which show the most conspicuous length variations are /i/ and /u/, which when short are very short indeed; but the lower vowels and the diphthongs too show readily observable differences of duration in such pairs as *race–raise*, *toss–cause*, *house* (n.) – *house* (vb). Another feature of vowel duration found in both Scots and SSE is that when a word ends in a stressed open syllable the addition of an inflexional morpheme does not affect the length of the vowel: thus *greed–agreed*, *brood–brewed*, *raid–rayed*, *pod–pawed*, etc., show unmistakable differences in duration. As between a vowel in a monomorphemic syllable closed with a voiced fricative and in one closed with an inflexional /z/, the latter is consistently longer to instrumental measurements, though the difference may not be readily perceptible in speech: *tease–teas*, *raise–rays*, etc. (McClure 1977).

Another effect of Aitken's Law on SSE is that whereas most other forms of standard English retain traces of the historical grouping of the English vowels into a 'long' and a 'short' set, the loss of this in SSE has led to the absence of several phonemic distinctions preserved in other accents of the language. *Cam* and *calm*, *cot* and *caught*, *pull* and *pool* are characteristically homophonous in SSE. It is interesting to note that Scottish accents which do incorporate one or more of those distinctions do so in a definite order. Scottish speakers who differentiate between two varieties of open vowel (i.e. make a distinction corresponding to the /æ/–/ɑː/ of RP) are not uncommon, a *cot–caught* distinction is notably rarer and always found in accents which also distinguish between the open vowels; a *pull–pool* distinction is very rare and usually restricted to accents which are markedly Anglicised in other respects too (Abercrombie 1979, whom see further for a systematic comparison between the vowel systems of SSE and RP). Such distinctions may be the result of direct English influence on the speech of individuals, but are not necessarily so; and when they are not this, but are institutionalised features of native Scottish accents (educated Edinburgh speakers, for example, quite commonly make a distinction between two open vowels), the differences are much less extreme than in other accents – *Sam* and *psalm* are [sam, saːm] rather than [sæm, sɑːm], *dawn* when distinguished from *Don* has nothing of the over-rounding characteristic of southern English accents – and, noticeably, do not always correspond in distribution: *salmon* and *gather* generally have the shorter rather than the longer vowel.

An effect of Aitken's Law has thus been to give SSE a rather smaller vowel system than most other accents of standard English. This remains true notwithstanding the transference to SSE from Scots of the phonemic split, also resulting from the Law, of ESc. /iː/ into /ae/ and /ʌi/ already discussed: *side* /sʌid/, *sighed* /saed/. Aitken (personal communication) reports a distinction heard among Edinburgh speakers between *cycle* /sʌikl/ (n.) and *cycle* /saekl/ (vb). (A further complication affecting the phonemic analysis of diphthongs of this type is that in many western and central accents the words *Bible*, *disciple*, *idol* and *Michael* (the present writer has found no other certain examples) contain a diphthong which is close in quality, like the /ʌi/ of *rice*, but long in duration, like the /ae/ of *rise*.)

Finally, the shortening of originally long vowels has resulted in what is perhaps the most instantly recognisable feature of Scottish accents of standard English: the retention of monophthongal pronunciation where the corresponding phonemes in other accents are realised as full or incipient diphthongs: *Dee*, *day*, *doe* and *do* are phonetically [diː, deː, doː, duː].

A marginal feature of the SSE vowel system is a phoneme of which the lexical distribution varies widely but even at its maximum is restricted to a few tens of words. It is most characteristically heard in the word *clever* – in the north-east it is virtually unique to this word – and is phonetically a front-central half-open (or rather less open) vowel, distinct from both the [ɪ] of *river* and the [ɛ] of *sever*. It has no accepted symbol: McClure (1970) suggests E. (This is still the most complete account of the vowel, but see also Abercrombie 1954 and Mather 1975.) Its distribution varies regionally and socially: in the south-west it can occur in at least fifty words, in the north-east it is almost absent; it is more common in professional-class than in working-class speech, where it is often replaced by /ɪ/. Among the words which commonly contain it are *never*, *clever*, *seven*, *eleven*, *twenty*, *breadth*, *earth*, *jerk*, *jerkin*, *heaven*, *shepherd*. A small piece of evidence that, despite its extreme lexical rarity, it is a fully 'live' member of the vowel system is that the present writer has heard Ayrshire schoolchildren use it in the name of the Swiss town of Vevey, where they were being taken on a school trip. The vowel appears not to be subject to Aitken's Law, remaining short despite the following /r/ in, for example, *earth*.

Scottish accents are uniformly rhotic (with a possible exception to be discussed later, p. 83), and the tendency to level certain vowels before /r/, though varying regionally and socially, is much less marked than in other rhotic accents (such as those of North America). In conservative middle-class Scottish accents *kirk*, *perk* and *work* are /kɪrk, pɛrk, wʌrk/. In regions where /ɛ/ occurs, it too may occur before /r/: *jerk* /dʒɛrk/ does not rhyme with any of the three words already cited. And – an oddity for which no satisfactory explanation is forthcoming – many speakers in western and central Scotland consistently divide words with orthographic ⟨ir⟩ into two groups, one being pronounced with /ɪr/ and the other with a central vowel distinct from all the others. In the present writer's speech, examples of the first group are *kirk*, *stirk*, *firth*, *girdle*; of the second, *first*, *birth*, *dirt*, *third*. Whereas in most other forms of standard English, that is, the triple merger of /ɪr/ /ɛr/ /ʌr/ has resulted in the appearance of a new phoneme /ɜ/, in some accents of SSE such a phoneme has arisen as the result of a phonemic split, unpredictable on phonetic or any other grounds, of /ɪ/ before /r/, some words retaining the original /ɪ/ and others acquiring a central vowel. This results in as many as five distinct vowels, in some people's speech, where most other accents of standard English have only one. This is rare, however – largely restricted to professional-class speakers of the west and south-west – and appears to be decreasing. A tendency in the western conurbation is to merge the /ɪr/–/ʌr/ distinction: as /ɜr/ in middle-class, /ʌr/ in lower-class speech. /ɛr/ in this region is invariably kept distinct. An Edinburgh shibboleth, by contrast, is the loss of all distinctions, /ɪr/, /ɛr/, /ʌr/ and the marginal /ɛr/ and /ɜr/ all being merged as /ɜr/. Characteristic of north-eastern accents is a very stable three-way distinction corresponding to historical and orthographic predictions: words with ⟨ir⟩ are pronounced with a front central vowel much lower than the normal realisation of /ɪ/, but this is simply its pre-/r/ allophone.

/ɔr/ and /or/ are also kept distinct in all accents which distinguish /ɔ/ and /o/ in any positions (as some, notably working-class accents, do not, merging them as /o/ [o]); and in such words as *fear*, *fair*, *poor* the pronunciation is /fir, fer, pur/. In some accents the following /r/ causes the vowel to undergo a slight breaking – [fiːᵊr, feːᵊr, puːᵊr] – but the emergence in some non-Scottish accents of new diphthongal phonemes resulting from a lost /r/ has not happened in SSE. The foregoing may be summarised as a statement that in conservative SSE the vowel system of stressed syllables is no more affected by a following /r/ than by any other consonant.

The development of a non-rhotic pronunciation has recently been observed in working-class speech of the Edinburgh area (Romaine

1978). Whatever the explanation of this, it is not influence from non-rhotic accents of English such as RP: such influence on speakers of this class is sociolinguistically impossible, and the accent contains no other features which could be attributed to it. The loss of post-vocalic /r/, which appears to have come via the intermediate stage of phar-yngealisation of the syllables, must be an independent development.

In the consonant system, two features which distinguish SSE are the retention of /ʍ/ (the usual realisation of the former /xw/ now written ⟨wh⟩) and of /x/. The latter is common in place-names and personal names, and has acquired some notoriety through the wearisome habit among English people of pretending to find names in *Auchen-* (field) and *Auchter-* (summit) both unpronounceable and wildly amusing; it is also used automatically by Scots in the pronunciation of biblical, classical and other foreign names such as *Enoch, Antioch, Arachne, Munich, Bach,* and by some people in Greek- and Hebrew-derived words such as *epoch, technical, patriarch.* Despite the status of this sound as a somewhat hackneyed Scottish shibboleth, however, its place in the system of contemporary urban accents is less secure than might be assumed: Macafee (1983: 32) reports its sporadic absence among Glasgow speakers, and the present writer has been startled to observe that Aberdeen working-class primary schoolchildren, whose accents are wholly Scottish in other respects, lack it entirely, pronouncing such names as *Murdoch* and *Docherty* with /k/.

A peculiar linguistic development associated with nineteenth-century urbanisation is an extreme social polarisation of the speech forms which emerged in the cities: a highly 'refined' accent cultivated by the middle class developed concurrently with a strongly marked urban demotic dialect. This phenomenon is particularly associated with Glasgow, where to a greater extent than in other cities an enormous population growth in the mid-nineteenth century resulted in rapid expansion of the city's boundaries and the unrestrained growth of appalling slums; but it is to some extent paralleled in Edinburgh. The 'refined' accents of the two cities take their names from the districts of Kelvinside and Morningside. These two accents differ considerably in intonation, Kelvinside contrasting with Morningside in having a characteristically narrow pitch range which is particularly noticeable in the shallowness of the fall in sentence-final contours, but some readily observable segmental features are common to both accents. These include an extremely close and fronted version of the /ʌi/ diphthong, which emerges as [ɛi] or even [ei], a high variety of /a/ approaching [ɛ], and a strongly fronted /ʌ/ approaching [ɜ] or [ë]. These accents appear to have originated in a deliberate attempt by socially prestigious private schools, particularly girls' schools, in Glasgow and Edinburgh to impose a 'pukka' London pronunciation model on their pupils; and it is interesting to note that the resulting accent has always been the target for some satire and ridicule: to this day, even when its status and its use are markedly lessening, the imitation of it is part of the stock-in-trade of theatre and television comedians (Johnston 1985). By contrast, the Glasgow working-class accent has always been strongly stigmatised. It too has features of which popular consciousness is very high: widespread use of the glottal stop as a substitute for medial and final /t/, replacement of medial /θ/ by [h] or [x] ([nʌhn̩, kɑhlʌk]), an extremely retracted /ɪ/, approaching [ʌ], and /a/, and a fronted /u/. (The last vowel is markedly centralised compared with cardinal [u], and under-rounded, in all Scottish accents; but in low-prestige speech of the western conurbation it approaches an under-rounded [ʉ] or even [ÿ].) All these are specific targets for criticism and attempts at 'correction' by traditionally minded schoolteachers; and many people show a high degree of skill in placing speakers on the social scale by reference to these and comparably marked features in their speech.

'Overt' and 'covert' Scotticisms

On the phonetic and phonological levels, it is very easy to demonstrate the distinctive nature of SSE. This is also true of other levels, but here it is more difficult to obtain precisely quantifiable data. There is no difficulty in listing an abundance of words, idioms and syntactic constructions which would mark their user as a Scot, in that they are not heard in the English of other countries. What is less easy, and in some cases impossible since the necessary research has not been carried out (see Sandred 1983 for the only published study), is to make non-impressionistic pronouncements on the status, frequency and pre-dictability of such usages. There are features of SSE which are naturally and unselfconsciously used by its speakers without any necessary recognition that there is anything particularly Scottish about them: in the terminology of Aitken (1979), 'covert' Scotticisms. There are others which are recognised as overtly Scottish, to be used in some but perhaps not all social contexts to give a definite national colouring to the speaker's utterances: these are 'overt' Scotticisms. This distinction, incidentally, was recognised long before the introduction of the terms.

John Sinclair, one of several eighteenth-century scholars who compiled lists of 'Scotticisms' to avoid (see McClure 1992), observed that whereas many 'broad Scotch' words in wide use are easily recognised, numerous expressions are liable to be innocently 'mistaken for English' – by which he meant that they were used in the belief that everybody spoke so – and need to be brought to the attention of people who out of concern for propriety of usage would prefer to avoid Scottish features. Besides speech habits known to be Scottish, there are other usages again which, though historically simply developments of Scots grammar which have influenced the English speech of Scotland, are thought of not as Scottish but as 'errors', and are therefore avoided. Attitudes of individual speakers vary widely and may be influenced by degree of education, social class, age and region: professional-class speakers in Aberdeen, for example, use far more Scotticisms on all levels than their counterparts in Edinburgh. Inconsistencies of attitude, readily explained as the result of educational conditioning, are very frequent: many middle-class speakers use traditional vocabulary items with some patriotic pride but would recoil at the thought of using a *grammatical* Scotticism like *a bit bread* or *I'll not can come*. In what follows, no attempt will be made in any but the most incontrovertible cases to comment on the conventional acceptability of the words and phrases cited: all that is claimed is that these are features which may be heard, and in some cases are characteristically heard, in the mouths of Scottish speakers who would describe their speech as English.

Lexis

Scottish vocabulary items abound. Some words which the present writer would judge to be 'covert' Scotticisms for most people are *ashet* 'large dish', *bramble* (the fruit as well as the shrub), *burn* 'stream', *byre* 'cowshed', *cleg* 'horsefly', *forenoon* 'late morning', *close* passageway between buildings, *granny* 'chimney cowl', *haar* 'sea mist', *mavis* 'thrush', *pinkie* or (in the north-east) *crannie* 'little finger', *rone* and *rone pipe* ('roof gutter' and 'down pipe'), *sort* 'repair', *stirk* 'bullock or heifer', *swither* 'hesitate', *skelf* or (in the south) *spelk* 'splinter in the skin' and *whin* 'gorse'. More 'overt' Scotticisms include *bonny* 'handsome', *blether* or *haver* 'talk nonsense', *chuckies* 'pebbles', *deave* 'deafen or exhaust', *dwaam* 'daydream', *fantouche* 'affectedly flamboyant', *jalouse* 'deduce', *kenspeckle* 'conspicuous', *peelie-wallie* 'sickly, weak', *Sasunnach* 'native of England', *shilp* 'insignificant person', *trauchled* 'overworked', *wersh* 'tasteless, insipid', *yokin-time* and *lowsin-time* (beginning and end of a working day). In a different category are peculiarly Scottish usages of general English words, especially in the fields of Church, education and law (three areas where the national institutions of Scotland are independent and distinctive): *beadle* 'church officer', *induction* 'installation of a minister', *intimation* 'formal announcement from the pulpit', *stipend* 'a minister's salary', *translate* 'transfer, of a minister'; *academy* 'senior secondary school', *bursary* 'scholarship', *Highers* 'school-leaving certificate examinations', *humanity* (Latin as a university subject), *natural philosophy* (invariably abbreviated to Nat. Phil.: 'physics', likewise), *rector* (headmaster of a secondary school, or in the universities, the official elected by the students as their representative on the university court); *advocate* 'a barrister', *deacon* 'officer of a guild', *factor* (officer who manages property for the owner), *inquiry* 'inquest', *probation* (hearing of evidence before a court), *writer* 'solicitor'. Words relating to Scottish culture with no exact equivalent in English naturally survive: *laird* (titled landowner), *first-foot* (first visitor to cross one's threshold after New Year has struck), *guising* (children's practice of visiting homes in disguise on Hallowe'en). Children preserve several traditional words in playground usages: *coalie-bag* 'ride on the back', *coxie-cusie* or *cockerty-hooie* 'ride on the shoulders', *leavie-o* 'a chasing game', *hi-spy* 'hide-and-seek', in which the seeker is *het* and 'home' is the *den* or *dell*. A number of words borrowed from Gaelic, mostly in recent times, have become common currency in SSE by virtue of referring to features of what has become the music-hall and travel-brochure image of Scottish culture: *philibeg* 'kilt', *sporran* (the ornamental purse worn in front of the kilt), *sgian dubh* (dirk worn in the stocking), *claymore* (a basket-hilted sword), *clarsach* 'harp', *ceilidh* (entertainment with traditional Gaelic music), *coronach* 'dirge', and even *bard*, re-introduced with romantic associations by Walter Scott.

Grammar and idiom

Features of syntax also characterise SSE. Prepositions often have distinctively Scottish usages: *angry at him, a game at rummy, among the snow, frightened for the dog, It's not for any use, Tell your father I was asking for him* (i.e. 'asking after his health'), *I'm for a drink, We got skelped from the teacher, Did you get it in a present?, Sit in to the fire, You'll be better of a rest, Shout on him to come in, She's married on to the doctor, He missed the bus with sleeping in, a fried egg to my tea, I got up through the night*. Several of the Scots syntactic features already discussed have found their way into SSE: scarcity of *shall, may, ought*; possible combinations of modal auxiliaries; recessiveness of the negative clitic, particularly in interrogatives (*it's not, you'll not* rather than *it isn't, you won't*; *Did you not tell him?*; *Why can we not go?*; *We've done that already, have we not?*); relative constructions of the form *the house that the window got broken*. Unobtrusive habits in phrasing, not always possible to discuss as examples of general grammatical rules, likewise mark SSE: *That's me finished now*, *Have you on your shoes?*, *He's away to the school* (similarly *the church, the hospital* and *to his bed*), *I doubt he'll not be coming*, *The likes of you*, *Mind and not lose it*, *The cat's wanting out*, *I'll walk the length of the post office*, *I'll tell him whenever he comes*. Idioms such as *go the messages* 'do the shopping', *put his gas at a peep* 'show him in an unflattering light', *when it comes up my back* 'occurs to me', *up to high doh* 'approaching panic', *Come and give us your crack* 'chat with us', *Does he always get Bandy?* 'Is he always known as Bandy?', more obviously Scottish ones like *set the heather on fire* 'make a sensation', *back to auld claes and porridge* 'routine daily work', *come into the body of the kirk* 'join the company', *Jock Tamson's bairns* 'common humanity' and phrases with recognisable literary antecedents such as *to gang agley* 'go astray', *auld lang syne* 'the old days', *aa the airts* 'all localities or directions' can also occur.

SSE at its least overtly Scottish, that is, will by definition have a Scottish phonological system, and some features of grammar, lexis and idiom which an outsider, though not necessarily a Scot, would recognise as Scottish. It may, and often does, have quite a large number of these: clearly the more that are present the more clearly will the speaker's usage approximate to the theoretical concept of Scots rather than SSE. In fact, though the opposing concepts of Scots and Scottish English are entirely clear in theory, they are much less so in practice. In areas where the local form of Scots is both highly distinctive and well preserved, such as the north-east and the Northern Isles, conscious bilingualism is observable among many speakers: together they use the full canon of the local dialect; with outsiders, regionally accented SSE. A more common situation is for the speech of individuals to show some degree – sometimes a very high degree – of variability, their utterances containing more or fewer Scottish forms (on all levels) depending on the social situation, the speaker's frame of mind, or on no observable factor at all. It has always been assumed without question that one of the main functions of the primary- and secondary-school system is to instil in all pupils a command of English, and most Scots can approach the SSE model on occasions; but by no means all habitually do: there is no question that the traditional assumptions and methods of the schools have merely served to implant in some pupils a reticence when confronted with SSE speakers, and in others an active hostility to the model and its users. An important sociolinguistic fact in non-Gaelic Scotland is that apart from SSE there is no standard model; and the speech forms which do not conform to the prescriptions of SSE show such wide diversity as to present difficulties not only of description but even of classification. The existence of regional dialects of Scots is universally recognised, and as already noted, is the subject of considerable popular interest. The degree of divergence between the dialects is sometimes exaggerated: a not uncommon experience among fieldworkers is to meet informants who claim to find the speech of other communities incomprehensible and demonstrate this by offering a list of words from their local dialect – many of which turn out to be general Scots words: none the less, distinctively local features on all levels of language certainly exist. Wide variations in sociocultural attitudes are also observable: a very common habit is to draw a contrast between what is perceived as 'good' or 'real' Scots and what is perceived as 'coarse' or 'slovenly' speech – the model so designated is often denied to be Scots – the two forms being in reality perceptions of traditional rural dialects and urban working-class speech (Aitken 1982). In the north-east, an almost universal practice is to contrast the dialect of Aberdeen unfavourably with those of the agricultural hinterland.

2.4 Language and culture in Scotland

Language adds a distinctive colouring to the contemporary Scottish cultural scene. For serious literature, all forms of Scots are regularly used. An important literary development in the early years of the twentieth century was the emergence of a poetic medium often referred to as 'Lallans' or 'synthetic Scots'. This movement is principally associated with the poet Hugh MacDiarmid, its greatest and most influential exponent; but in the essential features of 'Lallans' – use of words taken from any region without regard for geographical consistency, and experimentation with lexical archaisms and words having strong and deliberately evoked literary associations – he was following precedents established by R. L. Stevenson and his own older contemporaries, Pittendreigh MacGillivray and Lewis Spence. The remarkable success of MacDiarmid's 'synthetic Scots' as a poetic medium led to the rise of a whole school of poets who shared both his determined commitment to Scots and his exuberant delight in experimenting with its phonaesthetic and semantic resources. This poetic movement continues in vigorous life to the present day.

In contrast to the 'synthetic Scots' movement, and even in some senses in opposition to it, local dialect poetry also continues to flourish, some writers of by no means negligible talent acquiring a high degree of popularity in their own areas. In the north-east, a new volume of poems or stories by a living writer such as Sheena Blackhall, and still more the reprinting of a collection by a 'classic' poet such as Charles Murray, is a guaranteed success. It is observable that though MacDiarmid and some of his 'Lallans' successors have far higher reputations, internationally and among literary scholars, than the dialect poets, they have nothing like the general appeal of the latter group. Readers who speak some form of Scots as their native tongue are often able to respond enthusiastically to the poetry of their own areas, but are puzzled or repelled by the artificiality of 'Lallans' writing. An interesting development of the last quarter-century has been the emergence of Glasgow demotic, written in a quasi-phonetic orthography, as a vehicle for both poetry and prose (Macafee 1983; Morgan 1983). Short stories in literary and dialectal Scots appear regularly, a number of literary magazines providing important outlets; and novels in which some form of Scots is the medium for part or all of the dialogue are published at a healthy rate. The themes and settings of these fictional works range from the romantic and nostalgic to the abrasively contemporary. A few tentative experiments have been made at using Scots for literary criticism and comments on the Scottish language situation; but it would be over-optimistic to suggest that these have so far even portended, let alone established, didactic prose in Scots as a viable genre.

One of the most remarkable works of Scots literature, in quality and range, of the twentieth century is a complete translation (from the original Greek) of the New Testament, by William Laughton Lorimer (1983). This version, produced after a lifetime's study of the original text, earlier translations in Scots and a wide variety of other languages, and the Scots tongue itself, is like Gavin Douglas' *Eneados* an unchallengeable confirmation of the full maturity of Scots as a literary language. Its critical and popular success has been enormous, and some individual ministers have taken to using it, at least on occasions, in regular services of worship.

A notable feature of Scottish artistic life is the presence of a number of small touring theatrical companies which perform experimental dramas, often with a strong element of topical sociopolitical comment, in which literary and/or colloquial Scots is prominent. On a more purely popular level, Scots plays a major part in the light entertainment scene. Summer variety shows and Christmas pantomimes regularly include performers of the genre known as 'Scoatch coamics': stand-up patter-merchants whose acts are given in the local dialect. Naturally their performances vary widely in quality, and the lack of discrimination among audiences is sometimes disconcerting; but there can be no question of their unfailing popularity. Songs by Burns and other Scots lyrics form part of the stock repertoire of music-hall singers. Guitar-playing folk singers, some of whom genuinely and not unjustly regard themselves as inheritors of the great tradition of Scottish balladry, often use language with at least some Scots features. Even the pop and rock scene in Scotland is distinctive, and includes some performers whose central-belt working-class accents are deliberately harnessed to the sociopolitical content of their songs. Newspapers regularly carry comic strips and cartoons in various forms of Scots: the best known are the weekly half-page strip stories in *The Sunday Post*, which have continued in a virtually unchanging format since the late 1930s: these were produced for many years by Dudley D. Watkins, a comic artist whose output was for quality and quantity remarkable by any standards, and who must be regarded as one of the architects of contemporary Scottish popular culture.

All this is spontaneous and self-generating: a case could indeed be made for suggesting that the enduring vitality of Scots is most surely manifested not in the 'Lallans' poetry of scholarly literati but in this intimate association of the language with popular entertainment.

In radio and television broadcasting, the Scottish linguistic presence ranges from an occasional SSE voice among BBC announcers, through a small number of contemporary dramas or documentaries with Scottish settings or dramatisations of Scottish literary classics, to a recent and very popular series of broadcasts by the presenter Billy Kay in which Scots-speaking practitioners of traditional crafts participated in extended interviews conducted entirely in their native dialects. Though not negligible, however, the use of Scots or even SSE in programmes made for Scotland is much less than could be reasonably expected; and both the BBC and the independent television companies are often criticised for their lack of support for the languages of Scotland. (Gaelic too, incidentally, has always suffered from a similar lack of attention, and the pointed contrast with the BBC's quite generous provision for Welsh has been frequently drawn: very recently, however, the central government, in a gesture of unprecedented generosity, has provided a huge subsidy for the production of Gaelic programmes. No plans have been announced for any comparable support to Scots.) The imminent changes in broadcasting regulations in the United Kingdom give grounds for anxiety that the Scottish content will be reduced still further, and an active campaign to guarantee the future of Scots and Scottish culture in broadcasting is in train at the time of writing.

English visitors to Scotland often report a gradual and increasingly surprised awareness that they have come to a different country, with institutions, attitudes and modes of behaviour that are very much its own. This is particularly true of the state of the language. A superficial glance would reveal nothing very startling. Gaelic and traditional Scots are spoken only by relatively small numbers, and most of the population conducts its daily business (or such of it as is shown to incomers) in what is in principle of a piece with the speech heard in England, Canada or New Zealand: the international English language with some local colouring in pronunciation. More intimate acquaintance reveals how pervasive has been the influence not only of the Scots tongue – which, even where apparently 'dead', haunts the scene with unshakable persistence – but of the enormous edifice of religious, legislative, scholarly and literary achievement which developed during Scotland's centuries of existence as an independent state.

FURTHER READING

The basic reference works on Scots are the *Scottish National Dictionary* (ed. W. Grant & D. D. Murison (Edinburgh: Scottish National Dictionary Association, 1931–76)), the *Dictionary of the Older Scottish Tongue* (ed. W. A. Craigie, A. J. Aitken *et al.*, current editor-in-chief H. Watson (Oxford: Oxford University Press, 1931-continuing)), and the *Linguistic Atlas of Scotland* (ed. J. Y. Mather & H. H. Speitel (London: Croom Helm, 1975–86)). The first, complete in ten volumes, contains entries for all distinctively Scots words and Scots usages of common English words attested since 1700: the last volume includes a Supplement (for the earlier letters of the alphabet, in effect a comprehensive updating) and a miscellanea section containing information on the pronunciation of Scottish place- and personal names, weights and measures, scientific names with Scottish connections, and other matters of Scottish cultural interest. The Introduction to the *SND* incorporates a detailed account of the phonological features which differentiate the various regional dialects.

The *Dictionary of the Older Scottish Tongue*, currently at letter S, is a comprehensive account of the language from the earliest period to 1700. Both these dictionaries originated in a plan to compile regionally and chronologically specialised complementary works to the *Oxford English Dictionary*, and the methods employed and standards attained are comparable to those of the parent work.

With the completion of the *SND*, the production team has applied itself to producing shorter and more readily accessible works, maintaining similarly high standards of scholarship. The *Concise Scots Dictionary*, editor-in-chief Mairi Robinson, is a one-volume abridgement of the *SND* and the *DOST*, but takes account of ongoing research, particularly on urban dialects of Scots, by including many items omitted from the large-scale dictionaries. The *Pocket Scots Dictionary*, ed. Iseabail Macleod *et al.*, is a simplified version of the *Concise Scots Dictionary* produced partly with the school market in mind: it omits most of the grammatical and phonological information contained in the entries for the *Concise Scots Dictionary*, though including general discussion of these aspects of the language in an introduction, but retains the detailed and clearly focused lexical definitions of the parent work. The *Scots Thesaurus*, ed. Iseabail Macleod *et al.* (1990), categorises the vocabulary of the *Concise Scots Dictionary* under such general headings as 'Birds, wild animals, invertebrates', 'Environment', 'Food and drink', etc., with numerous subsections; this novel application of Scots lexicography provides a highly informative introduction not only to the vocabulary but to all aspects of traditional Scottish life and culture.

The first two volumes of the *Linguistic Atlas of Scotland* contain information on the geographical distribution of dialect words for various entities or concepts: animals and birds, games, farm work and implements, weather conditions, parts of buildings, physical ailments, are among the semantic fields covered. The information is presented in two forms: maps with hatchings, and in the second volume also symbols, show a general picture of the distribution of some of the more widespread lexical items, and supplementary lists give each word elicited by researchers from the numerous informants. The third volume, on the phonology of the dialects, applies an original method of analysis involving the introduced concept of the *polyphoneme* to present the extraordinarily complex dialect variations in Scotland as a coherent overall picture.

3 ENGLISH IN WALES

Alan R. Thomas

3.1 Introduction

The social factors which brought about the dominance of English in Wales, and which have set in motion the process of language shift, have been political, economic and educational. The process of language planning – for political, rather than educational aims – effectively began with the political Acts of Union in 1536 and 1542, which were, ostensibly, to ensure equal rights for the Welsh with the English under the Tudor monarchy. The Welsh gained representation in Parliament, while Welsh laws and customs were abolished in favour of those of England. With this political and legal uniformity came the imposition of English as the official language of Wales. The Acts denied office under the Crown to all who had no mastery of English. Many Welsh people took advantage of the opportunities for advancement thus opened to them, becoming prominent courtiers and scholars who saw the adoption of the English language as a prime route to the cultural, social and political emancipation of the Elizabethan Age (see Hughes 1924: 11–15). The process was to be continued with the dominance of English in the development of industrialisation, and with conscious educational policy, which sought further to secure the position of English, to the exclusion of Welsh, as the language of commerce, government and education during the nineteenth century.

However, the English language had been making inroads into the indigenous Welsh-language speaking community since the fourteenth century, initially through the settlement of English colonies in the major townships. At this time, Royal Boroughs were established in north Wales, from which the Welsh were excluded by charter. In Anglesey, for instance, the English town of Beaumaris was built from the stones of a nearby village whose indigenous inhabitants were removed and resettled in the new, aptly named village of Newborough nearby. Trade became largely the province of the English-speaking townspeople, a fact which was a source of power and prestige both for the occupying community and its language. As others have observed (e.g. Mathias 1973: 38), the status which the English language increasingly acquired in Wales owed less to the numerical settlement of English speakers *per se* than to its establishment as the language of trade and commerce at this early time. Consequently, the towns, as trading centres, continued to be powerful sources of Anglicisation in later centuries, setting up a pervasive linguistic divide which was essentially that between the trading centres and the rural areas, paralleled by – and supporting – one which separated a small, influential section of the gentry from the mass of the peasantry.

The Acts of Union of 1536 and 1542 ensured that the Welsh people would have the same rights as the English in Wales, provided that the English language alone would have legal and administrative status:

> all justices... shall proclaim and keep... all... courts in the English tongue;... all oaths shall be given... in the English tongue;... no person or persons that use the Welsh speech or language shall have... any office... within this realm of England, Wales or other the King's Dominion... unless he or they use and exercise the English speech or Language. (Act of 1536, quoted in D. Williams 1950: 38)

The strong government of the Tudor period unified the kingdom, and literary, commercial and political interests elevated the English of the east midlands as the most influential tongue. Commerce had been essentially in the hands of the English settler communities from the thirteenth century onwards: following the Acts of Union, the power of the law was added to the forces promoting the English language, and, increasingly up to the twentieth century, education was mobilised in the effort to encourage the promotion of the English language as a unifying political and commercial factor, and to bring about the intended demise of Welsh. These were crucial developments: the thirteenth-century settlements (as in Beaumaris) introduced varieties of English which had no more status in the ears of the Norman hierarchy than had the Welsh language. The settlements were affairs of convenience – Edward I had Provençal as his first language, and his concern was to ensure the obedience of Wales (see Mathias 1973: 38–9) as a governed entity rather than to bring about linguistic uniformity in a language (English) for which his court had little regard. In the sixteenth century, the developing standard variety of east midlands English was endowed with the prestige of governmental and legal authority within what was to be the principality of Wales, as it was in England (see further Leith 1983: ch. 6). Its spread was to be helped by the fact that interpreters ('latimers') were to be allowed only for a limited time.

It should be noted, however, that there was very probably an existing base for the cumulative Anglicisation of Welsh society. There is evidence that a minority of educated gentry were already functioning as 'representatives' for the uneducated and monolingual peasantry. Llinos Smith (1987), for instance, describes a Commonplace Book, put together by one John Edwards in north-east Wales at the end of the fifteenth century. Edwards came of a cultivated and prosperous Welsh family which provided patronage for poets in the bardic tradition: she describes him as 'a literate layman of the upper stratum of Welsh society in this period' (p. 175). The Book contains a variety of materials, in French, English, Latin and Welsh, including vocabularies of Latin words with their English equivalents, and an elementary Latin grammar. Smith points out that 'the medium of instruction evidently preferred by John Edwards was the English language', and goes on to suggest that 'the use of English as a medium of instruction was already firmly established in the north-east March of Wales by the end of the fifteenth century' (pp. 181–2). Speaking generally of such collections of documents in the fifteenth century, Smith describes them as 'the practical and unstudied gleanings of busy men of affairs, lettered, cultured and entrusted with responsibilities for the business of their neighbourhoods' (p. 184). The infrastructure, then, was already in place for establishing English as the language of administration, represented by this section of the gentry which was in a position to grasp the opportunity of personal furtherance in the patronage of the English Tudor court.

Within Wales, the dominance of the English language in matters of law and government led to a new distinction between that part of the gentry which acquiesced in the new order, who became increasingly bilingual, and the peasantry and, no doubt, some of the gentry who remained largely monolingual Welsh for a time. However, by the late seventeenth century, English had made significant inroads into the Marches, as indicated by the need increasingly to hold church services in the language, particularly in Radnorshire, Breconshire and Monmouthshire (see further Mathias 1973: 45–52). This dominance of the eastern edge of the country was facilitated by the ease of communication provided by the Severn, Wye and Usk valleys. Outside Wales, the Welsh gentry went diligently to the service of their compatriot Tudor rulers in positions of reward in the Inns of Court, and ensured that their children were prepared for continued social enhancement through education (in English as well as Latin) in the new grammar schools in both Wales and England. This was a matter of great significance: those of the gentry who 'went' were the entrepreneurs, the potential innovators in the developing fields of science and commerce; those who 'stayed' were the ones who reasoned from the inertial position of regard for traditions of high culture which intersected little with the processes of 'modernisation' which were emerging in Europe in the sixteenth and seventeenth centuries. They continued the conventional role of the gentry in providing patronage for the Welsh literary tradition, but English became the instrument for advancement for the Welsh in the emerging world outside.

The nature of the bilingualism introduced by the Acts of Union, however, was of a particular kind, as was anticipated above. Bailey (1985: 14) captures it succinctly:

> The only persons likely to be awarded 'office or fees', of course, were anglicized Welsh people or English appointees, and thus the statute did little to disseminate the use of English among the majority of the population ... the government in London supported Protestantism by passing an Act for the Translation of the Bible and the Divine Service into the Welsh Tongue in 1563. Church politics thus was given primary attention and the politics of English a distinctly secondary role, with the consequence that the use of Welsh in religious services helped to maintain the language.

The perceived 'secondary' role of 'the politics of English' was only apparent. In its religious function, the Welsh language was granted a primary role in an area which isolated it from the political mainstream of the effort to establish a strong, unified kingdom – a classic diversionary tactic. The effect of the Act was to isolate the peasantry through its linguistically independent religious institutions, and to reinforce the social, political, economic and religious divisions already existing in Wales between the advantaged gentry and the disadvantaged peasantry. The established Church was an instrument of state, and needed to have little regard for the Nonconformism which ultimately became the champion of the Welsh language. By granting a religious role to the Welsh language, while withholding a secular role for it, the state created what was to be an effective language buffer between the gentry and the peasantry (and, later, between the governing industrialists and the working class) for two centuries.

Indeed, Anglicisation of the peasantry had made little territorial advance, even by the end of the eighteenth century. It was contained along the eastern edge, separated from the mass of the country, which was monolingual Welsh, by a narrow strip where both languages were in use. The eighteenth century, however, was the predominant period of English incursion on this eastern rim, the Marches. By 1750, church services were almost entirely in English in the eastern half of Radnorshire, where the progress of the language was not disadvantaged by its being within the English diocese of Hereford. Along the west bank of the Wye there was a strip where Welsh was understood until the end of the nineteenth century, but it had been bilingual since the middle of the eighteenth century: John Wesley had preached in Builth, on the banks of the Wye bordering Breconshire and Radnorshire, with no linguistic difficulty (attracting large crowds) as early as 1745 and 1746, whereas he had needed interpreters in places where the English language had not penetrated among ordinary people.

A similar situation is described by Pryce (1990: 51), when he describes the linguistic situation in Monmouthshire in the later decades of the eighteenth century, again on the basis of such factors as the pattern of need for church services in the two languages, as recorded in a survey ordered by the Bishop of Llandaf in 1771 (NLW Mss. Church in Wales Records LL/QA/4-5; SD/QA/182 (1762)): 'the major language divides between Welsh and English co-incided with the north–south orientation of the River Usk. Within this narrow sinuated zone it can be assumed that Welsh and English enjoyed roughly equal currency'. Pryce's characterisation of the bilingual area is interesting:

> the bilingual areas…were communities where Welsh and English enjoyed equal status in public activities [*though not in legal matters – author's gloss*]. This should not be taken to mean…that every resident spoke both languages. Rather, within the bilingual areas it was much more likely that individuals spoke either Welsh or English and the parish churches sought to meet the needs of different language congregations…Moreover, as anglicisation proceeded, this medial bilingual zone shifted steadily westwards.

This statement might be modified in the light of our knowledge of the linguistic development of communities with two languages at their disposal, to point up the potentially transient nature of bilingualism in such circumstances as Pryce describes. When two separate groups, speaking different languages, coexist and are involved in regular interaction as social equals (e.g. in work, leisure and religious observance), communication requires that a medial group of interpreters emerges with knowledge of both languages. Such a community is likely to have a more complex linguistic profile than that suggested by Pryce for Monmouthshire. The mediators function as a means of accommodation between the two distinct monolingual groups with each of whom they interact. The alternative would be a form of pidginisation as a means of communication, for which there is no evidence in Wales, and which would involve unidirectional linguistic innovation on the part of both language groups, and the emergence of a novel variety.

The social mechanism for Anglicisation of ordinary people was different from that of Anglicisation of the gentry, who sought office and favour under the Crown, and learned English as a self-interested intellectual exercise, frequently through the medium of the grammar schools. For the peasantry, knowledge of English arose from contacts in daily life with people from neighbouring communities who were monoglot English. It was a matter of language diffusion through the accommodation process as described, towards the language of people of the same social ranking as themselves, in the contact communities. But the result would be the same in both cases: a growing set of bilingual individuals, rather than communities – who would mark successive points on the scale of language shift.

The important point is that, at the social level of the pre-industrial peasantry, the progress of English at this time was one of westward geographical encroachment, whereas Anglicisation of the gentry had no such geographical pattern. Recent work on the transmission of dialect features between social groups of similar social status supports the crucial function of face-to-face interaction (particularly Trudgill 1986, building on Giles 1973). This assumes that, in day-to-day interaction, speakers will accommodate to the speech patterns of others whom – although of similar socio-economic status as themselves – they perceive as having social prestige (in this case, the prestige conferred on the interpreters by their linguistic range and extended social contacts). They adopt them as models, approximating to their speech mannerisms; this process is controlled by the frequency of direct contact, and mediated by social encounters, in market-places and other centres of day-to-day business. This is well illustrated by Trudgill for interacting groups of dialect speakers, and it is difficult to conceive of a community with two languages at its disposal functioning differently from one in which the modified behaviour involves dialect diffusion or stylistic adaptation – indeed, language shift involves both simultaneously.

This seems to be an apt model for the locally motivated, graduated movement from Welsh monolingualism through bilingualism to English monolingualism which these border areas displayed in the eighteenth century. What would be modified, in the language repertoire of Welsh speakers, would be the pattern of language choice in varying social contexts, cumulatively expanding from the public ones of the market-place to the private ones of the home environment.

This gradual geographical pattern of encroachment of English on the ordinary people of Wales was to be replaced during the eighteenth century by a more dynamic vehicle for the language, more effective in its power of diffusion. Henceforth, its target would be the entire industrial working class, and not simply the communities which happened to come into contact with it because of their proximity to others which were already English or Anglicised.

3.2 Modernisation, industrialisation and education

The nineteenth century, culminating in the spread of formal primary education following the Education Act of 1888, was the period which saw the tipping of the linguistic scales in Wales. It was the turn of the working class – numerically the major part of the population and soon to become politically dominant internally in Welsh affairs with the development of unionisation in the industrial south-east – to become increasingly Anglicised. Pressures of education and commerce, and the industrial expansion in the south-east of the country, gave the English language an unmatchable position of public prestige, coupled with economic power. Jones (1980: 62) says that 'In 1852 only one industrial school in South Wales used Welsh as a normal medium of in-struction … Twenty years later the social scientist, Ravenstein, failed to find a single Welsh school in Glamorgan.' The Education Act also led to direct promotion of the English language in the schools, and the deliberate neglect – even denigration – of Welsh.

During this period of industrial expansion, the need to expand the work-force in the south-east led to significant changes in the patterns of in-migration. At first, the largest proportion of migrants came from the strongly Welsh-speaking areas of west, and, later, north Wales. It is clear that, initially, they were instrumental in reinforcing the strength of the Welsh language in the south-east, helped by their allegiance to the

Table 3.1. *Population present on census night aged three and over 1921–81: proportion of population speaking Welsh*

Area	Percentage of all persons speaking Welsh					
	1921	1931	1951	1961	1971	1981
a	b	c	d	e	f	g
WALES	37·1	36·8	28·9	26·0	20·8	18·9
Counties						
Clwyd	41·7	41·3	30·2	27·3	21·4	18·7
Dyfed	67·8	69·1	63·3	60·1	52·5	46·3
Gwent	5·0	4·7	2·8	2·9	1·9	2·5
Gwynedd	78·7	82·5	74·2	71·4	64·7	61·2
Mid Glamorgan	38·4	37·1	22·8	18·5	10·5	8·4
Powys	35·1	34·6	29·6	27·8	23·7	20·2
South Glamorgan	6·3	6·1	4·7	5·2	5·0	5·8
West Glamorgan	41·3	40·5	31·6	27·5	20·3	16·4

Source: Census 1981: Welsh Language in Wales. Note that the new county names correspond to the old county territories as follows: Clwyd = Denbighshire and Flintshire; Dyfed = Pembrokeshire, Carmarthenshire, Radnorshire and Breconshire; Gwent = Monmouthshire; Gwynedd = Anglesey, Caernarfonshire and Merionethshire; Mid, South and West Glamorgan = Glamorgan.

Nonconformist religious denominations, whose Sunday Schools were the prime source of Welsh language maintenance. This was, however, a strongly bilingual community: Welsh was frequently the language of hearth and chapel, but English quickly became the dominant language of the work-place, even among the work-force.

This was reinforced by the pattern of migration. Throughout the nineteenth century there was massive repopulation of the south-eastern industrial area. Initially, it drew heavily on the Welsh heartlands in the north and the west, but those sources of labour were soon exhausted. Between 1861 and 1871, 22 per cent of migrants into the county of Glamorgan came from outside Wales; during the following decade, the figure had risen to 57 per cent; by 1901–11, the proportion had risen to 67 per cent, mainly from the south-west of England and the Anglicised Marches (see further Lewis 1978: 275ff.). Mathias (1973: 51) describes the linguistic consequences of this growing deluge of English speakers succinctly:

> After 1850 an immigrant Englishman had no need to learn Welsh as his predecessors had often had to do. The language of the bosses was

Table 3.2. *Population present on census night aged three and over 1921–81:*
proportion of population speaking Welsh, by age

Age last birthday	Percentage of all persons speaking Welsh					
	1921	1931	1951	1961	1971	1981
a	b	c	d	e	f	g
All ages 3 and over	37·1	36·8	28·9	26·0	20·8	18·9
3–4	26·7	22·1	14·5	13·1	11·3	13·3
5–9	29·4	26·6	20·1	16·8	14·5	17·8
10–14	32·2	30·4	22·2	19·5	17·0	18·5
15–24	34·5	33·4	22·8	20·8	15·9	14·9
25–44	36·9	37·4	27·4	23·2	18·3	15·5
45–64	44·9	44·1	35·4	32·6	24·8	20·7
65 and over	51·9	49·9	40·7	37·2	31·0	27·4

Table 3.3. *Proportion of Welsh people speaking only English 1921–81*

Age	1921 (%)	1981 (%)
3–4	73	87
5–9	70	82
10–14	68	82
15–24	65	85
25–44	63	85
45–64	55	80
65+	48	73

English: the commercial language was English: the language of
opportunity was English. And for their children the language of
school was English too. Many streets were wholly English-settled and
no other language was ever spoken there. One did not have to be a
genius or an astrologer to discern with which language the future lay.

Also, ultimately, the increasing frequency of mixed-language marriages
accelerated the generational dilution even of the bilingual stock.

The rise of the English language in Wales can be expressed as the
reverse of the fortunes of the Welsh language, and the irrevocable
advance of English is clear from the census figures for Welsh-language
speakers during the course of the present century (see tables 3.1 and 3.2).

The growth in the proportion of monolingual English speakers is
significant, up from about 63 per cent in 1921 to 81 per cent in 1981. The

generational increment shows a comparable pattern (table 3.3; figures rounded). There was a slight increase in the number of bilinguals of school age between 1971 and 1981, reflecting the expansion of Welsh-medium teaching, but this does not alter the fact that 100 per cent of the population effectively speaks English.

3.3 Language and social function

The critical occurrence of the twentieth century, however, is not the numerical decline of Welsh-speakers of itself, but the change in the character of the linguistic situation in Wales. The situation in Wales was essentially diglossic at the beginning of the century – possibly until the outbreak of the Second World War in 1939, which led to enormous social upheaval throughout the country, and was followed after the war by changes in agricultural practice which led to depopulation of rural areas with subsequent weakening of the communities which were, and remain, the bastions of the Welsh language. The English language functioned as the language of commerce, law, government and education – the major social institutions, admittedly – but Welsh had its prestigious institution in the Nonconformist religion of the chapels. If this identification of function for each language did not actually guarantee stability in the linguistic situation (there was a substantial monoglot English population which did not identify itself with Welsh-language institutions), it did at least help to retard the decline of the Welsh language. Social change has now robbed the Welsh language of the support it drew from this special association with religious institutions, simply because of the decline of the institutions themselves. Speakers of Welsh today are in the stage of transitional bilingualism. Whether this process can be halted will be a matter of political and economic management. What is certain, however, is that – whatever the fortunes of the Welsh language may be – the English language must, henceforth, be increasingly the dominant one in the Welsh community: dominant, because it must be learned and taught of necessity and not from choice. Its character, too, must change substantially over the next half-century. Two hundred years ago, the spread of English into Wales was still, to a considerable extent, a matter of geographical encroachment, the tide of English moving inexorably westwards. Today, the proliferation of media sources – press, radio, television, film – has removed any geographical constraints on the spread of English. This is illustrated by an interesting instance of word geography in Radnorshire, where the eastern parts of the county have the English dialect-word *oont* for 'mole', reflecting the encroachment of neighbouring English dialects: the west of the county, however, more recently Anglicised, has the standard form *mole* (Parry 1964).

3.4   Pembroke and The Gower

The southern part of the old county of Pembrokeshire has been Anglicised since medieval times. The cause of this is obscure. The traditional explanation is that it followed the establishment of a Flemish settlement there by Henry I in 1108. It is confusing that the northern boundary of the area is known by the Norse name *landsker*. It does run in a straight line, however, following no natural geographical contours, which suggests a politically imposed frontier and supports the notion of the plantation of a colony. Mathias (1973) points up another anomaly, in the frequency of place-names with the English element *-ton* (e.g. *Picton*, *Wiston*), and suggests that there must have been a preponderance of English-speakers amongst the settlers, particularly since south Pembrokeshire was English-speaking within a century of the plantation. The best guess, then, is a plantation of Flemings and English, in which the English dominated – not surprising, since it was a plantation of the English Crown. The source of Norse *landsker* remains a mystery, though it must have connections with the much earlier occupation of the area by Norsemen, which is attested, for instance, by the Norse-derived place-name *Haverfordwest*. One might surmise that the plantation occupied an area which already excluded the Welsh – the problem lies in what it did include in the twelfth century.

The Gower peninsula was similarly Anglicised before the fifteenth century. Mathias, again, proposes a substantial English settlement, on the basis of the early date of Anglicisation, suggesting that the earliest indication of trade links with the West Country (another possible source for Anglicisation), through the lime trade, came considerably later and could only have reinforced an existing situation.

In neither case is there surviving evidence for the gradual process of Anglicisation which is attested in the rest of Wales. Furthermore, the English communities in both these early enclaves of Anglicisation must have been in positions of political independence and economic isolation from their immediate neighbours, through self-sufficiency. Both have resisted the intrusion of Welsh, despite the strength of neighbouring dialects of Welsh – in Pembrokeshire until this century and in The

Gower until the Anglicisation of its industrialised hinterland – and seem not to have influenced the English which their Welsh-speaking neighbours have adopted. They appear to be linguistic cul-de-sacs in the development of the English language in Wales, now subject to the same universal influences as 'indigenous' dialects of English in Wales. If the argument suggested earlier for the function of accommodation through face-to-face contact in social contexts, for language shift within comparable social groupings, has validity, then it would seem that these two communities were essentially isolated communities for much of their history.

3.5   Attitudes to Welsh and English

There are some indications of the favourable perceptions held of English, in relation to its significance for the people of Wales, which emanate both from within and outside Wales itself: for instance, the report, published in 1847, of a government commission to enquire into the state of education in Wales, asserted that the Welsh language was 'a manifold barrier to the moral progress, as to the commercial propensity, of the people' (D. Williams 1950: 256). West (1983/4: 389) quotes from *The Times* of 1866: 'the Welsh language … is the curse of Wales … its prevalence and ignorance of the English language have excluded the Welsh people from the civilisation of their English neighbours'; and from J. Hughes (1822), who, while advocating the use of Welsh (in contradistinction to educational practice in the eighteenth century), considered English to be the superior language because of its status as 'the general language of the Empire'. And Jones (1980: 62) quotes Lord Powys, at the Rhuddlan Eisteddfod of 1850, who described the advantages of English as 'the highest objects of ambition'.

There are instructive reflexes of this regard for the social utility of the English language in the attitudes of present-day adults and children. Sharp *et al.* (1973), summarised in Lewis (1978), report a survey of language attitudes amongst 2,110 primary- and secondary-school pupils, spread through areas of varying Welsh-language density. Except for those schools which used Welsh as a teaching medium, in which parents and children had a conscious commitment to the maintenance of the Welsh language, Thurstone tests indicated that attitudes towards English became increasingly favourable as children got older. Their attitudes combine a high degree (between 60 and 80 per cent) of tolerance for the Welsh language with general approval of the need to know English, and recognition of its economic and educational importance. A parallel study of 200 adults, aged between twenty and thirty, revealed that this cumulative, age-related favouring in attitude towards English formed a progression consistent with that of the children, though balanced by increased tolerance for Welsh among monoglot English, which correlated with their length of stay in Wales.

There is, however, an apparent firming up of loyalty to the Welsh language among one group of adults. Williams, Roberts & Isaac (1978; see also Thomas 1980) investigated the motivations of two groups of forty working-class parents, in the heavily Anglicised Rhondda Valley, for preferring bilingual or monolingual medium education for their children at the primary level. It was hypothesised that those parents who chose the bilingual school would have expectations of their children which would involve upward social mobility without geographical mobility – that the parents were 'burghers', social introverts seeking opportunities for economic and social advancement within their native community. Those parents who chose monolingual-medium education would be 'spiralists', social extroverts prepared to look beyond and outside their immediate community for advancement. It is suggested that burghers take the utilitarian view, perceiving the Welsh language, alongside secondary and tertiary education, as an instrument of intergenerational social mobility, while spiralists see no such necessary potential for it in their aspirations for their children.

In response to questions about the value of a bilingual education, those who opted for the bilingual school claimed that it creates wider job opportunities; the kind of employment associated with these wider opportunities is connected with the media, local government, tourism and teaching. This is reflected in the ideal occupational aspirations for their children of parents who made the choice of a bilingual school. Their aspirations were overwhelmingly professional, involving social mobility. At the same time, these 'wider' opportunities were just that – additions to, rather than replacements of, other opportunities which might come as a reward of education. The parents who chose the English-medium school were more realistic: half denied the value of Welsh in terms of employment potential, pointing out that the number of jobs available which required a knowledge of Welsh were limited, and claimed that a knowledge of Welsh without intellectual ability was of little value. The majority saw their ideal occupations for their children as being in skilled and semi-skilled jobs. This reflects the fact that, for the overwhelming majority of non-professional adults (and for many of the professionals, as the census figures clearly imply), the English language is increasingly seen as the one which has the economic advantage. The differential in the areas of social utility of the two languages is clearly pointed up: Welsh language alignment is focused on a minority, elite range of occupations, while English is not subject to such narrowing of range to any significant extent (see further Thomas 1980).

3.6 Early Welsh English

There is evidence, even in the sixteenth century, of an awareness of there being regional variants of the English language other than the indigenous dialects of England (see also Russ 1982). In a general sense, this is reflected in literary practice of the time, whereby vernacular or colloquial speech is combined with dialectal features as an aid to dramatic characterisation. The identification of particular dialectal features and their assignment to specific regions is, however, problematic on two counts. First, few of the non-standard features which occur are so localised in their distribution as to make narrow regional assignment possible; dialect features do not belong exclusively to any dialect, nor do they commonly form patterns in identifiable clusters over homogeneous territories. Second, as is shown by Blake (1981), playwrights of the sixteenth and seventeenth centuries drew on conventions of colloquial speech to reflect lowly social status or comedic role rather than regional affiliation. In Shakespeare's delineation of his Welsh characters, we find both dialectally locatable features which can be characterised as 'Welsh', and others which belong to more general vernacular usage.

In *Henry V* (4.vii) Fluellen is given features of usage which can confidently be interpreted as 'Welsh'. His pronunciation frequently has *p* for *b*, 'I think it is in Macedon where Alexander is porne... that the situations looke you, is both alike... it is out of my praines.' In *The Merry Wives of Windsor* (1.i), as noted by Blake (1981: 90), this representation of voiced consonants as being voiceless is extended to include an *f* for *v* in 'fery', and *t* for *d* in ''ort' ('word') in the speech of Sir Hugh Evans. This feature derives from a hearer's subjective perception of pronunciation – both voiceless and voiced plosives in native English are weakly aspirated, so that the strongly aspirated voiced plosives of Welsh English are interpreted, by an ear attuned to native English, as voiceless ones. Sir Hugh's loss of the initial *w* in 'word' can also be seen to derive from the structure of Welsh, which has no sequences of semi-vowel followed by a homorganic or near-homorganic vowel; in this case, however, the form reflects objective observation by the hearer.

We find, also, a non-standard verb form in examples like

> 'your Maiestie *is take* out of the Helmet of Alanson [*sc.* Alençon].'
> 'I hope your Maiestie *is peare* [*sc.* bear] me testimonie.'

The italicised forms are structural correlates of the periphrastic verb forms of Welsh, in which the lexical verb is uninflected, with inflections for tense carried on the appropriate form of the verb *bod* 'to be' (see Jones & Thomas 1977: ch. 3). The contrast for tense, in Welsh sentences corresponding in structure to those above, is neutralised, and the verb *bod* occurs in its uninflected form; in Welsh English the neutralisation is carried over in the form of invariant present-tense selection rather than the uninflected *be*. Such forms are not uncommon today in the usage of early learners of English and occasionally of elderly speakers who have imperfect control of the language.

Fluellen's use of the archetypal idiom 'look you' is interesting in that it reflects the word order of Welsh, in which the verb precedes its subject, and Blake (1981: 84) points out that parallel idiomatic usages, like *tell you*, *see you* are also found; as does *mark you*, which is of general occurrence.

Other features, though typical of Welsh English, are of wider geographical provenance. Lack of concord between a verb and its plural subject is common,

> 'Ay, *leeks is* good.'
> 'Your *shoes is* not so good.'

This feature accords with the structure of Welsh, which has no singular/plural contrast in the verb when it has a lexical noun (singular or plural) for its subject: on the other hand, it is also a common feature of English vernacular usage.

Another feature, though again typical of Welsh English, owes nothing to interference from the structure of Welsh. It is the use of unstressed forms of *do* as auxiliary tense carriers, in contexts like

> 'a garden where leeks *did* grow'

Dialectally, such forms are widespread in the south-west and west midlands of England, and are part of the composite linguistic repertoire of one lowly or comedic character type.

Similar features are found in other Elizabethan dramatic texts; see, for instance, references to George Peele's *Edward I* (1593), Henry Chettle's

Patient Grissel (1603) and Ben Jonson's *For the Honour of Wales* (1619) in Hughes (1924), in all of which the speech of Welsh characters is uniformly marked by features like those described above.

This caricature of Welsh English captures – though irregularly (note that, in the first quotation above, 'is porne' is followed by the regular form 'is both') – features which are evidenced today, particularly in the less-developed varieties. This very fact warrants the salience of this variety of English in sixteenth- and seventeenth-century dramatic performance. Its salience, for author and audience alike, must hold, even allowing for the role of convention in the dramatist's delineation of character, and for that of compositors of printed texts, who might well have generalised their own preconceptions of usage types over the language of regional and rural caricatures.

However, first-hand evidence for the nature of Welsh English before the twentieth century is very limited, and awaits further investigation. West's quotation (p. 105) comments on the general lack of fluency in English among the Welsh populace as late as the mid-nineteenth century. This is supported by other observers of Welsh society of the time. De Quincey (1856), for instance, records a visit to a home in Merionethshire in 1802, when he wrote letters for the younger members of the family, 'about prize money for one of the brothers, and more privately two letters to sweethearts for two of the sisters' (quoted in Hughes 1924: 96). Such comments point up the social imbalance in the diffusion of English which was earlier noted. It was adopted primarily by the gentry, who belonged to the politically more sophisticated stratum of society, and understood the potential of English as an instrument of social advancement within the framework of the British (English) polity. They were agents of government in Wales, and the documented use of English which survives is constrained either by the needs of public administration, the law and politics, or by the social and educated status of its users. Similarly, there is no 'Anglo-Welsh' literary usage to compare with the, admittedly skeletal, 'external' representations of 'Welsh English' which we find in the works of Shakespeare and his contemporaries. The English language documented in the usage of native Welsh writers is that of standard English, seldom distinguishable from that of England. Thus, while spoken English in Wales un-doubtedly carried over distinctive features of the phonological system of Welsh, the model for written usage was overwhelmingly that of standard written English.

At the same time, De Quincey's comment illustrated an acute social dilemma. It was the growing tension between the generally perceived functional status of English as a medium of communication – not only in administration, but for letter writing, seemingly even for private purposes – and the lack of literacy in English (as in Welsh, at this time, for the majority) amongst the peasantry. The use of English for written communications, both formal and personal, was to remain a mark of language use in Wales to the present day.

Wills, by their nature, are made up by formula, and a sample drawn from the sixteenth century onwards, from the archives of the National Library of Wales and of the University of Wales, Bangor, reveals few regional features of language beyond the very occasional intrusion of words from the Welsh language. In the will of John Thomas ap Robert (St Asaph R6: Copies of Wills 1620–3, fol. 147d, UW Bangor), the word *cerwyn* (< Latin *cerena*) 'a small tub' occurs, and both male *ap* and female *ach* patronymics, as in 'my Wief Elizabeth ach Morgan and Robt. ap Thomas my granndchild'. In this will, too, there is one instance of an adjective following its headword, after the pattern of Welsh, in the phrase 'on [*sc.* one] hefer black'. A will of 1661 made by 'Lewis Thomas, smith Llanllwchaearn, Cards' (NLW mss.), leaves 'To daughter Ellinor her mother jest': the omission of the possessive pronoun in 'mother jest' is a common feature which has no obvious source, while the representation of initial *ch* by ⟨j⟩ is so common as to be of no significance. The will of 'Llikie Howell, Betws, Cards' (1661, NLW mss.) has a loan from Welsh *ŵyr* 'grandson', 'To James David my eldest *wooere* one cow'. The remainder of a sample of wills dating from 1582 onwards likewise used the formal conventions of the genre without exception, and with little interference from Welsh or general vernacular usage.

The orthography, as the examples indicate, is irregular and internally inconsistent, but not in ways which differ from those of similar documents of the time from England. At the same time, they give no indication of influence from the orthography of Welsh, itself a complex of competing systems until the twentieth century. Legal documents from the seventeenth century relating to Cardiganshire are similarly formal in style and undistinctive in orthography.

Personal letters have some evidence of Welsh influence, though it is not extensive even in the nineteenth century. *Llythyron Sion Gymro* (National Library of Wales, Ms. 8623 C) has letters from W. Davies. In one to Dr Friend, written from Canerw, 10 July 1826, there are some instances of translation of Welsh idiom:

> 'I am *against* you *to come*', from 'wyf yn erbyn ichwi ddod' (lit. am(-I) in by for-you come)

carrying over the prepositional idiom which takes the uninflected form of the verb in Welsh;

> 'I *think to be* at Newtown...', from 'wyf yn meddwl bod yn...' (lit. am(-I) in think be in...)

where the semantic field of Welsh *meddwl* encompasses that of *think*, *expect*, *intend* in English.

However, the same letter has numerous other examples of vernacular or mistaken usage which could occur in a contemporary letter from any region of Britain, in the genre of personal letter writing not constrained by formula.

Roberts 1976, a volume of letters written between 1840 and 1935 between members of an Anglesey family, offers many examples of non-standard English, most of which cannot be distinguished from general vernacular usage. A letter dated 26 August 1852 (p. 37) is typical of the set, which the editor describes (p. 8) as 'being written in the Welsh idiom'. The omission of the preposition from the phrasal verb *wait for* in the following sentence cannot be identified with Welsh structure, for instance: 'He is only waiting his clothes to be ready' (p. 37, 1.9). In the same letter, however, we again find the ubiquitous uninflected verb 'Your dear mother most humbly *desire* if possible for you to prevent him from *go* to sea', which certainly derives from the structure of Welsh. Though the style of these and other letters is a distinctive genre, the extent to which the distinctiveness is unequivocally 'Welsh' is less clear. Where a feature might fortuitously be interpreted as being ambiguous between 'Welshness' and vernacular, I have opted for the latter.

Letters from tenants to the Voelas Estate (NLW mss.) as recently as the early twentieth century similarly show little evidence of intrusion by Welsh structural features:

> Voel C760 (4 Dec. 1902) has *has been ask me* which contains a confused English perfective element '*has __en* +verb' with an uninflected verb form, in place of the standard '*has* verb + *ed*'. This suggests interference from the corresponding Welsh structure *wedi gofyn imi* (lit. after (PERFECTIVE) ask to-me), in which perfectiveness is marked by preposition, and all verb forms are left uninflected; Voel C782 26 Dec. 1902 also has an uninflected lexical verb in a perfective verbal phrase,

'The police *have* not *catch* the person who fired the hay'; in Voel C763 5 Dec. 1902, there is an indirect question without inversion of word order, 'Will you kindly let us know *can we get it*', another example of influence from the structure of Welsh (see later section on syntax); on the other hand, Voel C728 (Tach. 11 (Nov.) 1902) has features which are of common vernacular occurrence in many varieties of spoken English. It has an unmarked plural in the quantitative phrase *3 Ton*, and an irregular past tense in the phrase 'But I did not *made* my mind up', in which there is dual marking of the past, an infrequent feature.

Other genres offer little scope for individuality because they are necessarily formulaic or abbreviated in character. The Abermeurig Account Book for 1758 (NLW mss.) shows no evidence of either Anglo-Welsh or vernacular usage. On the other hand, the Diary of Howel Harris for 1795 (NLW mss.) is more discursive, and has some features which are typical of general vernacular usage, like the lack of subject–verb agreement in the entry for February 19, 'Williams Langinid & Margaret his Wife *was broke out*'; this also has the past-tense form *broke* as past participle, and the translated Welsh idiom *torri maes* (lit. 'break out'), in the sense 'expel from chapel membership'.

Welsh English, in its less formal historical genre, seems to be marked by general vernacular features more than by those which are specifically 'Welsh'. Their provenance can only be hinted at in the absence of extensive archival research.

3.7   Modern Welsh English

In the south – particularly in the industrial south, in the Glamorgans – and in the eastern counties which border with England, there are already indigenous English dialects which have strong affinities with the English dialects of the west midlands and the south-west of England, superimposed on distinct substratal Welsh influences (see Parry 1972; Thomas 1983, 1984). These dialects are now independent of contemporary Welsh influence, and we must expect them progressively to shed indigenous Welsh characteristics since their model, in the realm of public prestigious usage, is that of RP and standard English (though see Coupland (1989) for a proposal for the emergence of a 'standard' form of Welsh English).

External dialectal influences on north-eastern Welsh dialects of

English stem from the north-western counties of England, and we must expect the extraneous standard model to have the same influence on the development of those dialects, too. In the western parts of Wales – where the Welsh language is at its strongest – less 'evolved' English dialects are found, with evidence of structural interference from the contemporary Welsh language. Note the difference between these western areas (Gwynedd and Dyfed), in which the Welsh language is a living influence on the English usage of bilinguals, and those eastern areas (much of Clwyd, most of Powys and the Glamorgans) in which the influence of the Welsh language is essentially substratal. The distribution of Welsh-speakers by percentage of population, as shown in tables 3.1 and 3.2 (see pp. 101, 102), point up the relatively sharp divide between these areas.

In the following discussion, I have taken a dialect in south Wales as a model, and indicated departures from it, noting two primary variants, those of the rural areas of the south-west and north. I have drawn on the items listed in the bibliography as well as on my own knowledge. To have acknowledged sources systematically would have incurred heavy intrusions on the text by annotation. The major published source for the dialects of Welsh English is Parry's *Survey of Anglo-Welsh Dialects* (1977, 1979); for further structural descriptions of specific varieties, together with discussions of their social status, see Coupland & Thomas (1990). Penhallurick (1991), a northern companion to Parry's work, came to hand too late for extensive use to be made of it.

In south Wales there are two major distinguishable varietal types. In the west, where the majority of speakers are bilingual in Welsh and English, there is interaction between the two languages which results in interference from Welsh in the structure of the region's English, in phonology, grammar and vocabulary; in the east – evidenced particularly from north Powys – there are substantial traces of the influence of neighbouring dialects of English in Shropshire, Hereford-and-Worcester and Somerset, alongside the substratal Welsh influence alluded to earlier.

For formal varieties of Welsh English, however, the determining models are those of standard English and RP. This is an indication of the extent to which Welsh English has been integrated into the overall sociolinguistic distribution pattern of English in Britain. It also reflects the sociological change which accompanies (indeed, causes) the shift from Welsh to English, which is inextricably linked with the expansion of middle-class occupations in Britain as a whole during this century. In grammar and vocabulary, formal usage must, of necessity, model itself on standard English usage; in pronunciation, Welsh English has adopted the class varieties of the English of England (with the expected regional modifications), as societal structure in Wales has changed with modernisation and industrialisation. Variety choice in the use of English in Wales observes a social patterning which is distinct from that which traditionally characterised variety choice in the Welsh language, in which it has been argued that 'lifestyle' connected with 'chapel' or 'pub' (to put the argument simplistically) were the determining factors (Rees 1950). For Welsh English, social class and professional status appear to be the determining factors, given the override one expects from features which have distinctive regional connotations, in terms of localised social affiliations. It also suggests a potential area of conflict for the bilingual speaker, whose social network allegiances may differ between the two language contexts, requiring different social conditions for varietal choice.

On colloquial usage, a significant influence is also that of 'general vernacular', which is regularly encountered through the media, in addition to more direct contact. I will give some exemplification of those features which are vernacular without being necessarily 'Welsh'.

3.7.1 Varieties

There are at least three varieties of usage, associated with the industrial south, the south-west and the north:

1   That associated with the industrial south. This is the more 'evolved' in that, although it clearly has substratal Welsh influence, it is probably isolated completely from contemporary interference from Welsh language features. This dialect – like those in the north of Powys which share its historical affinity with neighbouring dialects in England – can be expected to develop independently of Welsh influence, since their models for prestigious usage are those of standard English and RP. They retain distinctively 'Welsh' features, but as residual or fossil items – and as markers of internal communal solidarity, and of national 'separateness' (see Giles & Powesland 1975; Coupland 1989).

2   In the south-west, where the dialects have overt influence from Welsh, at all levels of structure, and have a distinctive verbal feature. It seems likely that this variety will increasingly come under the influence

of the dialects of the south-east, the industrially and commercially dominant region.

3 The northern varieties which are, to our knowledge, the most dependent upon Welsh for explication of their distinctive characteristics, though the status of Liverpool as an industrial and commercial centre has led to increasing penetration by the dialects of Merseyside along the north Welsh coastline, as in the occurrence of hypercorrect /ə/ for short /ʊ/ in words like *butcher*. The current development of the A55 coastal route as an expressway in this region will doubtless enhance communication with the north-west of England, and the influence of its dialects.

3.7.2 *Phonology*

I will describe the major distinctive dialectal features under structural headings, assuming as a base reference what may broadly be described as an 'evolved' variety of the industrial south. Prominent dialect variants follow.

Pronunciation

The chart below shows the vowel and diphthong phonemes of a typical South-Welsh English dialect – the dialect of the Swansea valley. Their precise phonetic values will be commented on where helpful, but their general values can be inferred from the IPA notation used.

Vowels							Diphthongs					
iː		uː	ɪ		ʊ		ɪu					
eː	ɜː	oː	ɛ	ə	ɔ			əu	ou	ei	əi	ɔi
	aː			a								

Welsh English differs from RP in a number of ways, which will be described in terms of the lexical sets proposed by Wells (1982), which are identified largely in terms of orthographic sets. 'These enable one to refer concisely to large groups of words which tend to share the same vowel, and to the vowel which they share.' For earlier descriptive comments, see Wells (1970).

KIT words uniformly have /ɪ/, as in

/bɪt/	/dɪg/	/wɪð/	/mɪə/	/prɪti/	/bɪld/	/wɪmɛn/	/bɪzi/
bit	dig	with	myth	pretty	build	women	busy

and DRESS words have /ɛ/, as in

| /nɛk/ | /ɛg/ | /sɛks/ | /brɛd/ | /ɛni/ | /frɛnd/ |
| neck | egg | sex | bread | any | friend |

TRAP words have /a/, as also can the LOT words *wasp* and *quality*, as in

| /tap/ | /mas/ | /mad/ | /and/ | /wasp/ | /kwalɪti/ |
| tap | mass | mad | hand | wasp | quality |

Otherwise, LOT words have /ɔ/:

| /rɔb/ | /ɔd/ | /dɔl/ | /ɔnɛst/ | /swɔn/ | /gɔn/ |
| rob | odd | doll | honest | swan | gone |

STRUT words have /ə/, as in

| /kəp/ | /bəd/ | /ənt/ | /kəm/ | /i'nəf/ | /bləd/ |
| cup | bud | hunt | come | enough | blood |

FOOT words have /ʊ/ as in

| /pʊt/ | /pʊl/ | /lʊk/ | /ʊmən/ | /kʊd/ |
| put | pull | look | woman | could |

BATH words form a mixed set:

1   the majority are not distinguished from the TRAP set, and have a short low central vowel /a/, as in

| /paθ/ | /gras/ | /nasti/ | /dans/ | /slant/ |
| path | grass | nasty | dance | slant |

2   some have the same vowel lengthened, having merged with the PALM set, as in

| /kaːf/ | /aːv/ | /laːf/ | /laːðə/ |
| calf | halve | laugh | lather |

CLOTH words have merged with LOT words in this dialect, and have /ɔ/:

| /ɔf/ | /sɔft/ | /mɔθ/ | /sɔri/ | /kwɔrɛl/ |
| off | soft | moth | sorry | quarrel |

The NURSE set has a long, half-close central vowel /ɜː/, with some degree of lip-rounding (see Wells 1982: 139) as in

| /ɜːt/ | /vɜːb/ | /tɜːm/ | /bɜːn/ | /gɜːl/ |
| hurt | verb | term | burn | girl |

FLEECE words generally have /iː/:

| /biː/ | /liːv/ | /driːm/ | /fiːld/ |
| bee | leave | dream | field |

FACE words maintain a contrast between the monophthong /e:/ and the diphthong /ei/. Words with an orthographic diphthong ⟨ai⟩, ⟨ay⟩, ⟨ei⟩ or ⟨ey⟩ have the phonetic diphthong /ei/, as in

/seil/	/sei/	/eit/	/prei/
sail	say	eight	prey

Those which have an orthographic correlate in ⟨a...e⟩, ⟨ea⟩ or ⟨a⟩ are represented by the monophthong /e:/:

/le:t/	/ke:k/	/gre:t/	/ste:k/	/fe:məs/
late	cake	great	steak	famous

PALM words have a central open vowel /a:/, with the length of its RP correlate:

/ka:m/	/sa:m/	/sɔ'pra:no/
calm	psalm	soprano

except for *almond*, which has the TRAP short vowel, /almənd/.

THOUGHT words are a mixed set. With orthographic correlates in ⟨au⟩, ⟨ou⟩, ⟨aw⟩, ⟨o⟩ and ⟨a⟩ before an historical ⟨r⟩, and ⟨a⟩ before an historical ⟨l⟩, it is long half-open /ɔ:/, as in

/bɔ:k/	/ɔ:t/	/lɔ:n/	/kɔ:d/	/wɔ:p/	/ɔ:l/
baulk	ought	lawn	cord	warp	hall

Before a retained phonetic consonant cluster, however, orthographic ⟨a⟩ and ⟨au⟩ usually have the short vowel /ɔ/:

/sɔlt/	/fɔls/	/ɔlso/	/fɔlt/	/vɔlt/
salt	false	also	fault	vault

Exceptions to the latter rule are

/tɔ:nt/	/bɔ:ld/
taunt	bald

GOAT words maintain a contrast between the long vowel /o:/ and the diphthong /ou/. Orthographic ⟨o⟩, ⟨o...e⟩, ⟨oa⟩, ⟨oe⟩ and ⟨ou⟩ occur as /o:/:

/so:/	/to:n/	/so:p/	/to:/	/ðo:/
so	tone	soap	toe	though

as do orthographic ⟨ore⟩, ⟨oor⟩, ⟨oar⟩ and ⟨our⟩ from the FORCE set:

/so:/	/do:/	/bo:d/	/po:/
sore	door	board	pour

Orthographic ⟨ow⟩, and ⟨o⟩ and ⟨ou⟩ before an ⟨l⟩ which is pronounced, occur as /ou/:

/blou/	/bould/	/soul/
blow	bold	soul

GOOSE words with orthographic ⟨oo⟩, ⟨o...e⟩, ⟨o⟩ or ⟨ou⟩ have /uː/, as in

/luːp/	/fuːl/	/muːv/	/duː/	/ɵruː/
loop	fool	move	do	through

those with ⟨u⟩, ⟨u...e⟩, ⟨eu⟩, ⟨ue⟩, ⟨ew⟩, ⟨iew⟩ and ⟨eau⟩ have the diphthong /ɪu/:

/dɪuk/	/tɪun/	/flɪu/	/fɪud/	/ɪu/	/fɪu/	/vɪu/	/bɪuti/
duke	tune	flu	feud	hue	few	view	beauty

Exceptionally, /jɪuɵ/ *youth* and /jɪu/ *you* have merged with this group, and are rare instances of a semi-vowel followed by a homorganic vowel, although it occurs only as a 'linking yod', when the preceding segment is a vowel: contrast these forms of *you*

/wɪl ɪu goː/	Will you go?
/aː jɪu goːɪn/	Are you going?

Less evolved dialects in west Wales, which preserve the post-vocalic /r/, would have the form /aːr ɪu goːɪn/.

PRICE words are uniformly /əi/:

/ləim/	/trəi/	/təi/	/təim/	/əit/
lime	try	tie	time	height

CHOICE words are uniformly [ɔi], always short:

/bɔi/	/nɔiz/	/kɔin/	/pɔint/	/ɔintmɛnt/
boy	noise	coin	point	ointment

In this variety, the words *choir* and *reservoir* have the diphthong of the CHOICE set, followed by /ə/: /kɔiə/; /rɛzevɔiə/.

MOUTH words are uniformly /əu/, as in

/ləus/	/əund/	/ləud/	/kəu/
louse	hound	loud	cow

NEAR words generally have the dissyllabic vocalic sequence /iːə/, as in

/diːə/	/biːə/	/fiːə/
dear	beer	fear

Those with ⟨e(e)⟩ or ⟨ea⟩ before ⟨r⟩ in the stressed syllable of a polysyllabic, however, have merged with the FLEECE set, giving forms in /iː/, like

/siːrjəs/	/piːrjəd/	/iːro/	/driːri/
serious	period	hero	dreary

SQUARE words are uniformly /ɛː/:

/fɛː/	/pɛː/	/vɛːry/	/skɛːs/
fair	pear	vary	scarce

except for /ðeiə/ *their*.

START words have merged with the PALM set, having a low central /aː/:

/faː/	/kaːv/	/paːti/	/faːm/
far	calve	party	farm

Both sets have, as their central membership, words with a vocalic nucleus followed by an historical orthographic liquid.

NORTH words have /ɔː/, as in

/bɔːk/	/kɔːz/	/kɔːd/	/ɔːl/	/lɔːn/
baulk	cause	cord	hall	lawn

except for /impoːtənt/ *important*, which has merged with FORCE.

FORCE words uniformly have /oː/, with the quality of the GOAT subset which has the same monophthong:

/moː/	/floː/	/soːd/	/toːn/	/koːt/	/foːə/
more	floor	sword	torn	court	fourth

CURE words behave in one of three ways. Some with orthographic ⟨oor⟩ or ⟨our⟩ have [uː], and are the only words which retain the *r* in word-final position for this dialect: thus

/muːr/	/tuːr/	/tuːrist/	/buːriʃ/
moor	tour	tourist	boorish

Others have the sequence /uːə/:

/puːə/	/duːə/
poor	dour

Those with ⟨u⟩ have the diphthong /iu/, followed by /ə/ when there is no following consonant:

/bɪuro/	/mɪural/	/pɪuə/	/manɪuə/
bureau	mural	pure	manure

Sure has /uː/ followed by /ə/ – /ʃuːə/.

Some general features

1   The front close vowels, for most varieties, are not strikingly different from RP, except that in a final unstressed syllable, with orthographic correlates ⟨i⟩, ⟨ie⟩, ⟨y⟩ or ⟨ey⟩, for instance, the vowel is always fronted to the position of the long vowel [iː], as in

/sɪti/	/pɪti/	/kwɪkli/	/məni/	/mɛni/	/taksi/
city	pity	quickly	money	many	taxi

2   Welsh English has no contrast between /ʌ/ and schwa /ə/: it has only the short vowel /ə/, so that both short vowels can be identical in forms like

/rənə/	/bətə/
runner	butter

3   The same short central vowel occurs as the first element of diphthongs in which RP has a glide from the fully open position to the fully close front or back. Thus

/məin/	/əus/
mine	house

This is unlikely to be a substratal vestige of the Welsh language, however, since Welsh has closely corresponding diphthongs to those which RP has in words like these (see Wells 1982: 383–4) – and the diphthongs of Welsh English are restricted in number in comparison with those which occur in the Welsh language. It seems clear that these diphthongs were fossilised in Welsh English before the shifts from /iː/ to /ai/ and /uː/ to /au/ were completed in varieties of English in England in PRICE and MOUTH sets, and represent the medial position of the lowering process.

4   Vowels followed by /ə/: of the three centring diphthongs of RP, /ɛə/, /ɪə/ and /uə/, /ɛə/ is represented by the pure long vowel /ɛː/, as in /pɛː/ *pear*. /ɪə/ (realised phonetically as [iːə]) and /uə/ are represented by a dissyllabic sequence of long vowel and schwa, with a strong tendency to develop a following /j/ or /w/ glide between the

two vowels, homorganic with the first one, as in [diːə] ~ [diːjə] *deer*; [puːə] ~ [puːwə] *poor*. Examples of the [uːwə] sequence are scarce in our specimen dialect, since most correlates of orthographic ⟨ure⟩ (a major source of the centring diphthong /uə/ in RP) are realised as a sequence of diphthong /ɪu/ + /ə/, as in /pɪuə/ *pure*, /kɪuə/ *cure*. These forms, like those above, can develop a homorganic /w/ glide, as in /pɪuwə/, /kɪuwə/.

5 Diphthongs followed by /ə/: the diphthongs in words like *mower*, *player*, may be followed by /ə/. In RP, the second element of the diphthong is frequently elided, with compensatory lengthening of the first element ('smoothing', after Wells, 1982: 238): for Welsh English, however, the diphthong is retained, often with the introduction of a homorganic glide as described already, giving parallel sets of forms like these: /mouə/ ~ /mouwə/; /pleiə/ ~ /pleijə/.

6 As in other varieties of English, the close long vowels /iː/ and /uː/ have considerably shortened variants before voiceless plosives and fricatives, as in

[liˑp]	[liˑf]	[luˑp]	[luˑs]
leap	leaf	loop	loose

7 Diphthongs closing to /i/ and /u/ have their second element approximating to the point of articulation of the long vowels [iː] and [uː], rather than that of their short correlates [ɪ] and [ʊ]. Similarly, the final unstressed vowel in words like *happy* and *city*, approximate to the position of [iː] rather that of [ɪ], and is retained in the plural, as in [sɪtiːz] *cities*.

Stress

In general, the stress system of Welsh English is not different from that of RP. Two distinctive features associated with Welsh English stress, however, derive from characteristics of the Welsh language. Long vowels, in the model we describe, occur only in stressed syllables – a feature of Welsh. Consequently, words like *expert* and *export*, which have a long vowel in the final syllable in RP, have a short vowel in Welsh English: /ɛkspət/, /ɛkspɔt/. In rhotic dialects, they have the forms /ɛkspərt/, /ɛkspɔrt/, and even in the process of accommodation to more standard varieties, in which post-vocalic /r/ is lost, there is no compensatory lengthening of the preceding vowel when it is unstressed.

Again, the intonation system of Welsh differs from that of RP in that pitch movement occurs on the syllables which *follow* a non-final stressed (tonic) syllable. Because of that, an unstressed syllable may have prominence equal to that of a preceding stressed one, or greater than it.

This phenomenon is carried over into Welsh English, and is the source of the resistance of unstressed final-syllable vowels to *reduce*. In this context, Welsh English has an unreduced vowel where RP has /ɪ/ or /ə/, giving forms like /ˈvilɛdʒ/ *village*, /ˈbəkɛt/ *bucket*, /soːfa/ *sofa*. A 'full' vowel is also retained in pre-stress syllables where RP has a reduced vowel, giving forms like

/aˈləu/   /ɔˈpoːz/
allow   oppose

It is tempting to suppose that investigation would again reveal a connection with the phenomena of stress and intonation – possibly a lesser differential between 'weak' and 'strong' syllables (in terms of prominence) than there is in RP.

At the same time, post-stress vowels in pre-final syllables resist *elision* for the same reason that post-stress final syllable vowels resist reduction, so that Welsh English has:

/ˈtɔlərɛt/   rather than /ˈtɔlreit/ (tolerate)
/ˈsɛpərɛt/   rather than /ˈsɛprɪt/ (separate)

Pilch (1983/4: 245) makes a related point about the intonation patterns of what he labels 'Cambrian English', when he comments on the unusual frequency of the rising pitch pattern, going on to say that 'This must have suggested the popular idea that the Welsh speak English on a very high pitch.'

Consonants

The inventory of Welsh English consonants is identical with that of RP except that our Welsh English specimen has no regular glottal fricative /h/, and consequently no aspirated semi-vowels /hj/ or /hw/; it also has two additional phonemes /ɬ/ and /x/, both with restricted incidence, which is illustrated in section 3.7.6.

Distinctive features of the Welsh English consonantal system include the following.

1   *Aspiration.* Plosives in Welsh English are accompanied by a much stronger aspiration feature than are those of RP. Indeed, the aspiration

which accompanies *voiced* plosives in Welsh English is almost as strong as that which accompanies *voiceless* plosives in RP. This feature is the source of one of the more common ways of caricaturing the phonetic characteristics of Welsh English speech in literature, in which voiceless plosives are made to substitute for voiced ones – thus reflecting the way in which an ear attuned to the relatively weakly aspirated voiced plosives of native English interprets the corresponding sounds in Welsh English (see the earlier comments on Shakespeare's rendering of Fluellen's accent). Examples are legion, and take the form of the following: *Pring the pottle, Petty* (for 'Bring the bottle, Betty'). Indeed, the phonetic opposition between the so-called 'voiceless' plosive series and the corresponding 'voiced' one in Welsh English is less one of voice than of the relative strength of the aspiration features which accompany them. In absolute initial or final position, the degree of voicing present may vary from the partial,

$$[_\circ^b\text{bɪn}] \qquad [\text{nɪb}_\circ^b]$$
$$\text{bin} \qquad\quad \text{nib}$$

to the totally voiceless,

$$[_\circ^b\text{in}] \qquad [\text{ni}_\circ^b]$$

Variations in the strength of aspiration, with both the voiceless and the voiced series, parallel those of the voiceless series in RP:

(a)   Aspiration is strongest initially as in RP:

       [pʰan] pan   [tʰɛn] ten   [kʰap] cap
       [bʰan] ban   [dʰɪn] din   [gʰap] gap

(b)   There is normally a strong release of a final voiceless plosive as well in Welsh English:

       [kapʰ] cap   [ratʰ] rat   [sakʰ] sack

       and, although aspiration is relatively weak, voiced plosives in final position are generally released, too, as in:

       [kɔbʰ] cob   [ladʰ] lad   [tagʰ] tag

(c)   Medially, between vowels, aspiration is relatively weaker for both series:

       [tɔpʰə] topper   [fɪtʰə] fitter   [θɪkʰə] thicker
       [rɔbʰə] robber   [sadʰə] sadder   [bigʰə] bigger

(d)   As in other varieties of English, a following /l, r, w, j/ is regularly devoiced after a 'voiceless' plosive, though not after a 'voiced' one:

[pₒˡiːz] please   [tₒʳiːz] trees
[kₒʳiːm] cream   [kₒˡəim] climb

but:

[bleːz] blaze   [briːz] breeze
[groːn] groan   [gluːm] gloom

(e)   Following /s/ (and other voiceless continuants), the plosives are very weakly aspirated, and are perceived by the native speaker (e.g. the present author) as being realisations of the 'voiced' series rather than of the voiceless series. Though the phones which occur after /s/ could be assigned to membership of either plosive series (they are always voiceless, and so could conveniently be interpreted as realisations of /p, t, k/ as is customarily done for RP), it seems to me that the awareness of the native speaker supports representation of them as realisations of /b, d, g/, thus /sbɪn/ *spin*; /sdiːm/ *steam*; /sgɪn/ *skin*.

It is clear that one of the main considerations in choosing how to represent the plosives which occur after /s/ for RP is orthographic practice for English. Orthographic practice for Welsh similarly lends support to the interpretation offered here for Welsh English. The contrast between voiceless and voiced plosives in this context is neutralised in the Welsh language, as it is in English. The orthographic conventions of Welsh, however, handle the neutralisations differently. Welsh selects the symbols for the corresponding voiced phonemes for the labial and velar ones, as in

/ˈsbiːo/   /ˈəsgol/
sbio 'to look'   *ysgol* 'school'

and it seems reasonable to project this same analysis on to Welsh English, as a substratal feature of Welsh phonology, and to extend it to the alveolar plosives, as is customarily done for Welsh.

2   *Release.* As was stated earlier, it is relatively untypical of Welsh English for plosives not to be released in absolute final position, whereas it is common in RP for plosives to be either unreleased or released only weakly.

   In clusters of stop consonants, too, Welsh English differs from RP in respect of the release stage of the first plosive in a cluster of two plosives, or of a plosive and an affricate, when they are not homorganic. In RP, the first plosive has no audible release, a smooth uninterrupted transition from one point of articulation to the next being achieved as the speech organs adopt the posture for the second closure before the release of the first. In Welsh English, audible (though often slight) aspiration occurs between the two stop consonants, as in:

['akʰdə] actor   [wəitʰ poːsd] white post
[tɔpʰ tʃap] top chap   ['tʃapʰdə] chapter

The same holds for a sequence of aspirated plosive + aspirated affricate, as in

['rapʰtʃə] rapture   ['sgripʰtʃə] 'scripture'

3 *Length*. Single consonants in medial position following a short stressed vowel are phonetically long in all varieties of Welsh English; this may be noted by doubling the appropriate consonant, as in:

[səppə] supper   [fɔllo] follow
[dɪnnə] dinner   [rəffə] rougher

It may well be that this feature is connected with the phenomenon of 'equalisation' of prominence over a stressed syllable and an unstressed one that follows it (see Stress, p. 121), in that a relatively prominent unstressed final syllable may require a stronger release of the medial consonants as onset to it.

4 *Glottal plosive*. The glottal plosive [ʔ] in Welsh English is not a phonemic unit; it is a non-significant phonetic phenomenon which occurs under predictable conditions. It serves two functions, which it shares with RP:

(a)   It may fill the hiatus between two vowels which belong to successive syllables, as in: [riˈʔakʃən] *reaction*; [riˈʔɔːdə] *reorder*.
(b)   It may reinforce an accented vowel under sentence-stress /ˈˈ/, as in: [ʃiːz ˈˈʔould] *she's* ''old''; [ɪts ˈˈʔɛvi] *it's* ''heavy''.

Under no circumstances does [ʔ] function in this variety, as it does in RP, to reinforce the articulation of final voiceless stops (see Gimson 1965: 162–3).

5 *Affricates*. Welsh English has the two affricatives /tʃ/ and /dʒ/ as in

/tʃɪn/ chin   /tʃein/ chain
/dʒɪn/ gin   /dʒeil/ jail

Phonetically, they are composed of a stop with delayed release which produces audible local friction. As in RP, the duration of the component of friction is shorter than it is for the fricatives proper, and there is a contrast between a close-knit medial affricate, as in /rəitʃəs/ *righteous*, with its short-duration friction, and a sequence of plosive /t/ + fricative /ʃ/, as in /ləitʃıp/ *lightship*, with friction duration typical of the fricatives, and comparable with that of a non-homorganic sequence of plosive + fricative, as in /flagʃıp/ *flagship*, both of which have plosive and fricative separated by syllable and compound word boundary, as opposed to the derivational morpheme boundary in *righteous*.

6   The English fricatives of Welsh English /f, v/ *fan, van*, /θ, ð/ *thin, then*, /s, z/ *seal, zeal*, /ʃ, ʒ/ *shin, leisure* have the same distributions as they do in RP. But /ʒ/ is replaced initially and finally by the affricate /dʒ/, as in /ruːdʒ/ *rouge*, /prɛsˈtiːdʒ/ *prestige*. It is worth noting that the affricates, and these fricatives except for /s/, do not occur initially in indigenous citation forms in the Welsh language. But the initial consonant mutation system of Welsh provided pronunciation models for all the fricatives but /ʃ/ in the shift from Welsh to English, in that they occur in Welsh as phonetic realisations of plosives under specified grammatical and lexical conditions (see S. J. Williams 1980: 174–7). /ʃ/ was a direct borrowing from English, as in /ʃiːr/ *shire*, /ʃɔp/ *shop*.

7   *Nasals*. Welsh English has the same three nasals as RP, with no differences of pronunciation or distribution: /man/ *man*, /nıl/ *nil*, /sıŋ/ *sing*.

8   *Voiced lateral liquid*. The voiced liquid lateral /l/ has the same distribution as it has in RP, and a 'dark' allophone before back vowels in medial or final position,

/lamp/	/fıl/	/fuːlıʃ/	/puːl/
lamp	fill	foolish	pool

9   *Voiced tapped liquid*. This is normally a tapped or rolled /r/, occurring initially and medially, except for the forms noted in CURE above, in which it occurs finally:

/reːs/	/kari/
race	carry

10   *Semi-vowels*. Both unrounded palatal /j/ and rounded labiovelar /w/ have the same distribution as they have in RP, except that, where the semi-vowel would be followed by a vowel of similar quality, the semi-vowel is lost. Thus *wood* and *hood* /ʊd/ are homophones, as are *yeast* and *east* /iːst/.

11 *Final consonant clusters*. The consonant cluster system of Welsh English is not distinctive, except that the historical process of simplifying homorganic final clusters of nasal + voiced plosive to a nasal, as in *climb* and *sing* is extended to the alveolar clusters after the diphthong /əu/,

/pəun/ /grəun/ /səun/
pound ground sound

and regularly when the cluster is followed by the voiced sibilant /z/,

/anz/ /ɛnz/ /pɔnz/
hands ends ponds

This is a common feature of vernacular varieties of English elsewhere in the British Isles.

3.7.3 Other accents of Welsh English

The type of pronunciation outlined above is representative of the speech of an industrial community in the south of the country; more precisely, the speech of a community in the western half of the urbanised south, in the Swansea valley. We will now briefly identify the major variants to this accent and note their principal pronunciation features.

Swansea. In the immediate environs of the city of Swansea, there is an accent variant wherein the normally short vowel of a stressed non-final syllable in a polysyllabic word is frequently lengthened before a single consonant:

/tʃaːpl/ /mɛːsɛdʒ/ /raːpə/ /bɔːbɪn/
chapel message wrapper bobbin

Cardiff. The most influential of the rival urbanised accents to our model is undoubtedly that centred on the capital city, Cardiff. Its most noticeable distinctive pronunciation feature – and the one usually chosen to caricature the accent – is its fronted and raised realisation of the phoneme /aː/, in words like /kæːt/ *cart*, /'kæːdɪf/ *Cardiff*. The accents so far described represent the most 'evolved' varieties of Welsh English, with their bases firmly established in extensive urbanised populations, where the Welsh language is spoken by a small minority of the population. Outside this urbanised area, there are two major accent types which owe their distinctive features to the fact that most of their speakers are bilingual in Welsh and English.

The west and the north: rhoticity. In the rural communities of the west and the north, the distribution of /r/ is extended regularly to post-vocalic position. Vowels other than /ə/ are usually long before a word-final /r/, as in /kaːr/ *car*, /boːr/ *bore*, /puːr/ *poor*, but /fər/ *fur*. Before clusters of /r/ + another consonant, a preceding vowel is usually short, as in /part/ *part*, /kɔrd/ *cord*. The occurrence of post-vocalic /r/ in the rural accents of the south-west and the north is clearly a feature of pronunciation which is carried over from the phonetic and phonological schema of the Welsh language, which is the first language of the majority who speak them. The retention of native English /h/ is facilitated in these dialects by its occurrence as a phoneme in the Welsh dialects of both areas, as in /hat/ *hat*, /həid/ *hide*. Speakers who have /h/ as a phoneme also have an aspirated, voiceless labiovelar semi-vowel /hw/ ([hw]), so that they have minimal pairs like:

/wɪtʃ/	witch	/hwɪtʃ/	which
/wəi/	Wye	/hwəi/	why
/weːlz/	Wales	/hweːlz/	whales

Speakers of this variety also have an aspirated voiceless /rh/ [r̥h] in words like: [r̥həin] *Rhine*, [r̥həim] *rhyme*, [r̥hɪðm] *rhythm*. This is an interesting example of spelling-pronunciation based on a characteristic of the indigenous language, Welsh, which has an opposition between [r] and [r̥h], in which the two segments are orthographically ⟨r⟩ and ⟨rh⟩.

The north. The English accent of north Welsh English has additional features which derive from the structure of the Welsh language. A distinctive consonantal feature of northern Welsh English is its dental realisation of the alveolar phonemes /t, d, n/, as in [t̪u] *two*, [d̪uː] *do*, [n̪əu] *now*. Another significant phonetic variant involves the realisation of intervocalic plosives following a short stressed vowel. In all varieties of Welsh English, consonants in this position are lengthened (another instance of interference from Welsh), but in northern Welsh English the release stage of voiceless plosives is more strongly aspirated, [rɪppʰər] *ripper*, [vɪkkʰar] *vicar*, and voiced plosives tend to be devoiced in their release stage, [rəb̥ɪʃ] *rubbish*, [dɪg̥ər] *digger*. Perhaps the most distinctive consonantal feature of northern Welsh English, however, derives from the fact that the Welsh language has no voiced sibilant /z/. This gap in the system carries over into northern Welsh English, so that for speakers of northern Welsh English the following pairs are homophones:

seal, zeal	/siːl/
sink, zinc	/sɪŋk/
pence, pens	/pɛns/
use (n., vb)	/ɪus/

Similarly /ʒ/ is realised as /ʃ/, as in *leisure* /lɛʃər/.

The affricates are not indigenous to Welsh either, and the voiced affricate /dʒ/ is likewise interpreted in northern Welsh English as a voiceless phoneme, so that the following, again, are homophones:

chin, gin	/tʃɪn/
choke, joke	/tʃoːk/
rich, ridge	/rɪtʃ/

Some varieties in the north-west also carry over a feature of the dialects of Welsh which are indigenous to the area. Welsh did not historically have a contrast between long and short close front vowels, having only a long variety. Consequently, in these dialects borrowed words with the short vowel of English have been assimilated to the Welsh system, which had a short close vowel in a retracted position, the 'barred *i*' of north Welsh. This occurs only in stressed monosyllables, such as /tip/ *tip*, /pit/ *pit*.

There is a related phenomenon to that immediately above in the north-west treatment of the orthographic diphthong ⟨oy⟩, in which the length of the first element is retained, and the second assimilated to the same vowel /i/ as in /boːi/ *boy*, /toːi/ *toy*. This again derives from the fact that Welsh has only this long diphthong closing to a front-to-mid close position, and it occurs only in unchecked, stressed monosyllables in the English dialect. Forms like *coin* /kɔin/, *quoit* /kɔit/ have the corresponding short diphthong of Welsh.

The principal vocalic difference between northern Welsh English and our specimen lies in the replacement of the diphthongs /ei/ and /ou/ by the pure vowels /eː/ and /oː/ respectively, so that whereas these two diphthongs have a restricted distribution in the southern specimen in comparison with RP, they do not occur at all in northern Welsh English:

| /leːt/ late | /weːt/ weight |
| /boːn/ bone | /boː/ bow |

The accent of the north-east of Wales has little published documentation as yet. Informal observation suggests that the dominant influence on its pronunciation is that of neighbouring Merseyside, and it is interesting that the hypercorrection /bətʃə/ for *butcher*, common in the north-east of England, is a regional feature in the area around the town of Wrexham. The same area also has the typical north-west England pronunciation /wɔn/ for *one*, but has a non-rhotic dialect.

One prominent innovation in the speech of teenagers in the Bangor area – regardless of social class – is the substitution of the glottal stop /ʔ/ for final /t/ and the flap /ɾ/ for medial /t/ in forms like /hɔʔ/ *hot*, /beɾə/ *better*. This cannot be a reflex of Welsh language structure, however, and may be a strong indicator of the extent to which young speakers of English, even in areas of dense Welsh-language usage, are prone to influences from general vernacular usage which are common in other parts of Britain.

3.7.4 Three special cases: the Welsh Marches, Pembrokeshire and The Gower

So far, attention has been confined to varieties of Welsh English in which the distinctive features can largely be attributed to interference from a substratal or coexisting Welsh language source.

There are three instances, however, in which local accents have affinities with regional accents within England. The Marches constitute the areas of Wales which border directly on the English counties Herefordshire, Shropshire and Gloucestershire – roughly the eastern edge of present-day Powys (centring on the old counties of Brecon and Radnor, and extending, in some cases, to Gwent). The Gower is an isolated peninsula west of Swansea, and the part of Pembrokeshire which interests us is that south of the landsker. Both these latter areas lie across the Bristol Channel from the western counties of Cornwall, Devon and Somerset, and had trading contacts with them in earlier times. As was previously described, these regions are ones of long-standing Anglicisation. Despite their being so widely separated, and the causes of Anglicisation in each case being different in kind and manner, it is striking that they share their major distinctive accent features, which derive from features common to the English dialects of the west midlands and the south-west – features which Parry (1972: 142) labels 'general western'. Though they are more distinct in their vocabulary than in their phonology, and distinguished from each other therein, some of the most obvious accent features will be exemplified which can be connected with neighbouring dialects in these western counties of England, drawing on Parry (1977, 1985) and *SED*.

1 In the Marches alone, and deriving from west midland speech, a fronted realisation [æ] of /a/ in [æpl̩z] *apples*, [kætʃ] *catch*. Note that this is a different phenomenon from the fronted realisation [æː] of /aː/ previously referred to in the Cardiff area, which is restricted to the long vowel, and is probably to be connected with a similar feature in the indigenous Welsh dialects of that area. This midlands-related fronted realisation of the short vowel also occurs in the Cardiff area, though fronting of the long vowel does not occur in Radnorshire.

2 [ʳ]-colouring (or retroflexion) of vowels, instead of the indigenous pattern, vowel + tapped [r]. Thus

       [ɜʳːθ] earth   [bɜʳːd] bird
       [kaʳː] car   [kɔʳːn] corn

This is very common in the Marches and Pembroke, but infrequent in The Gower.

3 In all three areas, pre-vocalic *r* – like that in general western – is the retroflex approximant [ɹ] (Parry 1985: maps 3.1, 3.2).

4 There are examples of the distinctive incidence of west of England features in specific words in all three areas, for instance

      the loss of the final /d/ in *second*;
      the form /trou/ or /troː/ for *trough*;
      /ɪ/ for /iː/ in forms like *feet, teeth, sheep*;
      initial /d/ in *thistle* in Pembroke and The Gower.

5 Voicing of initial voiceless fricatives:

      initial /v/ in forms like *fields* and *five* in all three;
      The Gower can have /z/ for *s* in words like *seven, silver, sow*, as did the south-west traditionally.

6 The Gower, like the south-west of England, has /ɪ/ in *feet, teeth*; /əu/ in *chewing*; and /ɪ/ in *kettle*.

7 Pembroke has /ʊ/ for RP /ʌ/ in *butter, suck, dust*, a feature which has a few parallels in the south-west, and is common in the west midlands.

Most of the features noted under 4–7 are by now relics of usage in general western usage in England (see Wells 1982: 343): it might be pertinent to ask whether, in those cases where all three Welsh areas share a feature which is missing from part of general western, the feature may have earlier been distributed throughout the general western region.

3.7.5 Accent and social class

The relationship of accent and class-status is much the same for speakers of English in Wales as it is for those in England. Standardisation of regional accent entails proximation to RP. Speakers of regionally modified RPs with a 'Welsh' substratum will have some of the features we have described, to varying degrees and in varying combinations: indeed, the fact that the description has been largely couched in absolute terms is not meant to suggest that speakers do not universally and continually vary their usage. I have put together a composite of features which are typical of the various accents, without aiming to be strictly representative of the usage of any individual or group.

Some general features of Welsh English, however, are clearly recognised as being non-standard, and are replaced early in the process of standardising. The lack of /h/ in the basic model has obvious prominence; and, as speakers adopt /h/, so do they also hyper-correctively adopt orthographic ⟨h⟩ in forms like /hwəi/ *why*, which (/hwɪtʃ/) – being foreign to RP – itself becomes a mark of a regional accent. This, along with the fact that southern speakers select a vowel or diphthong in FACE and GOAT words along orthographic conventions (see p. 117), suggests that speakers of this more 'evolved' dialect have a clearer awareness of the orthographic systems of English than do those of other Welsh varieties (see the similar implications of a suggestion in Parry 1985: 65, in regard to the diphthongs *ai* and *ei*). And, as with native varieties of English, the selected form has to meet the current accepted pan-dialectal norm for formal usage in England and Wales.

Post-vocalic /r/ is also lost on the path to standardisation; this is accompanied by lengthening of the preceding vowel, where appropriate.

One interesting feature of educated north Welsh usage in English appears to be 'interdialectal' (in the sense of Trudgill 1986). Educated speakers from the north-west frequently have a rhotic quality which is transitional between the indigenous post-vocalic tapped /r/ and the r-less standard variety, in that they have an otherwise untypical r-colouring of vowels, as in

[foʳ:] *four*   [biːəʳ] *beer*
[bɜʳ:d] *bird*   [baʳ:d] *bard*

– a feature which belongs neither to conservative north Welsh English, nor to Welsh, nor to RP. This, again, may indicate an awareness of spelling patterns among speakers of Welsh, a language which has a closely phonemic orthographic system.

Northern speakers adopt the distinction between /s/ and /z/ (see p. 128). This can lead to hypercorrection in educated speech, when an orthographic voiceless sibilant is wrongly realised as /z/, as in /feiz tu feiz/ *face to face*. Such forms are again examples of 'interdialect' in the sense of Trudgill (1986).

As one would expect, Welsh English has some general vernacular features, such as replacement of the final /ŋ/ of the verbal suffix *-ing* by /n/ in forms like *singing, running*, and glottalisation of word-final /t/ (see p. 130). In these features, Welsh English is no different from any other form of regional English.

However, the Welsh English accent fits into its own localised area of group dynamics. Public figures clearly find it no disadvantage to retain – possibly to cultivate – regional features. This applies particularly to politicians and popular broadcasters, who need to establish solidarity with a local constituency – a strong dynamic influence which is well described, in relation to Welsh public figures, in Coupland (1988, 1989), and is, of course, just one regional reflex of power dynamics in Britain generally. Public figures adopt regional and social-class features within limits which do not exclude them from the conventions of public usage which dominate their particular areas of activity.

3.7.6   *Welsh proper names*

For bilinguals, Welsh sounds are retained in the pronunciation of proper names in Welsh English. The voiceless lateral fricative /ɬ/ and the voiceless velar fricative /x/ (phonetically uvular) occur commonly, as in

/ɬanvairpʊɬgwiŋgiɬgogɛrixxwirndrɔbʊɬɬandəsiliogogogox/
Llanfairpwllgwyngyllgogerychchwyrndrobwllllandysiliogogogoch

and /x/ in the expression of displeasure /ax a viː/, best translated as *yuk*!

With increasing Anglicisation, these sounds are sometimes realised as follows:

initially, /ɬ/ can be replaced by the voiced lateral /l/, or by the
sequence /kl/ as in /lan/, /klan/ *Llan*; medially, it can be
replaced by the sequence /əl/, as in /lanɛəli/, /klanɛəli/
Llanelli;

/x/ is most often replaced by its corresponding velar plosive
/k/, as in /bʊlk/ *Bwlch*.

The diphthong /ai/ (comparable with RP /ai/ (PRICE), which is /əi/ in
Welsh English) occurs, as in /tai'baːx/ *Taibach*.

In north Wales, the high-mid-spread vowel /ɨ/, and the long
diphthongs /oːɨ/ and /aːɨ/ occur, as in /brɨn'dɨː/ *Bryndu*, /pɛnə'kaːɨ/
Penycae, /tanə'koːɨd/ Tanycoed. With Anglicisation, the diphthongs
proximate to the RP diphthongs /ɔi/ (CHOICE) and /aɪ/ (PRICE); the
short /ɨ/ becomes /ɪ/, and the long variant /ɨː/ becomes /iː/. For a
discussion of the pronunciation of Welsh place-names in an Anglicised
urban environment, see Coupland (1985).

3.7.7   *Grammatical features*

Dialects of Welsh English are significantly less distinctive at the level of
grammar than they are in phonology and lexis, but their structure will be
examined in terms of the three major determinants of the features of
Welsh English which have been identified:

1   the Welsh substratum;
2   general western dialects of English;
3   standard English usage, the determining model for the formal
        varieties.

Additionally, for grammatical features, we need to take account of
features of colloquial Welsh English which are less clearly dialectal,
being features shared with vernacular usage in many parts of Britain.
The following discussion will illustrate these conflicting formative
influences on the dialect.

3.7.8   *Formative influences in syntax: the Welsh language, and neighbouring*
dialects of English (see also Thomas 1985)

Aspect

Welsh English does not differ from standard English in major respects,
as far as its syntax goes. Its most characteristic feature is a particular use
of the auxiliaries *do* and *be*, both of which are evidenced fulfilling the

same function in the southern varieties which we have chosen to describe. They can both occur as periphrastic forms of the present habitual, alongside the standard use of the inflected form of the present tense. Thus, we find parallel occurrences like the following:

> He *goes* to the cinema every week (inflected present)
> He *do go* to the cinema every week (*do* + uninflected verb)
> He's *going* to the cinema every week (inflected *be* + inflected verb)

In the non-standard forms in the second and third examples, the auxiliaries *do* and *be* are always unstressed, and *do* is always uninflected; *be* is always regularly inflected for person and number. (These are matched by a set of past-tense contrasts,

> He *went/used to go* to the cinema every week
> He *did go* to the cinema every week
> He *was going* to the cinema every week

which similarly represent habitual usage in the past.)

All three forms are regularly attested, and it is clear that the inflected form of the lexical verb is the most prestigious (because of its status as the standard English form), and it is the most frequent in formal styles. What is not clear – because there has been no comprehensive survey of usage in any single community of speakers – is the precise socio-linguistic distribution of the competing non-standard forms. However, it is possible to tease out of the data in Parry (1977, 1979) a plausible interpretation of their geographical dispersal. The data are less complete than might have been expected. One or other of the forms certainly occurs regularly throughout the southern region, but there are frequent gaps in the data as recorded, probably reflecting the dialectologist's constant dilemma of collecting a disproportionate number of non-vernacular responses to a formally administered questionnaire. Their overall distribution is clear, however: in the industrial areas of Gwent and the Glamorgans, and the rural areas of Brecknock and east Radnor, the exclusive response is that with *do* as auxiliary; it also occurs sporadically elsewhere, in Pembroke, Cardigan and west Radnor. But, in these latter areas, the most frequent response is that in *be*. This division directly reflects that between areas of 'early' and 'late' bilingualisation (and ultimate Anglicisation). Parry drew attention to this distinction in his MA dissertation (1964), when he pointed out that early intrusion of English typically involved diffusion of the dialect forms of the English counties neighbouring Wales – later Anglicisation, however, involved spread of the current standard English form. Interestingly, his illustration centred on Radnor, where early infiltration of English had brought the neighbouring dialectal form *oont* (for *mole*) into the eastern parts of the county: in the western regions, however, more resistant to Anglicisation, the intrusion came later, and in the form of the StE *mole*. That distinction between borrowing from dialect and from standard is reflected here, in that the 'core' industrial areas of Gwent and the Glamorgans, and the eastern parts of Radnor – with the longest history of Anglicisation of the areas which concern us – have forms which are typically evidenced in neighbouring English counties. In this case, however, the distinction is not between dialect and standard within the English language, but between areas of intrusion of English dialect influence (the 'core' industrial areas referred to above), and those of resistance to it. The 'resistant' areas are broadly those which have the less 'evolved' variety of English, in which traces of the influence of the Welsh language are most evident. These are the western areas in which the majority of speakers are bilingual, and Welsh substratal influences are strong in the emerging English dialect. The periphrastic construction with *be* can be directly correlated with its correspondent in Welsh, in which the verb *bod* 'be' is followed by a subject nominal, a predicator *yn* (related to the preposition *in*) and an uninflected verb–noun, as in

> Mae ef yn mynd i'r sinema bob wythnos
> is he in go to-the cinema every week
> 'He goes to the cinema every week'

It seems clear that there is a peripheral western area in which the structure of the Welsh language is still a dominant influence on the emergent dialect of English. At the same time, we have to recognise the fact that the form with *do* occurs alongside that with *be* in this area and is spreading westwards: this suggests that the most immediate external dialectal influence on the western 'less evolved' dialect of English is that of the industrial heartland of south Wales – the area which is economically dominant. This is only to be expected; and, in turn, the dominant influence on the eastern dialect, and indeed on all dialects in their more formal styles, is that of standard English. There is interesting support for this in Coupland (1989), which demonstrates that public usage of politicians in Wales responds not to localised norms but to those which are common to standard usage throughout Britain.

Thus, in respect of this specific grammatical feature, it seems that the *do* pattern is characteristic of dialects of the west midlands – that is, they fit into a dialect subcontinuum which reaches out from neighbouring English counties; and the *be* pattern is characteristic of the speech of those who have a dominant Welsh-language influence, in being either bilingual or first-generation monolingual English speakers. The fact that the more conservative western areas show instances of forms in *do* alongside those in *be* suggests that we are witnessing a redeployment of the distribution of the forms, from the geographical to the social, in that they are becoming marked stylistically, as more or less 'evolved' varieties, rather than regionally.

Fronting

One of the more familiar distinctive features of sentence structure in Welsh English is the fronting of a constituent, when attention is focused upon it: the fronted constituent is accompanied by emphatic stress (marked '' in the following examples):

> ''*Coal* they're getting out, mostly
> ''*Singing* they were
> ''*Now* they're going

Sentences such as these are equivalent to both cleft and pseudo-cleft sentences in other varieties of English. The first two examples have more acceptable correlates in the pseudo-cleft variants

> What they're getting out mostly is coal
> What they were doing was singing

and the third in the cleft variant

> It's now that they're going

The Welsh language does not make the distinction between clefting and pseudo-clefting which is necessary for the analysis of English, since 'clefting' in Welsh universally involves fronting of a constituent (see Jones & Thomas 1977: 363, fn. 3). It seems probable that this feature of Welsh English is best accounted for as an instance of interference from Welsh.

Expletive *there*

The set of exclamations which, in other varieties, would typically be rendered *How* + adjective/adverb + subject + verbal form are introduced in Welsh English by the adverb *there*, as in

There's tall you are! (How tall you are!)
There's young she looks! (How young she looks!)
There's strange it was! (How strange it was!)

This, again, appears to be best interpreted as adoption of a construction which is a feature of Welsh, and which is the direct correlate of the above Welsh English examples, except for the order of subject and verb, which is the reverse of that in English. The adverb involved is the equivalent of English *there*, namely *dyna*, as in

Dyna dal wyt ti! (lit. 'There's tall are you')
Dyna ifanc mae hi'n edrych! (lit. 'There's young is she in look')
Dyna od oedd ef! (lit. 'There's strange was it')

Indirect question word order

In standard English, in an indirect question in a subordinate clause, the verb inverts with whatever constituent would immediately follow it in the corresponding direct question, as in

Is there anyone there? (direct question)
I don't know if *there's* anyone there (indirect question)

In Welsh English the word order of the direct question is maintained in both environments, giving parallel examples of direct and indirect questions such as

(1) a.   *Is it* true or not?
b.   *Would* there be any there now?
(2) a.   I'm not sure *is it* true or not
b.   I wouldn't know *would there* be any there now

This, again, appears to derive from the structure of Welsh, in which the order of the verb and what immediately follows it is always identical in direct questions and their related indirect ones. The elision of the conjunction (*if/whether*) is also facilitated by the Welsh rule of eliding the corresponding conjunction (*a/os*) in similar environments in the vernacular.

Infinitive for participle

Parry (1979: 155) records an interesting use of the infinitive where standard English would employ a present participle. The main clause object of the verb *stop* is followed by an infinitive in a subordinate clause, when it is simultaneously the subject of that subordinate clause,

> To stop the wood to wear out
> (StE To stop the wood wearing out)

It is plausible to suggest that this, again, is an interference feature which derives from the structure of Welsh, in which the equivalent form to the present participle in English is not marked by inflection, but by a particle *yn* preceding the uninflected form of the verb (the equivalent of the infinitive in English).

Possession

Welsh is essentially a nominal language (see e.g. Awbery 1976), and the notion of possession (see Jones & Thomas 1977: 54–5) is expressed by a prepositional phrase preceded by an existential use of the copula, rather than by a verbal construction, as in English. In Welsh English possession is expressed by a direct translation of this construction, in which we have expletive *there* + *be* + noun possessum + preposition *with* + noun possessor replacing the standard English noun possessor + *have* + noun possessum. Thus we have such examples as *There's no luck with the rich* as opposed to StE *The rich have no luck*. This is an instance of an idiomatic calque which entails syntactic variation from standard English as a secondary effect.

Anticipatory *it*

A frequently occurring construction has an anticipatory *it* with apparent extrapolation of a sentence embedding at subject nominal position, as in

> It depends on the intensity of the fire what action we take.

The relationship between the apparently extrapolated clause *what action we take* and the rest of the sentence is better seen as one of apposition, however, since the sentence can be paraphrased by inserting *namely* before it, as in

> It depends on the intensity of the fire – namely, what action we take.

Morphology

There seem to be no morphological forms which can be related to a Welsh language source, but there is one use of the modal auxiliary *will* which the *EDG* describes as peculiar to the English spoken in the Celtic countries. This is its use instead of *will be*, in contexts like

> I've always been poor, and I think I always will
> Is he ready yet? – No, but he will in a minute

General vernacular features

A full description of the grammar of Welsh English would take account of numerous other features, as the data in Parry (1977, 1979) confirm. We may list a number of typical examples:

1   Double negatives occur frequently, as in *I haven't been nowhere* and negation of a past-tense verb often takes the form *never* + past-tense verb form (*I never done it*) for standard past tense *do* + *not* + lexical verb (*I didn't do it*). As an emphatic response, *never* can function as a negated auxiliary, as in *I ''never!* for *I ''didn't!*

2   Numerals from *two* upwards are frequently followed by the singular form of the noun, as in *two pound, five mile.*

3   Present and past participles can be preceded by the clitic *a-*, as in *I'm a-going, She's a-doing something else.*

4   The relative pronoun occurs in the forms *as, what* and *which* following a human antecedent, as in

> the chap as works in the garage
> a man what likes to travel
> the women which went (as) a nurse

5   Generalisation of the third person singular suffix *-s* throughout the present-tense forms of the lexical verb, as in

> I knows that
> They plays football
> They wants us out of a job

and of the *-s* suffix in the past tense of the verb *to be*, as in

> We was laughing
> They was playing hard

But for auxiliary *have*, the third person singular form in the present tense is unified with other person forms as *have*, as in

> They're coming to film what have been done.
> There's no other place in South Wales have had to pay for the removal of tips.

The latter example, heard during a radio interview, shows zero realisation of the relative pronoun as well.

6   Strong verbs, in some cases, have adopted weak past-tense forms, as in *bringed, catched, drawed, growed*. This is common to general western dialects, as is the occurrence of common forms for the past-tense and past-participial forms in strong verbs like *eat, steal, take, break, speak*:

> It was all *ate*
> Something was *stole* from the shop
> He was *took* bad
> The window was *broke*
> Not a word was *spoke*

Past and present tenses are often undifferentiated in the same verb set, as in

> He come yesterday
> He run it last year

7   The objective reflexive pronouns *his self, their selves*, as in

> He hit *his self*
> They hit *their selves*

are of common occurrence in dialects in England, generalising the possessive pronominal form throughout the paradigm, on the pattern of *myself, yourself, ourselves, yourselves*.

8   *Too* can replace *either* as a tag to a negative sentence, as in

> I can't do that, too
> Nor me, too

and the tag *isn't it?* occurs commonly to replace person reference, in sentences like

> You're going home now, isn't it?
> She's coming home today, isn't it?

The reference of this tag is to the sense of the whole sentence, rather than to its subject nominal.

Again, in north-west Wales, the tag *yes?* with rising intonation is used with a declarative sentence to form a question, as in

> You're at university, yes?
> It's a nice day, yes?

9   In Radnor dialects, Parry (1972: 151) records the west-midland negative auxiliaries

inna	doona	anna	munna	shanna
(isn't)	(doesn't)	(hasn't)	(mustn't)	(shan't)

as common in casual speech. The present writer recalls these forms as common in the lower Swansea valley in the 1950s.

10 Obsolete or obsolescent features, recorded by Parry in the south-east during the 1960s, include the following:

(a)   disjunctive possessive pronouns *yourn, ourn, theirn, thine, hisn, hern* – forms which are historically general western;

(b)   some forms which have had wide distribution in dialects in England:

   (i)   on the eastern rim of the south-eastern Welsh area, the pronouns *thee* and *thy* were attested in 'familiar conversation between intimates' (Parry 1972: 152);

   (ii)   the third person singular feminine pronoun was recorded as *her* in the subjective, along the eastern rim while in northern Radnor, subjective and objective forms of the first person plural coincided in *we*;

   (iii)   the use of *be* was attested for all persons in the present tense, as in *be I?; bist thee?; be her?*; together with confirmatory negatives like *bistn't thee?; binna we?*

Many of these features occur commonly throughout Britain, and must be seen as features of general vernacular usage. They represent what might be termed the 'vernacularisation' of Welsh English, as it moves from being the usage of bilingual speakers to that of monolingual ones. They have the same distribution – linguistic and social – as they have in other varieties of English in Britain.

Vocabulary

Few items from the Welsh language have entered the vocabulary of Welsh English (see further Parry 1972, 1985). There are less than a handful with general currency, mainly ones which it was not plausible to translate for political, emotional or commercial reasons:

   eisteddfod /əistɛðvɔd/, a festival of the arts;

   hiraeth /hiːraiə/, a unique concept of 'longing for place or person';

   hwyl /huɪl/, gusto, enthusiasm, spiritedness;

   penillion /pɛnɨɬjɔn/, a form of singing in which the accompaniment does not coincide with the vocal melody;

   cymanfa /kəmanvə/, a chapel singing festival;

   Caerffili /kəˈfɪli/, the cheese of that name;

bara brith /bara briːθ/, bread loaf made with currants;

llymru /fləm(ə)ri/, 'flummery', a kind of porridge, and surely an archaism;

/tiːˈbaːx/ (south), *tŷ bach* tiːˈbaːx/ (north), 'little house' is retained as a euphemism for 'lavatory, toilet' (Parry 1985: 53).

A few other words have restricted geographical distribution:

In the Marches, the form *cardydwyn* /kaᵊdədwɪn/ stands for 'the weakest pig in a litter'; *dôl* /doːl/, 'meadow' occurs in north Powys.

In the south-east, *taflod, dowlod* /tɔlət/ 'a hayloft' and *twmp* /təmp/ 'hillock', both of which have spread into neighbouring western dialects in England; *gwas* /wəs/, a familiar form of address to a male, as (*h*)*ey wuss*!. *Bwbach* /buːbəx, buːbək/ 'scarecrow' occurs sporadically in the south, even in The Gower, as does *pentan* /pantən/ 'hob' (Parry 1972: 150) – rare instances of borrowing from Welsh into this early-Anglicised area; *carthen* /karθɛn, kaːθɛn/, a woven woollen coverlet for a bed.

In the north *del* /dɛl/ is a cross-sexual term of endearment for men, and a general one for women, while in the south *bach* /baːx/ is a sex-independent one for women, and used by men for women and children.

In Buckley, Clwyd, just on the wrong side of Offa's Dyke, *calennig* /klɛnɪg/ (New Year's gift), an allowance of money; *trefn* /dreːvɛn/ 'untidiness'; *glasdwr* /glastə/, a drink made of water mixed with milk; *gwachul* /waki/ 'unwell'; *mochyn* /mɔkɛn/ 'pig' (Griffiths 1969).

Broch /brɔk/ 'badger', dialectal in the north of England and sporadic elsewhere (*SED*), is not evidenced in Welsh English. Borrowings from the west midlands are frequent in various parts of the Marches, as evidenced in Parry (1972); *askel* 'newt'; *cratch* 'hay-loft'; *bing* 'gangway in a cowshed'; *hopper* 'seed basket'; *bodge*, make a mess of a job; *pleach*, to lay a hedge by weaving the branches around upright poles; *simple*, in poor health.

From the south-west come *dap* 'bounce', *pine-end* 'gable-end of a house', both of general occurrence in the south-east of Wales. In the Gower and Pembroke, we find *nestlestrip* 'weakest pig in a litter'; *voriers* headlands in a field; *pilm* 'dust'; *culm* 'slack coal'; *frithing*, wattling used in making hurdles.

Words which occur today, or have previously had currency in both the west midlands and the south-west (which Parry (1972: 142) called 'general western' words) and which are found in the south-east of Wales are *oont* 'mole'; *sally* 'willow'; *clem* 'starve'; *quist* 'woodpigeon'; *dout* 'put out a light or fire'.

A few forms which are clearly not of Welsh derivation are not evidenced in England, either: *lattergrass* 'aftermath', occurs in both The Gower and Pembroke. In Pembroke only, we find *byholt* 'hired pasturage'; *preen* 'to butt'; *labbigan* 'a female gossip'.

There are many lexical items and idioms which are regarded as being typical of the English of South Wales, some of which have a source in Welsh: *He's lost the bus*, from Welsh *colli* ('miss, lose'); *Rise money from the Post Office*, from Welsh *codi* ('rise, raise'). Others are of indeterminate source:

delight, meaning 'interest', as in *He's got a delight in cricket*;

the adjective *tidy* as one of general approbation, as in *He's got a tidy job*;

off, meaning 'angry', as in *He was off!*;

repetition of an adjective for intensification, as in *She was pretty, pretty*;

the discontinuous adverb of place *where ... to*, as in *Where's he to?*, meaning 'where is he?'

For a lighthearted account of Welsh English sayings, there is no better source than Edwards (1985). The distribution of English dialect words for this discussion was confirmed from *EDD* and *SED*.

3.8   The future of Welsh English as a dialect

Some aspects of the structure of Welsh English are uniquely 'Welsh': in other respects, its development has been determined by immediate contact with neighbouring dialects of English, with vernacular English of a more generalised kind, and with standard English.

A striking feature of this instance of language contact and shift is the extent to which the two languages have kept their distance from each other at the grammatical level, and very largely maintained their structural integrity. In contrast with the more mutable structure at the level of phonology, there are comparatively few grammatical features which require us to invoke the Welsh language to explain them. Indeed, there is relatively little localised idiosyncratic usage at the grammatical level: most features are characteristic of generalised non-standard usage which is evidenced, to varying degrees and with varying localisation, within the indigenous territory of the English language, as revealed by *SED* and *EDG*.

The same is true of English interference with Welsh. Though there has been massive relexification of vernacular Welsh through borrowing from English, bringing with it a transformation of Welsh phonology, only incidentally does the appeal to interference from the structure of English throw necessary light on historical change and regional variation at the level of grammar in Welsh (see Thomas 1982, for discussion and illustration). It is clear, and not unexpected, that linguistic systems more effectively resist interference and more nearly retain their integrity at the higher level of organisation within the grammatical domain than in others.

The change in the formative influences on the development of Welsh English is reflected in the fact that the dominant influence on its grammar appears now to be standard English, with an apparently growing tendency to adopt features which are more generally typical of vernacular, rather than regionally restricted usage. The spread of English is no longer simply territorial in nature; it now has blanket penetration through the media, and so does not offer major models which are dialectally restricted. Rather, we have – as in other parts of Britain – re-alignment of variation along the formal–vernacular continuum, with truly regional variation being less evident in grammar than it is in phonology and lexis.

As the use of English expands in all social circumstances in Wales, it comes increasingly under the influence of standard English for its formal varieties, and of more prestigious 'England-based' vernaculars for its non-standard ones, given the role of the media in disseminating vernacular English, particularly through television and radio situation comedies.

Welsh English, as a distinct dialect, is a transitional phenomenon which is particularly associated with dominantly bilingual communities, like those in the south-west and the north. Increasing monolingualism, removing productive interference from Welsh, reinforces the tendency evidenced within the 'English' model, towards a general erosion of dialect differences in grammar. Welsh English will increasingly come to be characterised as a distinct accent, rather than as a dialect, though its vocabulary and idiomatic usage will no doubt continue to be significantly distinguished from other varieties of English in Britain – at least in speech.

At the same time, we can expect varieties of English in Wales to continue to interact with regional varieties of native English, where they are in close contact. This contact potential is of two kinds. Along the border with England, commercial links with major market towns in the west midlands, along the Dee, Severn, Wye and Usk valleys will continue to provide 'local' input to the dialects of the Marches from dialects relatively homogeneous in their structures. Along the 'Costa Geriatrica' of the north coast, the input will be as varied as the regional backgrounds of the huge numbers of in-migrant retirees who are settling in the seaside townships – though predominantly from the English midlands and north-west (on an impressionistic judgement, the most important influence appears to be that of Merseyside). Within south Welsh English, the dialect of the south-east seems to be a dominant 'localised' force (see the comments above on the distribution of aspectual variants). This is to be expected, given the concentration of government, commercial and media investment around the capital city of Cardiff. For an authoritative analysis of migration patterns as revealed in the 1981 Census, and of the changing interface of Welsh and English in Wales generally, there is no better authority than Aitchison & Carter (1985); see also Bellin (1984).

Giles and Powesland (1975), in a social–psychological survey which covered attitudes towards the southern Welsh English accent and towards RP in Wales, identified key components in the determination of the future role of each variety in the social and public life of the country. The Welsh-English-accented speaker was judged highly for the expected factors of being trustworthy, sociable and friendly – those for which dialect speakers conventionally rate their peers highly; for arrogance, conservatism and snobbishness, the RP-accented speaker for Wales was the higher rated. Along with the latter values go influence, success and social mobility. Usage in the public sphere will increasingly favour RP and standard English, rather than a variety of Welsh English.

This is not to deny the fact that there are some areas of public usage where RP is not exclusively considered the most useful accent to have. Politicians, for instance, who must have an ear to a local constituency as much as to a national one, can have varying degrees of 'Welsh-modified' RP – for an interesting discussion of the 'Welshness' of prominent contemporary 'Welsh' politicians, see Coupland (1989). The same goes for those in the entertainment industry. It is likely that there will be an increasing consolidation of the use and status of a Welsh accent, in tandem with political and economic development, and media growth, and the dominant variety will be that of the dominant region within Wales.

FURTHER READING

The most extensive data on the dialects of Welsh English are to be found in three publications based on a general survey which was closely modelled on the *Survey of English Dialects* (ed. Orton *et al.*, 1962–71). David Parry covers the south in two volumes published under the rubric *The Survey of Anglo-Welsh Dialects*, vol. I *The South-east* (1977) and vol. II *The South-west* (1979); the north is covered in R. J. Penhallurick's *The Anglo-Welsh Dialects of North Wales* (1991). A major urban variety of Welsh English is described in Nikolas Coupland's *Dialect in Use: Sociolinguistic Variation in Cardiff English* (1988). Coupland has also edited (with Alan R. Thomas as associate editor) a wide-ranging volume, *English in Wales: Diversity, Conflict and Change* (1990), which discusses the demography of Anglicisation and the emergence of socially differentiated varieties, together with a set of descriptive sketches of a range of dialects, urban and rural.

4 ENGLISH IN IRELAND

Jeffrey L. Kallen

4.1   Introduction

A complex series of population movements and language contacts lies at the heart of the history of Irish English. Included in this history are the establishment of Viking shipping and trading towns in the ninth century, the first arrival of English-speakers in 1169, and the subsequent English and Scottish plantations of the seventeenth century which culminated in an overall shift during the nineteenth century from Irish to English as the most common vernacular language. The effects of this population movement and linguistic contact on both the internal linguistic structure of Irish English and on the development of sociolinguistic attitudes provide a background against which most analyses of Irish English take place. The development of English in Ireland, then, is seen in this chapter from two points of view: the external history of the diffusion of English is discussed in section 4.2, while internal linguistic developments are examined in section 4.3. Further topics arising from this discussion are treated in section 4.4.

The term *Irish English* is used here simply to denote the English language as spoken in Ireland. Henry (1958, 1977, 1986) suggests a division between *Anglo-Irish* as the term for English spoken in areas which have only recently become predominantly English-speaking and *Hiberno-English* as a term denoting urban varieties with a longer history. Todd (1989a) uses these two terms with virtually the opposite signification. 'Anglo-Irish' also commonly refers to the variety of English spoken in Ireland in the Middle Ages (see Irwin 1935; McIntosh & Samuels 1968), while 'Hiberno-English' often denotes both the English language in Ireland generally and the field of research into this variety (see Barry 1981b; Harris 1985a; Filppula 1986). Though many

Map 4.1   Ireland

writers attach no particular analytical significance to the choice of term for English in Ireland (note especially Montgomery 1989: 269; Wall 1990: 9), the choice may still retain a deeper significance for some: see Croghan (1988) for an example. In order to avoid confusion, *Irish English* is used here as a general term without any further implications: see also Ó Baoill (1985).

The term *Ulster English* as used here refers to the English spoken in the traditional Ulster counties of Antrim, Armagh, Down, Derry, Fermanagh, Tyrone, Cavan, Donegal and Monaghan (though see O'Rahilly (1932) for discussion of the wider extent of historical Ulster). *Northern Ireland* refers to the first six counties named above, now part of the United Kingdom, as distinct from the 26-county Republic of Ireland (see map 4.1).

4.2 External history

4.2.1 *The twelfth to the sixteenth centuries*

Though the Viking presence in Ireland, lasting roughly from the ninth to the early eleventh century, had little direct impact on the development of Irish English (see Curtis 1919: 234; Irwin 1935: 17–18; Barry 1982: 84), the establishment of coastal towns during this period was crucial for the development of relations between Ireland and the rest of Europe. Martin (1987b: 53) points to 'substantial trade between Dublin and the Normans in Wales, England, and France' from a time not long after 1066, and argues that the coming of Anglo-Norman soldiers in the twelfth century was an outgrowth of secular and ecclesiastical contacts which had been developing for some time previously. (For a discussion of ecclesiastical contacts, see Henry 1972: 136ff.) Though the coming of the Anglo-Normans to Ireland is frequently described as an 'invasion' (see Curtis 1919; Bliss 1977b; Martin 1987b: 44fn.), Martin's interpretation accords with the major contemporary source material from this period, the *Expugnatio Hibernica* of Giraldus Cambrensis (Scott & Martin 1978) and the fragmentary 'Song of Dermot and the Earl' (see Seymour 1929). Thus when a 'very motley crew' (Curtis 1919: 235) of 300–400 soldiers from Pembrokeshire and South Wales arrived in Wexford in 1169, there was, in Martin's view (1987b: 44) 'no intrusion or intervention' comparable to that of William in 1066, 'nor was there a conquest' by the Anglo-Normans.

Despite the number of Flemish surnames among the early settlers, many of whom came from the Flemish colony settled in Pembrokeshire by Henry I in the first part of the twelfth century, there is no evidence that either Flemish or Welsh was spoken in Ireland as a result of the Anglo-Norman settlement (see Russell 1858; Curtis 1919; Irwin 1935; Bliss 1979). In fact, Irwin (1935: 44–5) has analysed early surname records suggesting origins for the original settlers not only in Pembrokeshire and South Wales, but in many parts of England as well as France and Scotland. That the bulk of English-speaking settlers should have come from South Wales and the south-west and south-west midlands of England, with lesser numbers coming from more scattered areas elsewhere, appears compatible with British political loyalties in the reign of Henry I (see Martin 1987a, 1987c) and sets the stage for dialect mixing early in the birth of Irish English.

Recent views of the role of French in Anglo-Norman England (see Legge 1968; Short 1980) and Ireland (Barry 1982: 84; Bliss & Long 1987: 710) contradict the traditional view expressed by Cahill (1938: 163–4) that 'leaders of the first group of invaders [in Ireland] ... did not know English'; rather, bilingualism is suggested, in which French assumed certain cultural and political functions, while English remained as a widespread vernacular tongue. Thus Latin predominates in Anglo-Irish law during the twelfth and thirteenth centuries, supplemented by French in the fourteenth century (see Gilbert 1889; Irwin 1935). Some private letters in French also date from the fourteenth century (Curtis 1932), as does a Waterford petition to Edward III in 1371 (Gilbert 1885a: 271). Irish literary works in French date to at least the thirteenth century, although the quantity produced appears to be small (see Seymour 1929; Bliss 1984b; Shields 1975–6; Bliss & Long 1987).

The earliest recorded use of English in Ireland apart from personal names dates from ca 1250, in an entry of the records of the Dublin Merchant Guildsmen (Irwin 1935: 28). English was used by the Corporation of Waterford from 1365–7 onwards (Gilbert 1885a) and in the late fifteenth century appears as the dominant language in the Statute Book of Galway (Gilbert 1885b), creeping as well into the French of the Irish Parliament (Morrissey 1939). Latin and French, however, continued as the major languages of administration nationally and in Dublin until they were supplanted by English under Henry VIII in the sixteenth century (Gilbert 1889: 142–4, 237ff).

Although English, then, gains ground in Anglo-Irish legal documentation in the fourteenth and fifteenth centuries, it is at just this time that it appears to have gone into decline as a spoken vernacular. As early as 1297, concern was expressed by the Anglo-Irish government that the community was assimilating into the native Irish culture and society (Berry 1907: 211). Evidence for language use during this time is indirect, but various measures were passed by the Irish Parliament to arrest the process of cultural assimilation, both by trying to foster unity within the Anglo-Irish community, and by prohibiting relations with the native Irish population: for relevant legislation, see Berry (1907: 412, 417–18) and Gilbert (1885a: 292).

The Statutes of Kilkenny, written in French and passed in 1366, illustrate the perceived loss of English as a vernacular among the Anglo-Irish of the time. The preamble (Berry 1907: 431) notes that 'many English...forsaking the English language, fashion, mode of riding, laws and usages, live and govern themselves according to the manners, fashion, and language of the Irish enemies'. Accordingly, it was ordained 'that every Englishman use the English language, and be named by an English name'. The bifurcation in which an attempt is made to preserve English within the Anglo-Irish community while recognising Irish as the natural language of the rest of the population is seen in a Waterford ordinance of 1492–3 (Gilbert 1885a: 323), which declared that

> no manere man...of the citie or suburbes duellers [dwellers], shall enpleade nor defende in Yrish tong ayenste ony man in the court, but that all they that ony maters shall have in courte...shall have a man that can spek English to declare his matier, excepte one party be of the countre; then every such dueller shalbe att liberte to speke Yrish.[1]

In a move which appears to indicate the difficulty in enforcing the language statutes, the Parliament of 1495, while generally reaffirming the Statutes of Kilkenny, specifically excluded from consideration those statutes which pertained to 'the language of Irish' (*Statutes* 1786: 77).

The picture presented to Henry VIII in 1515 of the 'state of Ireland' (*State Papers* 1834, II, iii: 8) illustrates the tenuous position of the Anglo-Irish community and administration at the time. Only six counties are counted as 'subjett unto the Kinges lawes', while even in the loyal counties, much of the territory is counted as disloyal and it is stated that 'all the comyn peoplle...for the more parte ben of Iryshe byrthe, of Iryshe habyte, and of Iryshe langage'. In the rest of Ireland, the people are similarly stated to be 'of Iryshe langage, and of Iryshe condytions', except within the walled cities and towns. Later, particularly from 1534 onwards, statutes and directives issued under Henry VIII attack Gaelicisation through reference to trade, dress, hairstyle, fraternisation, recreation and language (see Hamilton 1860: 17, 32; Gilbert 1885b: 380; *State Papers* 1834, II, iii: 309; *Statutes* 1786: 119ff.).

The proclamation of Henry VIII as King of Ireland at the Irish Parliament of 1541 is frequently cited as revealing the extent of Gaelicisation among the Anglo-Irish nobility. Antony St Leger's account of the parliamentary session at which Henry was recognised as King of Ireland (a title not previously assumed by the English monarch) clearly describes the assembly of Irish lords as a grand and solemn event 'as the like thereof hathe not bene seen here of many yeris'. St Leger also reports the agreement of the lords to the statement of praise of Henry and to the bill naming him as king which were both read out and declared in Irish by the Earl of Ormond following their initial presentation in the House (*State Papers* 1834, III, iii: 304). Most recent writers (e.g. Cahill 1938; Ó Cuív 1951; Ó Murchú 1970; Bliss 1976) accept the position, as Ó Cuív (1951: 13) phrased it, that the use of Irish on this occasion 'was...sheer necessity, for it seems that the Earl of Ormond alone of the Anglo-Irish Lords knew English'.

Neither St Leger's account nor the evidence of other contemporary documents, however, supports the view that Irish was used on this occasion out of 'necessity'. Rather, an understanding of this event as part of what Bradshaw (1979: 238) terms a 'milestone in Irish constitutional history' shows it to be not a measure of language usage among the Anglo-Irish nobility, but a symbolic act in which a unique effort was made to incorporate the traditional Gaelic nobility within a newly styled kingdom of Ireland. There is no evidence, for example, that Irish was used at any other time during the Parliament of 1541 (see *Statutes* 1786; *State Papers* 1834; Hamilton 1860; Brewer & Bullen 1867). Actual evidence of the linguistic choices of early sixteenth-century Gaelic and Gaelicised nobility is indirect and often hidden by the status still accorded to Latin: most of the documents in which various Irish leaders swear loyalty to Henry at this time are in Latin and make no other reference to language (see Brewer & Bullen 1867, *passim*).

Yet other glimpses of language use and language loyalty are available from this period. In 1541, St Leger praises the loyalty of McGillapatrick of Carlow, whose son had spent time in the English Pale and is described as speaking 'good Inglisshe'. The elder McGillapatrick was, on St Leger's recommendation, made a lord and was present at the Parliament of 1541 (*State Papers* 1834, III, iii: 289, 304). One may also cite the letters in English from O'Reilly to Henry VIII (*State Papers* 1834, III, iii:

559–60) and from William de Burgo in professing his loyalty in 1541 (*State Papers* 1834, III, iii: 290–1). Although Con O'Neale's submission and creation as Earl of Tyrone in 1542, written in Latin, contains a commitment for O'Neale and his heirs to 'use ... to their knowledge the English language', the earl is recorded as having thanked Henry in Irish on receipt of his letters patent (Brewer & Bullen 1867: 198–9). Later, in 1568, O'Connor Sligo, in presenting himself to Elizabeth I, professes his loyalty in Irish through an interpreter (Brewer & Bullen 1867: 378).

The overall picture, then, which emerges during this crucial transitional period in Irish linguistic history is one which is significant on two levels. At the level of language use, there is some evidence of a transition towards English within the nobility to the extent that political loyalties outside the traditional Gaelic power structure are maintained. At the symbolic level, Irish is maintained as a symbol of Irish identity, evidenced in the deliberate use of Irish as a unifying medium at the proclamation of the kingship of Henry VIII, and in the continued use of Irish among at least some nobles who nevertheless professed loyalty to the English Crown. The retention of Irish at this level is also indicative of its status as a traditional prestige language, alongside Latin, in the domains of education, culture and law (see Ó Murchú 1970, 1985).

The picture of bilingualism and the encroachment of Irish into the Anglo-Irish community presented in anecdotal reports of the sixteenth century (see *State Papers* 1834, II, iii: 445ff.; Brewer & Bullen 1867: 76ff.) is brought into focus by the chronicle of Stanyhurst (1577). Stanyhurst lamented the contraction of the English-speaking Pale and noted (pp. 3–3v) that 'the Irish language was free dennized in ye English pale', objecting that familiarity between the Irish population and the colonists had brought about 'the utter decay and defoliation of Ireland'. Stanyhurst had a particular interest in Fingal in north Co. Dublin and in the baronies of Forth and Bargy in south Co. Wexford, where he stated (p. 3) that the residents spoke 'the dregs of the olde auncient Chaucer English' (see section 4.3.1 below). Nevertheless, he implies an intimate bilingualism in these districts, stating (p. 2v) that the speakers of this older English 'have so acquainted themselves with the Irishe, as they have made a mingle mangle, or gallamaulfrey of both the languages'.

Miscellaneous late sixteenth-century evidence of Gaelicisation and the attempt to support English include the efforts of Dominicke Linche in 1569 to establish a school in Galway in which English could be taught (Kelly 1897), a land grant from 1583 awarded on the basis that the recipient was 'a modest man and that speaks English' (Hamilton 1867:

464), bilingual sets of letters to and from Cormac O'Conor in 1567 (Hamilton 1860: 328) and the Mayor of Galway in 1583 (Hamilton 1867: 441), and the report of Fynes Moryson, based on his travels to Ireland between ca 1599 and 1613, that

> the meere Irish disdayned to learne or speake the English tongue, yea the English Irish and the very Cittizens (excepting those of Dublin where the lord Deputy resides) though they could speake English as well as wee, yet Commonly speake Irish among themselves, and were hardly induced by our familiar Conversation to speake English with us, yea Common experience shewed ... the Cittizens of Watterford and Corcke having wyves that could speake English as well as wee, bitterly to chyde them when they speake English with us.
>
> (Hughes 1903: 213; see also p. 481)

In interpreting the historical record up to the seventeenth century, most linguistic histories concentrate on the complaints and signs of loss of English at the expense of noting evidence of bilingualism. Thus Henry (1957: 16) states that English in Ireland 'became early extinct in all rural areas' except for south Wexford and Fingal. According to Bliss (1977a: 26), 'through most of the country Mediaeval Hiberno-English was effectively extinct' by the end of the sixteenth century. Similarly, Barry (1982: 86) maintains that 'at the opening of the sixteenth century, English was almost a dead language' except in Wexford and Fingal, while 'by 1600, Irish was probably the normal language even of most of the eastern coastal region'.

The contemporary reports cited thus far, however, hardly support a view of the 'extinction' of English. Anecdotal reports and comments such as Moryson's confirm that English was spoken within the Anglo-Irish population, though it may not have been the only language used and may not have corresponded to the contemporary English of England. A telling comment is found in the narration of the visit of Christopher, Lord of Howth, and other Anglo-Irish aristocrats to the court of Queen Elizabeth, contained in the late sixteenth-century 'Book of Howth' (Brewer & Bullen 1871: 201). Here resentment is evidently expressed at English misrepresentations of Anglo-Irish linguistic abilities in the anonymous chronicler's comment that 'the Queen asked the Lord of Houthe whether he could speak the English tongue. Belike, such was the report of the country made to the Queen.' Thus Irwin (1935: 32–3) has maintained that 'there is no strong evidence that in the 15th century English disappeared entirely from the manors and villages', while Canny (1980) has attacked Bliss' portrayal of the demise of English, citing historical evidence to suggest (p. 170) that 'far from being the feeble plant that Bliss has described, indigenous Hiberno-English was ... a vital and expanding language throughout the sixteenth century'.

4.2.2   The seventeenth century onwards

Two waves of 'plantation' in seventeenth-century Ireland have profoundly affected both the social and the political history of the country and its resulting linguistic development. Following some minor attempts at sixteenth-century plantation by Queen Mary, the 'Plantation of Ulster' began in earnest under James I after the 'Flight of the Earls' in 1607, in which much of the Gaelic aristocracy left Ireland following their submission to British forces in 1603.

Further plantation followed the Irish rebellion of 1641 and the ultimate defeat of the Irish in 1649. The aims of securing a greater hold on the country and of rewarding soldiers and merchants under Cromwell were in part served by allowing a significant number of 'planters' to occupy land in various parts of the country. The effect of plantation in Ireland was thus to introduce further varieties of English (especially Scots in Ulster and various seventeenth-century English dialects more generally) and to push the exclusive domain of Irish into more isolated areas, particularly to the south and west.

The settlement pattern of the Plantation of Ulster is complex: for detailed reviews see especially Braidwood (1964) and Robinson (1984). Roughly speaking, Scottish settlers tended to predominate in the north-eastern parts of Ulster, with settlers from England predominating in mid and south Ulster districts. Two qualitative factors in the settlement of Ulster had a bearing on subsequent linguistic developments: first, that the plantation population was spread thinly in many areas, failing to displace the native farm labouring population; and second, that a cross-section of agrarian labourers, planters and traders was settled rather than a single landowning class as had been the case in the original Anglo-Norman settlement.

The developing pace of English-speaking settlement and the use of English is reflected in contemporary comments. Sir John Davies, while repeating the customary lamentations concerning the historical Gaelicisation of the original colonists (see Davies 1613: 30, 182ff.), expressed the view (pp. 271–2) that the Anglo-Irish community found 'a great inconvenience in moving their suites by an Interpretor ... [and] do for the most part send their Children to Schools, especially to learn the English language'. Accordingly, Davies expressed the hope (p. 272) that 'the next generation, will in tongue and heart, and in every way else becom *English*'. From within the Gaelic tradition, Conell Ma Geoghagan, who translated the 'Annals of Clonmacnoise' into English in 1627, prefaces his translation with the observation (Murphy 1896: 7–8) that those who should be preserving Irish traditions 'set naught by the sd [said] knoledg, neglect their Bookes, and choose rather to put their children to learne eng: than their own native Language'.

The Census of 1659 (Pender 1939), commissioned as part of the Cromwellian plantation, is not to be taken literally as a modern census, yet it may provide a partial guide to linguistic distribution, particularly in those areas where English administration was most effective. The census appears to have used linguistic criteria to return the population as 'Irish', 'English', 'Scots' and, in Bargy, 'Old English'. Despite reservations about the definitions of these categories and the evident incompleteness and inaccuracy of some material (see Pender 1939: xiii fn., xviii), the data from the Census provide at least some quantity of information which is not available elsewhere.

The predominance of the 'Irish' population and the effects of plantation are both evident in the 1659 Census. Of the twenty-seven counties for which records exist, only Antrim in Ulster shows an 'English' majority, with 54 per cent of the population returned as 'English and Scots'. ('Scots' and 'English' are only occasionally differentiated in the data.) In Ulster the counties of Derry, Down and Armagh show substantial English and Scots populations (45, 43 and 35 per cent respectively), while the more outlying counties of Donegal and Fermanagh show English and Scots populations of 28 and 25 per cent respectively. In the rest of the country, only Co. Dublin with an 'English' population of 45 per cent shows a proportion of 'English' that is greater than 20 per cent. In 11 counties, the proportion of 'English' population is no greater than 10 per cent, falling to as low as 3 per cent in County Clare. At least two counties for which returns are not available (Galway and Mayo) could have also been expected on the basis of subsequent history to have shown extremely low levels of 'English' settlement in the census.

Given the importance of towns as possible sites of linguistic diffusion in many historically attested situations (see Trudgill 1974), the concentration of English settlement in the towns of the 1659 Census is significant. The typical pattern is for a given town to contain an inner

Table 4.1. *English population and percentages in towns, 1659*

Town	N	Urban (%)	Suburban (%)	Area (%)	English (%)	Co. (%)
Carrickfergus[a]	1,311	84	43	63	12	05
Belfast	3,852	62	51	53	29	13
Coleraine	2,750	NA	NA	56	35	16
Derry	1,052	NA	NA	54	13	06
Cork[b]	4,826	62	28	33	25	04
Kinsale	2,197	43	28	38	13	02
Limerick	3,105	53	06	26	41	03
Waterford	1,607	57	14	39	47	05
Carlow	1,517	48	13	26	52	07
Dublin	21,827	74	25	45	66[c]	30[c]
Kilkenny	1,722	39	13	25	30	02
Dundalk	2,536	29	07	13	18	03
Drogheda[d]	1,605	NA	NA	60	53	10
Wexford	902	44	18	38	21	02
Athlone[e]	948	40	14	56	NA	NA
Sligo	1,398	27	09	15	39	03

[a] Includes 349 soldiers and wives (97 per cent English).
[b] Includes 338 soldiers (93 per cent English).
[c] Urban English percentage of county totals.
[d] Includes 374 soldiers and wives (95 per cent English).
[e] Includes Westmeath (Leinster) and Roscommon (Connaught); including 430 soldiers, wives and servants (83 per cent English).

area which is largely or predominantly 'English' (sometimes including a settlement of soldiers and their wives), surrounded by liberties and suburbs which are more substantially Irish, leading in turn to the countryside which outside of Ulster is overwhelmingly 'Irish'. In some cases, this inner urban core constitutes the bulk of the 'English' population of the entire county. In others, the total English population will be more diffused. Outside of Ulster and Dublin, the English population of any given town will not constitute a large part of the population of the county as a whole, but the concentration of English in towns of importance for trade and administration could be expected to give this small population a linguistic significance, mediated by bilingualism, beyond its numerical strength.

Table 4.1 illustrates the pattern of urban English distribution in the 1659 Census. For each town, following the total population of the urban area and surrounding suburbs (*N*), the percentage is given for 'English' or 'English and Scottish' returned (a) in the urban area proper (*Urban* %), (b) in the suburbs and liberties (*Suburban* %), (c) in the total urban and suburban area (*Area* %), (d) as a percentage of the English total for the county (*English* %), and (e) as a percentage of the population of the country as a whole (*Co.* %).

The seventeenth and eighteenth centuries in Ireland saw the continued development of bilingualism and language shift towards English alongside the retention and even the development of Irish in new domains. Pointing towards the use of Irish are the report of Francis Ó Molloy (Froinsias Ó Maolmhuaidh) in 1676 that 'no language is well understood by the common people except Irish alone' (Ó Cuív 1951: 18); the recommendation to the Irish Revenue Commissioners in 1674–5 that riding officers at Wexford and Waterford should have the 'linguo of the country' in order to gain necessary information (McNeill 1930: 178); and Thomas Dinely's observation several years later that 'several English themselves' had become 'meer Irish', showing 'neglect & scorn of the use of their own propper language English' (Shirley 1856–7: 187). Protestant recognition of Irish as the language of the mass of the Irish people led to efforts to translate the Bible and to preach in Irish, and to a related interest in Irish grammar and literature (see MacLysaght 1979: 306–7; N. Williams 1986). Alongside the Anglo-Irish literary and cultural circle of Jonathan Swift in late seventeenth- and early eighteenth-century Dublin, there existed a vibrant Irish-language literary and scholarly circle: Ó Háinle (1986) demonstrates the nature of contact between these two literary groups via translation of Irish work into English and by the personal contacts of bilingual individuals.

Contrary evidence of the spread of English at this time is seen in the observation of Albert de Rochefort, who came to Ireland in ca 1660, that 'in the greater part of the towns and villages on the sea-coast only English is spoken' (Irwin 1935: 361–2) and in Eachard's account (1691: 16–17) that among the native Irish population 'the English Tongue is very frequently used among 'em, and in some places (particularly in the County of *Wexford*) they make use of a mungrel sort of speech between English and Irish'. Even Dinely also observed that 'they that do speake English here throughout the whole kingdom speake it generally better and more London-like then in most places of England' (Shirley 1858–9: 22).

Among eighteenth-century indications of language use are the observations of Bush (1769: 34) that 'English is the universal language of the country among people of any fortune', and that 'very few of the lowest class are met with that cannot speak' English, while 'thousands of the lowest rank ... speak both English and Irish' as well as the report of a bilingual trial in Galway in 1739 (MacLysaght 1944) which features a bilingual defendant whose compatriots are bilingual or monoglot Irish speakers. Arthur Young, who toured Ireland in 1776 (Young 1780), gives brief accounts of the older pockets of English speakers in Forth and Bargy (I, i: 108, 113), Fingal (II: 106), and a part of north Co. Dublin (I, i: 141) which was, in Young's view, 'more intermixed with Irish in language &c' than the Forth community. Young also refers to Lord Shannon's policy in Co. Cork of giving 'encouragement' to labourers 'only ... such as can speak English' (I, ii: 51), and to seasonal migration between Newfoundland and Bargy (I, i: 112) and Curraghmoor, Co. Limerick (I, ii: 177).

Local bilingualism in the early nineteenth century is well, if incompletely, illustrated in the parochial survey compiled by Mason (1814–19). Though this survey, compiled from a questionnaire distributed to Protestant clergymen throughout the country, is necessarily subjective and lacks reports for many areas (including such heavily Irish-speaking counties as Galway, Mayo and Kerry), the picture of language shift in progress which emerges from it is sufficiently borne out by later developments to suggest its validity as an indication of patterns of language use at the time (see further Mac Aodha 1985–6).

Of the seventy-seven parish reports considered here from Mason's survey, only four show Irish as the dominant language. On the other hand, eighteen parishes, including eight in Ulster and one covering Forth and Bargy, show English as the dominant or exclusive language. Fifty-five parishes appear as bilingual: in twenty-four, English is the major language, as opposed to sixteen in which Irish assumes priority, with a further fifteen showing socially stratified bilingualism. This social stratification, as well as the importance of towns in the diffusion of English, age stratification showing English as the language of younger speakers, and the presence of distinct 'Scotch' elements in Ulster may be seen in the following representative reports:

> *Kilgeriff, Co. Cork.* 'the language of the common Roman Catholic peasantry is Irish; Protestants of the lower order speak both English and Irish; in town [Cloghnakilty] English is frequently spoken by both' (II: 311).

Table 4.2 *Percentages of Irish speakers in selected age cohorts*

Area	1771–81	1801–11	1831–41	1861–71	to 1916	1937–46	1957–66
TOTAL	45	41	28	13	13	30	46
Gael[a]	NA	NA	NA	NA	21	05	03
LEINSTER	17	11	03	00	09	26	41
Gael[a]	NA	NA	NA	NA	00	00	00[b]
Kilkenny	57	45	14	01	08	29	47
Wicklow	01	01	00	00	07	29	37
MUNSTER	80	77	57	21	13	34	52
Gael[a]	NA	NA	NA	NA	12	03	02
Kerry	93	93	86	45	21	36	54
Gael[a]	NA	NA	NA	NA	35	12	10
Tipperary	51	45	16	02	09	33	52
CONNACHT	84	80	63	40	20	40	56
Gael[a]	NA	NA	NA	NA	38	18	13
Mayo	95	94	89	60	21	38	56
Gael[a]	NA	NA	NA	NA	44	19	14
Leitrim	52	43	19	01	07	32	51
ULSTER	19	15	08	04	19[c]	29[c]	43[c]
Gael[a]	NA	NA	NA	NA	63	29	19
Donegal	56	53	40	29	29	33	43
Gael[a]	NA	NA	NA	NA	74	47	35
Derry	10	07	04	01	NA	NA	NA
Monaghan	33	28	11	01	06	24	42

[a] Percentage of Irish speakers in Gaeltacht areas.
[b] 493 Gaeltacht speakers statistically insignificant.
[c] Includes only Donegal, Cavan, and Monaghan.

> *Athlone, Co. Roscommon.* 'Most of the natives of this parish speak English; there are only a very few, and these the oldest grandmothers, who speak nothing but Irish...; all the children speak it [English], and many of them cannot speak Irish' (III: 71–2).
>
> *Fuerty, Co. Roscommon.* 'The inferior orders of the people here seem indifferent as to their choice of the English or Irish language; among themselves, indeed, Irish is more commonly used' (I: 403).
>
> *Finvoy, Co. Antrim.* 'The language of the inhabitants of this parish is English, with some Scotch words used by the dissenters, and Irish by the natives' (I: 391).

The ultimate shift to English as the dominant vernacular in Ireland may be seen in census returns only if the data which are available are analysed with caution. It is generally accepted that the early census returns under-represented the level of Irish usage, due both to low prestige attached to Irish (particularly in areas undergoing language shift) and to the low prominence given to language questions on census enumerators' forms in 1851 and 1861. Data for Ireland as a whole are complete only until 1911, as the census in Northern Ireland does not include language questions. Most importantly, whereas the earliest census figures include as Irish-speakers mostly native bilinguals and a significant number of monolingual Irish-speakers (running to 72 per cent monolingualism in some areas; see Fitzgerald 1984: 152–3), the current levels of usage for Irish are much more reflective of language maintenance efforts. Thus recent surveys show the level of native speaker ability in Irish at a mere 3 per cent in 1983 (Ó Coileáin n.d.: 21; see also Ó Riagáin 1988a). For detailed discussion of these and other aspects of Irish language census data, see Ó Cuív (1951), Adams (1964a, 1973, 1976), Fitzgerald (1984) and Ó Murchú (1985).

Using the analysis of the 1881 Census presented by Fitzgerald (1984) and the data provided by the 1981 Census (*Daonáireamh* 1985), table 4.2 illustrates the decline of Irish usage from the end of the eighteenth century and its increase under different conditions during the twentieth century. Levels of Irish-speaking for age cohorts (i.e. the group born in a given decade which survives to the taking of the census) in the 1881 and 1981 Censuses are provided, with subtotals for each province and for a range of counties within each province.

The pattern of language shift which emerges from the census is not simply one of decline and modified revival, but one of levelling. Irish usage is now less localised in so far as fewer areas show very high levels of usage, while more areas show an Irish-speaking figure approaching the national average of roughly 36 per cent. The use of Irish in schools is a factor in considering the high percentage of young Irish-speakers: there are no particular implications for the continued use of Irish by this age group. The low level of native speaker ability in Irish is suggested by the low proportion of Irish-speakers in *Gaeltacht* (specially designated Irish-speaking districts) areas as a percentage of the total number of Irish-speakers. Proportions of Gaeltacht speakers among those speaking Irish are included from the 1981 Census where appropriate in Table 4.2.

Though the data of table 4.2 do not even show the full nature of local variations in the pattern of shift to English (see particularly Fitzgerald

1984), nor the complex role played by factors such as trade routes, geographical features and religious affiliation (see Adams 1958, 1964a; Ó Snodaigh 1973), they do make it clear that the spread of English in Ireland has been prolonged, geographically irregular and bound up with the overall status of the Irish language. Though the precise effect of bilingualism and language contact on the internal linguistic development of Irish English is still open to question, it is against this background that the linguistics of Irish English, discussed in the following section, must be understood.

4.3   The linguistic history of English in Ireland

It is convenient, if not entirely accurate, to separate the linguistic history of English in Ireland into two phases based on the external history: a medieval phase, leaving only traces in the archaic dialect of Forth and Bargy; and the modern phase based on the resurgence of English (including Scots) in the sixteenth and seventeenth centuries. The degree to which these varieties overlapped in historical times, and the question of intermediate stages between them, has never been explored in detail, and it is only possible here to follow a broadly chronological outline.

In the following subsections, discussion focuses on linguistic features which may be held as characteristic of Irish English at different times. The term 'characteristic' does not necessarily mean 'unique'. It is often difficult to ascertain whether or not a feature is actually unique to a particular language variety: in addition to the obvious problem of gaps in the information available for cross-dialectal comparison, there is the more subtle problem presented by forms which appear on the surface to be shared between dialects but which actually have different conditions of use or different values within their respective language systems (for relevant examples see Milroy 1984; Harris 1985b; Montgomery 1989; Filppula 1991). Moreover, while a given linguistic feature may not be unique to any particular variety, noting of the feature may nevertheless be typologically useful in order to illustrate general affinities between varieties. It is also realistic to include non-unique features of a dialect as yielding in combination a distinct configuration of features. Hence the treatment which follows seeks to reflect a representative view of what is characteristic of Irish English without trying to apply a strict criterion of uniqueness.

4.3.1 Early Irish English and the English of Forth and Bargy

An early fourteenth-century manuscript which contains material traditionally referred to as the 'Kildare Poems', edited by Heuser (1904), constitutes the essential starting-point for the linguistic history of Irish English. Sixteen major items in English, generally of a religious or satirical nature, are found in the manuscript alongside other items in Latin and French. Though little is known about the manuscript, Benskin (1990) has produced evidence that it is largely written by a single hand; linguistic and external historical indications lead Benskin to characterise the material as 'Waterford copies of originals apparently from Kildare' (Benskin 1989: 60; see also Henry 1972 and Bliss 1984b).

Further literary works from the fourteenth and fifteenth centuries include some song fragments from the 'Red Book of Ossory' (see Stemmler 1977), three poems edited by Seymour (1932–4) and some miscellaneous poetry as well as a treatise on the virtues of herbs (see Wright & Halliwell 1841–3; Heuser 1904; Bliss 1984b; Bliss & Long 1987). Fifteenth-century material is more given to translation, including James Yong's free rendition of the *Secreta Secretorum* (Steele 1898) and translations of Giraldus' *Expugnatio Hibernica* (Furnivall 1896). The register of Archbishop Swayne of Armagh (Chart 1935) contains a number of letters and a satirical poem on women's clothing (p. 139), while Irwin (1935) documents several other letters and short pieces in manuscript collections.

Legal material in English begins with isolated place-name and lexical entries in the Latin text of Justiciary Rolls from 1295 to 1303 (Mills 1905), yet it is only with the appearance of local ordinances, as mentioned in section 4.2.1, and with the use of 'some English' in the Ormond deeds from around 1350 (Curtis 1932: viii) that significant legal material becomes available. The fifteenth century provides more English documentation, including the *Liber primus* of Kilkenny and the records of the Dublin Merchants Guilds (see Bliss & Long 1987: 714–15), various deeds of the Blake family from 1430 to 1502 (Hardiman 1846; Blake 1902) and some miscellaneous items in the records of Dublin Corporation (Gilbert 1889). By far the most comprehensive listing of literary and legal material from this period is presented by McIntosh, Samuels & Benskin (1986: 270–9). Though many of the items listed are fragmentary and may show the influence of British norms, they demonstrate ample room for further linguistic analysis than the small amount which has been undertaken thus far.

Although early immigration from South Wales and the south-west of England discussed in section 4.2 would suggest an affinity between early Irish English and the English dialects of these areas, the geographical diversity also noted for this time appears to have brought about phenomena which are frequently ascribed to dialect mixing. Irwin (1935: 91) notes, for example, that while south-west midlands English at this time showed alternation between *heom* and *hom* for the equivalent of ModE *them*, contrasting with the south-west English alternation between *ham* and *hom*, Irish English reveals neither system of alternation but instead exhibits only *ham* in attested texts. McIntosh & Samuels (1968: 6–7) cite the use of *swa* 'so' and *hame* 'home' in Ireland as evidence of northern English influence, leading them to suggest (as do Bliss & Long 1987) that, while the basis for early Irish English may have lain with south-west and south-west midlands English, the influence of English from as far north as south Lancashire, perhaps coming via the Isle of Man, must not be underestimated.

Perhaps the most dramatic and commonly noted aspect of medieval Irish English which illustrates the role of dialect mixing is the loss of morphological significance for final unstressed *-e* (see Hogan 1927; Irwin 1935; McIntosh & Samuels 1968). This loss is manifested in the deletion of *-e* where it would be historically required and in its insertion in etymologically unjustified environments. Irwin (1935: 70) thus cites forms such as *met* (OE *mete*) 'food', *nam* (OE *nama*) 'name' and a converse spelling of *fleisse* (OE *flæsc*) 'flesh, meat'. McIntosh & Samuels (1968) note that northern and north midland speakers possessed a different distribution for the use of final *-e* from that of southern speakers, and suggest (p. 9) that conflicting norms could readily have led to the loss of this marker at an earlier time in Ireland than in the south of England. As evidence of the conservatism of Irish English at this time, McIntosh & Samuels (1968: 4) cite the preservation to a later date than in England such southern forms as *-y* and *-i* infinitive suffixes and the use of *oþir*, *othyr* for the equivalent of ModE *or*; Bliss & Long (1987: 709) cite the frequency of *hit* and *hyt* for later *it*. Despite this conservatism, the loss of morphological significance for final *-e* is relatively innovative within the context of general English.

Other characteristics of early Irish English phonology in so far as it can be reconstructed from spelling evidence include variation between ⟨w⟩ and ⟨v⟩, between ⟨th⟩ and ⟨t⟩, and in the use of final ⟨d⟩. Although McIntosh & Samuels (1968) and Bliss (1984b) simply note that words spelt with ⟨v⟩ in general Middle English are often spelt in medieval Irish English with ⟨w⟩, Irwin (1935: 77–9) has pointed out that the interchange between these two spellings is in fact quite complicated. In the earliest texts, according to Irwin, the English spelling ⟨wh⟩ was realised in Ireland as ⟨fw⟩ (perhaps indicating phonetic [φ]), while English ⟨v⟩ was spelt by ⟨w⟩. In the fifteenth century, however, the ⟨w⟩/⟨v⟩ replacement was reversed as well, while the Irish ⟨fw⟩ spellings were replaced by simple ⟨f⟩. Spellings thus to be noted include *John Fwyt, Edussa Fwyte* ('Whyte'), *foo so* 'who so', and *woyde, wapours, werry* 'void, vapours, very' alongside *vyntyr, voman, vif* 'winter, woman, wife' (Irwin 1935: 79, 109–10).

Interchange between ⟨th⟩ and ⟨t⟩ spellings may be noted here as in *tis* 'this', *tred* 'third' (Bliss 1965: 35), *set* 'seethe (boil)' (Britton & Fletcher 1990: 60), and *dynge* 'thing', *day* 'they' (Hogan 1927: 29) in contrast to *thyme* 'time', *plainth* 'plaint' (McIntosh & Samuels 1968: 5), *thedynge* 'tiding', *onther* 'under' (Hogan 1927: 29), and *rathel* the plant-name 'rattle' (Britton & Fletcher 1990: 62). In comparable, though not strictly parallel, fashion, many texts show stop spellings in place of English fricative spellings in the third person singular and plural endings: thus cf. *fallit* and *wringit* (Irwin 1935: 80) alongside the more common *-ith* and *-eth* endings.

Early Irish English texts also show spellings with final ⟨d⟩ contrary to historically expected patterns. Irwin (1935: 110–11) notes that the loss of historical ⟨d⟩ after ⟨l⟩ and ⟨n⟩ is more widespread by the end of the first quarter of the fifteenth century and continues into the sixteenth, at times including a lesser tendency to omit ⟨t⟩ after spellings indicative of palatal or velar fricatives. Examples here include Irwin's *blyne* 'blind' and *growyn* 'ground' vs *felde* 'feel' and *sermonde* 'sermon' as well as McIntosh & Samuels' citations (1968: 5) of *sune* 'sound', *hell* 'held' alongside *fynder* 'finer' and *wand* 'when'.

Some miscellaneous characteristics of early Irish English may also be cited which, while not necessarily unique to Ireland, may combine to suggest an Irish provenance for Middle English material (see Benskin & McIntosh 1972) or may help to put Irish English into comparative perspective with other dialects. Although it may be desirable ultimately to reconstruct a coherent phonological system for early Irish English, the lack of authoritative published transcripts of early manuscripts, as well as the considerable geographical and textual diversity of those which have been analysed suggests that such an attempt would be premature (see McIntosh, Samuels & Benskin 1986 and the reanalysis by Britton & Fletcher 1990 of material considered by Bliss 1965).

Some salient features of early Irish English thus include the following: (1) loss of ME ⟨ċ⟩ or ⟨g⟩ before ⟨d⟩, ⟨t⟩, ⟨þ⟩, resulting in frequent spellings such as *strenþ* and *leinþ* ('strength', 'length'); (2) realisations of 'burnt' as *brand* or *brant*; (3) fifteenth-century interchange of ⟨ch⟩ and ⟨ge⟩ spellings as in *privelech*, *churgh*, *villache* and *visache*; and (4) glide insertion and metathesis yielding spellings such as *haryme* 'harm' and *fryst* or *frust* 'first'. Interchange of ⟨s⟩ and ⟨sh⟩ spellings relative to expected Middle English patterns is seen in words such as *grasshe* 'grass', *wash* 'was', *devyshe* 'device', *sarpe* 'sharp', *sortely* 'shortly', *Englys* 'English' and *irismen* 'Irishmen'. Finally, one may note the appearance in Irish manuscripts of initial ⟨quh⟩ and ⟨qhu⟩ spellings for words with OE initial ⟨hw⟩, as in *qhuetmel* 'wheatmeal' (Britton & Fletcher 1990: 64; see also McIntosh & Samuels 1968: 6).

The constraints imposed by poetic and legal forms limit the amount of syntactic analysis which may be made of early Irish English: apart from some comments of Henry (1958: 62ff.), there is virtually no discussion of syntax in this period. The early Irish English lexicon has also received little attention, although Irwin (1933, 1934) published a number of etymological notes prior to the appearance of his more exhaustive 1935 study. In the latter work, Irwin (pp. 205–330) establishes eleven categories to account for nearly 200 words which show special significance for Irish English. By far the largest category is that of Irish loanwords (about fifty entries), including legal and technical terms as well as those related to farming and related pursuits (e.g. *collop* 'unit of cattle for levying taxes, etc.' and *garran* 'gelding'). Other major categories include words of Old English origin obsolescent or unattested outside Ireland (e.g. *outcomen/outcomes men* 'strangers', *alewyk* 'alehouse', *bredwik* 'breadshop') and words of Scandinavian origin such as *haggard* 'stackyard' and *farcostes* 'boat, ship'. Benskin (1988) presents a more detailed etymological and phonological analysis of some fifteenth-century lexical items, understanding, for example, the word *co(u)ntre* 'country' in a 'primarily social sense' to refer to Irish social loyalties and not simply to territory (pp. 44–6), commenting on the distribution of characteristic *mut(e)* 'unless, except' in relation to ME *but* and to Irish phonology (pp. 51–6), and examining socially important terms such as *keheryn ty(e)* 'household troops', *spen* 'exact food subsidies from' and *ravaynnour* 'extortioner, plunderer, abductor'.

The archaic nature of the Forth and Bargy dialect has attracted attention since the time of Stanyhurst and has inspired subsequent antiquarian work such as that of Vallancey (1788), Fraser (1807), Jacob

Poole (Barnes 1867; Dolan & Ó Muirithe 1979), Russell (1858) and others. Though the related Fingallian dialect and the use of the Forth/Bargy dialect in Bargy had gone into decline before the nineteenth century, there was enough recollection of the dialect in Forth to enable the compilation of word-lists and some song and poetry texts during the late eighteenth and early nineteenth centuries. More recently, Ó Muirithe (1990) has updated the Forth and Bargy glossary with material collected in 1978: although many classic features of the early dialect are no longer to be found, some remain.

The glossary compiled by Poole illustrates the conservatism of Forth and Bargy English in features such as the use of *-en* plurals (*ashen* 'ashes', *been* 'bees', *kyne* 'cows', *pizzen* 'peas') and past participles with *y-* (*ee-drowe* 'thrown', *ee-smort* 'smothered', *ee-sarith* 'served'). Velar fricatives appear preserved in words such as *nickht* 'night' and *reicht* 'right'. Of these characteristics, only *ashen* is listed for the contemporary dialect by Ó Muirithe (1990); both he and Poole, however, also cite *ayenst* 'against' with [j] rather than the [g] of mainstream Modern English. The tendency in Poole's glossary to use ⟨f⟩ spellings in words such as *fan* 'when', *faade* 'what' and *fidi* (or *vidi*) 'where' is reminiscent of earlier Irish English and parallels developments discussed below. No such examples are listed by Ó Muirithe (1990), though labial consonant variation is seen in the pair *bolach/folach* 'rapeweed' (⟨Ir. *bólach*).

In so far as vocalic phonology can be ascertained from glossary spellings and the notes provided by William Barnes (Dolan & Ó Muirithe 1979: 10–12), the Forth and Bargy dialect appears to have retained many words unaffected by the Great Vowel Shift and subsequent related changes. Thus, for example, [iː] is evidently intended by Poole in entries such as *breed* 'bride', *deemes* 'times', *heeve* 'hive' and *threeve* 'thrive' which have become diphthongised under /aɪ/ in general Modern English. Similarly, Poole's spellings of *rooze* 'rouse', *shrude* 'shroud', *jooudge* 'judge', and *gooun* 'gun' all suggest an /uː/-type vowel rather than modern /aʊ/ or /ʌ/. Although these pronunciations appear to be lost from the contemporary dialect, Ó Muirithe (1990) joins Poole in citing the form *spone* 'spoon' using /oː/ rather than modern /uː/.

One further aspect of Forth and Bargy English which bears comparison with subsequent developments in general Irish English is the use of a front /aː/ vowel in words now taking /iː/ or /eɪ/ in most Modern English varieties. Using the lexical sets suggested by Wells (1982), one may note FLEECE words given by Ó Muirithe (1990) as *aager* 'eager' and *baam* 'beam' with /aː/ rather than /iː/, and FACE words such as *baake* 'bake', *braave* 'brave' and *graashoos* 'gracious' using Forth and Bargy /aː/ rather than /eɪ/. Comparable examples are common in Poole's glossary.

The Forth and Bargy lexicon shows strong links to Old and Middle English, with considerable carry-over from the Irish language as well as from other, sometimes obscure, sources. In this first category may be considered Poole's form *kunnife* 'knife' and the lexical items *attercop* 'a spider', hence also 'small, insignificant person', *poustee* 'power, ability, bodily strength' and *mawen* 'a woman, a wife' alongside *helt* 'covered' and *barse* 'the fish, bass' cited by Ó Muirithe (1990). Irish words cited by Poole include *booraan* 'a drum' (cf. Ir. *bodhrán*), *garraane* 'a working horse' in this dialect, *muskawn* 'a large heap or lump' (cf. Ir. *meascán*), and *saalvache* 'a slut, sloven' (cf. Ir. *salach* 'dirty'). Other items include the distinctive *paugh-meale* 'the harvest home' (derived from Ir. *póg* 'kiss' + *mael*, cf. OE 'time', literally 'kissing time'; see Poole's glossary and Ó Muirithe 1977a), *chi* 'a small quantity' (listed by Poole and by Ó Muirithe 1990; I have heard this term from a Wexford speaker in the related sense of 'an armload'), and *craueet* 'the danger of choking for want of a drink in eating', listed by Poole, for which no etymology has been suggested.

4.3.2   The rise of Modern Irish English

From the sixteenth century onwards, population movement into Ireland is generally assumed to have brought Irish English into contact with linguistic developments in England and Scotland. It is difficult to make a clear separation between 'old' and 'new' Irish English, in that many of the features of early Irish English, such as the merger of ⟨th⟩ and ⟨t⟩ spellings, substitution of ⟨fw⟩ or ⟨f⟩ for English ⟨wh⟩, etc. are also present in the 'new' variety. Rather than positing a discrete break between varieties, then, it is more realistic to suggest a transitional period in which modern Irish English developed in a situation of interdialectal as well as interlinguistic contact.

Textual materials for early modern Irish English include a variety of letters and legal documents, some original literature, and representations of Irish speech in drama and poetry. Much of the formal writing shows the influence of standardisation from England and thus offers limited insight into the spoken English of the time. Three major literary works may be noted: the 'Book of Howth' cited above, and the seventeenth-century works entitled *An Aphorismical Discovery of Treasonable Faction* (Gilbert 1879) and the *Siege of Ballyally Castle* (Croker 1841). The 'Book of Howth' is a collection of transcripts of other manuscripts, original commentary, genealogy and other material presented in a relatively lively style and reflecting the literary and political interests of its compilers. The other two works are historical narratives of recently completed events: the *Aphorismical Discovery* has attracted attention due to its reflection not only of Irish English usage but of continental literary norms (see Irwin 1935; Bliss 1979).

Literary representations of Irish speech begin in English drama in the mid-sixteenth century, developing a mixture of realism and convention which becomes increasingly conventionalised in the late seventeenth and eighteenth centuries (see Bartley 1942, 1954; Bliss 1979). Other genres which may be noted include the highly conventionalised collections of 'Irish bulls' (malapropisms and other linguistic 'blunders' written in a supposedly Irish dialect orthography) which flourished in the seventeenth and eighteenth centuries (see Bartley 1947), satirical poetry in English and Irish-language writings such as the seventeenth-century *Pairlement Chloinne Tomáis* (Williams 1981) and later *Stair Éamuinn Uí Chléire* (Ó Neachtain 1918) and *Suirghe Mhuiris Uí Ghormáin* (Murray 1912–15) which satirised the efforts of Irish speakers to learn English.

This literary dialect material must be interpreted with due regard to its original background and purpose. Many playwrights who used Irish characters had not, as far as is known, been to Ireland, yet the speech of Irish servants, costermongers and similar individuals in England could have provided not only a model for writing but a frame of reference for English audiences. How representative this speech would be of general Irish English is open to question. In considering the satirical purpose of much of this material, the possibility that accuracy may have been sacrificed for effect cannot be ruled out. Thus while Bliss (1979) was inclined to accept most of the representations in his study of twenty-seven texts at face value for linguistic analysis, Canny (1980) and Henry (1981) have taken issue with Bliss' approach, echoing the concern of Irwin (1935) that most of the literary material relies too heavily on convention or peculiarity to be representative of typical speech patterns. Much of the information from literary texts, then, is best seen as complementary to the primary evidence of other works.

Many of the most characteristic features of Irish English phonology between the sixteenth and eighteenth centuries are familiar from the earlier period. Illustrated below are old and new consonantal alternations from this period (see Hogan 1927; Irwin 1935: 164 ff.; Henry 1958; Bliss 1979).

Major consonantal variations, sixteenth to eighteenth centuries

1   elision of ⟨g⟩ (*leynthe* 'length', *streinthen* 'strengthen')

2   loss of final ⟨d⟩ (*brone* 'brand', *greyons* 'greyhounds')

3   ⟨w/v⟩ alternations (*dewidit* 'divided', *wirgen* 'virgin', *wometted* 'vomited'; *vit* 'with', *vilt* 'wilt')

4   ⟨th/d⟩ or ⟨t⟩ alternation (*trone* 'throne', *wordy* 'worthy'; *oathes* 'oats', *thell* 'tell')

5   ⟨f⟩ and related spellings (*fome* 'whom', *furle* 'whirl', *faat* 'what', *phit* 'with')

6   ⟨s/sh⟩ alternation (*sheldom* 'seldom', *shuche* 'such', *firsht* 'first'; *sullynges* 'shillings', *sow'd* 'showed')

7   ⟨ch/sh⟩ alternation (*chylver* = shylver 'silver'; *porsh* 'porch', *shaine* 'chain')

8   ⟨sh⟩ spellings for historical [dʒ] (*shantleman* 'gentleman', *shudge* 'judge')

As with the Forth and Bargy dialect, the characteristic Irish English of the sixteenth to eighteenth centuries appears to show only a partial adoption of the vowel shifts and splits associated with general Modern English. Spelling evidence for the reconstruction of syllabic phonology in this period is difficult to interpret, given the diversity of text types and the influence of perception on the depiction of Irish speech by non-Irish writers. Irwin (1935) and Bliss (1979), for example, show different interpretations of the ⟨aa⟩ spellings common in literature from this period. These spellings may be grouped as (a) *aafter* 'after', *phaat* 'what', *waanity* 'vanity', (b) *plaash* 'place', *faash* 'face', *naame* 'name', alternating with *tawke* 'take' and *plaushes* 'places', and (c) *graat* 'great', *shpaaking* 'speaking', alternating with *bate* 'beat' and *spake* 'speech', where groupings roughly represent ME /a/, /aː/ and /ɛː/ respectively. For Irwin (1935: 152–4), the ⟨aa⟩ spellings of groups (a) and (b) suggested a merger under [aː], with group (c) simply showing an overextension of literary convention arising partly from developments in England. For Bliss (1979: 208 ff.), however, a more complex set of mergers and reanalyses is suggested. In either case, the use of a vowel such as /aː/ in FACE words does not appear as part of modern Irish English apart from the Forth and Bargy items as indicated above.

While the evidence of ⟨ea⟩ spellings to suggest either /e:/ or the more modern /i:/ in this period is equivocal, the failure of historical /i:/ to diphthongise in Ireland appears characteristically in the data: note *preyd* 'pride', *reepe* 'ripe' and *deereful* 'direful' from non-artistic texts of the sixteenth and seventeenth centuries in addition to dramatic representations such as *creesh* 'Christ' and *leek* 'like' (Irwin 1935: 157). Similarly, while Irwin (1935: 157–9) suggests that ME /o:/ appears to have followed the Great Vowel Shift pattern in raising to /u:/ no later than the early sixteenth century in Ireland (cf. *bloud* 'blood', *lusing* 'losing'), spellings such as *hue* 'how', *shoowre* 'sour' and *fundation* 'foundation' suggest that ME /u:/ had not undergone diphthongisation at a comparable time.

Among the miscellaneous phonological developments which may also be mentioned here are the lowering of ME /i/ to /ɛ/ and the raising of /e/ to /ɪ/. Irwin (1935: 161–2) notes the first change in sixteenth-century documents, as in *ventadge* 'vintage', *Lessmore* 'Lismore' and *brege* 'bridge', while Bliss (1979: 203) understood the second process as a forerunner of modern Irish English, citing spellings such as *min* 'men', *gitt* 'get' and *ilse* 'else'. Characteristics not unique to Irish English but generally seen to demonstrate the dialectal affinities of English in Ireland at this time also include the frequent favouring of ⟨ar⟩ spellings in words such as *sarvant* 'servant' and *clarge* 'clergy' (see Braidwood 1964: 54) as well as the apparent retention of [w] before [r] in sixteenth-century *wourytyng* 'writing', *worytten* 'written' (Irwin 1935: 174–5).

Bliss' (1979) material displays several distinctive morphological characteristics, yet it is difficult to know the extent to which these features constitute genuine aspects of the grammar of Irish English rather than stereotypical language-learning phenomena. Most noticeable here is variation in the use of plural marking (*foot(e)s*, *mans*, *gooses* vs *sheldrens*, *mens*, plural *seeps* 'sheep'), the loss of past-participle morphemes (*rob* 'robbed', *undoo* 'undone', *break* 'broken'), and the loss of pronouns as in *Vas he soe hot is cou'd no quench / De flame* '... that he could not quench the flame' (for commentary on pronoun loss see Guilfoyle 1986). Despite the widespread use of these and related features in literary writing, the lack of these elements in other works of the time makes the interpretation of the literary evidence inconclusive.

Syntax characteristic of Irish English begins to emerge in this period. The use of *after* as a marker of tense/aspect is perhaps the most noticeable characteristic, yet it is one for which modern usage may obscure the nature of historical developments. (Rather than suggest a rigid distinction between tense, modality and aspect, I follow Dahl (1985) by referring to 'TMA categories' more generally in the following discussion.) Shadwell's *I will be after reconciling thee* from 1681 (Bartley 1954: 130) appears to be the earliest example of *after* as a TMA marker; this construction becomes characteristic of representations of Irish speech during the eighteenth century. In Shadwell's usage and in most of the examples in the texts of Bliss (1979), *after* is used in a sentence which refers to a future state of affairs, typically marked with the modal verb *will*. In modern Irish English, however, TMA-marking *after* is a perfective marker and never takes a future sense (*I'm after missing the bus* 'I have missed the bus'; see section 4.3.3 below).

Though Bartley (1954: 130) tends to dismiss uses of *after* with future reference as mistakes by writers unfamiliar with genuine usage, Bliss (1979: 302–3) saw the frequency of these uses as suggesting an independent sense of *after* in early texts. Kelly (1989) has suggested that *after* may have had a regular status as a future marker, relying for her position not on the rather complicated analogy with Irish prepositions advanced by Bliss (1979), but on related uses of *after* signalling intention or imminence of action found in other English dialects. In Kallen (1990), it is suggested that the early Irish English use of *after* in sentences referring to future or non-actual states of affairs arises from the merger of inherent features of English *after* with universal principles of TMA systems under conditions of language contact and variability. The modern restriction of *after* to perfective uses is thus seen as a sort of decreolisation in which the variable range of significance for *after* is limited in accord with the demands of the English TMA system.

The Irish use of *do* as a verbal auxiliary apparently becomes perceived as distinctive at some time in the eighteenth century (see also section 4.3.3). Auxiliary uses of *do* are well documented in general English for this period (see Visser 1969–73) and the choice of using *do*, at least in Shakespearian drama, appears to have been conditioned by both linguistic and sociolinguistic factors (see Salmon 1965). The abundant use of auxiliary *do* in some representations of Irish speech suggests a caricature, as in the following passage from John Michelburne's 'Ireland preserved' (Bartley 1954: 111):

> By my fait, Dear joy, I do let de Trooparr ly wid my wife in de bad, he does ly at de one side and myself ly at de toder side, and my wife do lye in de middle side; for fen I do go out to work in de cold morning, to thrashe my Corne, he doth cover her, and keep my wife fery faarme, and she does leave to get up, and look after de House, and fen de

> Trooparr do get up, he does go and bring home de Seep and de Muck ['pig', Ir. *muc*], and de Shucking Pigg, and we do Eat togeder.

Lexical items coming into Irish English between the sixteenth and eighteenth centuries are mostly of Irish origin, though some terms have English or obscure origins. Some, such as *grey merchants* 'merchants going out in Irish dress' and *callodor*, evidently a Dublin name for a person in charge of the death cart in times of plague (cf. *call-o-door*), show only local or short-term use (see Irwin 1935: 213ff.). Many Irish terms could be listed from this period, including *bother* 'deafen' or 'bewilder with noise' (cf. Ir. *bodhar* 'deaf'), *cosher* denoting 'feasting' of a traditional type, and *kerne*, *galloglass* and *rapparee*, all terms connected with soldiering: see Bliss (1977a) and lexicographical references in section 4.3.3.

4.3.3   *English in modern Ireland*

Difficulty arises in tracing the transition from early modern to today's Irish English. Non-literary texts of the eighteenth century generally show the influence of standardised spelling and syntax similar to that of England, while realism is largely lost in conventional representations of Irish characters on stage. Despite some indications from eighteenth-century dictionaries and prescriptive works (e.g. Sheridan 1780, 1781; Walker 1802 [1791]), it is not until the development of more realistic literary portrayals and the beginning of systematic dialect study in the nineteenth century that a picture of spoken Irish English becomes available.

The dialectological record which is examined here points to complex relationships between Ulster English and the English of the rest of Ireland. Three commonly accepted categories of Ulster English will be referred to (see Adams 1964b, Harris 1984a for details): *Ulster Scots*, the most clearly related lexically and phonologically to Scots (found primarily in Antrim, north-east Down and part of Derry and Donegal); *South Ulster English*, the variety most similar to Irish English outside of Ulster (typical in south Armagh, south Monaghan, north Cavan, south Fermanagh and south Donegal); and *Mid-Ulster English*, generally seen to combine influences from the other two varieties (found in Antrim, including Belfast, south Tyrone, north Monaghan, north Fermanagh and part of south Donegal). For geographical discussion and maps, see Milroy (1981) and Harris (1984a, 1985a). These labels should not be taken to suggest predominance of one variety over another in any given area: local migration and language history militate against the establishment of zones of dialectal exclusivity on a wide scale (see Braidwood 1964). Moreover, the positing of well-defined dialect boundaries in Ulster does not imply either a total cleavage between northern and southern varieties or uniformity in the south. Although Ulster Scots shows the greatest divergence from other varieties of Irish English, South and Mid-Ulster English share many features with southern Irish English, and there is no evidence to support the suggestion (see Barry 1982: 110) that southern Irish English is more uniform than that of Ulster.

General characteristics of Irish English which demonstrate something of its historical development, either in a comparative or more local context, include the following: (1) the retention of historical /r/ in all positions; (2) the use of non-velar /l/ in all positions, counterbalanced in some locations by a tendency to use velarised [ɫ] noted by Wells (1982) and Harris (1985a); (3) retention of the historical /hw/–/w/ contrast, sometimes lost in Mid-Ulster English (see Harris 1984a); (4) traditional use of monophthongs /o(ː)/ and /e(ː)/ in words of the GOAT and FACE set; and (5) the use of epenthetic [ə] in clusters consisting of a liquid followed by a nasal in word-final position, as in ['fɪləm] *film*, ['harəm] *harm*, ['lɪŋkalən] *Lincoln*, etc. Feature (4) shows variation in so far as diphthongisation of the /oʊ/ and /eɪ/ type is found throughout Ireland today, while Milroy (1981: 77) demonstrates that in Belfast, at least, other diphthongs such as [e·ə] and [ɪ·ə] may also represent /e/. Feature (5) may be related to processes cited in section 4.3.1; it was also noted in the eighteenth century (Walker 1802 [1791]; see also Irwin 1935) and may be related to common metatheses such as ['mɑdrən] *modern*, ['sʌd̪ðərən] *southern*, ['pætrən] *pattern*, and so on. This feature is not unique to Ireland, though the lexical incidence of it may differ from that found elsewhere.

Significant vowel patterns in Irish English include the potential merger of words such as *meat*, *sea* and *decent* with *mate* and *say* in the FACE category using /eː/ rather than the /iː/ of *fleece*, *sleep*, *keep*, etc. A full discussion of the potential for a three-way distinction between *meat*, *meet* and *mate*, the theoretical implications of various merger possibilities, and the diachronic shift from historical [ɛː] in *meat* to [iː] is found in Harris (1985a). For data concerning the distribution of [ɛː] and [e] in *meat* words in rural Ireland, see Henry (1958: 110–11); for documentation in Dublin, note Bertz (1987).

Though Barry (1981c, 1982) suggests that southern Irish English differs from Ulster English in merging words of the PRICE and CHOICE sets with an unrounded diphthong, the actual dialect record does not support such a simple generalisation. While mergers have been reported in the south under unrounded vowels such as [ɛi] and [ʌi] (Nally 1971) and [ɑ + ɪ] or [ɑɪ], rounded diphthongs such as [ö̞ɪ] are also found, and the PRICE/CHOICE distinction may be preserved in various ways. The distribution of lexical items in either set, however, may differ within Ireland and from the distribution found elsewhere (see Henry 1958; Wells 1982; Bertz 1987). In conservative Ulster Scots, sensitive to the Scottish vowel-length rule often referred to as Aitken's Law (see Aitken 1981), Early Scots /i:/ gives rise to modern [ə̆i] in the so-called 'short' environments (e.g. *ripe*, *guide*, *mice*, *line*, *wild*), while [ɑ·ĕ] is favoured in 'long' environments as seen in *five*, *tire*, *trial*, *tie* and *tied* (Harris 1985a: 27–8). Lexical distribution and the effects of other sound changes, however, mean that these two diphthongs are not in simple complementary distribution; moreover, one may note Scottish-type lexical realisations as in the use of [i:] in *die* and [æ] in *blind*. Southern Ulster English, on the other hand, has a radically different system, basically using [əi] in *my*, etc. and [ɑi] in words of the *boy* type. For details, see Harris (1985a: 20ff.).

Independent Irish development of the 'FOOT–STRUT' split in general English (Wells 1982: 196–9) becomes evident in the eighteenth century and today illustrates the variation possible within a single area of Irish English phonology. Though there are still diverging views on the historical sequence of development in the FOOT–STRUT split (see Harris 1990 for a review), it may be roughly assumed that the basic pattern for this split involves five lexical categories, the first three of which stem from ME /o:/ while the others arise from ME /u/: (1) the *mood* group with modern /u:/; (2) *blood* lowering to /ʌ/; (3) *good* raised and shortened to /ʊ/; (4) the *cut* group also undergoing lowering to /ʌ/; and (5) *put* now realised with /ʊ/. Scottish developments have taken a different path, as Braidwood (1964: 57) points out, with the consequence that Early Scots /o:/ may now be realised with [ɪ] or [e:]. This pattern is found in conservative Ulster Scots, for which Harris (1985a: 20) notes *cool* and *foot* with [ï], contrasting with [ʌ] in words of the *cut* type.

Generally in Ulster English, but not in the south of Ireland, the potential distinction between *mood* and *good* words may be lost, in that both word sets use the high central vowel [ʉ]. The *mood* class in the south, I have noted, may include words taking [ʊ] in many other varieties (e.g., *book, hook, brook, cook, cooker, Tootsie, cookie*) and for at least some speakers may merge with undiphthongised /uː/ rather than /aʊ/ in *pouch* and possibly other words. In addition to the vowels associated with southern English or Scots, Irish English makes extensive use of a vowel intermediate between [ɔ] and [ʌ], described by Wells (1982: 422) as 'mid centralized back somewhat unrounded' and generally transcribed as [ɔ̈]. This vowel is usually, though not exclusively, found in the STRUT category, potentially including both words of the *blood* and *cut* type.

The Irish assignment of words to the STRUT group with [ʌ] contrasting with assignment to the FOOT group with [ʊ] as in England is noted by Walker (1802 [1791]: 16), who lists nine words (most with preceding labials) in which Irish English [ʌ] contrasts with usage in England: *bull, bush, push, pull, pulpit, cushion, pudding, foot*, and *put*. (See also Sheridan 1780.) In contemporary Irish English, most of Walker's list could be realised with [ʌ] or [ʊ] and possibly with [ɔ̈]. Henry (1958: 153–4), for example, demonstrates considerable variation in this area. In south-west Leitrim, *bush* and *pluck* appear with a slightly centralised version of low and advanced [u] in Henry's transcriptions [bʊʃ] and [plʊk], while *birds, turnips* and *double* appear with [ɔ̈], transcribed by Henry as [bɔ̈rdz], ['tɔ̈rnəps] and [dɔ̈bl]. In Westmeath, on the other hand, uncentralised low and advanced [u] appears in *turf* [tʊrf], *birds* [bʊrdz], etc., while *buck, thumb* and *wool* appear in the *mood* class with [u] and the vowel [ɔ̈] is not listed.

In Ulster, the /u/–/ʊ/ neutralisation and other factors yield a different, if related, configuration. For the Ulster Scots dialect of Braid, Co. Antrim, Henry (1958: 153–4) lists *cut, lugs, bushes* and *much* with [o], while *school, how, house, too, cow* and *good*, are all roughly united under [ʏ] or [ʉ]. In Belfast vernacular, Harris (1985a: 150–1) distinguishes three lexical classes: a BOOT class with categorical /ʉ/ (*boot, food, good*), a BUT class categorically taking /ɔ̈/ (*but, cud, blood*), and a PUT/FOOT group in which [ʉ] and [ɔ̈] may alternate according to sociolinguistic or other factors (*put, foot, full, look, pull, took, butcher, shook*). (See also Milroy & Milroy 1978: 25–7.)

The most significant consonantal variations in Irish English centre around the realisation of general English /t, d, θ, ð/ and palatalisation processes affecting in particular alveolar and velar consonants. The dental/alveolar group is discussed here in detail, with palatalisation treated primarily as it relates to this group.

A broad generalisation, often taken as indicative of the north–south

Jeffrey L. Kallen

dialect division in Ireland (Barry 1981c; Harris 1985a), sees [θ] and [ð] regularly only in Ulster, with southern varieties typically using the non-strident affricates [t̪θ] and [d̪ð] or alveolar and dental stops. A strict dialect separation, however, is not indicated: Henry (1958: 122–3) notes the variable use of [t̪θ] and [d̪ð] across his nine Ulster dialect points, while the fricatives [θ] and [ð] are also noted for some speakers in southern urban varieties (see Wells 1982; Hickey 1986).

Phonological oppositions may be maintained in the absence of [θ] and [ð] with a dental/alveolar distinction as in [t̪ʰɪn] *thin* vs [tʰɪn] *tin* (Wells 1982: 428–9). Yet fricatives may appear in the position of historical stops, particularly before /r/: Henry (1958: 124–5) notes [ðrɑ·ɪ] *dry*, [ˈprɛhɪz] *praties* 'potatoes', etc. in Ulster as well as southern [ˈwɒθər] *water*, [əðə ˈðrum] *of the drum* and [ˈlahəd ˈbɒhəmz] *latted bottoms*. (Dental realisations for /t/ before /r/ are also widely reported, though evidently declining at least among some younger speakers: see Milroy & Milroy 1978.) Glottal varieties of /t/ in Dublin include [ʔ] (Bertz 1987) and [h] as in [ˈdʒækəh] *jacket*, [(h)wɑh] *what?* and [ˈskærləh] *scarlet* 'embarrassed' in my observation.

The lenition of /t/ and, less commonly, /d/ to an alveolar fricative has been noted since the nineteenth century (Hume 1878) and is also found in Irish English speech in Newfoundland (Clarke 1986). The lenited segments are represented here by [t̞, d̞] (Wells 1982: 429); for further discussion and suggested transcriptions see Henry (1958: 123), Barry (1981c: 68), Conrick (1981: 73), Harris (1984a: 130), Hickey (1984: 235) and Bertz (1987: 45). Henry (1958: 123–7) shows the lenited segments to be well distributed geographically, although he sees them concentrated in south Leinster and the midlands: note [ˈgʲɛtəm] *get him* (Co. Cavan), [dɪd̞] *did* (Co. Mayo), [bleːᵊt, ˈbleːtən] *bleat, bleating* (Co. Clare), where Henry's [t̞] = [t̞] and [d̞] = [d̞]. While Barry (1981c) sees the absence of final lenited stops as a defining characteristic of Ulster English, Harris (1984a: 130) points out that despite the general lack of final [t̞] in Ulster, intervocalic position may yield an intraregional distinction in which Mid-Ulster English shows a voiced flap in *pity*, etc. while southern Ulster English uses the lenited [t̞] in this position.

Neutralisation of the *tin/thin* opposition may occur in several ways: (1) overlapping of realisations, as in [ta>tʃ] *thatch*, [wiˈdout̚] *without* vs [h] or [t̪θ] in *letters* and [t̞] or [t̪θ] in *butter* (Henry 1958: 123–7); (2) dentalisation before /r/ resulting in homophones such as [t̪riː] *tree, three* or [ˈbriːd̪ər] *breeder, breather* (Wells 1982: 431), although dentalisation is generally blocked before a morpheme boundary so that, for example, *matter* contrasts with *fatter* (Harris 1984a: 130); and (3) loss of dentalisation before alveolars such as /l, s/ (e.g. [feːts] *faiths, fates*) for speakers who would otherwise use [t] or [t̪θ] in words of the *thin* group (Wells 1982: 431).

Palatalisation processes also complicate the distribution of dental, alveolar and velar segments. Words of the *tune, Tuesday* type showing [tʲ] in many non-Irish varieties most often show [tʃ] in Irish English; Irwin (1935: 422) dates this development to the eighteenth century. The use of palatalised [k̟] and [g] rather than palatalised alveolars was early noted by Burke (1896: 698) in spellings such as 'opportkunity' and 'forkune' to characterise the speech of Meath, Kildare and Carlow; cf. similar data from Antrim (Henry 1958: 127–9) and Westmeath (Nally 1971). Palatalisation of velars (e.g. [kjɑrt] *cart*, [kʲap] *cap*) is also widely noted (described by Henry (1958: 115) as 'a Northern and Eastern feature fading to the West and South') and may be compared with an inverse use of alveolars as in [tlutʃ] *clutch*, ['tleˑᵊnənz] *cleanings* and [tlamp] *clamp* (Henry 1958: 129).

Salient features of Irish English syntax include (a) systems of clause conjunction and embedding, (b) the use of topicalisation and clefting, (c) a variety of prepositional and adverbial constructions, and (d) a distinctive set of TMA markers. These features are generally taken to demonstrate either affinities to other English dialects or the influence of an Irish-language 'substratum': the following discussion simply describes the most commonly cited elements, while section 4.4 addresses the substratum question. Material cited below under '(JK)' is taken from my fieldwork in Dublin.

Co-ordinate structures such as *He wouldn't give me a penny an' he rotten with money* (Burke 1896: 787) or *The size of er and she barking!* (JK) are widely reported in works on Irish English, while embedded clause types often noted are illustrated by *You would wonder what colour was the horse* (Shee 1882: 372), *I wonder was the horse well bred* (Hayden & Hartog 1909: 938), *What's the cause you didn't go?* (Henry 1957: 123), *They laughed at you in a way that you'd nearly turn against the Irish language* (Lunny 1981: 139), and *… to show them pictures and see is there any difference between the deaf children and the others* (JK).

Topicalisation and related phenomena have been examined in detail by Filppula (1986). Filppula points out that topicalisation in Irish English may fulfil a variety of discourse functions such as contrast, reassertion and specification (e.g. *Cold as ever it were*; *In splints it would come off*, where *splints* refers to an established topic; and *In some building he is working with the couple of weeks* 'for a couple of weeks', respectively) in addition to the emphatic function usually ascribed for English (as in *Aye, in the middle of the night they'd probably arrive*). By comparison with a British English corpus and with the use of intuitive judgements and geographical analyses, Filppula (1986) further establishes that the range of topicalisation types and frequency of topicalisation in discourse is greater in Irish English than in the British data, and that within Ireland the use of this device appears to increase in inverse proportion to the amount of time over which English has been spoken in a given locality.

Among the many prepositional and adverbial structures which have been commented on in dialect studies may be noted the following: (1) the use of *on* as a dative of disadvantage (*When the rent was doubled on me* (Shee 1882: 373); *I bought an ice cream and she rubbed it in my hair on me* (JK); and in various possessive uses (*There's no loss on him* 'he has nothing to complain about', *What's on you?* 'what's the matter with you?' (Henry 1957: 148)); (2) prepositional marking of possession (*The body is very small with a crow* 'A crow's body is very small' (Henry 1957: 133); *I scalded the hand o meself* 'my hand' (JK); *It was a custom by them to go out on Christmas Eve* 'their custom' (Lunny 1981: 140)); (3) other prepositional uses (*He's dead now with many a year* 'for many a year' (Lunny 1981: 139); *He's in his chest* 'bare chested', *She's in her health* 'healthy' (Henry 1957: 146)); and (4) the use of *in it* to denote general existence, as in *There are no horses in it* (van Hamel 1912: 286), *There's a good wind in it, today* (Ní Ghallchóir 1981: 157–8), and *Is there any jeans in it?* 'available' (JK).

Distinctions of tense and aspect in Irish English, referred to in their earlier stages in section 4.3.2, have been widely noted since the nineteenth century. The use of habitual markers to denote recurrent or generic states of affairs and the variety of means for marking a perfective TMA category have received particular attention and are discussed here.

Habitual or generic time categories may be grammatically marked in Irish English in three ways: (1) inflected *do*, (2) inflected *be*, and (3) inflected *do* plus non-finite *be*. Geographical distribution for these forms is unclear. Bliss (1984a), Guilfoyle (1983) and Harris (1984b) have associated inflected *be* forms with Ulster, while Dublin-based studies (Kallen 1986, 1989; Bertz 1987) show no such realisations. Yet inflected *do* has been reported throughout Ireland, while data from Co. Meath (Henry 1958: 133) and Co. Dublin (O'Neill 1947: 264) also reveal inflected *be*. Henry's (1957) Roscommon study and Todd's (1984) Ulster survey show all three realisation types.

Henry (1957), Harris (1984b) and Todd (1984) discuss the use of these three markers with slightly different semantic feature specifications for each one: in Kallen (1989) it is argued that these semantic shadings are best subsumed by a single 'generic/habitual (GH)' category, designating that a state of affairs 'holds true either as an inherent quality of a class of objects or due to the recurrence of particular actions, processes, etc.'. (Cf. generic *do* in Somerset English, noted by Ihalainen 1976.) Examples of generic/habitual *do* are given below. In all cases, *do* is not stressed and may be elided to [də] or a syllabic consonant. It is not to be confused with emphatic *do*.

Generic/habitual markers in Irish English
1 Inflected *do*
 He does come when he hears the noise (Henry 1957: 171)
 Me ma does tell me I'm livin on my nerves (Kallen 1989: 6)
2 Inflected *be*
 There bees no partition between the cows (Henry 1958: 133)
 Well there be's games in it and there be's basketball, darts and all (Harris 1984b: 306)
3 Inflected *do* plus *be*
 (a) With auxiliary *be*
 He diz be singin' (Todd 1984: 171)
 He does be weighing things out for me for when I'm on me own (Kallen 1989: 7)
 (b) Copular *be*
 That's how the master does be (Henry 1958: 133)
 Those pancakes do be gorgeous (Kallen 1986: 135)

The perfective TMA category in Irish English may be marked in a number of ways which differ from the general Modern English pattern using *have* plus *-en*.[2] Most analyses have concentrated on these alternative markers, obscuring the extent to which the general English *have* pattern is used in Ireland as well as the converse use of other patterns outside of Ireland: for comments see Hayden & Hartog (1909), Henry (1957), Harris (1983, 1984b), Milroy (1984) and Kallen (1989, 1990). Perfect marking with *after*, discussed in section 4.3.2, has attracted considerable attention as an Irish form: traditional accounts suggest that *after* perfects denote the recency of an event (van Hamel 1912: 276) or the conclusion of an action (Henry 1958: 64, 177). Harris (1984b: 308) uses the 'hot news' label of McCawley (1971) to encapsulate such notions. An Extended Present perfect form with a tensed stative verb such as *be* or *know* is taken by Harris (1984b: 308–9) to refer to a 'situation initiated in the past and persisting into the present', while an Accomplishment Perfect said to show a 'preoccupation with state' (Henry 1957: 177) and perfects with *be* plus 'mutative verbs such as *leave, change, die, go*' (Harris 1984b: 308) have also been cited.

It should be noted, however, that these four perfect-marking devices do not refer exclusively to any well-defined semantic category. In Kallen (1989: 10–11), for example, uses of *after* are shown across all of McCawley's categories of the perfect and are thus not limited to 'hot news'; conversely, other perfect markers are seen in 'hot news' contexts. In Kallen (1990), an attempt is made to match McCawley's categories with Irish English perfect markers: this attempt runs counter to the data, and it is suggested instead that the choice of perfect marker reflects a complex interaction of factors such as recency, transitivity, dynamism and lexical selection in addition to semantic considerations. Regardless, then, of the factors which influence the selection of general English *have* or any other device for perfect marking, the list below provides examples of the broadly perfective TMA markers of Irish English, using the category labels of Kallen (1989; see also Younge 1923–4 and Bliss 1979).

Perfect markers in Irish English

1   Perfects with *after*
     I am after writing a letter (Hayden & Hartog 1909: 933)
     Children can't believe they can take their coats off in this weather; they're after bein inside so many times (Kallen 1989: 11)

2   'Extended present' perfects
     He's working these years on it (Henry 1957: 172)
     We're living here seventeen years (Harris 1984b: 309)
     I know him for a long time (Kallen 1989: 15)

3   'Accomplishment' perfects
     She's nearly her course finished (Harris 1984b: 307)
     Have you your tea taken? (Henry 1957: 177)
     He has my heart broken (Taniguchi 1956: 59)

4   *Be* perfects
     I went back to school and all, but I'm not too long left (Harris 1984b: 308)
     Miriam is just gone asleep about two minutes ago (Kallen 1989: 19).

Interest in the Irish English lexicon is generally focused on the incorporation of words from Irish or on the historical retention and development of words of English or Scots origin. There is no Irish English dialect dictionary, and most of the work done in this area consists of word-lists either in bare form or with cross-references to the *EDD, OED* and Irish dictionaries.

Ulster vocabulary has inspired a number of compilations (e.g. Patterson 1860; Patterson 1880; Bigger 1923; Traynor 1953), although all such works demonstrate an overlap between the Ulster lexicon and that found in the rest of Ireland. Ulster terms with etymological connections to Scotland or the North of England include *whitrit* 'weasel, stoat', *ferntickles* 'freckles', *stroup* 'spout of a kettle', *elder* 'udder', *skelf* 'splinter (n., vb)', *lith* 'segment of an orange', while terms apparently restricted to Ulster include *champ* 'colcannon' (a traditional Irish food), *coggelty-curry* 'see-saw', *street* 'a farmyard', *diamond* 'town square' and *libbock* 'a small piece of anything' (see Patterson 1880; Traynor 1953; Henry 1958; Gregg 1972; Adams 1977; Robinson 1984).

Within Ulster, further divisions may be noted so that, for example, typically Scots grammatical constructions such as *dinnae, cannae, hinnae* and *maunae* are frequently noted for Ulster Scots, while Gregg (1972: 113) notes a dialect division between Ulster Scots use of *bag* vs general Ulster *elder* 'udder', and *cassey* or *close* 'farmyard' in place of general Ulster *street*. Traynor (1953) cites many words as belonging to Donegal only, although such a strict geographical restriction must be regarded cautiously: examples include *subs* 'footwear, especially old', *pook* 'the grain in wood; temper in a person', and *prashlach* 'odds and ends; rubbish, as small sticks and stones'.

The division between 'Irish' and 'English' components in the general Irish English lexicon is not always clear. A word like *grig, greg* 'tantalise, make jealous, annoy' has an English history (see the *OED*), yet shares a cognate Irish verb *griog*: in any given location, it may be difficult to assess whether the use of the word represents a retention from English, a carry-over from Irish, or a combination of the two factors. Word-internal code-switching is common as well, in that, for example, the Irish diminutive suffix *-ín* may attach to many English nouns (*maneen, girleen, houseen*, etc. are frequently noted), while Irish words may assume English nominal or verbal morphology (e.g. *cipíns* 'little sticks of wood' < Ir. *cipín* + E *s*; *ráiméising* 'speaking nonsense' < Ir. *ráiméis* 'nonsense' + E *-ing*). Lexical reanalysis showing interaction between Irish and English is exemplified in the most general meaning 'naughty' (in the sense of a child's behaviour) for *bold* in Irish English, evidently acquired from the translation of Ir. *dána*, which has both this behavioural sense and that of general English 'brazen, audacious', etc. In the following selection of lexical items, many may have only local distribution or may take different senses in different speech communities: appropriate patterns of distribution have not been charted systematically.

Material in the Irish English lexicon which stems from English or Scots sources is not necessarily unique to Ireland, but may be cited if (a) found in a different sense from that used elsewhere, (b) retained more generally than in England (either geographically or socially), or (c) retained in Ireland past a date when it is considered to have become 'obsolete' in England. Material of this kind includes the following, cited from Ua Broin (1944), Traynor (1953), Braidwood (1964), Bliss (1972b, 1984a) and my own observations: *cog* 'cheat in school, examinations', *chisler* 'child', *bowsey* 'disreputable drunkard; troublemaker', *cod* 'joke, hoax (n.); tease, playfully deceive (vb)', *mott* 'girlfriend, girl', *press* 'cupboard', *beholden to* in the sense 'depending on' (Ua Broin (1944: 164) *I'm not beholden to that* 'I have other resources to fall back on'), *power* 'a great many, a great deal', *airy* 'lively, fond of pleasure', *odious* ['oːdʒəs] (also *wodious*) 'exceedingly, exceedingly great' and *oxter* 'armpit'. The term *mitch* 'play truant' is widely reported; Ua Broin (1944: 147) also notes *jerring*, while I have informally noted *dossing* (general), *daubing* (Belfast), *scheming* (Galway, Donegal, Clare; see also Traynor 1953), and *go on the lang* (Cork). Probably the best-known coinings apparently native to Ireland are *hames*, as in *makes a hames of this* 'a ludicrously unsuccessful attempt to perform some action' (Bliss 1984a: 143; cf. also *a horse's collar* used in the same way) and *yoke* 'a thing' in general. Both terms are widely used, and Bliss (1984a) suggests derivations for both from terms related to the harnessing of animals.

The Irish-based material in Irish English shows multiple layers of historical derivation and geographical variation which may reflect local conditions of bilingualism and language shift. Terms such as *garran*, as noted above, belong to the earliest Irish English yet are reported relatively recently as well (Henry 1958). Others, such as *poitín* (a traditional illicit distilled spirit), *dillisk* (a type of seaweed) or *piseog* 'a traditional superstitious belief or practice', have been thoroughly integrated into the Irish English lexicon in the absence of any vernacular English-based lexical equivalent. While some such terms may be seen as borrowings, many others are more accurately described as retentions or *apports* in the sense of Allsopp (1980: 93ff.): *apports* typically accompany large-scale language contact and shift, and may exhibit what Allsopp terms 'slips, shifts, and innovations' which reflect 'intimate L_2 [second language] cultural survivals' not found in the regular borrowing processes of more settled languages.

The extent of Irish lexical retention at various times is well documented in local and more general studies. Lists published in *Irisleabhar Na Gaedhilge* ('Irish words' 1900–1), *An Sguab* ('Comórtas' 1922–3, 1923–5), and by Lysaght (1915) documented hundreds of Irish words commonly used in areas which had become English-speaking many years previously. Ó hAnnracháin (1964) provides a lexicon of over 500 Irish words from a part of Co. Kerry in which the Irish language had become essentially lost over the preceding 100 years. This list is particularly significant in that it contains many entries not found or no longer used in vernacular Gaeltacht Irish or in the standard literary language. Nally (1971) also refers to the existence of over 250 Irish words in the local district of a part of Co. Westmeath which had become Anglicised between 1750 and 1800.

Any selection from such a large potential Irish sublexicon is necessarily arbitrary. Many terms have no standardised spelling and appear in word-lists either in an Anglicised form (often highly idiosyncratic) or in Irish orthography. While some words have near-universal distribution, others are more restricted to particular localities or domains such as agriculture, animal life, etc. Words such as *blather* 'nonsense (n.); talk nonsense (vb)', *reek* 'mountain' and *gob* 'mouth' show the kind of multiple or obscure etymology illustrated above for *grig*.

With these reservations in mind, a selected list of Irish words is included below, cited from sources noted thus far, including also Henry (1958). Irish orthography is used unless otherwise noted, for example where common usage dictates English or joint entries. Thus note: *neanntóg* 'nettle', *castarbhán* 'dandelion', *bairneach* 'limpet'; *blathach* 'buttermilk', *tormas* 'carping at food' (*She had a tormas against eggs*, Ó hAnnracháin 1964: 89), *crubeen* (E) 'pig's foot'; *ciotóg* 'left-handed person, left hand', *amadán* 'fool', *stríopach* 'whore', *duine le Dia* 'innocent fool' (lit. 'person of God'), *flaithiúlach* 'generous, good-hearted', *balbh* 'indistinct or stammering in speech', *straoill/streel* (E) 'slovenly girl (n.); trail about (vb)', *gombeen* (E) 'a profiteer'; *breillis breallis* 'nonsense', *cabchaint* 'proud, arrogant talk', *canran* 'complain, grumble', *plámás* 'smooth talk, flattery', *cogar* 'whisper'; *glaum* 'snatch, grab', *bacaidí/*

bockedy (E) 'unstable, unsteady', *grá* 'love', *meas* 'respect', *púca* 'spirit, apparition', *cáibín* 'an old hat'. Other terms have more pragmatic significance than lexical content: *acushla* (E) 'my dear', *a mhic* 'son' (both terms of address); *mar dheadh/moryah* (E) literally 'as it were', an ironic tag ending; *sláinte* literally 'health', a toast for drinks; and so on.

4.3.4   Sociolinguistic perspectives in Irish English

Much of the political history of Ireland is reflected in the ideological status attached to the English and Irish languages. The foundation of organisations such as the Gaelic Society in 1807 and the subsequent development of a national Irish-language movement (see Ó Murchú 1985) coincided with political movements for Irish independence to the extent that the language policy of the independent government established after the partition of Ireland in 1921–2 was firmly orientated towards the support of the Irish language. Though complicated by political and economic considerations (see Commins 1988; Tovey 1988), policy in the Republic of Ireland is reflected in the comments of a 1965 White Paper (*Athbheochan* 1965):

> The Irish language is an integral part of our culture... Down the centuries it has moulded and given expression to the thoughts and feelings of the Irish people. English, of course, has also contributed to our national heritage but the English we speak still bears the imprint of the attitudes of mind and modes of expression which prevailed when Irish was the language of general use. It is through Irish as a living language that we and those who come after us can most surely retain a lively sense and understanding of the unique and essential elements of the Irish character.

In a similar vein, Henry (1974: 32–3) contrasts the two languages as follows:

> The only possibility for a national future as a distinct or distinctive people that Ireland can have lies in conserving, strengthening, renewing the Irish Gaelic tradition... The monoglot English-speaking Irishman is dominated by the manner of England either immediately or ultimately... In other words, an Irishman speaking English is not in the same category as an Englishman. The language has only been rented out to him.

The view of Irish English as not only alien but in some sense less valued than 'standard' English, referred to by Croghan (1986) as 'brogue-speak', comes through in various treatments. Burke (1896: 702), for example, explains the separate development of the Irish English lexicon as 'partly owing to our imperfect grasp of English', while the comments of Clery (1921: 552) could hardly be more blunt: 'we certainly have not learned how to speak English, for we have not acquired its sounds... Like the Chinese with their "pidgin" English, we have merely learnt how to make ourselves understood by a system of mis-pronounced English words, incapable of literary development.'

Counterbalancing the deprecation of Irish English are both the historical view that the English-speaking peasantry of Ireland possessed an English 'superior' to that of their English counterparts (see Dinely quoted above, Bush 1769: 34–6, and Edgeworth 1848 [1801]: 150) and a belief in the greater expressive power of Irish English. Writers such as J. M. Synge, Lady Gregory, W. B. Yeats and others in the 'Irish literary revival' of the late nineteenth and early twentieth centuries made conscious use of language based on that of rural speakers from districts only then undergoing Anglicisation. Sean O'Casey and James Joyce among others made use of Dublin vernacular and more general Irish English, while Edgeworth (1848 [1801]), Shee (1882) and Stockley (1927) registered complaints against both the unrealistic representation of Irish English in satirical or stereotyped portrayals and the rejection by others of Irish English as a valid medium of expression. The estimation of Dublin vernacular by Krause (1960: 234–5) in discussing the works of O'Casey is illustrative:

> Most Irishmen, but particularly the proud and garrulous people of the Dublin slums, have an instinctive love of word-play... Their characteristically emphatic speech is coloured with archaisms, malapropisms, puns, invectives, polysyllables, circumlocutions, alliterations, repetitions, assonances, and images. Such a word-hoard of colloquial rhetoric suggests that there may be a relationship between the spoken language of Elizabethan London and the spoken language of modern Dubliners.

This debate between those who have found Irish English vernaculars to be both linguistically and culturally expressive and those with other views, either through loyalty to Irish or by the sense of 'standard' English lying somewhere outside of Ireland, has rarely surfaced overtly. It remains, however, an important part of the overall sociology of language in Ireland: see Ó Riagáin (1988b) and Kallen (1988) for further discussion.

In Northern Ireland, macro-level sociolinguistics has taken a distinctive turn. Despite the effects of English-speaking plantations, Irish continued to be spoken as a vernacular in much of Ulster in the nineteenth century, and has continued in some parts of Northern Ireland to recent times (see Adams 1964a; Ó Dochartaigh 1987). During the eighteenth and early nineteenth centuries, Protestant religious activity in Ulster included Bible translation and publication, the establishment of schools and public preaching aimed at the Irish-speaking Catholic population. This activity often worked together with an antiquarian, cultural and nationalist interest in Irish which spanned religious divisions: for details, see O Casaide (1930), Ó Snodaigh (1973), and a critical analysis by the British and Irish Communist Organisation (1973).

In later years, however, with the growth of Irish nineteenth-century political nationalism, the Irish language in Ulster ceased to play a unifying function in so far as it became associated with the drive for Irish independence. Pritchard (1990: 30) documents the popularity of Irish as a secondary-school subject in Northern Ireland, noting an interest in Irish that has been 'growing in the Nationalist community from the 1960s onwards' (see also Hamill 1986), yet it would be an over-simplification to suggest that the use of Irish in Northern Ireland today is limited to the 'nationalist' population. Ó Glaisne (1981: 870), for example, cites a loyalist assertion that 'Ulster Protestants have as much claim, if not more in some cases, to the Gaelic culture as the Roman Catholic population', while Pritchard (1990: 30–1) discusses Irish-language organisations in the North which cite the historical common usage of Irish in trying to 'nail the myth that Irish is the property only of the Nationalists and Catholic community'.

In addition to the issue of relations between Irish and English, Ulster macro-level sociolinguistics is distinguished by a unique Ulster Scots literary and folk tradition: see Adams (1958, 1977) for discussion and Adams (1989) for an extensive bibliography. Thus the issue of language loyalty in Northern Ireland (cross-cut by divisions of political, ethnic and personal loyalty and status), while not yet investigated in detail, can be expected to differ fundamentally from that in the Republic.

Perhaps not coincidentally, it is in Northern Ireland that the study of socially conditioned language variation has taken hold. The works of Milroy (1976), Milroy & Milroy (1978) and others (see Milroy 1986 for a synopsis) have investigated phonology in Belfast vernacular English in detail, while related work such as that of Milroy (1980), Milroy & Harris (1980), Pitts (1985, 1986) and Milroy & Milroy (1985) has examined both the phonology of surrounding areas and a host of theoretical issues

Table 4.3 /a/ *variation in a Belfast speaker* (*Milroy 1986*)

Words	ɛ	æ	a	ä	ɑ	ɔ
bag	+					
back		+				
cap				+		
castle				+		
dabble				+		
map					+	
passage					+	
cab						+
grass						+
bad						+
man						+
passing						+

concerning the relationship between variation and historical change, fieldwork methodology in sociolinguistics and models of socially motivated variation and change.

Of the many variables examined in the Belfast studies, variation within the lexical set with /a/ may illustrate the dynamic involved. Within this set, two contrary tendencies may be noted: raising towards /ɛ/, particularly before velar consonants, and backing or backraising towards /ɔ/ in other environments (see Milroy & Milroy 1978: 27–9). The set of realisations for a working-class male Belfast speaker reading a word-list is shown by Milroy (1986: 40), seen in table 4.3, where a '+' represents use of a value. Milroy (1986: 40–1) contrasts this broad range of realisations with those of two middle-class speakers, one of whom shows only two words for which [ɑ] is not the realisation, while the other uses [a] in all cases.

Faced with such complex variation, the Belfast studies have moved away from an attempt to rely on a single linguistic dimension (such as vowel height or backness) correlating directly with a speaker variable such as socio-economic class, towards the analysis of factors which lead speakers to 'move away from the most highly localised usage, containing as it often does alternations, overlaps and near-mergers that normalised varieties avoid' (Milroy 1986: 44). The movement towards 'normalised' varieties in Belfast is not necessarily in the direction of an institutional 'prestige' value. In the Clonard district of West Belfast, for example, younger females use backing of /a/ more frequently than their male counterparts and far more frequently than their female counterparts in the East Belfast working-class district of Ballymacarrett. Style-shifting away from backing in formal speech and higher use of backing among male speakers in Ballymacarrett, however, suggests that backing is a low-prestige variation in this location: nevertheless, it is this value which Clonard females are adopting (see Milroy & Milroy 1978: 28–9).

Sociolinguistic research on Ulster syntax has examined syntactic variables which may be widespread outside Ulster, but which have not featured in traditional examinations of Irish English. Finlay & McTear (1986: 176) list eleven syntactic variables in a study of Belfast schoolchildren, including (1) the use of vernacular past tenses (e.g. *I seen*), (2) demonstratives as in *I love them sweets*, (3) negative concord (e.g. *I didn't feel nothin*), (4) singular concord (e.g. *Me and Denise was playin*), (5) 'Ins-suffix' (e.g. *themins/yuzins*), (6) *for-to* complements (e.g. *I went for to see him*), and (7) *whenever* used to denote a single definite event (e.g. *Whenever he came back in* 'when he came...'). Finlay & McTear's set of variables is geographically mixed. Features such as points (1)–(4) and (6) above occur readily throughout Ireland. Others, such as (7), are less widespread (though note *I was kind of really surprised whenever I got the first one* (JK)), and some may not occur in the south of Ireland. Finlay & McTear show a strong relationship between social class and the use of vernacular variants, with the only substantial middle-class use of vernacular forms occurring with *whenever* and negative concord among female speakers. The *for-to* structure was found only among working-class male speakers, while variables such as demonstratives appear with a roughly even distribution between the sexes in this social class.

Social divisions between Catholic and Protestant speakers have raised the question of ethnolinguistic differences in Ulster. While Milroy (1981: 44) argues that 'there is as yet no persuasive evidence to show that the two ethnic groups in Belfast (and Ulster) can be clearly identified by differences in accent', and that 'the differences that do exist are mainly regional', Todd (1984) has attempted to muster such evidence on the basis of a rural sample. (See also Todd 1989a.) Millar (1987) has vigorously rejected Todd's hypothesis on historical, methodological and empirical grounds, demonstrating considerable interpenetration of features between the two putative subdialects. O'Neill's (1987) research in Armagh similarly shows only quantitative variation, rather than categorical difference, in the frequency of vernacular phonological realisations across the two communities. Table 4.4 compares the use of

Table 4.4 *Realisation of* /k, g/ *before* /ar/ *in Armagh* (*O'Neill 1987*)

	Formal speech (%)			Informal speech (%)		
	Velar stop	Palatal stop	Glide insertion	Velar stop	Palatal stop	Glide insertion
Catholic						
Males	38	52	10	10	40	50
Females	80	20	0	15	55	30
Protestant						
Males	79	20	1	13	54	33
Females	90	10	0	43	40	17

three phonetic values in the realisation of /k, g/ before /ar/ in words such as *car* and *care*. These realisations (velar [k, g], palatal stop [k̟ g̟], and velar plus glide [kʲ, gʲ]) demonstrate the importance of style shift and sex-linked variation no less than any other factors (data based on O'Neill 1987: 23–5; see also Pitts 1985, Milroy 1980, and for related issues Milroy 1987).

4.4 Related studies in Irish English

The theoretical significance of Irish English as a contact vernacular, displaying both generations of language contact and isolation from historical sources in England, was perhaps first noted by van Hamel (1912). Interest in this topic was also expressed by Antoine Meillet (see Vendryes 1937) and later linguists such as Sommerfelt (1958), Hill (1962) and Breatnach (1967–8). Arguments concerning the origins of Irish English features such as the phonology of the dental/alveolar group of consonants, perfective forms in syntax, and various aspects of the lexicon have tended to be framed in either *substratumist* or *retentionist* terms. Substratumist explanations rely largely on the notions of 'transfer' or 'interference' from Irish to English (see e.g. Henry 1960–1, 1977; Bliss 1972a, 1977b; Hickey 1982), while a retentionist position seeks support from the history or dialectal distribution of English itself (as in Burke 1896; Harris 1983; Kallen 1986; Lass 1987, 1990; Kelly 1989).

Substratumist arguments may be readily illustrated with examples from syntax. The perfect with *after*, discussed in section 4.3, is often attributed to the influence of a comparable structure in Irish. Thus, for example, Harris (1984b: 319) cites the parallel between Irish and Irish English as follows (see also Lunny 1981: 137ff.):

> *Irish*: Tá   sí   tréis   an   bád   a dhíol.
>   be + non-past   she   after   the   boat   selling
> *Irish English*: She is after selling the boat.

Similarly, Harris (1984b: 319) notes the parallel usage in the Accomplishment Perfect and Irish TMA-marking, citing

> *Irish*: Tá   an   bád   díolta   aici.
>   be + non-past   the   boat   sold   at-her

The Irish English generic/habitual use of *do* is also commonly compared to Irish, which marks a distinction between punctual and non-punctual categories, as in examples from Todd (1984: 171):

> *Tá mé tuirseach* (BE I tired)
> *Bíonn mé tuirseach* (BE + regularity I tired)

Hickey (1982: 40) also notes the Irish English dative of disadvantage in comparison with Irish, citing

> *Irish*: Chuaigh   an   t-anraidh   thar   fiuchadh   orm.
>   went   the   soup   over   boiling   on-me
> *Irish English*: The soup boiled over on me.

Yet traditional substratumist claims, based largely on simple comparisons between isolated sentences of Irish and Irish English, often meet with compelling counter-evidence. Harris (1984b), in fact, while noting the Irish parallels with Irish English, also examines historical British English syntax and concludes (p. 320) that, except for the *after* perfect, forms such as the Accomplishment and *be* perfects 'far from being...innovations with an exclusive background in substratum interference, are actually retentions of older English patterns' (see also Harris 1983). Possible English sources for perfects with *after* have been noted in section 4.3.2; the rarity of the comparable Irish construction in historical and contemporary language corpora has been pointed out by Greene (1979) and is used by Kelly (1989) as part of the argument for an English source. Comparisons between the Irish and general English TMA-marking systems establish an asymmetry with regard to generic/habitual states of affairs; they do not, however, account for *do* as the Irish English lexical marker of the generic/habitual category. Here the nature of periphrastic *do* in sixteenth- and seventeenth-century English may be invoked as a crucial factor: see Kallen (1986) for details. Concerning the dative of disadvantage, Lass (1986) has argued against Hickey's interpretation, noting the availability of this construction in American English as well as parallel constructions in German and Latin.

A more recent trend in analysis puts Irish English in a global perspective, either by comparing developments in Ireland with those in other speech communities or by examining the role of linguistic universals in developing Irish English. Clarke (1986), for example, examines the phonology of Irish English-influenced speakers in Newfoundland, while J. Williams (1986) and Rickford (1986) have drawn connections between the external history of Irish settlement in the Caribbean and shared linguistic features of Irish and Caribbean English. Harris (1986) concentrates on possible links between Irish English habitual markers and those found in Atlantic creoles and Caribbean English as well as in American black English vernacular. In later papers, Harris (1987, 1990) concentrates on phonological reconstruction and historical development, again using a data base which includes Ireland alongside Caribbean and other Englishes.

In perhaps the most far-reaching undertaking of this kind, Montgomery (1989) traces possible connections between Appalachian English and the dialects of Scotland, England and Ireland (especially Ulster). Montgomery examines variables such as 'positive *anymore*' (e.g. *Wool is so expensive anymore* 'nowadays' (JK); see also Milroy 1981: 4), the use of auxiliary *do* and inflected *be*, single concord (see section 4.3.4), the use of relative pronouns (e.g., *Who is this was telling me...*) and characteristics of auxiliaries and modal verbs. In examining the data, Montgomery (pp. 235–40) proposes a set of linguistic and external criteria for testing the possibility of historical connection between geographically separated language varieties. This work is thus significant not only for placing the debate about the origins of Irish English within a wider framework, but for examining the overall history of syntactic variation in English.

The possibility that features of Irish English arise from neither substratum nor retentionist influences, but from a third source of language universals made manifest in the contact situation has been explored particularly by Filppula (1990); related suggestions concerning *after* (Kallen 1990) have already been mentioned (see also Kallen 1981). Filppula (1990) presents a systematic account of these three sources of derivation for Irish English topicalisation, making use of both typological and psycholinguistic universals in his analysis. Ultimately, for Filppula, no source can be completely ruled out and it is suggested (p. 52) that 'a combination of two or more factors ... is indeed the most likely alternative'.

Also of more general application, the work of Milroy (1980) uses Irish English data to enrich sociolinguistic theory and methodology in its own right. In particular Milroy demonstrates the value of *social network* as a conceptual tool in sociolinguistic research, demonstrating its clearer articulation, at least in some cases, with patterns of linguistic variation than that possessed by measures such as socio-economic class. Harris (1985a) uses Ulster data to expand theories of lexically governed phonological change and to query some well-known concepts of the phonetics of phonological merger. Problems of sociolinguistic field-work have been discussed in considering the effect of a non-local interviewer on the use of vernacular speech in a rural Co. Derry town (Douglas-Cowie 1978) and in assessing the sociolinguistic and grammatical distribution of perfective *after* in Dublin (Kallen 1991).

Issues in cross-dialectal language comparison have been discussed by Milroy (1984) in the light of evident conflict between Irish and other English varieties (see also Harris 1984a, 1985b). Focusing on grammatically based misunderstandings occurring in discourse, Milroy (1984) demonstrates that superficial similarities between syntactic constructions may mask deep-seated differences at the level of grammar. Filppula (1991) illustrates a similar point in considering the Irish English use of *and* as mentioned in section 4.3.3. Although this Irish English pattern resembles some marginal constructions in British English, Filppula's grammatical and quantitative approach suggests that the Irish and British systems are fundamentally different, with the Irish English use of 'subordinating *and*' representing an independent development.

Studies of the linguistic aspects of Anglo-Irish literature are rare, although van Hamel (1912), Taniguchi (1956), and Goeke & Kornelius (1976) all use literary samples for their analyses. Sullivan (1980) examines the changes in the literary representation of Irish English from the sixteenth to the nineteenth centuries, critically analysing these representations and their reflection of changes in Irish English during periods of intensive language contact. More general reviews of language and literature are found in Garvin (1977), Kiely (1977) and Todd (1989b), though none of these treatments benefits from the linguistically motivated research of recent years. Bliss (1972b) offers a glossary of Irish English in the work of J. M. Synge, while Wall (1986) examines James

Joyce's work (see also Kallen 1987). Reminiscent of the observations of Milroy (1984) and others, Wall (1990) discusses the apparent lexical similarities between Irish and other English varieties, revealing profound dissimilarities of meaning or connotation which editors and translators unfamiliar with Irish English often miss.

There is as yet no reference grammar of Irish English varieties, no phonological atlas or even a published set of detailed phonetic descriptions, and no dialect lexicon: in short, the working tools of linguistic description are still being developed. Note that many more fragmentary accounts have also been published in addition to the works discussed thus far, and that unpublished theses and other material (here referred to sparingly) also provide valuable information. Apart from more general English or Irish bibliographies, one may note as an aid to further enquiry the major bibliography of Aldus (1976), as well as the Ulster-based compilation of Corrigan (1990). Dolan & Ó Muirithe (1979) and Ó Muirithe (1977a) consolidate most of the material on the Forth and Bargy dialect, while Dolan's introductions to the recent editions of Joyce (1910) provide a historical account of the study of Irish English. The work of the Tape-Recorded Survey of Hiberno-English is surveyed in Barry (1981a, 1981b) and Tilling (1985), while further historical and bibliographical material is also found in Adams (1964b), Quin (1977) and Kallen (1985).

FURTHER READING

There is no published comprehensive overview of Irish English. Though having aims which differ from those of modern linguistic study, the works of Patterson (1860), Hume (1878), Burke (1896), Hayden & Hartog (1909), Joyce (1910), van Hamel (1912) and Hogan (1927), in particular, are still useful for a general orientation and for primary linguistic material. Henry's 1958 'linguistic survey' yields a great deal of raw data pertaining to syntax, phonology and lexicon, and is one of the few sources to discuss prosody systematically.

General treatments of Irish English, then, are mostly to be found in volumes of collected papers. The earliest of these collections, Adams (1964c), arises from the creation in 1960 of the Ulster Dialect Archive in the Ulster Folk Museum. An anthology of Adams' work on Ulster dialectology, together with a full bibliography, was published after his death in 1982 (Adams 1986). The 1974 Thomas Davis radio lectures on 'The English language in Ireland' have been published under the editorship of Ó Muirithe (1977b). Papers arising from the Tape-Recorded Survey of Hiberno-English Speech are assembled by Barry (1981a), while Ó Baoill (1985) presents papers from a 1981 conference on Irish English, together with two new introductory chapters. The work edited by

Harris, Little & Singleton (1986), based on the 1985 First Symposium on Hiberno-English, is the largest collection of papers on the subject published thus far. Eleven papers on Irish English are also contained in a 1990 edition of the *Irish University Review* (vol. 20, no. 1) dedicated to the memory of Alan Bliss.

Important monographs cover different aspects of Irish English. The most comprehensive survey of the medieval language is found in the unpublished thesis of Irwin (1935). Irwin's examination extends to the early nineteenth century, thus complementing in part the analysis by Bliss (1979) of seventeenth- and eighteenth-century literary texts. Straightforward dialect studies are relatively rare; note, however, the extensive Donegal glossary of Traynor (1953), Henry's (1957) study from Roscommon and Milroy's (1981) review of Belfast English, which focuses on phonology and phonological variation. Milroy (1980) gives a major treatment of Belfast vernacular and related sociolinguistic issues, while Harris (1985a) examines Ulster English phonology within a historical and sociolinguistic context. The substratumist hypothesis is put to a rigorous empirical test in Filppula's (1986) analysis of topicalisation.

NOTES

1 In historical quotations I have preserved the original spellings except for modernising the use of ⟨u⟩ and ⟨v⟩.
2 My use of the terms 'perfect' and 'perfective' implies no theoretical distinction between the two: 'perfect' is used as a noun, 'perfective' as a modifier.

5 THE DIALECTS OF ENGLAND SINCE 1776

Ossi Ihalainen

5.1 Some early observations

Our knowledge of the dialects of England from about 1500 till the first systematic description towards the end of the nineteenth century comes from a variety of sources: occasional regional spellings that continued into written documents, comments (usually derogatory) by the orthoepists, grammarians and lexicographers, glossaries of 'provincial words', occasional references to local speech in travel literature, fictional texts written to illustrate regional speech, and the use of dialect in literary works. Dialect in fiction is particularly interesting because it places regional speech in a social context. For instance, from Fielding's *Tom Jones* we gather that in the eighteenth century there were members of the landed gentry in the south-west who voiced their initial fricatives, used *un* for *him*, *thee* for *thou* and dropped the second person singular subject in questions, as in *Dost fancy I don't know it as well as thee*; they had the third person singular present-tense marker *-th* with auxiliaries, but *-s* with main verbs. What we do not find is the earlier common southern and south-western use of *ich* for 'I', and we are left in the dark as to whether this form had become obsolete in the type of language described, was not used by the type of people the writer had in mind, or was simply not chosen by the writer to give local colouring. Generally speaking, the picture that emerges from the early evidence is patchy, difficult to interpret and open to conjecture.

Although some dialectologists have been rather pessimistic about defining dialect areas with any precision, recent research carried out within the framework of perceptual dialectology[1] has shown that people are aware of dialectal differences in their mother tongue and have a general idea of what the main dialect areas are.[2] People are often even able to illustrate the main varieties by quoting shibboleths like the Cockney *lidy* 'lady', the Geordie *doon* 'down' or the 'Zummerset' *zider* 'cider'. One of the first English writers to exploit this awareness was Chaucer, whose clerks in *The Reeve's Tale* use such northern features as *I is* 'I am', *sal* 'shall' and an unrounded reflex of the Old English long *a*, as in *twa* 'two'.[3] We also discover that from very early times onwards regional speech carried a certain social evaluation: at least by the sixteenth century, speaking certain types of regional English was a definite handicap. Thus, Puttenham (1589: 121) points out that those who want to speak good English should in particular avoid imitating the English spoken by 'Northern-men beyond the riuer Trent'. Besides showing a lot about the social evaluation of northern English, this is a remarkably accurate localisation.[4]

One of the most interesting eighteenth-century occasional observers on regional speech is Defoe. In his *Tour thro' the whole Island of Great Britain* (1724–6) he specifically comments on Somerset and Northumbrian English. Somerset English is found particularly puzzling:

> It cannot pass my Observation here, that when we are come this Length from London, the Dialect of the English Tongue, or the Country way of Expressing themselves is not easily Understood … [I]t is so in many Parts of England besides, but in none in so gross a Degree as in this Part; This way of Boorish Country Speech, as in Ireland, it is call'd the Brogue upon the Tongue; so here 'tis call'd Jouring … It is not possible to Explain this fully by writing, because the Difference is not so much in the Orthography of Words, as in the Tone, and Diction; their abridging the Speech, *cham* for *I am*; *chil* for *I will*, *don*, for *put on*, and *Doff*, for *put off*; and the like. (p. 219)

He also went to visit a school in Martock, Somerset, where he listened to 'one of the lowest Scholars … reading his Lesson to the Usher':

> [H]is Lesson was in the Cant. [Song of Solomon] 5.3. of which the Words are these, 'I have put off my Coat, how shall I put it on, I have wash'd my Feet, how shall I Defile them?'
> The Boy read thus, with his Eyes, as I say full on the Text. 'Chav a Doffed my Cooat, how shall I Don't, Chav a wash'd my Veet, how shall I Moil'em?' (p. 219)

Defoe is also the first writer to comment on the Northumbrian 'burr':

> I must not quit Northumberland without taking notice, that the Natives of this Country, of the antient original Race or Families, are distinguished by a Shibboleth upon their Tongues namely, a difficulty in pronouncing the Letter R, which they cannot deliver from their

> Tongues without a hollow Jarring in the Throat, by which they are plainly known, as a Foreigner is, in pronouncing the Th: This they call the Northumbrian R, and the Natives value themselves upon that Imperfection, because, forsooth, it shews the Antiquity of their Blood.[5]
>
> (p. 662)

Defoe notes here an aspect of dialect that modern sociolinguistic studies have come across repeatedly: because they are seen as an integral part of the values and lifestyle cherished by a specific group, non-standard features may have covert prestige, which explains their resistance to change.

In addition to casual observations, there are also surprisingly early systematic treatments of English dialects. One of the earliest listings of dialect areas was made by Alexander Gil (1564/5–1635), High Master of St Paul's School. Although his prejudices against dialectal speech appear to have been less strong than those of his colleagues in the following century, his interest in dialectal and vulgar speech probably stemmed less from his love of philology than it did from his desire to eradicate provincialisms from the language of his young scholars. Gil lists the following six dialects, with the caveat that he 'does not know all the idioms of these': the general, the northern, the southern, the eastern, the western and the poetic (1619: 102). Gil does not explain the geographical boundaries of these, which suggests that people already had some kind of general idea of where these varieties could be heard. However, he does say that his own home county, Lincolnshire, is part of the north. This squares with Puttenham (1589), who appears to regard northern Lincolnshire as part of the north.

Gil goes on to discuss the main characteristics of each of these dialects. He says that in northern English *both* is *beath*, and attests thus the northern failure to round the original long *a*. Other northern characteristics are *hez* 'hath', *sal* 'shall' and *sen* for 'self', all features that were still recorded by the *SED* in mid-twentieth-century northern English. The *SED* shows that *sal* or its contracted form *'s* (also mentioned by Gil) was still common in parts of Yorkshire in the 1950s among the elderly rural working-class speakers (*LAE* M47). Gil also singles out contractions like *I'l* instead of *I will* as characteristically northern forms. This suggests that these forms originated in the north. The northern origin of these forms would explain the wide use of contractions in northern English even today. These include the main verb *have*, as in *He's a car*, and such negative forms as *He'll not do it* (rather than *He won't do it*). Of particular interest are Gil's comments on diphthongisation in northern English. These suggest that diph-thongisation of earlier long vowels was more advanced in the north than in the south (Wakelin 1988b: 133).

Gil's southern English shows voicing of initial fricatives and the use of proclitic *'ch* as in *chil* 'I will' and *cham* 'I am'. Contractions like these contrast sharply with the forms in the north, where the verb rather than the pronoun contracts. Gil's western dialect shares with southern English the voicing of initial fricatives, but it has its distinctive vocabulary (*nim, nem* 'take', *vang* 'take, accept') and morphology (e.g. *i-do* 'done'). Although Gil's case for the south–west distinction is not particularly convincing, and he fails to point out the obvious fact that *'ch* was a common western characteristic, it is nevertheless significant that the west is seen as distinct from the southern region.

One of the characteristics of Gil's eastern variety is the merger of ME *a*: (*name*) and *ai* (*pay*) as in modern standard English. On the basis of this, Kökeritz (1938/9) concludes that Gil probably had in mind Essex English, where these sounds merge, whereas they are kept separate in Suffolk and Norfolk. Equally important is his observation that in the eastern dialect *fire* has a long monophthong *i*: rather than a diphthong which probably represents [əɪ]. He thus spots one of the developments of OE *y*. The *SED* material for *lice* (IV.8.1) and *mice* (IV.5.1) shows that the present-day /i:/-area is generally confined to East Anglia and the south-east of England. Another historically interesting point is that, in addition to the south and west, the east, too, has voiced initial fricatives. Voicing of initial fricatives was later to recede to the south-west, and Gil's observation helps us in determining the chronology of this change: for instance, the 1640 edition of Jonson's *English Grammar* specifically states that the letter Z 'never [occurs] in the beginning [of words], save with rustick people, that have, *zed, zay, zit, Zo, zome*'.

5.2 Early glossaries and collections of dialect words

Important early evidence for reconstructing dialect areas comes from dialect dictionaries. These started appearing in the seventeenth century. The first real dialect dictionary was compiled by John Ray in 1674 and was entitled *A Collection of English Words Not Generally Used*. John Ray was a member of the Royal Society, a botanist and zoologist, who became known for his systems of classification. In fact, one gets the impression that he became interested in dialects partly because of the regional variation in names of plants he was studying. Although it is difficult today to agree with Walter Skeat (*EDS* 6, 1874) that 'Ray's is the most important book ever published on the subject of English dialects', John Ray's *Collection of English Words* (especially its second, augmented edition of 1691) is an important work in many ways. Ray does not say anything particularly specific about dialect areas in England, but his regional labelling of the entries gives us some kind of picture of what he thought were the main areas. Ray distinguishes between 'North-Country' words and 'South and East-Country' words. Most of Ray's provincial words come from the north. There are forty-eight pages of north-country words but only nineteen pages of south- and east-country words. This probably reflects the distance of northern English from the variety that Ray regarded as standard English.

When entries are localised they are usually localised by county, sometimes by town, or a large area such as the West Country, 'Essex, as well as Norfolk and Suffolk', or 'Somerset and elsewhere in the West'. His 'South and East-Country' words have references to Norfolk, Essex, Sussex, Surrey, Kent, Cambridgeshire, Northamptonshire, Leicestershire, Wiltshire, Somerset, Devon and Cornwall. Of the 184 'South and East-Country' words localised, only twenty-six are localised in the west. The most popular county is Sussex, which has fifty references. Ray's own home county, Essex, also has a high number of references; thirty-eight words are given as Essex words. In contrast with his more detailed treatment of northern areas, he does not, however, refer to specified towns in Essex. Sometimes a word is assigned to two areas, with one of them predominating, as in the case of the north-country word *murk*: '*murk*, adj. "dark"'. This word is also used in the South, but more rarely.'

Ray's 'North-Country' section has references to Westmorland, Cumberland, Cheshire, Yorkshire, Derbyshire, Lincolnshire, Lancashire, Northumberland, Worcestershire, Warwickshire and Shropshire. Sometimes specific towns such as Sheffield are singled out.

Although there is no systematic attempt to distinguish a specific midland area, Ray occasionally refers to the midlands. Thus the distribution of *nash* or *nesh* 'washy, weak, tender, puling', is given as 'North-West part of England and also in the Midland, as in Warwickshire'. But there is no attempt to distinguish between east and west midlands. It would appear that Ray's linguistic map consisted basically of two main areas, the north and the south, and that he regarded the Wash–Bristol Channel line as the main linguistic divider in England rather than the Humber–Ribble line.

Ray does not necessarily try to indicate the pronunciation of a word and he does not seem to be interested in local pronunciations *per se*. Thus, some northern pronunciations like *mack* 'make', which appear to have been common in northern English in Ray's day (and indeed continued to be so until quite recently), do not attract Ray's attention, probably because this word was used more or less the way it was used in other parts of the country.

Ray notices the word *sull* 'plough' and lists it under his 'South and East-Country Words', but unlike Marshall (1796), which gives the pronunciation *zule* and localises it as a west Devon word, there is no indication that it might be pronounced with a voiced initial fricative. However, there are entries suggesting voicing of initial fricatives in the south (e.g. *vollow* 'a fallow', Sussex, and *vang* 'to answer for at the font as godfather', Somerset; but there are no entries with an initial *z* or *zh*). And at one point Ray actually states this feature explicitly. After the entry '*Vollow* s. a fallow. Suss.' Ray adds: 'Generally in the West-Country, they use *v* instead of *f*, and *z* instead of *s*.'

5.2.1 *Characteristics of Ray's south- and east-country*

Ray's evidence is mainly lexical such as *mawther* 'girl' (Norfolk), *seel* 'time' or 'season' (Essex) and *sidy* adj. 'surly, moody' (Sussex). He does not usually show how the words were used in phrases and sentences. But, as we saw above, Ray records the southern voicing of initial fricatives in his general statement and there are stray instances of the voicing of initial *f* among the entries.

5.2.2 *Characteristics of Ray's north-country*

Despite Ray's apparent lack of interest in pronunciation, the examples that he gives to illustrate usage nevertheless often contain significant phonological features: for instance, *so* is not listed as a separate entry, but it appears in the phrase *yable sea* 'possibly so' showing the characteristically northern lack of rounding. Some consonantal features figure prominently in the north-country section. Yod-formation appears in words like *yance* 'once', *yane* 'one' and *yoon* 'oven', which incidentally are all pronunciations attested by the *SED*. L-vocalisation, too, is well represented by entries like *aud* 'old' and *caud* 'cold'.

There is not much grammatical information in Ray's *Collection*: for instance, he does not usually list function words, although this is a striking area in northern English not only lexically but also mor-phophonemically, as can be seen from texts like Meriton's 'Yorkshire Dialogue' (1684). Nor does Ray mention such obvious features as *at* 'that' or the use of the present-tense marker *-s* with plural and second person singular subjects, as in *All things runs wrang* or *Tha knows* and *Tha is*. But he does make the important observation that 'in the North-west parts of England' *hoo* and *he* are 'most frequently' used for *she*. This suggests that this pronominal form was in Ray's day already restricted to the area where it is found today, although his 'North-west parts of England' gives the impression that the area where *hoo/he* 'she' occurred was larger than it is today (see *LAE* maps M68 and M69). And again, certain salient points of northern grammar emerge from the examples given to illustrate the use of individual words. Under *dazed* is given the sentence *I's dazed* 'I am very cold', which shows *is* instead of *am*. *Sell* is listed as a pronoun meaning 'self', but it emerges from the examples given elsewhere that both *sen* and *sell* are used for *self* (*I'll go tull 'um my sen* 'I'll go and tell them myself', *You clean all the wite off your sell* 'You clear yourself of all blame').

5.2.3   Ray's lexicon

To those with some knowledge of Scandinavian languages Ray's northern section sounds strangely familiar, with entries such as *leeten* 'pretend', *murk* 'dark', *neive* 'fist', *reek* 'smoke' and *toom* 'empty'. The area in the north where Scandinavian influence was specifically strong is now known as the great Scandinavian belt. Samuels defines this as follows: 'a belt stretching from Cumberland and Westmorland in the west to the north and East Ridings of Yorkshire in the east, often including part of Lincolnshire but excluding the old kingdom of Bernica in Durham and Northumberland' (1985: 269). We shall see in the section on Ellis' classification of English dialects that the north-western part of the north is not only 'exceptional' from the viewpoint of Scandinavian vocabulary but there are other characteristics, too, that distinguish it from the rest of the north. Kolb (1965) shows that the Scandinavian belt can also be seen from the distribution of Scandinavian words in present-day dialects. This is another indication of the conservatism of northern English.[6]

As an illustration of how well Ray covers the northern vocabulary of his day, a representative sample of common northernisms was collected from early dialect texts such as Meriton's 'Yorkshire Dialogue' (1684) and checked against Ray's dictionary. The following list summarises the findings.

	listed by Ray
addle 'earn'	yes
barn, bearn 'child'	yes
deer 'door'	yes (i.e. northern fronting of *oo*)
dubler 'platter'	yes
flay 'frighten'	yes
gate 'way'	yes
ken 'know'	yes
kern 'churn'	yes
laer 'barn'	no
late 'seek'	yes
leer 'empty'	yes
leeten 'pretend to be'	yes
lite on 'rely on'	yes
mun 'must'	no
murk 'dark'	yes
owr (= over) 'too'	no
reek 'smoke'	yes
sark 'shirt'	yes
sell, sen 'self'	yes
skeel 'milk-pail'	yes
throng 'busy'	yes
wark 'ache'	no
wonne, wun 'dwell'	yes
yan 'one'	yes
yoon 'oven'	yes

Attached to Ray's *Collection* are Brokesby's observations on the pronunciation of the dialect of the East Riding of Yorkshire. Brokesby notes the lack of rounding in northern English ('So for *both* we say *bath*; for *bone*, *bane*; for *work*, *wark*'), /k/ instead of /tʃ/ ('So for *chaffe* they say *caffe*; for *churn*, *kern*'), *l*-vocalisation ('as for *cold* they say *caud*; for *old*, *aud*'), the fronting of the vowel in words like *fool* ('In some words, for *oo*, we pronounce *eu*, as *ceul*, *feul*, *eneugh*, for *cool*, *fool*, *enough*'). Before *r*, *oo* becomes *ee*, as in *deer* 'door'. The pronunciations of *go*, *no* and *so* are given as *ge*, *ne* and *se* (as in *se throng* 'so full of business'). The *eu* in words like *feul* 'fool' may represent an intermediate stage between the northern ME /yː/ and the modern /iə/, perhaps /iy/ or /iu/. (Meriton has *eau* in *deaun* 'done', *neaun* 'noon', *fleaur* 'floor'.) Brokesby also comments on yod-formation: 'They place y before some words beginning with vowels; yane, yance; as in some other parts of England, yarely for early; yowes for ewes.'

Brokesby makes only two grammatical points. He notes that East Yorkshire speakers omit the -s genitive ending and say *Jackson wife* instead of *Jackson's wife*. The other point is that the -en ending found in some words is not necessarily the plural marker found elsewhere in England.

Ray's *Collection* shows characteristics that were strengthened in later dialect dictionaries. One of them is that the northern English variety provides a considerable number of entries under the letters *k*, *wh* and *y* as opposed to the southern, later south-western variety, which favours the letters *v*, *ʒ* and *dr*.

5.3 Awareness of dialect areas from 1776 till the late nineteenth century

Although it is probably true that no radical changes took place in English dialects in the post-1776 period until the second half of the twentieth century, there are certain things that justify the choice of the late nineteenth century as marking the end of an era. It would seem that from 1776 till the second half of the nineteenth century dialects were stable, and although regional English was seen as an obstacle to social advancement and therefore as something to be avoided, there appears to have been no actual educational policy at work to create a unified 'polite' English, although there had been individual attempts to codify a spoken standard such as Sheridan (1780) and Walker (1791). However, in the second half of the nineteenth century, an active policy to eradicate regional features appears to have been adopted in public schools. Honey (1988: 213) suggests that this started in the 1870s. And the Education Act of 1870 of course must have exerted a certain levelling influence, although this may have been much smaller than one might gather from comments like Elworthy (1886) and Heslop (1892: xx–xxi, quoted in Beale 1987: 3), resenting the interference of what was called Book English with pedigree local varieties.

Generally speaking, dialects appear to have been far more conservative than ever believed possible by scholars. A good example of this tenacity is the *th'* [θ] realisation of the definite article in Cheshire folk speech. Darlington (1887) reports that 'one scarcely ever hears this from persons under twenty years of age', and in his judgement the standard form *the* [ðə] was rapidly superseding the indigenous forms of the article. However, the *SED* shows that both *th'* and the stop realisation *t'* for *the* were still common in Cheshire English in the mid-twentieth century (e.g. IX.2.3 '...till the sun sets'). In the same way, many northern words that Marshall (1788) thought were becoming obsolete were still recorded by the *SED*. In fact, one of the sentences that Marshall used to illustrate northern English, *Aa mun gan* 'I must go', actually appears in a tape-recording that Hedevind made in 1967. Joseph Wright virtually gave up dialectology after the publication of the *English Dialect Dictionary* (1898–1905), very probably because he believed that traditional dialects would soon disappear. The following passage from Wright's Preface (1898) to the *English Dialect Dictionary* is revealing: 'It is quite evident from the letters daily received at the "Workshop" that pure dialect speech is rapidly disappearing from our midst, and that in a few years it will be almost impossible to get accurate information about difficult points' (p. v). The real problem and cause for worry, of course, was not that the language situation had become hopelessly complicated, but that dialectologists had no tools for handling the new complexity. These tools were not developed until the latter half of the twentieth century by such scholars as William Labov in the United States and Peter Trudgill, James Milroy and Lesley Milroy in Britain. Nevertheless, statements like Wright's suggest that some kind of change was taking place towards the end of the century, and that the earlier part of the century is best regarded as a continuation of the former situation.

There was also a change in attitudes towards rural varieties of English in the latter half of the nineteenth century, which suggests that an era had ended. Whereas earlier there had been a general rejection of 'provincial' or 'vulgar' English, now rural (but not urban) dialects were seen as having a certain justification in that they were in many ways 'purer', of greater ancestry and better pedigree than was standard English (Ihalainen 1990a).

There were certain linguistic developments in the late nineteenth century, too, that suggest the end of an era. Well-known dialect features like the south-western present-tense marker *-eth*, *ich* for *I*, *n*-less participial forms (*i-do* 'done'), and Cockney *w/v* commutation became practically obsolete in the late nineteenth century. On the other hand, new features arose. These included such Cockney features as diphthong shift ('the lidies in the bowt'), *t*-glottaling and *th*-fronting (*nuffink* 'nothing').

Eighteenth- and early nineteenth-century writers on language appear to be less interested in the regional distribution of dialect features than grammarians were in the previous century. There is nothing to match the detail of Gil's 'northern', 'southern', 'eastern' and 'western' dialects. Of specific interest to those who touch upon 'vulgar' English are Cockney, Irish and Scottish English. The existence of a great variety of regional dialects is recognised, but they are lumped together under 'provincial English' or covered by statements like 'every county has its own dialect' (Walker 1791). A coherent picture of the dialectal structure of England does not arise until Ellis (1889).

5.3.1   Marshall's glossaries of provincialisms

Some of the most helpful observations on eighteenth-century regional English come from William Humphrey Marshall (1745–1818), although one should remember Skeat's caveat that Marshall's prefatory remarks 'cannot wholly be relied upon' (1873, *EDS* 1, iv). Marshall wrote about several 'rural economies', to which he attached glossaries of local words used in the area he was surveying. These glossaries also have comments on phonology and grammar although Marshall's main interest, of course, was the local agricultural names of implements, work methods, geographical features, types of land and so on.

Marshall's interest in dialect was not simply antiquarian but also practical: he believed that it was not possible to communicate effectively with the local peasantry without being familiar with their variety of English. Naturally, Marshall is mainly interested in words directly related to agriculture. The Marshall glossaries cover North of England (1781), East Norfolk (1787), East Yorkshire (1788), the Vale of Gloucester (1789), the Midland counties (1790) and West Devon (1796). His most extensive and helpful work is his 'Provincialisms of East Yorkshire', which is part of his *Rural Economy of Yorkshire* (1788).

5.3.2   Marshall on northern English

Marshall's 'Provincialisms of East Yorkshire' (1788) is particularly valuable, for here he is describing his own native variety. Besides lexical, phonological and grammatical information, Marshall's East Yorkshire glossary has comments on stylistic differences in dialect: he reports that the northern word *throng* 'busy' (which can still be heard at least in a *SED* recording made in Golcar in the 1950s) is pronounced in two ways: *throng* and *thrang*. The latter is called 'vulgar'. A similar stylistic distinction between what Marshall calls 'mid. dial.' and 'vulg.' is made in the case of *mickle* and *mitch* 'much'. This appears to be the first observation on stylistic variation within a dialect. One is reminded here of the words of a Somerset speaker recently that the difference between *ain't* and *ben't* is that the former is 'more polite' (*CCDE*: J. M. 1982, Somerset).

Unlike Ray, Marshall frequently illustrates the use of a word in an idiomatic sentence. This gives us much valuable grammatical information. Thus, to illustrate the use of *mun* 'must' he gives the sentence *Aa mun gang* 'I must go', which shows not only the local word *gang* but also that *I* was pronounced with a monophthong in precisely the way that it is pronounced today. Under *very* another instance of a monophthong occurs in the illustrative phrase *varra faan* 'very fine'. Marshall also notes here the northern lax quality of *-y* in *very*. This contrasts sharply with John Walker's observation that final *-y* could actually be written *ee*, which shows that polite London speech at that time had a tense vowel in this position (Walker 1791: 35).

Some morphophonemic processes characteristic of northern English are also discussed. These include the use of linking *v*, as in *gang tiv 'em* 'go to them', and the encliticisation of *it*, as in *pud sum mare to't* 'put some more to it'. Both of these are still common. Yet many striking structural features used in dialect texts like Meriton's 'Yorkshire Dialogue' (1684) do not occur in Marshall's glossary. The most obvious of these is the regular northern realisation of *the* as a stop, called 'suspended (t')' by Ellis (1889: 10*, 18, 832–3), and usually spelt *t'* in dialect texts, as in *t'oad riddle* 'the old riddle'.

Marshall also comments on the frequency and currency of certain words. He points out that *leer* 'barn' is 'growing into disuse', and *wun* 'live, abide' is 'nearly obsolete', whereas *thou* is 'still much in use'. It is highly significant that Marshall should specifically comment on *thou*; this pronoun had become obsolete in standard English and was felt to be a 'provincial archaism', as dialectal words were often called in eighteenth-century glossaries. Occasionally, one detects almost a certain surprise in Marshall's observation that an old northern form was still being used, as when he says about *kirk* that it was 'still pretty common in the vulgar dialect' (Marshall's 'vulgar dialect' refers to the most marked variety of northern English). Marshall might have been delighted to learn that *kirk* was still used by some Yorkshire speakers in the mid-twentieth century in phrases like *They gan to the kirk* 'They go to church'(*SED* VIII.5.1).

Marshall also notes some northern words that were not listed by Ray, the most obvious of these being *ken* 'know' and *wark* 'ache'. And he elaborates on some points introduced by Ray: for instance, when Ray gives simply *throng* 'busy', Marshall distinguishes between *throng* and the vulgar form *thrang*.

5.3.3 Marshall on south-western English

In his *Rural Economy of Glocestershire* (1789), Marshall has a section entitled 'Provincialisms of the Vale of Glocester', where he discusses a number of linguistic characteristics of the English spoken in the area. He points out the use of accusative forms of pronouns, as in *Her said so* 'She said so', the use of *he* instead of *it*, and the reduced form of the third person singular pronoun, spelt *ou*, which can be used for *he, she* and *it*. He correctly points out that these features, together with the voicing of initial fricatives, are common to the western counties in general. Other features of the Vale of Gloucester English which Marshall finds 'the most noticeable' include the use of *be* for *is*, *do* for *does* and *have* for *has*, all features still attested by the *SED*. He also notices that the Vale of Gloucester reflex of ME *ai* is pronounced /ai/ or /oi/.

Marshall's main point, that the linguistic evidence suggests that the 'inhabitants of the western side of the island are descended from one common origin' (p. 56), will probably appeal to few today. At the same time one must nevertheless note that he is perhaps the first one to recognise the significance of what is now called 'pronoun exchange' as a dialect marker, and that his arguments based on the linguistic unity (as opposed to the 'common origin' view) of the west are quite convincing.[7]

Another south-western variety that Marshall comments on is west Devonshire English (1796). Lexical entries include such words as *pook* 'a cock of hay', *shippen* 'ox-house', *vetty* 'suitable', *vinny* 'mouldy' and *wants* 'moles'. The words *vetty* and *vinny* show the characteristic southern voicing of initial fricatives, and the *e* of *vetty* probably stands for a lax *i*, which is still one of the hallmarks of south-western English, frequently exploited by dialect writers. Marshall also reports that the *-eth* present-tense marker is in 'common use'.

The fact that Marshall regards the *-eth* present-tense marker, as in *He go'th* and *They go'th*, as a striking Devon feature shows how far west this former southern characteristic had receded. Its last stronghold, before its disappearance toward the end of the nineteenth century, was Devon and west Somerset. It is probable that about the time Marshall made his observations, the -s suffix had already replaced -eth in many parts of the south-west: for instance, there is early nineteenth-century evidence in Halliwell (1881) to suggest that, while Devon still had *he go'th*, Wiltshire had *he goes*.

5.3.4 *Francis Grose's* A Provincial Glossary, with a Collection of Local Proverbs, and Popular Superstitions (*1787, corrected edition 1790*)

Grose relied heavily on Ray's *Collection*, the dialect texts published in *The Gentleman's Magazine* and Bobbins' *Lancashire Dialect*. However, because of his work, he travelled extensively and was thus able to make first-hand observations about dialectal speech in various parts of the country. He also consulted many of the county histories for new evidence.

Grose localises his words by using the labels 'North', 'South' and 'West' or the name of a specific county. However, he points out that words are seldom confined to a single county. Words used in several counties are labelled 'Common'. What is striking about Grose's classification is that, unlike Gil or Ray, Grose does not have a category 'East', the reason being that 'The East country scarcely afforded a sufficiency of words to form a division.' This suggests that, as far as the vocabulary was concerned, to Grose eastern English was not clearly differentiated from standard English.

5.3.5 *Halliwell's* Dictionary of Archaic and Provincial Words (*1847; 10th edition 1881*)

Perhaps the most useful general treatment from the viewpoint of the late eighteenth and early nineteenth century is Halliwell's *Dictionary of Archaic and Provincial Words*. In the introduction Halliwell gives samples with notes of English spoken in each county, but he does not attempt to group these into actual dialect areas or to study to what extent the Middle English division of English dialects into northern, midland and southern varieties was still justified. He points out that the available authentic evidence is too scanty for such a treatment and has 'led to an alphabetical arrangement of the counties in the following brief notices' (1881: xi). However, he notes that the original southern dialect is in his day 'retained in the Western counties' (1881: xi). Ellis (1889) makes a similar observation when he says that the earlier southern dialect forms are being preserved in the west (his area 10).

Although Halliwell does not attempt to classify dialects, he makes

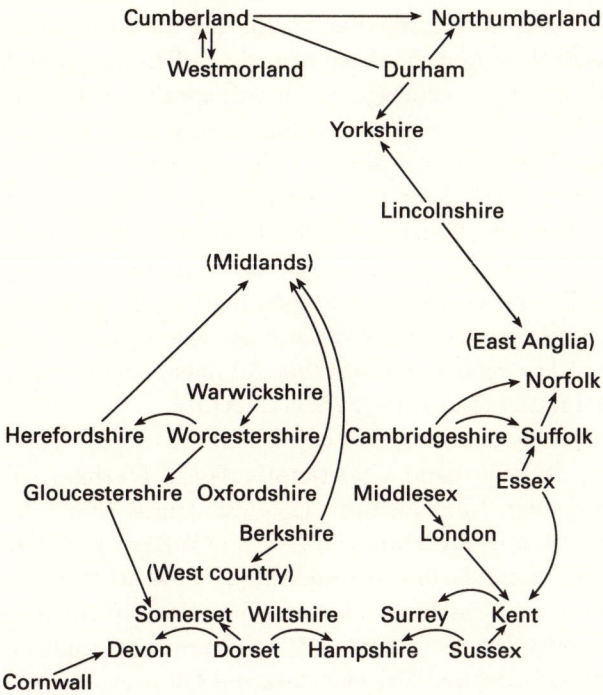

Figure 5.1   Connections among dialects, redrawn from Halliwell's *Dictionary*. (Unconnected counties: Lancashire, Cheshire, Derbyshire, Nottinghamshire, Staffordshire, Shropshire, Leicestershire, Rutland, Northamptonshire, Huntingdonshire, Buckinghamshire; Rutland connects to Leicestershire, but Halliwell does not try to link this bundle to a larger area.)

several observations about group relationships, such as 'There is little to distinguish the Cambridgeshire dialect from that of the adjoining counties. It is nearly allied to that of Norfolk and Suffolk' (1881: xi). The Berkshire dialect is said to belong partly to the western, partly to the midland, 'more strongly marked with the features of the former in the South-West of the county' (1881: xi), a comment which thus recognises the transitional nature of Berkshire. Wakelin (1986a: 1), studying the situation in the light of mid-twentieth century evidence, calls Berkshire a 'marginal area'. The connections that Halliwell makes in his 'brief notes' to the samples given are summarised in figure 5.1.[8] The arrows indicate that Halliwell connects the areas involved linguistically. The arrowhead indicates the direction of the connection. Thus, Cambridgeshire → Norfolk means that Cambridgeshire is related linguistically to Norfolk. The specific link connecting Worcestershire to

Herefordshire and Gloucestershire is the use of *which* as a sentence connector, as in 'I bought the sheep of a man at Broomsgrove fair, *which* he is a friend of the prosecutor's, and won't appear; *which* I could have transported the prosecutor ever so long agoo if I liked' (said by a butcher accused of sheep-stealing; Halliwell 1881: xxxiii). However, this feature has recently been reported at least in Lancashire, Somerset and Tyneside English (Shorrocks 1980; Ihalainen 1980; Jones 1985) so that its significance as a regional diagnostic is questionable. On the other hand, Halliwell's 'notes' in the introduction of his dictionary show that Worcestershire, Warwickshire and Gloucestershire also share pronoun exchange (as in *Her's going for a walk with she*), which definitely suggests a south-western rather than a northern connection.

Five specific clusters emerge from Halliwell's 'notes': (1) the north (Cumberland, Westmorland, Northumberland, Durham, Yorkshire with a link to north Lincolnshire); (2) East Anglia (Norfolk, Suffolk with links from Cambridgeshire and Essex); (3) Kent with links to and from Surrey, Sussex and a link to London; (4) the south-west (Cornwall, Devon, Somerset, Wiltshire, Dorset with links from Hampshire, Oxfordshire and Gloucestershire); (5) southern west midlands (Worcestershire, Herefordshire, Warwickshire and Gloucestershire, which is also connected to the West Country). Middlesex has a special position, closely connected to London. Halliwell simply states that 'The metropolitan county presents little in its dialect worthy of remark, being for the most part merely a coarse pronunciation of London slang and vulgarity' (1881: xxiv).

Halliwell also attempts to characterise the broadness of various dialects. This probably measures the difference between the variety concerned and what was regarded as standard English. Thus, Derbyshire English is described as 'broad' (p. xiv), whereas Buckinghamshire speech, which Halliwell does not link with any other variety, is characterised as being 'not very broad', (p. xi) which suggests closeness to standard English. The counties that Halliwell found difficult to structure are the northern west midland counties, and most east midland counties.

Halliwell's view of the dialectal structure of England probably very well reflects the contemporary awareness of dialect areas. Northern, south-western, East Anglian and London varieties of English were better known than the midland varieties. A similar picture arises if we look at the amount of scholarship produced by the time Ellis started his work on dialect areas in England.

5.4 Dialect markers in the late eighteenth and early nineteenth century

This section summarises the main dialect features that appear in the literature from the late eighteenth century up to about 1870. Most of the relevant sources were reprinted by the English Dialect Society in the late nineteenth century and are easily available.

Quite a few of the features listed below appear in Halliwell's Dictionary, either in the samples and comments published in the preface or under the dictionary entries. Skeat's *Nine Specimens of English Dialects* (1896, *EDS*, 76) has good samples of northern, south-western, southern and East Anglian English. Further samples can be found in Skeat (1911). Elworthy's edition of the *Exmoor Scolding* and the *Exmoor Courtship*, two eighteenth-century texts, has extensive comments on south-western English, including historical developments. Short samples of dialect texts from the seventeenth and eighteenth centuries are analysed in Wakelin (1988b). Together Forby (1830), Jennings (1825), Elworthy (1875, 1877/9 and 1886), Barnes (1886), Heslop (1892) and Darlington (1887) give a good idea of the structural characteristics of some of the main regional varieties.

The features listed below (followed by comments on their regional distributions) are not only typical of late eighteenth-century and early nineteenth-century dialect but they also figure prominently in later treatments of English dialects like Ellis (1889), Wright (*EDD*, *EDG*), Wakelin (1977) and Trudgill (1990).

Linguistic characteristics of late eighteenth- and early nineteenth-century dialects

Northern features

Northern lack of rounding	*ste'an* [stɪən], *wark* 'work'
Northern *oo*-fronting	*me'an* [mɪən] 'moon', *se'an* [sɪən] 'soon'
Northern long *a*	*ne'am* [nɪəm] 'name'
/ai/-monophthongisation	*Ah* [aː] 'I', *faan* 'fine', *insard* 'inside'
yod-formation	*yan* 'one', *yak* 'oak'
l-vocalisation/dropping	*au'd* 'old'
linking *v*	*tiv another* 'to another'
soom 'some'	*some* pronounced [sʊm]
hoose 'house'	*house* pronounced [huːs]
second person singular verb	*Tha knows* 'You know'

y-laxing — *Jerra* 'Jerry', *verra* 'very'

at 'that' — *a chap at knaws hauf as mich as me* 'a chap that knows half as much as me'

t' for *the* (i.e. the realisation of the definite article as a stop) — *Nea doot thoo knaws t' oad riddle* 'No doubt you know the old riddle'

sal, 's 'shall' — *Ah' se be forced te gang yam* 'I shall be forced to go home'

I is 'I am' — *Ah's seer* 'I'm sure'

universal -*s*, subject to the northern subject rule — *They peel them and boils them, Birds sings*

West midland features

West midland *ngg* — *strong* [stɹɔŋg]

rounding before nasals — *mon* 'man'

ai-rounding — *roit* 'right'

same/seem switch — *dee* 'day', *way* 'we'

hoo — 'she'

-*na* negation — *inna* 'isn't', *winna* 'will not'

second person singular verbs — *Hast seen it?* 'Have you seen it?'

pronoun exchange — *Her told I* 'She told me'

plural present indicative marker -*en* — *They sayn* 'They say', *They'n do it* 'They'll do it'

plural *am* — *How-r am jo?* 'How are you?'

South-western features

periphrastic *do* — *They da* [də] *peel them*

universal -*th* — *He go'th, Folks go'th*

universal -*s* — *They makes them, Farmers makes them*

plural *am* — *They'm nice* 'They're nice'

pronoun exchange — *Her told I* 'She told me'

Ich 'I' — *Ich say* 'I say'

proclitic *'ch* 'I' — *cham* 'I'm', *chall* 'I'll'

second person singular verb — *Thee dost know/Thee's know* 'You know'

uninflected *do, have* — *He don't know, It have happened*

otiose *of* — *Whot's er a-düing ov?* 'What's he/she doing?'

voicing of initial fricatives — *zay, vinger, ʒhilling*

retention of ME *ai* — *day* [dai]

r for *gh* — *fought* pronounced [fɔɾt]

East Anglian features
Norwich *a*   *Rabbin* 'Robbin', *Narwich* 'Norwich'
that for *it*   *That's raining* 'It's raining'
uninflected present-tense   *He know*
  form of a main verb
uninflected *do*, *have*   *He don't know, It have happened*
otiose *of*   *She's ollas a-eating o' thapes* 'She's always
                                           eating gooseberries'

South- eastern/Cockney
  features
interchange of *v* and *w*:   *wery* 'very', *vet* 'wet'
diphthong shift   *lidies in the bowt* 'ladies in the boat'

'*Common vulgarisms*'
r-dropping   *farm* pronounced *fahm*
hyper-rhoticity   *fellar* 'fellow', *Belindar* 'Belinda'
intrusive *r* (called 'euph-   *saw-r-it* 'saw it'
  onic' *r* in early studies)
h-dropping   *'ammer* 'hammer'
y-tensing   *charitee* 'charity'

Some of the features listed above were well-established dialect characteristics in the late eighteenth and early nineteenth century; others were unsettled, in the sense that their social status was not quite clear. For instance, while it was obvious that it was vulgar to say *Tha knaws* or *Thee'st know*, it was not quite clear what was generally thought of pronunciations like *fahm* 'farm'. The social significance of *r*-dropping remains unsettled in the twentieth century. Thus, although Walker (1791) said that *r* should always be pronounced, he observed, without censure, that *r* was nevertheless often silent and words like *farm* and *storm* were pronounced as if written *faam* and *stawm*. Sheridan (1762), on the other hand, seems to regard *r*-dropping as a provincial feature, characteristic of northern English specifically. Börje Holmberg (1964: 73) observes that although Henry Sweet's description of English pronunciation from 1888 shows few differences between present-day standard English and the pronunciation Sweet describes, there is the striking difference that Sweet still seems to have pronounced *r* in final position (but not before consonants). However, Jones (1909), who clearly purports to describe a pronunciation standard, a variety used by 'educated people in London and the neighbourhood', describes a non-rhotic variety. One of the first writers using rhoticity as a dialect marker must surely be John Read in a story entitled 'Dicky Paine in London'.

The story appeared in 1927 in the *Somerset Yearbook*, but Read says that the story was written in 1906 and 'refers to an episode which goes back to 1900'.

Other problems connected with *r* are hyper-rhoticity (*fellar* 'fellow') and intrusive *r* (*She saw-r-it* 'She saw it'). Hyper-rhoticity refers to an *r*-sound that is induced by a final schwa. Sheridan (1762) regards this as a Cockney feature, Walker (1791) simply calls it vulgar. Walker comments on the pronunciation of the final *ow* in words like *window* and *fellow* as follows: 'The vulgar shorten this sound, and pronounce the *o* obscurely, and sometimes as if followed by *r*, but this is almost too despicable to notice' (1791: 46). Halliwell (1881: xxix) reports hyper-rhoticity from Sussex and Bedford but does not regard it as a strong regional diagnostic. Wells (1982, II: 343) gives hyper-rhoticity as a modern West Country characteristic. The *SED* data on *meadow* and *yellow* (displayed in *LAE* maps Ph206 and Ph207) show a final [əɾ] or [əɹ] from Cornwall, Devon, Somerset, Dorset, Wiltshire, Monmouthshire, Herefordshire, Worcestershire, Warwickshire, Shropshire, Northamptonshire, Hampshire, Sussex, Surrey and Kent. Hyper-rhoticity probably accounts for the merger of the masculine and feminine enclitic subject pronouns in present-day south-western English, as in *Don' er?* 'Doesn't she/he?' The feminine pronoun derives from *her* whereas the masculine pronoun comes from the weak form *a* [ə], which induces an *r* in final position. This interpretation is supported by the fact that in some varieties of south-western English, most notably in Devon, the masculine enclitic is *a*, whereas the feminine pronoun is *er*.

Intrusive *r* refers to an *r*-sound induced between two vowels in contexts like *Anna-r-is at home* and *law-r-and justice*. Forby, referring to his native East Anglian English, comments: 'We constantly use it. It is even sometimes heard from the mouths of persons of education and refinement' (1830: 102). To Forby, intrusive *r* is a vulgarism rather than a dialectal feature. By this he probably means that it is distributed over a large area, as suggested by the present distribution. The *SED* reports intrusive *r* from the west midlands, for instance.

H-dropping is another feature that has attracted a great deal of attention. Walker regards it as a characteristically Cockney 'fault' (1791: 11), whereas Sheridan describes it as a common 'rustic defect' which was 'gaining ground amongst the politer part of the world' (1762: 34). *H*-dropping was, of course, in no way restricted to London. Thus Ellis gives it as a common midland feature: 'The aspirate is altogether neglected in the M. div. ... This absence of aspiration penetrates to well-educated classes, and may be even heard from the pulpit' (1889: 295). The *SED* shows that in the mid-twentieth century only East Anglia and the north-east of England were *h*-pronouncing. Because of its wide distribution, *h*-dropping has not played a particularly important role as a regional diagnostic in traditional dialectology. Its sociolinguistic implications, however, are highly significant.

5.4.1   *West midland characteristics*

Rounding before nasals: *mon* 'man'

Rounding before nasals is one of the striking features of west midland texts like the 'Conversation between a Staffordshire canal boatman and his wife' dating from 1823 (Halliwell 1881: xxviii). Rounding before nasals seems to have become an exclusively west midland feature towards the end of the nineteenth century, when it disappeared from south-western English. The *Exmoor Courtship* (1746) still has rounding in *hond*, but Elworthy (*EDS* 25, 1879: 76) says it is obsolete, 'but only recently so'. Rounding before nasals is one of the characteristics used in such recent classifications of English dialects as Wakelin (1983) and Trudgill (1990).

-ngg

Although there is evidence for the loss of /g/ after /ŋ/ in unstressed contexts in certain dialects from the fourteenth century, this has been the accepted pronunciation only from about 1600 (Dobson 1968, II; section 399). Today *g*-ful pronunciations are found in the west midlands. *G*-fulness has been used as a classificatory criterion for both traditional (Wakelin 1983; Trudgill 1990) and modern dialects (Trudgill 1990).[9] *G*-dropping spread from eastern dialects (including London English).

Walker (1791) describes a distribution of *ng* and *ngg* in stressed positions (as in *strong*) that is basically the distribution of this feature today: no *g* in the base form *strong*, *g* in the comparative and superlative forms *stronger*, *strongest*. However, he allows for two pronunciations for the *-ing* ending: *-in'* if the base ends in *-ng* (e.g. *singin'*), but *-ing* elsewhere (e.g. *sinning*), so that the usage still vacillated in the eighteenth century.

same/seem switch

This refers to the interchange of the diphthong /eɪ/ and the long vowel /iː/ in some varieties of west midland English. There is evidence of this in a Staffordshire text published in 1823 and entitled 'Conversation between a Staffordshire canal boatman and his wife' (Halliwell 1881: xxviii). Gibson (1955) regards the *same*/*seem* switch as one of the most striking characteristics of Stafford English. One gets the impression from Ellis (1889: 461) that this feature was widespread in the midlands. The *SED* shows a rather restricted area with north Staffordshire as its centre.

Present indicative plural in -en: *They sayn* 'They say'

The present indicative marker *-en* is reported by the *SED* in Lancashire, south-west Yorkshire, Cheshire, Derbyshire, Staffordshire and north Shropshire (see especially VIII.5.1. 'They go to church'). In broad outline, this area is very close to the distribution given by Ellis, who regards the verbal plural in *-en* as 'the chief constructional peculiarity' of the midland division (Ellis 1889: 295–6). Lowth (1762: 31) says that the *-en* ending 'hath long been obsolete', and passes no social judgement on it.

-na negation

The samples published in Halliwell (1881) show that *-na* negation is the regular way of forming negation in much of the west midlands. Thus *cannot* is *conner* (with the characteristic rounding before nasals) in the Derbyshire sample. The Lancashire sample has *hoo cou'd naw* 'she couldn't' and the Bilston Folk (Staffordshire) sample *thee cost'na* for 'you can't' (with pronoun exchange on *thou*). Darlington (1887: 77) discusses *-na* negation in Cheshire English at some length, which suggests that it was a prominent feature. The *-na* negative particle seems to induce an intrusive *r* in Cheshire English. Thus, *wunna* 'won't' becomes *wunnur* (as Darlington spells it) in contexts like *I wunnar 'av it* 'I won't have it'. The focal area of *-na* negation as shown by the *SED* includes Cheshire, Staffordshire, Derbyshire and Shropshire. This area is practically the same as the present indicative *-en* area.

hoo 'she'

This feature has been noted as a dialect marker since Ray's *Collection*. *Hoo* appears under Ray's 'North-Country Words', but he specifies that it occurs in the 'North-west parts of England', where it is 'most frequently used for *she*'. Ray, of course, as was pointed out above, does not differentiate between the north and the midlands, which he regards as one area. With reference to Middle English dialects, Samuel Moore

(1964: 123) remarks: 'An important morphological criterion for distinguishing between the East Midland and the West Midland dialects is that the feminine nominative singular *ho* is frequently used in West Midland texts but does not appear to be used in East Midland texts.' Halliwell gives *hoo* as a Lincolnshire word, but this is probably a slip of the pen for Lancashire. Localisation in Lincolnshire is certainly not supported by the evidence he publishes in his introduction. His Lincolnshire sample has *she*, whereas the Lancashire sample has *hoo*. The *SED* still shows a rather large *hoo*-area in the northern west midlands (covering parts of Lancashire, Cheshire, Yorkshire, Derbyshire and Staffordshire).

5.4.2 Northern characteristics

Failure to round

The late Old English rounding of long *a* stopped, roughly, at the river Humber, so that even today north-of-the-Humber pronunciations of words like *stone* can be heard that are reflexes of *a:* rather than *o:*. Thus, in northern England a common pronunciation of *stone* is [stɪən]. These are now being replaced by pronunciations like [stɔːn], but were still reported from older and middle-aged speakers in the 1970s (Tidholm 1979). The Humber–Lune/Ribble line has, until quite recently, been the most important linguistic border in England, separating the north from the rest of the country. This boundary has proved very stable. A comparison of the isogloss that appears on Moore's map of Middle English dialects and the one on the *LAE* map based on the *SED* data on *one* (*LAE* Ph125a) shows an almost identical area: an unrounded vowel is retained north of the line running from the Humber to Morecambe Bay. However, looking at the situation in 1990 Trudgill states: 'Here we can see that what was the most important British dialect boundary of all in the Traditional Dialects – the one that descended from Anglo-Saxon times and started on the east coast at the mouth of the Humber – has disappeared completely' (1990: 76). But in eighteenth- and nineteenth-century northern texts the failure to round, together with some other northern vowel developments (such as the *name* and *moon* vowels), are prominent and regular features.

Soom 'some'

Unrounding of *u* may have occasionally occurred in dialectal English as early as the fifteenth century but was still regarded as vulgar in the early seventeenth century (Dobson 1968, II: section 93). The first orthoepist to regard the unrounded pronunciation of *u* as a standard English sound is Simon Daines in 1640. Marshall (1788) does not list unrounding as a northern provincialism, but says that *u* has its 'accepted power'. (Interestingly, he also claims that the letter *a*, as in *man*, has its 'accepted power' in North Yorkshire English.)

One of the earliest attempts to mark off this pronunciation is evidently shown by the author of *York Minster Screen* (1833). In this text the spelling *oo* is used for *u* in words like *oother* 'other', *poot* 'put', *soom* 'some', *book* 'bulk' (with the characteristic loss of *l*) and *coom'd* 'came'. (But *book* is spelt *beuk*, suggesting a long sound. The same spelling is used for *seun* 'soon'.) Rounded *u* is really both a midland and northern feature, but the lack of midland texts, especially east midland texts from the early period, makes it impossible to comment on *u*-unrounding in this area. We know from the modern distribution that the unrounded vowel is found south of the Wash–Severn line, which is now a major dialect boundary in England.

t' for *the*

The stop realisation of the definite article, as in *t' axle's bent*, is a regular feature of early northern texts like the *York Minster Screen* (1833). The *t'* definite article has a number of phonetic realisations depending on the linguistic context and the dialect involved. These are discussed in detail in Jones (1952). One of the possible realisations of the *t'* form was called 'suspended (t`)' by Ellis. The ` accompanying the *t* here 'marks suspension of the organs of speech for a sensible time' (1889: 88*). Jones (1952: 87) feels it highly probable that the 'suspension' consists of both glottal and oral closure. Suspended (t`) plays an important role in Ellis' classification of English dialects.

Barry (1972) surveys the present distribution of the *t'* definite article, but is unable to say anything specific about its origin. Hedevind (1967: 227) believes that in some parts of the north, in the Dent–Sedbergh–Westmorland area, the original [θ] was replaced by *t'* forms only a century ago, so that in the early nineteenth century the *t'* may have actually been on the increase. Tidholm (1979: 126) suggests that the replacement of [θ] by /t/ started in the seventeenth century. Hedevind's transcriptions of Dentdale English show the use of the *t'* forms to be the rule. They are also common in the *SED* material. Question V.6.6 'in the oven' shows instances of *t'* in Cumberland,

Durham, Westmorland, Lancashire, Yorkshire, Derbyshire and, one instance, in Nottinghamshire. Other *SED* questions add instances from Cheshire. More recent studies have reported a sharp decline in the use of the *t'* forms amongst younger speakers. Tidholm (1979) comments on Egton (North Yorkshire) English: 'The Egton definite article /t/ is fairly frequent in age group Old (36·7 per cent) and Mid (39·7 per cent), but it is of rare occurrence in the Young age group (5·6 per cent). His data are summarised as follows:

The definite article

	Old (%)	Mid (%)	Young (%)
t'	36·7	39·7	5·6
the	63·3	60·3	94·4
instances:	215	170	196

Tidholm's percentages are based on a fairly large population. His 'Young' refers to speakers born after the Second World War. Tidholm believes that the *t'* forms will have disappeared in two generations. Lodge's analysis of present-day Stockport (Greater Manchester) English also points to the recent disappearance of *t'* forms (Lodge 1984). Riitta Kerman's study of the language of four elderly speakers of Lancashire English shows that *t'* forms were used with any regularity by only one of the informants (Kerman 1991). However, David Storey still used *t'* to mark the dialect of the older generations in his 1982 novel *A Prodigal Child*.

at 'who'

The use of *at* as a relative pronoun appears to have been the rule in northern dialect literature since its beginnings. Ellis (1889) uses the relative pronoun to differentiate between northern and midland English. The relative pronoun is *at* in the north, but *as* in the midlands. The *SED* (III.3.7) shows that this distribution still held in the mid-twentieth century.

The northern subject rule: *They peel them and boils them*

According to the northern subject rule, plural present-tense verbs take *-s*, unless they are immediately preceded by a personal-pronoun subject, as in *They peel them and boils them* and *Birds sings*. This separates northern dialects from *s*-marking dialects where no such restriction obtains and sentences like *They peels them* and *Farmers makes them* occur freely. This is the situation in the south-west today. The earlier south-western *-eth*, which was replaced by the *-s* ending during the nineteenth century, did not have any restrictions either (with the exception that it was not used to mark the second person singular), and we find forms like *I go'th*, *He go'th*, *They go'th*, and so on. The operation of the northern subject rule in present-day dialects can be clearly seen by comparing the *SED* responses to questions VIII.7.5 'Burglars steal' and VIII.5.1 'They go to church'. The *Burglars steals* area is much bigger than the *They goes to church* area. The shrinkage is accounted for by the northern avoidance of *They goes to church*. The same tendency can be seen in the responses to the *SED* questions on 'They keep hens' (IV.6.2) and 'Bulls bellow' (III.10.2; III.10.7).

5.4.3   South-western characteristics

ich: *Chill pick you teeth*, *zir*

One of the popular dialect markers used by Elizabethan dramatists was *ich* 'I', often appearing as a proclitic *'ch*. At that time it appears to have been a common form throughout the south of England. Perhaps the most famous instance of the use of *ch* as a marker of southern rusticity is Edgar in *King Lear* masquerading as a Kentish 'base peasant'. His *Chill not let go*, *zir*, *without vurther 'casion* looks like eighteenth-century south-western English, but the scene is 'the Country near Dover' and the dialect probably Kentish.

A poem called 'A ride to London zitty' written by an anonymous writer some time between 1561 and 1666 has *Ice* for *I* with main verbs and *ch* with auxiliaries, *have* and *am*: *Ice stood*, *Ice tould*, *Ice zmeled*, *chad* 'I had', *chil give* 'I'll give'. 'The Somerset man's complaint' (said to be written by Thomas Davies between 1614 and 1684) has *ch* as a proclitic with auxiliaries, *have* and *be*, but the full form, used with true verbs, is *I* rather than *Ice*, so that one finds *chill sell my cart* but *I goe* instead of the earlier *Ice goe*. In the *Exmoor Scolding* and the *Exmoor Courtship* (1746) the form of *I* is *'ch* with the verbs *have* and *am* and the auxiliaries (with the exception of *do*): *cham* 'I am', *chave* 'I have, *chont* 'I won't', etc.); elsewhere the form for 'I' is *es*, i.e. *us* (spelt *ees* once).

Ich seems to have become a fossil and locally very restricted by the latter half of the nineteenth century. Elworthy does not regard *'ch* as a living form of west Somerset English in the late nineteenth century (Elworthy 1875, 1877–9 and 1886). In the 'Preface' to his 1879 edition of *An Exmoor Scolding and Courtship*, he points out that *'ch* 'is now completely obsolete, and has been so, longer than the memory of the oldest inhabitant' (p. 15). However, Ellis (1889: 84–5) found evidence of *ich* in a small area in Somerset near Montacute. He calls this area the Land of Utch. There seems to have been some confusion in people's minds between *utch* and *us*, which was also used for 'I', as shown by Ellis' Montacute sample. L. L. Bonaparte made a special effort to attest *ich*. He reports from Cannington, near Bridgwater, that *itchy* was still used by old people. His informant was a 94-year-old man called Edward Wills (Bonaparte 1875–6: 579). As late as 1951, Peter Wright, one of the *SED* fieldworkers, recorded [ɪtʃ] two or three times on tape in conversation with a Somerset farmer in his forties. This was at Merriott, just west of Montacute, in Ellis' Land of Utch (Wakelin 1977: 165). These comments show that compared with the seventeenth century, *ich* was exceptional in the nineteenth century. That *ich*, in spite of its frequency in contemporary dialect literature, probably was rare and locally restricted even in the eighteenth century is suggested by the fact that Fielding does not use it as a dialect marker in *Tom Jones* although this work is rich in West Country pronominal forms. For all practical purposes, then, *ich* had become obsolete by the end of the nineteenth century. According to the *OED*, I 'in the forms *ich*, *utch*, *ch-*, *che*, or *utchy*, remained in s.w. dialects till the 18th or first half of the 19th c.'. As we have seen, this chronology is not quite accurate, but is close enough if 'remained' is replaced by 'remained in general use'.

The other form of 'I', spelt *es* in south-western dialect texts like the *Exmoor Courtship*, Elworthy believes to be *us* used for the singular (*us* was in fact pronounced something like /es/ in north Devon English in Elworthy's time). This sounds reasonable considering that *us* is still used as a subject in Devon and there is a widespread tendency in non-standard (and also sometimes in standard) English, not restricted to the south-west, to use *us* for the first person singular, at least in the object position. I have heard *bona fide* sentences like *Excuse us* for *Excuse me* quite recently even from young speakers.

Finite *be*: *They be nice* 'They're nice'

Halliwell (1881) notes both *be* and *ben* for 'am', 'is' and 'are', but simply labels them as dialectal without trying to locate them. His samples suggest a south-western distribution: finite *be* shows up in the Sussex, Hampshire, Gloucestershire, Devon and Wiltshire samples. Halliwell's reluctance to localise finite *be* suggests that at that time it had a much wider distribution than it has today. However, it is prominent as a dialect marker in eighteenth-century south-western dialect texts, and in the nineteenth century *I be* even ousts the former *'cham*. Thus, the *'cham* of *Exmoor Courtship* (1746) shows regularly as *I be* in ' Jim an' Nell' (1867), both representing Devon dialect.

Lowth (1762: 36) still lists *I/we/you/they be* as possible finite forms in 'polite' English, but adds that *be* with singular subjects is obsolete and 'is become somewhat antiquated in the plural'. The distribution of finite *be* reported by the *SED* is displayed on *LAE* maps M1–M19: for instance, the map for 'I am' shows an area west of a line running from Sussex to south Cheshire, with the north-western tip of this area having *I bin* rather than the suffixless *I be*. According to *EDD*, however, *be* was formerly much more widespread, occurring in the entire east up to Lincolnshire and Nottinghamshire, as well as in the south and south-west. Ellis (1889) reports limited use of finite *be* from Norfolk and southern east midlands, but, by and large, regards finite *be* as a characteristically south-western feature.

Plural *am*: *They'm nice*

This is a common south-western and west midland feature today. The history of plural *am* has not been worked out, but it appears to be a post-Middle English development (Wakelin 1975). One early dialect text to use this feature is ' Jim an' Nell' (Rock 1867), where forms like *they be* and *they'm* for *they're* alternate. In the south-west plural *am* is contracted; in the west midlands a full form is also used. Darlington (1887) gives forms like *How-r am jo?* 'How are you?' (with an intrusive *r*) to illustrate Cheshire English. The syntax of plural *am* is complicated by many other factors that to my knowledge have never been properly studied: for instance, although plural *am* occurs with the pronoun *we* in Devon English, the form *us'm* does not seem to occur. There is no such restriction on pronoun exchange with finite *be*: *us be* is a common Devon form.

The present indicative marker *-th*

During the eighteenth century the *-th* present-tense marker continued to be used in formal styles in standard English, but appears to have become regional in everyday speech. Lowth (1762) lists both *he loveth* and *he loves* in his verb paradigm without further comment. However, in his auxiliary section he points out that '*hath* properly belongs to the serious and solemn style; *has* to the familiar' (p. 35). His own usage appears to have been variable, with the *-th* suffix mainly appearing with auxiliaries.

Marshall, a northerner, was struck by the use of the *-th* ending in Devon English (1796). For Marshall the *-th* ending appears to have been a definite provincialism. Fielding's *Tom Jones* has *-th* with auxiliaries, whereas true verbs take the *-s* ending. Elworthy (1886) already regards *-th* forms as marginal in west Somerset. Here Somerset seems to differ from Devon, where Chope (1891) still finds it productive. Ellis (1889: 157–8) too reports the *-th* ending from Devon, especially in north Devon. The samples in Halliwell (1881) show a mixed situation in the south-west: for example, in Wiltshire people already said *They works* whereas the Devon form was *They work'th*.

The *SED* still reports stray instances of the *-th* ending from the south-west (Cornwall 1, Devon 9 and 10; Wakelin 1977: 119); but these are rare examples and *-th* seems to have been widely replaced by the *-s* ending or periphrastic *do* during the nineteenth century. The south-western *-th* present-tense marker was, as the more modern *-s* marker still is, used with all grammatical persons of the verb except the second person singular, which takes *-st*. The use of forms like *They likes it*, common in earlier educated varieties of English, appears to have become dialectal in the eighteenth century: for instance, Lowth (1762) allows only uninflected plural present-tense forms. The only plural ending he refers to is the present indicative *-en*, which he says 'hath long been obsolete' (p. 31).

The retreat of earlier southern features like the *-th* present tense marker and *ich* 'I' appears to have been to the south-west, Devon and Somerset in particular.

Periphrastic *do*

The use of periphrastic – that is, unstressed – *do* in affirmatives appears to have become obsolete in polite English in the eighteenth century. Samuel Johnson (1755: 8) notes it but discourages its use: '*do* is sometimes used superfluously, as in *I do love, I did love*: but this is considered a vitious mode of speech'. Charles Coote (1788) simply says such usage is archaic. Although Halliwell does not list *do* as a provincialism, his Somerset and Dorset samples show it. Periphrastic *do* is spelt *da*, as in *Birds da look*, to distinguish it from the true verb *do*. Another difference between periphrastic *do* and the true verb *do* is that the auxiliary does not take the -s suffix. This restriction still holds in south-western English: I recently recorded sentences like *I still dos* [duːz] *a bit of gardening* and *She da* [də] *live by the pub* from Somerset (*CCDE*, Somerset). Jennings (1825) lists a number of south-western, particularly Somerset, features. These include *Har'th a doo'd it* 'She has done it', *I be* 'I am', *they'm* 'they are', but not periphrastic verb forms. For Ellis (1889), however, periphrastic *do* is one of the hallmarks of south-western English. Wakelin (1984: 83) shows an area roughly covering Dorset and parts of Cornwall, Wiltshire and Somerset. But Klemola (forthcoming b) shows that the *do* area is much larger and (with the exception of Devon) covers approximately the area where initial fricatives are voiced. The grammar of periphrastic *do* is discussed in Ihalainen (1976) and Weltens (1983).

5.4.4 East Anglia

Early nineteenth-century East Anglian characteristics include such grammatical features as uninflected present-tense forms (*He say*), *that* and *ta* 'it' (*That rain* 'It rains'), otiose *of*, as in *She's ollas a-eating o' thapes* 'She's always eating gooseberries'. Otiose *of* is also found in south-western texts from that period, but it seems to have had a less prominent role as a dialect marker in people's minds there, although it has persisted even to the present day, as can be heard from the *SED* and *CCDE* tape-recordings. The reason for the prominence of this feature in East Anglian texts may simply be that there were fewer dialectal characteristics for writers to choose from than for writers using south-western English.

The term 'Norwich *a*' refers to the unrounding of the vowel in words like *top* and *dog* and *straw*. It is one of the features exploited by Larwood in his 'Norfolk dialogue' (1800). Norfolk *a* was still common enough in the late twentieth century to be used by Peter Trudgill as a socio-linguistic variable in a study of Norwich English (Trudgill 1974). However, the unrounded vowel is being replaced by a rounded vowel (Trudgill 1986: 42).

Larwood's *Dialogue* also shows a monophthong, probably [ɛː], in *sa* 'say', *da* 'day'. Kökeritz (1932) reports [ɛː] in these words in Suffolk English, but Wakelin (1988b: 172) calls spellings like *sa* 'doubtful'. However, Larwood's spelling practice that 'omitted letters indicate omitted sounds' suggests a monophthong. Larwood's spelling practice also suggests a monophthong [ɛː] in *par* 'pair'. There is also evidence that [ɜ] was realised as [aː], as in *barn* 'burn' and *har* 'her'. However, there is no evidence for the present-day *beer/bear* merger (i.e. *bear* and *beer* are pronounced [bɛː]) in Larwood's *Dialogue* or in Forby (1830). Judging from Trudgill (1974) and Trudgill & Foxcroft (1978), this merger is of quite recent origin. Nor is there evidence of modification of the pronunciation of the vowel in words like *moon*. Ellis seems to have regarded the *moon* vowel as an important characteristic of Norwich English. He calls it, rather hesitatingly, 'French (y)', but admits that 'the exact analysis of this curious sound is still to be made' (1889: 260–1). The sound is probably a centralised [uː], a modification that is very difficult to represent in conventional spelling.

5.4.5   The Cockney interchange of v and w

The interchange of *v* and *w*, as in *winegar* 'vinegar' and *voif* 'wife', was censured as a Cockney feature by both Sheridan (1762) and Walker (1791). However, it is in no way restricted to Cockney only. It appears to have been common in East Anglian English (Forby 1830: 102) and can be found in various other parts of the south-east (Wakelin 1977: 95). The interchange of *v* and *w* became very popular in literary Cockney, where it lived long after it had become obsolete in real Cockney. One of the best-known confusers of *v* and *w* is Dickens' Sam Weller, who calls himself Veller. The interchange of *v* and *w* seems to have disappeared towards the end of the nineteenth century (Ellis 1889: 230; Wells 1982, II: 333) although the *SED* still reports stray instances from the south-east of England.

What is interesting about the situation is that there are no signs in the early nineteenth-century evidence of such striking characteristics of present-day Cockney as *lidy*/laɪdɪi/ for *lady* and *bowt* /bʌʊt/ for *boat*.[10] These pronunciations were first attested in the late nineteenth century, about the same time the interchange of *v* and *w* disappeared from descriptions of Cockney (Ellis 1889: 226–34). Nor is there any sign at this stage of *th-* fronting (i.e. *wiv* 'with', *fink* 'think'), *t*-glottaling or *l*-vocalisation, as in [mɪək] 'milk'.

5.4.6   The south-east

As in the case of the east midlands, there appears to be very little evidence for the reconstruction of south-eastern English in the early nineteenth century. Halliwell correctly notes that south-eastern areas such as Kent belonged to the linguistic south, but former characteristics like the voicing of initial fricatives or *ich* for 'I' had subsequently receded to the West Country. There are references to the interchange of *w* and *v*, but not, for instance, to *I are* 'I am', attested by Ellis (1889) and the *SED* in the mid-twentieth century.

5.4.7   Some general characteristics

The evidence shows that some of the basic structural characteristics of present-day dialects had already established themselves by the early nineteenth century. For instance, present-tense marking distinguishes between the following areas:

(1)   The north
   a. He makes them.
   b. They make them.
   c. Farmers makes them.

(2)   Northern west midlands (e.g. the Potteries)
   a. He makes them.
   b. They maken them.
   c. Farmers maken them.

(3)   East Anglia
   a. He make them.
   b. They make them.
   c. Farmers make them.

(4)   The south-west and the south
   a. He makes them.
   c. They makes them.
   d. Farmers makes them.

Parts of the south-west have periphrastic *do* in addition to the universal *-s* marking:

(5)   a. He da make them.
   b. They da make them.
   c. Farmers da make them.

The distribution of the present-tense forms of *be* in the early nineteenth century also shows a pattern that resembles the present-day situation, with the reservation that we do not actually know the details of the distribution of *I are* until Ellis (1889). *I is* was found in the north, *I be* in the south-west and southern west midlands (although stray instances are reported from southern east midlands and northern East Anglia) and *I are* in the south-east. Cullum's glossary (1813) suggests that the *are* area extended at least to Suffolk in the east.

Second person singular forms

Another important feature that characterises much of England and helps us differentiate between the major areas is the use of second person singular forms. These forms appear to have been completely lost in standard English in the eighteenth century. Lowth (1762: 34) states quite categorically: '*Thou* in polite, and even in the familiar stile is disused, and the plural *you* is employed instead of it; we say, *you have*, not *thou hast.*' (Lowth differentiates between the subject pronoun *ye* and the object pronoun *you* in his paradigm, but uses only *you* himself.)

Marshall (1788: 41) lists the use of *thou* as a Yorkshire provincialism and comments on it as follows:

> *Thou.* This pronoun is still much in use. Farmers in general 'thou' their servants; the inferior class (and the lower class of men in general), frequently their wives, and always their children; and the children as invariably 'thou' each other. Superiors in general 'thou' their inferiors; while inferiors 'you' their betters. Equals and intimates of the lower class generally 'thou' one another. These distinctions are sometimes the cause of awkwardness: to 'you' a man may be making too familiar; while to 'thou' him might affront him.[11]

The *SED* data displayed on *LAE* map M67 show a wide area where the second-person pronoun was still used in the mid-twentieth century. The area covers the north, the west midlands and the south-west. However, the usage is not unified in this area. To simplify the matter slightly, there are two systems: the northern and the west midland/south-western system.

In the northern variety the subject/object, or *thou/thee*, distinction is preserved. Usually the subject pronoun also has a separate enclitic form, as in *Ista ready?* The verb in this system usually takes an -*s* ending, as in *Thou/Tha knows.*

The west midland/south-western system shows object pronoun generalisation, as in *Thee'st know all about it* 'You know all about it' and *I'll let thee have some tools.* At least in the south-west, tense in these constructions is indicated periphrastically by using *dost*, phonetically realised as [s] (which may be voiced in a voiced environment). The -*st* may stand for other second-person auxiliaries like *shouldst*, *wouldst*, but not *can*, which has the forms *cass* 'canst' and *cassn* 'canst not'. A subject form *thee* occurs in the south-west and south- and mid-west midlands up to north Shropshire.

In the early 1970s, on my very first day of doing fieldwork in

Somerset, I was asked by an old man at John's Lodge *Cassn ʒee un, cass?* 'You can't see it, can you?' (I was looking for a bicycle valve cap that I had dropped.) This kind of language came to me as quite a shock. I knew from Elworthy's *Grammar of West Somerset* that second-person forms like this were used in the south-west in the late nineteenth century, but I did not expect to hear them in the 1970s. However, it turned out that in intimate style, when you talk to someone you are 'pally wi'', the second-person pronoun was still used. In 1982 I had a rare chance of talking to a number of Somerset speakers who had this pronoun in their own speech. It turned out that in Somerset *thee art* and similar forms were still used in the intimate style. The *CCED* tape-recordings show forms like *Thee's had me rabbits, What's say?* 'What do you say?', *I ha'n' had thee rabbits* 'I haven't had your rabbits', *They say 'tis, thee, Jack. I said, What's say? Well, they say 'tis thee, He said, 'Thee art a man'.*

However, there are indications that the use of second person singular forms is being restricted not only by stylistic but also by linguistic factors. This produces highly mixed grammars. Examples of this mixed usage are reported in Ihalainen (1986, 1991) and Wright (1989). One characteristic usage concerns emphasis and emotion, as in the following interchange from Somerset, where *thee* appears as a salient form of *you*:

> A: How old are you, Bert?
> B: Gone seventy-six.
> A: Gone seventy-six! Thee! Thee! (Ihalainen 1986: 376)

Peter Wright (1989: 239) notes mixed usages like *Hey up* (= *Hello!*), *you're right up there, aren't thou?*, but does not comment on the possible conditioning factors regulating the choice of the pronoun. Wright's personal impression is that *thou* has disappeared quite dramatically from South Yorkshire and north-east Derbyshire.

Tidholm's 1979 study of Egton (North Yorkshire) English finds that *thou* is disappearing. What is interesting about this development is that although young speakers use *you* instead of the earlier *thou* they nevertheless retain the *-s* ending, as can be seen from Tidholm's transcriptions (p. 171). This, of course, produces forms that seem to violate the northern subject rule.

Pronoun exchange

Pronouns in dialect show two distinct tendencies. One is the development of two markedly different sets of pronouns, full and weak forms; the latter are usually enclitic, as the pronoun *us* 'we' in Somerset sentences like *Didn's get it?* 'Didn't we get it?' The other tendency is to exchange pronominal forms. The term 'pronoun exchange' refers to a complex area of pronominal morphosyntax, but one way of defining it is to say that it refers to cases where subject forms of pronouns are used for object pronouns and object forms for subject pronouns, as in *Her told I* 'She told me', a sentence that I heard over the phone recently (1991). Traces of pronoun exchange can of course be found in standard English, where the oblique form *you* has replaced the earlier subject pronoun *ye*, but in dialect its use is extensive. One early comment on pronoun exchange comes from Marshall. In his 'Provincialisms of the Vale of Glocester' (attached to *The Rural Economy of Glocestershire*), Marshall notes that in Gloucestershire pronouns are 'abused, the nominative and the accusative cases being generally reversed' (1789: 56). Judging from Marshall's strong reaction, pronoun exchange appears to have been quite unknown to this Yorkshireman. He calls this phenomenon 'misapplication', 'abuse' and 'deviation'. These are very strong terms from someone who otherwise shows a great deal of understanding for regional variation. Somewhat unexpectedly, Marshall's 'Provincialisms of West Devonshire' (1796) makes no reference to any pronominal 'abuse' although there is every reason to believe that Devon deviations were even more marked than the ones Marshall heard in Gloucester. Perhaps by the time he got to Devon he had already got used to these. Early dialect literature and glossaries show a complete absence of pronoun exchange in northern English, but make frequent reference to it in the west midlands and the south-west. The *SED* shows a distribution similar to this. Judging by the *SED* material, the most widespread case of pronoun exchange is the use of *her* for *she*. It can be found in an area extending from the east of Sussex up to Derbyshire and Lancashire (where *hoo* occurs alongside *her* as a subject pronoun; *LAE* maps M68 and M69). Pronoun exchange is interesting in that it is one of the few features that divide the country up in an east–west direction.

5.5 Awareness of dialect as reflected by the number of writings in and on English dialects up to 1877

The English Dialect Society bibliography, which covers dialect texts and studies of dialect up to 1877, gives an idea of the amount of attention various regional varieties had attracted. The ten most popular counties are Lancashire, Yorkshire, Cumberland, Cornwall, Northumbria, Devon, Westmorland, Dorset, Somerset and Norfolk. By far the most popular dialect is northern English, followed by south-western and East Anglian English. Of particular interest here is the large figure for Lancashire. Intuitively, one would have guessed that the variety that has attracted the greatest deal of attention would be Yorkshire.[12]

There is one important development in the awareness of non-standard speech which is not obvious from the dialect stories, glossaries and studies on dialect listed in the *EDS* bibliography. This is the emergence of Cockney as the prototypical vulgar form of English. The importance of Cockney from the late eighteenth century onwards can be seen from the fact that it is the only non-standard English variety that Sheridan (1780) and Walker (1791), the leading authorities on spoken English, discuss in any detail. 'Provincial' Englishes are simply lumped together with comments such as 'almost every county has its own dialect'. Cockney is also promoted as a literary dialect at the expense of the earlier rustic southern variety of the 'Chill not let go, zir, without vurther 'casion' type, now rapidly being confined to the West Country.[13]

The change of interest from rural to urban varieties of English would appear to reflect the massive urbanisation going on in Britain about that time. Liverpool increased its population tenfold from 1680 to 1760; Manchester multiplied fivefold between 1717 and 1773. The growing interest of writers and grammarians in urban varieties of English has a natural explanation.

5.6 Ellis' survey of English dialects (1889)

Alexander Ellis' *On Early English Pronunciation*, Part V, *The Existing Phonology of English Dialects* (1889) is the first survey of English dialects based on rich, systematically collected evidence. Before Ellis, His Imperial Highness Prince Louis Lucien Bonaparte had published a classification of English dialects in 1875–6, and it was Bonaparte who gave Ellis his 'first conceptions of a classification of English dialects'. Bonaparte also provided Ellis with a number of specimens for his survey. However, Ellis' work far surpasses anything done before him. In spite of criticism directed towards it, Ellis' collection continues to be an important source of data for English dialectology.[14] Equally important are Ellis' comments on a number of historical developments and his first-hand observations on contemporary folk speech. Passages like the one depicting Dr Ellis checking his fieldworkers' transcriptions against the shouts of fishmongers in a Norwich street give one an idea of his dedication. A good example of Ellis' detective work on language change is his tracing of the loss of the v/w commutation from Cockney and the rise of the modern 'lidies in the bowt' shibboleth towards the end of the nineteenth century.

Ellis developed three data-gathering tools: the comparative specimen (c.s.), the classified word-list (c.w.l.) and the dialect test (d.t.). The comparative specimen was a text of fifteen sentences to be read by informants. The purpose was to obtain 'dialect renderings of familiar words in various connections and some characteristic constructions'. Ellis' instructions to those who administered this test in the field call attention to seventy-six specific points in these sentences. The classified word-list had 971 items. Numbers 1–712 were 'Wessex and Norse' words; 713–808 were 'English' words; 809–971 were words of Romance origin. The dialect test was a short reading passage of seventy-six words. The three tools developed at different stages of research between 1873 and 1879. Not all of these three tools were necessarily employed at each locality investigated. Nevertheless, usually enough data were collected to give a reasonable picture of the dialect concerned.

Ellis also recognised the importance of pitch and intonation differences as dialect markers and he refers to these in his various descriptions, although in rather vague terms. He attached to the 'classified word-list' notes on intonation. The helpers are instructed to do the following: 'Try to characterise the nature of the singsong of the speech, underlining as may be, rough, smooth, thick, thin, indistinct, clear, hesitating, glib, whining, drawling, jerking, up and down in pitch, rising in pitch at end, sinking at end, monotonous' (1889: 25*).[15] Not much useful information was gathered by this method, though, besides the fact that we learn in general terms where intonation was a striking feature (the western division, Scotland) or where it might actually differentiate between related dialects (Norfolk and Suffolk). Even today, although the relevance of intonation as a dialect marker is clearly recognised (Wells 1982, I: 91) our ignorance in this area is considerable.

Ellis' 811 voluntary helpers gathered data from 1,454 localities, seventy-five of these being in Wales or Scotland. Most of the data were in modified orthography, which Ellis, assisted by Hallam, converted into a home-made transcription called 'palaeotype'. Thomas Hallam was one of Ellis' most significant helpers; his employment on the railways made it possible to cover much of the midlands and the north. He was one of the few of Ellis' assistants who were able to render responses directly into palaeotype.

Below is an example of the response that Ellis' dialect test sentence no. 5 'We all know him very well' elicited from Upper Cumberworth (6 miles south-east of Huddersfield; Ellis' district 24, variety V, i). The informant was Mrs Ann Littlewood (born 1824). The response was rendered into palaeotype by Hallam in 1881.

(6)   wi ʌʌl noon ɪm vári wiil 'We all know him very well'   (Ellis 1889: 380)

The difference between the lower case 'i' of 'wi' on the one hand and the italic lower case *i* of 'ɪm' and 'vári' on the other, is that of a tense and lax vowel, that is [i] vs [ɪ]. Doubling indicates length. Thus the vowel of 'wiil', although longer than the vowel of 'wi' is identical with it in quality. The grave accent (`) indicates an intermediate length between long and short. Thus the lax *i* of 'ɪm' is longer than the lax *i* of 'vári'. The ʌʌ of ʌʌl 'all' is a raised [ɒ]. The phonetic value of the italicised double *o* of 'noon' is [oː]. The acute accent (´) is used to characterise stress. It is particularly useful for the description of diphthongs and complex vowels. Of grammatical interest here is the plural indicative marker *-en* in *we known*, an old midland characteristic.

What is obvious from even this short sample is that interpreting Ellis' transcriptions requires a lot of effort. A useful, critical discussion of Ellis' palaeotype with IPA renderings of a number of his symbols can be found in Eustace (1969).

5.6.1   Ellis' dialect areas

Ellis divides England into five major divisions on the basis of ten 'transverse lines' (i.e., isoglosses): southern, western, eastern, midland, northern. These were further divided into 'districts', which in their turn were divided into 'varieties'. Ellis' divisions and districts can be seen from the map on page 236.

The ten transverse lines (1889: 15–22)

Ellis' main classificatory criteria were phonological. Only four features were used: the pronunciation of words like *some*, the pronunciation of *r*, the pronunciation of the definite article, the pronunciation of words like *house*. The application of these criteria to his evidence, then, resulted in 10 'transverse lines' or isoglosses. These are the following:

Line 1: the n. *sum* line or northern limit of the pronunciation of *some* as [sʌm] in southern England. The pronunciation [sʌm] re-appears north of line 8. Ellis regarded the unrounded variant as a 'modernism and an encroachment'. He comments on its dialectal status as follows: 'Hence we may expect to find that it is not a sufficient mark of a difference of district, because all other characters may remain and the modern (ɜ) [i.e. [ʌ]] may have only partially prevailed. Also intermediate forms may prevail arising from the encroachment being still incomplete.' It is interesting to note a hundred years later, while Ellis' latter 'anticipation' still held, dialectologists found that the *sum*/*soom* line had actually become the primary boundary in England, with the line for such earlier main diaglosses as the northern lack of rounding retreating towards the Scottish–English border (Chambers & Trudgill 1980: 129–37; Trudgill 1990: 76).

Line 2: the s. *soom* line. This is the southern limit of the pronunciation of the word *some* as [sʊm] in England. The northern limit is line 9.

Line 3: the reverted *ur* (ʀ) line. The northern limit of the pronunciation of *r* as a 'reverted' (i.e. retroflex) or a 'retracted' sound. The reverted sound is written (ʀ) and the retracted (rʹ). (Retracted is defined as an *r* pronounced 'with retracted instead of reverted tip of the tongue, which approaches the hard palate', p. 85*.)

Ellis comments on this isogloss as follows: 'Sporadically and through natural defects of pronunciation, reverted *ur* (ʀ) may be heard still more northerly, and even to the w. in D 13. But it ceases to be the regular pron. at this limit, and even in D 9 the *ur* frequently sinks into the common received vocal *er*.' It appears that the pronunciation, incidence, regional distribution and social status of *r* was unsettled in Ellis' day and this situation continued for a long time. A good idea of the complexity of the *r*-phenomena can be gained from Eustace (1969).

The *SED* shows a reverted *r* area that is considerably larger than Ellis' (see *LAE* map Ph11 'arm' for the mid-twentieth-century distribution of [ʈ]). But the *SED*, of course, shows only a small number of citation forms and it is unable to show whether the usage was variable or categorical in spontaneous speech, which was Ellis' criterion for placing line 3.

Line 4: the *teeth* line. This is the southern limit of the use for the definite article of 'suspended (t‛)' (commonly written *t'* in dialect books) or of the hiss '(th)', that is, [θ], as heard at the end of *teeth*. Ellis chose the word *teeth* as the name for this line because *teeth* contains both [t] and [θ].

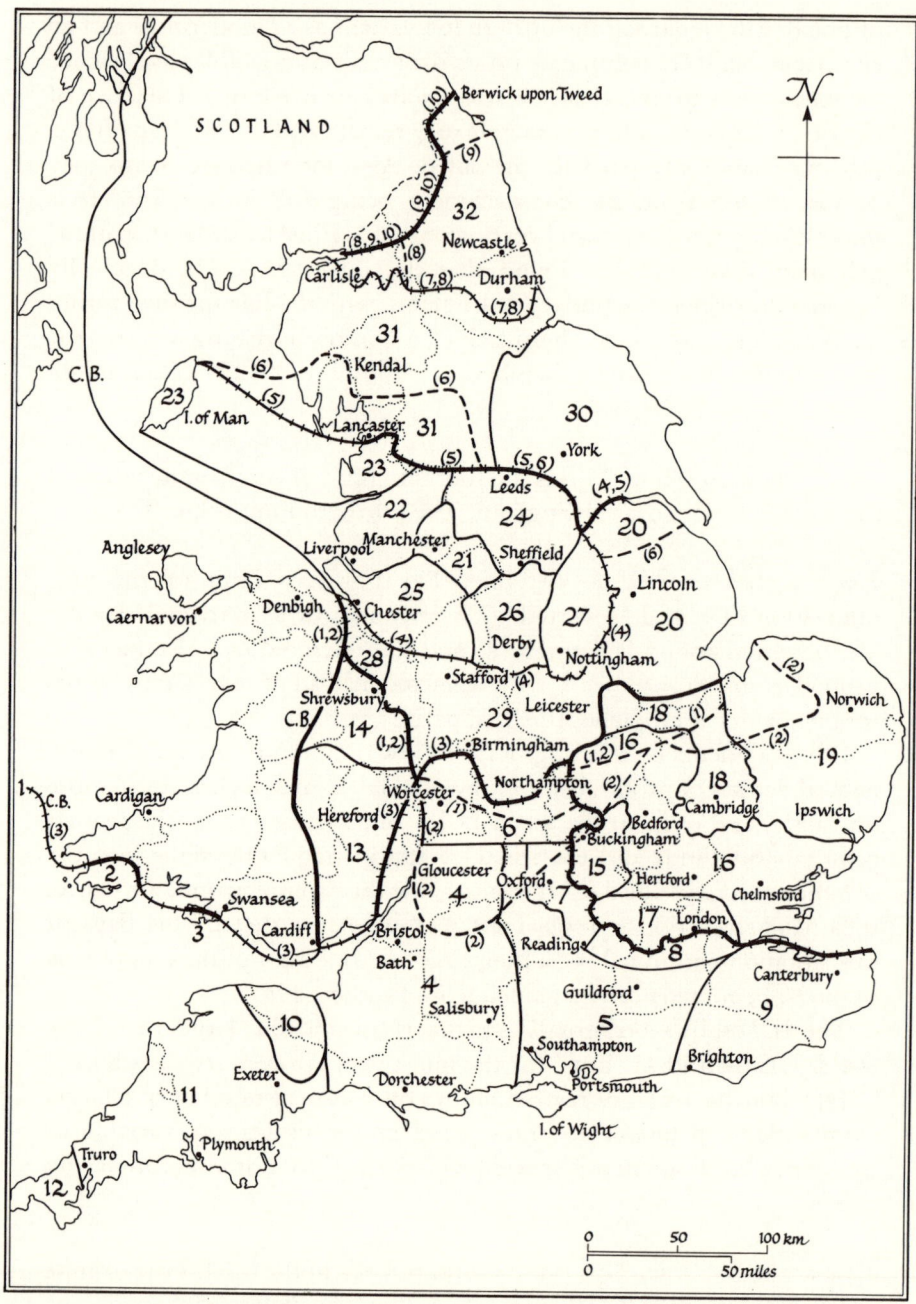

Map 5.1   English dialect districts, 1887 (redrawn from Ellis' map in his *On Early English Pronunciation*, 1889)

Line 5: the *theeth* line. The northern limit of the use of the standard form of *the* and the hiss (th), i.e. [θ], in conjunction with suspended (t`) as the definite article, till *the* returns to the north of line 7.

Line 6: the s. *hoose* line. The southern limit of the pronunciation of the word *house* as [hu:s]. The *hoose* line is also the northern limit of the [haus] pronunciation of *house*.

Line 7: the northern *tee* line. The northern limit of the suspended (t`) for the definite article.

Line 8: the southern *sum* line in northern England or the southern limit of the unrounding in words like *some*. Here the direction is 'travelling from Scotland into England'.

Line 9: the northern *soom* line. The northern limit of any variety of the [sʊm] pronunciation (which may be mixed with unrounded pronunciations), 'on proceeding from the Midland counties to Scotland'.

Line 10: the limit between 'L [Lowland] Scotch and N [Northern] English speech'. The linguistic border is 'not precisely coincident with the political boundary of England and Scotland': for instance, 'Berwick-on-Tweed and its Liberties, extending 2 to 4 miles into Bw.[Berwickshire], are linguistically part of England', whereas parts of Cumberland and Northumberland are assigned to Scotland (Ellis 1889: 21). Where the linguistic boundary should run seems to have been a controversial question. In this matter, Ellis' views differed from those of Murray and Bonaparte (see Glauser 1974: 49–55 for a discussion). This suggests that the linguistic situation around the border was rather complex, with spill-overs into the neighbour's territory. Since Ellis' day the political border seems to have become linguistically more important, with northern England becoming linguistically more sharply differentiated from Scotland.

5.6.2   Ellis' divisions

On the basis of the ten transverse lines, Ellis divides the dialects of Great Britain into six principal divisions, which are further divided into forty-two districts. The districts are further divided into varieties. The divisions and districts, but not the subdivisions, are indicated on a map attached to Part V of Ellis' *On Early English Pronunciation* (1889). The divisions and districts are the following:

I	The southern division: districts 1–12
II	The western division: districts 13 and 14
III	The eastern division: districts 15–19
IV	The midland division: districts 20–9
V	The northern division: districts 30–2
VI	The lowland division: districts 33–42

The main divisions and the districts in England and Wales are shown in map 5.1 from *On Early English Pronunciation*, Part V. Districts 1 to 3 of division I represent the 'Celtic Southern', that is Welsh, English, and division VI English as spoken in the Lowlands of Scotland. These will not be discussed here. In addition to the 'transverse lines' that are used to differentiate between the principal divisions, Ellis lists a number of other characteristics that he found within each division. Some of these will be discussed below. The following chart summarises the criteria used to differentiate between the divisions, that is, the main dialect areas.

Ellis 1889	Reverted *r*	*soom*	*t'*	*t'* and *th'* [θ]	*hoose*
South	yes	no	no	no	no
West	(uncertain)	no	no	no	no
East	no	no	no	no	no
Mid	no	yes	no	yes*	no
North	no	yes*	yes*	no	yes

The asterisk (*) indicates that the feature characterises much of the area but not necessarily all of it. Thus much of the north-west of England does not have the *t'* realisation of the definite article, and there is a small area in Northumberland where *some* is *sum* rather than *soom*. Further differences between the general north and Northumberland include such lexical oppositions as *summat* vs *something*, *thou* vs *ye*, *seet* vs *sight*, *slape* vs *slippy* 'slippery', *nor* vs *than*, *wool* vs *ool* 'wool'. The '*t'*' in connection with *th'*' realisation of the definite article does not occur in the east or the south midlands.

Perhaps the most surprising anomaly here is that, besides the fact that these areas are geographically separated from each other, there is nothing to separate Ellis' west from his east. Both are 'straight no' dialects. On a lower level of abstraction, of course, the differences are striking. Problems like these pinpoint the difficulty of finding classificatory criteria that support our judgements about linguistic areas, are general enough to cover large areas and yet have considerable discriminatory power.

That a small number of criteria do not identify areas that are mutually exclusive simply shows something about dialect areas in general and should not give us concern. For instance, Ellis' *soom* and *sum* areas overlap in the east midlands (as they still do) to form a mixed area, a transition zone (Chambers & Trudgill 1980: ch. 8).

Ellis admits he is not quite happy with the reverted *r* line in the west. He says that it exists in his district 13 (the southern part of the western division), but adds that it is 'generally inconspicuous and often uncertain, so that it would not be possible to correct line 3' (1889: 176). The north Herefordshire sample immediately following this passage shows that reverted and non-reverted realisations of /r/ alternate. The *SED* reports *r*-retroflexion in almost the whole of Ellis' western division (*LAE* map Ph11 'arm').

The distinction between the south and the west division is further justified by the observation that some important southern and southwestern (i.e. 'Wessex') characteristics (such as the retraction of the *r*-sound or the retention of ME *ai*) are non-existent or weakened at best in Ellis' western division (D 13 and D 14). There is, of course, a lot to connect the southern part of Ellis' western division to at least the mid southern variety – both have finite *be* and periphrastic *do*, for instance – but Ellis' observations about the western division fractures in such words as *they*, *road*, *write* and *doubt* and their connection to standard English rather than any indigenous English dialect support his view that underlying much of the western division English is some type of 'Book English' rather than a 'pure' dialect. The main characteristics of Ellis' main divisions will be briefly discussed next.

The southern division

The defining characteristic is the 'reverted' or 'retracted' *r*. Southern districts 1–3 are called 'the Celtic Southern'. Since this variety occurs on what Ellis calls 'Celtic territory' – that is, in parts of Ireland and Wales – it will not be discussed here.

Although he still seems to use this label in its historical sense, Ellis is aware that the south is linguistically less unified than it used to be. The reverted *r* still prevails over the southern division, 'but the older main characters, as shewn in D 4, all of which were probably characteristic of the whole division, fade out gradually to the e. of D 4, and become complicated with other characters to the w.' (Ellis 1889: 23). To Ellis, then, the mid southern variety of southern English, which occupies 'the principal seat of the Wessex tribe' (Ellis 1889: 36), is a paradigmatic, historically pure representative southern variety of English.

LINGUISTIC CHARACTERISTICS OF THE MID SOUTHERN (I.E. 'WESSEX') VARIETY D 4

Linguistic features of the mid southern variety of southern English include 'reverted' or 'retracted' *r*, voicing of initial /s/ and /f/, the realisation of *thr-* as *dr-*, the use of /ai/ in words like *hay* and *way* and the centralisation of the first element in the diphthongs /au/ and /ai/. (The first element is said to be Bell's vowel number 22.)

The main grammatical characteristics are: finite *be* (*I be* 'I am'), prefixed participial forms (*a-done* 'done'), periphrastic *do* (*I do go* 'I go'), pronoun exchange (*Her told I* 'She told me'), *ən* for 'him' and 'it', *he* 'it' (as in, *Where's the knife? He's in the kitchen – where you left un*), *utch* 'I'. A point of historical significance about this list is that the older south-western *n*-less participial forms, as in *i-do* 'done' and *i-go* have been replaced by an *n*-ful form.[16]

Ellis' western division (districts 13 and 14)

Ellis characterises the western division type of English as basically Southern English with Welsh influence (D 13), giving in the west the impression of being 'book English spoken by foreigners or a mixture of S. and M. (D 14), where Southern forms are much used'.

The western division is bounded by the reverted *r* line and the *sum* line; that is, this variety does not retroflex the *r*-sound and has *sum* rather than *soom*.

The samples included show that Ellis' western dialects are rhotic, but the *r* is not exclusively the retracted or reverted variety of Southern English. As was pointed out above, Ellis nevertheless felt that there was not enough evidence to make it possible to correct line 3 in the west.

The western division covers portions of Monmouthshire, Herefordshire, Shropshire in England, and of Breconshire, Radnorshire and Montgomeryshire in Wales. Hereford is divided: South-Eastern Hereford belongs to D 4 (the mid southern), and the west of Hereford English becomes more like Welsh English. The western division 'represents on the east comparatively late, and on the west very modern invasions of the English language on the Welsh' (1889: 175).

Ellis finds D 13 an 'imperfect dialect' with a considerable amount of Welsh influence: 'In D 13 the groundwork is S. English, which has been altered by Celts in a different way from D 10, 11" (i.e., Cornwall, Devon, West Somerset).

PHONOLOGICAL FEATURES OF DISTRICT 13

Among the phonological characteristics of D 13 Ellis mentions the 'fine (ö)' for [ʌ] ('fine (ö)' is a central, schwa-type vowel) and the diphthongs /ai/ and /au/, which have a 'fine (ö)' as their first element. (For a phonetic interpretation of Ellis' (ö), see Eustace (1969)). Furthermore, Ellis finds the use of [ai] for Middle English *ai*, a south-western characteristic, 'uncertain', and initial *ʒ* and *v* (i.e. voicing of initial fricatives) almost extinct; *dr-* for *thr-* (as in *three*) is lost. In other words, some of the strongest south-western characteristics are doubtful here. As a regional idiosyncrasy Ellis mentions the form /əθ/ 'with'. This may seem like an irrelevant detail at first sight, but it is worth noting that *with* is usually realised as *wi'* in the south-west. The samples show forms like *I be*, /jənt/ 'isn't' and *her's* 'she is'.

Ellis finds Welsh intonation 'influential' in parts of the western division. For instance, Monmouthshire English is described as 'book English with Welsh intonation and Herefordshire or Gloucestershire tendencies' (1889: 183). Pitch movements in Welsh-influenced English, as in the pronunciation of the word *likely*, are likened to pitch movements in Norwegian. These intonational features are noticeable even today; they create a strange impression of West Country grammar being spoken with the 'wrong' accent.

The samples illustrating the varieties of English spoken in District 13 actually suggest to the reader clear grammatical affinities to south-western English. But this aspect of the data is not elaborated on by Ellis.

DISTRICT 14 OF THE WESTERN DIVISION

According to Ellis, the reverted *r* is totally absent. Unlike in D 13, where this feature was 'uncertain', 'Southern' /ai/ (i.e., /ai/ for Middle English *ai*) in words like *day* does occur in D 14. The *SED* data on Middle English *ai*, published in *AES* maps 119 to 130, shows that this pattern still obtains. What is interesting here is that D 13 separates D 14 from the larger /ai/-pronouncing area to the south of the western division. It is possible, then, that D 14 is a residue of an earlier larger area cut off from it by some later developments. As in D 13, /ai/ and /au/ have the 'fine (ö)' as their first element. On the other hand, features like the plural present indicative *-en* (*We bin* 'We are', *We do-en* 'We do') and negations of the type *bina* 'aren't' clearly point to the Midlands and thus distinguish D 14 from D 13.

The eastern division (districts 15–19)

The eastern division covers the whole or greater part of Bedfordshire, Buckinghamshire, Cambridgeshire, Essex, Hertfordshire, Huntingdonshire, Middlesex, Norfolk, Northamptonshire, Rutland, Suffolk and the London metropolitan area. According to Ellis, eastern division English has 'a closer resemblance to received speech than in any other division' (p. 188). The pronunciation in this area is not quite uniform, but the differences are 'so slight that it has been found extremely difficult to obtain satisfactory information'. This is basically a non-retroflex, *sum*-area, but in the north there is a mixed *sum/soom* region. This mixture seems to have persisted to our days, as can be seen from Chambers & Trudgill (1980: 129–137). Cockney, which is described as eastern and east metropolitan in origin, is treated as part of district 17 ('South Eastern'), but its independent status is recognised by Ellis' division of the south-eastern varieties into 'Metropolitan English' or 'London Town Speech' and 'Rural Speech'.

District 19 is East Anglia, one of the areas that, as we have seen, had attracted the attention of early writers on English dialects. Ellis points out that Norfolk and Suffolk English are widely known for their intonation, but regrets that there is no way of describing these characteristics. Another salient point is the so-called 'French (y), of which every one speaks' (p. 260). This is the sound in words such as *moon*. He concludes that the Norfolk sound is of recent origin and different from the Lancashire *moon* vowel. Ellis' symbol for the East Anglian *moon* vowel is a lower-case upright y with the subscript $_1$. This is defined as 'a modification of Fr[ench] *u* in a direction not precisely ascertained' (1889: 87*). The sound is apparently often fractured by beginning with the mouth too open. Ellis concludes his discussion of the *moon* vowel by stating that 'the exact analysis of this curious sound is still to be made'. Dialect writers represent this sound by *ew*, as in *tew*, or by *u* as in *mune*. More recent transcriptions of East Anglian English show a centralised vowel, which may be diphthongised (Kökeritz 1938/9: 41–8; Lodge 1984: 110–20). Kökeritz, however, finds that in Suffolk English the *moon* vowel shows a great deal of variation and that it is often diphthongised, as in [jɛu] 'you'.

Other East Anglian characteristics referred to by Ellis are the following: words like *name* have a monophthong /e:/ (at least in Norfolk) and words like *boat* (i.e. words with an original OE *a:*) have /o:/. The *ride* and *house* vowels show considerable variation. *W* and *v* are commutable, but Ellis believes only the use of *w* for *v* to be indigenous, whereas *v* for *w* is a hyperurbanism resulting from an attempt to speak received English. East Anglian English has a 'euphonic *r*', that is, an *r* sound in contexts like *draw-r-ing* 'drawing'. It is one of the few local dialects that do not drop aitches. (For the subsequent spread of *h*-deletion to East Anglia, see Trudgill (1974, 1983: 76–7, 1990: 50).)

Considering how common the glottal stop is in this area today, it is somewhat significant that Ellis makes no mention of it. If this is not inattention, the development of the glottal stop in this area must have been recent and very rapid.

A distinctive grammatical characteristic is the use of uninflected third person singular forms like *He know it*. Interesting from the viewpoint of the development of dialect areas is Ellis' observation that, although positive forms of finite *be*, as in *I be tired* did not occur, negative forms did. This shows that the present finite *be* area was much larger in Ellis' day. It also shows that the retreat of finite *be* was gradual, with certain contexts retaining older forms longer than others. There are similar observations by Ellis from the east midlands, where finite *be* is obsolete today. The samples given by Ellis also show traces of the *a-* participial prefix. But these appear to be exceptional and the prefix was apparently being more and more confined to the south-west.

The midland division (districts 20–9; west midland 22, 25, 28)

The midland division, which is bounded on the south by the northern *sum* line (line 1) and on the north by the northern *theeth* line (line 5), covers all Cheshire, Derbyshire, Leicestershire, Lincolnshire, Nottinghamshire, Staffordshire, the north of Worcestershire and most of Warwickshire, south and mid Lancashire, the north-east of Shropshire. It also extends into Wales, covering 'all detached or English Fl. [i.e. Flint], a small part of main, or Welsh Fl., and of Dn. [i.e. Denbigh]'.

Dialectally the midland division falls into two distinct and apparently unrelated sections, an eastern comprising D 20 (Lincolnshire) and a western comprising the rest (p. 290).

Ellis points out that the midland area is not homogeneous and one cannot look for 'any one pervading character', but it must be 'defined by negatives': it does not have southern, western, eastern or northern characteristics. The linguistic points that Ellis regards as particularly significant include short *u*, *œ* for [u:], the diphthongisation of [i:], which according to Ellis is 'the first step in the change of [i:] to [aɪ], and the development of OE *uː* (standard English [au]), which in some part of the west midlands has undergone a further development to a monophthongal [a:]. Ellis finds *r*, when not before a vowel, totally vocalised in D 20, although he admits that this sound caused great difficulty even to phoneticians, and reliable information from lay assistants (who could not always keep spelling and pronunciation apart) was hard to get. Finally, Ellis found that in the midland division *h* was universally dropped.

Grammatical forms of interest are the definite article, the present indicative plural marker -*en*, the form for *I am*, *hoo* and *shoo* for *she*. The definite article has four forms, [ðə, ð, θ] and suspended (t') in D 21–D 27, but there is much variation in their use. The plural marker, as in *you know-en* 'you know', is universal in D 21, D 22, D 25 and D 26. In D 23 it occurs in a few contracted forms (*An yo?* 'Have you?' *Dun yo?* 'Do you'?). In D 24 it is only found at the borders of D 22 on the west and D 26 on the south. In D 27 it seems to be practically lost, but Ellis feels this is a recent development. In D 28 it is 'plentiful'. In D 29 it chiefly exists in contracted forms, and 'more in the west than east, but even in Leicestershire there are traces of it'.

The form *I am* separates the midland division from the northern division, which has *I is*. Invariant *be*, as in *I be* 'I am', is seldom used, and most frequently in the negative *I ben't*; it is confined to the parts of the southern midlands which border on the south division. The pronoun *hoo* 'she' is prevalent in D 21, D 22, D 25 and D 26, although here also *her* may be used for *she*. The form *shoo* occurs in district 24.

The above features can still be found in various degrees in the *SED* material. The present indicative marker -*en* shows an area that is basically the area given by Ellis. Thus the *SED* shows that with true verbs (*SED* VIII.5.1. 'They go to church', IV.6.2 'They keep hens') the stronghold of the -*en* suffix is Cheshire, northern Staffordshire and west Derbyshire, although it occurs in the adjoining parts of Lancashire, Yorkshire and

Shropshire. The use of *-en* with true verbs like *go* and *say* appears to be confined to the north-west midlands. But the *-en* suffix with *be*, as in *they bin, I bin*, is centred further south on Shropshire.

The northern division (districts 30–2)

The northern division is bounded on the south by the northern *theeth* line (transverse line 5) and on the north by line 10. The area covers the entire North and East Ridings with some of the West Riding of Yorkshire, northern Lancashire, most of Cumberland and Northumberland, all Westmorland and Durham. Much of this is characterised by the following features. ME *uː* is retained, as in *o't wrang house* /ot raŋ uːs/ 'of the wrong house' (1889: 520). With the exception of the area north of line 7, the definite article is the suspended (t`). *I is* is the regular form for *I am* in most of the northern division. Words like *nose* and *moon* have [ɪʊ] or [ɪə]. 'The letter *r* occasions considerable difficulty', but Ellis concludes that in the east post-vocalic *r* 'practically disappears' and even in the west 'its power is very small'. R is retained post-vocalically in Northumberland, where it is realised as a uvular sound (as opposed to the more usual 'gently trilled' *r* of northern English). This is the 'Northumbrian' burr, first commented on by Daniel Defoe in his *Tour thro' the whole Island of Great Britain* (1724–6). It is perhaps of some interest that Ellis believes the uvular *r* to be 'rather a defective utterance than a distinctive dialectal pronunciation' (p. 495). The distribution of post-vocalic *r* that emerges from the *SED* material is surprisingly similar to Ellis' description (see e.g. *LAE* map Ph11 'arm').

Of historical interest is Ellis' observation that 'the guttural (kh) [i.e. the voiceless velar fricative] has practically vanished from the N.' However, on passing the Scottish–English border, both the guttural (kh) and *r* become 'strong'.

Finally, Ellis feels that parts of 'north Cumberland' and 'north Humberland' belong to Scotland linguistically. Ellis' view of the geography of the Scottish–English linguistic border differs from those of Murray and Bonaparte.

5.6.3   *Realisation of Ellis' test sentence 'You see now (that) I'm right' in the main divisions*

As an illustration of some of the differences revealed by Ellis' evidence, I list realisations of 'You see now (that) I'm right', which is part of the dialect test. The phonetic exegesis applied to Ellis' palaeotype is that of

Eustace (1969), but it should be borne in mind, as Eustace reminds us, that the palaeotype is often ambiguous, occasionally intentionally vague and never easy to interpret. In several places Ellis himself points out that the rendering is doubtful or arbitrary or the symbol ambiguous.

> Division I, the southern division, district 4 (Montacute, Somerset; Ellis 1889: 85)

[ði: dɜ zi: nʌʊ ðət/ʌɪ bi: ɹʌɪt]

> Division I, the southern division, district 9 (Wingham, East Kent; Ellis 1889: 142)

[je̯ʊ si: ne̯ʊ dət/ɔɪ a̤:ɹ ɹɔɪt]

> Division II, the western division (Lower Bache Farm, near Leominster, Herefordshire; Ellis 1889: 176)

[ju si· nɜʊ ɜɪ bi· rɜɪt]

> Division III, the eastern division, district 19 (Great Yarmouth, Norfolk; Ellis 1889: 278)

[jə si: nɛʊ ʌim rʌɪt]

> Division III, the eastern division, district 19 (Stanhoe, near Wells-next-Sea, Norfolk; Ellis 1889: 264)

[jʌʊ si: nəʊ ðət a̤:ɪm ɹəɪt]

> Division IV, the midland division, district 28 (Hanmer, English Flint; Ellis 1889: 453)

[jə si:n nɜʊ əz ɜɪm ri·t]

> Division V, the northern division, district 30 (Goole and Marshland; Ellis 1889: 522)

[jʊ si: nu: ət a̤:z ri:t]

Some important linguistic characteristics of the main divisions are brought into sharp relief by this simple sentence. For instance, 'I am' is realised in different ways (I be, I are, I am, I is), there are differences in verb agreement with see, and different forms of that appear (northern at vs west midland as). There are differences in the pronunciation of and incidence of /r/, differences in the pronunciation of diphthongs and so forth. The following points are worth specific comment. Speakers of Somerset English who have periphrastic do today find it obligatory to mark the second person singular present indicative form with -st, realised as [s], as in *thee 's know* 'you know'. Therefore, it is likely that the [ði: dʒ ziː] realisation of 'thee dost see' in the Somerset sample above is an instance of assimilation. Ellis also has doubts about the precise phonetics of the diphthong of the Montacute *now*. However, this is a particularly problematic region from the viewpoint of /au/. I have also heard diphthongs with fronted first elements of different heights in this part of Somerset and it seems that Ellis' reluctance to take a stand on the 'pure' pronunciation of this sound is a sign of good judgement.

5.7 Wakelin on Ellis' divisions: the extent to which Ellis' areas are still recoverable

Wakelin (1977: 102) believes that 'when English dialects are classified again (if they ever are) their remnants will be seen to correspond remarkably well with Ellis's results'. The data of the *SED* would in fact make it possible to look at the present form of some of Ellis' districts. Unfortunately, not much work along these lines has been done. However, research on south-western English done by scholars like Fischer, Wakelin, Viereck and Klemola suggests that Ellis' districts could still be captured from the *SED* material, although possibly reduced in size. In his study of Stafford English Gibson (1955: 306) compares the relevant *SED* data with Ellis' and concludes that 'the dialect situation has not altered a great deal since 1889'. And to give one quite specific example, the area where Ellis found the plural present indicative -*n* suffix with true verbs (i.e. verbs other than the auxiliaries, *have* and *be*) is practically identical with the area that emerges from the mid-twentieth-century *SED* material, with Cheshire and northern Staffordshire as its heartland (Ihalainen forthcoming b).

5.8 Dialect areas today

Our knowledge of the various dialect areas in the late twentieth century is largely based on the evidence provided by the *SED*. The *SED* data have been interpreted from the viewpoint of dialect areas by Wakelin (1977, 1983), Fischer (1976), Viereck (1986), Lass (1987) and Klemola (forthcoming a). Glauser has studied the Scottish–English linguistic border by using evidence he collected specifically for this purpose. Rohrer (1950), too, collected his own evidence for a study of the border between the north and northern midlands. Viereck (1980) interprets Guy Lowman's corpus from the 1930s to establish boundaries in the south-east, south-west and East Anglia. The complexity of what is arguably the most important modern isogloss, Ellis' *sum/soom* line, was investigated, in the Wash area, in great and revealing detail by Chambers & Trudgill (1980: 129–37). Their analysis clearly shows how far abstracted from reality lines drawn on maps can be.

5.8.1   *Classificatory criteria*

Criteria used in classifications of dialects are mainly phonological, but Glauser (1974), Fischer (1976) and Viereck (1986) show that, in spite of occasional reservations by dialectologists, lexical material can be used to define dialect areas. The emphasis on phonological criteria derives naturally from the fact that the greatest amount of variation can be found in phonology, and phonological criteria can be used to differentiate between quite small areas as against grammatical and syntactic features that may unite areas showing a great deal of phonological differentiation. For instance, the area where *be* is used as a finite verb, as in *They be tired* 'They're tired' (south-west and south-western midlands; see *LAE* map M1) the vowel of *five* has at least seven different realisations, ranging from [fæːv] to [fɔiv].

Table 5.1 compares the main criteria used by Ellis, Wakelin and Trudgill to define English dialect areas. The capital letters indicate the feature concerned.

5.8.2   *Studies of specific dialect boundaries*

Three linguistic borders have been extensively studied: the Scottish–English border (Glauser 1974), the south-western border (Fisher 1976; Wakelin 1986a) and the border between the northern and north midland dialects (Rohrer 1950).

The north

The Scottish–English linguistic border was investigated by Glauser (1974). On the basis of lexical evidence he concludes that the English side that used to share features with Lowland Scotland is now assimilating with northern England, with dialect words receding north. The political border has thus become a strong linguistic barrier. Glauser believes that the importance of the geographic boundary as a linguistic divider will increase in the future.

Rohrer (1950) investigated the border between the northern and northern midland dialects by asking eighty-three questions of more than

Table 5.1. *Criteria used to define English dialect areas*

Feature	Ellis 1889	Wakelin 1983	Trudgill 1990/Traditional	Trudgill 1990/Modern
sOme	x	x		x
paRK	x	x	x	x
riNG		x		x
hOUse	x	x		
gAte				x
lOng			x	
nIght			x	
mAn		x	x	
pAst		x		
bAt			x	
Seven		x	x	
blInd			x	
fEW				x
coffEE				x
Hill			x	(x)
miLk				x
the	x			
finite be		x		
periphrastic do		x		

a hundred informants from seventy-four villages in Yorkshire. He found that the border between the north and north midlands runs along the Wharfe, roughly. This was later confirmed by the *SED* material (Hedevind 1967: 38). The differences between the two varieties are shown in features such as the following:

	Midland	Northern
foal	[fɔɪl]	[fʊəl]
eat	[ɛɪt]	[iət]
cow	[kaʊ]	[kuː]
bone	[bʊən]	[biən]
spoon	[spʊɪn]	[spiən]

The south-west

Depending on the features that they have regarded as significant, various scholars have defined the south-west slightly differently. Yet they seem to agree that this is typically an area where people say *I ben't sure* instead of *I'm not sure*, *vinger* (with a prominent retroflex *r*) for 'finger', *Where be em to?* (*Where be mun to?*) for 'Where are they?' and *What's do that for?* for 'Why did you do that?' They use *he* and its object form *en* to refer to things as well as persons. It might be noted in passing here that, although phonological, lexical, morphological and syntactic features seldom co-occur to form clear-cut dialect boundaries, it appears that the *vinger*-pronouncing area is more or less identical with the area where people say *What's do that for?* for 'Why did you do that?'

In his book *The Southwest of England* (1986a), Wakelin includes in the south-west, 'with its several sub-varieties', Cornwall, Devon, Somerset, Dorset, Wiltshire and South Avon. Avon north of Bristol and the western extremities of Gloucestershire, Berkshire and Hampshire are regarded as forming a marginal area. This seems to be a conservative estimate in that some scholars might extend the south-west slightly further east and north, but the differences are not great (see Viereck 1980; Wells 1982). Lass (1987: 220–3) defines a set of 'core' south-western counties. These are: (part of) Cornwall, Devon, Somerset, Wiltshire, Dorset and Hampshire (as opposed to the south-eastern counties of Berkshire, Surrey, Kent, Sussex and southern East Anglia).

Interestingly, voicing of initial fricatives, the stock linguistic device of Elizabethan dramatists to mark rusticity, is still found to be an important dialect feature. However, today it characterises south-western English rather than southern English in general.

Fischer (1976: 358) analyses lexical evidence provided by the *SED* with the aim of establishing the dialect areas in the south-west of England. The results are summarised as follows:

> The South-West as a dialect area comprises the region lying southwest of a line running approximately through Gloucestershire, western Oxfordshire and Berkshire, and eastern Hampshire. A great many dialect words used everywhere in the South-West or in large parts of it confirm its homogeneity and coherence and separate it from other speech areas further north and east. Yet despite this unity the region as a whole must be subdivided into three smaller areas, namely Area 1 (West Cornwall), Area 2 (East Cornwall and Devon) and Area 3 (the remaining zone).

Fischer also recognises transitional areas. His '2/3' is a transitional belt between west Somerset and east Devon, closely resembling Ellis' district 10. Roughly, the relationships between Ellis' and Fischer's findings can be seen from the following equations: Ellis 12 = Fischer 1, Ellis 11 = Fischer 2, Ellis 10 = Fischer 2/3, Ellis 4 = Fischer 3 (Fischer's maps 305 and 308).

Fischer finds that his area 2 is the *Kernlandschaft*, the most homogeneous area of the whole region. He does not elaborate on this, but it is perhaps worth pointing out that this area also stands out from the rest of the south-west on phonological and grammatical grounds: for instance, it is unique in the south-west in that it uses *us* freely as a subject pronoun, has [ʏ:] in words like *food*, has a monophthong [æ:] in words like *knife*, just to mention the most striking unique characteristics.

A comparison with Ellis' classification shows a striking resemblance between the late nineteenth and the mid-twentieth centuries (compare Fischer's maps 305 and 308 in particular). In the actual development of dialect vocabulary Fischer finds two kinds of recession in the south-west. There is evidence of a westward recession, something that we have already seen in phonology and grammar with southern features like the voicing of initial fricatives, the present-tense *-th* marker and the pronoun *'ch* 'I' retreating to the south-west. Perhaps somewhat unexpectedly, Fischer also discovers dialect words receding eastwards, with older forms being replaced by standard vocabulary in Cornwall and Devon. Fischer feels the reason for this is the late arrival of English in his area: dialect is less deeply rooted here than elsewhere in the south-west and thus more susceptible to influence from standard English. On the whole the south-west is a retreat area.

5.8.3   General surveys of contemporary dialect areas

Wakelin (1983), on the basis of phonological evidence provided by the *SED*, argues for four dialect areas, which appear to be basically those of the Middle English period. These are the north, the south-west, the west midlands and the east midlands. The line that separates the north from the rest of the country is the Humber–Ribble line based on the pronunciations of the words *cows, goose, loaf, coal, eat, ground, blind* and *wrong*. Typical pronunciations of these north of the Humber are [ku:z], [gɪəs], [lɪəf], [kʊəl], [ɪət], [grʊnd], [blɪnd], [raŋ].

The south-west is seen, rather vaguely, as the area west of Watling Street, a view that Wakelin modifies in his *Southwest of England*, as was seen above. Characteristics of the south-west are rhoticity, voicing of initial fricatives, lack of *w* in words like *woman*, and *be* or *bin* for *am*. Wakelin finds periphrastic *do* (*They do go to work*) in a restricted area in the central south-west, but he believes periphrastic *do* to have occurred in the area bounded by Watling Street although its distribution is now limited to the central south-west. Klemola (forthcoming b) has recently studied the unpublished incidental material in the *SED* fieldworkers' recording-books and found evidence for a *do* area that roughly coincides with the area where initial fricatives are voiced.

Viereck (1986) searches for bundles of isoglosses based on dialect words ('heterolexes') in the *SED* material. He discovers evidence for the following lexically differentiated (recessive) areas: the north (with the extreme north-west of England emerging as a separate area), Lincolnshire, East Anglia, the extreme south-east of England, the south-west and the west midlands. The Home Counties do not emerge as a clearly focused area on the basis of lexical evidence, which can be accounted for by the close affinity to standard English. The solid lines on map 5.2 indicate heavy bundling of dialect words and can be interpreted as major dividers. The blank, unbounded areas indicate lexical closeness to standard English. There is a clear-cut blank in the Home Counties. One is reminded of Puttenham's statement that the 'best' type of English was 'the vsual speach of the Court, and that of London and the shires lying about London within lx. myles, and not much above' (*The Arte of English Poesie*, 1589). Viereck's analysis would thus appear to support Görlach's conclusion that 'the geographical basis of good English has not really changed over the last 400 years' (vol. III, of *CHEL*, forthcoming).

Trudgill (1990) differentiates between 'Traditional Dialect' and 'Modern Dialect' and sketches the distributional patterns of each in a way that makes it possible to draw conclusions about recent changes in English dialect areas. Trudgill's Traditional Dialect is the type of rural, mid-twentieth-century, working-class English surveyed by the *SED* (1962–71). The term Modern Dialect is not clearly defined, but it is used to cover rural, working-class English today. Trudgill's criteria are phonological. They are listed below:

Traditional dialect	*Modern dialect*
1 Long: *lang* vs *long*	1 *but* vs *boot*
2 Night: *neet* vs *nite*	2 *arrm* vs *ahm*
3 Blind: *blinnd* vs *blined*	3 *singer* vs *singger*
4 Land: *lond* vs *land*	4 *few* vs *foo*
5 Arm: *arrm* vs *ahm*	5 tense vs lax *ee* in *coffee*
6 Hill: *ill* vs *hill*	6 *gate* vs *geht*
7 Seven: *ʒeven* vs *seven*	7 *milk* vs *mioo(l)k*
8 Bat: *bat* vs *bæt*	

Expressed another way, his key words for Traditional Dialects are LONG: *lang* vs *long*, i.e. [laŋ] vs [lɒŋ]; NIGHT: *neet* vs *nite*, i.e. [niːt] vs

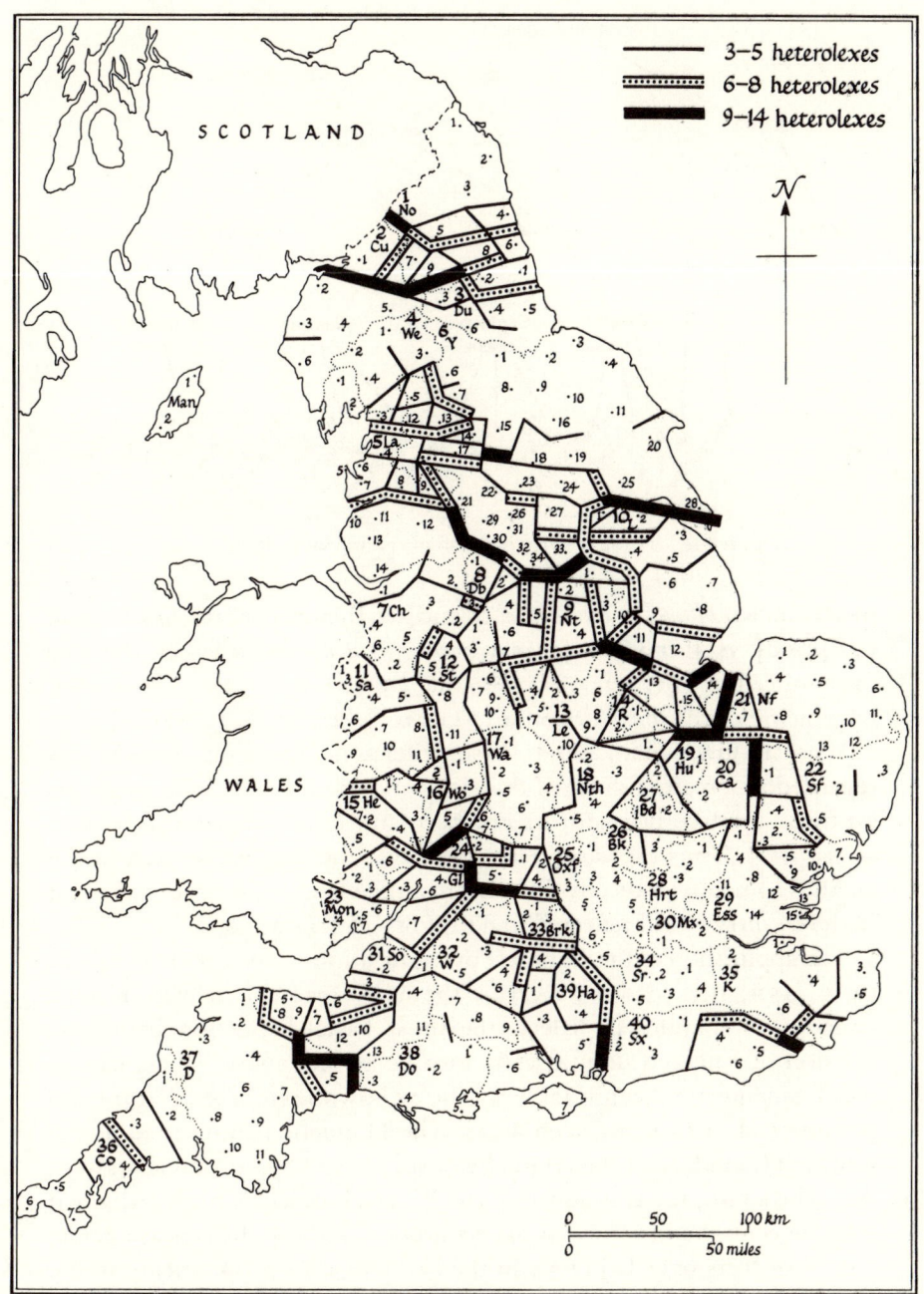

Map 5.2   Bundles of heterolexes in England (redrawn from Viereck 1986: 734)

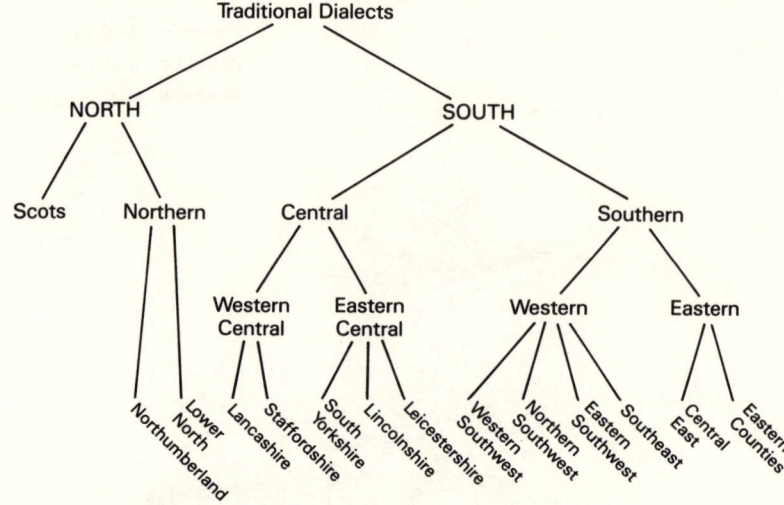

Figure 5.2   Trudgill's classification of traditional dialects.

[naɪt]; BLIND *blinnd* vs *blined,* i.e. [blɪnd] vs [blaɪnd]; LAND *lond* vs *land,* i.e. [lɒnd] vs [lænd/land]; ARM *arrm* vs *ahm,* i.e. whether the *r* is pronounced or not; HILL: *ill* vs *hill,* i.e. *h*-deletion; SEVEN *ʒeven* vs *seven,* i.e. voicing of the initial fricative; BAT *bat* vs *bæt,* i.e. [bat] vs [bæt].

What is interesting about these criteria is that Ellis' *some* is not regarded as a main divider of divisions and there is a definite emphasis on items that are northern or northern and north midland (*lang, neet, blinnd, lond*). Thus the early perception that the English spoken in the north is somehow radically different from the English spoken in the rest of the country is still reflected in Trudgill's classification.

The application of the eight test pronunciations (LONG, NIGHT, BLIND, LAND, ARM, HILL, SEVEN, BAT) to the *SED* material defines thirteen varieties of traditional dialect, the most basic distinction being the division of England linguistically into north and south. These can be seen from figure 5.2, while table 5.2 shows how the eight test features are pronounced in these thirteen areas. The linguistic feature used as the southern boundary of the linguistic north is the /laŋ/ pronunciation of *long.* The south, the area south of the River Humber, is further divided into the central and southern dialect areas. Southern dialects as against central dialects have [æ] in *bat* in the east and are *r*-pronouncing in the west. An additional feature that distinguishes between these two varieties is the pronunciation of the vowel in words like *path.* The vowel is short in the central dialects and long in the southern dialects.

Table 5.2. *The pronunciation of Trudgill's eight diagnostic features in the thirteen Traditional Dialect areas (from Trudgill 1990: 32)*

	Long	Night	Blind	Land	Arm	Hill	Seven	Bat
Northumberland	lang	neet	blinnd	land	arrm	hill	seven	bat
Lower North	lang	neet	blinnd	land	ahm	ill	seven	bat
Lancashire	long	neet	blined	lond	arrm	ill	seven	bat
Staffordshire	long	nite	blined	lond	ahm	ill	seven	bat
South Yorkshire	long	neet	blinnd	land	ahm	ill	seven	bat
Lincolnshire	long	nite	blinnd	land	ahm	ill	seven	bat
Leicestershire	long	nite	blined	land	ahm	ill	seven	bat
Western Southwest	long	nite	blined	land	arrm	ill	zeven	bat
Northern Southwest	long	nite	blined	lond	arrm	ill	seven	bat
Eastern Southwest	long	nite	blined	land	arrm	ill	seven	bat
Southeast	long	nite	blined	lænd	arrm	ill	seven	bæt
Central East	long	nite	blined	lænd	ahm	ill	seven	bæt
Eastern Counties	long	nite	blined	lænd	ahm	hill	seven	bæt

Interestingly, using a totally different set of criteria, Trudgill comes up with major dialect areas that resemble those of Ellis. That is, the major dialect boundaries divide the country into northern, central (that is, midland) and southern areas. There is a close resemblance between Trudgill's traditional dialect areas and Ellis' English dialect districts.

Trudgill uses traditional spelling (supplemented by a number of diacritics) to show pronunciations. One cannot help noticing that many of these are remarkably similar to the spellings found in early dialect texts: for instance, such northern pronunciations as 'the rang spee-oon' (*the wrong spoon*), 'a stee-an hoos' (*a stone house*) could have come from Meriton's 'Yorkshire Dialogue' (1684).

Trudgill's criteria for classifying Modern Dialects are the following pronunciations: the vowel in *but*, *r* in *arm*, *ng* in *singer*, *ew* in *few*, *ee* in *coffee*, *a* in *gate* and *l* in *milk*. These features are incorporated in the test sentence 'Very few cars made it up the long hill'. The diagnostically interesting realisations of these variables are [ʌ] vs [ʊ] in *but*, rhoticity, [ŋ] vs [ŋg] in words like *singer*, *y*-dropping in words like *few* (i.e. [fjuː] vs [fuː]), tensing of the final vowel in words like *coffee* (i.e. [kɒfɪ] vs [kɒfiː]), monophthong in *gate* (i.e. [geɪt] vs [geːt]), /l/ in words like *milk* (i.e. [mɪlk] vs pronunciations where the *l* has acquired a short [ʊ]-like vowel in front of it or is realised as a vowel, as in [mɪʊlk], [mɪok]). As in the case of traditional dialect, *h*-retention is also used as a diagnostic, although its

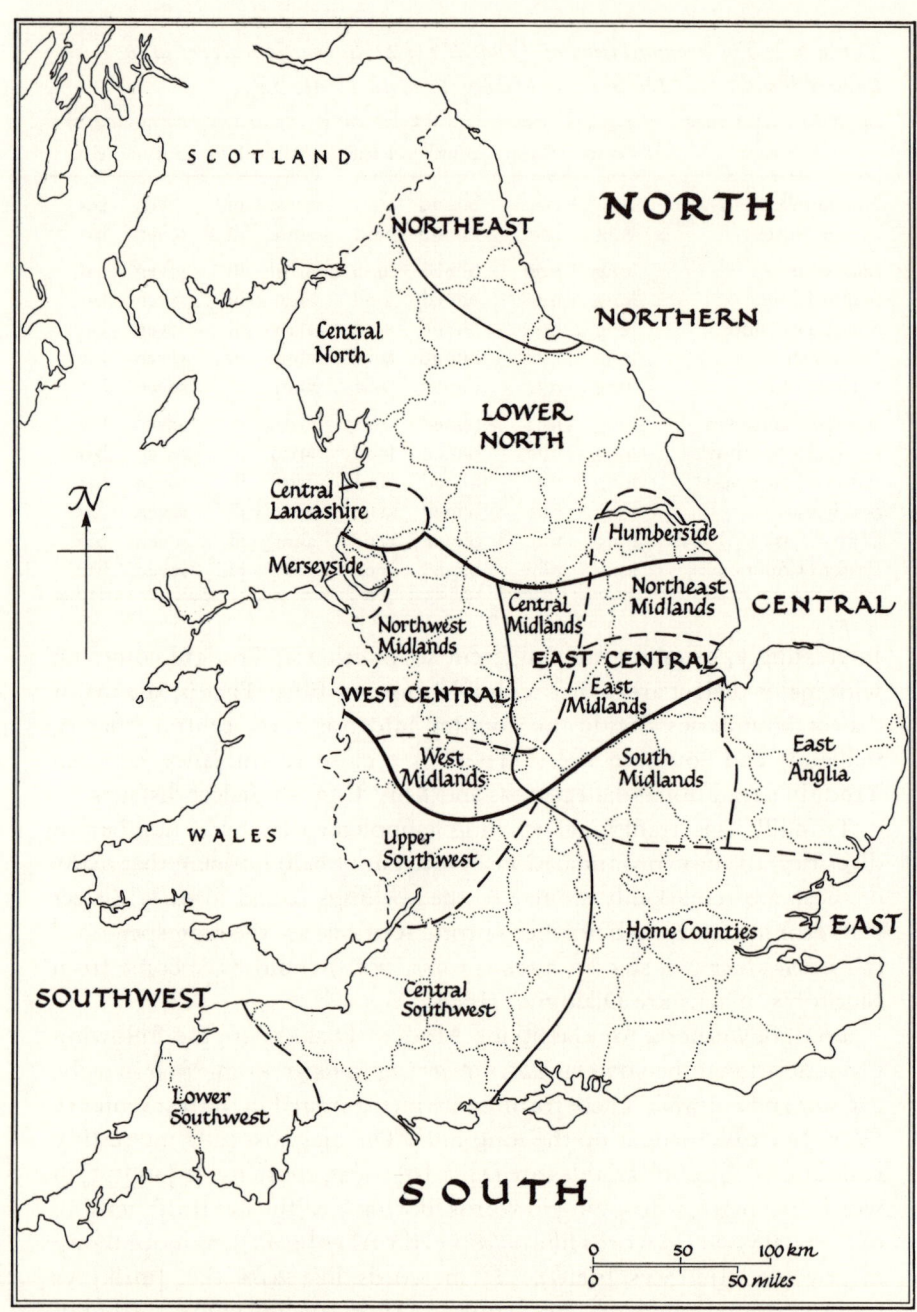

Map 5.3   Trudgill's modern dialect areas

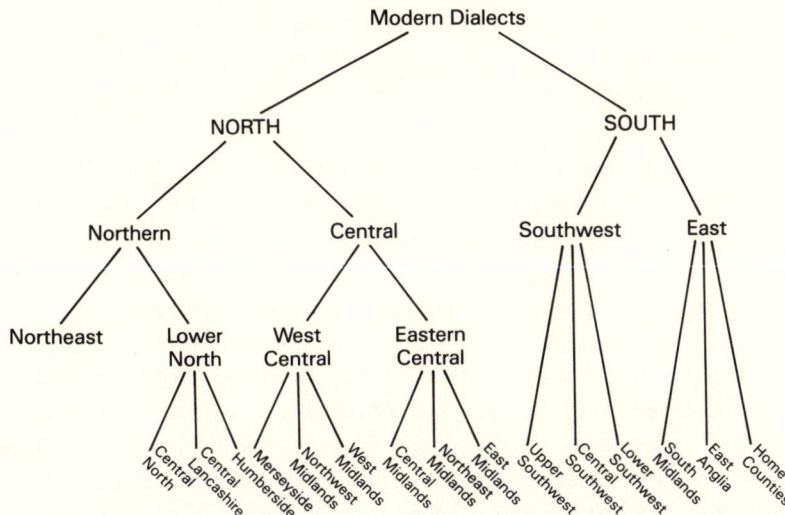

Figure 5.3   Trudgill's classification of modern dialects.

distribution today appears to be quite restricted, with former *h*-pronouncing areas like East Anglia becoming *h*-less (Trudgill 1990 : 50).

The most basic criterion in Trudgill's classification is the 'but/boot' distinction. This is, of course, Ellis' 'sum/soom' boundary. One is reminded of Ellis' prediction that this may turn out to be the most important contemporary linguistic divider in England. Trudgill's classification of Modern Dialects can be seen from map 5.3. How the various Modern Dialects are grouped together is shown by figure 5.3. The following list shows how Trudgill's test sentence 'Very few cars made it up the long hill' is realised in sixteen Modern Dialect areas:

Very few cars made it up the long hill:

Northeast	Veree few cahs mehd it oop the long hill
Central North	Veri few cahs mehd it oop the long ill
Central Lancashire	Veri few carrs mehd it oop the longg ill
Humberside	Veree few cahs mehd it oop the long ill
Merseyside	Veree few cahs mayd it oop the longg ill
Northwest Midlands	Veri few cahs mayd it oop the longg ill
West Midlands	Veree few cahs mayd it oop the longg ill
Central Midlands	Veri few cahs mayd it oop the long ill
Northeast Midlands	Veree few cahs mayd it oop the long ill
East Midlands	Veree foo cahs mayd it oop the long ill
Upper Southwest	Veree few carrs mayd it up the long ill
Central Southwest	Veree few carrs mayd it up the long iooll
Lower Southwest	Veree few carrs mehd it up the long ill

South Midlands	Veree foo cahs mayd it up the long iooll
East Anglia	Veree foo cahs mayd it up the long (h)ill
Home Counties	Veree few cahs mayd it up the long iooll

(Trudgill 1990: 65–6)

As can be seen from works like Wyld (1956) and Dobson (1968), the features Trudgill uses for the classification of Modern Dialects may have long histories in spite of their relatively recent status as diagnostic features. In what follows the emphasis will be on recent developments and possible future changes in dialects and dialect features.

Three of the Modern Dialect markers, the final vowel of *coffee*, *y*-dropping (i.e. the *dook* realisation of *duke*) and *mehd* for *made*, will be briefly discussed here; *ngg* for *ng* in words like *strong* was dealt with on page 217. Because of their wider implications, the remaining 'modern dialect' markers, with some additional features, will be discussed in sections 5.8.4 and 5.8.5.

The [iː] realisation of the final *ee* in *coffee* – called y-tensing by some scholars – was in fact regarded as a standard feature by Walker. He points out that words like *vanity* might as well be written *vanitee* (1791: 24). In early northern dialect texts, on the other hand, the final -*y* was often spelt *a* (*verra* 'very', *Jerra* 'Jerry', *Sunda* 'Sunday'), which not only suggests that the vowel was lax but also that it was markedly northern. The *SED* shows that in the mid-twentieth century the country was about three-quarters -*y*-laxing in words like *every* and *ready* (*LAE* maps Ph203, Ph204). In rural dialects tensing appears to have been indigenous especially in the south-west. Trudgill feels that the tense vowel is now spreading rapidly into the lax -*y* territory. It has already reached such northern urban centres as Liverpool and Newcastle, where it has jumped over the intervening lax -*y* territory (Trudgill 1990: 77).

Yod-dropping, as in *duke* /duːk/ was observed and censured by Walker (1791), who compares it with assibilation:

> There is a slight deviation often heard in the pronunciation of this word [i.e. *duke*], as if written *Dook*; but this borders on vulgarity; the true sound of the *u* must be carefully preserved, as if written *Dewk*. There is another impropriety in pronouncing this word, as if written *Jook*; this is not so vulgar as the former, and arises from an ignorance of the influence of accent.

The spread of the /eː/ pronunciation, Trudgill's 'mehd' and 'geht', in words like *made* and *gate* in northern English at the expense of the traditional [ɪə] can be seen from Tidholm's study of Egton English

(1979). Tidholm provides the following figures for his three informant categories Old, Mid and Young (Tidholm's 'Young' informants were born after the Second World War):

name, made, etc.	Old	Mid	Young
ɪə	12·2	18·6	5·4
eː	84·8	61·4	59·5
ei	3·0	20·0	35·1

Tidholm explains the [eː] pronunciation in words like *made* [meːd] as an approximation of the standard English sound. Trudgill feels this sound is 'destined to spread into Humberside, Central Lancashire and the Lower South-West in the not too distant future' (1990: 78).

5.8.4   Recent developments in dialect areas

Like Ellis (1889), Trudgill uses the pronunciation of *r* as a main classificatory criterion.[17] However, there is a difference. While Ellis was interested in the phonetic realisation of *r* (whether *r* was 'reverted' or not), Trudgill is concerned with the question of whether varieties of English are rhotic or non-rhotic, a rhotic dialect being one where *r* is pronounced in non-prevocalic positions, as in *car* and *park*. There was, of course, a good reason for Ellis not to use rhoticity as such as a criterion for classifying dialects: rhoticity, at least variable rhoticity, appears to have been 'accepted' up to the twentieth century. Ellis' remarks on the pronunciation of *r* suggest a situation that Gimson and Eustace were able to document as late as 1965. They recorded the speech of Miss Flora Russell (the niece of the ninth Duke of Bedford), whose speech they regard as a 'good example of a certain kind of Victorian English' (Eustace 1969: 34). The transcription of Miss Russell's speech shows that she has an *r* (phonetically realised as a velar or bunched *r*) before non-vowels (i.e. in words like *German*) in six cases out of the possible twenty-two (Eustace 1969: 73). Eustace regards the *r* of Miss Russell's type of English as a weakening of an earlier retroflex *r* before its disappearance in pre-nonvocalic contexts. However, the variety described in Jones (1909) is non-rhotic. Jones characterised this as a variety used by 'educated people in London and the neighbourhood', and clearly intended it to provide a pronunciation standard. That rhoticity was seen as regional about that time is also supported by evidence from dialect literature. (See, for example, the reference to a story by John Read on p. 215.)

Although Ellis was more interested in the phonetics of *r* than in rhoticity as such, his transcriptions suggest that the 'reverted' *r* area was rhotic. Assuming this to be the case, we can compare Ellis' reverted *ur* area with Trudgill's southern 'Modern Dialect' *r*-pronouncing area. This comparison shows that rhoticity has disappeared from the southeast of England and shows a south-westerly recess movement. Because of this rapid retreat, Trudgill concludes that rhoticity is 'unlikely to survive for longer than a century or so' (1990: 77).

Since Ellis' 'reverted' *r* area is more or less the *r* area that emerges from the *SED* evidence, it is reasonable to conclude that the recession of *r* in the south of England is a post-1950s development. Combined with the evidence about recent changes in Yorkshire English from Tidholm (1979), it would seem that English dialects were rather stable till the generations born after the Second World War.

Comparing the *SED* material with his modern evidence, Trudgill (1990: 76) concludes that the northern limit of rounding of OE *a:*, the so-called Humber–Ribble line, which separated northern England from the rest of the country, has disappeared completely. The distinction between rounded and unrounded reflexes of Old English *a:* is still an important dialect boundary, but it has receded northwards and now divides Scotland from England. Glauser's study of northern vocabulary shows the same kind of recession into Scotland. The political boundary between England and Scotland has thus increased its importance as a linguistic divider, with northern English becoming more English and more clearly differentiated from Scottish English than before.

The earlier primary linguistic boundary in England, the Humber–Ribble line, Trudgill argues, has now been replaced by the 'pahst' vs 'passt' and 'up' vs 'oop' isoglosses, which run, roughly, from the Wash to the Severn and separate the linguistic south from the linguistic north (i.e. the north proper and the midlands): 'this is a line which most English people are very well aware of and which they use informally to divide "southerners" from "northerners"' (1990: 76).

These two dialect markers, as opposed to the northern failure to round Old English *a:*, are of relatively recent origin and they show the modern trend for innovations to spread from the south-east.

In words like *past* and *dance* the original short sound shows signs of lengthening towards the end of the seventeenth century, and the lengthened vowel is further lowered to /ɑː/ (Dobson 1968, II: section 50). However, the relative social status of the short and long vowels appears to have been still unsettled even in the late eighteenth century.

Such an influential authority on pronunciation as Walker (1791) actually says that 'the short *a* in these words is now the general pronunciation of the polite and learned world ... and every correct ear would be disgusted at giving the *a* in these words the sound of the *a* in *father*'. He assigns the *a* in *fast* the value of *a* in *fat*. Jones (1909: 18), who identifies the short vowel in *past* as northern, nevertheless points out that the short sound is also heard in southern English. Jones calls these pronunciations affected but adds that some elocutionists nevertheless recommend the short vowel in these cases (Holmberg 1964: 78). The short *a*, on the other hand, seems to be quite unthreatened by the southern long sound even today. Thus, Tidholm (1979: 61) finds that even younger speakers of Egton English use only a short *a* in words like *path*, *fast* and *staff*. He concludes: 'It is probable that /a/ in this position will withstand RP /ɑ:/ for several generations.'

Unrounded *u* was regarded as vulgar till about 1640, when Simon Daines, a Suffolk schoolmaster, described it as the accepted pronunciation. Like the long retracted *a* of *past*, this change appears to have been south-eastern in origin. Unrounded *u* spread only to the area south of the Wash–Severn line, so that much of England still has [ʊ] in words like *duck*. Unrounded *u* appears to be well established in northern English even among younger speakers (Tidholm 1979). Northern adherence to [ʊ] has resulted in a widespread linguistic change where traditional pronunciations like [dɪən] 'done' are being replaced by [dʊn] rather than [dʌn]. As a result of this development (and changes in other contexts where northern English has [ɪə]), the importance of [ɪə] as a dialect marker has been considerably weakened and [ɪə] will probably disappear in the near future.

Besides the northward recession of such traditional isoglosses as the northern failure to round OE long *a*, there is a distinctive south-westerly retreat, as can be seen from the recession of early southern English characteristics like the voicing of initial fricatives, *ich* for *I* and the *-eth* present-tense marker. While the voicing of initial fricatives still covered a large area in the south-west in the mid-twentieth century (roughly, the area west of the line from Portsmouth to Gloucester), *ich* for *I* and the present-tense marker *-eth* had retreated to a small area in the south-west (Devon and Somerset) by the latter half of the nineteenth century and had virtually become obsolete by 1900.

Another important recession takes place in the midlands, where one of the most important Middle English midland characteristics, the plural present indicative suffix *-en*, retreats to the north-western corner of the west midlands. The conservativeness of this area is also shown by the retention of the *hoo* 'she' pronoun.

What emerges from these developments is the conservativeness of the north, the south-west and the west midlands as opposed to the innovativeness of the south-east.

5.8.5   *The importance of London and the south-east*

Although standard English, especially standard English pronunciation or RP, can be argued to be a social rather than regional variety, its linguistic roots are in southern English. This was made quite clear by Daniel Jones, when he characterised the type of pronunciation he was describing in the first edition of his *Pronouncing Dictionary* (1917) as the pronunciation 'most usually heard in everyday speech in the families of Southern English persons whose men-folk have been educated at the great public boarding-schools'. He actually called it 'Public School Pronunciation' but changed the label in the 1926 edition into 'Received Pronunciation', a term that had been popular in the previous century. The idea that the type of English that could provide a standard is of a southern type and spoken by the 'educated' and 'polite' goes at least as far back as Puttenham (see p. 252), who added that the English of 'Northern-men... whether they be noble men or gentlemen, or of their best clarkes' is less elegant than southern English (1589: Book 3, chapter 4).

A clear indication of the growing importance of London English is the fact that by the eighteenth century the earlier-stage dialect based on rustic southern English had been replaced by Cockney. Although Walker in his highly influential *Critical Pronouncing Dictionary* (1791) castigates a number of what he feels are faults of Cockney pronunciation, he nevertheless argues that polite London speech is superior to all other varieties; and it was this type of speech that Walker codified in his dictionary to be imitated as a standard.[18]

The importance of London and its environs as the source of linguistic innovations is also emphasised by Ellis, who even predicts that such recent Cockney and northern metropolitan developments as *tike* for *take* and *bowt* for *boat* may work their way up in the social scale and become 'polite' pronunciations 'in another hundred years' (1889: 236). Judging by such recent reports on RP as Ramsaran (1990b) these two pronunciations have not made much headway in late twentieth-century received speech. However, Walker might be delighted to hear that his *charitee* pronunciation, known as *happy* tensing in the twentieth century, is not only a significant marker of south-eastern English, as we saw from Trudgill's analysis of Modern Dialect, but is also advancing in 'polite' circles (Ramsaran 1990b).

Another recent indication of the linguistic influence of the south-east is the spread of *l*-vocalisation, as in [mɪək] 'milk'. A rapid spread of this change from the south-east to the midlands has been reported by Knowles (1987: 83) and Trudgill (1990: 60–2). Trudgill calls *l*-vocalisation 'a relatively recent change', but it appears to have occurred in several dialects and at different times in the history of English. Ray (1674) quotes several instances in the 'North-Country' section of his dictionary, and Marshall (1788) regards it as one of the defining features of East Yorkshire English. Spellings like *o'ad/oad/aud* 'old', *cov'd* 'calved', *book* 'bulk', *faut* 'fault' and *awmeast* 'almost' are also frequent in seventeenth- and eighteenth-century dialect texts illustrating York-shire English, whereas Tidholm (1979) shows that in the 1970s there was a definite tendency to restore *l* in these words. It is even conceivable that the *l*-ful pronunciations now being restored in northern English will become dialectal if the *l*-vocalised forms become generally accepted.

Where *l*-vocalisation has been firmly established, it has already had some interesting consequences for vowels generally:

> In the heart of this area – London itself – words ending in -*ill* and -*eel* such as *fill* and *feel* may now be pronounced identically: 'fi-oo(l)'. And in all of this region there is a tendency for short 'o' and long 'o' to become the same before an *l*: *doll* 'do-ool', *dole* 'do-ool'. Words such as *dull* may even acquire the same pronunciation 'do-ool', and there is also a tendency for words like *pull* and *Paul* to become the same. We are probably seeing here the beginnings of a whole new change in the language that will lead to the disappearance of 'l' in these words altogether in the same way that 'r' began to disappear 200 years ago in words like *arm*.   (Trudgill 1990: 61–2).[19]

There are thus reasons to expect that London and its environs, the south-east, will continue to be a source of linguistic innovations. More and more southern English is likely to end up as 'Received English'. However, as can be seen from Tidholm's analysis of the English of younger-generation speakers in North Yorkshire (1979), it is also likely that certain regionalisms will resist outside influence. There may be structural reasons for a variety to resist a specific prestige feature, but cultural, social and economic differences may turn out to be an even more efficient wall against southern influence.

Appendix

List of localities in the national network (as given in the *SED*)

A superior [r] attached to the name of a locality in the lists below means that one or more of the informants concerned was tape-recorded either at the time of the field-investigations or later.

1 Nb
  1 Lowick[r]
  2 Embleton[r]
  3 Thropton[r]
  4 Ellington[r]
  5 Wark[r]
  6 Earsdon
  7 Haltwhistle[r]
  8 Heddon-on-the-Wall[r]
  9 Allendale[r]

2 Cu
  1 Longtown[r]
  2 Abbeytown
  3 Brigham[r]
  4 Threlkeld[r]
  5 Hunsonby[r]
  6 Gosforth[r]

3 Du
  1 Washington[r]
  2 Ebchester
  3 Wearhead[r]
  4 Witton-le-Wear[r]
  5 Bishop Middleham
  6 Eggleston[r]

4 We
  1 Great Strickland[r]
  2 Patterdale
  3 Soulby[r]
  4 Staveley-in-Kendal[r]

5 La
  1 Coniston[r]
  2 Cartmel[r]
  3 Yealand
  4 Dolphinholme[r]
  5 Fleetwood[r]
  6 Pilling
  7 Thistleton
  8 Ribchester[r]
  9 Read[r]
  10 Marshside[r]
  11 Eccleston[r]
  12 Harwood[r]
  13 Bickerstaffe
  14 Halewood

6 Y
  1 Melsonby[r]
  2 Stokesley[r]
  3 Skelton[r]
  4 Egton[r]
  5 Dent[r]
  6 Muker[r]
  7 Askrigg
  8 Bedale[r]
  9 Borrowby[r]
  10 Helmsley
  11 Rillington[r]
  12 Burton-in-Lonsdale
  13 Horton-in-Ribblesdale[r]
  14 Grassington
  15 Pateley Bridge[r]
  16 Easingwold[r]
  17 Gargrave
  18 Spofforth
  19 York[r]
  20 Nafferton[r]
  21 Heptonstall
  22 Wibsey
  23 Leeds[r]
  24 Cawood[r]

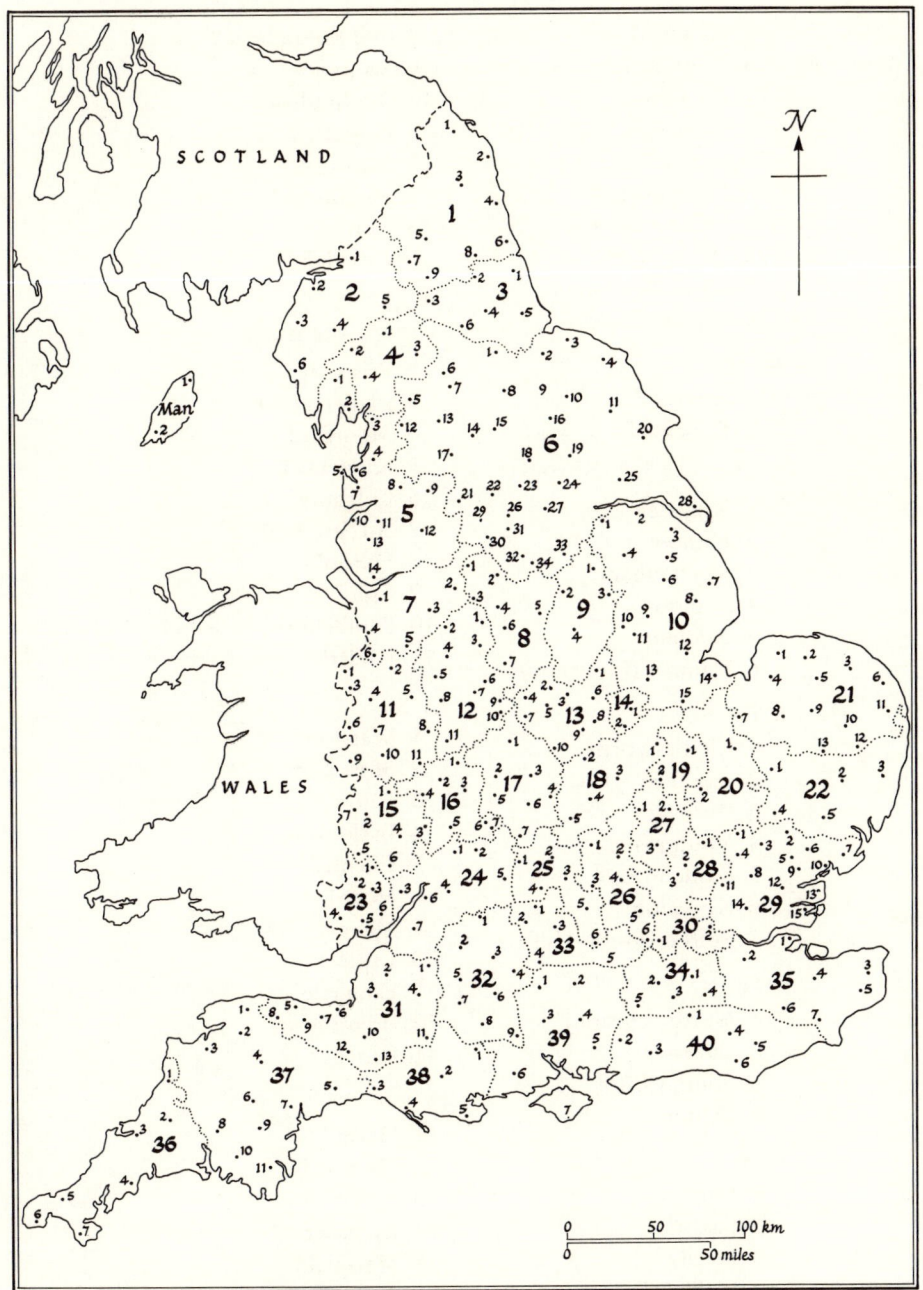

Map 5.4   *SED* localities

25 Newbald
26 Thornhill[r]
27 Carleton
28 Welwick[r]
29 Golcar
30 Holmbridge[r]
31 Skelmanthorpe[r]
32 Ecclesfield
33 Tickhill
34 Sheffield[r]

6a Man
1 Andreas[r]
2 Ronague[r]

7 Ch
1 Kingsley[r]
2 Rainow
3 Swettenham[r]
4 Farndon[r]
5 Audlem
6 Hanmer (Flintshire)

8 Db
1 Charlesworth
2 Bamford
3 Burbage
4 Youlgreave[r]
5 Stonebroom[r]
6 Kniveton[r]
7 Sutton-on-the-Hill[r]

9 Nt
1 North Wheatley[r]
2 Cuckney
3 South Clifton[r]
4 Oxton[r]

10 L
1 Eastoft[r]
2 Saxby[r]
3 Keelby[r]
4 Willoughton[r]
5 Tealby[r]
6 Wragby[r]
7 Swaby

8 Old Bolingbroke[r]
9 Scopwick[r]
10 Beckingham[r]
11 Fulbeck[r]
12 Sutterton[r]
13 Swinstead
14 Lutton[r]
15 Crowland[r]

11 Sa
1 Weston Rhyn[r]
2 Prees
3 Llanymenech
4 Montford[r]
5 Kinnersley
6 Chirbury[r]
7 All Stretton[r]
8 Hilton[r]
9 Clun[r]
10 Diddlebury[r]
11 Kinlet[r]

12 St
1 Warslow[r]
2 Mow Cop[r]
3 Alton[r]
4 Barlaston
5 Ellenhall[r]
6 Hoar Cross[r]
7 Mavesyn Ridware[r]
8 Lapley[r]
9 Edingale[r]
10 Wigginton
11 Himley[r]

13 Lei
1 Harby[r]
2 Hathern[r]
3 Seagrave[r]
4 Packington[r]
5 Markfield
6 Great Dalby[r]
7 Sheepy Magna[r]
8 Goadby
9 Carlton Curlieu

10 Ullesthorpe[r]

14 R
  1 Empingham[r]
  2 Lyddington[r]

15 He
  1 Brimfield[r]
  2 Weobley[r]
  3 Cradley[r]
  4 Checkley[r]
  5 Longtown[r]
  6 Whitchurch[r]

16 Wo
  1 Romsley[r]
  2 Hartlebury
  3 Hanbury[r]
  4 Clifton on Teme[r]
  5 Earls Croome[r]
  6 Offenham[r]
  7 Bretforton[r]

17 Wa
  1 Nĕther Whitacre
  2 Hockley Heath
  3 Stoneleigh
  4 Napton-on-the-Hill[r]
  5 Aston Cantlow[r]
  6 Lighthorne
  7 Shipston-on-Stour

18 Nth
  1 Warmington[r]
  2 Welford[r]
  3 Little Harrowden[r]
  4 Kislingbury[r]
  5 Sulgrave[r]

19 Hu
  1 Warboys[r]
  2 Kimbolton[r]

20 C
  1 Little Downham[r]
  2 Elsworth

21 Nf
  1 Docking[r]
  2 Great Snoring[r]
  3 Blickling[r]
  4 Grimston[r]
  5 North Elmham[r]
  6 Ludham[r]
  7 Outwell[r]
  8 Gooderstone[r]
  9 Shipdham[r]
  10 Ashwelthorpe[r]
  11 Reedham
  12 Pulham St. Mary[r]
  13 Garboldisham[r]

22 Sf
  1 Tuddenham[r]
  2 Mendlesham[r]
  3 Yoxford[r]
  4 Kedington[r]
  5 Kersey[r]

23 Mon
  1 Skenfrith[r]
  2 Llanellen[r]
  3 Raglan[r]
  4 Cross Keys
  5 Llanfrechfa
  6 Shirenewton[r]

24 Gl
  1 Deerhurst[r]
  2 Gretton[r]
  3 Bream[r]
  4 Whiteshill[r]
  5 Sherborne[r]
  6 Slimbridge[r]
  7 Latteridge[r]

25 O
  1 Kingham
  2 Steeple Aston[r]
  3 Islip[r]
  4 Eynsham[r]
  5 Cuxham

6 Binfield Heath[r]

26 Bk
1 Tingewick[r]
2 Stewkley[r]
3 Long Crendon[r]
4 Buckland[r]
5 Coleshill
6 Horton

27 Beds
1 Turvey[r]
2 Great Barford[r]
3 Harlington[r]

28 Herts
1 Therfield[r]
2 Codicote[r]
3 Wheathampstead[r]

29 Ess
1 Great Chesterford[r]
2 Belchamp Walter[r]
3 Cornish Hall End[r]
4 Henham[r]
5 Stisted[r]
6 West Bergholt[r]
7 Little Bentley[r]
8 High Easter
9 Tiptree
10 East Mersea[r]
11 Netteswell
12 Little Baddow[r]
13 Tillingham
14 Doddinghurst[r]
15 Canewdon

30 Mx and London
1 Harmondsworth
2 Hackney

31 So
1 Weston[r]
2 Blagdon[r]
3 Wedmore[r]
4 Coleford[r]

5 Wootton Courtenay[r]
6 Stogursey[r]
7 Stogumber[r]
8 Withypool[r]
9 Brompton Regis
10 Stoke St. Gregory[r]
11 Horsington[r]
12 Pitminster[r]
13 Merriott[r]

32 W
1 Ashton Keynes[r]
2 Sutton Benger[r]
3 Avebury[r]
4 Burbage[r]
5 Steeple Ashton[r]
6 Netheravon[r]
7 Sutton Veny[r]
8 Fovant[r]
9 Whiteparish

33 Berks
1 Buckland
2 Uffington[r]
3 West Ilsley[r]
4 Inkpen[r]
5 Swallowfield[r]

34 Sr
1 Walton-on-the-Hill[r]
2 East Clandon[r]
3 Coldharbour[r]
4 Outwood[r]
5 Thursley

35 K
1 Stoke[r]
2 Farningham[r]
3 Staple[r]
4 Warren Street[r]
5 Denton[r]
6 Goudhurst[r]
7 Appledore[r]

36 Co
  1 Kilkhampton[r]
  2 Altarnun[r]
  3 Egloshayle[r]
  4 St Ewe[r]
  5 Gwinear[r]
  6 St Buryan[r]
  7 Mullion[r]

37 D
  1 Parracombe[r]
  2 Swimbridge
  3 Weare Giffard[r]
  4 Chawleigh
  5 Gittisham[r]
  6 South Zeal
  7 Kennford
  8 Peter Tavy
  9 Widdicombe
  10 Cornwood
  11 Blackawton

38 Do
  1 Handley[r]

2 Ansty[r]
3 Whitchurch
  Canonicorum[r]
4 Portesham[r]
5 Kingston

39 Ha
  1 Hatherden[r]
  2 Oakley[r]
  3 King's Somborne[r]
  4 Alresford
  5 Hambledon[r]
  6 Burley[r]
  7 Whitwell[r] (I.o.W.)

40 Sx
  1 Billingshurst
  2 Harting
  3 Sutton
  4 Fletching[r]
  5 Horam
  6 Firle[r]

FURTHER READING

The following works, together with the information provided by Ellis (1889) and the *SED* (1962–71), are good sources of information on the main varieties of English dialects from the early modern times to the present. Much information on English dialects can be found in general surveys like Wakelin (1977, 1984), Wells (1982, vols. I–III). The tape-recordings made in connection with the *Survey of English Dialects* and the original fieldworkers' notebooks (with a considerable amount of unpublished material) are deposited in the University of Leeds. *The Computer Developed Atlas of England 1* (Viereck & Ramisch 1991) displays important lexical, morphological and syntactic data from the *SED* in a way that makes it easy to see the actual amount and nature of variation involved without consulting the *SED* basic-material volumes (which is not usually the case with more traditional dialect maps).

Hughes & Trudgill introduce ten urban varieties: London, Norwich, Bristol, South Wales, west midlands (Walsall), Bradford, Liverpool, Tyneside, Edinburgh and Belfast (1979, with tape-recorded samples). Lodge (1984) discusses the phonology of the following varieties: Stockport (Greater Manchester), London, Peasmarch (Sussex), Coventry, Norwich, Edinburgh. Milroy & Milroy (1987) discuss the syntactic characteristics of modern

Tyneside and Northumbrian English, southern English, Scottish English and Irish English.

Good bibliographical sources are Skeat & Nodal (1877), Wright (*EDD*, vol. VI), Viereck, Schneider & Görlach (1984) and Edwards & Weltens (1985).

Northern English: Meriton (1684), Marshall (1788), Seward (1801), Brown (1833), Wright (1892), Orton (1933), Jones (1952), Viereck (1966), Hedevind (1967, with samples on gramophone records), Melchers (1972, with samples on tape), Viereck (1975, with samples on tape), Tidholm (1979, with samples on tape), Hughes & Trudgill (1979, with samples on tape), Rydland (1982), Jones-Sargent (1983), Petyt (1985).

The Midlands: 'Tim Bobbin' (Hole, *A View of the Lancashire Dialect*, 1746), Halliwell (1881), Darlington (1887), Peacock (1889), Gibson (1955), Sykes (1956), Viereck (1975), Campion (1976), Shorrocks (1980), Hughes & Trudgill (1979, samples on tape), Lodge (1984).

East Anglia: Larwood (1800), Forby (1830), Spurdens (1840), Kökeritz (1932), Trudgill (1974, Norwich), Viereck (1975, with samples on tape), Hughes & Trudgill (1979, samples of Norwich English on tape), Lodge (1984).

The South-West: Hole (1746), Jennings (1825), Barnes (1886), Rock (1867), Elworthy (1875, 1877/9, 1886), Chope (1891), Hewett (1892), Wilson (1913), Widén (1949, with samples on gramophone record), Harris (1967, 1969), Viereck (1975, with samples on tape), Wakelin (1975; 1986a; 1988a, with samples on tape), Hughes & Trudgill (1979, with samples on tape), Ihalainen (1987), Gachelin (1991).

Cockney and Southern English: Sheridan (1762), Walker (1791), Ellis (1889), Matthews (1938/72), Viereck (1975, with samples on tape), Sivertsen (1960), Hurford (1967), Hughes & Trudgill (1979, with samples on tape), North (1979), Cheshire (1982).

Dialect in literature has been discussed by Brook (1963: ch. 8), Page (1973: ch. 3), Blake (1981) and Wakelin (1988b *passim*).

Attitudes towards non-standard English and the social evaluation of regional English: Giles & Powesland (1975), Trudgill (1983, chapters 11 and 12), Milroy & Milroy (1985), Honey (1988, chapter 4), Giles, Coupland, Henwood, Harriman & Coupland (1990).

NOTES

1 A good introduction to folk dialectology is Preston (1988), who assesses the value of folk accounts of dialect differences as follows: 'The study of folk dialect boundaries has been of limited interest to traditional dialectologists, but more recent concentration on ethnographic and attitudinal language facts makes such studies an important part of determining the boundaries and composition of speech communities' (p. 373). Preston works on

American English dialects. For further discussion, see also Preston (1990). So far folk accounts of dialect areas in England have not been studied.

2 For instance, Skeat (1911: 107) expresses these reservations as follows: 'No map of dialects is here given in illustration, because it is practically impossible to define their boundaries accurately. Such a map was once given by Dr Ellis, but it is only arbitrary; and Prof. Wright expressly says, that in his work also, the boundaries suggested are inexact; they are only given for convenience, as an approximation to the truth. He agrees with Dr Ellis in most of the particulars.' Recent research on isoglosses clearly shows that these nice and clear-cut lines on the map actually stand for complex and messy transitional zones. But at the same time it is true that there are focal areas that are sharply differentiated from other areas around. Bearing this in mind, I find Ellis' classification of English dialects perhaps less objectionable than Joseph Wright did. In particular, the comparisons that I have been able to make between the picture given by Ellis and the picture that arises from the *SED* material have convinced me that Ellis' work, including his map of the dialect areas of England, deserves serious consideration by future scholars.

For a survey of transition and focal areas in England, see Glauser (1991).

3 Blake (1981) is a good survey of the use of non-standard language in English literature. The use of dialect by Chaucer and his contemporaries is discussed by Blake in chapter 1.

4 Northern English has turned out to be remarkably conservative. A good illustration of this is that both *I is* 'I am' and *sal* 'shall', which were used by Chaucer to characterise northern speech, were still the forms reported from the north by the *SED* in the mid-twentieth century.

5 As can be seen from Påhlsson (1972), the 'burr' was still in the mid-twentieth century a significant sociolinguistic marker.

6 Studies like Tidholm (1979) and Rydland (1982) suggest that really significant changes in northern English can be detected only in the speech of those born after the Second World War (Ihalainen forthcoming a).

7 The *SED* data on 'She is' (question IX.7.7.3) show that *her* is used as a subject pronoun west of the line running from Portsmouth to south Derbyshire, covering the south-west and most of the west midlands.

8 Halliwell makes the following observations about the relationships between various counties:

> *Bedfordshire*: no link.
> *Berkshire*: south-west, midland.
> *Buckinghamshire*: no link, but is characterised as being 'not very broad' (xi), which suggests that it was close to standard English.
> *Cheshire*: no link.
> *Cornwall*: no link as far as English is concerned, but Cornwall is linked to Devon historically.

Cumberland: 'The dialects of Cumberland, Westmoreland, North-umberland, and Durham may be considered to be identical in all essential peculiarities, the chief differences arising from the mode of pronunciation' (xiii).

Derbyshire: no link, but characterised as being 'remarkable for its broad pronunciation' (xiv). (Halliwell quotes Dr Bosworth here.)

Devon: linked to the West Country: 'The West Country dialect is now spoken in greater purity in Devonshire than in any other county' (xiv).

Dorsetshire: similar to 'most of the Western parts of England' with 'essential features...which are not heard in Surrey or Hants' (xv). (Halliwell quotes Mr Barnes here.)

Durham: 'The Durham dialect is the same as that spoken in Northumberland and the North Riding of Yorkshire, the former being more like Scotch, and the latter more like English, but each in a very slight degree' (xvii).

Essex: 'The dialect of Essex is closely allied in some parts of the county to that of Kent, and in others to that of Suffolk, though generally not so broad, nor spoken with the strong Suffolk whining tone' (xvii).

Gloucestershire: 'The dialect is more similar to that of Somersetshire than of the adjoining counties, though not so strongly marked as a Western dialect' (xviii).

9 The terms 'Traditional Dialect' and 'Modern Dialect' are used by Trudgill (1990) to refer to the type of dialectal English described by the *SED* and dialectal English as it appears today.

10 The phrase 'ladies in the boat' plays an important part in Ellis' discussion of Cockney pronunciation. His attention was first attracted to these two diphthongs when he heard this phrase in Hyde Park. Changes in diphthongs also attracted Skeat's attention: 'We must also remember how pro-nunciation changes; for I can testify...that I was not accustomed to hear, half a century ago, the now familiar pronunciation of *skate* with the sound of *i* in *kite*, as if it were *skite*' (1896: xiv).

11 Marshall's comments on the social complication, on how to determine the proper social distance, are perceptive. Many Finns were equally confused in the 1960s and 1970s when there was a lot of social pressure to abandon the *you*-form in Finnish and use *thou* in all speech situations.

12 Below is a list of counties under which at least one pageful of entries (about 12 entries) was listed in the *EDS* bibliography (1877):

	Number of pages
Lancashire	32
Yorkshire	18
Cumberland	14
Cornwall	7
Northumberland	5
Devon	4
Westmorland	3
Dorset	2
Somerset	2
Norfolk	1·5
Durham	1
East Anglia	1
Essex	1
Gloucestershire	1
Hampshire	1
Kent	1
Lincolnshire	1
Suffolk	1
Sussex	1
Wiltshire	1

13 For a discussion, see Blake (1981: ch. 6).

14 This criticism is briefly discussed by Petyt (1980: 75–6).

15 Walker (1791: 10) had observed that besides the 'mispronunciation of single words', vulgar speech uses 'slides' or 'inflections', Walker's terms for various tunes, that differentiate it from polite speech. He actually recommends drills to help people to get rid of these unwanted 'inflections'.

16 A recent study based on tape-recorded Somerset speech found that of the grammatical features listed by Ellis, *ich* 'I' and the prefixed participial form are extinct; the rest are still common (Ihalainen 1991).

17 Wyld (1956: 298) suggests that *r* may have begun to be lost or vocalised in certain phonological contexts as early as the fifteenth century, 'at least in Essex and Suffolk'. Both Sheridan (1780) and Walker (1791) recommend that *r* should always be pronounced; but while Sheridan regards *r*-lessness vulgar, Walker lists pronunciations like *baad* 'bard' and *caad* 'card' without too much censure. There is a tradition in the literature that assumes the loss of *r* to have been completed by 1800. As we have seen, this dating cuts a long story short.

18 The importance of Walker's *Dictionary* is assessed by Bronstein (1990: 138) as follows: 'Walker's *Critical Pronouncing Dictionary* became the arbiter for most dictionary users of the time, meeting the demand for logic, order and linguistic regularity. Nor did his influence end with that century.' And furthermore: 'Walker's work was considered the more authoritative and

Sheridan's pronunciation entries succumbed, in later, other lexicons, to the dictates of Walker.'

19 Sounds resulting from *l*-vocalisation show a considerable amount of variation. The following are possible realisations of the mergers referred to by Trudgill: 'feel/fill' [fɪo], 'doll/dole' [doʊ]/[dɒoˑ], 'pull/Paul' [poː]. For further discussion, see Sivertsen (1960), Wells (1982, II: 313–16) and Gimson (1989: 205). Frogley (1983) gives a good picture of the extent of this phenomenon in one specific regional variety.

PART II

ENGLISH OVERSEAS

6 ENGLISH IN AUSTRALIA

George W. Turner

6.1 Introduction

6.1.1 Dialects in contact

Australian English had its beginnings in the late eighteenth century in a convict settlement where people of diverse speech were brought together. Some levelling of dialects had probably already taken place in England or even at sea. The first settlers were especially important in setting the direction of linguistic development in the new land. The vocabulary of the language grew by borrowing from Aboriginal languages or by retaining or borrowing from English dialects, by extending the reference of existing resources or by conjoining existing elements in compounds or set phrases. The controlling force in directing the actual development of the language from these potential sources was the social experience of the inhabitants of Australia.

The people who established European settlements in Australia had no thought of changing the English language. Yet even before the Union Flag was raised at Sydney Cove on 26 January 1788 the forces of change had been at work. Most of the involuntary passengers had already left rural England for cities, accommodating their speech to their new neighbours there, and in some cases learning the ways of urban crime, though not all who were caught, perhaps in a single minor theft, were professional criminals. Then they were again thrown among people of varying background to learn the ways of prisons or to adapt to the new experience of a sea voyage lasting more than eight months. Finally the passengers of the several ships in the *First Fleet*, as it is always called, were brought together in the small settlement at Sydney Cove.

Though the new settlement was a small community, it can hardly have been small enough for any individual to influence the general speech, as happened in a rare instance in Pitcairn Island (Ross & Moverley 1964: 137–8). It was a situation of 'dialects in contact', the bringing together of differing forms of English leading to a mutual adjustment or accommodation of speakers in particular encounters with consequent mixing, levelling and simplification of language (Trudgill 1986: 2–4, 127). How far such mutual adjustment and the formation of a new variety of English had already taken place before the First Fleet arrived has been a matter of debate (see especially Blair 1975; Collins 1975; Hammarström 1980), but since some mixing of dialect in English cities must be conceded, and since, no language ever being quite uniform, a koine tolerating a fair amount of residual variation may be assumed as a basis for fuller Australianisation, the debate is perhaps somewhat artificial.

We may assume that, as in America (Baugh 1951: 416), the first comers established (or brought with them) the main form of a local speech and that later generations were assimilated to it. Experience was valuable where all was novelty and the hierarchies of prison life reinforced a tendency to conform to the new traditions being developed. There is evidence for this in the Australian English terms *old hand* and *new chum* with connotations both in their prison context and in wider use of respect for the old hand or expert and amused contempt for the new chum or novice. New models of authority were replacing the values brought from the old country. Individual parents might attempt to impose more traditional values on the manners and speech of their children but children are less influenced by parents than by peer-groups (Labov 1978: 304–7) so that conformity was predominantly to a socially, not individually, determined norm.

There was, however, a counter-tendency. The new society was rigidly divided by class. Tench (1961: 297) thought the 'flash' language of the convicts 'deeply associated with depravity'. Clearly there was no amiable mixing there. Nevertheless, though the adjustments of language made in face-to-face interaction are more important than the passive understanding of such authoritarian speech as present-day broadcasting or the eighteenth-century pulpit in guiding linguistic change, standard language probably had a greater influence than the small number of its speakers in early Australia might suggest. It was one among the regional and social varieties brought into the melting pot, and to master it could be a measure of making good in the colony. To take an example from the later levelling society of the goldfields, the Bulder brothers in *The Miner's Right* no longer speak dialect after living in Australia while their old friend back in England says such things as 'Moind ye bain't took by them kangaroos, Miss' (Boldrewood 1890: 343). It is an upper-class view which describes the difference as 'different degrees of development', but undoubtedly a good deal of upward social mobility had linguistic leverage to help it.

People who in their conversation adapt their speech to meet different expectations in a hearer need not be conscious of the changes they are making. Linguists are sometimes surprised at how prominent a linguistic item or feature may seem and still be overlooked (Labov 1978: 309). Speakers of varying dialect may even, if few actual misunderstandings occur, be unaware that there is a difference. Even unusual terms may be understood in context, and might have the appeal of novelty or colourful expression and be imitated in ways of varying friendliness, so that whereas the usual result of dialect mixture is the loss of untypical elements, especially in pronunciation, there is a counter-tendency, especially in vocabulary, to adopt 'certain highly salient linguistic features such as new words and idioms' (Trudgill 1986: 40). This explains the retention from English dialect of such Australianisms as *chook*, *cobber* or *dinkum*.

6.1.2 *Languages in contact*

The mechanism of linguistic borrowing between languages may be examined in the early history of the word *kangaroo*. It is first mentioned by Banks in 1770 as a native word. Cook three weeks later referred to 'the Animals which I have before mentioned called by the natives *kangooroo* or *kanguru*' (Cook 1968: 367). In 1788 the sentence (quoted by the *AND* s.v. *kangaroo*) 'Near one of these huts we found the bones of a kangaroo' anticipates the modern spelling and accepts the word as part of English.

The borrowing is not a single event but a process passing through a series of phases. First there must be contact, some sort of bilingualism or sharing of understanding, the very minimum being an understanding of the significance of pointing. If Banks and the influential speaker of the Guugu Yimidhirr language communicated by pointing, the animal observed was presumably a large black or grey kangaroo, probably a male of the species *Macropus robustus*, since that is a current meaning of Guugu Yimidhirr *gaɲurru*. Then, stripped of its original connotations, the word took on a widened English meaning and an English plural (*Kanguroos* Phillip 1789: 104). It was given a spelling, or two spellings, by

Cook, which would have meant nothing to its original speakers, and began its long history of entering into English compounds (*kangaroo-rat*, Tench 1961: 269).

Borrowings begin as quotations ('so-called by the natives'), and social attitudes and prejudices may inhibit or facilitate the passage of a term from 'so-called' to adoption. Because of such prejudices, recourse to Aboriginal languages was infrequent in the nineteenth century.

Recourse to other languages or dialects was not necessary in adapting English to its new and very different environment and social experience. Even so novel a creature as the kangaroo was described in English before its present name was established. Cook reported 'an animal something less than a greyhound' (Cook 1968: 351). It was compared to a goat (*ibid.*: 352), a hare (*ibid.*: 359) and a few years later to a jerboa (Phillip 1789: 104). A midshipman with the First Fleet, Newton Fowell, wrote 'their head very much resembles that of a fox, their forelegs very short with a hand like a Monkeys' (*Advertiser*, Adelaide, 17 December 1987, p. 6). A few years later still, the poet Barron Field sees a combination of the squirrel and the hart. Joseph Banks discovered a name for one kind of kangaroo when Cook's party put in for repairs in the Endeavour River area, modern Cooktown, in North Queensland, and the name *kangaroo* was extended to cover similar marsupials and soon supplanted the menagerie of English descriptive titles.

6.1.3 Semantic change

Kangaroos were strange animals but hardly more strange than the traditional absurdity, the *rara avis in terris nigroque simillima cygno*, the black swan. The collocation of *black* with *swan* was not quite unprecedented; Richard Brome's play *The Antipodes* (1640), for example, links black swans with other antipodean absurdities (I.vi.158), but in Australia the collocation became more frequent, or, if the adjective *black* was omitted, the term *swan* took on new connotations. To complicate matters further, the earlier image of white swans persists in literary and traditional contexts, so that an Australian hearing that Annie Laurie's 'throat is like the swan' does not imagine a black throat.

Whether a language used in a new situation borrows new terms or extends the use of existing ones, change is equally real and inevitable. Even borrowed words do not bring with them their native conceptual structure intact but enter into a new structure of semantic elements. Different languages borrowing an international word emphasise different aspects of the potential semantic complex. To Australians a kangaroo is the animal that moves rapidly with a leaping movement. A leaping kangaroo is the logo of Australia's international airline QANTAS. With less emphasis on speed and elegance, a car *kangaroos* when it starts with a series of jerks. To the French a kangaroo is the animal that carries its baby in a pouch, and so a *wagon kangourou* is a railway 'piggyback' truck. Similarly in Italian *canguro* is an aeroplane lifting a smaller craft for launching in the air, though it is also a colleague promoted more rapidly than his competitors think fit (Turner 1976: 54–5).

In each language the distribution of the new word is affected by competition from semantically related words. *Kangaroo* in English is affected by the presence of its hyponyms such as *wallaby, wallaroo, euro, pademelon*, etc. Where an Australian specifies a wallaby, a Dane may simply say *lille kænguru*.

The description of novelty allowed three possibilities, all illustrated in the naming of the dingo. Cook simply referred to *dogs* ('Tame Animals they have none but Dogs' – Cook 1968: 367); Phillip noted that a specimen sent to England 'laps like other dogs, but neither barks nor growls if vexed and teized' (1789: 274). It seems (to us) quite natural to call this medium-sized dog-shaped frequenter of human company a *dog*, though we think it quaint when by a similar semantic extension Aboriginal people called pigs *wombats* (Reynolds 1982: 41) or the unicorn on a coat of arms the 'dingo' (*AND* s.v. *dingo*).

Dingoes could also be given their native name, *dingo*, in English, at first with such phrases as 'as the natives call them' but by 1835 used without such fencing off from the general vocabulary. In fact, by then *dingo* could be used to translate a less familiar word ('three dingos, or native dogs, the "warrigul" of the aborigines' – Bennett 1834, I: 231).

Dingo is now in fact the usual term except in special collocations such as *the dog fence*, a fence over 8,000 km. long that is *dog-proof* 'proof against dingoes', or *dogger* 'dingo-hunter'. This allows a polarisation of connotations to accumulate around each of the words *dog* and *dingo*. *Dog* retains its general English associations, many of them favourable memories of the faithful household pet. The dingo is the dog given a bad name. The *AND* refers, with the support of numerous quotations, to the 'characteristics popularly attributed to the dingo, esp. cowardice, treachery'. The collocation 'the sneaking dingo' is as early as 1869. The connotations of the word *yellow*, the colour of the dingo, unfortunately for him reinforce the connotations of cowardice attached to him. A 1901 quotation harnesses the two together: 'The dingo I will never show; – that is I won't turn up the yellow.' As a verb, *to dingo* has come to mean 'to behave in a cowardly manner'. It can suggest betrayal *Don't dingo on your mates*.

6.1.4 Compounds and combinations

There is a third possibility in naming *Canis familiaris dingo* in English; it can be called *native dog*, a natural collocation attested as early as 1788. If the collocation is frequently used, the 'motivation' (in Saussure's sense) or awareness of the meaning of the separate elements, fades and the term operates as a unit, gathering its own connotations (mainly of theft, it seems, in the case of *native dog*).

In an extreme case an attribute may do nothing except cancel the essential connotation of another word, as in *false sarsaparilla*. Usually the much commoner attribute *native* includes this negating function. A *native bear* is not only 'not northern hemisphere' but also not a bear or even a mammal. In both cases the attribute may sometimes be dropped so that one semantic element in the residue *sarsaparilla* or *bear* is 'not a sarsaparilla' or 'not a bear'. This pervasive negativity in our Australian nomenclature may foster a feeling that truth and standards reside in the northern hemisphere.

Semantic change of this kind is especially common in names of flora and fauna, but any kind of semantic change can be described in terms of the shedding and gaining of semantic elements. Thus the word *muster* loses the feature 'military' and gains the feature 'agricultural' when applied to mustering cattle.

But why does *muster* change in just this way? Social pressures, in this case the organising of agriculture in military convict stations, provide the motive force. Semantics indicates possible directions of change; sociolinguistics explains the actual realisation of these potentialities.

Even in phonology, morphology and syntax, though they are less immediately sensitive to continuing social pressure than lexis, we are taken back to the origins of settlement and the social composition of the initial European population of Australia, and, to a lesser extent, to later migrations. These developments are examined in sections 6.2 and 6.3; a detailed history of lexis is given in section 6.4.

6.2   Phonology

6.2.1   *Origins*

We are reminded when we notice the rhymes in an early ballad 'Botany Bay' (Clark 1957: 75–7) that the language brought to Australia was late eighteenth-century English. There is evidence from general English that the rhymes in the following couplets were good in their day:

> Ye worst of land-lubbers, make ready for sea,
> There's room for you all about Botany Bay.

> Commercial arrangements give prospects of joy,
> Fair and firm may be kept ev'ry national tie

Australian and English speakers have changed *pari passu* in these pronunciations as, at a less standard level, both have discarded the pronunciation which is associated with the Wellers ('Be wery careful o' vidders') and was captured in Peter Cunningham's comment on an emerging colloquial speech among 'currency' youths (those born in the colony): 'Even the better of them are apt to meet your observation of "A fine day" with their *improving* response of "*Wery* fine indeed"' (Cunningham 1827, II: 60).

In the context Cunningham makes some perceptive remarks about the origin of a local pronunciation founded, like the English of the north of Ireland or the United States, on the speech of the first settlers. He notes a predominance of a London background in those who first formed a local pronunciation, though he gives no details apart from the striking Wellerism.

Most of the writers who have commented on Australian speech are less helpful than Cunningham. They are usefully summarised by Baker (1966: 431–6) and the earlier comments, before 1855, are summarised and discussed by Blair (1975). Hill (1968) stressed the importance of manuscript sources for the study of early pronunciation but the result was to bring to light only the unsystematic and often contradictory observations of lay observers (Delbridge 1970: 24).

There is so much diversity among the printed comments that they afford the historian of phonology little help. Some hear Cockney everywhere, others note a remarkably pure speech. Shortly after Cunningham, George Bennett, another usually reliable observer, writes:

> It has often been mentioned by writers upon the United States of America, that a purer and more correct English is spoken in that country than in the 'old country' where it is corrupted by so many

different provincial dialects. The remark respecting the United States of America will equally apply to Australia; for among the native-born Australians (descended from European parents), the English spoken is very pure; and it is easy to recognise a person from *home* or one born in the colony, no matter of what class of society, from this circumstance. (Bennett 1834: 331–2)

The purity in this context seems to imply an absence of dialects among those born in the new colony. An earlier writer, James Dixon, in 1820 similarly supports the theory that dialects mingled and were levelled early in the new colony when he writes: 'The amalgamation of such various dialects assembled together, seems to improve the mode of articulating the words' (Dixon 1822: 46).

With the goldrushes in the mid-nineteenth century came a fresh influx of linguistic variety. One writer, Samuel Mossman, mentions the 'Cockney drawl of the hucksters' which he enjoyed as 'thoroughly English' (Blair 1975: 22) but a New South Wales School Commission of 1854–5 viewed with alarm an 'inattention' to 'vicious pronunciation' in schools which tended to 'foster an Australian dialect' which bade fair 'to surpass the American in disagreeableness' (Baker 1966: 431). Thirty years later, nevertheless, J. A. Froude again discovered 'pure English', specifically contrasting it with the American (Froude 1886: 84).

Without phonetic training an observer can hardly be expected to detect significant details of speech, and, if he or she could, general language affords very vague terms to describe them. 'Pure' to one person might simply mean 'not American', to another 'without regional variation', to another again 'not Cockney'. The speech referred to might be cultivated, general or broad Australian.

6.2.2   McBurney's testimony

One observer did have some training in accurate listening and detailed reporting. Samuel McBurney, a school principal in Victoria, travelled widely in Australia and New Zealand in the 1880s examining large classes of tonic sol-fa singers in schools. While doing this he made careful and detailed notes on the pronunciation of a number of words, used as types, among the children in each centre that he visited. He had studied Melville Bell's *Visible Speech* and A. J. Ellis' *Pronunciation for Singers* and his work remains valuable as the first detailed description of Australian English pronunciation (Horvath 1985: 8). His findings were summarised in an article in the *Press* (Christchurch, NZ, 5 October 1887) and more widely disseminated in Ellis (1889: 236–48).

McBurney found Australian pronunciation 'purer than can be found in any district at Home' (1887: 81). The qualification 'in any district' shows that the 'purity' in this case is not just an absence of regional variation. Perhaps a comparative absence of social differentiation is implied. He also recognises the levelling effect of dialects in contact:

> So great has been the intercourse and intermingling of the many parts of which we are made up that the distinction [marking colonials] is not nearly so great as might be expected. Indeed for months after I had commenced my investigations on this subject, the unfailing answer to my enquiries in the different Australian colonies was 'We can hear no distinction between ourselves and visitors.' (*ibid.*)

McBurney discounts parental influence as a source of change or stability: 'In the bush, where children hear only their parents, we may find broad Scotch, Irish, or provincial English, but in almost all other circumstances the influence of parentage is very slight, and generally acts by modifying the *general* usage, not by conserving the original type of speech' (*ibid.*: 82).

Among features of Australian speech already current a century ago and noticed by McBurney are 'linking [r]' (*the idea-r-of*) against a generally non-rhotic background (pronouncing no [r] in *farther* or *world*, even when parents produced 'a very loud trill'), and similarities to Cockney, which surprised him, as he considered, with Ellis, that Cockney was a recent phenomenon and thought few Australians were emigrants from Kent (*ibid.*). McBurney describes speech that is recognisably Australian. It seems that the outlines of Australian English pronunciation were established by the end of the first century of European settlement.

Nobody doubts that the origins of Australian English are to be sought in south-east England. Unlike northerners, Australians distinguish the vowels of *put* and *but*; they do not sound historical [r] except before a vowel (Trudgill 1986: 130). An earlier fusion of predominantly south-eastern modes of speech produced RP, which is also part of the input into the later fusion of speechways in Australian English or its popular origins in England. It is not then surprising that:

> Phonologically, all Australian English is very close to RP; phonetically, it is not. That is to say, the Australian vowel system can be set in one-to-one correspondence with the RP system (which is also that of the south of England in general, if we ignore certain recent developments). Furthermore, the lexical incidence of these vowels in

stressed syllables is virtually identical with that found in RP. The correspondence in unstressed syllables breaks down mainly because of the Australian avoidance of unstressed [ɪ] in favour of word-internal [ə]...and word-final /iː/.

(Wells 1982: 595)

6.2.3   The Mitchell era

Just before the end of the nineteenth century Australian vocabulary was seriously recorded in dictionaries by Morris (1898) and Lake (1898), but the serious study of pronunciation had to wait almost another half-century for the pioneering work of Mitchell (1946). The Australian accent had 'long been a favourite subject of inconclusive discussion' (Mitchell 1946: 1). The search for order was helped by the correspondence between RP and Australian English in phonology though not in phonetics. It was, without the technical phoneme theory that was making its controversial beginnings in Europe and the United States, possible simply to list the sounds of RP, as described by Daniel Jones, and compare their realisation in English and Australian speech, a procedure usual until about 1970 (Pilch 1971: 269).

Since there was clearly some variation among speakers of Australian English, Mitchell distinguished popular from educated speech (1946: 13), later, following Baker (1966: 436), making a tripartite division into Cultivated, General and Broad Australian (Mitchell & Delbridge 1965a: 14) which is now generally accepted (e.g. Wells 1982: 594), though some have felt it necessary to emphasise that a particular speaker need not be confined to one variety (Horvath 1985: 174) and that such divisions are a convenient segmentation of a cline or gradation, not a series of three discrete groups (Hammarström 1980: 62). This is no damaging criticism; it is of the nature of language to partition continua.

In a revised edition with Arthur Delbridge of Mitchell's 1946 book, the authors remark that 'if the book were now being written *de novo*...the writers would not feel, as Professor Mitchell did then, that it was necessary to describe Australian speech by comparing it, point by point, with Educated Southern English' (Mitchell & Delbridge 1965a: x). It was nevertheless an obvious way to proceed. Since the most cultivated Australian accents are close to RP, it would make little difference whether an analysis of the other variants took the form of a comparison with Cultivated Australian or RP.

In either case egalitarian Australians tend to be embarrassed by the suggestion of an elite. This attitude gives Broad, or at least General,

Australian a 'negative' (Labov 1966: 495) or 'covert' (Trudgill 1972, 1984) prestige especially among males. The terms *basilect*, *mesolect* and *acrolect* could be used to avoid the popular connotations of 'broad', 'general' and especially 'cultivated' or 'educated', though the new terms mean much the same to the etymologically sophisticated. The term *acrolect* does, however, avoid a suggestion that an upper variety is produced (by cultivation or education) from a pre-existing general or broad stock. It may be, but should not merely be assumed by the pressure of terminology.

A genuine case of 'cultivation' in its literal sense is what has been called a 'modified accent' (Mitchell & Delbridge 1965b: 1–2), one that has been deliberately, artificially and unsystematically tinkered with in the direction of a fancied upper-class style. Even 'cultivated' speakers call such speech 'affected'.

It was the merit of Mitchell and his successors to bring order into the description of the infinite variety of sounds people make to communicate in Australia. The generalised units that are distinctive, the phonemes, and the most basic levels of social difference were clarified. To do this, detail had to be sacrificed to outline. Recent trends have been to increase the complexity of the description by elaborating sociolinguistic methods and investigating and quantifying the detail masked out in phonemic analysis. Topics such as gender differences, ethnicity and social class are increasingly prominent in current studies, sometimes based on implications of details in a survey by Mitchell & Delbridge (1965b) themselves that were not brought out. Horvath points out (1985: 19–21; cf. Elliott 1977) that from their results it was clear, for instance, that a broad accent is much more likely in a working-class male than in a girl from a private school. Nevertheless their work is still the basis on which Australian phonological study is built (Horvath 1985: 8).

6.2.4 The vowel system in stressed syllables

Wells has argued (1982: 181) that the basis of a typology of accents of English must be based upon vowels, a view in accordance with that of Mitchell & Delbridge (1965b: 9), who asked speakers in their survey to read aloud the diagnostic words *beat, boot, say, so, high, how* at the close of each interview.

In order to describe Australian English vowels in detail we may conveniently divide them into four sets, based on Wells (1982: 168–78, 596):

1   a set of traditionally short stressed or stressable monophthongs;

2   a set of traditionally long vowels and diphthongs with a front mid to close quality or (if diphthongal) endpoint;

3   a set of traditionally long vowels and diphthongs with a back mid to close quality or (if diphthongal) endpoint;

4   a set of traditionally long vowels and diphthongs which have a relatively open quality or (if diphthongal) endpoint.

In addition there is schwa, /ə/, the indeterminate vowel at the end of *comma*, always unstressed, variable in realisation, an anomalous entity, for some the most frequent phoneme, for some absent because not found in contrast with unstressed /ɪ/.

The term 'traditionally short' (or 'long') indicates that the sound is the reflex of a historically short (or long) vowel. Probably, in fact, the set 1 vowels are indeed short and the other sets still long but all differ in quality as well so that length may be left out of account (is not contrastive or phonemic) in describing Australian English vowels. There have been counter-suggestions, that length alone distinguishes *banner* 'one who bans' from *banner* 'flag' with a shorter vowel (Bernard 1963, but cf. Burgess 1968 and the summary of the discussion in Delbridge 1970: 23–4). If there is in fact an audible difference (whether in the stressed vowels or in the following consonants), it seems better to treat the distinction as one of morphology, as we would presumably leave some speakers' pronunciation of *grown* and *thrown* as /grʌʊən/ and /θrʌʊən/ contrasting with *groan* and *throne* as /grʌʊn/ and /θrʌʊn/ to morphology rather than try to fit a new triphthong into the sound system of English. A similar argument applies to those Australian speakers whose *shared* and *shed* differ only in the length of a monophthongal vowel.

Set 1 of the Australian English vowels consists of the stressable monophthongs in the words *kit*, *dress*, *trap*, *strut*, *lot* and *foot*. These vowels are short but, more important, are always 'checked' or followed by a consonant in Australian English. Perhaps some speakers who monophthongise the centring diphthongs in *here* and *there* do in fact display lengthened variants of the vowels in *kit* and *dress*, and since the vowel of *cut* and the vowel of *cart* or *car* may differ only in length for some speakers, a system recognising real short vowels contrasting with long equivalents could be devised for these subvarieties, but for most Australian speakers length as a criterion is unnecessary if we define the set 1 vowels as necessarily checked.

Compared with other accents of English (except New Zealand English), Australian English, especially in the broader end of the social spectrum, is marked by a raised pronunciation of the front short vowels in *trap*, *dress* and *kit*. Wells (1982: 598) found the vowel of *dress* strikingly different from that heard in most other accents. Mitchell (1946: 32), however, thought the difference between the Australian and English realisation of this sound 'not easily heard' and one that 'calls for a keen ear and careful listening'. An Australian may be struck by some English speakers' pronunciation of a word like *exit* with its marked impression of closing, where the vowels of an Australian version /eksət/ tend to be level or falling.

The vowel of *strut* is fronted, possibly as a drag-chain effect of the raising of /æ/, /e/ and /ɪ/ (Wells 1982: 599), though since the pronunciation of this sound by younger English-speakers is forward of the more conservative older pronunciation (Gimson 1962: 102), it seems that the same tendency to fronting is found there. It is also found in London Cockney (Wells 1982: 599).

The pronunciation of /ʊ/ in *foot* appears not to vary between Australian English and RP, while /ɒ/ in *lot* 'tends to be a little closer than the English vowel' (Mitchell & Delbridge 1965a: 36).

Set 2 of Australian vowels contains traditionally long vowels and diphthongs with a front mid to close endpoint. Key words are *fleece*, *face*, *choice* and *price*. Set 3 is the corresponding set with a back mid to close endpoint. The key words are *goose*, *goat* and *mouth*. Together the two sets make a superset of closing diphthongs, since even in cultivated Australian English the vowels of *fleece* and *goose* are slightly diphthongal, phonetically [ɪiː] and [ʊuː], while in general or broad speech a more markedly lowered first element approaches schwa in quality (so [əiː] and [əuː]). It will be noticed that all of Mitchell & Delbridge's main diagnostic sounds in *beet*, *boot*, *say*, *so*, *how*, *high* belong to the superset of closing diphthongs. These six are also the vowel variants discussed by Horvath (1985: 13–15). The seventh closing diphthong, not matched by an equivalent with a back endpoint, is the diphthong in the key word *choice*. The Australian English pronunciation is not distinctive except that its initial element may be somewhat raised as it is always kept separate from the diphthong in *price*.

The six diagnostic long vowels and diphthongs merit separate discussion.

/iː/, the sound in *beet* or *fleece*. The vowel in Cultivated Australian

English may be near a monophthong, at least in citation forms. In General and Broad accents the initial element is one of the closer variants of schwa, the opening being greater and the glide longer towards a high front target as the accent becomes broader. The high front target of the glide may not be reached, especially in Broad accents. This seems to differentiate Australian English from Cockney, which has a similar realisation of the *fleece* vowel but whereas, according to Eva Sivertsen (1960: 49), 'there can be no lengthening of the initial element' in Cockney, it seems to me that a broad drawled pronunciation /ət 'sə:ɪmz tə 'mə:ɪ/ is possible in Australian English. When Gough Whitlam and Billy Snedden dominated the Australian television screen such pronunciations in deliberate speech were heard from the highest in the land, in accents not otherwise, or not consistently, broad. A variant [eɪ] with fronted first element is sporadically heard but is not common in Australia.

/u:/, the sound in *boot* or *goose*. This parallels /i:/ in having a possible monophthongal pronunciation, made rather more likely by the possibility of fronting the /u:/ instead of diphthongising it. The spectrum of variation in the diphthong, from [ʊu] to [əʊ], and the length of glide as accents become broader also parallels the variation in /i:/ but seems to be less marked. The existence of Mitchell's [əʊ] has been doubted, but perhaps a marked opening to something like [əʊ] seems not impossible after yod, as in *you beaut* [jə:ʊ bjə:ʊt]. To Hammarström (1980: 11) the fronted version of /u:/ recalled the vowel of Swedish *hus*, but without its rounding.

/ʌɪ/, the sound in *face*, *say*. The starting-point is the Australian /ʌ/ of *but*, between half open and open and a little forward of central. Cultivated has a somewhat higher and fronter starting-point, near cardinal [ɛ].

/ʌʊ/, the sound of *goat*, *so*. Many variants for the pronunciation of this vowel have been noticed (e.g. Hammarström 1980: 16; Horvath 1985: 14). Mitchell (1946: 35) represented the broad version as /ʌʊ/, the phonemic transcription used by Wells (1982: 596). (The symbol /əʊ/ used by some English phoneticians is unsuitable for Australian English as it suggests a broad pronunciation of the vowel in *goose*.) The target may be an unrounded sound (a somewhat fronted [ɯ]). Mitchell & Delbridge (1965b: 84) found a variant of this sound, the only regionally distinctive sound in their survey, among Adelaide girls in independent schools (Hammarström (1980: 16) thought the restriction too exclusive). A sound like [ɒʊ] was able to be clearly heard on the accompanying gramophone record, especially in a phrase *where the overflow goes*. My impression is that this pronunciation was commoner in a generation of female students in Adelaide at about the time of the survey than it is now.

/ɑɪ/, the sound of *price, high*. Wells chooses a phonemic notation with [ɑ], emphasising the maximum differentiation of the starting-points of the diphthongs in *price* and *mouth*. A more phonetically accurate choice would be /ɒɪ/ since there is usually rounding of the first element. Cultivated speakers may favour a more forward starting-point, [aɪ].

/æʊ/, the sound in *mouth, how*. A Cultivated accent may exhibit a diphthong [aʊ] close to its equivalent in RP. In General and Broad there is a clear [æ] in the onset, the Broad having a longer onset than the General, or a higher one.

The final set of stressed or stressable sounds is the set of centring diphthongs, the sounds in *near, square* and *cure*, and the open vowels in *start, palm* or *bath, north* or *force* and *nurse*. Details are given in the following paragraphs.

/ɪə/ and /eə/, the sounds in *near* and *square*. The phonetic realisation of all the centring diphthongs tends towards the monophthongal, especially before an /r/ which is pronounced or finally. When that happens, usually in the broadest accents, length alone distinguishes *vary* (ve:ri:) or *Mary* (me:ri:) from *very* (veri:) or *merry* (meri:), and the rule that stressed /ɪ/ and /e/ occur only in checked syllables no longer applies.

/ʊə/: monophthongisation is particularly common in the *cure* diphthong, /ʊə/ then being merged with /ɔ:/, the vowel of *north*. Many speakers make this change in some words and not others, especially in *your* (and *you're*), *poor* and *sure*. It is possible to mistake a pronunciation of *endure* as *enjoy*. Those retaining a diphthong tend to lengthen its onset to [u:ə].

/a:/ the sound in *start, palm, bath*. This is a front sound in Australian

English, nearer cardinal [a] than [ɑ]. This sound especially distinguishes Australian from South African English, and even in British English the equivalent sound in an announcement that *Staff cars park in the staff car park* has been known to strike strangely on antipodean ears.

/ɔː/ the sound in *north*, *force*, the only true back vowel in Australian English (Wells 1982: 599) since /uː/ and /ɜː/ tend to be fronted.

/ɜː/ the sound in *nurse*. Besides being fronted, this sound is rounded and is closer in Australian English than in RP. An Englishperson's *bird* may sound like a *bard* to an Australian. A collection of Australian poems with the title *Bards in the Wilderness* makes a sort of pun, since a bird of the wilderness figures in an old song, though of course the Australian *bard* is distinguished both from RP and from Broad AustE *bird*. The hesitation phenomenon spelt *er* in English texts would be better spelt *ar* or *ah* for Australians.

In discussing Australian long vowels in relation to RP (or discussing the grades of accent within Australia), the broader sounds can consistently be described as raised versions, or, in the case of already higher vowels, diphthongised versions, of the more cultivated sounds. By displaying this array of observed differences against a time-scale it is possible to translate them into successive stages in an evolutionary process. Usually in such assumptions the broader pronunciations are taken to be less conservative (more advanced) than the cultivated ones, especially if they represent a general historical tendency or 'drift' in which 'it is the uncontrolled speech of the folk to which we must look for advance information as to the general linguistic movement' (Sapir 1921: 167). Sapir did not develop this insight or quite escape the prejudice of his time against the 'uncontrolled' spoken vernacular, especially that of the cities, but in his remark is a hint of a procedure for reconstructing the history of Australian English vowels. Vowel change is particularly well suited to such study since the available space in the classic vowel quadrilateral allows gradual change (Samuels 1972: 32). If one item changes, it may either leave a space which another sound may fill (a drag-chain effect) or crowd an articulatory space making it necessary for another sound to change in order to preserve its distinctiveness (a push-chain effect) (Bynon 1977: 82–8; Wells 1982: 98–9).

A classic systematic change which can be interpreted either as a push-chain or drag-chain is the Great Vowel Shift of early Modern English, and the similarity between that change and the variation in Australian vowels interpreted as a diachronic process has been noticed (Mitchell 1946: 32; Turner 1960; Wells 1982: 256). In an ideal case such a change may replace every sound with a different sound and yet preserve the system intact, as in musical transposition each note may change and the tune be considered the same.

Though in general Australian English and RP, or the variants of Australian English within Australia, agree phonemically if not phonetically, there is not always correspondence in particular words (Wells 1982: 78, 597). In some cases only an isolated word is affected, as when *maroon* (the colour) is pronounced /mə'roʊn/; sometimes a pair or group of words is affected, as when *auction* and *caustic* are pronounced only with /ɒ/, not a choice between /ɒ/ and /ɔː/, or *aquatic* and *quagmire* have /ɒ/, not /æ/. Sometimes a more deliberate pronunciation is favoured in Australia (*immediate* as /ə'miːdiːət/ not /ɪ'midʒət/); sometimes there are differences in stress as in /dʒuːbə'liː/, not /'dʒuːbɪliː/ for *jubilee*. Extensive lists of such departures from RP can be found in Mitchell (1946: 38–46). They apply to all levels of Australian English.

One set of variants seems to mark a rare regional difference within Australian English. Words like *dance, plant, sample* and other words (listed in Wells 1982: 135), where an RP /ɑː/ is followed by a nasal plus another consonant, are usually pronounced as in RP in Adelaide but with the /æ/ phoneme of *trap* in Sydney. Since recent research is reported (Bradley 1989: 262–3) to have confirmed what Adelaide people always believed, that Adelaide has a higher-than-usual proportion of Cultivated speakers, it is generally assumed that the pronunciation as in *start* is more traditional or correct. Sydney people coming to Adelaide to live cannot bring themselves to adopt the Adelaide pronunciation because it 'sounds affected'; if Adelaide people were to try to adopt the Sydney pronunciation they would perhaps feel that they were assuming a dinkum-Aussie-ness to which they are not entitled. A similar ambivalence of attitude towards a variation in a set of words including *dance* is reported from Chicago, where the back variant was also 'higher class' (Bloomfield 1935: 48).

It may come as a surprise, then, to find that the *trap* vowel appears to have been the more refined variant in England in Australia's early years. The preliminary 'Principles of English pronunciation' in Walker's pronouncing dictionary (Walker 1791: 11) was firm in its condemnation of the Adelaide (and RP) variant of the word *plant*, in which 'pronouncing the *a*... as long as in *half*, *calf*, etc. borders very closely on vulgarity', and under the word *plant* itself in the main body of the dictionary, Walker renews the attack on 'a coarse pronunciation of this word, chiefly among the vulgar, which rhymes it with *aunt*'. He recommends the same /æ/ pronunciation for *dance* and *sample* but the element *-mand* in *demand* and *command* is given the long sound.

6.2.5   *Vowels in unstressed syllables*

The most striking differences in the lexical distribution of phonemes in RP and Australian English are found in unstressed or weakly stressed syllables. In the word *trinity* an RP pronunciation is analysed as a succession of three syllables each containing the vowel phoneme /ɪ/, the sound in *kit*; an Australian pronunciation of the same word is analysed as a succession of three syllables containing three different vowel phonemes, /ɪ/, /ə/ and /iː/. Differences of this sort are pervasive, so that words with the same pronunciation in one variety may be distinguished in the other. *Surplice* and *surplus* are usually distinguished as /ˈsɜːplɪs/ and /ˈsɜːpləs/ in RP but are both /ˈsɜːpləs/ in all levels of Australian English, whereas *taxes* and *taxis*, not distinguished in RP, are always /ˈtæksəz/ and /ˈtæksiːz/ in Australian English. Further examples are given by Wells (1982: 601–3).

A partly parallel variation effects /ʊ/ in a word like *educate*, RP /ˈedjukeɪt/, AustE /ˈedjəkeɪt/. Neither /ɪ/ nor /ʊ/ remains short in an open syllable so that *medium* is /ˈmiːdiːəm/ and *gradual* is /ˈgrædjuːəl/ in Australian English. This is in accordance with the general rule that traditionally short vowels are checked, without having to confine the rule to stressed syllables as Wells (1982: 119) does for RP.

One result is the often remarked terminal /iː/ in words like *happy*, a trait also associated with near-RP by Trudgill & Hannah (1982: 11–12) and with Irish English by Thackeray (1959, I: 159), who reports the speech of Captain Costigan: 'He was quitting a city celebrated for its antiquitee, its hospitalitee, the beautee of its women, the manly fidelitee, generositee, and jovialitee of its men.' An Australian would have added *citee* and *manlee* to these pronunciations.

The distribution of /ɪ/ and /ə/ before a consonant in unstressed or partially stressed syllables in Australian English is complex. In a paper more important than its modest title and publication might suggest, J. R. L. Bernard (1975) investigates the accepted view of the time that in these cases the usual Australian preference is for /ə/, the British, especially in RP, for /ɪ/. The following 'well-worn' examples are given: *roses*, AustE /'roʊzəz/, RP /'roʊzɪz/; *wanted* AustE /'wɒntəd/, RP /'wɒntɪd/; *defeat*, AustE /də'fiːt/, RP /dɪ'fiːt/. While this is 'all very true', Bernard examines the effects of variation in stress on the quality of these vowels.

With main stress (*hit* as /hɪt/) or secondary stress (*risibility*, AustE /ˌrɪzə'bɪləti:/, RP /ˌrɪzɪ'bɪlɪtɪ/), 'the two march as one'. One might add that it is a standing joke among Australians that New Zealanders differ in this, merging /ɪ/ and /ə/ to a schwa-like sound (see Wells 1982: 606). New Zealanders in Australia have to put up with questions like *Dud you brung your fush and chups in a chully bun?* (a *chilly bin* is an insulated container usually called by the trade-name *Esky* in Australia), or look at graffiti like *New Zealand sucks – Australia seven*. Recent research, however, suggests that the trend in the Sydney pronunciation of stressed /ɪ/ is moving in the New Zealand direction (Bradley 1989: 265).

It is when the stress is less than secondary that the one-to-one correspondences between Australian and English and RP, or between Broad and Cultivated Australian English, begin to break up. The group of words affected are those with traditional spellings in *-ing*, *-ive*, *-ic*, *-ish* and *-age*. Thus *running*, *massive*, *antic*, *garnish* and *cabbage* might for some speakers of Cultivated Australian English be realised as /'rʌnɪŋ/, /'mæsɪv/, /'æntɪk/, /'gɑːnɪʃ/ and /'kæbɪdʒ/.

It is not claimed that these pronunciations are universal even among speakers of Cultivated Australian English. The most convincing example is the *-ing* of *running*, already exempted from the change in earlier accounts. Evidence for a high variant before /k/ is added to by literary writers who hear *paddock* as *paddick* (Furphy 1903: 5) or *bullock* as *bullick* (Wood 1953: 51). Since Cockney has a similar incidence of a high vowel before /k/, rendering *haddock* as /'ædɪk/ (Sivertsen 1960: 52), we have to be on guard against possible literary conventions, but the literary spellings may at least count as further evidence.

Bernard (1975: 32) thought that the varying incidence of /ɪ/ and /ə/ in closed syllables without main or secondary stress might be accounted for by assuming a tertiary degree of stress in educated varieties of Australian English, absent in the Broad varieties. He confesses that 'the notion of tertiary lexical stress is not especially appealing and it is a difficult thing to demonstrate instrumentally or with minimal pairs'. Since he also confesses the tertiary stress 'must be a subjective item', it might be best simply to state that either the /ɪ/ set or the /ə/ set is the result of an unexplained combinative sound change in the stated environments. The concept of 'shading', 'the development of different allophones conditioned by the place of articulation of the following consonant' (Wells 1982: 128), may be useful in dealing with the problem, or another approach might be to see the whole pattern as an example of (incipient) vowel merger (Wells 1982: 85; Trudgill 1984: 88–101).

The Macquarie Dictionary makes use of Bernard's guidelines, which were in fact devised to guide those making its phonemic descriptions. That there was some difficulty in applying rules of tertiary stress is suggested by the decision to use /ɪ/ in the first syllable of *pistachio* and *mistook* but /ə/ in *mysterious, moustache* or *mistake*. If this represents a genuine difference for some speakers, it is a very fine one.

6.2.6   Prosodic characteristics

The incidence of main stress within words in Australian English does not usually differ from that of RP. Occasionally a word with the option of even stress (e.g. *hillside* as /ˈhɪlˈsaɪd/) in RP has only initial stress in all levels of Australian English. In sentence rhythm stresses seem to occur rather more frequently in Australian English than in RP (Mitchell 1946: 47; Turner 1966: 90–1). Mitchell cites a pronunciation of *half a pound of butter* with two stresses (on *half* and *butt-*) in RP against three (*half, pound* and *butt-*) in all levels of Australian English.

Intonation (Adams 1969) is allied to stress (Wells 1982: 89–91). In practice, it is often intonation that guides us in recognising stress. Australian intonation resembles what Wells called (p. 92) 'the low pitch range of a Texan drawl'. It is intonation especially that makes a difference in the general impression given by Australian and English, especially Cockney, speech. There are more stresses in an Australian utterance than in a corresponding English one and so more steps before a moving tone. The steps vary little in pitch, approaching a low-pitched monotone, and the pitch of the moving tone has a narrow range (Mitchell 1946: 49–51; Turner 1966: 92–3).

One detail of intonation has recently attracted a good deal of scholarly attention. When J. A. Froude in 1885 admired the 'pure English' of Australia, he particularly remarked 'They do not raise the voice at the end of a sentence as the Americans do, as if with a challenge to differ from them. They drop it courteously like ourselves' (Froude 1886: 84–5).

There are signs that this situation is beginning to change. When analysing interviews conducted in 1958 for their survey of adolescent speech, Mitchell & Delbridge (1965b: 56) noticed 'an abnormal type of speech contour' which they called 'the interview tune'. The interviewee was 'inclined to end with a rising terminal a sentence which would normally fall away to a low terminal'. The investigators took it to mean 'I've finished with that. What are you going to ask me next?'

As the new intonation became more widespread and more prominent, it attracted the writers of theses, was given a name 'high rising tone' or HRT (McGregor 1980) and is given a whole chapter in Barbara Horvath's study of Sydney speech (Horvath 1985: 118–32). Its social distribution was studied by McGregor, its meaning by Guy & Vonwiller (1984) and Allan (1984).

Horvath found that the social characteristics most likely to be associated with HRT in Sydney were teenagers, females, lower working class and either Greeks or Anglos (1985: 122). She finds that the underlying meaning of rising tones is to request the heightened participation of the listener (p. 132).

Of the other prosodies, nasality and voice quality (Wells 1982: 91–3), little that is conclusive can be said. Australian speech is popularly supposed to be generally nasal, but serious examination of the question does not support this belief. Mitchell & Delbridge (1965b: 58–9) distinguish pervasive and contextual nasality, the former affecting all vowels, the latter occurring only in the neighbourhood of nasal consonants. They found that /æ/ was the most likely vowel to be nasalised. Nasality was mainly found in Broad Australian English, but only 14 per cent of the whole sample showed noticeable nasality.

Mackiewicz-Krassowska (1976) confirmed these findings in so far as she found no evidence to support the popular conception of a 'nasal twang' in Australian English, and observed the propensity of /æ/ to nasalisation, but contrary to usual phonetic theory she suggested that high vowels are the more easily nasalised.

Wells (1982: 91) instances voice quality as an area 'where our ignorance of the facts is considerable'. It is possible that laymen claiming to be able to tell Sydney from Melbourne people 'by their accents' and being right more often than according to theory they should are responding to differences in voice quality, but this topic awaits research.

6.2.7   Consonants

Recent study of Australian English, especially by Barbara Horvath, has focused attention on variations in consonants, which were comparatively neglected in earlier studies. Consonants subject to variation are:

1   /h/ subject to variation in incidence.
2   /ŋ/ in the morphemes -*thing* or -*ing*, varying with /ŋk/ or /n/.
3   /θ/ and /ð/ subject to replacement by /f/ and /v/.
4   /l/ subject to vocalisation.
5   /t/ subject to allophonic variation especially in its degree of aspiration or (along with /d/, /s/ and /z/), palatalisation.

Details are given in the following paragraphs.

/h/: Froude (1886: 85) found 'the aspirates in the right places' in the 'pure English spoken in Australia'. McBurney, on the other hand, found 'the omission of the aspirate, and its occasional wrong insertion' was 'of frequent occurrence' in Australia (McBurney 1887). Obviously the two observers listened to different people, and now variation in the incidence of /h/ is seen as one of a number of variables defining the sociolinguistic varieties of Australian English. The omission of /h/ is especially associated with working-class males (Horvath 1985: 102) and, not surprisingly considering the phoneme inventories of their first languages (Bradley 1986: 283), with Italian migrants more often than Greeks. The total incidence of *h*-dropping is not high in Australia (about 10 per cent in Horvath's sample), enough, however, for Wells (1982: 603) to consider that it supports 'a general impression of Englishness rather than Americanness'. One peculiarity is the pronunciation of the name of the letter 'h' with initial aspirate as /hʌɪtʃ/, a pronunciation not considered deviant in many Catholic schools, though stigmatised by many people outside them. It can hardly be considered 'uneducated' when a graduate discusses his P. Haitch D. on D. Haitch Lawrence. The origin of the variant is Catholic Ireland (Wells 1982: 432).

/ŋ/: The variant /-ŋk/ in the pronunciation of *something, nothing, anything* is very much stigmatised by guardians of standard English, though Shnukal (1982: 205–6) found it 'not overtly stigmatised' in a study in Cessnock, New South Wales. Horvath (1985: 102) noticed that this variant stands out as one that does not distinguish male from female speech. She found it mainly among upper-working-class Anglo adults.

Mrs Clacy noticed it on the gold diggings in 1852–3: 'they couldn't cook nothink fresh' (Clacy 1963: 30).

With the substitution of /n/ for /ŋ/ in the *-ing* morpheme in *running*, *walking*, etc., the vowel is centralised so that the variation is between /ɪŋ/ and /ən/. The /ən/ variant is male and teenage, especially in working-class speakers (Horvath 1985: 103). There may be constraints of stress and following consonant; when I pronounce a sentence beginning *I'm going to buy*… as /'aɪŋənə 'baɪ/ in a phonetics test, students do not sense any departure from educated style.

/θ/ and /ð/: Hammarström (1980: 20) noticed the variants /f/ and /v/ in the broadest Australian varieties where most Australians have /θ/ and /ð/, but heard it only on rare occasions. The early twentieth-century poet C. J. Dennis uses *wiv* etc. but there is such a strong literary Cockney tradition in such writing that it must be used with great caution as evidence for Australian speech (Turner 1966 [1972]: 175–6). Horvath (1985: 102) agrees that /f/ and /v/ variants are rare and found in the speech of lower-working-class males. As with /h/, the /θ/ and /ð/ forms give the Greeks no trouble, so that in migrant English it is found chiefly among Italian speakers.

/l/: Wells (1982: 594) and Trudgill (1986: 131) agree in classifying Australian English as a variety without *l*-vocalisation, but there appears to be some evidence for the vocalising of /l/ in South Australian speech. Students from Victoria find South Australians 'funny' when they have a 'babyish' pronunciation of *milk* (as /mɪʊk/. A South Australian speaker beginning an answer to a question with a hesitant *Well*… may pronounce little more than a prolonged 'w' sound. Incidentally, if we are to take the word *Strine* seriously as a possible Australian English pronunciation of *Australian*, there appears to be some *l*-vocalisation even in 'the University of Sinny'.

/t/: The replacement of /t/ by a glottal stop, characteristic of Cockney, does not occur widely in Australian English. As in RP, it is only before a consonant (especially /m/) that /t/ is glottalised, e.g. *fit them*, *footman* (Trudgill & Hannah 1982: 13, 18).

Horvath (1985: 103) drew attention to a flapped variant of /t/ especially in male and perhaps especially teenage speech. The written form *bewdy*, sometimes used in order to spell an enthusiastic interjection of *beauty* in its Australian English adjectival use, seems to be an acknowledgement of this phenomenon. An extremely aspirated, even affricated, /t/, on the other hand, is prestigious and associated with female speech.

The alveolar consonants /t, d, s, z/ when followed by yod as in *tune, dune, assume, resume*, pronounced /tju:n/, /dju:n/, /əˈsju:m/, /rəˈzju:m/ have the variants /tʃu:n/, /dʒu:n/ /əˈʃu:m/ and /rəˈʒu:m/ showing palatalisation. The phonetic details are complex, as is the distribution of forms among speakers. Thus *sugar* always shows palatalisation, *suit* in the form *shoot* (as in Barefooted Bob's 'another shoot of toggery', Furphy 1948: 104) hardly ever, dropping its yod instead. Bernard (1975) suggested that such palatalisations became fewer as one moved up towards the Cultivated end of the sociolinguistic scale, a view confirmed by Horvath (1985: 117), who finds it more frequent among males and teenagers and somewhat disfavoured by the middle class. The phenomenon is not recent; McBurney noticed *Jeer me*? for 'Do you hear me?' over a century ago (McBurney 1887: 82).

6.2.8 *Sociolinguistic patterns*

The uniformity of Australian English has often been emphasised (Mitchell 1946: 11; Bernard 1969; Pilch 1971: 274; Wells 1982: 593) but the uniformity described is regional rather than social. The chief detailed investigation, the survey by Mitchell & Delbridge (1965b), though regionally far-reaching, had a narrow social range, being confined to schoolchildren who had not dropped out before their final year. Though social stratification was acknowledged, it was clear that an educated or standard variety enjoyed most prestige (Eagleson 1989: 156).

A cultivated or educated variety, accepting minor differences in pronunciation in the interests of a growing sense of national identity, could still function as a standard in the interests of the educational and administrative forces in a unified modern community (see Thuan 1973, 1976).

The phonemic linguistics of the earlier twentieth century allowed a tidy description of variation in Australian English, and the development of acoustic phonetics by G. R. Cochrane, J. R. L. Bernard and O. N. Burgess gave exactness to its detail, but in its generalising it swept a certain amount of information under the rug. More recent research, with the influence of Labov and Trudgill, has investigated differences in gender, age or occupation by using statistical methods and by taking subphonemic detail, or details of the incidence of phonemes, into account to refine the description of sociolinguistic variation (Shopen 1978; Martino 1982; Horvath 1985). Even regional variation may prove to be more prevalent than previously supposed when finer methods are used (e.g. in Jernudd 1973) and social variation taken into account. Work on Melbourne English is currently being advanced by D. and M. Bradley (see Bradley 1979, 1989; Bradley & Bradley 1979).

It is an important question how far the acrolect, Cultivated Australian English, is passively understood by most Australians. To make it so is an aim of education, and the results of public examinations may be regarded as expensive large-scale research projects to quantify the success of this aim. In its written form the acrolect approximates to standard written English, opening an immense world of experience to those who master it. But such understanding, even of the spoken forms, varies in thoroughness and cannot be taken for granted. Australian soldiers in 1915 are said to have found the 'high-falutin' speech of their British officers 'hard to understand' and 'got into a lot of strife' (that is 'trouble') for laughing at their commands (Facey 1981: 249).

Broadcasting has probably brought increased passive familiarity with variation in accent, though in general Australians are not much consciously aware of such differences. Few make the efforts many English do to change from one type of accent to another. Donald Horne (1975: 201) was an exception but there is an ironical intention in his account of his feeling that 'it seemed a negation of education to speak "like an Australian"' and in the description of his private practising of diphthongs until from the security of an achieved acrolect he could defend the view 'that there was nothing wrong with the Australian accent; it was just that some of us did not happen to use it'.

6.3   Morphology and syntax

6.3.1   General

Morphology and syntax have been comparatively neglected in Australian English studies. Comments tend to be sporadic: for example, Australian -ie/-y and -o terminations (e.g. *Johnny/Johnno*) are discussed by Ridge (1984: 336–8), and there is a small Australian input into Matsuda's (1982) study of variation between *out* and *out of* in such contexts as '*looked out (of) the window*', but in general there appears to be much the same range of formal and informal choices as in southern England. Variations are easier to record than phonological variants but the likelihood that literary preconceptions will colour the observations of literary informants is greater. Did Mrs Clacy really hear a waterman say in 1852 'times isn't as they used to was' (1963: 15) or a man on the goldfields cry out "'Ere's happles, happles, Vandemonian happles, and them as dislikes the hiland needn't heat them' (*ibid.*: 86)? Catherine Helen Spence (1971: 63–4) is more plausible describing a woman in Adelaide about 1854 whose 'accent and manners were unmistakeably vulgar' (and whose daughter was accordingly denied access to a good Adelaide school) saying 'she cries dreadful' or 'in the bush people gets so rough'. Such literary evidence could be multiplied. It is evidence of the variety of grammatical forms brought to the mixing bowl in the new country and presumably surviving to an extent that is only beginning to be measured.

Research using computers and quantitative methods is beginning to address this question. A survey of speech in Queensland was already made over a quarter of a century ago (Flint 1964; Turner 1966: 123–7). More recently Corbett & Ahmad (1986) describe a corpus of texts from *The Age* (Melbourne) amounting to 100,000 words, being editorials from September 1980 to January 1981 and available from ICAME, the International Computer Archive for Modern English in Bergen, Norway. In Sydney, David Blair and Peter Collins are compiling a data base designed to be comparable with a corpus of a million running words made at Brown University in the United States, and a matching corpus, built on the same mix of varieties, at the University of Lancaster in England. The mix of varieties can be matched except that there is a time lag of some quarter of a century between the Brown corpus and its Sydney counterpart.

6.3.2   Morphology

As already noticed, there is a problem of demarcation between morphology and phonology in accounting for forms like /grouən/ for *grown* but not *groan*, or *spanner* 'a wrench' and, with lengthened vowel, 'something that spans'.

There may be variation between past-tense and past-participle forms with the use of a standard past-participle form as a finite verb *I seen him*, or conversely *He might've took them*. These and other variants in inner Sydney speech were studied statistically by Edina Eisikovits (1987).

6.3.3   Syntax

Like morphological deviants, unusual syntactic patterns are normally noticed (though many people are unaware of the difficulty of parsing the frequently heard *If I'd've known*; which is not the Dutch and German English *If I would have known* since, asked to expand, speakers are apt to fumble with *If I had have …*).

The Melbourne survey (Corbett & Ahmad 1986) brought to light an interesting variation between British and Australian use of the optional concord between nouns of multitude like *committee* and their verbs (*the committee has/have decided*). Plural agreement in such instances was found to be markedly less common in Australian than in British English. Is there a social insight here? Do we tolerate varying views less and like our political bodies to be monolithic?

A much-noticed syntactic feature of Australian English is sentence-terminal *but* as in 'Funny old bag. I quite like her but' (Jolley 1983: 102). Trudgill (1984: 26) found that this construction is not even understood in southern England, though it is known in many dialects in Scotland, Northern Ireland and the north-east of England.

6.4   Lexis: history

6.4.1   The Aboriginal languages

If the history of language in Australia, currently thought in the more conservative estimates to span about 40,000 years, is reduced in imagination to a period of twenty-four hours, the share of English, on the same scale, is about seven minutes. Yet in that short time the language of the pink strangers has replaced most of the original languages, usually without even recording them.

The first English settlers in Australia neglected to name the human part of the landscape. Cook refers to the original inhabitants as 'Natives', Tench as 'natives' or 'Indians'. As the Australian-born descendants of European settlers later appropriated the name *natives* for themselves and in 1871 formed an Australian Natives' Association with a tendency to a 'white Australia' policy and advocacy (too late to save the Aboriginal people) of restricted immigration, no term was left. The general English term *aboriginal* or *aborigine* was commandeered, often until recently without even a capital letter. Now the Australian government's *Style Manual* recommends the forms *Aboriginal* (singular noun), *Aboriginals* (plural noun) and *Aboriginal* (adjective). *Aborigines* is given as an alternative plural, but the singular use of *Aborigine* is not recommended (though in fact it is not uncommon). The Aboriginal people themselves seem not to favour the name *Aboriginals*, which now takes on a suggestion of government, and in practice seem to use the whole phrase *Aboriginal people* however often it occurs in discourse. It is not ideal since seven-syllabled terms in common use tend to be slurred or abbreviated. Some Aboriginal people prefer the term *Koori* (adjective and noun) for an Aboriginal but it is especially an east-coast word. In south-west Australia, for example, the equivalent word would be *Nyungar*. The term *gubba* for 'white man' is colloquial and derogatory so that *Koori and gubba* cannot pretend to unite the races in the way that the phrase *Maori and Pakeha* attempts to do for New Zealand. Perhaps the best we can do at present is the crude two-colour spectrum separating the bronzed from the rubicund as *blackfellow* and *whitefellow*.

There were about 200 Aboriginal languages (Dixon 1980: 1). It is not easy to count them; sometimes differences are small enough to suggest dialects rather than separate languages, but the differences are important to Aboriginal people as they indicate tribal affiliation (Dixon 1980: 33). A language might be named by a distinctive word, as if we were to label Scots as 'the language with *bonny*'. If the word for *no* is *wira*, the language is *Wiradhuri* '*wira*-having' (Donaldson & Donaldson 1985: 77). In the Western Desert a language distinguished by having *pitjantja* as the word for 'come' is distinguished by the name *Pitjantjatjara* (*pitjantja*-having), and neighbouring *Ngaanyatjara* is distinguished by its word for 'this', *ngaanya*. The word for 'this' in Nyanganyatjara is *nyanganya*. *Guugu Yimidhirr* is literally 'the language having *yimi* "this"' (Dixon 1980: 41–2).

These names may be used in English contexts but most are not common except in the works of anthropologists and linguists. Sometimes a tribal name is well enough known to have a standard form different from the modern linguists' more accurate rendition of the native word. Examples are *Aranda* and *Kamilaroi* which, if spelt in accordance with the modern spelling of these languages, would be *Arirnta* and *Gamilaraay*.

Like classical European languages, Aboriginal languages usually have inflections showing case, tense and mood, but there are differences, notably in the frequent presence of an ergative case marking what is in our terms the subject of a transitive verb. Some sounds which seem to be almost universal in better-known languages are missing in most

Aboriginal languages, for example the sounds represented by *f*, *s*, *sh* or *z* in English. Thus a Western Desert word for a (nursing) sister disguises its English origin in the form *tjitja* (Douglas 1977: 3) where *tj* represents a palatal stop. No distinction is made in most Aboriginal languages between voiced and unvoiced stops (*b*, *d*, *g* against *p*, *t*, *k*), so that a given word might variously be spelt in the Roman alphabet or Anglicised with *b* or *p*, *d* or *t*, *g* or *k*. The place-name *Coober Pedy* can be derived from the Gugada language *guba bidi* 'white man's holes', and *Gugada* itself can equally well be called *Kukata* (Platt 1972: 1). Similarly *Pitjantjatjara* or *Pitjantjara* may appear as *Bidjandjara* (*ibid.*). Anthropologists in the Eastern States tend to favour spelling with *b*, *d*, *g* while South Australians favour *p*, *t*, *k* (Dixon 1980: 138).

Words in most Aboriginal languages have to end in a vowel. When the English word *missus* is borrowed as a word for 'white woman', it takes the form *mitjitji* (Douglas 1977: 3). The words quoted in the previous paragraph follow the rule of the terminal vowel, as do a number of words borrowed into English, *kangaroo*, *woomera* 'a "throwing stick" used to launch a dart or spear', *brolga* 'a large crane', *bora* 'a male initiation site', and such place-names as *Wagga Wagga*, *Gundagai*, *Wodonga*, *Ernabella* or the fictitious *Bullamakanka*. There were exceptions, however, and these seem to have been especially numerous in areas where the main cities were destined to arise, the areas best known to later Australians. In New South Wales words could end in a velar nasal, so that *boomerang* or *currawong* 'a crow-like bird', or *billabong* 'a cut-off pool in a river branch', or the name *Goolagong*, 'sound Aboriginal'. The name of an Aboriginal protégé of Governor Phillip, *Bennelong*, commemorated in the name *Bennelong Point*, now the site of the Sydney Opera House, is another example. In Victoria names like *Ballarat* or *Mordialloc* end in consonants. In south-western Australia many names end in *-up*, so that the name *qualup bell* for a shrub, based on a local name in that area, has an authentic local flavour. Another fictitious name for a remote outback locality, *Woop Woop*, sounds Aboriginal in its reduplication but it is not especially associated with Western Australia and so is dubiously Aboriginal in flavour. A possible source is *Whoop-up*, the name of a backwoods American goldmining town in E. L. Wheeler's once popular *Deadwood Dick on Deck*, a form, oddly enough, which might, if unchanged, have fitted the Western Australian pattern quite well.

It is a general principle that when two languages come into contact, words borrowed by one language from another 'show a superiority of the nation from whose language they are borrowed, though this superiority may be of many different kinds' (Jespersen 1922: 209). In accordance with this principle, just as their ancestors learned little from the despised Celts and their remoter ancestors on the continent contributed little to the superior Romans, the technologically dominant English took from the Aboriginal languages less than they gave. The earliest borrowings were from the languages first encountered in the area round Port Jackson. Examples from the Dharuk language of this area include *boobook* 'a type of owl', *boomerang*, *cooee*, *dingo*, *gibber* 'stone, rock', *gin* 'Aboriginal woman', *gunya* 'Aboriginal hut', *hielamon*, 'shield', *koala*, *koradji* 'tribal doctor', *kurrajong* 'a tree, especially of the genus *Brachychiton*', *nulla-nulla* 'an Aboriginal club', *wallaby* 'small kangaroo', *wallaroo* 'mountain kangaroo', *waratah* 'red-flowering tree', emblem of New South Wales, *warrigal* '(especially wild) native dog or dingo', *wombat* 'burrowing marsupial', *wonga-wonga* '(1) a kind of pigeon, (2) a vine' and *woomera*. As settlement advanced there were further borrowings from the more easterly languages. From Wiradhuri come *billabong* and *corella* 'white cockatoo' and from other New South Wales sources *bilby* 'rabbit bandicoot', *budgerigar*, *mulga* 'an acacia', also 'the outback', and (from Kamilaroi) *yarran* also 'an acacia'. Other words were borrowed in Victoria (*bunyip* 'mythical river monster', *lowan* 'mallee-fowl, a large mound-building bird', *luderick* 'black-fish', *mallee* 'scrubby eucalypt', *mia-mia* 'an Aboriginal hut', and *yabby* 'a freshwater crustacean') or from Queensland (*barramundi* 'giant perch', *humpy* 'Aboriginal hut', *yakka* 'work') or from South Australia (*callop* 'golden perch', *wurley* 'Aboriginal hut'; there is a detailed account of South Australian borrowings in Knight 1988), or from Tasmania (*lubra* 'Aboriginal woman', *boobialla* 'large shrub, a species of *Myoporum*') or Western Australia (*jarrah* 'Western Australian eucalypt', *kylie* 'boomerang'). Though the listed words are fairly generally known, they are not universally known to Australians and there is some regional variation in such knowledge (Ramson 1964). Except for one or two striking items like *boomerang* and *kangaroo*, which have become international, the words have little semantic complexity.

It will be noticed that the first contact, with coastal New South Wales, was the chief source of borrowing and the source of the best-known words (other than *kangaroo*), though some of them (e.g. *koala*, *dingo*) did not fully displace English descriptions (*native bear*, *native dog*) until a period of growing nationalism a century after their first appearance. It will also be noticed that most of the words borrowed from Aboriginal languages related to the flora and fauna of the new country and Aboriginal weapons and customs.

Influence the other way, from English to Aboriginal languages, is much more pervasive. A pidgin means of communication between newcomers and the Aboriginal population developed, perhaps aided by the previous experience in Tahiti and elsewhere of seafaring visitors to the colony (Mühlhäusler 1991: 169). Even some Australianisms in English may have passed via Aboriginal pidgin from English back into English. This is a likely source for *jumbuck* 'sheep', perhaps from *jump up* (Ramson 1966: 107). At present *whitefellow* from Aboriginal pidgin is nudging its way into general English, and *walkabout*, originally an Aboriginal period of wandering in the bush, now has royal patronage.

Some Port Jackson words were spread to other districts, where they were accepted as part of a pidgin English. Horses made a profound and rather frightening impression on the Aboriginal people and names spread ahead of the animals. *Yarraman* is possibly from Dhurga, the language spoken in Bateman's Bay on the east coast (Ramson 1966: 107). It may relate to the word *yira* 'teeth' (Blake 1981: 107) as horses were feared for their power to bite. In South Australia the horse was called *pindi nanto* 'the newcomers' kangaroo' (Teichelmann & Schürmann 1840: 27). Both *yarraman* and a form of *nanto* reached Central Australia as words for 'horse' (Reynolds 1982: 13; Knight 1988: 155).

Along with such words, and not distinguished from them since etymology is not part of a user's current knowledge of the language, were genuine English words, not always without change of meaning. The word *wheelbarrow* became a general word for 'a vehicle'; 'a fire-wheelbarrow' is a literal translation of the word for 'train' in one area (Dixon 1980: 122).

Borrowing reflects the words current in the source language at the time and among the people that the native people were likely to meet. Thus *gammon* 'humbug', a marginal word in current English, is a very frequent word in pidgin forms of English. Again, the use of a word might precede contact with its ultimate donors. The Pitjantjatjara *makiti* 'gun' derives its name from *musket* but though a form *mukkety* is recorded by Ernest Giles as used to describe a cartridge by an Aboriginal boy at Ross' Waterhole, 90 miles from Peake, in 1873 (Giles 1889, I: 141), it seems safe to assume that muskets had been superseded by rifles when Europeans made significant contact with the people of the Western Desert. Mühlhäusler (personal communication) has used the metaphor of a weed, which spreads without the deliberate agency of

Europeans even to areas where Europeans have not been themselves, to describe the similar spread of English linguistic elements through a region. It is becoming increasingly evident (Holm 1989: 540–1; Mühlhäusler, personal communication) that Australian pidgin had far-reaching influence on pidgin languages, even further afield in the Pacific region.

A pidgin language is nobody's first language. It is used in a situation of contact between speakers of different languages, the main adjustment being made by the people assuming the inferior status. Thus pidgin English is largely English in vocabulary. A pidgin language may become creolised, replacing the first language of one group of its speakers. This has happened in the Roper River area of the Northern Territory of Australia (Sandefur 1979; Holm 1989: 542–3). A development of this kind can be rapid, children developing a form of language unintelligible to their parents (Mühlhäusler forthcoming). The tendency is always towards a metropolitan standard language (Mühlhäusler, personal communication). Only recently has the variety of contact languages and restructured English been properly realised and much research remains to be done. Mühlhäusler sets out a list of tasks at the end of his paper (forthcoming).

A creole language is to be distinguished from Aboriginal English, a form of English with varying amounts of influence from an Aboriginal substratum (Douglas 1976: 10–12; Dixon 1980: 74–7; Blake 1981: 68). Holm (1989: 538) uses the term 'restructured English in Australia' to refer to 'a continuum of varieties spoken by Aboriginal people, ranging from contact jargon, pidgin, and creole to post-creole Aboriginal English' remarking that 'today most Aborigines speak some form of restructured English and many also speak standard or regional Australian English to varying degrees of proficiency'. The teaching of standard English to speakers of Aboriginal English is an important application of linguistic theory in present-day Australia (Gardiner 1977). Recently Kriol (Australian creole) has been adopted for oral work and initial literacy in some Aboriginal schools (Holm 1989: 543).

6.4.2 The convicts

There is argument whether the founding of a prison was the chief or only motive for founding Australia (Tench 1961: 118–19; Blainey 1966: 27–33), but for the historian of language it is one that is unlikely to be overlooked. Prisoners and their keepers have a language of their own, able to cope with the technical subtleties of crime or its prevention. Like other technical languages it is characterised by very general terms and very particular terms. One word describes a complex of attributes; prudence, economy in acting, abilities arising from long experience, the accomplishing of a project in a masterly manner, are all semantic elements in one word, *judgement*; on the other hand a special condition 'having been divested of one's watch' has its own term *unthimbled* (Vaux 1964: 247, 277). As in other occupational sublanguages, words acquired enhanced precision of meaning. In strict usage *traps* were not just any policemen but officers or runners. Some words belonged to the language of the police rather than their prey. To *weigh forty* referred to a practice of letting a *prig* ('thief') *reign* ('follow his career') unmolested until he committed a capital crime when his arrest might bring a reward of forty pounds (Vaux 1964: 279). It seems, however, that sometimes the convict was a better linguist than the keeper, and that an interpreter was necessary to translate the deposition of a witness or the defence of a prisoner in the courts (Tench 1961: 297).

Much of the language of the prison was sheer exuberant slang with no purpose beyond asserting group solidarity, perhaps disguising intentions from a victim, or delight or competitiveness in communal verbal art. There was no other need to say *lag'd for his wind* rather than 'transported for life'. It is the classic example of an anti-language (Halliday 1976), the language of an anti-society, acting out a different social structure with its own hierarchies.

The above and other examples of *flash language* (or *kiddy language*, Tench 1961: 297) were recorded by a convicted petty thief in 1812 while he was in Newcastle, New South Wales. James Hardy Vaux was not intending to record a regional (Australian) form of English but an occupational one. Many of the technicalities of criminal life would later disappear or remain the speciality of thieves, and much of the slang would be as ephemeral as most slang is, but some relics of the convicts' jargon recorded by Vaux have found their way into general Australian English.

Perhaps best known are the pair *new chum* and *old hand*. Vaux (1964: 232) tells us that a *chum* was 'a fellow prisoner in a jail, hulk &c' so that there were *new chums* and *old chums* as they happened to have been a short or a long time in confinement. Both terms continued in use long after the convict era, and *new chum* is still current as a contemptuous or patronising term for 'a tyro or novice'. *Old chum* has been mainly replaced by *old hand*, itself with convict associations once as it referred to an ex-convict, but now with the general English overtones of respect for a practical workman or experienced person.

Another well-established word is *swag*, originally 'a bundle or package', particularly 'a thief's loot', now given a different specification in the *swag* 'rolled-up belongings' carried by a *swagman* or 'tramp'. These words are historical now, but *swag* lives on in the sense 'large quantity' (*a swag of letters to answer*). *New chum* and *swag* appear to be known throughout Australia (and New Zealand, which until it failed to participate in Federation in 1901 belonged to a loose community of Australian colonies), as do some other originally cant expressions such as *throw off at* 'ridicule' with its variants *sling off at*, *chuck off at*. *Togs* 'bathing suit' appears to be confined to the Eastern States (where it competes with *cossie* and, recently, *swimmers*), the word being *bathers* in South Australia and Western Australia, but *togs* has remained in general use in New Zealand.

Not perhaps surprisingly, the words deriving from convict use are best known in the states which were once convict settlements. South Australians or New Zealanders might not share in such accepted Australianisms as *ding* 'throw away', *drum* '(confidential) information or advice' perhaps, though early citations are lacking, from *drummond* 'an infallible scheme', based on *Drummond & Co*, a bank in Charing Cross (Vaux 1964: 238), *grey* 'double-headed or double-tailed coin', *lag* '(vb) transport', '(n.) transported criminal', *molly-dooker* 'a left-handed person' from *mauley* 'a hand', *push* 'bunch of larrikins', later 'group of like-minded people', *ridge*, *ridgie-didge* 'good, genuine' from *ridge* 'gold', *serve* 'a reprimand' (Vaux *serve* 'maim, wound'), *shake* 'steal' or *traps* 'police'.

A similarity between items in Vaux's list and modern Australian idiom does not guarantee a direct or continuous link between the convicts and the present day. In many cases there is a large gap in time between Vaux and the first dictionary record of a word. A *serve*, for example, is dated only from 1974 (or 1967 in the meaning 'thrashing'). We can accept that words like *grey*, connected with two-up (gambling) schools, or *lag* or *trap* or *school* itself 'a party of persons met together for the purpose of gambling' (Vaux 1964: 263) might survive in underworld slang, and even more general slang does not easily find its way into writing, but other possible channels for cant terms to pass into everyday use have to be kept in mind. Some terms (*beak* 'magistrate', *lark* 'prank', *split* 'betray by informing', *put-up job*, *stow it* 'be quiet' as well as *swag* 'loot' and *prad* 'horse') are found, for instance, in *Oliver Twist*.

No one would dare tell the Australians that their treasured corpus of slang is of English literary origin, but, even in our slang, we cannot ignore the general currents of development in the English language, especially those in Britain and, to a lesser extent, in the United States. Much of the underworld language described by Vaux has now become general English, with or without its original colloquial flavour. In some cases Vaux perhaps erred in including terms which were already more general than he implies (*pinch* 'steal', *toddle, toddler, dummy* 'half-wit', *grub* 'food', *sound out, his nibs, sticks* (of furniture), *weed* 'tobacco', *out and out, bring to light* (already in the Bible) and others) but, even if we rule these out, early cant terms that have become part of general English far outnumber those that are especially Australian. It is almost as if Australians were especially sensitive to convict words and avoided them until they became purified by British associations. Some of the words occurring both in Vaux and in general English are *cadge, awake to, bash* (as in *wife-bashing*), *croak* 'die', *dollop, grab, job* 'robbery', *judy* (derogative) 'woman', *fancy woman, frisk, move* 'action', *mug* 'face', *pigs* 'police', *put* (someone) *up to* (action), *quod* 'prison', *rattler* 'coach' now 'train', *Romany* 'gypsy', *seedy* 'shabby', *sharper, snooze, stink* 'furore', *swell* 'gentleman', *try it on, dressed to the nines, whack* 'share', *wanted* (of criminal) and *yokel*.

Sometimes American English is the channel for underworld terms to reach general English. *Racket* as 'organised crime' or, in weakened sense, 'noise' or 'commotion' brings an American flavour. *Bang-up* remains American, and the American *ringer* is a *ring-in* 'substitute' in Australia. *Pull* 'advantage' though chiefly American is known elsewhere too. *Galoot*, originally 'a soldier', especially 'an awkward soldier', has lost its American flavour and is just a somewhat derogatory word for a person.

Vaux sometimes helps us with an etymology. The entry *steven* 'money' suggests an origin for the general English phrase *even Stephen* 'equally', and the information that *danna-drag* 'night cart' was commonly pronounced 'dunnick-drag' supports a linking via *dunny-ken* (Hotten 1872: 128) with the Australian *dunny* 'outside privy'.

6.4.3   Discovery

Borrowings into general English from Aboriginal languages or from the professional jargon of convicts were, like any linguistic borrowings anywhere, part of a response to a felt need to communicate new experience. All was novelty and discovery in a new land, which at first did not even have a settled name.

Speakers of English were not the first visitors to the island continent. Australians might have been speakers of Portuguese and looked to Portugal and Brazil for natural allies, or Dutch might have overspread the land. The word *balanda* 'a white man' in some northern Aboriginal languages can be traced to the word *Hollander*, perhaps brought to Australia by Macassan traders (Dixon 1980: 238). Spanish navigators also were attracted by a legend of *Terra Australis Incognita*, the undiscovered south land which Pedro Fernandez de Quiros thought he had reached in 1605. He gave his discovery the name *Austrialia del Espiritu Santo*, combining a reference to the *terra incognita* with a compliment to Philip III of Spain, who was of the Austrian Royal House, along with a more prominent one to the Holy Ghost. In the following year, after Quiros had abandoned the expedition, Luis Vaez de Torres, commander of a second ship accompanying Quiros, sailed round Espiritu Santo proving it to be an island (part of modern Vanuatu) and passed through the strait which now bears his name. It seems unlikely that he actually saw any part of Australia.

The Dutch penetrated further. Abel Janszoon Tasman is especially remembered for naming the continent *New Holland* and discovering the island to the south which he named *Van Diemen's Land* after the Governor General of the Dutch East Indies, Anthony Van Diemen. The name *New Holland* survives only in a few faunal names like *New Holland honey-eater*, and *Van Diemen's Land* and its adjective *Vandemonian* only in literary and historical use, but Tasman is remembered in the renamed *Tasmania* and the *Tasman Sea*, while one of his ships, the *Zeehaen* ('seacock') is commemorated in the name of the Tasmanian town of *Zeehan*. An Englishman, William Dampier, touched briefly on the north-west shore of Australia in 1688, but his tercentenary in 1988 was eclipsed by the bicentenary on the east coast.

The spelling *Australia* seems first to have been used in a Dutch translation of Quiros' *Memorial* and to have occurred sporadically in literature during the seventeenth and eighteenth centuries (*Australian Encyclopaedia* 1983, I: 141–2). By Cook's time *New Holland*, especially for the west coast, and *New South Wales* for the east coast, so named by Cook after first suggesting *New Wales* (Cook 1968: 388), were the current names. Matthew Flinders in 1814 called the account of his voyage of discovery *A Voyage to Terra Australis* and explains:

> There is no probability, that any other detached body of land, of nearly equal extent, will ever be found in a more southern latitude; the name Terra Australis will, therefore, remain descriptive of the geographical importance of this country, and of its situation on the globe: it has antiquity to recommend it; and, having no reference to either of the two claiming nations, appears to be less objectionable than any other which could have been selected. (Flinders 1814, I: iii)

In a footnote Flinders adds 'Had I permitted myself any innovation upon the original term, it would have been to convert it into AUSTRALIA; as being more agreeable to the ear, and an assimilation to the names of the other great portions of the earth.'

By 1827 Peter Cunningham could write 'the climate of Tasmania is generally cooler than that of New South Wales (or *Australia* as we colonials say)' (Cunningham 1827, I: 9), attesting the growing acceptance of both names, *Australia* and *Tasmania*, though not including Tasmania within Australia.

In 1829 the founding of the Swan River Colony and the claiming for Britain of New Holland, the area west of 135° longitude (cf. Flinders 1814, I: iii), confirmed the need for a term to refer to the country as a whole.

6.4.4   Early days

The beginnings of contemporary Australia are inevitably associated with the landing at Port Jackson on 26 January 1788 and the founding of a penal settlement designed to relieve the overcrowded gaols of England so that, in the words of a writer some ninety years later, 'by expelling all the wicked, England would become the model of virtue to all nations' (Dunderdale n.d.: 2).

The differences between the old country and the new were (literally) astronomical. The seasons and stars were different. E. E. Morris has been criticised (Baker 1966: 5) for including the word *Christmas* in his *Dictionary of Austral English* (1898) but, as his quotations (not mentioned by Baker) show, the climatic connotations of the word in Australia are so diametrically different that it serves as a good example of the inevitability of linguistic change in a changed environment, in connotations if not in lexicon. There is a further difference, a difference in collocations; *Christmas* enters into compound names for summer-flowering plants, *Christmas bells*, *Christmas bush*, *Christmas tree*, as well as *Christmas* (summer) *holidays*.

In a land where Orion's sword hangs upwards and the burden

traditionally carried by the man in the moon lies at last at his feet, the pole-star is absent from the visible sky, but we have our *pointers*, α and β Centauri, and they point to the *Southern Cross*. In Britain the phrase *with the sun* could mean 'clockwise' and *withershins* could mean 'against the motion of the sun, and therefore eerie or unnatural', but in the southern hemisphere the sun runs against the clock-face based on a northern sun. The south was no longer Keats' 'warm south' but the source of a *cool change*, a sudden squally wind, the *southerly buster*, whereas the north wind was 'like the blast of a heated oven'(Tench 1961: 265 – the simile is not a hyperbole in Australia) and blew hot at Christmas time. On 27 December 1790 the temperature in Sydney reached 109°F in the shade.

The sun still rose in the east but it was now observed from a different place so that the *Far East* was now closer and to the north. Escaped convicts sometimes tried to walk to China, believing it to be close at hand, but they never tried to walk to the East Indies, because east was over water (Cunningham 1827, II: 202). We smile, but continue to use the misleading terms. When a notable architect calls Sydney 'the ugliest city in the Western world', it is only the word *ugliest* that is disputed.

At least the officers among the founders of Australia came not without some knowledge of the country and the area that was to become Sydney. In neighbouring Botany Bay, named for its vegetation (Cook 1968: 310), Cook had described a promising land, but with less than his customary accuracy, it seems, if indeed no natural disaster intervened between 1770 and 1788. His description of 'woods, lawns, and marshes' seems accurate enough since the only meaning of *lawn* in the usage of the time was 'an open space between woods' (Walker 1791), and he noted the sandy soil near the sea. The 'much richer' land further inland with 'in many places a deep black soil' and 'as fine meadow as ever was seen' (Cook 1968: 309 and footnote) seemed to promise more than Phillip's party could find when they arrived to found a settlement eighteen years later. The area they explored was swampy, exposed to the easterly wind and without a usable water supply (Phillip 1789: 45–6). Accordingly Phillip sailed north to explore Port Jackson, which Cook had named after one of the secretaries of the Admiralty but had not explored, and there he discovered a more suitable site for a settlement, naming it Sydney Cove in honour of Lord Sydney, Home Secretary in the British cabinet (Phillip 1789: 48). The modern city of Sydney, never officially named, takes its name from Sydney Cove. So the convicts did not set foot in *Botany Bay* though its name long remained as a synonym for transportation.

Some idea of what animals and plants to expect was gained from Cook. He had described (1968: 365–8) kangaroos, wolves (perhaps as Beaglehole suggests (Cook 1968: 369) the thylacine or Tasmanian wolf, now confined to Tasmania; but possibly dingoes) and a tame dog (certainly a dingo) and mentioned 'Possums', a reminder that England was not the only source of vocabulary for sailors and travellers. Our possum somewhat resembles the American *opossum* (with a pronunciation 'reduced in common speech ... to *possum*' (Mencken 1980: 104). Australians have followed Cook in adopting the aphetic form.

For the most prominent of the trees in the new land a name was available. The word *gum-tree* was established at least as early as 1676 to refer to trees in North America. Dampier found trees in north-western Australia which exuded gum resembling gum dragon and supposed they were dragon trees (Clark 1957: 24–5) but perhaps they were acacias. Cook described 'the gum Tree' as the largest in New South Wales, apparently describing a eucalypt (Cook 1968: 393), though, strictly speaking, eucalypts produce a kino rather than a gum. Phillip (1789: 107) appears to use *gum-tree* in the same way, a way now standard, but also mentions a plant producing *yellow gum*, which from the accompanying plate and the description is clearly the *grass-tree* or *blackboy* (genus *Xanthorrhoea*) (Phillip 1789: 60) which was later to be exploited for its resin.

It is difficult for a modern Australian to realise the isolation of the first settlers. A ship which had been only four months and twelve days on its passage from England in 1791 was worthy of remark (Tench 1961: 240). Captain Tench was one of a party that rowed out 6 miles to meet that very ship, so hungry were they for news of the outside world. Unfortunately the master had not anticipated their interest in the world they had left and when asked about events in France or Russia could only answer 'As to that matter I can't say' or 'That you see does not lie in my way; I have heard talk about it but don't remember what passed'. Asked by the exasperated enquirers why he had not brought newspapers, the master replied 'Why, really, I never thought about the matter, until we were off the Cape of Good Hope, when we spoke a man of war, who asked us the same question, and then I wished I had' (Tench 1961: 241).

The most serious aspect of the settlers' isolation was uncertainty about food supplies. Attempts to grow food locally were not very successful. The seasons and climate were unfamiliar, the soil was sandy and poor and its capabilities not yet discovered. Because of the open spaces between trees, initial cultivation was easier than in America, but the ground lacked the effect of the mulch associated with a closer covering. Most of the convicts were city people; Tench (1961: 65) desiring that some practical farmers should be sent out implies their absence (cf. Mudie 1964: 10). Later in 1788 a Government Farm was established with a hundred convicts and their officers some 24 kilometres west of Sydney Cove at a place named *Rose Hill* after a British Treasury official, George Rose. Later the native name *Parramatta*, the first place-name with an Aboriginal source, was adopted, but not before Rose Hill had given its name to the *Rosehillers*, colourful parrots whose name is now Latinised as *rosellas*, possibly through the influence of its homonym naming species of hibiscus, including a native one, the source of *rosella jam*.

The early organisation of agriculture in Australia had a profound effect on rural vocabulary. The urban convicts would bring no rich rustic dialect to describe country activities, and even the standard English topographical words, the loss of which has been deplored by sentimentalists from time to time, would be much less familiar than words describing the routine of a convict camp on the edge of an unfamiliar landscape. What a countryman might have called a *flock* of sheep would remind the city-bred of the 'tumultous rout' (Walker 1791) or *mob* of London, a word disapproved of by Addison (*Spectator* 135), cautiously allowed by Walker in its English sense, but both were too far away to matter. A count of sheep would recall the *muster* of prisoners or soldiers or the early equivalent of the modern census. The *superintendent* of the *station* and the *huts* of the men became the models for the sheep and cattle *stations* of the pastoral industry of later years.

Early Sydney was a coastal settlement. The outlets of the small streams of the area into the sea were called *creeks*, in accordance with general English usage, but it is difficult to say exactly where a creek ends and the stream begins. It seems that streams explored upwards from the coast remained *creeks* as far back as they were explored and English words like *stream* (except in figurative use), *beck*, *burn*, *rivulet* and so on were forgotten or rarely used, except in literary contexts. Australian creeks are often without water; if Arabs had named the Australian countryside a creek would be called a *wadi*.

The replacement of the British *woods* by *bush* was already part of a general colonial usage and the words *coppice*, *copse*, *spinney* and *thicket* perhaps hardly suited the scattered trees that were first encountered. They disappeared. The loss of the geomorphological words *dale*, *glen*, *vale, coomb* and *glade* is mourned but the words are not entirely dead since they live on as elements of place-names. Wine buffs know of *Rutherglen* and *McLaren Vale*. Indeed *glen* appears so often in names that Les Blake's *Place Names of Victoria* lists fifty-one names beginning with *Glen-*. Most are of places named after localities in Scotland or Ireland though some are named after people (*Glenmaggie, Glenthompson* and even *Glenpark*, after a local storekeeper named *Glen*), and some are descriptive (*Glenfern*, or the intriguing *Glencreek* in the Shire of Yackandandah). *Glen Waverley* commemorates the nineteenth-century admiration of Scott's novels and *Glenrowan* has its own fame as the scene of Ned Kelly's last stand. In Central Australia the explorer Ernest Giles named fourteen places with the element *Glen*, his usual word for a ravine, or what might be called a *gully* in current Australian English.

The meaning of the place-name elements is often lost. *Evandale* is a suburb in a completely flat part of Adelaide. *Moor* and *heath* are lost words less often noticed. Nothing in the landscape round Sydney would call for their use but they might have been extended in reference a little to cover hot dry spinifex country in the interior. As it is, the word *desert* is used, a misnomer according to the explorer Warburton's editor (Warburton 1875: 212) who thought *wilderness* would have been a better term.

The unanswerable question 'How long is a creek?' is matched by another, 'How big is a paddock?' In Britain a *paddock* is a small field, especially near a stable. The relation of the words *paddock* and *field* in Britain is well brought out by George Meredith in chapter 2 of *The Tragic Comedians*, when he remarks of Clotilde and Alvan, 'They were not members of a country where literature is confined to a little paddock without influence on the larger field (part lawn, part marsh) of the social world.' In Australia the (literal) larger field, part lawn, part marsh, was unfenced and its flocks tended by shepherds or *crawlers* as they came to be contemptuously called. Paddocks remained *paddocks* but as a fenced area was extended the name remained unchanged so that by 1832 a paddock might contain 100 acres and sixty years later 12,000 acres (Morris 1898: 336). Even 64 square miles is not a big paddock according to a writer in 1937 (*OED* Supplement, III: 207).

6.4.5   *The pastoral era*

As the settlement began to prosper, three industries, whaling, timber-cutting and sheep, became prominent. Whaling was worth more than wool as an export until 1833 but has not contributed much to Australian vocabulary. *Bay whaling* and the *bay whalers*, the boats participating in it, were based on shore stations near bays where female southern right, or *bay*, whales were caught when they came in to breed. Whalebone rather than oil was the prize. Some place-names containing the element *Lookout* recall whaling days. The colloquial *gallied*, as in Furphy's 'looked a bit gallied on it' (Furphy 1903: 185) meaning 'hesitant, uneasy about a risky action', is associated with whaling idiom (*OED* s.v. *gally*). Whalers may have helped the spread of pidgin forms of English along the coast (Mühlhäusler, forthcoming).

Settlement along the coast of New South Wales was preceded by the *cedar-getters*. The Australian *cedar* is not of the boreal genus *Cedrus*. Most of the trees cut in coastal New South Wales were *red cedar* (*Toona australis*), which provides light, soft wood, easy to polish and resistant to white ants and borers. Now rare, the wood is still much prized for cabinet work. *Cedar-getting*, like whaling and, later, mining was exploitative and exhausted its supplies. It had little effect on language but its workers, working in pairs, provide a prototypical example of the growing Australian ideal of *mateship*. The word *mate* as a vocative among males is obviously not confined to Australia, but its tone differs. In England it can be aggressive but in Australia it represents the legendary egalitarian male friendship and interdependence, initially in the workplace and then more generally, that is illustrated by two men at the ends of a cross-cut saw – if we overlook the advantage of being *topman* (or *top-notcher*) above the *pitman* (Harris 1953: 88, 89) who is showered with dust in the sawpit (Hughes 1988: 21).

With the growth of the pastoral industry, the Australian connotations of the word *squatter* began to develop. The first squatters were people with little claim to a fixed abode, mostly *ticket-of-leave men* (convicts having served part of their time and given liberty with certain restrictions) and *emancipists* (ex-convicts who had served their terms). Such men *squatted* for pastoral purposes on land unoccupied except for Aboriginal owners, who were ignored. Gradually the term *squatter* applied to any occupier of public land without a title (with no implication of dishonesty), later still to those who held Crown land under lease or licence, or as freehold. The term took on class overtones and came to suggest wealth and prestige (Twopeny 1883: 91), though eventually it has given way to *pastoralist* or *grazier*.

The reality of the 'pastoral era', the period between the early settlement and the goldrushes, along with its continuing importance after the goldrushes, must be disentangled from two very different myths which have arisen from it, one aristocratic, an attempt to transplant the ideals of a British landed gentry, the other democratic, based on the mateship, militant unionism and life and work of shearers and *overlanders* (drovers, especially in the *outback*, the regions remote from the coastal settlements where most Australians live).

The aristocratic myth was earlier and is now popularly supposed to be the less real. In actual fact, as the splenetic James Mudie Esq. noted (Mudie 1964: xiii), many 'in the condition of' gentry were felons now undergoing or who had already undergone their sentences. Mudie coined the term *felonry* (on the analogy of *gentry*, *peasantry*, etc.) for this class of people, comprising convicts, ticket-of-leave men, emancipists (a name he thought absurd for emancip*ated* prisoners) including conditionally pardoned convicts, fully pardoned convicts and *expirees* (whose sentences had expired) together with runaway convicts subdivided into *absentees*, a name he thought 'foolish for its mildness' and bushrangers (*ibid.*). Despite Mudie, wealthy emancipists came to be accepted by the rival *exclusives* as allies against the mob, and in favour of re-introducing a policy of *assignment*, the allocation of convicts as cheap labour (Crowley 1980, II: 108), virtually a form of slavery.

The nemesis of the aristocratic movement came with an attempt in 1853 to establish a permanent *squattocracy* in the form of a colonial nobility, based on the landed gentry, to provide an upper house in the New South Wales legislature. The suggestion was ridiculed by the orator Daniel Deniehy as a *Bunyip aristocracy*, drawing on two contemporary meanings of *bunyip*, both attested by G. C. Mundy (1852: 214), first as 'a fearful name' for a sort of '"half-horse, half-alligator"' haunting the wild rushy swamps and lagoons (small freshwater lakes) of the interior' and secondly as an 'imposter, pretender, humbug and the like'.

Looking to Britain, the *Angipodes* as the *Bulletin* called it on 21 January 1888, as a model or norm was in the eyes of later democrats a major failing of the early gentry. James Mudie Esq. thought the new settlement should be 'distinguished by a British spirit and character, as well as by the British language' (Mudie 1964: 30), and his property, Castle Forbes, was praised for its 'British-like aspect' (*ibid.*: 195). Peter Cunningham wished for some British birds to enliven the Australian countryside (1827, I: 327). Even the democrats did not break the link with Britain entirely. Urging support for a London dockers' strike in 1889, a speaker declared that 'while being Australians first of all', they were 'Britons still' (*Sydney Morning Herald* 16 September 1889, in Crowley 1980, III: 277).

The nostalgia for Britain was manifested in the novels that depicted the languid gentleman who proved to be 'an overmatch for half-a-dozen hard-muscled white savages' (Furphy 1903: 33) but had little effect on the detail of language except a conservative one and an impulse to share in developments of English in Britain. Raymond Williams (1961: 13) has traced the profound and complex changes in meaning undergone in the words *industry, democracy, class, art* and *culture* since the last decades of the eighteenth century. This is precisely the time that Australia has existed as a separate English-speaking country but an Australian needs to make no adjustment on this account to understand Williams. Australians have shared in a general British development in these words and similar cultural vocabulary.

Where nostalgia for Britain has had a profound and less admirable effect is on Australian attitudes to those linguistic features they recognise as their own, especially an accent and an indigenous, now somewhat fossilised, thesaurus of slang. Both are regarded as oddities, departures from a boreal norm, like the duck-billed platypus. A serious dictionary of Australian usage is likely to be reviewed under a heading such as 'Fair dinkum cobber, take a dekko at this yabber' (where *dekko* is one of a large number of colloquialisms, conveniently listed in Wilkes (1985: 463–90), wrongly thought by Australians to be their own, and the massing of the other words is simply caricature).

The opposing democratic myth promotes the local element but might betray its own insecurity with concoctions not unlike the headline above. No one having experienced it would want to give up the direct and laconic way of speaking common in Australia but there is a danger of ignoring the feminine component of humanity, accepting the *ocker* (uncouth Australian) image and interpreting the moral and the higher life entirely in terms of *Rules* (Australian National Football) or surfing. The 'offensively Australian' Furphy, an unexceptionable Australian with his refusal to seek a British publisher in accordance with his slogan *aut Australia aut nihil*, had to remind his compatriots of 'a fact which we are, perhaps, too prone to lose sight of – namely the existence of a civilisation north of Torres Straits' (Furphy 1903: 270).

The democratic myth re-interprets the pastoral life, no longer in terms of gentlemen who learned their farming from Theocritus, but in terms of shearers whose nuances of vocabulary (the *board* 'floor of a woolshed', the bare-bellied *joe* 'ewe', the *ringer* 'fastest shearer', the *blow* 'stroke of the shears', *snagger* 'rough shearer') are known to every city dweller who can sing 'Click go the shears', though many of them could not tell you which breeds of sheep are bred for meat and which for wool.

The democratic myth has promoted useful research into the colloquial reaches of language (Baker 1966) and special interests such as shearing (Gunn 1965, 1971) and Australian Rules football (Eagleson & McKie 1968–9).

In an odd way the democratic myth is at one with the gentry; it emphasises from its own point of view the large farming unit, the *station*. Bush songs celebrate the *stockman* 'man in charge of livestock' or the *jackaroo* 'apprentice on a station'; the name suggests the influence of the word *kangaroo* but since it also appears in the American west it may well be from Spanish *vaquero* (Wentworth & Flexner 1960: 283). Both myths neglect the small farmer, the *cocky* managing by enlisting the help of his whole family, another form of slavery, or the country women savagely revealed in the bush stories of Barbara Baynton. They neglect, too, the divisions within the station, the contempt of the stockman for the crawler or shepherd and the gradation from the *house* of the owner or manager via the *barracks* occupied by overseers and jackaroos to the *hut* for lesser workmen (Wilkes 1981: 36–7).

It is open to debate whether there are traditional hierarchical social divisions in Australia. That there have been identifiable groups is beyond doubt (Cunningham 1827, II: 116). As soon as a generation of native-born Europeans became prominent, they were identified as *currency lads* and *lasses*, recalling the *currency* (Spanish dollars, barter, Irish banknotes and various foreign coins used in the first years of the colony) as opposed to *sterling* (which was also used to refer to settlers born in Britain). The settlement was founded on a distinction between bond and free. Those who were free comprised *free emigrants* (colloquially, especially the wealthy ones, called *pure merinos*), who had never been convicted, and those who had been convicted and later pardoned or had served out their sentences. This distinction between the free and the freed became blurred as time went on, as it became accepted that a crime was expiated by its punishment and euphemisms (*government men* rather than *convicts*, *the System* rather than *transportation*) softened the acerbities of early rivalries. Descendants of both groups can now unite against later immigrants from Britain, the *poms* or *pommies*; the name apparently comes from playful variants of *immigrant*, *jimmygrant*, *pomegranate* and now frequently refers to those who live in Britain with no thought of emigrating.

The kinds of social division imported into Australia even by free emigrants are well described in chapter 5 of Trollope's *John Caldigate* or in the description of the 'cabbage-tree-hatted' lad in chapter 33 of Henry Kingsley's *Geoffry Hamlyn*. Trollope notes the rapid formation of 'separate sets' of passengers on an emigrant ship and the distinctions between those with 'saloon' or 'second-class' antecedents. Kingsley depicts the young Australian 'amusing himself by looking round Mrs Buckley's drawing-room, the like of which he had never seen before'. The scene recalls visits to a grand house in Mrs Gaskell's *Wives and Daughters*, even the romantic 'mysterious domain' of Alain-Fournier's *Le Grand Meaulnes*. But Kingsley's book, it may be argued, appeared in 1859. Yet Patrick White in *The Vivisector* describes a poor woman's vision of a visit to a big house in equally glowing detail (White 1973: 28). Her son, later adopted by the pastoralist family, had to 'learn the language' they spoke (*ibid.*: 90). The difficult part, he found, 'was to know what you leave out' (*ibid.*: 87).

Now that dress no longer visibly distinguishes social classes and the costly *belltopper* 'top hat' and the humble *cabbage-tree* 'wide-brimmed hat woven from cabbage-tree leaves' have alike disappeared, a tradition of not enquiring too closely into antecedents allows an egalitarian mateyness, aided by immediate use of first names, inner privacy being maintained by protective slang or an assumed common interest in sport. First names may be abbreviated or given the Australian diminutive in -o (*Stevo* from *Stephen*) or the distinctive Australian change of /r/ to /z/ in *Bazza* for *Barry* or *Tez* for *Terence* (Poynton 1989: 62). Another change converting *Maurice* to *Mocker* or *Oscar* to *Ocker* explains the origin of *ocker* 'uncouth Australian' from the name of a character in a television series.

6.4.6 The goldrushes

In 1849 Alexander Harris considered that opportunities of large gain offered by the cedar trade were then at an end and could never be renewed (Harris 1953: 226). It must have seemed that the country was settling into a stability where the pastoral rich and poor were unchangeably established. But two years later the goldrushes were in full swing.

Before the goldrushes, the population of Australia was less than half a million. By 1860 Victoria alone had a population which had risen from 76,162 in 1850 to 521,072. Employers were concerned as their employees rushed off to the diggings, though ultimately, as the alluvial deposits were worked out, newcomers to the country tended to remain, so that there was an ultimate gain in the work-force.

Once again dialects were in contact. Different classes, different regions and different countries met on the goldfields. Bull (1884: 315) writes:

> Take a picture perfectly true. Here are four gentlemen working a claim; next claim on one side four Tasmanians (coarse fellows) and not far off a party of Melbourne men. All these men are on an equality as to their pursuit. Did the well-bred men descend to the general manners of their surroundings? As a rule, no... The roughest of the men see and adopt, as far as they can, the manners of the gentlemen.

That not all adopted the idiom of the gentlemen is suggested by William Howitt's account (Keesing 1967: 144) of 'language not to be repeated' on the goldfields. Two diggers passing his tent and seeing a thermometer on the post had this conversation:

> 'What d——d blasted bloody thing is that now?'
> 'Why I'm blowed if it ain't a d——d blasted bloody old weather-glass'.

There were complaints about 'Vandemonian slang' and the 'Vandemonian gentry' that used it (Crowley 1980: 202, 218).

Boldrewood (1890: 44) describes the goldfields as very English 'as if the concourse of adventurers had been located in Surrey or Kent', but another writer (Keesing 1967: 164) depicts a cosmopolitan scene:

> The German camps are strong in music, but they lapse into silence when stirring martial strains are commenced on the bagpipes by enthusiastic Highlanders, who are numerous on Bendigo... In Golden Gully we find a party of four full-blooded negroes entertaining a group of miners... A party of four Britishers or Americans are seated around a camp fire.

The accents in such a community must have been very diverse and the diversity would continue with little modification as diggers stayed on after the goldrush. Furphy (1903) is probably realistic enough in recording northern and southern Irish, Scots, a rustic form of southern English and nautical language, as well as strong Dutch, German, French and Chinese accents in the area north of the Murray, though such medleys are a literary tradition going back to Shakespeare's *Henry V*. But just because such accents are prominent and noticed (and thought funny) they would not influence mainstream English. To accommodate to such noticeable accents would be impolite – as indeed Tom Collins in *Such is Life* (Furphy 1903: 155–60) does in a highly comic scene (pp. 155–60) in which he assumes a Scots accent in reply to a man from Ecclefechan, but in so doing earns the disapproval of another Scot (*ibid.*: 168).

Gold-mining brought a spate of technical terms; in one page J. E. Erskine (in Crowley 1980, II: 199) uses *cradle* 'rocking box for separating gold from gravel etc.', *prospecting pan* 'a flat vessel of tin, like a milk-dish', *prospectors*, *claim*, *new colour* (describing a vein of thin blue clay) and *nuggets*, not to mention *grog shops* selling liquor. Some mining terms survived the excitement of the time and added to general metaphor; *to get down to bedrock* and *to pan out* are not confined to Australia but are perhaps commoner where gold has been mined.

6.4.7   *The modern period*

The prosperity of the era of gold brought improvements in transport and advanced the development of political independence. The exploration of the country was completed.

In the early days transport was especially by sea. Each day newspapers reported coastal shipping movements and included passenger lists valuable now for genealogists. The terms *cleared out coastwise* for departing ships, or *intercolonial* (to other Australian colonies) and *extracolonial* (to destinations such as Ceylon or Britain) were daily words (*Adelaide Register* 1855 *passim*).

Railway practice in Australia generally followed that in Britain, so that railway vocabulary in Australian English follows a British rather than an American precedent, *railway* rather than *railroad*, *goods train* rather than *freight train* and *guard's van* rather than *caboose*, but *cowcatcher* is American and *fettler* 'workman maintaining railway tracks' is in this sense Australian. Railways now have competition from *road trains* consisting of a prime mover and several trailers on the *beef roads*, built for trucking cattle in the north. Like the Americans, Australians have *semi-trailers* (often abbreviated to *semis*) rather than *articulated lorries*. The word *lorry* itself is giving way to *truck* in Australian English and *station wagon* has replaced *estate car*. In transport American terms enjoy prestige, perhaps because it is another big country.

Telegraphic communication was also in the news when railways began and popular interest in it is attested by the metaphor *bush telegraph* 'source of rumour, grapevine' first cited in 1864 in the *AND*. Contact with Britain was still by ship until the completion in 1872 of the *Overland Telegraph Line* crossing Australia from Port Augusta to Darwin.

Less dramatic but far-reaching in its effects was the development of corrugated iron (colloquially *galvo*), which became the commonest roofing material in Australia, and galvanised wire, which economically replaced the older *post and rail fence* 'a strong wooden fence with upright posts and horizontal rails' or the *dog-leg fence* made from horizontal logs and crossed uprights, and at the same time replaced the *crawler* or *shepherd*, though *boundary riders* had to be employed to keep fences in order.

The increased population and development of the country after the goldrush years led to political change as the colonies were given representative and then responsible government. A vocabulary of politics has grown up, as genuinely Australian in its way as the more self-conscious 'bonzer cobber' slang.

With *Federation* on 1 January 1901 the *Colonies* became *States* and *intercolonial* became *interstate*, also an American word, of course, but with a special additional use in Australian English as an adverb (*They were married interstate*) or with the meaning 'taking place in another state (*an interstate wedding* – not necessarily between participants from different states).

The federal administration was supported by *Federalists*, watched more suspiciously by *State-righters*. It was given a two-chambered Parliament, an Upper House or *Senate* and a lower *House of Representatives*. The states retained their various names for their houses of parliament, the upper house (except in Queensland, which abolished it in 1922) being called a *Legislative Council* and the lower house (or only house in Queensland) a *Legislative Assembly* in Queensland, New South Wales, Victoria and Western Australia, or *House of Assembly* in South Australia and Tasmania.

The early use of a secret ballot in Australia gave American English the term *Australian ballot*. Within Australia the adoption of a preferential voting system gave rise to the *donkey vote* 'simply numbering the names in order down the sheet'. The word *electorate* in Australian English has narrowed reference to what in Britain is called a *constituency*, and voters who vary their allegiance are *swinging* rather than *floating* voters. A spoiled vote is called an *informal vote* in Australian English.

The Overland Telegraph Line was made possible by J. M. Stuart's previous exploration of the land it traversed. Explorers named the countryside, nostalgically with British names or by finding 'the' name from the natives. Later explorers opened up the outback to the imagination and provided models of heroism. They also developed a topographical vocabulary of Australian English. This vocabulary runs obsessively on what for the explorers of the interior was *not* a pervasive feature of the landscape, namely water. In ten pages taken at random Warburton (1875: 151–60) uses the word *water* twenty-eight times and also uses the related words *drink, drinkable stream, flood, channel, lake, clay hole, watercourse, rock hole* (twice), *soakage, spring, pool* and (three times) *creek*. The following few pages add *water-hole, running water, native well, drainage hole, clay hole* (again) and *surface water* (twice).

Lexicon is a relatively unstructured part of a language, each word tending to have a history of its own. The important detailed study of words is found in dictionaries. Morris (1898) reflected the growing nationalism which led to Federation. Baker later added much detail especially from the informal registers of the language. The use of computers has facilitated the proliferation of Australianised versions of overseas dictionaries. The bicentenary in 1988 was celebrated by the launching of the *Australian National Dictionary: a Dictionary of Australianisms on Historical Principles* edited by W. S. Ramson.

Dictionaries are at the interface of prescriptive and descriptive language study. Setting out to record language, they record precedents which others follow. More direct standardising is sought by fisheries boards or boards drawing up standard terms for the timber trade. International committees and the demands of trade determine that a *crayfish* shall be called a *rock lobster* (Turner 1966 [1972]: 93). There is regional variation in the lexicon (Bryant 1989); even a technical language may show regional variation (Gunn 1971) so that the visiting linguist may know more shearing terms than the individual shearer working in a particular area. New technicalities bring new variation but multinational manufacturers tend to work against regional variation. The same is true of the media, where, especially in broadcasting, prestige models tend to be American (Leitner 1984; Sussex 1989).

Asked about their language, Australians are apt to think of the slang recorded by Baker, much of it already beginning to have a flavour of Old and Middle Australian now. He might note a propensity to hypocorisms (*blowie* 'blowfly', *mossie* 'mosquito', *tinnie* 'can of beer', *coldie* 'a cold beer'). These childish forms may seem to accord ill with the predominantly male image of the chief users of Australian slang, but there seems to be a parallel in the Roman soldiers who spread diminutive forms from Latin into the Romance languages of Europe.

In pronunciation the average Australian will probably think of Strine and be apologetic about it. Occasionally Strine catches an Australian feature but it is mainly a bit of fun about the mismatch of writing and speech, and the assimilations and elisions made in rapid speech (probably less in Australian English than in RP if tests were made).

Horvath reports (1985: 176) that General pronunciation is being favoured among the young against both Cultivated and Broad forms. This suggests a standardising trend, though it must be remembered that speakers often have a range of accents and a standard one is not necessarily the prestige model for everyone. Eagleson (1989: 156) reports that among an Aboriginal community anyone speaking the dialects of educated whites in the home would be accused of using *flash* language. So the word *flash*, referring two centuries ago to the lowliest form of English brought to Sydney Cove, has come to be applied to the acrolect. Standard Australian English is not, however, condemned; it is merely kept in its place. It is a reminder that even monolinguals might preserve within themselves, in Australia as elsewhere, a complex of linguistic variation.

FURTHER READING

6.1 *General. The Australian National Dictionary* (1988) is for Australian English what its model, the *OED*, has been for general English-language studies, the indispensable reference for the history of individual words. Earlier general studies of Australian English, except for Baker (1966) (the Mencken of Australian English studies) are now out of print, for example, Turner (1966, much revised in 1972), or the collection *English Transported* (Ramson 1970). Current trends can be studied in the collection edited by Collins & Blair (1989). The Sydney University Australian Language Research Centre published a set of *Occasional Papers* on special topics. Within Australia the main journal is *The Australian Journal of Linguistics. AUMLA* occasionally has articles on Australian English. Overseas journals such as *English World-wide* also publish papers on Australian English.

6.2 *Phonology.* The classic studies of Australian pronunciation are Mitchell & Delbridge (1965a, 1965b). The most influential recent work so far published is Horvath (1985). For background theory Wells (1982) and Trudgill (1986) are recommended.

6.4.1 For Aboriginal languages, Dixon (1980) is the major general account.

6.4.2 For the convicts, Vaux (1964) indicates the kind of language drawn on.

6.4.3–7 Crowley (1980) is a useful collection of documents illustrating Australian history. For the goldrushes, Keesing (1967) is a collection of social documents. For a historical study of the vocabulary, see Ramson (1966).

7 ENGLISH IN THE CARIBBEAN

John A. Holm

7.1 Introduction

The history of English in the West Indies is unlike that of other former colonies like Australia, Canada, New Zealand and South Africa. There, English was spoken from the start predominantly by settlers from the British Isles, who passed it on to their descendants and others largely through the normal processes of language transmission: infants learned it from their elders and adults learned it through fairly close daily contact with native speakers. In the West Indies this way of transmitting English predominated only in the early seventeenth century, during the first generation of settlement of a few islands like Barbados. After that period the massive importation of slaves from Africa brought about a restructuring of English (see sections 7.1.1 and 7.1.2) that resulted in Creole, a distinct language system with words derived from English but with phonology, semantics and morphosyntax influenced by African languages and other forces. After it became established as the first language of entire communities, this creolised English was transmitted like any other language. Over the years, because of language contact phenomena, Creole came to influence (and be influenced by) the standard and regional varieties of English brought from Britain. These uncreolised varieties survived among a few relatively isolated groups made up largely of whites, and standard English survived as the language of administration and education in all the territories that remained British colonies. But to understand the forces that created the folk speech of most of the Anglophone West Indies, it is necessary to understand the social and linguistic forces that resulted in creolisation.

7.1.1 Pidginisation

Pidginised English was used in the slave trade in West Africa and brought to the Caribbean by African slaves and the British slavers and settlers who dealt with them. A pidgin is a reduced language that results from extended contact between groups of people with no language in common; it evolves when they need some means of verbal communication, as in the slave trade, but, for social reasons that may include lack of trust or close contact, no group learns the native language of any other group. Usually those with less power (speakers of substrate languages) are more accommodating and use words from the language of those with more power (the superstrate), although the meaning, form and use of these words are influenced by their first languages. When dealing with these groups, native speakers of the superstrate language adopt many of these changes to make themselves more readily understood, and no longer try to speak as they do within their own group. They co-operate with the other groups to create a make-shift language to serve their needs, simplifying by dropping unnecessary complications such as inflections (e.g. *two knives* becoming *two knife*) and reducing the number of different words they use, but compensating by extending their meanings or using circumlocutions. By definition a pidgin is restricted to a very limited domain such as trade, and it is no one's native language (e.g. Hymes 1971 : 15). European expansion led to pidgins based not only on English but also on Portuguese, French and other languages.

7.1.2 Creolisation

A creole results when a pidgin is adopted as the first language of an entire speech community. Creolised varieties of a number of European languages arose in the Caribbean in the seventeenth and eighteenth centuries when African slaves from diverse ethnolinguistic groups were brought to European colonies to work together on sugar plantations. For the first generation of slaves in such a setting, the conditions were often those that produce a pidgin. Normally the Africans had no language in common except what they could learn of the Europeans' language, and access to this was usually very restricted because of the social conditions of slavery. The children born in the New World were usually exposed more to this pidgin – and found it more useful – than their parents' native languages. Since the pidgin was a foreign language for their parents, they probably spoke it less fluently; moreover, they had a more limited vocabulary and were more restricted in their syntactic alternatives. Furthermore, each speaker's mother tongue influenced his or her use of the pidgin in different ways, so there was probably massive linguistic variation while the new speech community was being established. Although it appears that the children were given highly variable and possibly chaotic and incomplete linguistic input, they were somehow able to organise it into the creole that was their native language, an ability which may be an innate characteristic of our species (Bickerton 1981). This process of creolisation or nativisation (in which a pidgin acquires native speakers) is still not completely understood, but it is thought to be the opposite of pidginisation: a process of language expansion rather than reduction (although a pidgin can be expanded without being nativised). For example, creoles have phonological rules (e.g. assimilation) not found in early pidgins. Creole speakers need a vocabulary to cover all aspects of their lives, not just one domain like trade. Where words were missing, these were provided by various means such as innovative combinations e.g. Jamaican Creole *hand-middle* 'palm'. For many linguists, the most fascinating aspect of this expansion and elaboration was the reorganisation of the grammar, ranging from the creation of a coherent verbal system (pp. 372ff.) to the development of complex phrase-level structures such as embedded clauses.

The creoles that developed in the Caribbean (called Atlantic creoles along with those of West Africa) have a startling number of phonological, morphosyntactic and lexicosemantic features in common which distinguish them from the European varieties of English, French, Spanish, Portuguese and Dutch which were the source of most of their lexicon. Comparative studies of their structure (e.g. Holm 1988) indicate that, despite their differing vocabularies, in some respects Jamaican Creole English, for example, is more similar to Haitian Creole French than it is to the English of Britain. As one might suspect, many of the Atlantic creoles' similarities can be traced to their common substratum of typologically similar African languages. However, it should be borne in mind that their superstrate European languages also share a number of typological features, and sometimes these happened to coincide with those of the relevant African languages (e.g. the predominant order of the main sentence elements: subject–verb–object). Furthermore, there seem to be some universal tendencies in the restructuring of languages since all adults appear to have certain strategies for learning another language. One of these is the tendency to convey grammatical information (e.g. tense) not with an inflection (e.g. *arrived*) but rather with a separate word (e.g. *did* arrive or arrive *already*). These universals affected the structure of the pidgins that later became creoles. Moreover, creoles – like all languages – can draw on their internal resources to produce innovations (e.g. via analogy), thus developing their own systematicity. Again, like all languages, creoles can borrow features (most often lexicon) from other languages with which they happen to be in contact (sometimes called adstrate languages, to distinguish them from superstrate and substrate languages): for example, Amerindian languages such as Arawakan contributed words to many Caribbean creoles. In sum, a creole's features – phonological, lexical, semantic and morphosyntactic – are influenced by its superstrate, substrate or adstrate languages, or by universals or internal innovation, or by the convergence of two or more of these factors.

The common features of the Atlantic creoles, whatever the source of their lexicon, suggest that they form a typological group of languages *sui generis*. While any claim of their genetic relatedness would have to rest on the genetic relatedness of their superstrates on the one hand and their substrates on the other, there would seem to be a strong case for their parallel independent development: they arose among speakers of partially similar African languages learning partially similar European languages under partially similar social conditions. For this reason, the Caribbean creoles based on English have a double identity: they have the structural features of Atlantic creoles, but also lexical and other features of regional dialects of English. Whether they themselves should be considered dialects of English is a complex question, depending in part on the degree to which they have been decreolised.

7.1.3   *Decreolisation and semi-creolisation*

In some areas where a creole has remained in contact with its lexical donor language (e.g. in Jamaica, where English is the official language), there has been a historical tendency for some of its speakers to drop its most noticeable non-European features if these are felt to be stigmatised, often (but not always) replacing them with European ones – or what are taken to be such. This process of decreolisation can result in a continuum of varieties, from those farthest from the superstrate (the basilect) to those closest (the acrolect), with mesolectal or intermediate varieties between them. After a number of generations some varieties lose all but a few vestiges of their creole features (i.e. those not found in the superstrate language) through decreolisation, resulting in post-creole varieties such as (according to some) American Black English. Others would call such varieties semi-creoles, which also means that they have both creole and non-creole features but does not imply that they were ever basilectal creoles, since both creoles and non-creoles (e.g. the English of the Cayman Islands) can become semi-creoles by borrowing features. Sometimes there is no way of determining with any certainty which way the development of a particular variety went. Although the verbal systems of English and Creole would seem to be irreconcilably different (p. 372), mesolectal varieties can generate intricate webs of revised syntax to bridge this gap. There is not always historical documentation of an earlier creole stage of a particular variety, and some may argue that it never existed.

While every English/Creole-speaking community in the Caribbean proper has a post-creole continuum of lects, each such continuum occupies a slightly different span on a larger historical continuum: for example, today basilectal Jamaican is farther from standard English than is basilectal Bahamian, but it seems likely that a century ago both were farther yet from the standard. Thus the problem of deciding whether a certain variety is more like Creole or more like a regional dialect of English applies not only to a particular lect but also to the span of lects found in a particular community. On structural grounds a good case can be made for basilectal Jamaican constituting a linguistic system quite different from English, while on the same grounds the acrolect is clearly the same language as English, with only negligible differences from the British standard in certain areas of lexis and intonation. Similarly, it is not at all clear that there is any significant typological difference between very decreolised continua such as American Black English and English dialects such as Cockney just because the former retain rather more foreign elements. These are all questions of degree which can only be answered somewhat arbitrarily.

The following will focus largely on those varieties farthest from English in each territory since it can be assumed that the standard variety in each locality differs minimally from that of Britain and that intermediate varieties combine features of both the basilect and the acrolect, as discussed above. Thus it should not be assumed that a particular linguistic feature is necessarily used by everyone in a given community. There are sociocultural correlates in that basilect speakers tend to come from poorer and often more isolated communities affirming more traditional African-American values, whereas acrolect speakers tend to come from wealthier and less isolated communities affirming European-American values, such as those emphasised in the educational system. In most territories the majority of speakers fall between these two extremes.

Creole English in the West Indies can be considered a single language, historically related to – but distinct from – both English (a parent language) and the creoles of Suriname (sister languages rather than dialects, if only because there is so little mutual comprehension). The various dialects of Creole English in the Caribbean proper (and to a lesser extent in certain adjoining areas such as the Bahamas, South Carolina and Georgia, the eastern coast of Central America, and Guyana) have remained in relatively close contact with both their European parent and one another as the language of maritime colonies which in the main had strong political and economic links. Diffusion of innovations on all linguistic levels has been an important force in the development of these dialects, as has their contact with uncreolised English.

7.2   The spread of English and Creole in the West Indies

It is difficult to gain a clear overview of how English and Creole spread in the West Indies – whether as standard or regional British, Caribbean or North American English, or as English-based pidgins and creoles. The general history of English in the region has been fragmented into dozens of histories of English in particular islands or territories. These histories are complex, with over three and a half centuries of dates of settlements, wars, economic upheavals and migrations. A further difficulty is that the story of the spread of English in the West Indies and surrounding area does not always coincide with the history of the spread of British political power in the region. There are former British colonies such as St Lucia or Dominica where English is spoken largely as a second language only, as well as areas that were never British such as Costa Rica or the Samaná peninsula of the Dominican Republic, where English *is* spoken as a first language. Another difficulty lies in the fact that even when British colonial history coincides with the spread of English, the focus of traditional historians was usually on political or economic events rather than on the spread of language varieties such as pidgins or creoles that were commonly held in as little esteem as the people who spoke them – usually slaves or peasants. It is only comparatively recently – that is, since the independence of most British islands, beginning in the 1960s – that histories have been written from the perspective of the colonised rather than the colonisers. The most valuable of these social histories for the present purpose are the sociolinguistic histories written by West Indian and foreign creolists which have focused specifically on the development of the local speech of particular islands or territories.

The problem here, then, is to tie these sociolinguistic histories together into a coherent whole providing a clear overview. In order to do this, the following will have to be confined to only the most important historical events in each area that had the most direct impact on language usage, with reference to more particular studies for further details.

The following history spans over 350 years and a good number of territories; to sharpen the focus in both time and space, the history is divided into fifty-year periods and discussion is largely limited to the main geographical areas into which English spread during each of these periods, although some earlier and later history of each area may be included to prevent the discussion from becoming too disjointed.

In references to its spread, 'English' is to be understood as including the metropolitan variety (usually non-standard) as well as restructured varieties. In early seventeenth-century settlements populated largely by indentured servants from the British Isles (e.g. Barbados until about 1640), 'English' generally meant regional forms of early Modern English, sometimes as spoken as a second language by Irishmen and Africans. In areas with developed plantation economies (i.e. most islands after the latter part of the seventeenth century) social conditions prevailed that were likely to produce pidgin and creole English among slaves, that is, there was increased social distance between whites and the fast-growing black population, which soon predominated numerically. The use of pidgin English as a second language was probably most common in the middle of the seventeenth century. It has been contended that before this period the small minority of Africans, who worked relatively closely with indentured servants from Britain, probably learned their regional English as a second language. After the establishment of Creole as the identifying language of the local community (or at least its slaves), newly arrived African slaves learned Creole as a second language if they had not already learned restructured English in Africa – as either a pidgin (Cassidy 1980) or a creole (Hancock 1980a). The language of most local whites was probably increasingly influenced by Creole by the end of the seventeenth century, with only a tiny minority of upper-class whites speaking anything approaching standard English (Le Page & DeCamp 1960: 115–16). In most population movements white settlers brought their slaves (who often outnumbered them), so the introduction of English-speakers into new areas of the Caribbean after the middle of the seventeenth century should be understood as entailing the introduction of Creole as well.

7.2.1   1600 to 1650

Although English smugglers and privateers had been active in the Caribbean during the second half of the sixteenth century, in 1600 Spain was still the only country with colonies in the Caribbean, but these were confined to the Greater Antilles (Cuba, Jamaica, Hispaniola and Puerto Rico) and the mainland. The English, French and Dutch, however, were seeking a portion of the wealth flowing from the Americas and began attempting to establish settlements in areas which the Spanish did not control. The first permanent English settlement in the New World was at Jamestown, Virginia in 1607. This was followed by the 1609 settlement of Bermuda, some 600 miles to the east. During this period the north Europeans were also trying to gain a foothold on the unsettled Guiana coast of northern South America but only the Dutch were successful, establishing a permanent settlement at Essequibo in 1618. However, it was this effort that led to the first permanent English settlement in the Caribbean.

The Leeward Islands

The Leeward Islands, which form the northern part of the great arc of the Lesser Antilles (map 7.1), include St Kitts. Englishmen returning from a failed attempt to form a colony on the Guiana coast established a settlement on St Kitts in 1624. The next year they were joined by some Frenchmen, whom they welcomed as allies against their common enemies, the Carib Indians who inhabited the island and the Spanish who claimed it. Surviving attacks by both, the English and French divided the small island (until the French were expelled in 1713) and eventually managed to drive out the Carib. They produced tobacco for the European market during the early decades of the colony, mainly with the labour of indentured servants. From St Kitts the English settled the nearby islands of Nevis and Barbuda (1628), Antigua (1632),

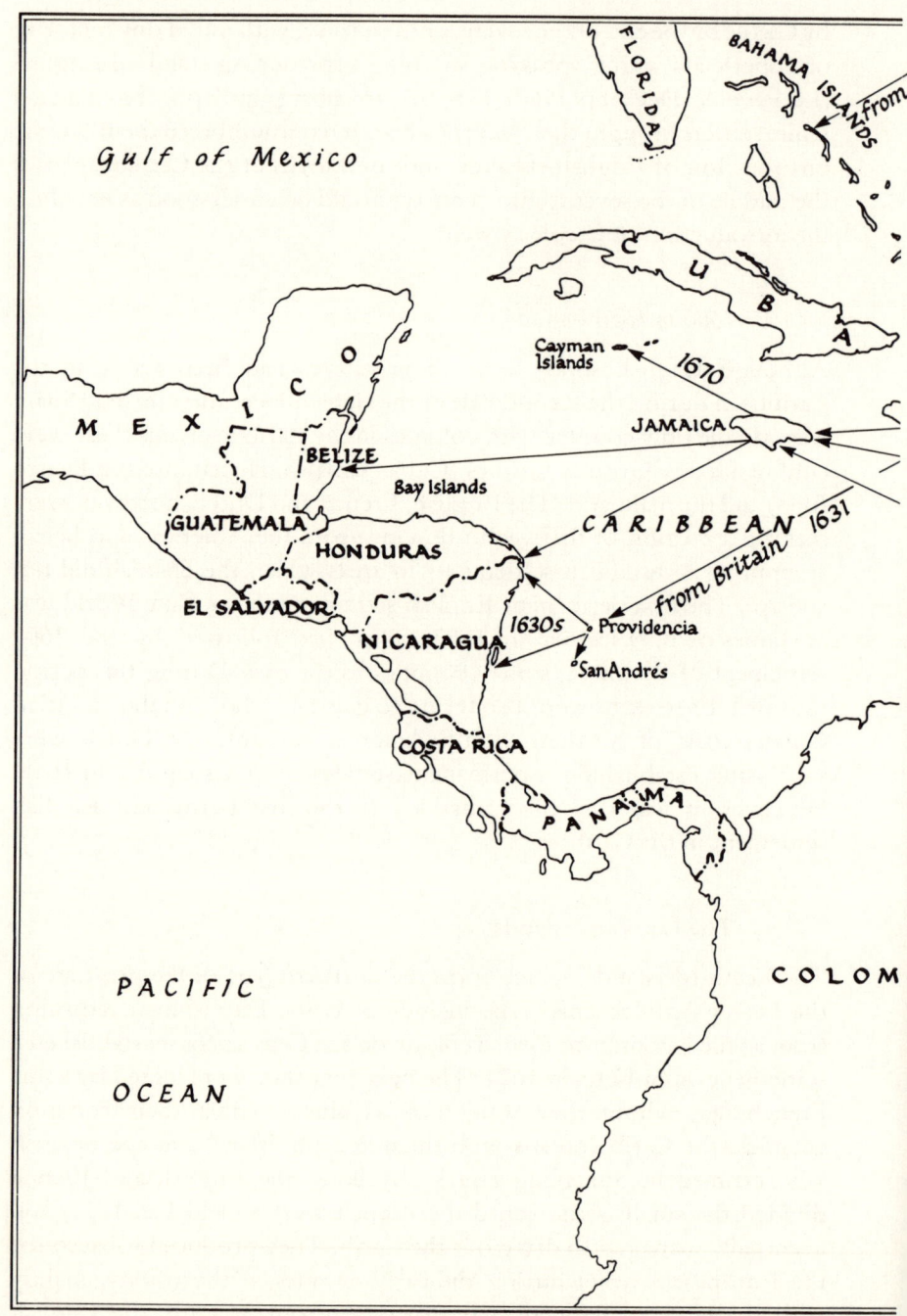

Map 7.1   Movements of English/Creole speakers in the seventeenth century

Montserrat (1633) and Anguilla (1650). Except for the last island, the cultivation of sugar spread throughout the Leewards from the 1640s onwards (Cooper 1982).

Barbados

Barbados lies to the east of the Windward Islands, which form the southern part of the Lesser Antilles. Although Barbados was the second island to be settled by the English (1627), it was the first in importance in the spread of English and Creole. During the first twenty years of settlement, most of the labour for growing tobacco was provided by indentured servants from Britain and Ireland. The island prospered and the number of colonists swelled from 4,000 in 1631 to 37,000 in 1642. During the English Civil War, Barbados became a convenient dumping ground for prisoners of war, Gypsies, Irish rebels, prostitutes and petty criminals. This white population speaking forms of regional English reached its peak in the 1640s but then suddenly declined as the consequence of a plague which swept the Caribbean from 1647 to 1649, and also because of the island's changing economy. The cultivation of sugar, which was more profitable than tobacco, was introduced in the 1640s. The labour required to produce sugar was much more gruelling and the indentured servants were not willing to do it. Their labour started to be replaced by that of African slaves; there were only a few hundred of the latter in Barbados in 1640, but by 1685 there were 46,000, while the number of whites had dropped to 20,000 (Parry & Sherlock 1974: 69). The former indentured servants who had smallholdings were forced off the land as the island was taken over by large sugar plantations. To be profitable, estates had to be big and have a large work-force to produce the great quantities of sugar needed to offset the initial investment of capital in the mill and other machinery as well as land and labour. The displaced white peasantry chose emigration over starvation during the second half of the seventeenth century, populating the new English settlements in Suriname, Jamaica and Carolina – and taking their Barbadian speech with them.

Providence Island

Providence Island (today called Providencia) lies at the opposite end of the Caribbean from Barbados, some 150 miles off the coast of Nicaragua. In 1631, just ten years after the founding of the Plymouth colony in New

England, a group of English Puritans established a settlement on Providence. At first settlers came from the faltering Bermuda colony, then from England and Massachusetts Bay (Parsons 1954: 8). Their aim was to establish an agricultural colony and to trade with the Indians on the mainland of Central America, whom they hoped to convert. The leader of the group that later came to be known as the Miskito eventually swore allegiance to the King of England. However, the colonists' crops were not successful despite help from the Indians; African slaves were bought from the Dutch and by 1641 they numbered about 450, with some 500 English indentured servants. However, after an attack by the Spanish in 1635, the colony became less of an agricultural settlement than the fortified headquarters of a privateering war against the Spanish. In 1641 the latter destroyed the colony and carried off its inhabitants, but the traders who had explored the mainland from modern Belize to Nicaragua remained in their outposts and a permanent English presence in the area had begun (Holm 1978).

The Dutch Windward Islands

St Martin, St Eustatius and Saba are three small islands scattered among the Commonwealth Leewards (p. 337). The Dutch made an abortive attempt to colonise St Martin in 1631, when they found it already inhabited by some fourteen French families. The Dutch returned in 1648 to settle the island, partitioning it with the French. In 1636 settlers from Zealand took possession of St Eustatius and started raising tobacco there. In 1640 some of these settlers went on to colonise Saba, which some shipwrecked Englishmen had reached eight years earlier. The three islands changed hands a number of times during the seventeenth century as different groups of settlers came and went; the islands ended up as Dutch possessions but English emerged as the dominant language. St Eustatius, an important entrepot in the slave trade, became a sugar colony. Today most blacks there speak Creole, but Creole-influenced regional English survives among the whites, who predominate on mountainous Saba (Williams 1983).

7.2.2   1650 to 1700

During the second half of the seventeenth century a creole with a structure quite distinct from English merged as the native language of a number of slave communities in the West Indies. While different varieties of Creole probably developed simultaneously on different islands, they did not develop in total isolation from one another because of the frequent movement of English settlers and their slaves. Barbadians played a key role in the spread of English and Creole during this period, introducing their speech into new areas.

Suriname

Suriname became an English colony in 1651 when the British governor of overcrowded Barbados sent a hundred men to found a colony on the Guiana coast of South America. Most were former indentured servants seeking land to establish plantations of their own. Within fifteen years there were 1,500 Englishmen in Suriname with 3,000 African slaves on small plantations averaging about twenty persons each (Voorhoeve 1964: 234–6). In 1665 some 200 Portuguese-speaking Jews from Brazil were permitted to settle in Suriname with their slaves. In 1667 Suriname became Dutch under the Peace of Breda, whereby New Amsterdam became British New York. By 1675 most of the English and their slaves had left Suriname for British islands in the Caribbean (particularly Jamaica), but in the short period between 1667 and 1675 the slaves imported by the Dutch apparently learned English Creole from the slaves of the British, possibly repidginising it. At any rate it was restructured English that survived as the lingua franca after the departure of the British slaves was virtually complete in 1680 (Goodman 1985). This early form of the modern creole (called Sranan) was then learned as a second language by newcomers from Holland as well as Africa. The Dutch used the English creole for contact with their slaves and reserved Dutch for use with one another. Sranan continued to develop without further contact with English; the Dutch treated it as a language in its own right, albeit one with little prestige until quite recently. Today it is a separate language that cannot be understood by speakers of English or the English creole of the Caribbean proper. It is worth noting that this did not happen to the English creole of the Dutch Windward Islands (p. 339). Although the language of administration there was also Dutch, as it was in Suriname after 1667, whites in the Dutch Windward Islands continued to speak English, which influenced the creole in much the same way as on neighbouring islands.

Jamaica

Like the other islands of the Greater Antilles, Jamaica had been settled by the Spanish in the sixteenth century but the colony failed to prosper. In 1655 the British, under Cromwell, planned to attack Spain by capturing Santo Domingo. A fleet left England and recruited 4,000 more men in Barbados and another 1,200 in the Leewards before attacking Santo Domingo, where they were thoroughly routed. In an attempt to save the expedition from total disgrace, the English attacked Jamaica, where the island's 1,500 Spaniards could mount little resistance (Le Page & DeCamp 1960). Their slaves, about equal in number, retreated to the mountains with them; most were eventually evacuated to Cuba except for some 250 who became Maroons. In 1656 settlers came from Nevis in the Leewards and began farming in eastern Jamaica under the protection of British soldiers. Of the original 1,600 settlers (including 1,000 slaves) about one-third were dead from disease within a year, but by 1658 further immigration brought Jamaica's population up to 4,500 whites and 1,400 blacks. In 1664 about 1,000 more settlers came from Barbados; in 1671 some 500 came from Suriname, followed by another 1,200 in 1675, at least 980 of whom were slaves (Cassidy 1961). These Surinamese slaves made up about a tenth of Jamaica's 9,500 slaves at this point, who had now come to outnumber the 7,700 whites. Since sugar was Jamaica's main crop almost from the beginning, the slave population quickly increased to 92 per cent of the total by 1734 (Reinecke 1937: 288).

The Bahamas

Carolina and the Bahamas formed a single colony in the seventeenth century. The first to be settled was the Bahamas: in 1648 some seventy religious dissenters from Bermuda established a colony on the island of Eleuthera. In 1656 'some troublesome slaves and native Bermudians and all the free Negroes' were sent from Bermuda to Nassau (Albury 1975: 45). In the 1660s other Bermudians, mainly seamen and farmers, began to settle the present site of Nassau on New Providence Island; of the two islands' combined population of 500 in 1670, about 60 per cent were white and 40 per cent were black. Because of its poor soil, the Bahamas never developed the large plantations found elsewhere; whites and blacks remained in approximately equal numbers over the next century and worked relatively closely together to make their living from small farming or from the sea (Holm with Shilling 1982). In 1678 salt was discovered on Turks and Caicos Islands south of the Bahamas, and Bermudians began coming to gather it and trade it to the North American colonies (Verdi 1984). In 1670 a patent granted to the Lords Proprietors of Carolina included the Bahamas, creating a single colony.

That year saw the first permanent English settlement in Carolina, near present-day Charleston. By 1672 there were some 800 British settlers and 300 slaves; almost half the whites and more than half the blacks had come from Barbados (Wood 1974: 24–5). Other settlers arrived from the British Isles and other North American colonies, as well as Bermuda, the Bahamas, the Leeward Islands and Jamaica (*ibid.*; Joyner 1984: 13). During its first twenty-five years, the colony's inhabitants traded with the Indians for deerskins and raised livestock, sending meat to Barbados in exchange for slaves and sugar. By the 1690s it became clear that the Carolina coastline was suitable for raising rice, for which there was a growing market in southern Europe and the Caribbean. The intensive labour needed to cultivate rice caused a great increase in the importation of slaves: by 1708 the colony's population of 8,000 was equally divided between white and black, but by 1740 there were 40,000 slaves as opposed to 20,000 whites. While this ratio of whites was high in comparison to that of the West Indies, it was low in comparison to the rest of the North American mainland. This may account for the fact that the Carolina coastland produced the continent's only true Creole English, called Gullah. Yet Gullah and Bahamian have apparently never differed as much from standard English as have creoles in the Caribbean proper, such as Jamaican: the higher ratio of whites – perhaps coupled with their closer working relationship with Africans than on Caribbean sugar plantations, providing a more accessible linguistic model – may have prevented the northern creoles from diverging as much from English from the time of their formation, then greater contact with the English of whites apparently accelerated decreolisation.

The Virgin Islands

Located at the north-west tip of the Lesser Antilles, the Virgin Islands attracted the interest of the Dutch after they had settled their nearby Windward Islands (p. 337). They claimed the eastern Virgin Islands in 1648 but ceded them to England in 1666. Meanwhile unsuccessful attempts to colonise St Thomas had been made by the Dutch, the English and the Danes, all looking for a Caribbean entrepot for the slaves secured at the outposts they had recently established on Africa's Gold Coast (modern Ghana). The Danish West India Company finally established the first permanent settlement on St Thomas in 1672, but so many of the Danish settlers died from disease that by the following year they made up only twenty-eight of the ninety-eight whites on the island

(Larsen 1950: 19). Because of their depleted numbers, the Danes allowed settlers of other north European nationalities to stay on. By 1688 Dutch speakers from the nearby islands made up nearly half the whites, followed by speakers of English (22 per cent) and Scandinavian languages (13 per cent) (Reinecke 1937: 395). At this time blacks constituted only 57 per cent of the population, but by the middle of the next century they had increased to 94 per cent (*ibid.*, 418). Plantations, however, were relatively small. Creole English apparently coexisted with Creole Dutch from the seventeenth century; the English-speaking slave owners seldom learned Dutch, so their slaves had to communicate with them in English. When St John was settled from St Thomas in 1717, both creoles were brought there as well, but when the Danes purchased St Croix from the French in 1733 English became established there to the virtual exclusion of Dutch. Danish remained the language of administration only.

The western Caribbean

The eastern coast of Central America attracted British settlers after the capture of Jamaica in 1655. The logwood that grew on Mexico's Yucatan Peninsula had been exploited by the Spanish since the sixteenth century; when the British realised its high value in Europe as a source of dye for wool, they began establishing settlements for cutting logwood along the coast of the peninsula in the 1670s, but these were recognised by neither Britain nor Spain. By 1705 the harbour at what is today Belize City was being used as the loggers' principal port. Meanwhile farther south along the coasts of what is today Honduras and Nicaragua, the posts for trade with the Indians that had been established in the 1630s from the ill-fated Providence settlement became centres for British buccaneers, who attacked ships laden with gold and silver from the Spanish Main. The buccaneers hid their ships in the coastal lagoons inhabited by the Miskito, their allies against the Spaniards. The British men formed conjugal arrangements with Miskito women in exchange for metal tools and arms, and they took Miskito men along on their expeditions to act as harpooners to help feed their crews. The Miskito became a culturally and genetically hybrid group, already having intermarried with escaped African slaves who came to their shores in 1641, quite probably from Providence Island. They retained their Macro-Chibchan language, which was never creolised, but adopted pidgin English as their second language (Holm 1978). In 1687 their

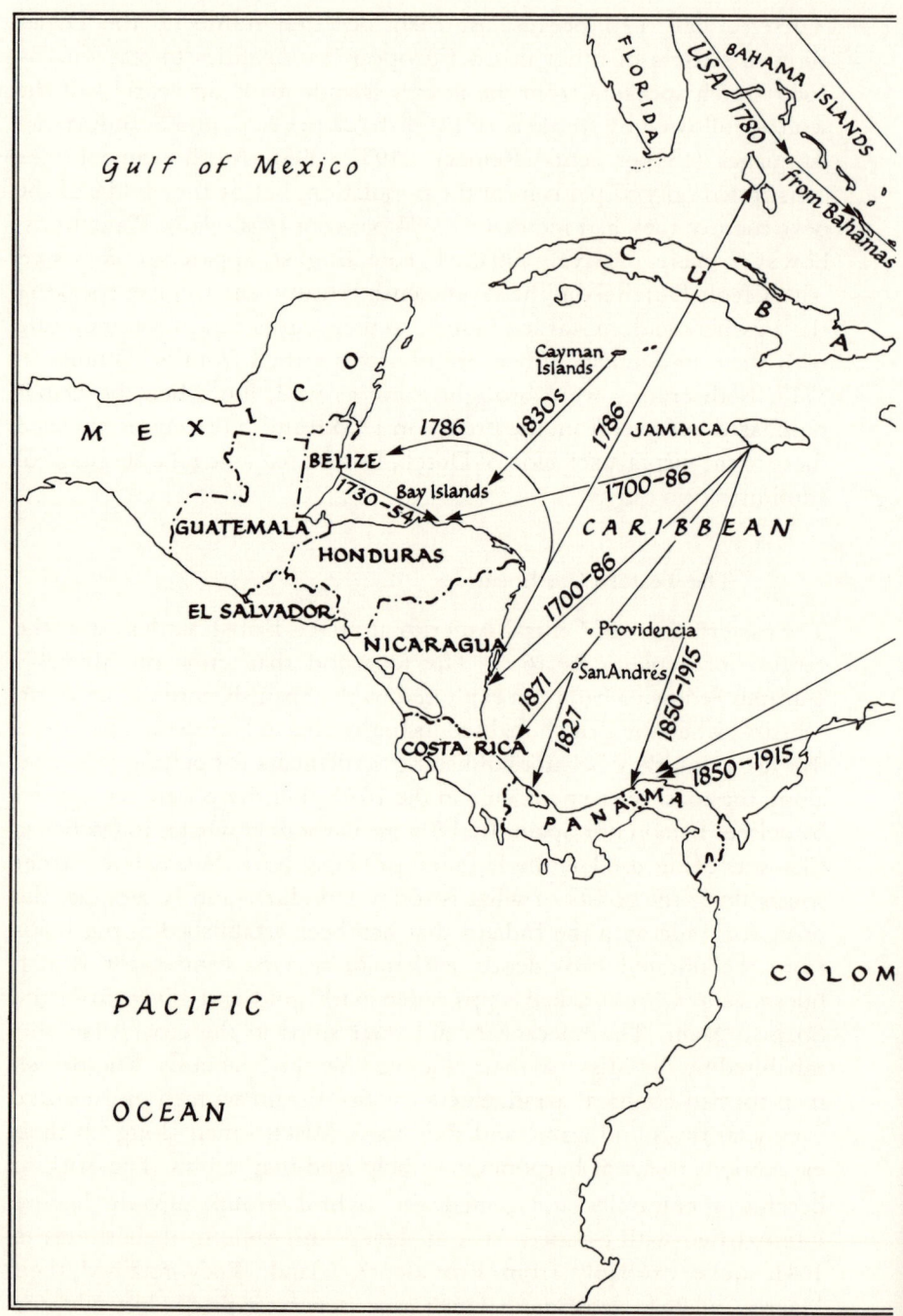

Map 7.2   Movements of English/Creole speakers after 1700

ATLANTIC

OCEAN

From USA 1917

From USA 1898

From USA 1824

VIRGIN
ISLANDS

Anguila
St Martin
Antigua
Montserrat
Saba
St Kitts
Nevis
Guadeloupe

HAITI
DOMINICAN
REP.

PUERTO
RICO

1800-20

LEEWARD
ISLANDS
1763

Dominica

Martinique

WINDWARD
ISLANDS

St Lucia

1850-1915

SEA

St Vincent

Barbados

Grenada

1800s

Aruba
Bonaire
Curaçao

Tobago
Trinidad

1740s–1800s

VENEZUELA

GUYANA

FRENCH
GUIANA

1680–1760
SURINAME

BIA

```
0          500        1000 km
0          500 miles
```

leader was brought to Jamaica, where he reaffirmed his allegiance to the English and was crowned King Jeremy I. Meanwhile the British claimed the Cayman Islands north of Jamaica in 1670. The first settlers were shipwrecked British sailors and army deserters, followed by immigrants from Jamaica. Their main occupations were turtle fishing and salvaging wrecked ships. Without plantations, the Caymans' population remained predominantly white and continued speaking regional British English, albeit with some influence from Creole (Washabaugh 1983).

7.2.3   1700 to 1750

By the first half of the eighteenth century the British had gained Spain's recognition of many of their Caribbean holdings, leading them to join in the suppression of buccaneering in order to protect their newly established colonies. The sugar plantations, which were being developed wherever possible, fostered a rigid social hierarchy in the form of a pyramid, with a small group of whites at the top and masses of field slaves at the bottom. This reinforced the isolation of most slaves from English, ensuring the predominance of Creole in nearly all British-held colonies in the region.

Suriname Maroon creoles

In Dutch-held Suriname distinct Maroon languages developed during the late seventeenth and early eighteenth centuries. Several hundred slaves had escaped from the coastal plantations (map 7.2) during the English period before 1667 (Voorhoeve 1973) but it is uncertain whether this group founded the ethnolinguistic group that came to be known as the Saramaccans. Revolts and escapes continued and by 1715 most of the fugitives who became Saramaccans had fled into the interior rain forests (Price 1975). The large portion of Portuguese-derived words in Saramaccan (37 per cent of the core vocabulary, as opposed to less than 5 per cent in Sranan and Ndjuka) was traditionally explained as originating on the plantations of the Brazilian Jews: 'Originally a corrupted Portuguese was spoken on the many Jewish-owned plantations, but it has now ... almost disappeared. It is spoken by only one tribe of the free Bush Negroes, the so-called Saramaccans on the upper Suriname River, most of whom originally came from these plantations' (Wullschlägel 1856: vi). Herskovits (1930–1) proposed instead that the words had been borrowed into African languages that were brought by the slaves to Suriname, but Voorhoeve (1973) suggested that the Africans actually brought a Portuguese pidgin whose relexification (or word-for-word replacement of Portuguese-derived lexicon by English-derived lexicon) on the coastal plantations was incomplete when the Saramaccans' ancestors escaped. Goodman (1987) argues that the traditional explanation was essentially correct. At any rate modern Sranan speakers find Saramaccan unintelligible, but not Ndjuka. The Ndjukas' ancestors apparently escaped during the half century following 1715 (Price 1975), when the Saramaccan settlements stopped accepting further fugitives. After a long series of guerrilla wars, the Maroons concluded a peace treaty with the Dutch which recognised their freedom but forbade them from harbouring any more fugitives. Later escapees, the ancestors of the Aluku, were finally driven into French Guiana in the 1790s. The language of their descendants is a dialect of Ndjuka, which in turn appears to be an offshoot of eighteenth-century Sranan.

The Miskito Coast

The Caribbean coast of what is today Nicaragua and Honduras became a more regular British settlement after the suppression of buccaneering by the early eighteenth century. However, the Spanish routed the British logwood cutters in Belize in 1730 and again in 1754; each time they retreated to join other British settlers at Black River on the coast of Honduras. This became the capital of the Mosquito Shore, which extended down to southern Nicaragua. The settlers and their Miskito allies were joined by more British traders, loggers and planters who brought African slaves with them from Jamaica. In 1740 the British organised the area into a protectorate with a superintendant appointed from Jamaica. In 1757 the population included an estimated 7,000 Miskitos and separate settlements of over 1,100 others; of the latter, 14 per cent were white, 15 per cent were mixed and 71 per cent were slaves (Holm 1978). It seems likely that the pidginised English spoken by the Miskito influenced – and was in turn influenced by – the Creole English of the slave and mixed population and the Creole-influenced regional English of the British settlers. During this period English-speakers started resettling the smaller islands off the coast of Central America, that is, the Bay Islands, Providence and St Andrews.

Guiana

During the eighteenth century the Guianas were held by the Dutch except for the French settlement at Cayenne in the east. In addition to the central section, Suriname, the Dutch had settlements in the western section (later British Guiana) dating from the early seventeenth century. There two varieties of creolised Dutch had arisen with the importation of African slaves to work on sugar plantations after 1640. The colony on the Berbice River prospered, but the colony on the Essequibo River to the west, which was on poorer soil farther inland, did not. By the 1740s the Demerara River between the two colonies had begun to attract English planters from Barbados and the Leewards, who were coming to settle on the mainland illegally to avoid the high taxes and difficult farming conditions on the islands (Edwards 1983). The governor of Essequibo recognised the value of the English planters for trading in slaves and other supplies that were needed by the Dutch, so he granted them permission to remain. By 1760 the British outnumbered the Dutch in Demerara (Rickford 1987).

7.2.4   *1750 to 1800*

The second half of the eighteenth century brought constant warfare to the Caribbean as Britain and France fought over the sugar islands, which were producing great wealth. Although the sociolinguistic dice determining the form of the region's creoles had already been thrown, these languages – now developed and stable – were brought into new areas with the shifting fortunes of war.

The Windward Islands

Forming the southern part of the Lesser Antillean chain (map 7.2), the Windward Islands were vigorously defended by the Carib Indians against European encroachment, but they were unable to stop the French settlement of Martinique and Guadeloupe in 1635. The Carib, joined by shipwrecked African slaves who adopted their language and culture, retreated south to the uncolonised islands of St Lucia and St Vincent as French planters unofficially settled these islands from Martinique during the first half of the eighteenth century. Britain also wanted these islands, but they were by treaty declared officially 'neutral' Carib islands (i.e. neither French nor British) until the British captured them all in 1763. The Caribs' resistance to the British (with covert French support) finally led to their mass deportation from St Vincent in 1797, when most were transported to the Bay Islands off Honduras. They took with them their language, leaving St Vincent a monolingual English/Creole-speaking island. Along with the other Windwards, it began to be settled by English-speaking planters and their slaves from the Leeward Islands. St Lucia was returned to France and received French-speaking planters and their slaves from the other Windward Islands. The islands changed hands a number of times again, but by 1815 all had become British. However, the folk speech of all except St Vincent remained largely French Creole.

The Bahamas

The Bahama Islands became a refuge for mainland loyalists and their slaves after the American revolution; the islands' white population doubled while the black population trebled. Some mainlanders created all-white communities on the small cays off larger northern islands like Abaco, keeping their slaves on the latter and not permitting them to stay on the cays. On New Providence the loyalists' slaves doubled the black population, but the island's white community grew as well. However, many loyalists took their slaves directly to the unsettled islands to the south to establish plantations for raising cotton like those they had had on the mainland. But this crop quickly exhausted the islands' thin soil, and by the early nineteenth century insects had destroyed what was left of the Bahamian cotton industry. Most of the owners abandoned their plantations, sometimes leaving their slaves to fend for themselves. During this period over 3,000 slaves (nearly a third of the slave population) were exported to other colonies such as Trinidad, despite the 1808 ban on such trade (Saunders 1978). The south-eastern islands of the Bahamas that were settled from the mainland became almost exclusively black; since the slaves' speech was considerably more isolated from that of whites than it was on the mainland, it seems likely that they preserved much of the decreolising plantation speech that gradually became Black English in the American South. This is supported by the presence on these islands of lexical items found in (and presumably originating from) the mainland, but not attested in the creoles of the Caribbean proper (Holm 1983a).

The Miskito Coast and Belize

The British used their Mosquito Shore protectorate to attack the Spanish Empire in 1780. The British lost and were compelled by the ensuing peace treaty to evacuate all settlers from this region, including the offshore islands. While some went to other British colonies such as the Bahamas (particularly Andros Island), most – some 2,000 settlers and their slaves – went to the Belize River area, where the Spanish stipulated that their activities were to be strictly limited to the cutting of logwood. Thus Belize Creole is an offshoot of Miskito Coast Creole, which continued to be spoken by the free people of colour and others who stayed on in what became eastern Nicaragua.

7.2.5   1800 to 1850

The French Republic's abolition of slavery in 1794 began the end of the old order in the West Indies. After great social upheaval in the French Antilles and elsewhere, Napoleon imposed slavery again, but the British abolished it permanently in their Empire in 1834. The ensuing economic changes brought new migrations of labourers and their languages.

Trinidad

Trinidad, the most southerly of the Caribbean islands just off the coast of Venezuela, remained a Spanish colony until the late eighteenth century. Worried by the British seizure of nearby Tobago in 1763, the Spanish authorities decided to bolster Trinidad's small population of some 1,400 by encouraging the immigration of Catholics from friendly countries with grants of free land and exemption from taxation for a certain period. This offer began a massive influx of French/Creole-speaking planters and their slaves, first from those islands that Britain had taken in 1763 (Dominica, St Vincent and especially Grenada) and then from the French colonies, where slavery was abolished in 1794 (particularly Guadeloupe, Martinique, and St Domingue – later called Haiti). When the English captured Trinidad in 1797, its population had mushroomed to 28,000; most of the 20,000 slaves spoke French Creole, as did over half the free population (Wood 1968). French had become the *de facto* language of law and commerce, which it remained throughout much of the nineteenth century. However, English was made the official language in 1823, and within a century the majority of the population spoke an English semi-creole. English-speaking immigrants included

British landowners and administrators as well as black veterans of the British army, including demobilised West India Regiment soldiers and escaped slaves from the United States who had fought on the British side in the war of 1812. Later these were joined by emancipated labourers from Barbados (Winer 1984).

The Virgin Islands

St Thomas and St John (then part of the Danish West Indies) began moving away from Dutch Creole and towards English Creole in the late eighteenth century as the warfare carried out by England and France in the Antilles made neutral St Thomas one of the few safe havens for commerce, bringing a great influx of foreigners who were much more likely to know English than Dutch. The position of English was further strengthened during the Napoleonic wars, in which Denmark sided with France. The British occupied St Thomas from 1807 to 1815 and the presence of 1,500 of their soldiers promoted the spread of English. After Denmark abolished slavery in 1848, the population shifted from the plantations (the stronghold of Creole Dutch) to the towns (the stronghold of Creole English). By the second half of the nineteenth century Creole Dutch was quickly losing ground and the Danish schools adopted English as the medium of instruction (Reinecke 1937).

Samaná

The Samaná Peninsula of what is today the Dominican Republic (map 7.2) was settled by speakers of Black English from the United States in the 1820s. In 1822 Haiti took advantage of the confusion created by the disintegration of Spain's American empire and seized Santo Domingo. Haitian rule, 'hostile to everything Spanish and white' (Parry & Sherlock 1974: 221) lasted until 1844. During this period Haiti attempted to strengthen its hold on Santo Domingo by bringing in not only Haitian peasants but also North American freedmen. The Haitian plan found support among various interest groups in the United States who favoured such emigration, including the freedmen themselves. Over 6,000 accepted and the first boatload arrived in the city of Santo Domingo in 1824. Although the Americans were decimated by typhus and some of their settlements were apparently Hispanicised early on (Poplack & Sankoff 1987), the 200 sent to Samaná prospered in their relative isolation. By the 1860s their numbers had increased to between

500 and 600 (DeBose 1983); they were mainly farmers and their churches and schools were the focal institutions of their language and culture, helping to maintain both (Vigo ms.). Today Samaná English, an offshoot of the decreolising American Black English of the early nineteenth century which has undergone some lexical and syntactic influence from Spanish, is spoken by some 8,000 persons, although the younger generation is becoming increasingly Hispanicised.

Eastern Caribbean

The abolition of slavery in 1834 had profound economic, demographic and linguistic effects in this region. Barbados, which had a high birth rate and a healthy climate, became an exporter of labour, helping to establish Barbadian speech (much less creolised than Jamaican) more firmly in the French Creole speaking Windward Islands and Trinidad, as well as in formerly Dutch Creole speaking British Guiana. To replace slave labour in the latter two colonies, the British imported indentured labourers from India, whose descendants today make up 36 per cent of Trinidad's population and 51 per cent of Guyana's. Their ancestral tongues still survive but they are being replaced by English Creole, to which they have contributed a number of words. Other immigrants during this period included indentured Africans (6,000 to Trinidad and 13,000 to British Guiana), many of whom had been liberated from the slave ships of various countries by the British navy; those who arrived via Sierra Leone were likely to bring with them a knowledge of that country's Creole English. Indentured labourers from India were also brought to the Windward Islands – although not in the proportion found in Trinidad and Guiana – to work on plantations, since migrant labourers from Barbados had a marked preference for the towns. English landowners and Barbadian administrators, schoolteachers and traders also tended to live in the main towns of the French Creole speaking islands, forming English/Creole-speaking enclaves. As the centre of government, Barbados became a kind of metropolis for the Windward Islands as the dispersal point for British goods, language and culture, having the only secondary schools in the region. Today St Vincent and Grenada are largely English/Creole-speaking countries, although Creole French survives among older rural people in Grenada. However, in the main English is spoken as a second language in both Dominica and St Lucia, although there are small communities of native speakers in both countries (Le Page 1977; Christie 1980; Carrington 1981).

Central America

Spanish settlement of the Mosquito Shore area evacuated by the British in the 1780s did not succeed, and English Creole remained the lingua franca. When Central America gained its independence from Spain in 1821, the weak federation could not control much of the Caribbean coast, creating a power vacuum into which the British gladly stepped. The Belizeans revived the protectorate of Mosquitia, which encouraged British settlers – both white and black – to reoccupy the offshore islands, where the evacuation of the 1780s had been spotty at best. Providence and St Andrews had become Colombia's Providencia and San Andrés, but their English Creole speaking populations continued to grow. In 1827 a group from San Andrés established a permanent settlement at Bocas del Toro in Panama, then part of Colombia (Parsons 1954). During the economic crisis following the abolition of slavery in 1834 a substantial number of Cayman Islanders moved to the Bay Islands off the coast of Honduras, transplanting their Creole-influenced regional English (Warantz 1983; Washabaugh 1983). Britain claimed the Bay Islands as part of Belize until ceding them to Honduras in 1856 under American pressure; English has survived there, however. The 2,000 Black Carib that the British had evacuated from St Vincent to the Bay Islands in 1797 had migrated up and down the Central American coast by the middle of the nineteenth century, taking with them their language (Garifuna) but also learning Spanish and English (Escure 1983; Holm 1983b).

7.2.6   1850 to 1900

Central America gained more English speakers during the second half of the nineteenth century even though British political influence waned there. The United States opposed Britain's plan to build a canal across the isthmus in Nicaragua; in 1860 a treaty between the two powers put the Miskito Coast under the protection of Nicaragua, which was allied with the United States. The latter's economic influence increased as North American companies built railways and established banana plantations and rubber and logging operations along much of Central America's eastern coast. The construction of a railway from Costa Rica's capital of San José to the port of Limón, which began in 1871, brought workers from Jamaica and the eastern Caribbean who stayed on, making Puerto Limón the centre of a Creole English speaking area (Herzfeld

1983). The migration of British West Indian labourers to Panama for the construction of railways from the 1850s onwards swelled with the building of the Panama Canal from 1904 to 1914; today there are large Creole English speaking enclaves in Panama City and Colón as well as Bocas del Toro. Meanwhile English Creole rather than Spanish was spreading to some Indian groups in this area. During this period the Rama of eastern Nicaragua began replacing their ancestral language with the Creole of the Miskito Coast, which they apparently recreolised (Assadi 1983).

7.2.7   1900 to the Present

The influence of North American rather than British English grew in the Caribbean area as the United States emerged as a world power at the beginning of the twentieth century. The Spanish–American War of 1898 brought Puerto Rico under American control with an 'English only' language policy in the schools until teaching in Spanish was reinstated with the Commonwealth constitution of 1952 (Zentella 1981). Today it is estimated that about half of Puerto Rico's 3.4 million inhabitants understand some English (Boswell 1980); 23 per cent have lived on the mainland for at least half a year (Zentella, personal communication) and some 100,000 were born there. North American English has also become the acrolect in the Virgin Islands purchased by the United States from Denmark in 1917, where 23 per cent of the population is now from the US mainland (Cooper 1983). In the Commonwealth West Indies standard American English is competing with southern British Received Pronunciation in influencing the emerging standard West Indian English and its regional variants. In many Commonwealth Islands the pronunciation favoured by television and radio announcers depends on where they as individuals received their higher education, although local pronunciation of standard English is finding increasing favour among the younger members of the new elite.

The story of the spread of English in the West Indies and the surrounding area is by no means over. The 350-year-old struggle between Spanish and English continues, with shifts in local balances of power resulting from continuing political and economic changes. While English seems to be gaining ground in Puerto Rico, the 1979 revolution in Nicaragua has brought more Spanish speakers to Bluefields on the Miskito Coast (now reportedly over 50 per cent Hispanic) and even Miami (now 64 per cent Hispanic). The struggle between English (in all its forms) and Creole is just as old; by all accounts English has been steadily winning, but any predictions of Creole's demise seem sure to be premature.

7.3   The restructuring of English in the West Indies

As outlined above (7.1.1–3), English was quite literally broken (jargonised), then partly rebuilt (pidginised) and then completely reconstructed (creolised) by Africans and Britons and their descendants in the West Indies. The original building blocks (words from the various social and regional dialects of early Modern English) were often reshaped (phonologically), re-interpreted (semantically) and recombined (syntactically) to erect a new structure: Creole English. The blueprint for this reconstruction was based on previous models (the English superstrate and the African substrate) and contemporary ones (adstrate languages) and guided by regulations (language universals) and creativity (creole-internal innovation). Later this modest house was partly remodelled (decreolised) again and again to make it more similar to a more imposing edifice: standard English.

Since French, Spanish, Portuguese and Dutch were similarly re-structured, the Atlantic creoles based on these languages share many features with Creole English in the West Indies. While the following overview of the structure of Creole English could focus on these similarities, comparative studies have already been done (e.g. Holm 1988) so the present study will include only one example, a comparison of the verb phrase (p. 374). Detailed studies of parallel African substrate features have also been done (*ibid.*); reference will be made to these from time to time to throw light on the origin of otherwise puzzling features.

7.3.1   *Lexicosemantics*

Creole English shares much more of its lexicon with English than it does with the Atlantic creoles based on other languages in so far as the *form* of its words is concerned, but all the creoles share certain traits in the *kinds* of words they retain (e.g. words that are today archaic or regional in Europe) and the *kinds of changes* these words underwent. Some of these changes are at least partly attributable to a common African substratum (e.g. calques, certain semantic shifts and reduplication) and some to the wholesale restructuring which is characteristic of pidginisation and creolisation (e.g. the reanalysis of morpheme boundaries). However, every kind of change described below can be found in non-creole languages as well. What is distinctive about creole lexicons is not the *kind* of changes that words have undergone, but rather the *extent* to which the vocabulary has been affected by them (Hancock 1980b).

British sources of the Creole lexicon

Creole English (CE) drew a considerable part of its vocabulary from English in forms virtually identical to those of Britain except for certain fairly regular sound changes (7.3.2). Even these often happened not to affect particular items, leaving words such as Jamaican CE *brij* virtually indistinguishable from standard English *bridge*. Moreover, all varieties of Creole that have remained in contact with English have continued drawing on it for terms needed in modern life (e.g. *televijan*), so that a great deal of the Creole lexicon is almost the same as English. The following, however, will focus on that part of it that is different.

Creole preserves many words that are today archaic or regional in Britain – or both. For example, CE *from* can be a conjunction with the temporal meaning of 'since': **From** *I was a child I do that*. This usage is archaic in standard English: the last recorded use of *from* with this meaning in the *Oxford English Dictionary* was in 1602, suggesting that it was still current – if somewhat old-fashioned – in standard speech when English began spreading throughout the Caribbean in the seventeenth century. However, *from* with this meaning was still current in the regional dialects of Ireland and Scotland when Wright's *English Dialect Dictionary* was compiled around 1900. Thus there is no way of knowing whether this usage of *from* was brought into West Indian Creole English by speakers of standard (but archaic) English or by speakers of regional British dialects. Of course many other words belong to only one of the two categories. Some examples are current Rama Cay CE *rench* and Sranan *wenke*, both 'young woman' from archaic *wench*. Another kind of archaism is the preservation of a pronunciation no longer current in Britain. For example, Miskito Coast Creole English retains the /aɪ/ diphthong in words like *bail* 'boil' and *jain* 'join'; this sound became /ɔɪ/ in standard English after about 1800. This makes the Creole English word for 'lawyer' homophonous with standard *liar* (but there is no confusion since in Creole English the latter takes the dialectal form *liard*, analogous to *criard* 'crier' and *stinkard* 'stinker' – cf. standard *drunkard*).

Creole also preserves forms, meanings and pronunciations that are now found only in regional British English, such as Miskito Coast

Creole (MCC) *krabit* 'cruel' from Scots *crabbed* or *crabbit* 'ill-tempered'. British pronunciations that appear to be regional have also been preserved in Creole, but again it is often impossible to determine whether these are in fact regional rather than archaic. Cassidy (1964: 272) points out that Sranan words reveal the state of flux of certain vowels and diphthongs in the seventeenth-century English on which Sranan is based. For example, at that time the shift from early ModE /ʊ/ to ModE /ʌ/ was apparently not yet complete; in some Sranan words /u/ preserves the earlier pronunciation, as in *brudu* 'blood', while in others /o/ preserves the later pronunciation, as in *djogo* 'jug'. However, this shift never took place in many midlands and north country dialects of England, where these words are still pronounced /blʊd/ and /dʒʊg/. Therefore, there is no way of knowing whether Sranan *brudu* or even Bahamian *shoove* /ʃʊv/ 'shove' preserve an archaic or a regional British pronunciation.

Nautical English was also a source of Creole lexicon since Britain's West Indian territories were maritime colonies long reached only by sea. Because of the mixture of dialects and even languages found among ships' crews, nautical speech has always constituted a distinctive sociolect; in the seventeenth century British sailors' speech was described as 'all Heathen-Greek to a Cobler' (quoted by Matthews 1935). Today in eastern Nicaragua kitchens or separate cooking huts are called *gyali*, from nautical English *galley* 'ship's kitchen'; as further examples *haal* 'haul' and *hib* 'lift from below' (cf. *heave*) and *hais* 'lift from above' (cf. *hoist*) are used much more frequently than in standard English.

Slang and vulgar usages also influenced Creole. The British brought the dialects of their social class as well as their region to the colonies, and for the urban poor, soldiers and many others who made up the early settlers, slang was an important part of daily speech. When such words became a part of Creole they often lost the connotations they had had in Britain. If the only Creole word for 'urine' was *piss*, this word became as appropriate as *urine* in any domain, shedding the vulgarity of its etymon.

African lexical influence

The portion of African-derived words in most creoles is quite small – usually under 5 per cent. The portion of non-European words in the pidgins out of which the creoles grew could not exceed a certain level without impairing communication with the Europeans, which was the pidgins' original function. Moreover, there is evidence that in the slave trade and on the plantations slaves were purposely mixed linguistically to make secret communication for a rebellion more difficult. Thus it seems likely that competence in ancestral African languages was usually not transmitted beyond a generation or two in the West Indies, despite the continuing arrival of newly imported slaves.

Of the limited number of African words that did survive, there are both retentions and loans. Retentions are those basic items that are today widespread in both African and Caribbean languages that were part of an early pidgin lexicon. Such words include *nyam* 'to eat' with cognates with related meanings in scores of Niger-Congo languages (Koelle 1854: 80–1) and *fufu*, a dish made of boiled and mashed starchy vegetables like cassava, plantains, etc. (Turner 1949: 193). If it is likely that such words were part of an early pidgin, they can hardly be called 'loans' into the creole any more than the vocabulary derived from English. However, it seems likely that other African-derived words were in fact loans, that is, borrowed well after the establishment of the creole. These may include the widespread words for Yoruba dishes such as *àkàrá* or cultural phenomena such as *èèsú* 'savings club', since the Yoruba were not brought to the Caribbean in large numbers until the defeat of their empire in the late eighteenth century, well after the formation of the creoles.

Although the number of Creole words derived from African languages is limited, the influence of the substrate languages on the semantic range of creole words is quite extensive. Alleyne (1980: 109) has suggested that this occurred via relexification: 'the historical development of the lexicon has been in terms of a substitution, massive and rapid in this case, of West African lexemes by English (and Portuguese, Dutch, etc.) lexemes, leaving the former residual in…the semantic structures which underlie the lexicon'. For example, Twi *dùá*, Ibo *osisi* and Yoruba *igi* all have a semantic range including 'tree, wood, stick'. In Creole English the word *stick* can also mean 'tree' (e.g. Bahamian CE *a stick name pine*) or 'wood' (e.g. *a piece o' stick*). Moreover, Twi *dùá* has the additional meaning of 'penis'; this is also an extended meaning of Jamaican CE *wood* (as it is of the equivalent Haitian Creole French *bwa*, Papiamentu Creole Spanish *palu*, and Brazilian Portuguese *pau*) but not of the corresponding words for 'wood' in the European source languages.

The Creole lexicon has also been affected by the syntax of Niger-Congo languages. For example, the notions expressed in English by adjectives correspond to verbs in basilectal varieties of Creole, such as MCC *If yu wud sief, yu wud ron* 'If you want to be safe, you had better run'. However, while in this instance a strong case can be made for the likelihood of the influence of West African languages (in which stative verbs often correspond to English adjectives), such changes of syntactic function often resulted from the general restructuring that took place during pidginisation (characterised by multifunctionality, in which a single word has many syntactic functions to compensate for the limits on vocabulary), for example CE *He **advantage** her* 'He took advantage of her'. Still other instances (e.g. *She **out** the light*, i.e. 'extinguished') can be traced to British dialects.

African languages also affected Creole lexicon by means of calquing, that is, the word-for-word translation of an idiom. Creole *big-eye* means 'greedy; wanting the biggest and best for oneself'. This metaphor is widespread in Africa: Twi *ani bre* or Ibo *aŋa uku*, both literally 'big eye' meaning 'greedy'. Calquing can also affect word-formation rules; in many creoles the sex of animate nouns can be indicated by juxtaposition of a word for 'male' or 'female', a pattern found in many West African languages. For example, CE *boy-chil'* means 'son', while *gyal-chil'* means 'daughter'; in Bambara, a Niger-Congo language, the word for 'son' is *dén-ce* (literally 'child male') and the word for 'daughter' is *dén-muso* (i.e. 'child female').

African languages also affected the Creole lexicon in the importance of reduplication as a mechanism for forming new words. Reduplication is the repetition of a word (or part of a word) resulting in a distinct lexical item with a slightly different meaning and an intonational contour different from iteration, or the simple repetition of a word for emphasis (e.g. *a long, long walk*). For example, in Miskito Coast CE *Bad-bad* is a boy's nickname (accented on the first syllable; note that *bad* can have a positive connotation, as in many African and creole languages). Creole *big-big* means 'huge', just like Yoruba *ńláńlá* or Kongo *múpátipáti*, both literally 'big-big'. In European languages such constructions are possible, if much less frequent, suggesting that the influence of the superstrate and language universals converged with that of substrate languages.

Other lexical sources

While English was the source of most Creole words and African languages provided a little lexical and a great deal of semantic input, there are two other sources of Creole lexicon that should be mentioned: Portuguese and adstrate languages. The Portuguese-based pidgin that evolved in West Africa from the fifteenth century onwards was well established as the language of the slave trade in the seventeenth century, when the Dutch, English and French began capturing Portuguese forts from the Gambia to the Congo to gain supplies of slaves for their colonies in the New World. It has been claimed that the Portuguese pidgin used around these forts (and possibly by the first generations of Africans brought to the New World) was, according to the monogenetic theory, relexified or changed word for word towards the language of the Europeans currently in power, leaving Portuguese words in the pidgins of these various languages as remnants which survived in the ensuing creoles. For example, *sabi* 'know' (cf. P *saber*) is found in many of the world's creoles, including Sranan, Ndjuka and Saramaccan, and even in the Caribbean proper (e.g. Jamaican *sabi-so* 'wisdom'). Cassidy (1964) points out some fifty words apparently from Portuguese that are shared by Sranan and Jamaican Creole English. Aside from the uncertainty of some of the etymologies, however, there are some problems in attributing these words to the remnants of an earlier Portuguese pidgin rather than the Portuguese brought to Suriname by the Brazilian Jews (pp. 346–7). The Surinamese creoles also have some Portuguese-derived function words like *ma* 'but' (cf. P *mas* 'but'), the general locative preposition *na* (from P *na* 'in the'; cf. Jamaican *ina* 'in the') and the verbal marker of completive aspect (p. 376) *kaba* (cf. P *acabar* 'to complete, finish', possibly converging with the completive marker of an African language like Bambara *ka ban*).

Words of Portuguese origin like Guyanese CE *preyta* 'person of African descent' (cf. P *preto* 'black') seem less likely to come from an early pidgin; they are probably later borrowings from Portuguese as an adstrate language spoken by immigrant labourers from Madeira and the Azores who were brought to the Caribbean area after emancipation in the 1830s. Other adstrate languages include Spanish (particularly in eastern Central America), Creole French (in the Windward Islands and Trinidad), Creole Dutch (in the Virgin Islands) and standard Dutch (in Suriname, where as the administrative language it took on a role in the development of the English Creoles almost comparable to that of English in the British West Indies). Amerindian adstrate languages contributed a variety of terms for flora and fauna to the Caribbean creoles, often via Spanish, such as Island Carib *mabi*, a species of tree whose bitter bark is used in preparing a drink called *maubi* in Eastern

Caribbean Creole English. Other such languages include Miskito and Nahuatl, which contributed words to Central American Creole English.

Morphological changes

Most basilectal Atlantic creoles have no inflectional morphemes to mark grammatical categories, like English *-ed* for the past or *-s* for plurals, although sometimes mesolectal varieties have borrowed such endings from the superstrate, for example Jamaican CE *waakin* 'walking', corresponding to basilectal *de waak* (p. 375). This loss of inflections seems likely to have resulted from a universal strategy of adults in acquiring a second language which affected the pidgins out of which the creoles grew, but it should be noted that many of the substrate Niger Congo languages also lack grammatical inflections and this could have influenced the creoles' morphology as well. Some English inflections did survive in certain Creole words as fossilised remnants devoid of grammatical meaning that had become a part of the word itself: for instance, in Creole one can speak of one *ants* or one *matches* or one *tools*, in which the English word and its plural inflection have become a single Creole morpheme with either singular or plural meaning. Such agglutination of an inflection often reflects the frequency of the source form in English. For example, some words are more likely to be heard in the plural such as *shoes*, which usually come in pairs; CE *shuuz*, meaning 'shoe' or 'shoes' can be made unambiguously singular with a quantifier: *wan **fut** a shuuz*. Similarly, some verbs may be more likely to occur in their past or present participial form, which serves as the etymon of the Creole verb: CE *to marid* 'to marry' or *to fishin* 'to fish'. Such reanalysis of morpheme boundaries can be found in all the Atlantic creoles.

An important Creole strategy for filling gaps in the lexicon was to create a new combination of morphemes to express a particular concept. In Trinidad, for example, the state of being well brought up is referred to as *broughtupcy*. Free morphemes are more likely to enter into such new combinations. In Miskito Coast Creole English, for example, two familiar words (*mountain cow*) were combined to refer to the unfamiliar tapir. Some such terms impose a cultural redefinition on their etyma, such as *fairy boy* 'ancestral spirit inhabiting the jungle'. Creole has also created a number of new phrasal verbs such as *dark up* 'turn dark', *drunk up* 'become intoxicated', *hug up* 'embrace enthusiastically' and *wet up* 'soak'. Some of these may actually represent survivals of archaic or regional British usages, but since lexicographers have largely ignored the status of phrasal verbs as separate lexical items until recently, such an origin for these terms is difficult to establish. However, when they include verbs based on English adjectives (e.g. *dark up*), the case for their being innovations is quite strong. Some Creole morpheme combinations like *han elbo* 'elbow' or *hed skol* 'skull' seem redundant, but reference to substrate languages often throws light on such puzzles. In most West African languages there is a single word for the lower arm and hand, the meaning of Creole *han* (similarly, *fut* refers to the entire extremity below the knee). Calquing may also have played a role in the development of *hed skol*: Yoruba *agbárí* 'skull' comes from *igbá* 'calabash' plus *orí* 'head'. English *skull* may have initially been interpreted as 'calabash', whence *hed skol* to distinguish it from other kinds of calabashes.

Semantic changes

Sometimes the difference in meaning between an English word and the corresponding term in Creole is due not to external influences but rather to internal developments taking place some time after pidginisation.

Semantic shifts are characteristic of any language used in a new geographical setting. When the European languages that provided the creoles' lexicons were first taken to tropical Africa and the Caribbean, they lacked words to refer to local plants, animals, customs, objects, etc., that were unknown in Europe. While some of these gaps in the lexicon were filled by borrowing or creating new words, very often old words were simply used for new referents. On the Miskito Coast, *lion* came to be used for the local cougar, and *tiger* for the jaguar. Such semantic shift represents an extension of a word's meaning with the loss of its earlier meaning. Semantic broadening is such an extension without the loss of the original meaning. For example, *tea* in most varieties of Creole English refers not only to the infusion made from various leaves, but also to any hot drink. A Bahamian can say, *I must have my tea before I go to bed – either coffee or cocoa.* The semantic source of this extension of the meaning of *tea* might be the calquing of monomorphemic words in West African languages meaning 'hot drink', a meaning transferred to *ti* as a loan in Twi, spoken in Ghana. The frequency of semantic broadening in the creoles suggests that in some cases this may have resulted from the retention of usages in earlier pidgins, noted for polysemy or the use of the same word for a variety of meanings to compensate for a limited vocabulary. Semantic narrowing, or the restriction of a word's meaning, seems to be less frequent. One example is MCC *stew*, which has acquired the specialised meaning of 'boiling meat and vegetables in coconut milk', while boiling them in plain water is to *run* them *down*.

There are several other kinds of semantic shifts, including metaphor. For example, the cutlass of seventeenth-century pirates has survived in the Caribbean as an ordinary gardening tool that can be purchased in any hardware store. Bahamians call one whose blade is sharp on both sides a *French knife*, which is also a term of abuse for a two-faced person. Hancock (1980b) also identifies playforms as further sources of semantic shift; these include phonological modifications, intentional puns and intentional etymologies. The last might include Bahamian *donkeyfy* 'not caring about social norms'; there is a slightly different alternative pronunciation, *don't-ca(re)-if I* (do or don't), but the first form carries the extra idea of a donkey's obstinacy. The final category of semantic change is that caused by using a word as a euphemism. In Bahamian *hip* is a euphemism for 'buttocks'; it is the only part of their anatomy that ladies ever fall on.

7.3.2 *Phonology*

The phonological differences between English and the creoles of the Caribbean and Suriname can be attributed to the factors in the genesis of the creoles discussed above: the influence of superstrate, substrate and adstrate languages, as well as language universals and creole-internal innovations, frequently with two or more of these converging. Phonological influence of the superstrate that differs from the modern standard includes that of archaic and regional British English (discussed on pp. 356–7). Substrate influence, discussed throughout the following, is far-reaching; the most obvious examples are the sounds in the Surinamese Creoles not found in English, the coarticulated and pre-nasalised stops (pp. 368–9). Moreover, an adstrate language, Dutch, has affected the phonotactic rules of one of these creoles (p. 365). Language universals play a role in the general patterns of possible phonological changes that creoles can undergo, such as in palatalisation (pp. 369–70), although here the converging influence of substrate languages is also evident. Creole-internal innovation can be seen in the systematisation of the phonological patterns that emerged.

Continua

As noted above, varieties of Creole in the Caribbean proper that have coexisted with standard English as the official language over a number of centuries today form a continuum of lects. The focus of the following discussion is the phonology of the basilectal end of those continua, the varieties least like English. Mesolectal and acrolectal varieties are unlikely to include many of these features. In Suriname, however, there is no continuum but rather a clear break between the creoles and the standard, which is a completely different language, Dutch. While there is some influence from Dutch, English has not influenced these creoles for over 300 years, except for recent lexical borrowings from English as a foreign language.

Phonotactic rules

Creole phonotactic rules, which determine the permissible sequence of sounds in a syllable, were clearly influenced by substrate languages. With few exceptions, the relevant African languages have a rule requiring a syllable to consist of a single consonant followed by a single vowel (possibly nasalised). This CV syllabic structure rule can be clearly seen in the Surinamese creoles, and remnants of it can be found throughout Creole English in the Caribbean proper.

In the earliest creoles sounds were dropped or added to maintain a pattern of CV CV syllables. This can be seen in Sranan words like *bigi* 'big' or *dagu* 'dog', with a paragogic vowel added to the end of the word. In the Caribbean proper such additional vowels survive only in proverbs (e.g. *Fowl drinky water...*; Powles 1888: 167), or in the speech of idiots or monsters in folk tales, for example *God hatee me* or *You want to eat allee* (Crowley 1966: 66). The CV pattern could also be achieved by dropping the first consonant in a word-initial cluster: Sranan *tan* (with a final nasalised vowel) from English *stand*. The absence of such consonants is stigmatised in decreolising varieties, leading to hyper-corrections in which there is a 'replacement' of an initial consonant (usually /s/) which is thought to be missing: *scrumbs* 'crumbs'. Decreolising varieties that developed a phonotactic rule tolerating a single final consonant may still omit the second element of a final consonant cluster in English, particularly when the consonants are both voiced or unvoiced: *roun'* 'round' or *des'* 'desk'. This coincides in part with a colloquial English rule permitting the dropping of a final stop in a cluster before a word beginning with another stop (e.g. *roun' table*), but post-creoles also allow final stops to be dropped before a vowel (*roun' apple*) or a pause (*It's roun'*). Since this loss of a final consonant can also be stigmatised, decreolising varieties sometimes develop hypercorrect forms that 'replace' the sound thought to be missing: CE *sinimint* 'cinnamon'.

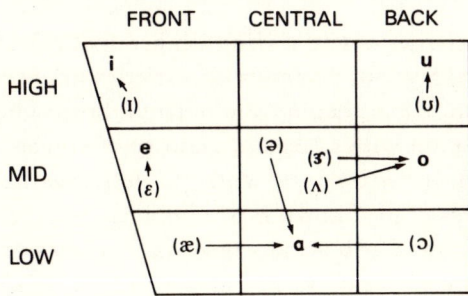

Figure 7.1   The convergence of English vowels in Creole English

In reshaping syllables to achieve a CV CV pattern, sounds could also be dropped within the word (e.g. Sranan *kosi* 'curtsy' or *sisa* 'sister'), or added within the word: for example, Ndjuka *sikoro* 'school' has such an epenthetic vowel to break up the initial consonant cluster. In coastal Sranan, which has been in closer contact with Dutch than the Maroon creoles, the modern form of this word is *skoro*, although *sikoro* is still heard in poems. This suggests that an earlier CV syllable pattern in Sranan was disturbed by borrowing words from Dutch without making them conform to this phonotactic rule: Sranan *skrifi* 'write' (with an initial consonant cluster) from Dutch *schrijven* 'write'. This development of a rule permitting consonant clusters in certain words (which may have carried prestige through association with the official language) appears to have led to the creation of new consonant clusters through the elision of earlier epenthetic vowels, as in the change of *sikoro* to *skoro* (Eersel 1976). Some cases of apparent metathesis or reordering of sounds like Sranan *wroko* 'work' may have resulted from original epenthesis (*wóroko*) followed by a shift of stress to the epenthetic vowel (*woróko*) and then the elision of the original vowel (*wroko*). However, other cases of metathesis may actually represent the survival of archaic or regional British forms: Bahamian CE *aks* 'ask' or *cripsy* 'crispy'.

Vowels

Pidgins tend to retain those sounds that occur in both superstrate and substrate languages, while all other phonemes tend not to survive in either the pidgin or an ensuing creole. Since English has some dozen vowels (see figure 7.1) and the substrate African languages usually have between five /i, e, a, o, u/ and seven (also /ɛ/ and /ɔ/, although these are often allophones of /e/ and /o/ respectively), it is not surprising that a number of English vowels did not survive in the creoles. It seems likely that the earliest varieties of Creole English had five vowels (as the Surinamese creoles do today) but decreolising varieties moved towards the English system through lengthening and outright borrowing. Semi-creoles may have started out with a larger inventory of vowels.

The English high front vowels /i/ and /ɪ/ fell together in the Surinamese creoles, for example Sranan *si* 'see' and *bigi* 'big'. Although the Creole English of the Caribbean proper has developed a clear opposition (cf. Jamaican *siit* 'seat' vs *sit* 'sit'), this may depend more on vowel length than vowel quality (Alleyne 1980: 41). The distinction between the mid front vowels /e/ and /ɛ/ as separate phonemes in Sranan is a matter of dispute, but in the Creole English of the Caribbean proper the two sounds are clearly separate phonemes. Standard English /e/, phonetically [ey] with an off-glide, corresponds to /ie/ with an on-glide in some territories (apparently due to the influence of regional dialects of northern England and Scotland) but to [e] (with neither on-glide nor off-glide) in others.

Of the English mid central vowels, unstressed /ə/ became /a/ in Sranan and Jamaican (e.g. *bita* 'bitter'), but not in less creole-like Bahamian and Gullah (/bɪtə/). English stressed /ʌ/ became /o/ in the Surinamese creoles (e.g. *koti* 'cut') but /ɵ/ in Jamaican [kɵt] (the vowel is 'short, centralized or mid-back, half-rounded' according to Cassidy & Le Page 1980: xxxix). In Gullah and Bahamian, this vowel is the same as that of standard English. The vowel in *first* (/ɜ^/ in rhotic varieties of English, /ɜ/ elsewhere) generally followed the same path as English /ʌ/ in the creoles, e.g. Sranan *fosi*, Jamaican /fɵs/, Gullah and Bahamian /fʌs/ or /fʌɪs/ (the latter following usage along the North American coast from Brooklyn to Texas).

The low English vowels /æ, ɑ, ɔ/ fell together in the Surinamese creoles, for example, *ati* 'hat; heart; hot', but in Jamaican there is a distinction between *hat* 'hat, hot' and *haat* 'heart'. Gullah and Bahamian distinguish between /hat/ 'hat' and /hɔt/ 'hot'. The /ɔ:/ vowel in *fall* (considerably higher in Britain than in North America) became /a/ in Sranan *fadon* 'fall (down)' and /aa/ in Jamaican *faal*, but remained /ɔ:/ in the eastern Caribbean and Gullah.

Regarding the high back vowels in English, the distinction between /u/ in *pool* and /ʊ/ in *pull* is not maintained in the Surinamese creoles (e.g. Sranan *lutu* 'root' and *furu* 'full') but it is in Jamaican (e.g. *fuul* 'fool' vs *ful* 'full'), although this may be a distinction more of vowel length than vowel quality. Alleyne (1980) postulates that Creole English vowels developed in three stages: first, there were distinctions in quality only, not length; next, distinctions in length only (e.g. /i/ vs /iː/) arose to approximate English distinctions in vowel quality; finally, off-glides developed to maintain the distinction between /e/ vs /ie/ and /o/ vs /uo/. Le Page holds that the latter arose due to the influence of northern English and Scots dialects. However, this identification of a source does not diminish the likelihood of the motivation suggested by Alleyne.

Of diphthongs, the merger of /ai/ and /oi/ in the Caribbean proper was discussed above (p. 356), but it should be noted that Sranan maintains a distinction (e.g. *bai* 'buy' vs *boi* 'boy'), although it is by no means regular (e.g. *wefi* 'wife', *bori* 'boil'). English /au/ often corresponds to /o/ in Sranan (e.g. *oso* 'house') and /ou/ (phonetically [ou]) in Jamaican (e.g. *hous* 'house'). Le Page notes that the Jamaican diphthong is close to seventeenth-century southern or later northern English usage (Cassidy & Le Page 1980: liv).

Like most of its substrate languages, Creole English has nasalised vowels. English has weak nasalisation of vowels on a phonetic level conditioned by the environment: the air stream producing an oral vowel (usually released through the mouth) is partly released through the nose in anticipation of a nasal consonant, as in [ĩn] 'in'. In some languages like French, vowels can be much more clearly nasalised and have phonemic status, contrasting with oral vowels in minimal pairs, for example /sã/ 'hundred' vs /sa/ 'that'. There is disagreement as to whether nasal vowels have phonemic status in any English-based creole or post-creole. There would seem to be minimal pairs, e.g. Sranan [brõ] 'to burn' and [bro] 'to breathe' (cf. English dialect *blow* 'to breathe'). However, this contrast does not exist before nasal consonants: in Ndjuka the word for 'sand' is [sãnti], which varies freely with [santi] and [sãti] but not *[sati]. But this suggests that there *is* a nasal phoneme that is realised phonetically as a nasal vowel, a nasal consonant or both. These may be in free variation, as in Ndjuka *santi*, or allophones conditioned by the phonetic environment, like American Black English /don/ 'don't', which is [don] before a a vowel (e.g. [don ai] 'don't I?') and [dõ] elsewhere, like French *bon*. Alleyne (1980: 37) postulates that in the earliest forms of the English-based creoles, English words with a vowel followed by a syllable-final nasal consonant (i.e. /n, m, ŋ/ before another consonant or a word boundary, e.g. *man*) were re-interpreted as ending with either a nasal vowel plus nasal consonant (*mãn*), or just a nasal vowel (*mã*), or an oral vowel (ma). Since /Vn/, /Vm/ and /Vŋ/ (where V represents any vowel) could all merge as /Ṽ/, the original form of the nasal consonant could not always be reconstructed later during decreolisation. This accounts for such hypercorrect forms as Miskito Coast CE *skriim waya* 'screen wire' and denasalised forms such as Bahamian CE /əbáras/ 'embarrassed'.

Finally, a number of West African languages have vowel harmony, in which there is a tendency for words to have vowels all of the same height or laxness or even the same vowel. Remnants of vowel harmony can be found in many Atlantic creoles, including those of Suriname, in which such rules appear to have played a role in determining paragogic vowels, for example Sranan *bigi* 'big', *dede* 'dead', *ala* 'all', *mofo* 'mouth', *brudu* 'blood' (Alleyne 1980: 67). Epenthetic vowels also seem to have been affected: Ndjuka *somoko* 'smoke'. There may also be remnants of vowel harmony in Jamaican, particularly in the epenthetic vowels in *simit* 'Smith' and *worom* 'worm' (although the latter may actually be a British regionalism).

Consonants

Alleyne (1980: 76) has postulated that the inventory of consonants of the earliest English-based creoles included some African sounds (the coarticulated and pre-nasalised stops discussed below) and lacked some English sounds (the voiced fricatives /v, z, ʒ/ and the interdentals /θ, ð/. Apparently basing his hypothesis on the Surinamese creoles, he further suggests that the English affricates /tʃ, dʒ/ were realised as palatals /tj, dj/ and that two pairs of English phonemes /s, ʃ/ and /r, l/ were each single phonemes with allophonic variants conditioned by the phonetic environment.

Pidgins and their ensuing creoles can be expected to have an inventory of phonemes representing the subset common to both their superstrate and substrate languages – although creoles are likely to preserve those phonetic realisations of a pidgin's phonemes that are most common among the group whose children are beginning to speak the language natively – that is, those of substrate rather than superstrate speakers. The preservation of some African phonemes in Saramaccan (and to some extent Ndjuka) is unusual and suggests the survival in Suriname of one or more African languages having those sounds, at least among those generations which developed the two Maroon languages. Like a number of West African languages, Saramaccan has labiovelar coarticulated stops; the voiceless phoneme is represented as /kp/ and the voiced one as /gb/, although each represents a single sound. They are articulated with the back of the tongue against the velum and the lips closed; the tongue is lowered and the lips open

Table 7.1. *Palatalised consonants*

	Alveolar	Alveopalatal	Palatalised alveolar	Palatalised velar	Velar
−Voice	t	tʃ	tj	kj	k
+Voice	d	dʒ	dj	gj	g
−Voice	s	ʃ	sj		
+Voice	z	ʒ			

simultaneously while air is expelled (or drawn in in the case of the labiovelar implosives). Saramaccan has both sounds, often in words of African origin for flora and fauna, such as *kpasi* 'vulture' or *gbono-gbono* 'moss'. Saramaccan /kp/ and /gb/ have the allophones /kw/ and /gw/ respectively; in some dialects of Ewe, an African language thought to have been brought to Suriname in the seventeenth century (Smith 1987), /kp/ and /gb/ correspond to /kw/ and /gw/ in other dialects of the same language (Boretzky 1983: 62). Only /kw/ and /gw/ occur in Sranan, often corresponding to Saramaccan /kp/ and /gb/; Ndjuka also generally has /kw/ and /gw/, but some speakers have variants of certain words with the coarticulated stops, for example *gwe* or *gbe* 'leave' (cf. *go away*). Alleyne surmised that [kp] and [kw] were allophones in the earliest creole, but only the latter survived in those varieties that remained in contact with Dutch, which lacked the coarticulated stop.

Pre-nasalised stops are also frequently found in the Atlantic creoles' substrate languages. They consist of stops preceded by homorganic nasals (e.g. /mb/, /nd/, /ŋk/) functioning as a single phoneme, that is, as C in languages permitting only CV syllabic structure. Saramaccan has four pre-nasalised stops – the above plus palatal /ɲdj/ – to which Rountree (1972: 22ff.) assigns phonemic status. Ndjuka also has such stops, as in the name of the language. However, Sranan has simple nasals where Saramaccan has pre-nasalised stops: *meti* instead of *mbeti* 'meat', *neti* instead of *ndeti* 'night', etc.

Palatalised consonants in the English-based creoles also appear to reflect substrate influence. Palatalisation is the raising of the tongue towards the hard palate, often as a secondary feature of articulation, as in the initial sound of the standard British pronunciation of *dew* as opposed to *do*. In some creole and African languages, the sounds in table 7.1 are related via palatalisation (/j/ is the palatal glide, English *y*). Alleyne

(1980: 56ff.) traces the /tj/ and /dj/ in the Surinamese creoles to two sources. First, /k/ and /g/ developed the palatalised allophones [tj] and [dj] before front vowels: *kina* or *tjina* 'leprosy', and *gei* or *djei* 'resemble'. Secondly, the alveopalatals /tʃ/ and /dʒ/ in English and Portuguese were re-interpreted as these palatalised alveolars: *djombo* 'jump' or *tjuba* 'rain' (cf. P *chuva*). Since these also occurred before back (i.e. non-palatalising) vowels, a phonemic split took place because the palatalised alveolars now contrasted with velar stops: e.g. Saramaccan *tjubi* 'hide' vs *kubi* 'kind of fish'. Later influence from English and Dutch established velar /k/ and /g/ before front vowels; sometimes these replaced earlier palatalised alveolars, as in *waki* 'watch' (earlier *watji*) or *wegi* 'wedge' (earlier *wedji*). There are some remnants of these phenomena in the Creole English of the Caribbean proper, for instance Jamaican lexical variants like *kitibu* or *tšitšibu* 'firefly', and *gaagl* or *džaagl* 'gargle'. Substrate influence appears to have reinforced the retention of archaic or regional British /kj/ and /gj/ before front vowels in Caribbean CE, as in *kyabaj* 'cabbage' and *gyaadn* 'garden'.

The Surinamese creoles generally have /s/ where English has /ʃ/ (e.g. Sranan *sipi* 'ship', *fisi* 'fish') but the allophone [ʃ] can occur before high front /i/ and the glide /j/, such as [ʃipi] 'ship' or [ʃjɛŋ] 'shame', much like allophones of /s/ in West African languages like Ewe and Ibo. Remnants of this can be found in Jamaican *laša* 'last year' or Gullah [ʃyiəm] 'see them'. English /ʒ/, which was just becoming nativised in the seventeenth century, normally corresponds to Jamaican /dʒ/: *pleja* 'pleasure'. In Gullah [ʒ] occurs only as an allophone of /z/, as in [ɪʒuː] 'is you', parallel to /s/ and its allophone [ʃ].

Although /l/ and /r/ are separate phonemes in English, they are related in a number of African languages, either as allophones or as the distinctive parts of allomorphs or as corresponding sounds in different dialects of the same language. In the Surinamese creoles these two sounds merged as /l/ in word-initial position: *lobi* 'love; rub'. However, /r/ can occur between vowels (e.g. *kaseri* 'kosher'), even when the etymon has /l/ in English (e.g. *furu* 'full') or Dutch (e.g. *eri* 'whole' from Du. *heel*). The English Creoles of the Caribbean retain only a few lexical remnants of this alternation, such as Jamaican *flitaz* 'fritters' or Bahamian *ling* 'ring for playing marbles'.

The English labial sounds /b/, /v/ and /w/ have tended to merge in the creoles. A number of African substrate languages have no /v/, and the earliest English creoles may have also lacked this sound. In the Surinamese creoles /b/ regularly corresponds to English /v/, as in *libi* 'live', but Saramaccan has acquired /v/ in loans from Portuguese (e.g. *vivo* 'alive'). There are lexical remnants of /b/ or /v/ in Caribbean Creole English: *beks* 'to be annoyed' (cf. E *vex*), *nabel* 'navel' or *hib* 'heave'. In Gullah and Bahamian /v/ and /w/ have fallen together as a single phoneme /β/, a voiced bilabial fricative, with [v] and [w] as allophones in apparently free variation. This feature is also found in the speech of whites in coastal South Carolina and the Bahamas (Holm 1980a) as well as in the Caribbean proper, for instance the Bay Islands of Honduras (Warantz 1983). It may be related to the alternation of /v/ and /w/ in some varieties of eighteenth- and nineteenth-century London speech.

Suprasegmentals

English speakers from Britain and North America are often struck by the distinctive intonational patterns of Creole English. There is increasing evidence that these patterns were influenced by the African substrate, which consisted almost exclusively of tone languages. These differ from intonational languages like English, which have three interrelated prosodic features: pitch (high vs low notes), stress (loudness) and length (how long a syllable is drawn out). These are linked in English in that syllables that receive primary stress also receive greater length and more prominent pitch. However, in tone languages each syllable has its own tone or relative pitch, which is not related to stress or length. In tone languages the relevant pitch pattern is that of each word or segment, while in intonational languages the relevant pitch pattern is that of the whole sentence (e.g. to convey emphasis, a question, an attitude, etc.). There is also an intermediate type of language, which is neither a tone nor an intonational language; this is the pitch-accent language, in which only one syllable per word can receive the tonal accent.

Saramaccan is a tone language, with minimal pairs such as *dá* (high tone) 'to give' vs *da* (non-high tone) 'to be'. Tone plays an important role in Saramaccan not only on the lexical level but also on the grammatical level by marking syntactic units: for example, the tones of the words *mí* 'my' and *tatá* 'father' are different in isolation from their tones when they occur as a noun phrase, *mí tata* (Voorhoeve 1961: 148). Saramaccan words normally have high tone on the syllable corresponding to the stressed syllables in their etyma, as in *fája tóngo* 'tongs for a fire'. Ndjuka is also a tone language, but Sranan is not, generally having stress where the Maroon languages have high tone.

Remnants of tone can be found in Jamaican Creole, which has a pattern of pitch polarity: each syllable is opposite in tone to the preceding one, that is, high tone is followed by low, then high, etc. (Carter 1982). Guyanese uses tone to distinguish minimal pairs displaying pitch-accent such as *turkéy* (the bird) vs *Túrkey* (the country), which makes it a pitch-accent language (Carter 1987). Studying the speech of West Indians in London, Carter (1979) concluded that creole intonation patterns consistently conveyed unintended connotations to speakers of British English; intonation patterns that conveyed a pleasant attitude in Creole English were almost without exception interpreted as unpleasant (e.g. surly, judicial, detached, cold, hostile, etc.).

7.3.3   *Syntax*

Like its lexicosemantics and phonology, the syntax of Creole English was influenced by its superstrate (e.g. the form of the habitual marker *does*, from archaic and regional English), by its substrate (e.g. much of its system of pre-verbal tense and aspect markers), by adstrate languages (e.g. the influence of the Dutch complementiser *dat* 'that' on the Sranan *taki* in noun complements like *a bribi taki...* 'the belief that...'), by language universals (e.g. the loss of case marking in the pronominal system), and by creole-internal innovations (e.g. the development of 'for him' from a prepositional phrase to a possessive pronoun (*iz fo im* 'it's his') to an emphatic possessive adjective (*iz fo im jab* 'it's *his* job'). However, syntax is the linguistic level on which the Atlantic creoles' similarity to one another and to their substrate is most readily apparent. If its vocabulary underscores Creole's identity as a variety of English, its grammar proclaims its African origins.

The verb phrase

While it is true that no particular set of syntactic features will identify a language as a creole without reference to its sociolinguistic history, it is also true that the structure of the verb phrase has been of primary importance in distinguishing creole varieties (e.g. Jamaican Creole English) from non-creole varieties (e.g. Caymanian English) of the same lexical base. In the Caribbean, the non-creoles have their European system of tense-marking (e.g. verbal inflections and auxiliary verbs) more or less intact, whereas the creoles have a radically different way of dealing with tense and aspect. Basilectal varieties of Creole English have no verbal inflections; instead, verbs are preceded by particles indicating tense or aspect. These often have the outer form of their etymological sources, the English auxiliary verbs which occupy a similar position and serve a similar function. But semantically and syntactically these particles are much more like the pre-verbal tense and aspect markers in many substrate languages. Table 7.2 (from Holm 1988, which provides sources) gives an overview of the following discussion of the Creole English pre-verbal markers, and also shows how the Creole English verbal system closely parallels that of other Atlantic creoles as well as that of substrate African languages.

The unmarked verb (with the zero marker $\emptyset$ in table 7.2) refers to whatever time is in focus, which is either clear from the context or specified at the beginning of the discourse. Not marking stative verbs (which refer to a state of affairs, e.g. *I* **know** *the way, I* **have** *a sister*, etc.) usually corresponds to using the simple present tense in English, whereas not marking non-stative verbs (referring to actions, e.g. *Wi* **kom** *doun hiir* 'We came down here') usually corresponds to using the past tense. In some Western Caribbean varieties of Creole English that do not mark habitual aspect (see below), unmarked non-stative verbs can also have habitual meaning. For example, a Miskito Coast Creole English speaker, discussing how each jungle spirit guides the animals under his protection to hide them from hunters, said the following: *Him a di uona. Him* **tek** *dem an* **put** *dem an dis wie ... die* **kom** *and him* **liiv** *dem aal hiia an* **guo** *de* 'He is their owner. He takes them and puts them on the right path ... They come and he leaves them all in that place and goes off' (Holm 1978).

Anterior tense markers (e.g. Jamaican (*b*)*en* in table 7.2) indicate that the action of the following verb took place before the time in focus (i.e. the time reference of the unmarked verb). The anterior tense can correspond to the English past or past perfect; unlike these, however, the anterior is relative to the time in focus in the discourse rather than the time of the utterance. While the earliest English creoles apparently had anterior markers derived from English *been*, decreolising varieties often have alternative forms derived from *did*, *had* or *was*; these frequently deviate less from standard usage and are thus less stigmatised.

Progressive aspect markers (e.g. Jamaican *de* in table 7.2) indicate that an action is in progress, such as *im* **de** *sing* 'he is singing'. Creole *de* (with variants *da* and *a*) may come from English *there*; it also means 'to be (located)' (see below). The development of the Creole construction could have been influenced by a language universal: many European,

Table 7.2. *Tense and aspect markers in various Creole and African languages*

	Unmarked	Anterior	Progressive	Anterior	Habitual	Anterior	Completive	Anterior	Irrealis	Anterior
São Tomé CP	Ø	ta(va) —	s(a)ka —	tava ka —	ka —	tava	za —		ka —	ka —
Cape Verde CP	Ø	— ba	ta —	ta — ba	ta —	ta — ba	ja —		ta —	ta — ba
Papiamentu CS	Ø		ta —	tabata —	ta —	tabata —	— kaba	a — kaba	lo S —	lo S a —
Palenquero CS	Ø		ta —	taba —	ase —	aseba —	a —	a — ba	tan —	tanba —
Negerhollands CD	Ø	(h)a	lo —	a lo —	lo ~ ka(n)	a ka —	ka —	a ka —	lo ~ sa(l) —	a sa —
Lesser Ant. CF	Ø	te —	ka —	te ka —	ka —	te ka —	— fin?		ke —	te ke —
Haitian CF	Ø	t(e) —	ap —	t-ap —	Ø ~ ap —	t(e)	fin — ?		(v)a —	t-a —
Sranan CE	Ø	ben —	(d)e —	ben e —	Ø ~ (d)e —		— k ə ba		(g)o ~ sa —	ben o —
Jamaican CE	Ø	(b)en —	(d)a ~ de —	(b)ena —	Ø ~ a	(b)en —	don — ~ — don	don — ~	go ~ wi —	wuda —
Gullah CE	Ø	bin —	(d)a — ~ — in	bina —	da ~ doz	doz —	don —	don —	gwɔ̃i —	wuda —
Yoruba	Ø	ti —	ń —	ti ń —	maa ń —	ti maa ń —	— tán	ti — tán	á ~ yíó —	yíó ti —
Bambara	Ø		bɛ —	tun bɛ —	bɛ —	tun bɛ —	ye — ka ban	tun ye — ka ban	bɛna —	tun bɛna —

African and other languages indicate that an action is in progress with a metaphor of location, for example early Modern English *I am on writing* or *I am a-writing*, or Bambara *A bε na tobi la* 'He *is* (at) cooking sauce'. In decreolising varieties, *de* can alternate with or be replaced by a more English-like construction with no auxiliary before the verb plus *-in*, as in this Miskito Coast Creole English passage: *Di gal no de briid, man. Di gal, shi **did** fiil laik shi wa briidin, bot shi no briidin* 'The girl wasn't pregnant. She felt as if she was pregnant, but she wasn't pregnant'. Note that the anterior marker can precede the progressive marker in nearly all of the creole and African languages in table 7.2, resulting in a meaning corresponding to English 'he was doing' or 'he had been doing'.

Habitual aspect markers (e.g. Gullah *doz* in table 7.2) indicate that an action occurs or recurs over an extended period of time. For example, a Nicaraguan Creole speaker used this marker to stress the fact that his seventy-year-old aunt was in the habit of rowing her canoe some forty miles to Bluefields to sell produce and buy supplies: *Shi aluon **doz** guo doun to bluufiilz bai kanu.* A number of African languages use the same marker to indicate both progressive and habitual actions, as do many creoles (table 7.2): for example, *da* is used this way in the Leeward Islands; in the Windwards (perhaps also under the influence of the local Creole French, in which *ka* marks both aspects) the verb plus *-in* can have habitual meaning, as in Grenadian CE *Gud children **goin** tu hevn* 'Good children go to heaven' (Le Page & Tabouret-Keller 1985: 163). Habitual *da* varies with *doz*, apparently influenced by the English auxiliary *does*. Like the simple present tense in general, this auxiliary conveys the idea of habitual action (e.g. *He does drink*) and in the seventeenth century it did not require emphasis as in the modern standard. Unstressed *does*, *do* and *da* survive in England's southern and western dialects with habitual force; similar forms, perhaps influenced by Gaelic, also survive in the English of Ireland with habitual meaning, such as *He does write* or *He does be writing* (Barry 1982: 109). Today habitual *doz* is found in mesolectal varieties of Creole English throughout the Caribbean, with the notable exception of Jamaica (Rickford 1974). This habitual *doz* has the reduced forms *iz* and *z*, for instance Bahamian *They **is** be in the ocean* (Holm with Shilling 1982: 111). Rickford (1980) suggests that the complete loss of these reduced forms left *be* itself with habitual force in some varieties: Bahamian *Sometimes you **be** lucky* or *They just **be** playing*. However, there is a good case for the convergence of a number of influences in the development of the latter forms, which are also found in American Black English. In addition to substrate influence on progressive/habitual *da* and the creole-internal innovation reducing and deleting *doz*, there is good evidence of the influence of regional varieties of the superstrate. Rickford (1986) suggests that habitual *be* in the English of northern Ireland influenced the development of habitual *be* in the Black English of North America (where the Scots-Irish predominated among Irish immigrants), whereas habitual *do be* in the English of southern Ireland influenced the development of *does be* in the Caribbean (where the southern Irish predominated in the seventeenth century). Finally, it should be noted in table 7.2 that in most of the creole and both of the African languages considered, the habitual marker can be preceded by a marker of anterior tense to refer to a habitual action before the time in focus in the discussion.

The completive aspect marker (e.g. Jamaican *don* in table 7.2) indicates that an action has been completed: MCC *Ai **don** giv im a dairekshan* 'I have (already) given him an address'. In the Surinamese creoles the completive marker *kaba* (see etymology above, p. 360) only occurs after the verb – as does that of a number of African languages – suggesting that it originated as a serial verb (see below). Jamaican *don* can occur either before or after the verb (but does not combine with other verbal markers), whereas MCC *don* occurs only before the verb (and can be preceded by the anterior marker), suggesting a development from serial verb to pre-verbal marker motivated by systematicity (via creole-internal innovation) rather than decreolisation (Bickerton 1981: 80ff.).

The irrealis marker (e.g. Jamaican *go* in table 7.2) indicates that the action of the following verb is not (yet) a part of reality. Used alone, it approximates in meaning the future tense, as in Guyanese CE *Fraidi awi **go** mek* 'Friday we will make [some]' (Bickerton 1975: 42). Used in combination with the anterior marker, the irrealis marker can impart the idea of the perfect conditional: Guyanese CE *Awi **bin go** kom out seef* 'We would have come out all right' (*ibid.*). This combination of markers and meaning is found in most of the Atlantic creoles, as well as Bambara; its development may reflect the influence of a linguistic universal as well. The Surinamese creoles have two other combinations of markers not indicated in table 7.2. First, Sranan irrealis *sa* can be followed by progressive *e* to produce a future progressive meaning: *a **sa** e go* 'he will be going'. Secondly, these two markers can be preceded by anterior *ben*: *a **ben sa** e go* 'he would have been going' (Voorhoeve 1957: 383).

Besides verbal markers, several other features of the Creole verb phrase bear mentioning. One is the complementiser, corresponding to the English infinitive marker *to*. The oldest form of the Creole complementiser is apparently *fo* (with variants *fu* and *fi*), as in MCC *a fried fo guo* 'I'm afraid to go'. This *fo* is from *for* in archaic and regional British dialects, such as *I came for see* in western England (*LAE*, S3), or *I came for to see* in archaic English. This *fo* has become stigmatised in some decreolising varieties and is being replaced by *to* or simply omitted: *ai niid_tes mai ai* 'I need to have my eyes tested'. Unlike English, however, Creole *fo* can be followed not by an infinitive but a clause with a subject and tensed verb: MCC *Dem sen dem for ai dringk* 'They sent them [i.e. the tea bags] for me to drink'. Saramaccan can actually mark the verb for tense: *Mi kë tsuba kai fu ma sa-go a wosu*, literally 'I want rain fall *so-that* I-not *will* go to house', that is, 'I want it to rain so I won't have to go home' (Byrne 1984: 102).

Creole verbs can come in a series without a conjunction (e.g. 'and') or complementiser ('to') between them, for instance MCC *Aal di waari ron kom bai mi*, literally 'All the wild-boars *ran came* by me', that is, '...came running up to me'. Serial-verb constructions are unusual in English (e.g. *Go get it*) but common in a number of West African languages and Atlantic creoles. They fall into several broad categories, based on the combined meaning of the verbs; one of these is directionality, as in the above example in which *kom* conveys the idea of 'motion towards'. Creole *guo* 'go' achieves the opposite effect: Jamaican CE *ron guo lef im* 'run away from him'. Another category is the instrumental, as in Ndjuka *A teke nefi koti a meti*, literally 'He *took* knife *cut* the meat', that is, 'He cut the meat with a knife' (Huttar 1981). Sranan *tjari kon* (literally 'carry come') means 'bring'; these can be combined with *gi* 'give' to show that the carrying was for someone (i.e. dative): *Kofi tjari den fisi kon gi mi* 'Kofi brought the fish for me'. Creole English verbs with meanings involving saying or thinking can be followed by the verb for 'say' introducing a clause: *A nuo se yu bizi* 'I know that you're busy'. This demonstrably African construction has survived in American Black English in *They told me say they couldn't get it* (Rickford 1977: 212). Finally, in some English-based creoles the verb meaning 'surpass' can be used after adjectives (a subcategory of verbs) to indicate a comparison, as in Gullah *I tol pas mi* 'He is taller than I' (Turner 1949: 215).

Creole English, like other Atlantic creoles and a number of West African languages, has several different words corresponding to English *be* whose use is determined by the following grammatical construction.

(1) If *be* is used before an adjective in English, no word for 'be' is usually needed in the corresponding Creole construction because the following word is actually a verb in most basilectal varieties, as in many African languages. For example, no form of 'be' is needed in Miskito Coast CE *Evriting chiip* 'Everything is cheap'; however, like other verbs, adjectival verbs can be preceded by the anterior marker: *Evriting **did** chiip*. (2) If *be* is used before a noun in English, an expressed word for 'be' (the equative copula) is needed in Creole: MCC *Mi **da** i anti* 'I am his aunt'. Decreolising varieties have a term more like English, such as MCC *Ai **iz** di straika* 'I am the harpooner'. (3) A different word for 'be' is used for location: MCC *Di gyorl-dem aal **de** pan di veranda* 'The girls were all (there) on the veranda'. Creole *de* is from *there*, but its development was influenced by the syntax of African languages, as can be seen in sentences like *Im **de** Manawa* 'He is in Managua'. (4) Finally, Creole has a particle that highlights or emphasises the following word to make it the focus of discourse (Todd 1973; Holm 1980b). As in African languages like Yoruba, the Creole particle highlights constructions that have been moved to the front of the sentence for emphasis, such as Jamaican ***A** di buk Mieri waan* 'It's the book Mary wants' (i.e. not the pencil) (Bailey 1966: 86). Since question words are also fronted, they are also highlighted: ***A** wa Anti sen fi mi?* 'What has Auntie sent for me?' (*ibid.*, 87). In decreolising varieties, *a* is replaced by *iz* (cf. English *it's* before fronted material, as in *It's the book*...), for example MCC ***Iz** hou Orl truo mi wie?* 'How could Earl have rejected me?' (Holm 1978: 271). Finally, like many West African and other Atlantic creole languages, Creole English can front verbs for emphasis, introducing them with the highlighter: Jamaican ***Iz tiif** dem tiif it* 'It was certainly stolen (not just borrowed)' (Cassidy 1964: 273).

The noun phrase

Basilectal Creole English nouns do not have English inflections to indicate plurality and possession; like substrate African languages and other Atlantic creoles, they do this with determiners and other particles as well as word order. In the earliest creoles, the definite article seems to be derived not from English *the* but from the demonstratives *this* (e.g. Saramaccan *di omi* 'the man') and *that* (e.g. Sranan *a man* 'the man') as in other Atlantic creoles. This may reflect a language universal, since articles have evolved from demonstratives in a number of cases of language change, such as the transition from Latin to the Romance languages or from Proto-Germanic to German and English; it may also reflect the frequent use of deixis during the early stages of pidginisation. Some Atlantic creoles form the plural (with an added idea of definiteness) with a plural form of the definite article (derived from the European plural demonstrative); the English-based creoles use a form derived from *them*, which could be either a dialect demonstrative (*them men*) or the third person plural pronoun, for example Saramaccan *dee omi* or Jamaican *dem man* 'the men'. The Jamaican pluraliser can also follow the noun, as in *di man dem*; it is usually used only with animate nouns. The basilectal creoles form the demonstrative by reinforcing the article with the word for 'here' or 'there', for instance Saramaccan *di omi **aki*** or Jamaican *dis man **ya*** 'this man (here)' – perhaps with converging influence from dialectal English *this here man*. The plural demonstrative simply changes the singular article to the plural: Saramaccan ***dee*** *omi aki* or Jamaican ***dem*** *man ya*, both 'these men'.

Possession is indicated without the inflection -*'s* by juxtaposition, as in MCC *di uman_biebi* 'the woman's baby'. This survives in American Black English *that girl shoe*. Some creoles can emphasise possession with the word for 'his' or 'her' (third person singular pronouns do not indicate gender in basilectal creoles or many African languages), for example Saramaccan *konu ala **en** moni* 'all the king's money', or *mi dadi **im** buk* 'my father's book' in the Krio of Sierra Leone (partly transplanted from Jamaica in the 1790s). Basilectal creole pronouns also lack case distinctions; Bailey (1966: 22) posits the following paradigm for early Jamaican Creole:

mi 'I, me, my'	wi 'we, us, our'
yu 'you, your'	unu 'you, your (plural)
im 'he, him, his; she, her; it, its'	dem 'they, them, their'

The second person plural *unu* (with variants *wuna* in Barbados, *yina* in the Bahamas, etc.) seems to have resulted from a gap in the English lexicon (lacking distinctive singular and plural forms of *you* by the late seventeenth century) filled by the convergence of some partly similar forms for 'you [plural]' in a number of Niger-Congo languages, for instance Ibo *unu*, Yoruba *nyin*, Wolof *yena*, Kongo *yeno*, Mbundu *yenu*, and Common Bantu **nu*. Decreolising varieties have borrowed various English pronouns, and with them grammatical distinctions of case and gender. Early creoles developed possessive pronouns with *fu*, perhaps from the English model *This is **for you***, which is nearly equivalent semantically to *This is **yours***. The Ndjuka possessive pronoun (e.g. *Na* *fu mi* 'It's *mine*') can replace the possessive adjective for emphasis, so that *mi osu* 'my house' becomes *a osu fu mi* '*my* house'. This can also precede the noun, for instance *du fu mi pikin* 'my child', as in some creoles of the Caribbean proper, such as MCC *fo-him jab* 'his job'.

Word order

Like English, Creole has SVO (subject–verb–object) word order; however, in Creole this word order has only one exception, the fronting of elements discussed above (p. 378). A similarly inflexible SVO order is found in many substrate African and other Atlantic creole languages. The English-based creoles have nothing like *do*-support in English; the negator simply precedes the verb (e.g. *Im no wier shuuz* 'He does not wear shoes') and there is no inversion of the subject and the auxiliary to form questions (e.g. *Im wier shuuz?* 'Does he wear shoes?'). Intonation alone can distinguish questions from statements in Creole, but there are also question markers for emphasis. One is derived from the English tag question, but has no syntactic relation with the main verb, for instance MCC *Das waz a swiit stuori,* **duonit**? 'That was a nice story, wasn't it?' There is also a sentence-initial negative question marker derived from *ain't*, which frequently begins questions in non-standard English, such as Gullah /ɛnti rɛbəl tɔim kʌmɪn bak/? 'Ain't slavery coming back?' (Turner 1949: 262) or MCC **Ent** *yu kud ton?* 'Couldn't you turn?' (Holm 1978: 245).

While basilectal varieties have no subject–auxiliary inversion for questions, in decreolising varieties such inversion frequently occurs: in Bahamian one finds *I can go?* varying with *Can I go?* This variation also occurs in embedded questions (which are not inverted in English): one hears *I don't know where* **I can** *go* varying with *I don't know where* **can I** *go*. Such variation is also found in American Black English.

Conclusion

Understanding the history and nature of English in the West Indies requires an understanding of Creole. The literary language of the Commonwealth Caribbean is much the same as that of Britain except for a relatively limited amount of lexicon; but the folk speech of most territories is a mixture of English and Creole, and it is the latter that is not well known outside the West Indies. It resulted from the different linguistic processes that were set in motion by language contact in

Africa and the Caribbean: pidginisation, creolisation, decreolisation and semi-creolisation. The structure of Caribbean Creole English reflects influence from a number of sources: superstrate, substrate and adstrate languages, as well as language universals and creole-internal innovation. But it is to social and historical factors that we have to look for explanations of the varying linguistic paths that English and Creole have taken in different parts of the Caribbean.

The study of Creole gives us the story of the birth of a new language. Such births are usually hidden and obscure, but this one is extraordinarily well documented. Creole has already taught linguists much about particular kinds of language contact. Historians and sociologists are also beginning to learn what it can tell us about the British and Africans and Creoles, as well as their language.

FURTHER READING

The past few decades have seen the growth and development of a substantial body of literature about the English-based creoles in the West Indies, often in connection with studies of the processes of pidginisation and creolisation. A landmark publication on this topic was the collection of articles edited by Hymes (1971). Discussion of more recent developments in theory can be found in Bickerton (1981), Boretzky (1983), Holm (1988) and Thomason & Kaufman (1988).

The models for the sociolinguistic history of Creole-speaking communities are Reinecke's survey (1937) and especially Le Page's detailed study of Jamaican (Le Page & DeCamp 1960). Both have had a profound influence on later work, such as Rickford's study of Guyanese (1987) and Lalla & D'Costa's recent study of Jamaican (1990).

The model for lexicographical scholarship on English-based creoles is Cassidy & Le Page's *Dictionary of Jamaican English* (1980), which benefited from the earlier work of Turner on Gullah (1949) and influenced later dictionaries on Bahamian (Holm with Shilling 1982) and Trinidadian (Winer forthcoming). Turner (1949) and the *Dictionary of Jamaican English* also provide important phonological studies, as does Alleyne (1980) in *Comparative Afro-American*, a book-length study of the English-based Atlantic creoles and their structure. Other major morphosyntactic studies include Bailey's classic study of Jamaican (1966) and books on Guyanese by Bickerton (1975) and Rickford (1987). A comparison of the structure of the English-based Atlantic creoles with those with lexicons from French, Spanish, Dutch and Portuguese can be found in Holm (1988).

8 ENGLISH IN NEW ZEALAND

Laurie Bauer

8.1 Introduction

8.1.1 The European settlement of New Zealand

New Zealand was first discovered by Polynesian explorers around AD 925, if Maori genealogies can be trusted, and was settled by AD 1150. It was rediscovered by the Dutch in 1642. The only linguistic result of that rediscovery is the name New Zealand, given not by Abel Tasman himself – he called it Staten Land, under the misapprehension that it was part of Australia – but by Dutch geographers later in the seventeenth century. James Cook visited New Zealand in 1769 and circumnavigated the islands. He was the one who claimed New Zealand for the British Crown, beating French interests by a matter of weeks. He was also the first to use Maori words in his written English.

From about 1792 onwards, whalers and sealers visited and operated from the coasts of New Zealand. There were some French ships involved, as well as British and American ones, but the lingua franca was probably English. In 1814 the arrival of Anglican missionaries was marked by a Christmas Day service conducted by the Reverend Samuel Marsden. Catholic missionaries from France arrived later, from about 1838, but do not appear to have had any linguistic consequences on New Zealand English.

There was a great deal of trade between New South Wales and New Zealand from about 1792 onwards. In the years 1826–39 some £768,000 worth of goods were exported from New Zealand to Australia (Lloyd Prichard 1970: 16). The reverse trade was usually in muskets, and it is estimated that some 40,000 of the 200,000 Maoris in New Zealand in 1769 were killed in internecine wars before 1840 (Sinclair 1959: 42). By the 1830s, land-hungry people from Australia were arriving in New

Zealand to buy land from the Maoris in exchange for muskets or axes. Quite apart from relative proximity, there are thus a number of good reasons why New Zealand was officially viewed as a dependency of New South Wales until 1841.

By 1838 there were some 2,000 Europeans in New Zealand, but that number was to quintuple by 1842. European settlement began in earnest with the arrival of the first ship of the New Zealand Company in Port Nicholson (later Wellington) in January 1840, just before the Treaty of Waitangi between the Crown and Maori chiefs was signed, ceding *rangatiratanga* (presented as a translation of 'sovereignty') to the Queen. For the rest of the century, immigration was largely upper working class or lower middle class (Sinclair 1959: 101) and largely British. There were several types of immigration, and it may be helpful to keep them distinct.

The first type, which had most influence from 1840 until the end of the 1850s, was largely fuelled by various organisations with idealistic goals, of which the most important is probably the New Zealand Company, and its offshoot, the Plymouth Company. Wellington and Nelson (see map 8.1) were founded by the New Zealand Company, and most of the original settlers in these areas came from London or counties nearby (Sinclair 1959: 91). The original settlers in Taranaki came from Devon and Cornwall under the auspices of the Plymouth Company, and founded New Plymouth. Otago, in contrast, was settled as a Scottish free-church settlement, and Canterbury was conservative Anglo-Catholic. Waipu was settled by highlanders who had become dissatisfied with life in Nova Scotia, and Puhoi by Bohemians. This type of settlement, in which specific groups settled in the same area, was, to a lesser extent, carried forward into the 1880s. There was an English purchase of a large block of land near Feilding, with 1,600 immigrants arriving in the years 1874–7, and there were 4,000 Irish immigrants to the Bay of Plenty in the years 1875–84 (Oliver 1981: 74).

The second type of immigration was the direct result of the discovery of gold. In the second half of 1861, the population of Otago jumped from 13,000 to over 30,000, with over half of the gain coming from Australia (Lloyd Prichard 1970: 80). The population of the West Coast of the South Island reached 29,000 in 1867, and for a time Hokitika (today a small town of some 3,400 inhabitants) was New Zealand's busiest port. At this period the West Coast was referred to as an 'Australian community' (Sinclair 1959: 107).

The third type of immigration was due to the assisted immigration of

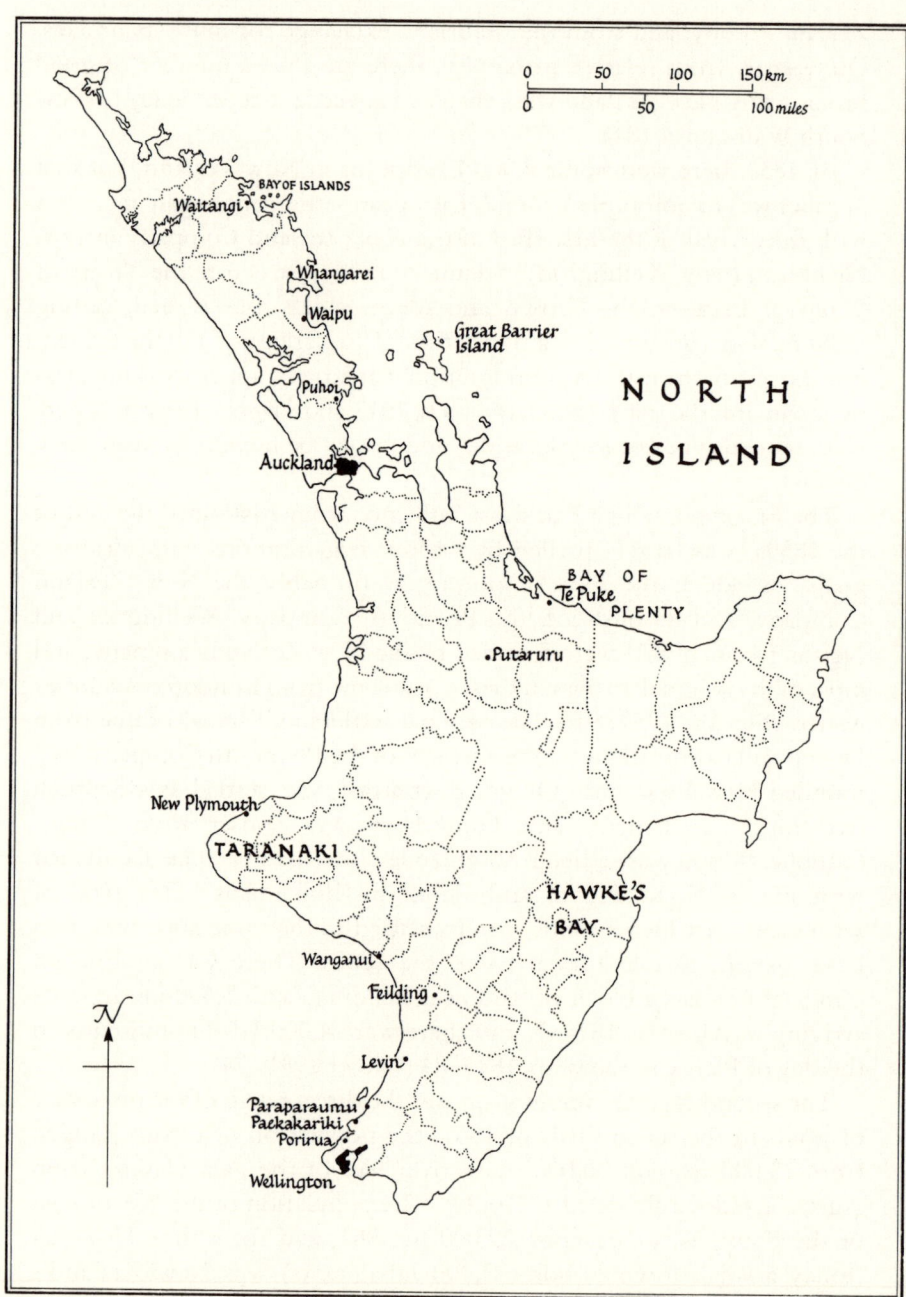

Map 8.1   New Zealand

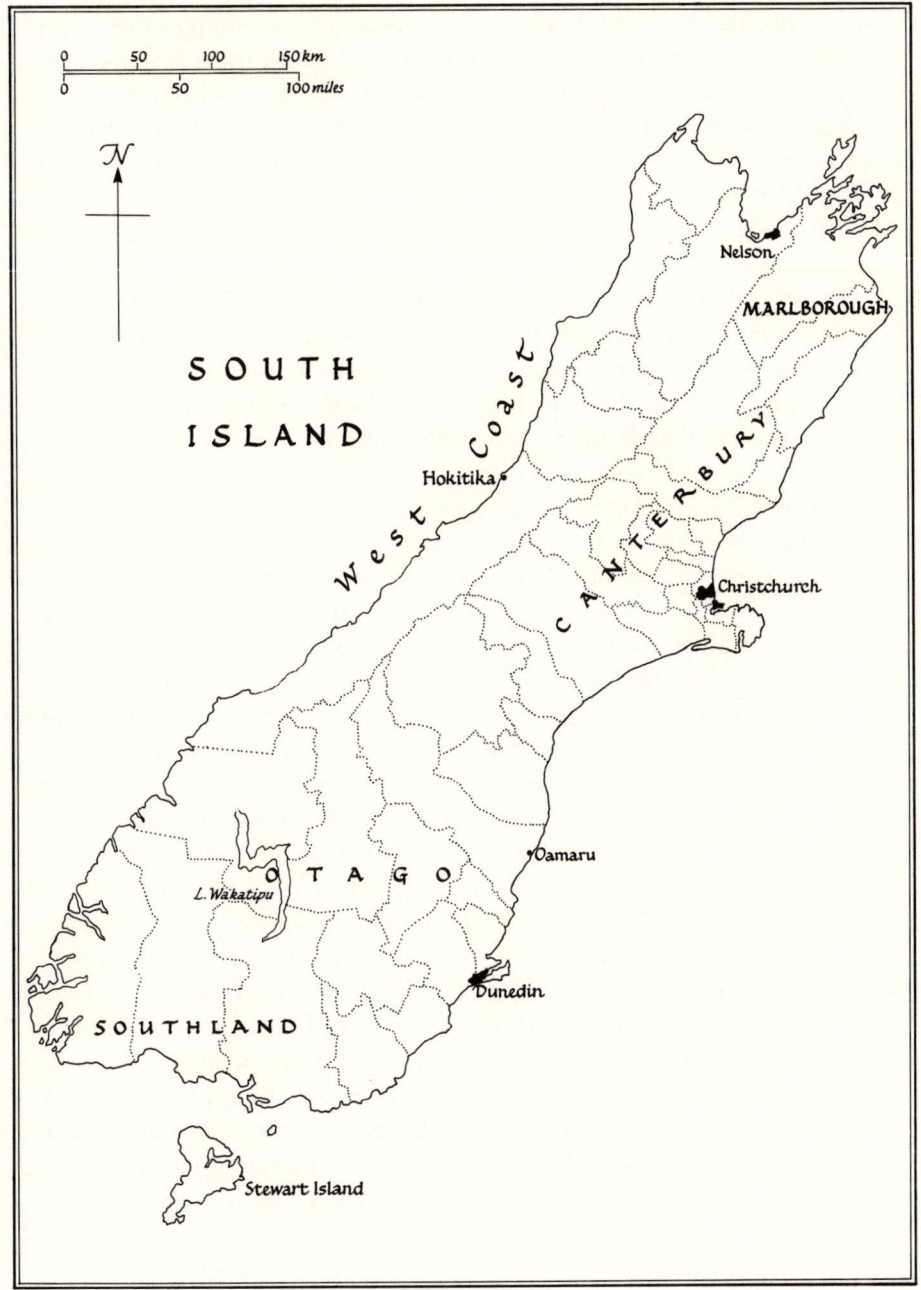

the 1870s. In 1874, which was the high point of this immigration, over 26,000 assisted immigrants arrived in New Zealand from Britain, over two-thirds of the immigrants for that year. Overall, about 10 per cent of the assisted immigrants came from Cornwall, with nearly all of them coming from south of a line between the Wash and the Bristol Channel (Arnold 1981).

Although immigration has continued to add greatly to New Zealand's population (about a quarter of the population growth in the years 1951–66 still came from immigration; Gibson 1971: 107), by 1890 there were more New Zealand-born Europeans in New Zealand than immigrants. We can probably take this date as a point after which the development of the English language in New Zealand reflected New Zealand rather than British or Australian trends.

There are two facets of this history to which I wish to draw particular attention. The first is the extent to which areas of New Zealand were settled by relatively homogeneous groups of immigrants from the same area outside New Zealand. This is not the kind of pattern that one would expect to lead to homogeneity of dialect within New Zealand; yet the traces of original dialects are so rare as to be virtually non-existent in present-day New Zealand. The second point is the strong influence of Australia on New Zealand in the early days of settlement. Talking about 1852, Sinclair (1959: 89) comments that 'Communications between the settlements were often worse than those of the individual settlements with Australia,' and Gordon (1988: 181) makes the same point even more vividly: 'For years the easiest way to travel between Wellington and Auckland [under 500 km. apart as the crow flies] was to travel via Sydney [about 2,200 km. from Wellington].' In the early days, all trade went through Australia, and the number of Australians in the country must have been large. To cite Sinclair (1959: 100) once again: 'In 1851 [Auckland's] population was thirty-one percent Irish, as compared with two percent in Wellington. Probably over half the population had come from Australia. William Fox, a Wellingtonian, thought it "a mere section of the town of Sydney transplanted".' Even if Fox may have exaggerated (there are Wellingtonians who might agree with the judgement even today!), the Australian influence ought to be clear.

8.1.2 Maori

The language spoken in New Zealand (Maori *Aotearoa*) at the time of the arrival of the Europeans (or *pakehas*) was a Polynesian language,

Maori (*Maori* 'ordinary, normal'). As might be expected with languages in close contact, there was a great deal of mutual influence between English and Maori, so that a few comments on the structure of Maori are relevant.

Maori is a VSO language, with modifiers generally following the heads they modify. Maori nouns are only exceptionally marked for plural, though determiners show number. Pronouns also show number, and there is an inclusive/exclusive distinction in the first person plural, and a dual in all persons. Tense/aspect is marked by preposed particles rather than by inflections on the verb.

The canonical Maori syllable has the structure (C)V(V). The two vowels may be identical, in which case the realisation is a long vowel, or distinct, in which case a diphthong is heard. There are five vowels in Maori, /i, ɛ, a, ɔ, u/ and ten consonants: /p, t, k, m, n, ŋ, f, h, r, w/. Vowels, especially close vowels, may be voiceless phrase-finally. The voiceless stops were, at the beginning of the period, unaspirated (though they are heard variably aspirated today, and affricated in some varieties), /t, n/ are variably dental or alveolar, /r/ is a voiced alveolar tap. The precise quality of the /f/ varies from dialect to dialect, and there is dispute about its original quality. The missionaries who first wrote Maori down spelt it *wh*, which implies that the variety they heard was [ʍ]. McBurney (in Ellis 1889) says that he heard a [ɸ] in the 1880s. Very different qualities, such as [ʔw] are heard in some dialects. [n] is heard rather than [ŋ] in some dialects. For more details of Maori dialectal pronunciations see Biggs (1989). The rhythm of Maori is mora-timed, rather than syllable or stress-timed: that is, every (C)V provides a unit of timing, and traditional Maori verse counts morae rather than syllables or feet (Bauer 1981).

As stated above, /f/ is spelt *wh*. /ŋ/ is spelt *ng*. In the public domain, vowel length has seldom been marked, but can be marked either with a macron or with double vowel orthography. So we find, for example, either *Maori*, *Māori* or *Maaori*, with the first by far the most common. Since stress placement is predictable only in the light of vowel length, it can be difficult to know where words are stressed when they have been met only in the written form. This matter is made more complex by the fact that different Maori dialects have different stress rules, and by the fact that Maori dialects show variation in vowel length in some words.

8.2 Pronunciation

This section begins with a description of present-day New Zealand English phonetics and phonology, and then goes on to discuss the history of the pronunciation of English in New Zealand.

In order to avoid giving transcriptions which require unnecessary effort to read, I shall use a phonemic transcription system which works for RP when giving a broad transcription of New Zealand English. However, to obviate the necessity for such nonsensical statements as /æ/ is pronounced [ɛ], I shall generally use Wells' lexical sets to define the phonological item to which I want to refer. Thus I shall say something like 'the TRAP vowel is pronounced [ɛ]', indicating that the vowel which appears in the lexical set designated as the TRAP set by Wells (1982) has that phonetic quality. In some cases, however, Wells provides several lexical sets which are all said with the same phoneme in New Zealand English (and in RP). In those cases I shall abbreviate, so that my lexical set START encompasses Wells' BATH, PALM and START lexical sets, and my lexical set THOUGHT encompasses Wells' FORCE as well as THOUGHT.

8.2.1 Synchronic structure

Phonologically speaking, New Zealand English is a variant of a southeast England system. With only two exceptions (both of which are subject to variation), it has the same vowel system as RP, although the realisations of the phonemes are different from the RP realisations. The consonant system, less surprisingly, is also basically identical to that of RP.

Where consonants are concerned, the main differences between New Zealand English and RP reside in the realisations of the phonemes rather than in a different phoneme inventory. /hw/ or [ʍ] is heard from some speakers, but while it is probably more common in New Zealand English than it is in RP, it is far from being as ubiquitous as it is in Scottish standard English. Coalescent assimilation of a sequence of an alveolar obstruent and /j/ is more prevalent in New Zealand English than in RP, especially in words like *assume*, *presume*, but also in words like *Tuesday*, *duty*. Yod-dropping is slightly more common in New Zealand English than it is in RP, with /j/ being dropped regularly following /θ/ and variably following /n/. Occasional yod-dropping after labial consonants is heard, but this is not standard except in loanwords like *début*. The major consonantal difference between New Zealand English and RP is the degree of vocalisation of /l/ heard in the former. /l/ is always darker than its corresponding RP allophone, and non-pre-vocalically it is frequently vocalised. The quality of the resulting vowel is variable in terms of backness, height and rounding, but can frequently be considered an allophone of the vowel phonemes in FOOT or GOOSE.

The two systematic differences between the vowels of New Zealand English and those of RP are (1) the lack of a phoneme /ə/ contrasting with the vowel of KIT in unstressed syllables and (2) the variable merger of /ɪə/ and /eə/. Where the FEAR and SQUARE vowels are merged, the phonetic result of the merger may fall anywhere in the range covered by the two vowels together. Some speakers who do not merge these two vowels nevertheless have a lexical distribution for the two phonemes which is very different from that in RP and other accents of English: for example, many distinguish *pier* on the one hand from *peer, pair, pear, pare* on the other.

The vowels of New Zealand English are realised as shown below. The values given here apply only when there is no following /l/ or /r/, for which see later. Where there is variation, more formal variants, or variants associated with higher social class, are listed before less formal or lower-class variants. Only stressed vowels are dealt with here, unstressed vowels require further discussion.

Lexical set	*Variants*
FLEECE	[iᴛi], [əi]
DRESS	[eᴛ], [ë˪]
KIT	[ë], [ə]
TRAP	[ɛᴛ], [ɛ˪]
STRUT	[ɐ], [a˪–]
START	[ɐ–:], [a˪–:]
LOT	[ɒ˪+]
FOOT	[öᴛ], [ÿᴛ]
THOUGHT	[oᴛ], [oə], [oɐ]
GOOSE	[ʉᴛ], [əi]
NURSE	[œ̈], [ö]
FACE	[æe], [ɐe]
PRICE	[ɑ+e], [ɒe]
CHOICE	[oe]
MOUTH	[ä˪ö], [ɛi]
GOAT	[ɐö], [ɐÿᴛ]
NEAR	[iᴛɐ] ⎫
SQUARE	[eɐ] ⎬ [iᴛɐ]
CURE	[ʉɐ]

Before /l/ (sometimes before /l/ followed by a voiceless obstruent, depending on the particular case) there are many cases of neutralisation of these contrasts. Below the maximal neutralisation patterns are given, though it must be recognised that not all speakers use all of these patterns, and that speakers do not necessarily neutralise all the time, even when their speech shows one of these patterns. Also, where more than two vowels are shown as neutralised below, some speakers will only neutralise some of the oppositions shown. Furthermore, some speakers may neutralise before vocalised /l/, but not before consonantal /l/. In the presentation below, an attempt has been made to put the neutralised contrasts in some kind of order of likelihood of neutralisation, but this has not been done on the basis of any formal research findings, merely impressionistically.

Oppositions neutralised	*Typical realisation*
FLEECE/NEAR	[əi]
DRESS/TRAP/STRUT	[ɛ], [æ—]
GOOSE/FOOT/KIT/STRUT	[u], [ɤ]
LOT/GOAT/THOUGHT/STRUT	[ɒo]

In addition there are cases of neutralisation before /r/, as shown below:

Oppositions neutralised	*Typical realisation*
FLEECE/NEAR	[əi]
DRESS/SQUARE	[eː]
GOOSE/CURE	[ʉː]

Where unstressed vowels are concerned, it is easier to treat them as a separate system. The unstressed vowel in the HAPPY lexical set is perceived as belonging to the same phoneme as the stressed vowel in the FLEECE lexical set. Phonetically, however, it is not identical. For most people, there is no distinction between an unstressed KIT vowel and a schwa, which is not surprising given the normal centralised realisation of the KIT vowel in New Zealand English, but this vowel only occurs in closed syllables. In final open syllables, a more open version is heard, which is frequently perceived as belonging to the same phoneme as the STRUT vowel. This variant is also heard when, by virtue of speech tempo or position in the utterance, a normally unstressed vowel is given more prominence than usual. A fourth unstressed vowel is provided by the result of vocalisation of /l/. The quality of this vowel is variable in New Zealand English. All these vowels are neutralised before a syllable-final /l/, and the vowel heard here is usually associated with the vowel phoneme in the FOOT lexical set.

Vowels are reduced to schwa less frequently in unstressed syllables in New Zealand English than in RP, with the result that the former can sound more syllable-timed than the latter. Also, the NURSE vowel is heard in unstressed syllables in New Zealand English, particularly in careful speech in words like *mastered*. The quality of the full vowel used in place of the schwa appears to be determined in terms of the orthography, although the influence of an underlying morphophonemic value cannot be ruled out.

As in South African English (Lass 1987: 307), *the* and *a* do not always have the same range of allomorphs in New Zealand English that they have in standard English. Rather, they are realised as /ðə/ and /ə/ independent of the following sound. Where the following sound is a vowel, a [ʔ] is usually inserted.

There is a small set of words such as *known*, *thrown*, which are regularly pronounced with two syllables, allowing distinctions between such pairs as *groan/grown*.

The intonation of New Zealand English is generally speaking rather flat, but the high rise terminal is used, as in Australian English, on statements to seek confirmation that one's interlocutor is following.

8.2.2   Development

As stated earlier, it is clear that New Zealand English derives from a variety of English spoken in the south-east of England. It has /ʌ/ rather than /ʊ/ in words like *cup*; it has /ɑ/ rather than /æ/ in words like *fast*; except in one regional dialect it does not, as a rule, have non-prevocalic /r/, and so on. The question which really needs to be answered about the origins of New Zealand English concerns not the general area of its origin, but the precise area of its origin, and the route by which the language travelled to New Zealand. Such questions will be discussed later, in section 8.9, once the nature of New Zealand English itself has been established. In this section, the development of pronunciation in New Zealand will be considered.

The earliest trustworthy account of New Zealand English pronunciation is that provided by Samuel McBurney, in an article in *The Press* of Christchurch (McBurney, 1887), later reprinted with other observations in Ellis (1889). McBurney was a Scot, and autodidact phonetician, who had been the principal at a Ladies' College in Geelong, and who travelled Australasia examining tonic sol-fa singers. His comments are, accordingly, comments on the language of the children of the period, not the adults, and presumably also in fairly formal styles, but they are none the less indicative.

The only consonants that McBurney gives us any information on are non-prevocalic /r/, post-consonantal /j/, /hw/ and /h/. Non-prevocalic /r/ appears to have been widespread pre-consonantally in the South Island (including Nelson and Christchurch) but not in the North. McBurney notes that it occurs 'generally' in *morning*, but in word-final position his evidence is apparently contradictory, showing /r/ as 'general' in Nelson and Christchurch in *more*, but no /r/ as 'general' in Dunedin. With *sure*, and *pure*, lack of /r/ appears to have been widespread, though /r/ was heard in *poor* and *floor*. The use of intrusive /r/ is also commented on as being 'pretty general', though from the detailed comments in Ellis (1889) it would appear that it was less general in New Zealand than elsewhere. Yod-dropping was heard in a few cases following an alveolar stop. /hw/ was 'general' from girls, and heard from many boys in Dunedin. /h/ was not generally dropped. The use of /ɪn/ rather than /ɪŋ/ in the suffix *-ing* is commented on as being of 'frequent occurrence', in New Zealand as well as in Britain.

Where the vowels are concerned, McBurney comments not only on features to be heard in New Zealand, but features which are heard in Australia but not in New Zealand. Those heard in New Zealand include the following:

1 variation between [ɐi] and [ɒi] in the PRICE vowel;
2 a short vowel, called that of *pull*, in the word *food*; it is not clear from McBurney's description how general a phenomenon this is in terms of the lexical items that are affected, but it appears to have been a minor pronunciation throughout New Zealand;
3 a very open vowel in STRUT;
4 great variation in the realisations of the MOUTH vowel, with front and raised starting-points more frequent than back and low starting-points for the diphthong;
5 variation between [ɪ] and [iː] for the HAPPY vowel.

Features stated to exist in Australia but not (or not widely) in New Zealand include:

1 the lowering of the starting-point of the diphthong in the FACE vowel;
2 the lowering and unrounding of the starting-point of the diphthong in the GOAT vowel;

3 a lengthening of short vowels, especially the TRAP vowel, and including the use of /ɔː/ rather than /ɒ/ in words like *dog, coffee* (though the description suggests that in some cases the vowel may not have been rounded).

In a number of publications (Gordon 1983; McGeorge 1984; Gordon & Deverson 1989) the evidence of written historical records, especially educational records, has been considered. These indicate an awareness of an 'Austral' pronunciation among New Zealanders (children in particular) from the turn of the century onwards. This coincides with the period when New Zealand-born children must have started to make up the majority of secondary-school children. Earlier comments are frequently self-congratulatory in tone, suggesting that the worst excesses of British regional dialects are being avoided in New Zealand. That is probably what is meant by the editorial in *The Press* (Christchurch) for 8 October 1887, when it is noted, on the basis of McBurney's earlier article, that 'the Queen's English is as well or better spoken in the colonies than in the Old Country'. From the early 1900s the tone changes, and complaints are made about the local New Zealand pronunciation. The following points are among those complained about before the First World War:

1 the lowering of the starting-point in the FACE diphthong;
2 the lowering and unrounding of the starting-point in the GOAT diphthong;
3 the raising and fronting of the starting-point in the MOUTH diphthong;
4 centralisation of the KIT vowel;
5 the raising of the TRAP vowel;
6 the retraction and rounding of the starting-point of the PRICE diphthong;
7 the use of assimilated forms /tʃ/ and /dʒ/ in place of /tj/ and /dj/;
8 the dropping of unstressed syllables.

In this period, however, complaints about /h/-dropping and the use of /ɪn/ for *-ing* become much rarer, perhaps surprisingly given that both these pronunciations persist to the present day: perhaps the purists themselves made the same 'errors' and thus no longer observed them in others.

Noteworthy in this list is that New Zealand appears to have caught up with Australia in the pronunciation of the diphthongs in a period of something like thirty years. Also, the centralised KIT vowel, today a diagnostic feature of New Zealand English, seems to have impinged on the general awareness very rapidly; it must be assumed that the tendency had been there before this period, but it cannot be dated accurately.

By the 1930s, the list of 'errors' in New Zealand speech appears to have grown. Wall (1938: 16–21) complains of the following matters:

1   the centralisation of /ɪ/;
2   the use of the a long vowel in HAPPY;
3   the fronted and raised vowel in the START lexical set;
4   the diphthongisation of the FLEECE vowel;
5   the diphthongisation of the GOOSE vowel;
6   the retraction and rounding of the first element in the PRICE diphthong;
7   the fronting and raising of the first element in the MOUTH diphthong;
8   the lowering and retraction of the first element in the FACE diphthong;
9   the lowering and/or fronting of the first element in the GOAT diphthong;
10   the use of dark /l/ pre-vocalically;
11   the reduction of /kw/ to /k/ word-initially;
12   the use of the TRAP vowel rather than the START vowel in words like *dance*;
13   the neutralisation of the STRUT vowel and the LOT vowel before /l/ and a voiceless obstruent: needless to say, the complaint is not phrased in these terms;
14   various spelling pronunciations, and the use of full vowels in unstressed syllables.

Of these, number 12 has now virtually vanished, pronunciations like /tʃæns/ being taken to be Australian in New Zealand, despite the fact that they can still be heard from (especially older) New Zealanders, and that they are not heard from all Australians, this pronunciation being rare from South Australians. The others remain. Wall also complains about the pronunciation of Maori words in New Zealand English, something which has become an abiding complaint in discussions of pronunciation.

The comment by Wall on the use of the LOT vowel to replace the STRUT vowel before /l/ is one of the earliest clear comments on the neutralisation of vowels in this environment. There is, however, one obscure comment in an earlier source, which may be worth noting. In a report on the activities of the Otago Institute in *The Otago Witness* for 9 August 1911 (p. 37), in a summary of a paper given by G. E. Thompson on 'The question of a New Zealand dialect', the speaker is reported to have commented on 'the distinct tendency, when uttering vowel sounds, to lower the tongue' with the result that the vowel in a word like *twelve* is mispronounced. Given the otherwise well-attested tendency to vowel-raising in New Zealand English, this may be a reference to (incipient) neutralisation of DRESS and TRAP before /l/. Gordon & Deverson (1985: 26) also cite Wall (no reference) as commenting on the neutralisation of KIT and FOOT before /l/. By the 1970s these neutralisations had started to impinge on the general consciousness of New Zealand English speakers, and we find letters to the editor of *The Listener* such as

Who is this newcomer? His name is Alec Tricity.   (31 March 1979)

Is it true that Radio New Zealand journalist Grant Woolliams's name is Grant Williams? [The editor answers no, but the point is made that the two are homophonous.]   (1 November 1986)

Here we see an increase in the amount of neutralisation and in awareness of the neutralisation over a forty-year period.

The merger of the NEAR and SQUARE vowels is another relatively recent phenomenon. Gordon & Maclagan (1989: 204) cite Turner (1966) as the first possible source of comment on this merger. Today it is one of the most distinctive features of New Zealand English pronunciation, although the merger is by no means complete, and the pattern of change is obscure. Certainly, it seems to be one area where younger speakers are more and more using the merged forms, with /ɪə/ being the preferred pronunciation, although there is some evidence that this has changed rapidly in the last few years (Gordon & Maclagan 1989).

Turner (1966: 155) comments that in a class of first-year English students at the University of Canterbury in 1964, about 50 per cent reported that they made a distinction between /w/ and /hw/. This figure is likely to show an over-reporting of the distinction, but may be taken as a guideline. My own observations suggest that far fewer students made such a distinction regularly in the 1980s, although many make the distinction sporadically. This feature is kept alive by overt teaching:

/hw/ is perceived as being a prestige pronunciation. However, such pressures seem to be slowing its disappearance rather than preserving it for posterity.

Finally, a note on intonation is required. Benton (1966: 71), in a discussion of the language of Maori schoolchildren in the early 1960s, makes the following comment:

> A distinctive rising intonation, especially marked in the speech of 5 to 8 year old children, but present in a modified form in the speech of older children too, was encountered in one Bay of Islands area, and in Hawkes Bay and Whanganui, as well as in one Tuhoe settlement. All but the latter were areas where the children's knowledge of Maori is negligible, and any European children attending the schools seemed to follow the Maori children's speech patterns.

This looks like a comment on the early stages of the introduction of the high rise terminal, which by 1980 had become so widespread as to count as fairly general New Zealand English. It would certainly not draw comment as a particular feature of Maori English today. If that is the case, it is a change which has taken place with remarkable speed. The origin of this change presents an interesting case. There is some evidence that the Australian English high rise terminal has its origin in the New Zealand one, which is found earlier and used more frequently (Allan 1990; Holmes & Bell 1990). Possibly it has its origins in Maori English, though reports of similar intonation patterns in varieties of American English, English regional dialects, as well as in French and German in recent years suggest that there may be some more widespread phenomenon at work here.

8.3   The pronunciation of Maori

Since Maori has provided New Zealand English with so many loanwords, and in particular with place-names, the pronunciation of Maori is an important facet of the way in which English is used in New Zealand.

It goes without saying that Maori is not pronounced by most pakehas in the same way as it would be pronounced by a native speaker of Maori. Many of the differences can be easily explained by the phonetic structure of the two languages: thus Maori /r/ is usually pronounced [ɹ] rather than [ɾ] by pakehas (white New Zealanders); /p, t, k/ are usually aspirated or affricated; /t, n/ are pronounced as alveolars rather than as dentals. Since Maori loanwords are generally perceived as monomorphemic entities in English (even where they contain several morphs in Maori), orthographic *ng* is treated as it would be in a monomorphemic English word, and Maori /ŋ/ is frequently realised as /ŋg/ in English when it occurs word-medially. Word-initially /n/ is used rather than /ŋ/ in English. Maori /f/ is realised variably as English /f/ (a formal and innovative form) or /w/, corresponding to the spelling *wh* which is most frequently pronounced /w/ in present-day New Zealand English.

Maori short vowels in word-final position are pronounced as long vowels in English. Thus, the Maori determiner *te* is usually pronounced /tiː/ or /teɪ/ in English. English speakers do not distinguish between the diphthongs such as /ai/ and /ae/, /ɔi/ and /ɔe/. Maori /uː/ following an alveolar is sometimes rendered as English /juː/. The monophthongs of Maori are usually assigned to English phonemes as shown below:

Maori phoneme	English phoneme
i	ɪ, iː word-finally
iː	iː
ɛ	e, iː, eɪ
ɛː	eɪ
a	æ, ʌ, ə, ɒ following w, and occasionally adjacent to other velars
aː	ɑː, eɪ
ɔ	ɒ
ɔː	əʊ
u	ʌ, ʊ, uː
uː	uː, juː (esp. word-initially)

In addition, vowels in unstressed syllables are reduced to /ə/ in English, although there is no /ə/ in Maori. The general pattern of diphthong replacement is listed below. Generally no distinction is made between a diphthong with a short first element, and one with a long first element. Maori diphthongs not listed below are treated in English as sequences of the individual vowels.

Maori diphthong	English vowel
ia	iə
iu	juː
ei	eɪ
ea	iə, eə
eu	juː
ai	aɪ

ae	aɪ
ao	aʊ or sequence of vowels
au	aʊ, əʊ
oi	ɔɪ
oe	ɔɪ
ou	əʊ, uː

Within this pattern, there is a certain amount of diachronic and stylistic variation apparent. Very early loans from Maori appear to have been borrowed from oral sources, later ones from written sources. So Maori *piripiri* gives English *biddy-biddy* and Maori *Otakou* gives English *Otago*, showing the unaspirated Maori stops being perceived as corresponding to English voiced stops, and the Maori tap being perceived as /d/ rather than /r/. Such words may have been borrowed before Maori spelling was standardised in the late 1830s and 1840s. In most Maori loanwords in English, Maori voiceless stops are rendered with English voiceless stops.

In many cases there is variation between an earlier version which interprets the Maori orthography in terms of English graphemic and phonemic conventions, and a more modern version which attempts to give a pronunciation which is closer to the Maori pronunciation. The latter version is heard from professional broadcasters and also from people who wish to show solidarity with Maori ideals in the use of the Maori language. For example, the /æ/ pronunciation of Maori /a/, the /iː/ pronunciation of Maori /e/ (especially, but not exclusively in word-final position) and the /aʊ/ pronunciation of Maori /au/ are now perceived as 'less accurate' than /ʌ/, /eɪ/ and /əʊ/ respectively. The reason for the last of these is the very front realisation of the first element of the /aʊ/ in New Zealand English, combined with the central quality of the Maori /a/ in the /au/ diphthong: it leads, however, to a merger of Maori /au/ and Maori /ou/ in the pronunciation of those speakers who use this value.

There is a well-established tradition in English for the abbreviation of Maori place-names: for example, Maori *Wakatipu* becomes English *Wakatip*, Maori *Paekakariki* becomes English /paɪkɒk/ and Maori *Paraparaumu* becomes English *Paraparam*. Some such abbreviations may be explicable in terms of the Maori devoicing of phrase-final close vowels (*Wakatip*, for example), but not all of them are, by any means. Such pronunciations may always have been fairly informal, but they are widely frowned upon today in the public domain.

The proper pronunciation of Maori is currently a controversial issue in New Zealand, and it is a subject on which feelings run high. The issue is at heart a political rather than a linguistic one, since it is clear linguistically that there is no good reason to expect native-like Maori pronunciation in words which are being used in English. None the less, it has the linguistic consequence that there is a good deal of variation in the way in which Maori loanwords are pronounced in English, with variants close to native Maori norms at the formal end of the spectrum, and much more Anglicised versions – sometimes irregularly Anglicised versions – at the other. To give some idea of the variation this can lead to, I present below a few place-names with a Maori pronunciation and one extreme English pronunciation. Variants are heard anywhere on the continuum between these two extremes.

Place-name	*Variant pronunciations*
Aotearoa	aːɔtɛːaɾɔa
	eɪətɪəˈɹəʊə
Putaruru	putaɾuɾu
	pəˈtæɹəɹuː
Te Puke	te puke
	tiːˈpʊkiː
Whangarei	faŋaɾei
	wɒŋɡəˈɹeɪ

8.4   New Zealand English grammar

It is only recently that any serious descriptive work on New Zealand English grammar has been carried out. It has generally been assumed that the morphology and syntax of New Zealand English is in-distinguishable from that of British English. Recent research shows that this is not the case, but that the differences are not categorical ones. It is usually the case that New Zealand English has the same constructions available as standard English English, but uses them slightly differently, giving preference to different options. When non-standard varieties are included, the pattern becomes even less clear. Much of the grammatical variation that can be observed in New Zealand can also be observed elsewhere in the English-speaking world. For example, the construction illustrated in *I wish he hadn't have done it* (alternating with *I wish he wouldn't have done it*) can be found not only in New Zealand but also in Australian, British and American English. It may be the case that this particular construction is heard more often in New Zealand in contexts which otherwise appear to be calling forth standard variants, but it is hard to judge, both because the situation in New Zealand is unclear and not properly researched, and also because comparative data are lacking. It is certainly the case that much of the grammatical variation that can be heard in New Zealand English can also be heard in other varieties of English, usually with similar social or stylistic effects. Such variants include the use of double comparison, double negatives, the use of *never* as a sentence negator, confused use of the case forms of pronouns, especially under co-ordination, use of *done* and *seen* as past-tense forms, use of *there's* with a plural subject, use of *was* with plural subjects and so on.

Some of the factors that seem to distinguish standard New Zealand English from standard British English are the following (where specific references are not given, see Bauer 1987b).

1   a preference for *-ves* plurals with words like *hoof, roof, wharf* rather than an *-fs* plural (Bauer 1987a);

2   a greater use of *proven* as the past participle of *prove* (Bauer, 1987a);

3   a greater use of *do*-support with *have* in questions and negatives (Bauer 1989a);

4   a preference for *didn't used to* rather than *used not to* (Bauer 1989b);

5   there may be a slight tendency for New Zealand English to prefer singular concord with collective nouns (Bauer 1988);

6   Trudgill (1986: 141) suggests that New Zealand English uses *will* rather than *shall* in a phrase like *Will I turn out the light?*, and that this might show Scottish influence;

7   the productive use of the *-ie* diminutive ending, as in (established) *sickie* 'day off work', *rellies* 'relatives';

8   the use of plural concord with certain nouns such as *measles* which end in *-s*;

9   switches from transitive to intransitive or vice versa with certain verbs: *We farewelled the retiring professor, We are meeting with the union later today, They protested the government's actions.*

Where non-standard New Zealand English is concerned, as well as those already mentioned, the following grammatical points are particularly noteworthy.

1   the use of plural *yous*;

2   use of supporting *ones* after possessives and demonstratives: *We can use my ones*;

3   the use of *she* as a neutral or non-referring pronoun: *She'll be right!*;

4   generalisation of the perfect to simple past contexts: *I have seen it last week*;

5   the use of tag *eh?*, probably to check comprehension, but partly as a solidarity marker (Meyerhoff 1990); note that this tag has falling intonation;

6   in some areas the use of the construction *son of Smith, brother of Sue* (Turner 1972: 137; Gordon & Deverson 1985: 60);

7   in some areas use of the past participle after *want*: *My shirt wants washed* (Bartlett 1990).

The origins of some of these constructions are clear: 1 is sometimes attributed to Maori, which has dual and plural second person pronouns, but the form must be Irish in origin; 7 is equally clearly Scottish in origin; 3 is shared with Australia, although it is not clear to me how it got into Australian English; 5 is again frequently attributed to influence from the Maori particle *ne*. The form /eɪ/ is also found in Canada, though not with the same intonation. This is the only one of these constructions which may be native to New Zealand.

Information is lacking on the diachronic development of these constructions, although we may guess that those of Scottish and Irish origins arrived in New Zealand early. In any case, since many of them involve the favouring (or disfavouring) of a construction already in general use in Britain, we would expect change to be slow and undramatic. In general, the similarities with British English are more striking than the differences, although New Zealand English grammar is not identical with British English grammar, in either standard or non-standard forms.

8.5   Vocabulary

Most of the vocabulary that is found in New Zealand English is general to all varieties of English. Clearly, this shared vocabulary tells us little or nothing about the history of English in New Zealand, so that the discussion below will be in terms of the small amount which does show a specific New Zealand (or, in many cases, a more general Australasian) flavour. Although an attempt is made below to break this vocabulary down into a number of categories, the categories are not always as distinct as this process might seem to imply.

8.5.1 *Maori vocabulary*

In one sense, the most clearly New Zealand vocabulary to be found in New Zealand English is the vocabulary that is borrowed from Maori. There are, however, problems with the status of these words: are they specifically New Zealand English, or are they general English? Is the word *kiwi* 'flightless bird' a word of New Zealand English, or is it the English word for the bird? With this particular example, agreement might easily be reached that the word belongs to general English, just as words like *kangaroo* and *armadillo* do. With a word like *taniwha* it is less clear that this is the case, if only because this mythical monster tends to be discussed only in a New Zealand context. Certainly it is the case that New Zealand English is characterised by a relatively high number of words of Maori origin, but this is largely because such words refer to things which are found predominantly in New Zealand. Secondly, it is not always clear whether a Maori word used in an English context is a word of New Zealand English, or whether it is a case of code-switching between English and Maori. This becomes particularly problematical in the speech of some Maoris. An utterance such as the following, from a seminar on Maori Language Education, given by a Maori, is almost certainly code-switching: 'The importance of the reo ['language'] was reaffirmed.' Other instances may not be so clear, even where they contain a relatively high number of Maori words. Consider the following literary passage from Ihimaera (1986: 111):

> Her act of assertion would have been regarded as a violation of the tapu of the marae and the tapu of the male. In most other tribes, excluding the matriarch's own and just a few others, the art of the whaikorero was the province of the male. Even in her own lands, the matriarch's rank had to be impeccable to allow her to speak. Wisely, on the marae in Wellington, a place strange and dangerous even to her mana, she at least followed the male orators of the ope.

The following passage is from a news broadcast (Mana News, Radio New Zealand National Programme, 19 November 1990):

> It's vital for kohanga whanau to keep in touch with their regional tino rangatiratanga units or their kohanga reo co-ordinator ... full funding of seven and two dollars, depending on the age of the tamariki, but kohanga who don't reach licensing standard will receive a dollar per child per hour of attendance.

It is certainly the case that among the Maori words used in New Zealand some are more generally recognised and more widely used than others. At one end of the scale, there are words such as *Kiwi* 'New Zealander' which are formally Maori, though not Maori in their meaning. These are used absolutely generally. A word such as *kiwi* 'flightless bird' is also the only possible word to describe the bird, and completely normal. A number of names of flora and fauna come into this category, though by no means all. To take tree names as examples, *kauri* and *pohutukawa* are absolutely normal; *manuka* (stressed on the first or second syllable, more usually the latter despite the Maori stress) is perfectly general, although *tea tree* exists as an alternative; *rimu* and *red pine* may vary dialectally, or for some speakers be distinguished, with *rimu* denoting the tree and *red pine* the timber (Orsman 1980: 41); *kahikatea* and *white pine* are both heard quite frequently, but *kahikatea* would not be as generally recognised as *rimu* is: there may also be differences of generation here, *white pine* being a commoner term among older speakers; *ti* or *ti palm* or *ti tree* is extremely rare, *cabbage tree* being the preferred variant (possibly because of homophony with *tea tree*). In all of these cases, there are English equivalents where the Maori term is not completely general, but when it comes to terms for Maori artefacts or cultural institutions, it may be the case that there is no precise English equivalent, but that the Maori words would still not be recognised by most pakehas.

The most obvious classes of Maori words in New Zealand English are words for flora, fauna and Maori cultural institutions. Examples of each will be given here, with comments on their generality and English alternatives where these exist.

Examples of flora names have been illustrated above. Other common tree names include *kowhai*, *matai*, *ngaio*, *ponga* (also spelt *punga*), *rata*, *tawa*, and *totara*. Of these, only *matai* has a common English name, *black pine*, but *matai* is quite general. *Toitoi* or *toetoe* 'pampas grass' is absolutely standard, but *raupo* 'bulrush' is far less common. *Kumara* (sometimes spelt *kumera*), a sweet potato, is also general. *Piripiri* 'sticky Willie' is almost never used, but the Anglicised form *biddy-bid(dy)* (which shows the early perception of Maori unaspirated /p/ as /b/, and of flapped Maori /r/ as /d/) is standard.

The only native mammals in New Zealand before the arrival of the Maori were the bats, and they are not generally referred to by the Maori name *pekapeka*. The Maoris brought with them two mammals: the dog, which, while distinct from the European strains of dog, is these days seldom referred to as a *kuri* or *gooree*; and the rat, again distinct from the European version, and sometimes referred to as a *kiore*, although the

English equivalent *Maori rat* is far more widely used and recognised. The only other native land animal of note, the *tuatara*, a lizard-like reptile, is always referred to by its Maori name. Frogs, geckos, etc. are not referred to by Maori names.

Where insects are concerned, the *weta* is always referred to as such, as is the *huhu grub*. Otherwise the only common Maori name in general use is *katipo*, the poisonous spider related to the Australian redback. The body louse or head louse (Maori *kutu*) used to be referred to as a *cooter* or a *cootie*, although in urban areas at least it is now most often a *louse*. Native wasps and bees, katydids, mantises, moths, etc. are not generally known by Maori names.

A few fish are given Maori names such as *tarakihi* (also spelt *terakihi*), *kahawai* and *warehou*. The *groper* is, in some regions, called the *hapuka* or in Anglicised form, the *harbooker* (Orsman 1980: 41). The *kokopu* is more usually Anglicised as *cockabully*. Shellfish, for some reason, are more generally known by their Maori names: *paua* (exported as *abalone*), *pipi*, *toheroa*, though *crayfish* (not *koura*) is now exported as *rock lobster*.

The largest number of Maori names for fauna are found among the names of birds. Here it is necessary to distinguish those bird names which are general from those which are rare. Birds which are regularly referred to by their Maori names include the *kea, kiwi, moa*. There are a number of birds which are now generally referred to by Maori names, although they also have English names, which used to be more common: *pukeko* (previously *swamp hen*), *takahe* (often previously known by its scientific name *notornis*), *tui* (previously a *parson bird* because of the white feathers on the front of the neck) and *weka* (previously *Maori hen* or *woodhen*). There are some birds which have both Maori and English names, but neither of them is particularly familiar because of the rarity of the bird itself: an example is *kokako*, previously *wattle bird* or *native crow*. Finally, there are a number of birds whose Maori names are almost never used: the *bellbird* rather than *makomako*, although the Anglicisations *mocker* and *mockie* used to be found; *fantail* rather than *piwakawaka* (or other similar names); *kingfisher* rather than *kotare*; *native pigeon* or *wood pigeon* rather than *kereru*. In the case of the *kotuku* or *white heron* the two names appear to be used interchangeably.

Where Maori cultural institutions are concerned, the picture is far less clear. There has been a marked increase in the use of Maori words in this category in the media over the last ten years or so, but it is not clear how many of them are understood by pakeha speakers, or how many of them will survive.

A few words for Maori constructions are generally recognised: *marae* 'courtyard of a meeting house', *whare* 'house', formerly much more common than today, and *waka* 'canoe'. *Pa* 'fortified village' is today used mainly in a historical sense, though it used to be used for what is now called a *marae*.

Words for Maori artefacts are recognised extremely variably. One of the best known is probably the *tiki* or *hei tiki* 'a good luck carving', and *poi* 'flax ball used in dancing' is also well known. Others such as *mere* 'war club', *putorino* 'flute', *piupiu* 'skirt made of dried flax' are heard, but not as widely.

Words for cultural events such as *hui* 'meeting, gathering' and *tangi* (from Maori *tangihanga*) 'ceremony of mourning, funeral' and *hangi* 'earth oven, food prepared in an earth oven, feast at which such food is eaten' are well known, but others are more variable. *Hongi* 'to press noses in greeting' is widely recognised, but *powhiri* 'ceremonial welcome onto a marae' is only now coming into general cognisance.

There are several words denoting people, again only a few of which are widely recognised by non-Maori speakers. *Pakeha* is the best known of these. Its precise meaning is difficult to pin down. Basically it means 'person of European descent', but it has for many Maoris connotations of power and cultural dominance. Some speakers are not sure whether Indian and Chinese New Zealanders count as pakehas or not. This word has also fallen into disfavour among some pakehas in recent years, because it is claimed to be a term of abuse. Various unlikely and uncomplimentary etymologies are postulated for it by such people. Its real etymology is obscure; even D'Urville in the early 1800s could not discover what it derived from (Legge 1989). It is probably about as abusive a term as *politician* or *student*: that is, how abusive it is depends on the person who is using it and the occasion. For the time being, *pakeha* seems likely to survive, since the alternative, *European*, is taken to imply European origin for the individual. The alternative *Caucasian* is too technical a term, and is not widely understood. *Wahine* 'woman' used to be quite widespread, but is no longer in general use. *Tohunga* 'wise man, doctor' is fairly frequently heard in a Maori context, but fell into disfavour among pakehas in the early years of this century. A word like *kuia* 'old woman, elder' is less widely recognised. Similar comments apply to *mokopuna* 'descendant, grandchild' and *rangatira* 'chief'.

Finally, there is a mixed bag of words. There are a number of relatively abstract words, such as *rangatiratanga* 'chieftainship', *taha Maori* 'Maori perspective or way of doing things', *taonga* 'treasure', which have become prominent in recent political debate. *Whanau* 'extended family', *hapu* 'subtribe' and *iwi* 'tribe' are discussed a great deal at the moment, in terms of current legislation, but have not been well known before now. *Mana* 'prestige, standing', sometimes understood by Maoris as 'power', which is one of its Maori meanings, is very well known and widely used. *Tapu* 'sacred', which is related to *taboo* but lacks the supercilious connotations attached to the Fijian word, is widely recognised, though used almost exclusively in Maori context. *Aroha* 'love', cognate with Hawaiian *aloha*, is not nearly as widely used or recognised as its Hawaiian equivalent. *Kia ora*, known in the United Kingdom as a drink, is a familiar salutation, common in English about the time of the First World War, and recently revived among pakeha New Zealanders. *Taihoa* 'wait!' (frequently pronounced /taɪhəʊ/) used to be used more frequently than it is today, though it is still heard, even in purely pakeha surroundings. Finally, *pakaru* 'broken' provides an interesting example. It is usually used in English in the form *puckeroo*, and seems to have achieved some of its force by being supported by English *buggered*, of which it could almost be a transliteration. It is another Maori word which is no longer as widely used as it used to be, perhaps partly because it is avoided by some Maori speakers because it is believed to be a transliteration.

While the examples I have mentioned here are, to a certain extent, random ones, and the list is very far from exhaustive, they provide some kind of idea of the range of words borrowed from Maori into New Zealand English.

8.5.2   Other Pacific languages

Given New Zealand's position in the Pacific, and the number of immigrants from Pacific nations in New Zealand, the small number of words from Pacific languages in New Zealand English is perhaps surprising. The only common words from Pacific Island languages are *lavalava* (also general English: see the *OED*) and *(pa)palagi* 'pakeha', from Samoan (the *g* is pronounced /ŋ/). Even that is not all that common except in discussions of the Pacific Islands. Burchfield (1988) also lists *afakasi* 'half-caste', *aiga* 'family', *faamafu* 'home-brewed liquor' and *faa-Samoa* 'the Samoan way of life', none of which is at all common except in discussion of things Samoan.

8.5.3   British dialect words

There are quite a few New Zealand English words which have their origins in British regional or non-standard dialects. Some of these are words relating to agriculture, or to special areas such as prospecting, but most of them are not so specialised. Some examples are listed below. Many of these are also listed as Australianisms in the *AND* and are thus more correctly viewed as Australasian words. These words are indicated with a parenthesised plus symbol in the list below. Other words not shown as New Zealandisms in *The Macquarie Dictionary* (and thus presumably recognised in Australia) are marked with a parenthesised †.

Here and below, the examples are not further classified in terms of semantic fields, since that might tend to imply that New Zealand words occur only in specific categories, which does not appear to be the case. Nonetheless, it may be worth noting that Burchfield (personal communication) estimates that about a quarter of distinctively New Zealand terms occur in farming contexts. These are not, of course, the words most frequently met by the visitor to New Zealand, or by the majority of the population, who live in the cities. *Billy* (+), *bobby calf* (†) 'calf intended for veal', *bowyang* (+) 'strap round trouser legs', *break in* (land) [for agriculture], *(give something a) burl* (+) 'try', *crook* (+) 'ill, angry', *dinkum* (+) 'genuine, truth', *fossick* (+) 'hunt around', *hogget* (†) 'sheep aged between one and two years used for meat', *lolly* (+) 'sweet', *pikelet* 'Scotch pancake, dropscone', *slater* (†) 'woodlouse', *sook(y)* (†) 'coward', *sool (on)* (+) 'to set [a dog] on', *spell* (+) (from work) 'a break', *wee* (†) 'small'.

It seems likely that these words are very old New Zealandisms, many of them probably crossing the Tasman from Australia with the earliest pakeha settlers. It is noteworthy how many of them are of Scottish or northern English origin, and this is one of the few areas where Scottish influence can be seen on New Zealand English. Given the importance of Scottish settlement, especially in the South Island, it is not a very strong influence.

8.5.4   Australianisms

Quite apart from the words listed in the last section, there are some words which clearly represent Australianisms, and yet which have, or have had, wide currency in New Zealand as well. *Cooee* is an obvious example. It is originally an Australian aboriginal call, but is current in

New Zealand both as a way of gaining attention and in the phrase *to be within cooee of*. *Cobber* 'friend, mate' is probably another, although the *AND* suggests a British dialect source for it. Less obviously, *bellbird*, *cabbage tree* and *morepork* (usually in the form *mopoke*) are also used in Australia, though not for the same tree/bird that are denoted by these words in New Zealand. All of these are very early borrowings into New Zealand English though *cobber* is now not used as much in New Zealand as it used to be, and is frequently perceived as being an Australian word by New Zealanders.

8.5.5 Changes of meaning

There are a number of *faux amis* in New Zealand English for speakers of other varieties of English. Some of these are more disturbing and confusing than others, but their use marks a particular regional variety. As previously, those which are also listed in the *AND* are marked with a plus symbol.

Bush (+) is used of very different country in Australia and New Zealand, but in both it indicates uncultivated country – in New Zealand it might be best glossed as '(rain) forest'; *caucus* (+) 'parliamentary members of a political party as a decision-making group'; *creek* (+) (also American English) 'stream'; *dairy* 'corner shop', must by law sell milk and ice-cream and be open certain hours; *fence* can be made of stone, concrete or brick as well as other materials; *footpath* (†) in a town means the 'pavement, sidewalk' – in the country they are called *walkways* or *tracks*; *home* (+) (also with an initial capital) 'Britain', now very dated; *jug* is now less confusing than it was, since electric jugs have appeared in Britain and kettles in New Zealand, but this used to be the equivalent of a kettle – it is also used as a measure of beer in a pub; *lay-by* (+) 'system of purchase whereby goods are put on one side, and paid off over a period of time'; *partner* 'the person, of either sex, with whom one lives in a sexual relationship, irrespective of marital status'; *paddock* (+) 'any field, including a football field'; *run* (+) 'grazing land'; *runabout* (†) '(extended to) small boat'; *station* (+) 'large farm'.

All the above are standard words. There are a few less formal words which fit into the same category, such as *hard case* (+) 'a character' and *hooray!* (+) 'good-bye'.

8.5.6 Changes of style level

In a few cases there are words of New Zealand English which mean the same as they do in other parts of the English-speaking world, but whose style level is very different. The two most striking examples are the relatively recent *untold* (stress usually on the first syllable) which is a very colloquial word in New Zealand English (and at one time was even used as a general slang indication of approval), and the well-established *varsity*, which has no upper-class connotations in New Zealand, but is a normal word for university.

There are also some words which, while they mean the same as in other varieties of English, are used more frequently in New Zealand English than elsewhere. *Mate* as a vocative is one such, and possibly also the phrase *not to know someone from a bar of soap*. Given names are used in address far more frequently in New Zealand than in British English.

8.5.7 Americanisms

Despite the fact that many New Zealanders have an ambivalent attitude to America and Americanisms (which will be discussed again later), there are a number of Americanisms in New Zealand English which are normal, and a lot more which are stylistically marked.

Among the normal New Zealand English words are *collect* (of a telephone call), *guy* (used in the plural and sex-neutrally), *kerosene* 'paraffin', *movie* 'film' (*flicks* is now obsolete slang, and urban people rarely go to the *pictures*), *muffler* 'silencer', *station wagon* 'estate car', *truck* 'lorry' (which gives rise to *truckie* 'lorry-driver'). Note the use of *sidewalk café*, as a counterpoint to *pavement artist* and the fact that the ordinary word for the place where both of them are found is the *footpath*. For further details see section 8.8 below.

8.5.8 New Zealand coinages

The remaining words are Australasian coinages. Again, many of these are shared with Australia, particularly informal or slang terms. For instance, all of the following slang terms are also Australian (though many are dated in Australia, New Zealand or both): *beaut, bonzer, bosker* all meaning 'good', *dag* 'character', *drongo* 'fool', *no-hoper* 'helpless person', *nong* 'fool', *off-sider* 'companion, helper', *pongo* 'Englishman', *sheila* 'woman', *sickie* 'day off sick', (*town*) *bike* 'woman of easy virtue', *wowser* 'spoilsport', *yacker* 'work'. Phrases include *give something away* 'to stop doing something', *to give someone heaps* 'to give someone trouble', *open slather* 'open to all comers', and *big bikkies* 'a great deal of money'.

Less informal words also shared with Australia include *bikie* 'biker', *bowser* 'petrol pump', *cocky* 'farmer', *compo* 'social security', *freezing works* 'meat processing plant', *kitchen tea* 'party for a woman about to be married', *marching girl* 'girl who takes part in displays of formation marching', *old identity* 'local character', *pavlova* 'meringue desert', *pom*(*mie*) 'English (person)', *sticky-beak* 'nosey-parker, to be curious', *wharfie* 'docker'. The list could be extended considerably.

There is a certain amount of reluctance in New Zealand, even today, to believe that New Zealand words are not either Maori words or slang. In fact there are a lot of words which are standard usage in New Zealand, but unknown (or virtually unknown) outside it. Some examples are given below. *Accredit* 'to pass someone for university entrance without making them take the examination', *bottle store* 'shop where beer, wine and spirits are sold', *cattle stop* 'cattle grid', *dark chocolate* 'plain chocolate', *dome* 'press-stud, popper', *dosing strip* 'place where dogs are treated for hydatids', *family benefit* 'cash allowance paid to a mother for each dependent child', *gib*(*raltar*) *board* 'plaster board', *government valuation* 'officially determined value of land', *health stamp* 'postage stamp, some of the revenue from the sale of which goes towards supporting health camps for children', *joint family home* (legal term), *lolly scramble* 'children's entertainment in which sweets are thrown in the air, and the children scramble for them', *main trunk line* 'the Wellington–Auckland railway line', *Plunket nurse* 'children's district nurse', *primers* /prɪməz/ 'first two years in primary school', *rail car* 'passenger railway vehicle', *section* 'building site, garden' (no longer used in Australia), *state house* 'council house', *Taranaki gate* 'makeshift gate', *tarseal* 'asphalted road surface' used in expressions such as 'quarter of an hour's drive from the tarseal', *unit* 'suburban train', *warrant of fitness* 'official declaration of a vehicle's fitness to be on the road'. Again, the list could easily be extended.

8.5.9   General observations

One of the striking things about discussion of New Zealand English vocabulary is how much of the non-Maori material is shared with Australia. This is fairly easily explained in terms of the close contacts with Australia in the early days of European settlement in New Zealand, and the continuing close cultural links. During the First World War, Australians and New Zealanders fought side by side. Nowadays, many New Zealanders spend time in Australia, either on business, or for leisure and recreation. New Zealanders make up approximately 10 per cent of immigrants into Australia at the present time.

It is particularly interesting to note how much of the shared vocabulary must have arrived in New Zealand very early on. The shared words with origins in non-standard British dialects fall into this category. In recent years, some of this vocabulary has been falling into disuse in New Zealand English, but there remains a very high concentration of shared words. Gordon (1988: 181) comments specifically that 'The earliest New Zealand colloquial vocabulary has much in common with that of Australia.'

8.6 Regional variation in New Zealand English

The surprising thing about regional variation in New Zealand English is how little of it there is. Given the way in which New Zealand was settled from Britain, it might be expected that traces of Scottish, Irish and West Country dialect features (at least) would be found in different areas of New Zealand. While there are some traces of Scottish (some of them even in the standard language: see above), those traces are minimal. In this sense, New Zealand is dialectally homogeneous, although there are social dialects of New Zealand English as there are of other varieties of English, and there may be at least differences of style between urban and rural speakers. In Britain you can drive from York to Newcastle in under two hours, and be unable to understand the locals when you arrive. In New Zealand you can take seven hours to drive from Wellington to Auckland, and not be able to hear any difference in the English that is spoken when you arrive. Given this general homogeneity, the points mentioned below are extremely minor. Pronunciation, grammar and vocabulary will be dealt with individually below.

8.6.1 Pronunciation

The only clear regional dialect feature in pronunciation that has been described by linguists is the presence of non-prevocalic /r/ in a shrinking area of rural Southland. We have McBurney's evidence that this feature was found throughout the South Island in the 1860s, so rhoticity has evidently been on the wane ever since. In only one place that I am aware of is the loss of rhoticity being reversed. The name of the letter R is frequently pronounced by otherwise non-rhotic speakers with a post-vocalic /r/. This pronunciation is particularly prevalent among children, but can also be heard from adults.

What is particularly surprising about this homogeneity of accents is that non-linguists do not believe it. Dunedin people are frequently said to 'drawl', Wellingtonians to have 'clipped accents' and Aucklanders to sound like Australians. No research has been done to see whether people can be identified as coming from particular regions by speakers who make such claims, and the evidence for such claims is never precise. If there are differences in voice quality, intonation, speech tempi, etc., these remain to be identified and described.

In areas with a high Maori population varieties are heard which are similar to (or identical to) what is otherwise called 'Maori English' (see section 8.7 below). Such varieties may simply be based on social class, but there is probably a regional element involved in them as well.

8.6.2 Grammar

Turner (1966: 137) and Gordon & Deverson (1985: 60), citing Durkin (1972), give the construction *the girl of Smith* as being one found on the West Coast. Bartlett (1990) cites constructions such as *This shirt needs washed* as being found in Southland, and as far north as Oamaru. He also comments on the existence of non-contracted forms of *not* in Southland, as in *You'll not manage it*.

8.6.3 Vocabulary

It is in vocabulary that most of the regional dialectal variation in New Zealand is found. The best-known example is *bach* 'holiday cottage' which is replaced by *crib* in Otago and Southland. And in the North Island, strawberries come in a *punnet*, while in the South Island, they come (or used to) in a *pottle*. Orsman (1980: 41) cites the fish-name *groper*, which is the Wellington term, but is termed a *hapuka* in Auckland and a *harbooker* in Marlborough. Gordon & Deverson (1985) cite *polony* as being the name for a saveloy in Auckland, but not in Christchurch (as does Turner 1966: 137), and *half-G*, *flagon* and *peter* as being regional names for a half-gallon refillable container for beer. Citing Durkin

(1972) again, they also mention terms such as *barber* 'a cutting wind', *bungy* 'punga', *crib* 'cut lunch' and *taipo* 'weta' as being words restricted to the West Coast. A bus *section* in Wellington corresponds to a *zone* in Dunedin.

8.6.4 The Australian connection again

Interestingly enough, some of the isoglosses distinguishing New Zealand English regional dialects cross the Tasman into Australia. Turner (1972: 137) comments that the construction *boy of O'Brien* is also found in Newcastle, New South Wales. *Crib* is also found meaning 'lunch' in Australia. Small red-skinned sausages are called *cheerios* in New Zealand, as they are in Queensland, but not elsewhere in Australia (Bryant 1989). *Polony*, mentioned above as an Auckland word, is also found in Western Australia (Bryant 1989). *Slater*, which is a widespread New Zealand English word, though originally from the South Island, is also found in New South Wales (Turner 1972: 137). *Blood nose* 'nose bleed' is normal in New Zealand, but restricted to Victoria and South Australia in Australia (Bryant 1989). New Zealand can thus be seen as part of a larger Australasian dialect area in more ways than just sharing vocabulary with Australia.

8.7 Maori English

There is generally assumed to be an ethnic dialect of English in New Zealand, which is called Maori English. This label is appropriate only if it is recognised that it is a stereotype. Many of those who speak this variety are Maori. However, not all Maoris speak this variety, and not everyone who speaks this variety is Maori. It is perhaps better described as a social dialect of New Zealand English, one of whose functions is to indicate solidarity with Maoris and/or their aspirations. Having said that, it should be noted that it is generally taken to be a contact variety of English, its form caused in part by the structure of Maori.

I have spoken of Maori English as being 'a variety', but very little is currently known about it, and there may in fact be several varieties involved. The label usually implies a variety belonging to a fairly low social class, and that is the variety I shall attempt to describe here, although it must be recognised that some middle-class Maoris have a pronunciation which retains some features of the variety described below.

8.7.1 Pronunciation

Maori English is most easily recognised by its pronunciation, in particular by the voice quality and the rhythm. The rhythm is more syllable-timed than that of other varieties of New Zealand English, with more full vowels in unstressed syllables.

Where segmental pronunciation is concerned, Benton (1966) comments that Maori schoolchildren in the early 1960s tended to merge /d/ and /ð/, /t/ and /θ/, and /s/ and /z/. All of these would be explicable in terms of the structure of Maori. He also says that they tend to use an apical or palatalised ('somewhat shriller': Benton 1966: 70) /s/ rather than the normal New Zealand English quality. /k/ and /g/ were also merged by some children. Benton also comments (1966: 71) on the use of a monophthong for the GOAT vowel, saying that it is replaced by the Maori /ɔ/ (presumably, although he does not comment, the long vowel).

8.7.2 Grammar

Benton (1966) also draws attention to a number of grammatical constructions, which he found to be typical of Maori children in the early 1960s. Among others, these include the constructions illustrated in:

> (1) Who's your name?
> (2) We collected the fire-woods.
> (3) He asked me if I will go.
> (4) I wish we are going to town tomorrow.

Of these, (1) might simply be a developmental problem, since it is heard from children with no exposure to Maori as well as from Maori children, although it looks like a translation of the Maori construction. It is not clear to what extent the others (and others Benton lists) are really features of Maori English, although (2) almost certainly is. McCallum (1978) finds little evidence of grammatical features of Maori English, but suggests that the use of *went to* as a past-tense marker may be one.

In a more recent study, Jacob (1990) compared the speech of Maori and pakeha women of similar age, social class and regional origin. She found a number of grammatical features which distinguished the two groups of women. These include:

1   greater use of the (standard) past participles *come*, *seen*, *rung* and *been* as past-tense forms among the Maori than the pakeha women;

2   greater use of an *-s* inflection on present-tense verbs of persons other than the third singular among Maori than among pakeha women;

3   variable deletion of the *be* in the expression *be going to* among the Maori women, but categorical retention by the pakeha women;

4   deletion of auxiliary *have* in a wider range of contexts by Maori women than by pakeha women, and to a greater extent: for example, it was categorically deleted by the Maori women in *had better*, but categorically retained by the pakeha women in that context;

5   greater use of double negatives among the Maori women than among the pakeha women.

While this evidence is not necessarily conclusive, since the numbers involved are fairly small (always a problem when dealing with corpus-based research), and since Jacob herself points out that some of the data might be explained by other factors, none the less this is of very great interest in that it is the first hard evidence we have that Maori English is not simply a class dialect, but might be a genuine ethnic dialect. In another analysis of the same data, Allan (1990) finds that Maori women also use more high rise terminals than do pakeha women.

One grammatical point that has drawn quite a bit of attention recently is the use of Maori unmarked plurals. In Maori, plurality is marked on determiners, not on nouns. English does not consistently mark plurality on determiners, but there is a feeling that when a Maori noun is borrowed, it should not have a foreign plural marker imposed upon it. Speakers who use this feature frequently say, for example, that Maori believe something, or that Maori are taking certain actions. Despite the fact that this pattern is a minor one in English, and despite the fact that the pattern is not constructionally iconic, it has become remarkably pervasive in a short time in the speech of pakehas as well as Maoris.

8.7.3   *Vocabulary*

It may be that a greater amount of Maori vocabulary is found in Maori English than in other varieties of New Zealand English, but this is not clear. The amount of Maori vocabulary seems to be determined by the subject of conversation rather than by the dialect in which it is spoken. A few words, such as *kai* 'food', do seem to be associated with Maori English, but this is not a clear trend. Rather there seems to be a new Maori-influenced variety of New Zealand English emerging in print and in the broadcast media which uses a large amount of Maori vocabulary. While this variety is produced by Maoris and for Maoris, it is not Maori English as this is generally understood, since it is a variety with greater mana than normal Maori English, and because it need not be pronounced with the typical Maori English accent.

8.7.4   Other points

Benton (1991: 194) suggests that 'there are differences at the semantic and especially the metaphorical levels which neither Maori nor Pakeha interlocutors may recognise... The figurative codes... may be very different.' If this is the case, it may be a matter of culture rather than strictly a matter of language, although it may cause problems of communication just as easily as a 'purely' linguistic matter. However, Benton is attempting to define Maori English in the face of research findings which have consistently failed to find a distinctively Maori dialect. Perhaps the problem for him, as for others, is defining Maori English as the English spoken by Maoris rather than as that variety of English which is stereotypically spoken by Maoris, but not by all Maoris and not exclusively by Maoris.

Another point which needs to be considered is whether the variety of Maori English spoken by Maoris whose first language is Maori is distinct from the variety spoken by other Maoris. Benton (1966) makes passing comment on such matters, but I know of no other research in this area.

8.7.5   Directions

In a passage which has been cited earlier, in a different context, Benton (1966) comments with some surprise on the high rise terminal intonation used by Maori school children in the early 1960s. That intonation pattern, clearly unusual in 1963, is widespread throughout New Zealand today. This gives rise to an interesting possibility: does Maori English show something of the direction in which New Zealand English is likely to develop? The use of the tag question *eh?* is generally attributed to Maori and then Maori English, but is today a general feature of New Zealand English. The heavy use of the sentence adverbial *to me* is typical of Maori English, but is also quite common in pakeha varieties. The use of syllable-timing is more marked in Maori English than other varieties of New Zealand English, but also distinguishes New Zealand English from, say, RP. It seems likely, given that change usually comes from below (in Labov's terminology) that many of the features that are today attributed to Maori English will later become general features of New Zealand English; we just do not know which ones!

8.8 North American influence

During the Second World War, American forces in New Zealand discovered that, although they ostensibly spoke the same language as their hosts, they were not always understood. Among the words which could not be understood were *bouncer*, *closet*, *cookie*, *elevator*, *hardware* and *truck* (anon. 1944). Today, it is inconceivable that an American would not be understood in New Zealand because of using these words. Yet at the same time there exists in New Zealand (as in Britain) an anti-American linguistic chauvinism which is entirely surprising in the light of the general use in the community of a number of forms which are American in origin. It is not clear how widespread these attitudes are in the community, but the fact that they exist is shown by the following extracts from Letters to the Editor of New Zealand periodicals:

> Most of our worst grammatical or pronunciatory [*sic*] errors stem from America.
> (*The Listener*, 10 November 1973)

> Why don't we improve our English instead of adopting a worse speech from a culture which branched off from England several centuries ago?
> (*The Listener*, 25 November 1978)

> We are not Americans, and I know I for one do not like the way this country is trying to carbon copy itself with American influence.
> (*The Otago Daily Times*, 12 September 1984)

8.8.1 *Pronunciation*

There are a few words where what might be viewed as 'the American pronunciation' is standard in New Zealand English. The clearest of these cases is *vitamin*, pronounced with the PRICE vowel in the first syllable. In cases like *either* and *neither* pronounced with the FLEECE vowel in the first syllable, *ate* pronounced with the FACE vowel and *frustrate* stressed on the first syllable, the relevant pronunciations are not so widespread, and it is, in any case, more difficult to be sure that the influence is indeed American. In a case like *harass* /həˈræs/, a Scottish origin for the pronunciation is perhaps more likely than an American one, even though the relevant pronunciation is heard in the United States today. It seems to be an innovation there.

In other cases, the influence is more clearly American. *Schedule* with initial /sk/, *lieutenant* with initial /luː/ and the letter ʒ called /ziː/ appear to be increasing pronunciations in current New Zealand English, with younger speakers leading the way (see Bayard 1987, 1989). The sudden switch of the first vowel in *dynasty* from the KIT vowel to the PRICE vowel is directly attributable to the American television programme, and may disappear again in another few years.

Perhaps more surprising, especially given the negative attitudes towards Americans mentioned earlier, is the fact that, at least for younger speakers, an American accent appears to have high prestige. Bayard (1990a) reports that for university students a North American accent (Canadian, in this case) is ranked highly in terms of power, and the same is true for high-school students, for whom 'The North American accent ranks highest in terms of three of the four solidarity variables' as well.

8.8.2   Grammar

Where grammar is concerned, it is difficult to say whether or not there is direct influence from American on New Zealand English or not. However, there are several variables where the innovative form coincides with the American English form, so it would be naive not to allow for American influence. The following constructions are all regularly heard in New Zealand English, and follow an American rather than a British pattern:

> (5) The government has decided to seek arbitration.
> (6) The students protested the government's action.
> (7) The prisoner will appeal this decision.
> (8) Union leaders will meet with the prime minister.
> (9) I've gotten used to it now. (See Bauer 1987a, 1989c)
> (10) I only play on the weekend.

The pattern with singular concord in (5) is particularly interesting, in that it is prescribed by the main metropolitan dailies, and appears to be used by university students as a standard form (Bauer 1988). However, it is used less in sports reports, and also used less in Radio New Zealand's

Mana News programme, which is presented by Maoris for Maoris. There is thus *a priori* evidence that this feature acts as a sociolinguistic variable. Examples (6)–(8) all involve transitivity. The use of the preposition is the factor in question in (10) , although this might be better classed as lexis rather than grammar. There is an alternative New Zealand English pattern with *in* (Bauer 1989d).

8.8.3 *Vocabulary*

Again, the problem with vocabulary is showing direct American influence, but the following terms are widely used in New Zealand with their American meanings: *collect call*, *eraser*, *kerosene*, *movie*, *muffler* (for a car), (*potato*) *chip*, (*school*) *principal*, *stroller*, *truck*. The list is exemplificatory rather than exhaustive.

One interesting use of American vocabulary in New Zealand English is to provide high-style advertising terms. Given a pair such as *torch* and *flashlight*, the British version is the one most likely to be used in everyday speech, and the American one is likely to be used commercially, to make the product sound more appealing. Thus one would normally pull the *curtains*, but the shop might sell you *drapes*. Other pairs with a similar relationship are *lift*/*elevator*, *nappy*/*diaper* and possibly (although there may be a semantic distinction here) *biscuit*/*cookie*. Bayard (1989) comments on such pairs in some detail, pointing out that for younger speakers, the American member of such pairs, even if it is not widely used, is considered to be 'better' English (a term Bayard deliberately does not define more closely).

8.8.4 *Conclusion*

The evidence here suggests a great deal of linguistic insecurity, with Americanisms being both hated and loved (possibly by the same people!) at the same time. If copying is the sincerest form of flattery, Americans need not feel insulted by the diatribes that are occasionally unleashed against their language in public or in private. Bayard (1987, 1989) suggests that the acceptance factor is conditioned by the large number of American television programmes broadcast in New Zealand. This may or may not be correct. If it is, the amount of grammatical change that this has caused is surprising. In any case, this American influence is a relatively new phenomenon, dating from no earlier than the 1950s.

8.9   The origins of New Zealand English

Discussions of the origins of New Zealand English are closely tied to discussions of the origins of Australian English. Indeed, in most cases, the discussion is the same, and it is assumed that New Zealand English is merely a form of Australian English, and that the same general points apply. It is not obvious that this should be the case. Australia was settled much earlier than New Zealand, the original settlers of Australia were convicts rather than the upper-working-class settlers of New Zealand, and the first Australian settlers did not come from the same areas in Britain as the first settlers in New Zealand came from. In the discussion below, I shall therefore concentrate on the New Zealand perspective, although I shall inevitably consider literature written about Australian varieties of English as well.

8.9.1   *Australasian as Cockney*

Hammarström (1980) argues on the basis of the close analysis of the phonetic evidence (particularly the evidence provided by the vowels) that Australian English is an exported variety of eighteenth-century London English, the precursor of Cockney. In support of this claim he points out, for example, that one-third of the convicts in Australia before 1819 were from London (1980: 53). This gives rise to the possibility that New Zealand is a separate development from London English (in the New Zealand case, it would have to be nineteenth-century London English, though it is not clear how important a difference this is). Such an explanation of the origin of New Zealand English would explain the similarities between Australian and New Zealand pronunciation: they both have the same immediate ancestor. Differences between Australian and New Zealand English might be due to changes in London English in the period between the start of Australian settlement and the start of New Zealand settlement.

The evidence in favour of a claim of this kind would be provided by the kind of analysis Hammarström carried out for Australian English. It is a truism that Australasian vowel qualities sound Cockney to British speakers. While there are clear differences between present-day Cockney and present-day Australian and present-day New Zealand English, these are not necessarily greater than might have emerged since the varieties split with emigration from London. I shall not argue the case in any more detail, since a comparison of the material in section 8.2 above with a description of present-day Cockney will make the point. Cochrane (1989) argues the case again with reference to Australian English and much of what he says also applies to New Zealand English.

The evidence against this position as far as New Zealand is concerned is demographic. While large numbers of New Zealand immigrants in the early period of European settlement were from the south-east of England, including London, there is little, if any, evidence that they were Cockneys. Indeed, what we know of their social class suggests not only that they were not Cockneys, but that they would have despised a Cockney accent. In any case, there were large enough numbers of immigrants from the West Country, the Home Counties west of London, Scotland and Ireland for the overwhelming dominance of London assumed in this vision of the development of New Zealand English to seem extremely unlikely.

8.9.2 Australasian as East Anglian

Trudgill (1986: 134ff.) suggests that a careful comparison of the phonetic features of Australian English with those of dialects in England might suggest that the former had its origins in East Anglia rather than in London. He points out, for example, that Australian English, unlike London English, but like the English of (southern) East Anglia, retains /h/, has a front vowel in the START lexical set and /ə/ rather than /ɪ/ in the unstressed syllable of words like *hundred*. The same points could be made about New Zealand English. However, Trudgill does not wish to argue that Australian (or New Zealand) English actually comes from East Anglia.

> It is highly unlikely, however, that Australian English actually *came from* Essex, particularly since, as Bernard (1969) and others have shown, there was a heavy preponderance of Londoners in the early Botany Bay colony. Much more reasonable would be a supposition that Australian English is ... a mixed dialect, incorporating mainly London features but also including features from elsewhere in south-eastern England, including especially perhaps Essex.
>
> (Trudgill 1986: 136–7).

This introduces the next possibility, that Australasian varieties of English are mixed dialects, and this will be taken up immediately below. It is, however, worth asking whether similar cases could not be made for the influence of other areas of Britain on the basis of a different selection of phonetic or phonological features, such as the use of /æ/ in *dance*, *example* in much of Australia and earlier in New Zealand, the use of the high rise terminal, and so on. In either case, it does not seem that too much weight should be given to the notion that East Anglia is specifically implicated in the development of Australasian varieties of English.

8.9.3   *The mixing bowl theory*

The preferred theory about the origins of both Australian and New Zealand English seems to be that they arise through dialect mixture. The idea behind this theory is that when speakers of a number of different varieties of (in this case) English are thrust together, a new mixed dialect emerges. This seems reasonable enough. What is perhaps in question is whether the different dialect mixes that went into the make-up of Australian and New Zealand English could produce such similar-sounding varieties.

Recall that large numbers of the early settlers in Australia were convicts from London. Whether the Australian English they spoke was simply a transplanted regional form of English, or whether it was a new mixed dialect, it appears to have been well enough established by the 1830s for the Irish immigrants who arrived at that period not to have had any great influence upon it. Bernard (1969: 65) makes the point that the fact that Tasmanian English is not demonstrably different from the English of New South Wales, despite the fact that no Irish convicts were sent to Tasmania, seems to demonstrate this conclusively. As has already been seen, New Zealand had large numbers of immigrants from Australia, from south-east and south-west England, from Scotland and from Ireland. Why should the mixture that these speakers produced resemble so much the mixture that arose in Australia?

This is the kind of question that Trudgill (1986) attempts to answer, but, as might be expected, the answer is not a simple one. He suggests that the features which are kept in a mixed dialect (he terms the setting up of such a dialect 'koineisation') are:

1   features to which people can accommodate easily; these tend to be

         (a) salient features, which are easily perceived, yet not judged to be too excessively marked;

(b) features which do not break any strong phonotactic constraints;

(c) features which are supported by orthography;

(d) features which do not impose great comprehension difficulties;

(e) features which involve phonetically 'natural' changes;

2 features which retain phonological contrasts; Trudgill is ambivalent about this point: on the one hand, speakers appear to avoid accommodations which involve making phonological mergers (1986: 17) and yet simplifications with mergers win out over distinctions in koineisation situations (1986: 105);

3 features which are not especially 'marked' in the context in which the koineisation is taking place.

Where the new koine retains variants from its input dialects, they may remain as socially determined variants, rather than dialectally determined variants.

This outline is, of course, an oversimplified version of Trudgill's discussion, but it provides sufficient background for some consideration of the claims with particular reference to New Zealand English.

First of all, consider what might have been thought 'marked in the context of the koineisation' in nineteenth-century New Zealand. The early comments we have, for example those from Samuel McBurney, suggest that people were pleased with the 'purity' of the English heard in New Zealand. The term 'pure' really signifies no more than people liked what they heard, and yet the context in which such observations occur suggests that what they like is the lack of 'barbarous' forms from the north of England. In such a context, it seems reasonable to suppose that a merger of /ʌ/ and /ʊ/ would have been excessively marked, and that in general there was an attitudinal bias in favour of variants which sounded as though they might come from the south-east of England. This may be the source of what Lass (1990) refers to as the 'swamping' of northern and western features by southern and eastern ones (see below).

The use of a voiced form for intervocalic /t/, especially in words like *beauty* used as an expression of approval, is explained by the change involved being a natural one, and the form being salient, and in one of the input dialects (south-western dialects, at least). The retention of [th] as a prestige form shows that forms from different input dialects can be retained as socially differentiated forms, as Trudgill argues. The rarity of an alternative variant, [ʔ], a widespread variant in south-east England, is not, however, explained. The lack of this in New Zealand English may be due to the fact that it is an innovation in the south-east of England, post-dating the establishment of the southern hemisphere colonies (Trudgill 1986: 131–2). However, this does not account for the fact that [ʔ] is now increasingly found in New Zealand English as a variant of /t/ (Bayard 1990b). This variant presumably has to be explained as a later borrowing from British English, imported by the twentieth-century immigrants, or copied from British television shows and popular songs.

But this hypothesis seems incapable of explaining the lack of non-prevocalic /r/ in standard New Zealand English. Recall that many of the nineteenth-century British immigrants came from rural areas west of London, that there were large numbers of Scots and Irish immigrants, and it seems likely that most of the speakers making up the early waves of settlers spoke rhotic varieties. Non-prevocalic /r/ cannot, then, have been a particularly marked feature of the early years of European settlement in New Zealand. Furthermore, it is supported by the orthography, which (nearly) always marks non-prevocalic /r/, and it is a salient difference between south-eastern English varieties and others. Loss of non-prevocalic /r/ can also give rise to a number of mergers which might be considered undesirable, such as *flaw* and *floor*, *sauce* and *source*, *baa* and *bar*. Trudgill (1986: 16) suggests that /r/ is lost in the mixed variety because there is a strong phonotactic constraint against /r/ except before a vowel for non-rhotic speakers; but this is not sufficient explanation. There is plenty of anecdotal evidence to support the notion that /r/-less English speakers visiting Scotland or the United States pick up /r/ more quickly than /r/-ful Scots or Americans visiting England (Australia, New Zealand) lose it. /r/-ful English is comprehensible to non-rhotic speakers, while /r/-less English is not always comprehensible to rhotic speakers. My own English becomes rhotic the moment I get north of Berwick-on-Tweed, and I have heard non-rhotic speakers who have visited the United States say that they had to learn to pronounce /r/ in order to be understood. We have McBurney's evidence that the whole of the South Island was (at least partly) rhotic in the 1860s, and that rhotacism could be heard in the North Island. Such gross loss of rhotacism is not, it seems to me, easily explained by the mixed dialect hypothesis. To explain this feature, we need a particularly strong form of 'swamping' (Lass, 1990) which obliterates non-southeastern forms in mixed dialects despite their prevalence in the input dialects. Such a phenomenon requires further explanation.

There is also some grammatical data which are not easily explained by the mixed dialect hypothesis. Trudgill (1986: 98ff.) suggests that levelling and simplification are typical of mixed dialect situations. In another passage (1986: 147) he suggests that the use of the regular past tenses of verbs such as *burn, lean, smell* in American English are the result of such levelling. That being the case, it has to be explained why such verbs retain the irregular forms *burnt, leant, smelt* in New Zealand English (Bauer 1987a). It would surely be expected that they would also be levelled in New Zealand English if that arose as a result of the same pressures as American English. Furthermore, in the case of the past participle of *prove*, New Zealand English uses the minority irregular form *proven* more than the regular *proved* despite the fact that the majority of the supposed input dialects must have had *proved*. 'Swamping' appears not to have worked uniformly in these cases, though Lass (1990) predicts this pattern.

While it must be admitted that New Zealand English does have levelled grammatical forms in other constructions, such as the preference for *She didn't used to read science-fiction* as opposed to *She used not to read science-fiction* (see Trudgill 1986: 147; Bauer 1989b), these may not come from the same source.

In summary, although dialect mixture might explain much about the form of New Zealand English there are some awkward forms which are not easily explained. Lass' 'Law of Swamping' might help these explanations, though it is perhaps worth commenting that the Law itself (that mixed dialects tend to prefer south-eastern forms) requires explanation.

8.9.4 New Zealand English as Australian

In this section, I shall suggest that the most likely origin of New Zealand English is as an exported variety of Australian English. There are a couple of obvious phonological difficulties with this hypothesis, which I shall have to explain. Perhaps more importantly, it is politically not a very welcome message in New Zealand. I shall thus try to present this material in a suitably tentative manner.

The first piece of evidence in favour of my hypothesis is the overwhelming phonetic and phonological similarity of Australian and New Zealand English. While these can be distinguished, many outsiders regularly fail to distinguish them, and even within New Zealand an Australian accent is not invariably picked up. While New Zealanders say they can always tell an Australian, I have spoken to Australians in New Zealand who say that they are not always (or even usually) identified as such. Bayard (1990a) comments that half of his high-school informants 'took the Australian as a New Zealander', and that percentage is indicative, even if one would expect adults to make fewer errors. While there are alternative explanations for the similarities, direct line of descent would certainly provide an explanation for it.

The difficulty with this hypothesis would not be the undeniable similarities, but the equally undeniable differences between Australian and New Zealand English pronunciations. In particular, the lack of the centralisation of the KIT vowel in Australian English, the different pattern of neutralisation before /l/ and lexical differences such as the use of the TRAP vowel in words like *example* in Australian English need to be explained.

There is some recent evidence that the KIT vowel in Australian English is becoming centralised as it is in New Zealand English, at least in Sydney (Bradley 1989: 265). It might thus be that both dialects are developing in similar directions, but that New Zealand is further down the track than Australian English.

The pattern of neutralisation before /l/ is interesting, since most of the neutralisations that are found in New Zealand English can also be found in Australian English but not in the same place. Thus Melbourne speakers tend to neutralise the DRESS and TRAP vowels before /l/, and Adelaide speakers tend to use a back vowel for the GOOSE vowel before /l/, while Sydney speakers neutralise the FOOT and GOOSE vowels before /l/ (Bradley 1989). All these features are found together in New Zealand English. There are several possible reasons for this, such as a mixing of Australian dialects in New Zealand, or again the hypothesis that the two varieties are changing at different speeds. Note that similar, though not identical, patterns of neutralisation before /l/ are also found in London English. Such neutralisation seems to be a natural concomitant of /l/-vocalisation.

Where the lexical choice of the TRAP or the START vowel in words like *example* is concerned, there is really nothing to explain. Both varieties are found in Australia, both are (or were until very recently) found in New Zealand. The New Zealand English selection of the START variant as standard is presumably related to the perception of England as 'Home' in the earlier years of this century, and the number of immigrants from areas of Britain where /æ/ had been lengthened in the appropriate environment. If it is true that the TRAP pronunciation lasted longer in Southland than elsewhere (Orsman 1966), this could be accounted for by the Scottish influence on the Southland dialect that we have seen elsewhere.

The second argument in favour of the hypothesis that New Zealand English is derived from Australian is the demographic one. New Zealand was first settled by Europeans from Australia. There always has been, and still is, close contact between Australia and New Zealand, in all kinds of trade, from the early trade in flax, through gold, to the present period of CER (Closer Economic Relations) and tourism. Recall that at one stage areas of New Zealand could communicate more easily with Australia than with other parts of New Zealand. Recall, too, that as well as the large numbers of Australian immigrants into New Zealand who show up in the immigration figures, there must have been others who came from Britain via Australia. The influence of Australia in all walks of life is ubiquitous in New Zealand.

The next argument is a linguistic one, based on vocabulary. The number of words which Australia and New Zealand share – virtually to the exclusion of the rest of the English-speaking world – is astounding if the two varieties have independent origins. The shared vocabulary is explained if New Zealand English is, in origin, a variety of Australian English. In particular, note that much of the shared vocabulary tends to be early vocabulary, and thus not easily explicable in terms of long coexistence. Words such as *cobber* seem to have appeared in New Zealand virtually as soon as they appeared in Australia (there are only three years' difference between the first dates given by the *AND* and the files for the forthcoming *Dictionary of New Zealand English*), while more recent words like *warrant of fitness* still divide the two countries. Gordon & Deverson (1985: 32) comment explicitly that 'The majority of Australasian terms were current in Australia first, spreading from the older to the younger colony in the 19th century.'

Where grammar is concerned, finally, it was pointed out earlier that there are some places where New Zealand English does seem to have some simplified grammar, such as might be expected from a mixed dialect. The example given there was the construction *NP didn't use(d) to V*. The use of *do*-support here is the preferred usage in Australian as well as in New Zealand English (Collins 1981: 27), and so the patterns found would still be compatible with the notion that the latter had its origins in the former.

8.9.5   *Conclusion*

If New Zealand is, in origin, a variety of Australian English, then the ultimate origins of New Zealand English remain obscure: is it a transported version of London English, a mixed dialect formed on British soil, or a mixed dialect formed in Australia? However, from the New Zealand point of view, the questions became of less immediate importance. This depends, though, on the arguments above being accepted. I do not believe that the arguments are cut and dried, but it does seem to me that, in the current state of our knowledge, the hypothesis that New Zealand English is derived from Australian English is the one which explains most about the linguistic situation in New Zealand.

FURTHER READING

The best general introduction to New Zealand English is Gordon & Deverson (1985), which is aimed primarily at secondary-school pupils in New Zealand. Its style is approachable, and it is not too technical, but it does contain some material that is not specifically restricted to New Zealand English. A good bibliography of writings is Deverson (1988), with addenda in subsequent editions of the *New Zealand English Newsletter*. The *New Zealand English Newsletter* provides a forum for discussion of various facets of New Zealand English. Most of the articles in it assume little background in linguistic studies. An older general study is Turner (1966), which views New Zealand English in the context of Australian English. It is now rather out of date.

The best general coverage of the phonetics and phonology can be found in Bauer (1986), although the present article provides slightly more up-to-date opinions in a few areas. Bauer (1986), in effect, provides a summary of work done on the pronunciation of New Zealand English up to about 1985. The most significant article since then is Gordon & Maclagan (1989). For an early study of pronunciation see Bennett (1943).

On attitudes to New Zealand English pronunciation and its development as shown by reports from educationalists, see Gordon (1983) and Gordon & Deverson (1989). More recent attitudes are discussed in Bayard (1989; 1990a), Holmes & Bell (1990). For an analysis of New Zealand English pronunciation in Labovian terms, see Bayard (1987), and subsequent publications.

A number of articles of mine provide the only detailed discussion of New Zealand English grammar, with Bauer (1987b) providing a non-technical overview. Kuiper (1990) makes some further suggestions, and hints at a fascinating distinction between real New Zealand English and its fictional portrayal. The same is possibly true of Maori English. The passage below, for example, seems to represent a fictional pidginised variety of English. It does not sound like a true representation of current Maori English (though earlier contact varieties might have been like this), even though it contains features (such as lack of third-person verbal concord) which do occur in Maori English:

> The horse gets a very big fright. My brother fly out in the air you see, because of the big kehua make his horse very wild. And down, down, and splash in the small water. And bang. His head break on that rock there with a big kehua on it. My poor brother, ka pakaru te upoko. (Grace 1986: 56)

Where vocabulary is concerned, the forthcoming *Dictionary of New Zealand English* will provide the first thorough coverage, and will allow careful comparison with Australian English vocabulary. Currently there are three pocket New Zealand dictionaries, all of which are overseas dictionaries with New Zealand material edited in. In my opinion, the best of these for its New Zealand content, as well as the earliest, is Orsman (1979). Gordon (1982) and Burchfield (1986) provide slightly different coverage. There are also some more popular publications, such as McGill (1988, 1989). For an early study of New Zealand English vocabulary, see Baker (1941).

On the American influence on New Zealand English see in particular Bayard (1987, 1989).

For papers on the sociolinguistic situation in New Zealand, see Bell & Holmes (1990). There is quite a large literature on the pragmatic use of language in New Zealand (in a number of papers by Holmes) and in the use of language in particular professional contexts, such as auctioneering and horse-racing commentaries (in a number of papers by Kuiper and his associates), but this is not of direct relevance to the subject of the history of English in New Zealand.

William Branford

9.1 Introduction

The sociohistorical context of English in South Africa differs in important ways from those of English in Australia and New Zealand. There are similarities, for instance that all three originated in the English of emigrant communities speaking several different dialects; but there are major differences too.

From 1795 onwards, the first British soldiers and later settlers at the Cape moved into a long-established 'white' community with its own language and its own powerful traditions and dynamics. Beyond this 'white' community – the 'Cape Dutch' – and indeed merging into it, were the original occupants of the subcontinent: the Khoisan peoples who had already lost their ancestral lands in the south to the Dutch and beyond them the black nations whose lands and destinies were to fall under white control during the next century. English thus moved into an already established symbiosis of languages and communities.

The South African Dutch culture of the eighteenth century flowered in the Trekker republics of the nineteenth and became the dominating Afrikanerdom of the twentieth. Much that is characteristic of South African English can be traced to the language and culture of the South African Dutch and their descendants, though there is of course a basic distinction between 'Afrikaans English' (a second language), and South African English (hereafter SAfrE), a mother tongue.

The Black and Khoisan peoples survived conquest in very large numbers (if we count some of the present 'coloured' population as descendants of the Khoi). 'Black Power', through the twentieth century, has gathered impressive strength. Khoisan and, later, Black ('Bantu') languages have from early times provided an important input to South African English. The Black press and Black literature are growth points for all English-speaking South Africans.

The 'contact languages' have strongly influenced the vocabulary of South African English and (to a lesser degree) its phonology and the syntax of informal styles. The weight of this influence is a matter of some dispute.

Lass & Wright (1986: 203) suggest that 'The normal condition for a language system is to be a self-contained structural network.' This does not seem to fit the case of South African English which appears to reflect the interpenetration between L1 and L2 varieties, the extent of speaker/hearers' experience of other languages and of their own, spoken by bilinguals of varying competence.

More appropriate is the kind of perspective that Le Page (1968) has established for English in the Caribbean, and the viewpoint of Hudson (1980: 13) that there are 'reasons for questioning the view that languages are discrete, identifiable entities', and that 'There is no such thing as a homogeneous grammar, whether for an individual or community, but that a speaker makes extraordinarily subtle use of the variability available to him in order to locate himself in society' (*ibid.*, 20).

The persuasive theory of Lass & Wright will be reconsidered in section 9.4. But particular patterns in the syntax and phonology of South African English can in many cases be traced to a possible *convergence* of influences, on the one hand from immigrant dialects, such as Scottish, and on the other from the contact languages, notably Dutch/Afrikaans.

South African English, however, has not been built up by a simple additive process of borrowed items and tendencies: whatever is 'borrowed' into a linguistic system becomes part of that system and takes on values of its own.

Thus the South African accent, though its phonology contains elements traceable to particular dialects of English and contact languages, is clearly distinguishable from that of other 'transplanted' Englishes and reflects a unique system or rather cluster of systems.

In the same way the vocabulary has undergone major transformations, as will be shown for some complex words (e.g. *comrade, location, springbok*) and for entire subsystems, for example the designations of 'peoples' as between 1795 and 1990. These transformations have been 'English' processes, though South African English can never be satisfactorily studied out of the context of its symbiosis with the other languages of the subcontinent.

This symbiosis is reflected most clearly in the vocabulary. It is, indeed, the vocabulary of South African English that distinguishes it most clearly from that of other 'transplanted' varieties.

A few historic words, such as *apartheid*, *Boer*, *trek* and *veld*, have, as it were, a special symbolic resonance and weight. This prompts a line of enquiry which will be touched upon in this chapter, suggested by two remarks by Basil Bernstein:

1   The real world is to a large extent built up on the language habits of the group (Bernstein 1973: 142).
2   Embedded in a culture or subculture may be a basic organising concept, theme or themes, whose ramifications may be diffused through the culture or subculture (*ibid.*, 184).

Two such themes in South African language and culture can be suggested by *apartheid* on the one hand and *the struggle* of resistance movements on the other. It is, however, important to guard against the views that

1   South African English is all about politics and oppression.
2   There is one kind of South African English or a single culture for all mother-tongue speakers of English in South Africa.

Alexander (1990: 139) claims indeed that 'in the political and cultural sense there is no nation in South Africa'. This is an extreme view. It illustrates, nevertheless, how the major challenge to the historian even of 'white' South African English is just the remarkable diversity of attitudes, viewpoints and subcultures which it encodes.

9.1.1   Historical landmarks

A thumbnail sketch of South African history since the first Dutch settlement may be useful at this point. For fuller treatments see Walker (1928), Davenport (1980), Peires (1981) and Maylam (1986). Six 'periods' can be fairly clearly demarcated.

Beginnings to 1795. The Dutch East India Company's settlement at the Cape was established in 1652 and reinforced in 1658 by the first contingent of African slaves and in 1688–9 by a small group of French

Huguenot refugees. By 1795 the Company claimed control of an area of about 170,000 square kilometres, most of it held in fact by a small and widely dispersed Dutch population.

Along the eastern border Dutch frontiersmen were already in contact with the 'Caffres', that is, the AmaXhosa, a branch of the Nguni-speaking group which includes the Zulu and Swazi peoples. Contact with people of the Sotho-Tswana groups north and east of the Colony had been relatively slight.

Within the Colony, the original Khoikhoi population ('Hottentots') had for the most part by 1795 been reduced to servitude or near-servitude, though the 'Bosjemans, or Wild Hottentots' (Somerville in Bradlow 1979: 25) still held out in desert or mountain areas against successive *strafcommandos* ('punitive expeditions').

Between white frontiersmen and the authorities at the Cape there was, by 1795, considerable tension, particularly over the treatment of indigenous peoples. There was already a considerable body of writings in English on the Cape.

1795–1838. This period spans the British occupation of the Cape from 1795 (with a brief return to Dutch control in 1803–6); the arrival of the English 1820 settlers, frontier warfare with the AmaXhosa, the emancipation of the slaves and the resultant exodus of Boer frontiersmen and others northwards and eastwards known later as the Great Trek.

The Cape Colony 'Population Return for 1818' (Bird 1823: 107) reflects roughly 43,000 'inhabitants' (including 1,900 'free blacks'), 23,000 Hottentots, 1,300 'apprentices' and 32,000 slaves, a total of about 101,000. (*Inhabitants* seems normally to have meant 'whites'.) Perhaps 5,000 of the 'inhabitants' at the time were English-speaking (Watts 1976: 42).

In 1820 the English-speaking population was roughly doubled when between four and five thousand 'settlers' were helped by the British government to establish themselves in the Eastern Cape. This brought up the total of mother-tongue speakers of English permanently resident at the Cape to about 10,000 at a time when there were perhaps 35,000 Dutch-speaking whites (Watts 1976: 43–4).

1839–69. The economy remained largely agricultural. This is the period of the foundation of the 'Dutch' Republics of Natalia, the Orange Free State and Transvaal, and in these of what might be called the *Volksraad* style of government. Article 9 of the Transvaal Constitution (1858) states explicitly: 'The people will permit no equality between coloured people and the white inhabitants, either in Church or State. "Het volk wil geene gelijkstelling van gekleurden met blancken ingezetenen toestaan, noch in Kerk noch in Staat"' (Eybers 1918: 364). A small English settlement in Natal dates back to 1824. In 1843 the British annexed the short-lived Dutch republic of Natalia, from which many Trekkers moved further north. In 1849–51, between four and five thousand British immigrants settled in Natal: 'They were drawn largely from the middle or upper-middle classes, and the Midlands, Yorkshire and Lancashire regions were strongly represented' (Norton 1983: 5). In 1860 the first indentured Indians were brought in to work the sugar plantations in Natal, and the Indian population has since increased steadily.

1870–1910. This period spans the mineral/industrial revolution associated with the discovery of diamonds and later gold which doubled the white population. In 1867, the year of the discovery of the first South African diamond, whites numbered about 330,000 with perhaps 65,000 speakers of English as L1 (Watts 1976: 42–3). It has been calculated that the 'mineral revolution', whose great foci were Johannesburg and Kimberley, brought over 400,000 immigrants to South Africa between 1875 and 1904.

Tensions between British and Transvaal authorities built up gradually. The first Anglo-Boer war (1881–2) left the Transvaal Republic independent, but disputes over Transvaal citizenship for white immigrants led ultimately to a second war (1899–1902), followed by the consolidation of former 'Dutch' Republics and 'English' colonies into the Union of South Africa (1910).

This period also saw the final subjugation of most of the African peoples and the beginnings of passive resistance by the Natal Indian Congress and other bodies. The step-by-step transference to white ownership and control of the ancestral lands of the African peoples relegated most Blacks to *locations* and *reserves*, which by 1913 had been reduced to about 13 per cent of the Union's territory. Blacks had little or no part in national (or municipal) decision-making.

1910–48. This period was one of steady economic and population growth: of Anglo-Afrikaner co-operation in the establishment of many of the basic institutions of the 'apartheid society' which followed it, the rise of the African National Congress, the consolidation of the National

Party as a party of the Afrikaner people, and of South African participation in the First and Second World Wars.

1948–89. This period saw further economic and population growth; the election victory in 1948 of the National Party, which has governed the country ever since; removal of 'coloured' voters from the common roll; secession from the Commonwealth; the renaming of 'apartheid' as 'separate development' and the attempt to establish for the African people *homelands*, some of which became 'independent'. South African forces became involved in long and costly operations against guerrilla forces in Namibia and elsewhere.

'The struggle' – resistance, initially passive, to white supremacy by the African National Congress and other bodies, notably the Pan-Africanist and Black Consciousness movements, despite 'bannings' and worse – gathered steady momentum. The Soweto uprising of 1976 was only one of many surges of black 'unrest'. 'The armed struggle' – sabotage and occasional attacks on civilian targets – was initiated by the military wing of the African National Congress, *Umkhonto we Sizwe*, 'spear of the people', familiarly 'MK' in the Black press.

The 1980s brought, nevertheless, some substantial moves towards desegregation and a more integrated society, for instance in some areas of industry, public and corporate life, and in the opening of a number of 'private' schools to all races. The year 1985 saw the first Tricameral Parliament, with separate houses for 'coloureds', Indians and whites, in which Africans remained unrepresented.

The new stance of the government of F. W. de Klerk, the 'un-banning' of the African National Congress early in 1990, Namibian independence and the release of Nelson Mandela and other political prisoners have initiated political processes whose consequences cannot at present be foreseen.

At the beginning of this century there were four major English-speaking groups in South Africa. There were the 'English' of Cape Town and the Western Cape, many with close contacts with bilingual 'Dutch' families; the largely rural community of the Eastern Cape inland of Port Elizabeth and East London; the 'Natal English'; and the English of the cosmopolitan mining and industrial centres of the Transvaal. This last group came from many parts of Britain, notably Ireland and Cornwall, and included refugees from eastern Europe with strong traditions of Yiddish.

The 1820 settlers had come from several dialect areas: nearly 1,900 from London and its environs, over 450 from Ireland and over 300 from Lancashire and Yorkshire (Morse Jones 1969 [1971]: 5–6). In the period 1819–20, about 300 came from Scotland. Scots were influential out of proportion to their original numbers; they were later recruited both as schoolmasters and from the Church of Scotland as ministers of religion for the Dutch Reformed Church. Nearly a century later A. G. Kidd (1910: 157) was to remark: 'As there are so many Scotch teachers in South Africa their influence must affect in time the average of English pronunciation.' A small sidelight on this is that a number of early borrowings into Xhosa (e.g. *tichela* for *teacher*) show traces of an original with post-vocalic /r/, possibly Scottish (J. S. Claughton, personal communication).

The 1820 settlers were of mixed social background. Pringle (1835 [1966]: 13) remarks: 'I should say that probably about a third part were persons of real respectability of character ... but that the remaining two-thirds were for the most part composed of individuals of a very unpromising description – persons who had hung loose upon society.' Given the operation of English justice about this time, the lower levels of settlers as described by Pringle may have differed but little, in point of social origin, from many of the Australian convict population. Lanham & MacDonald (1979) trace certain prestige variables in South African English pronunciation to Natal origins, though the so-called 'private schools accent' is a class manifestation with several points of origin. The general mobility of the South African population has done much to obscure regional differences.

9.1.2   Languages in government and education

Until 1795 the language at the Cape both of government and of such education as was given was naturally Dutch. Early British governors interfered only mildly with the *status quo*, but in 1822, a proclamation decreed *inter alia* that from 1 January 1827: 'The English Language be exclusively used in all Judicial Acts and Proceedings either in the Superior or Inferior Courts in this colony' (cited in Eybers 1918: 23). This was repealed just in time, on 13 December 1826.

For the complex history of later discrimination by British authorities against Dutch in the 'colonies' and by the Republican authorities against British in the Transvaal the reader should consult Malherbe

(1925, 1977). There, were, however, many counter-currents of 'openness'. Thus one of the principal Transvaal newspapers, *Die Volkstem* ('Voice of the people') was for many years bilingual, and English teaching in much of the Free State was of a high standard for several generations.

The Act of Union (1910) laid down in an entrenched clause that 'Both the English and Dutch languages shall be the official languages of the Union, and shall be treated on a footing of equality and possess and enjoy equal freedom, rights and privileges.' 'Afrikaans' replaced 'Dutch' in this clause in 1925. There is no reference in the Act to African languages.

The distancing of Afrikaans from Dutch and the conversion of Afrikaans from a language of 'hearth and home' to one fully capable of satisfying the requirements of a modernised society are largely beyond the scope of this chapter (but see also section 9.5.2). So is the enforced use of the Afrikaans medium in African schools (since abandoned) which was a major cause of the Soweto uprising of 1976.

From quite early in the century most white children learned both English and Dutch or Afrikaans as school subjects, though it was only in 1946 that both became compulsory examination subjects in the Transvaal.

From 1911 onwards there was strong support by government for dual-medium instruction in 'white' schools. Malherbe (1966: 15) notes that in the Cape in 1924 the media of instruction were Afrikaans for 27,000 children, English for 37,000 and both for 69,000. Of the dual-medium group, many are likely to have grown up as competent bilinguals.

The National Party victory of 1948 was followed by a long period of Afrikaner dominance in education, the phasing out of dual-medium instruction and an increasing shortage of English-speaking teachers in provincial schools (Malherbe 1966: 14–17). Thus schools have often provided even English-speaking children with more extensive exposure to Afrikaner teachers speaking English as L2 than to teachers whose L1 is English.

9.1.3 *Bilingualism and 'language gaps'*

The principal agent in language contact is the bilingual speaker (Weinreich 1953: 72), a key figure in the interpenetration of languages reflected in South African English. But *bilingual* in South Africa has typically meant 'bilingual in English and Afrikaans'. Shuring & Ellis (1987) estimate from census figures of 1980 that in that year 92 per cent of whites 'did not know' a Black language.

Census figures indicate a steady rise in the proportion of whites returning themselves as able to speak both English and Afrikaans. In 1918, for those over seven years of age this was 42 per cent, in 1936, 64 per cent, and in 1951, 73 per cent (Malherbe 1977: 33). Shuring & Ellis (1987) calculated from the census returns of 1980 that nearly 80 per cent of whites reported themselves able to read and write both English and Afrikaans.

Estimates of those claiming to use both languages at home vary considerably. In 1938 a survey involving over 18,000 white school pupils in three provinces indicated that 43 per cent were from homes 'bilingual in varying degrees' (Malherbe 1977: 57–9). Later, in a report on a stratified sample of 659 English-speaking informants, Watts (1976: 79) found that 'Fifty-eight percent said that they could speak Afrikaans "freely and fluently" while four-fifths said they could "personally understand it".' To the question 'State the language(s) most commonly spoken at home' in the census of 1970, 18 per cent of the white population responded 'Both Afrikaans and English'. (For further details see Malherbe 1977: 65–7.)

Intermarriage, furthermore, is often likely to produce competent bilinguals. On his 1976 survey, Watts reports that 'Fifty-two percent of the sample have Afrikaans-speaking close relatives or family members, while 36 % had Afrikaans-speaking ancestors' (Watts 1976: 78). Shared work and military experience – the latter in particular since the conscription measures of 1957 – have involved men of both language groups in months of close contact. While the 'social distance' between English and Afrikaners is often still considerable, many factors and situations have favoured the emergence of competent bilinguals in significant numbers.

9.1.4 *Population: English as minority language*

The figures of Bird and Watts quoted in section 9.1.1 suggest that after the settlement of 1820 speakers of English as L1 numbered about 10 per cent of the total population of the 'Colony'. For South Africa as a whole, this proportion seems to have remained fairly constant. An informed estimate of the total South African population for 1987, including 'homeland' citizens, is 35·2 million: African 26·3 million (74·7 per cent); Coloured 3·1 million (8·7 per cent); Indian 0·9 million (2·6 per cent) and White 4·9 million (14 per cent) (*Race Relations Survey*, 1987–8: 11). Of these, speakers of English as L1 probably number about 10 per cent (3·5 million). Unfortunately there are no reliable contemporary census data for languages. For the 'white' languages K. P. Prinsloo's extrapolation from the census data of 1980 gave 4·9 million for Afrikaans and 2·8 million for English in a 'total' population for that year of 24·5 million. This figure excludes several million African citizens of 'independent' homelands, and is ten years out of date.

Among those reporting English as their mother tongue in 1980, whites numbered about 1·76 million, 'coloureds' about 0·32 million and Indians 0·7 million, with about 77,000 Africans. Thus in 1990, of people calling themselves 'English-speaking South Africans' probably at least one in three is not 'white'. Rough estimates for 1988 for African languages in the Republic and its associated territories place Zulu first with 6·4 million speakers and Xhosa second with 6·2 million, though speakers of the languages of the Sotho-Tswana group together totalled 7 million.

9.2   The vocabulary: overview

9.2.1   *South African* English?

Let us first consider briefly which vocabulary items 'count' as South African English or not. Some critics of Branford (1978) and subsequent editions of her *Dictionary of South African English* (particularly Afrikaners) have complained that too many entries are for Afrikaans words which do not properly belong to South African *English*. But in the South African situation the borderlines between languages may not be easy to draw. Loanwords (e.g. *gaar* [xaːr], 'cooked' or, usually, 'not sober'), common in the English of many speakers, may be unintelligible to many others. Donaldson (1988) reports a similar problem in deciding which of many English loanwords used in Afrikaans count as *ingeburger* ('fully assimilated') or not. Some borrowings, of course, are nonce-words, others marginal.

Among loanwords in South African English, those most fully assimilated are probably items like *smous* ('pedlar', from South African Dutch). Such words

1 have a history of use in English over a long time and from many different sources: the Rhodes Dictionary Unit has 116 contexts for *smous* from eighty-four different texts, from 1786 ('a species of old-clothes men') to African writers of the 1980s;

2 are regularly used in English texts on their own, without glosses, (as is *smous*);

3 where appropriate, are regularly used with English affixes (e.g. *smouses* and *smousing*).

Smous, significantly, was not replaced by English *pedlar*, though their meanings are similar. As in many other cases, the established local word has here lived on and been fully assimilated into English; perhaps often as a kind of gesture of solidarity with speakers of Dutch/Afrikaans (cp. Trudgill 1983: 103).

It would serve no purpose to claim South African origin for words or senses that have become distinctively South African despite non-South African origin and use in other varieties. *Assegai* is from Berber *al-zagayah*, 'the spear', of which a reflex appears in Chaucer. *Bioscope* ('cinema') first appeared in Britain about 1901, but lived on in South African English long after it had vanished from British. *Dropper*, 'a batten stapled to fencing wires to keep them apart' (Baker 1966, cited in J. Branford 1987: 93) seems to have appeared almost simultaneously in Australia and South Africa about 1897 (Ramson 1988: 214; Silva & Walker 1976: 275). *Assegai*, *bioscope* and *dropper* are typical of words with special associations with South African experience which simply cannot be counted out of South African English.

Some more 'marginal' words are of major historical or social importance: for example, *amaphakathi*, the inner circle of councillors of a higher chief, the plural of Nguni *umphakathi* 'councillor'. This in South African English texts, usually glossed, dates back to 1829 or earlier. Modern African writers, such as Matshoba (1979), may use it unglossed. Its frequency and importance make it, perhaps, a 'marginal' item of South African 'English', though it is clearly beyond the fringe of what Murray might have called 'common words'.

Amaphakathi, incidentally, illustrates a general property of the vocabulary. This is the division, in almost every domain, between 'black' vocabulary and 'white'. Thousands of contemporary whites do not know *amaphakathi* and scores of other words of equal importance both in traditional and in more recent 'Black' culture, such as *impimpi* 'informer', *kwela-kwela* 'pirate taxi' and *sangoma* 'diviner'. Yet all four of these are in regular use in *English* contexts today, for example in the columns of the widely read *Drum*, *Pace*, and *Learn and Teach*. And they are known and actively used by a large number of speakers of English as L1.

Finally, examples in this text are not limited to the works of writers or speakers of South African birth. A treatment of 'South African English' which excluded, for example, Lady Anne Barnard, Thomas Pringle and Rudyard Kipling, would, as we have argued elsewhere (W. Branford 1976b; 1984) be excessively limiting.

9.2.2 Stereotypes and senses

The popular image of the vocabulary, as late as the 1970s, was highly selective. In 1970 the magazine *Personality* sponsored a competition for the Rhodes University Dictionary Project for the best list of 'South African' words submitted by a reader. This drew 166 entries from all parts of the country and mostly from whites. Sixteen words each occurred in thirty entries or more. These are as follows, with the number of competitors citing each one: *Ag* (39); *biltong* 'dried meat' (44); *braaivleis* 'barbecue' (66); *donga* 'dry watercourse' (33); *eina* 'ouch!' (33); *gogga* 'insect' (32); *ja* 'yes' (39); *koeksister*, a kind of doughnut (37); *kopje* 'small hill' (44); *lekker* 'nice' (49); *mealies* 'maize, Indian corn' (41); *ou* 'chap' (39); *spruit* 'stream' (33); *stoep* 'verandah' (56); *stompie* 'cigarette stub' (32); *vel(d)skoen* 'rough shoe' (45). The image is one of informality, *die lekker lewe* ('good living') and the great outdoors. There is not one 'sociopolitical' word in the list, not one item of 'township' vocabulary, not one reminder of the racial tensions and 'iron laws' which concern such writers as Brink, Fugard and Paton. In 1990, after the Angola, Namibia and Soweto experiences, the stereotype has probably changed, and work in progress will be testing this.

The real vocabulary is more diversified. This was shown in a study by John Walker, reported in W. Branford (1976a), of 1,006 items of relatively high frequency from the materials of the Rhodes dictionary project. Of these, predictably, most (868) were nouns or noun phrases; constituents of other kinds (e.g. adjectives and verbs) numbered 138.

For the 868 nouns and noun phrases there were 1,021 'significations' (roughly: senses). Thus 'nouns of multiple signification were relatively few' though later work has revealed more of the semantic complexity of words like *baas*, *boer*, *trek* and *veld*. Walker made a rough analysis of the senses in terms of semantic features. This began with the contrast of 'Abstract' (e.g. *apartheid*) vs 'Concrete' (*minedump*). 'Concrete' was subdivided into 'Non-living' (*backveld*) vs 'Living' (*wildebeest*), 'Non-living' into 'Natural' (*kloof*) vs 'Material culture' (*stoep*), 'Living' into 'Plant' and 'Animate' and 'Animate' into 'Non-human' (*springbok*) and 'Human' (*predikant*). Thus 'Non-Human' here implies 'Animate'. The results are summarised below:

Noun-significations: N=1021

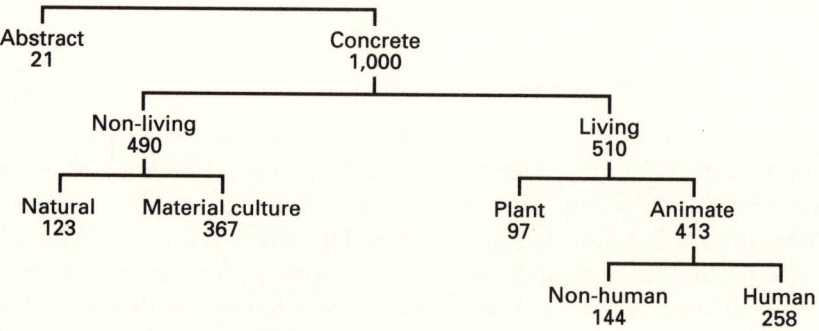

Some comments are called for:

1.   The analysis is of a sample of 'common words' only; it excludes specialised terminologies, such as those of botany, mining or traditional beer-drinking. Some of these terminologies are very large; thus Smith (1966) has over 6,500 entries, but few of these are 'common words' in Murray's sense.

2.   The exact figures are unimportant and would doubtless differ for a different sample or for different conventions of grouping.

3.   The picture does, however, contrast sharply with the popular stereotype of 1970, reflecting 'a very extended and diversified engagement of words with experience' (Branford 1976b: 313).

4.   Very few of the senses recorded are abstract, and about half of these are political, for instance *apartheid* and *separate development*. This point will be followed up in 9.5.2. Here it illustrates the dependence of South African English on the international standard for nearly all such terms as *equality, civil, faith, justice, privilege, right* and *truth* and the kinds of thinking they encode.

The materials of the Dictionary Unit include some citations recorded from speech but most are from printed sources. However, many words rare in print are common in speech. *Boy* and *Native*, for instance, for an African, disappeared many years ago from the press, but are still in common use (for example) among older East Cape speakers. There is as yet no adequate data-based study of the vocabulary of contemporary speech, and most of the everyday speech of the past is simply not recoverable.

9.2.3 Languages of origin

About half the present vocabulary of the South African component of South African English is of Dutch–Afrikaans origin. This proportion will vary between individuals and groups, but dictionary holdings present a fairly consistent picture. Two estimates follow, one based on 500 items chosen at random from Pettman's *Africanderisms* (1913) the other on 2,549 drafts in the holdings in 1988 of the *Dictionary of South African English on Historical Principles* (*DSAE:Hist.*) at Rhodes University. The second listing is of *all* items for which the Unit had at that time drafted entries. The normal criterion for inclusion as an entry in *DSAE:Hist.* is at least five contexts from different sources over a five-year period. On *Bantu* and *Sintu* see Note, p. 496.

	Languages of origin (%)	
	Africanderisms (1913)	*DSAE:Hist.* (1988)
Dutch–Afrikaans	50	48
English	28	29
Bantu	5	11
Other	17	12

Items of Khoisan origin were unfortunately counted only for *DSAE: Hist.*, in which they numbered just over 1 per cent (included among 'Other' in the tabulation above). The two estimates agree quite closely, though the proportion of items of Bantu-language origin has doubled between the 1913 and the 1988 samples.

For the 1988 sample only, numbers and percentages were calculated separately for each of the six 'periods' outlined in section 9.1.1. In table 9.1 N indicates the *number* of items for each period. The figures for each language or language group are *percentages* of this number. (These were rounded to the nearest integer, so do not always add up to 100. Thirty-

Table 9.1. *Languages of origin by period*

Period	N	Dutch/Afrikaans (%)	English (%)	Bantu (%)	Other/unknown (%)
Before 1795	(202)	64	23	—	13
1795–1838	(470)	52	21	15	10
1838–69	(219)	44	27	19	9
1870–1909	(456)	45	34	10	10
1910–47	(426)	53	25	7	14
1948–88	(776)	39	35	11	14

two Khoisan items are included under 'Other'. Nineteen of these appear first in the first two periods.)

Overall, the figures suggest a somewhat decreasing intake from Dutch–Afrikaans and a somewhat increasing proportion of items of English origin. But since items like *Bushman* (from Dutch *Bosjesman*) were counted as 'English', the Dutch–Afrikaans influence may be somewhat understated. For 1948–88 the proportions from Afrikaans and from English are nearly equal, which suggests a 'creative' thrust in the last half-century by English-speaking South Africans.

As between 1795–1869 and 1870–1947, there is a drop in the numbers (114 vs 77) as well as the percentages of new items of Bantu-language origin. This suggests, perhaps, an increasing 'social distance' between black and white from about 1870 onwards, with a movement into the more impersonal relations of city and industrial life and towards stricter segregation. It is as if by 1870 the 'white' vocabulary had absorbed most of the basic items of African-language origin that white speakers needed. But 1910–47 vs 1948–88 shows a reversal of this tendency; in 1948–88 the Bantu-language percentage rises from 7 to 11, and the number of new items from 31 to 83.

Of a total of 274 items of Bantu-language origin in the holdings, 76 per cent are of Nguni-language origin and 24 per cent from Sotho-Tswana. This may reflect data-gathering problems but clearly relates also to the longer, more intimate and better-documented contacts of English with Nguni-language speakers especially of Xhosa and of Zulu. The very small proportion of items of Khoisan origin reflects the early submergence of Khoisan cultures as such.

For items cited in later sections, the language of origin can be taken to be Dutch or Afrikaans except for obviously English items or unless another language of origin is specifically mentioned. The abbreviations used for languages of origin are listed on pages xxi–xxiii. Between 'Afrikaans' and South African Dutch there is of course a grey area. Only those 'Dutch' items of South African origin appearing in English before 1875 will be marked 'South African Dutch', e.g. '*Kloof* (1731; SAfrDu.)'. The year 1875 is chosen as cut-off point as the date of the manifesto of the Genootskap van Regte Afrikaanders (see section 9.4.3).

9.2.4   *'Domains', oppositions and themes*

The outline of the vocabulary that follows will sketch a series of 'domains' or topic areas, such as landscape and topography, 'peoples and tongues', 'some human types and relations'. Within each topic area there will be a rough division into subtopics, for instance for 'human types and relations' the language of solidarity, the language of master and servant, and phatic and formulaic items.

Within each subdivision a rough historical progression will be followed. The focus will usually be on 'common words'. There are brief discussions of a few 'major words', such as *boer*, *comrade*, and *veld*. Preference has also been given to 'active' rather than merely 'decorative' vocabulary used for special effects in literary texts.

A problem for the description of a vocabulary is the choice of unit of analysis. Alternative units might, for example, be 'period' or 'semantic field'. A 'period', for instance 1795–1838 (British occupation to Great Trek), is an unsatisfactory unit because domains overflow periods so that a description by periods runs the risks of repetition and of segmentation at the wrong points. 'Semantic field', on the other hand, is a limiting concept which means different things to different writers.

Domain has here the rough sense of 'topic area' or 'field of experience or activity', as in Baker (1966, e.g. 'the soil'; 'the bush'; 'the city yesterday') or J. Branford (1976) rather than the strict sociolinguistic senses outlined, for example, by Fishman (1972) or Downes (1984: 49).

Approach in terms of 'domains' in this informal sense will, it is hoped, show with reasonable clarity how some major themes of South African cultures and subcultures are encoded in the vocabulary (see Bernstein cited in section 9.1). Between and within domains there are frequently oppositions, often of an obvious kind, such as that of what Paton called 'the beloved country', to its desecration by soil erosion and overcrowding (the oppositions symbolised by *veld*, *donga* and *shackland*).

A second opposition might be symbolised by *apartheid*, once official, vs *the struggle* of the resistance vocabulary, a third perhaps by that of the *lekker lewe* ('living it up') to the counter-cultures to which the *lekker lewe* sometimes relates. These, of course, are 'givens' of experience, but reflected in substantial and contrasting clusters of vocabulary. An important set of contrasts involves the vocabulary of 'black' vs 'white' experience, e.g. of *struggle* to *separate development* (9.5.2).

For other themes it may be difficult to find adequate verbal labels or formulae. But granted the 'untidiness' of much of history and sometimes of language itself, too neat a thematisation will fail to capture important concepts and facts.

9.3   The beloved country

Stand unshod upon it, for the ground is holy   (Paton 1948 [1983]: 7)

This section will sketch the vocabularies of landscape (including some human modifications of the landscape as represented, for example, in *shackland*), of weather and 'living things'. South Africa has a wealth of kinds of terrain and of 'living things', and African, Afrikaans and English traditions agree on a certain reverence for these, reflected above in the epigraph from *Cry, the Beloved Country*. Only a brief sampling will be possible here.

Some basic items of the vocabulary of landscape and weather appear in English texts well before 1795. Medley (1731) has *kloof* 'deep valley or ravine' (SAfrDu.); *kraal*, an African or Khoikhoi village, later also an enclosure for farm animals (SAfrDu., from P *curral*) and *tablecloth* for the famous spread of clouds on Table Mountain. Somewhat later are *Karroo*, the semi-desert inland plateau of the Cape hinterland, or countryside of this type (1776, from Khoi); *krans* 'cliff' (1785) and *platteland*.

Many 'new' topographical words appear in English between 1795 and 1838. These include *berg* 'mountain' (1823); *bushveld* from SAfrDu. *bosveld* (1822); *dorp* 'small town' (1801); *drift* 'ford' (1795); *land* 'a cultivated field' (1815); *poort* 'narrow pass' (1796); *rand* 'ridge' (1822) and *veld* 'open country' (1835). Most of the basic topographical vocabulary is current in English by 1838 and most of it is of Dutch origin.

Platteland (1785, literally 'flat country'), is the first South African term for the 'outback' and has come to symbolise a mentality as well as a terrain (*This won't go down well on the platteland*). In the same set are *backveld*

(1905) 'back country', from Dutch *achterveld*. Pettman (1913: 42) glosses *backvelder* as 'a not very progressive class of farmer'. Others are *bundu* 'wild country', as in *dry river beds and trackless bundu* (Shona?, 1939), hence *bundu-bashing*, getting through rough country (cf. British *yomp*) and *Blikkiesdorp* (1970) 'the fictitious prototype of a dreary one-horse town' (J. Branford 1987: 31; *blikkies* are 'little tins').

One will be lucky to find even a Blikkiesdorp in the *gramadoelas* (1970) 'the wilds, the back of beyond', perhaps from Nguni *amaduli* ('hills'; J. Branford 1987: 121). This small set fulfils an important expressive need in South Africa and elsewhere.

With *Blikkiesdorp* we are close to the theme of man's desecration of the environment, and can thus comment briefly on *location*, *reserve* and the vocabulary of urbanisation. As in Australia (Ramson 1988: 372) a *location* was originally an area of land granted for settlement. Sophia Pigot notes in her *Journal* for 25 December 1820 'Went to mr Bailey's location for a dance.' But the word soon took on the sense of 'district set aside for blacks', as in 'The plan Government devised was to preserve the native distinct from the whites, and for this purpose large tracts of country were set aside, under the designation of '*locations*' for the natives' (Holden 1855: 176). Quite early, however, *location* began to take on its later sense of 'segregated urban area for blacks', so that by 1870 'A Lady' writes: 'About nine hundred of these poor people were then living at what is now called the 'Location' – a double row of huts and cottages, extending for nearly two miles out of town – and were almost in a state of barbarism' (Ross 1870 [1963]: 36). This sense and image of 'location' persists into the mid-twentieth century and beyond: 'the usual mess, the location, of sacking and paraffin tins' (Jacobson 1956: 12). Hence the gradual replacement of *location* by *township* (1934), which has a longer history in South Africa in its ordinary English sense.

Location and *township* are key members of the vocabulary of black urbanisation. Alongside officially recognised black 'townships' and sometimes far beyond them, are *shacklands*, usually squalid and sometimes of enormous extent. The *pondoks* (1801, 'hovel', perhaps Malay) of rural slums are replicated in many black townships but alongside many hectares of *matchboxes* (small uniform housing units but, unlike *pondoks*, usually brick). Population movement has changed many a *dorp* (Du. 'village; country town', 1801) into a city, and left many more dorps smaller than they were.

Bioscope ('cinema', 1908), not originally South African, lives on, particularly in the phrase *go to bioscope*. The *general dealer*, the smallish all-purpose country shop (1832) is steadily losing business to city hypermarkets and township *spaza shops* – small outlets often in Black peoples' private houses, perhaps from Zulu *isphaza*, counterfeit. The sharp contrast of black township and white suburb, the latter with its neatly separated *erfs* ('urban building lots', 1812) is one of the most vivid symbols of *apartheid*.

The period 1840–80 saw the creation on a large scale of *native reserves* as rural areas set apart for blacks: 'To segregate the black races from the whites is the whole object of the foundation of native reserves' (Goold-Adams 1936: 31). Since most reserves were too small for the populations crowded into them, they soon became areas of drastic soil erosion and of *dongas* ('dry watercourses', Ng. 1875). All this is in grim contrast to the traditions of the *veld* as national symbol.

Veld appears early in the Dutch record. Van Riebeeck (*Daghregister* for 1 March 1653) has 'met de beesten ende schapen in 't velt' ('with the oxen and sheep in the open country'). This reflects one of the major senses of *veld* in Dutch. A second is that of 'field of battle' (Van Dale 1904: 1730) and it is in this sense that it enters *Veld-Kornet*, and hence *Field Cornet* (see p. 464).

In the 'open country' sense *veld* appears on its own in English texts rather later than might be expected. Greig's *Cape Almanack* (1831) has for February: 'Farm: the field may be burnt, but it is late.' Steedman (1835 in Silva & Walker 1976: 837) has 'And here for the first time we bivouacked in what is called the Veld.'

Compounds like *bushveld* (1822), *sweetveld* (1812) and *zuurveld* 'sour veld' (1801) had appeared much earlier. Other compounds include, for example, *grassveld*, *Karroo veld* and *thornveld*, besides (for instance) *veldkos* 'food such as the veld may furnish' (J. Branford 1987: 395) for Bushman and other hunter–gatherers. *Veld* is an important place-name formative as in *Highveld* ('the Transvaal grasslands'). For fuller treatment see J. Branford (1987: 394–8).

Veld, moreover, has become a powerful poetic symbol, in texts ranging from Hardy's 'Drummer Hodge' (1899?)

> His landmark is a kopje-crest
> That breaks the veldt around

to Percival Gibbon 'The veldt' (1903?)

> Cast the window wider, Sonny,
> Let me see the veldt

and Roy Campbell's satirical *Veld Eclogue* (1930) on 'The witching whatdyecallum of the veld'.

The immense South African vocabulary of 'living things' can be only briefly sampled here. Branford (1988) has suggested that the processes by which explorers or settlers can build a vocabulary for the creatures of a 'new world' include:

1   transference of existing 'common' names from their L1 (analogy with the known);
2   descriptive terms reflecting appearance, habit or habitat;
3   borrowing indigenous vocabulary;
4   adopting scientific terms, such as *erica, protea, Watsonia*.

Existing names, most of them Dutch, were used for many new species and frequently borrowed into English. Thus, for example, *kabeljou* (1731: now often shortened to *Kob*) is from Dutch *kabeljauw* but is 'a fish of a totally different order and family from that of the northern hemisphere cod' (Branford 1988: 71). Among indigenous trees, *essenhout* (1785) is from Dutch *essen* 'ash'; *boekenhout* (1790) is 'beech' in Dutch, but the species are again distinct.

Among animals, *tiger* (1708, 'leopard') is from Dutch *tijger* 'tiger'. Several antelope species have names taken directly from Dutch: *eland* (1786, Du. 'elk'); *rhebok* (1731, Du. 'roebuck') and *steenbok* (1775, Du. 'ibex').

Descriptive coinages, reflecting appearance, habit or habitat are very common. Among fish, *jakopever* (1727), a large-eyed reddish species, is said to commemorate a Captain Jacob Evertson. *Springer* (1797) names several jumping species; Lady Anne Barnard found it 'the very best fish I tasted in all my life'. The esteemed *galjoen* (1843) commemorates the galleons of earlier days.

Among trees, the valued hardwoods *stinkwood* (1731) and *yellowwood* (1790) are from the Dutch coinages *stinkhout* and *geelhout*. *Fynbos* ('delicate bush', 1881, originally *fynbosch*) is the collective term for a Cape coastal vegetation type ('macchia') in which evergreen small- and narrow-leaved species predominate. *Fynbos* is now a key environmental term.

Among animal species, *boomslang* ('tree snake', 1795) *bushbuck* (1825, from Du. *bosbok*) and *wildebeest* (1824; Du. 'wild ox') also called *gnu* (1777, Kh.) are just three of scores reflecting habit or habitat.

Names from indigenous languages include *buchu* (1731, Kh.) for certain plant species used medicinally; *dagga* (1670, Kh.) 'wild hemp' (cannabis) smoked as a narcotic, and names of several antelope species, such as *impala* (1801, Zu.), *inyala* (1891, Zu.), *kudu* (1776, Kh. or Xh.) and *oribi* (1795, Kh.).

Some 'common names' of plants are from scientific terminology, for instance *agapanthus* (1789) and *protea* (1751) for a genus of evergreen shrubs (also Australian) 'Protean' in their multiplicity of forms.

A count of 100 names of living things taken at random from Branford (1987) indicated languages of origin as follows: Dutch–Afrikaans 56; English 25; Nguni 7; Khoi 3; Tswana 1; other 8. Just over 80 per cent of these names are of Dutch–Afrikaans or English origin; only 11 per cent are from indigenous languages.

In recent years, it has been the custom to give animal names to armoured fighting vehicles or military aircraft, notably the *hippo*, an armoured police vehicle (1976); the *Impala* jet aircraft (1970) and a fast armoured troop-carrier, the *ratel* ('honey badger', 1977).

The most significant transference of an animal name is, however, that of *springbok* (1775), a particularly graceful and agile gazelle, now a potent national symbol. Early human *springboks* were the national rugby team who toured Britain in 1906: 'A crowd of 9,000...accorded the springboks a great welcome as they walked onto the field' (*South African News Weekly*, 3 October 1906). The name, now internationally known, has been extended to players accredited to represent South Africa over a wide range of sports. (See Note, p. 496.)

The First World War brought into being another kind of springbok. The *Star* of 5 April 1916 has the headline SPRINGBOKS IN EGYPT: DECENT BAPTISM OF FIRE. The military Springboks figure prominently in records of the Second World War as in 'The Springboks whipped off their sunhelmets and gave three rousing cheers for the king' (Birkby 1941, in J. Branford 1987: 341) but are now figures of the past: for contemporary military vocabulary see section 9.5.3.

9.4 Peoples and tongues

> The term *Caffer*, like that of *Hottentot*, is entirely unknown in the
> language of the people to whom it is applied.
>
> (Pringle 1835 [1966]: 265)

9.4.1 Naming and renaming

The ethnic diversity of the South African population and the social
significance in South Africa of ethnicity make the names of peoples bulk
large in the South African lexicon. Renaming of peoples, moreover, for
example of *Dutch* as *Afrikaners* or of '*Bantu*' as *Blacks*, reflects social
change.

Any group or individual, at any given time, will probably have more
names than one. Thus in a single chapter of Fitzpatrick's *Jock of the
Bushveld* (1907) Jim Makokel, one of the author's favourite characters, is
called *boy*, *Kaffir*, *nigger*, *wagon-boy* and *Zulu*. We can only estimate the
relative frequencies of names in actual use; but major changes over long
periods of time stand out clearly.

To the British at the Cape in (say) 1814, there were five conspicuous
'peoples' in or near the Colony: those typically then called 'the Caffres'
(variously spelt), 'the Dutch', 'the English', 'the *Bosjesmen*' and 'the
Hottentots'. Four of these have since been renamed, and 'the English'
now means 'the South African English'.

A significant and fairly new practice, however, is that of 'no-naming'
in terms of ethnic group. Thus a press report of the 1970s, 'Two whites
and five Africans were injured', would in 1990 be more likely to read
'Seven people were injured' and the same practice – anticipated in parts
of Paton's *Cry, the Beloved Country* (1948) – is, in certain circles, gaining
ground in speech.

9.4.2 Caffre to black

Kaffir, one of the best-hated words in South Africa, is from Arabic *Kafir*
'non-Muslim; infidel'. It probably began among Arab traders as a word
for non-Muslim indigenous peoples of south-eastern and southern
Africa. Initially in this general sense, it was borrowed into Portuguese
(see Hakluyt 1599, cited in *OED* at *Caffre*), Dutch and later into English
in various spellings, such as *Cafar*, *Caffre*, *Kaffir*.

The Dutch at the Cape, however, from early times distinguished
clearly between 'Hottentots' and 'Kaffirs', the latter being the Nguni-

speaking peoples of the eastern frontier and in particular the Xhosa (Medley 1731). The English adopted *Kaffir* in this narrowed sense, though a number of early writers pointed out that this was an unfortunate and offensive designation. Thus Lichtenstein (1812–15, 1: 390) points out 'These people are exceedingly offended at being called Caffres.'

Somerville (in Bradlow 1979: 124) remarks of the Tswana ('Boot-shoonanas'): 'The boors have already begun to call this people by a misnomer, *Caffers*.' This is an early reflection of the extension in South African Dutch of *Kaffer* to signify any non-Khoisan African. English was quick to follow, and by 1879 the *Cape Times* (1 January) was reporting of a Zulu uprising 'In Natal, the Kaffirs are up.'

Many tribal names were of course well known. They begin to appear in large numbers in 1795–1838: *Barolong*, ST 1824; *Basotho*, ST 1833; *Bechuana*, ST 1801; *Mashona*, Ng. 1835; *Matabele*, Ng. 1835 and *Zulu* (Ng., in various guises – *Zoola, Zoolah, Zooler, Zooloo*) 1824. Schapera (1937: 445ff.) lists over 260 of these for South Africa as a whole.

The extension of *Kaffir* was probably stimulated by the mineral/industrial 'revolution' of 1870–1900, which brought together members of many different indigenous peoples in overcrowded mining compounds and 'locations'. The same process would have favoured the generalised *native*.

Many white South Africans have used *Kaffir* neutrally and without overtones of contempt, as does Olive Schreiner in *The Story of an African Farm* or Selwyn (1891, in Silva & Walker 1976: 415):

> The jungle may close o'er the desolate grave
> Of the Kaffir evangelist, humble and brave.

But all too often, *Kaffir* carries explicit signals of contempt as in 'No ways I work under a Kaffir' (Slapolepszy 1985: 60). Though in the 1970s *Kaffir* had become an actionable insult (J. Branford 1987: 160) it lives on, regrettably, in non-standard spoken usage. Significantly, the National Place Names Committee has resolved to approve no new names (e.g. *Kafferskraal*) in which *Kaffir* is a component.

Kaffir stood as modifier in a large number of compounds and two-word lexemes, now (1990) nearly all obsolescent. In many, such as *Kaffir plum* (1844), it meant simply 'wild' or 'indigenous'. *Kaffir beer* (1837) had a short life as *Bantu beer* (1972) and is now *sorghum beer*, or sometimes KB. The *Kaffirboom* (1827) is now again the *coral tree*. *Kaffir corn* ('millet', 1786) has been officially replaced by *grain sorghum* (Walker & Silva 1976:

427). *Kaffir pot* (a black iron pot on three legs, 1896) has proved difficult to replace, though *potjie* (Afrik. 'little pot'), *black pot* and even *tripot* are being used instead. *Kaffir sheeting*, a coarsely woven cloth, is now usually *K-sheeting* or *Bhayi* (Xh. *ibhayi*, cognate with 'baize'). The numerous *Kaffir wars* of school history-books are now *Frontier Wars*.

Kaffir, for many decades, designated an African language (usually but not always Xhosa) as well as the people who spoke it. The missionary Shaw records 'a sermon in Caffre' for 28 June 1828 (cited in Silva & Walker 1976:416). The first *Grammar of the Kafir Language* (1834) was the work of W. B. Boyce. *Xhosa* has replaced *Kaffir* in the titles of its modern successors.

Alongside the major Bantu languages of southern Africa are a number of pidgins and koines. *Kitchen Kaffir*, a pidgin of white employers and black servants, usually English-based, is first mentioned about 1862. Another contact language was *Isikula* (Zu. 'coolie language') used between Zulus and Indian traders early in this century (Cole 1964: 548). A third is *Fanakalo* (perhaps from Zu. *Kuluma fana kalo* 'speak in this way') used extensively in the mines even in the 1980s, though condemned by many mineworkers and by their union. More important are the township varieties known (for example) as *flytaal* (English slang *fly* 'cunning, smart' and Afrik. *taal* 'language'), *mensetaal* ('people's language') or *tsotsi-taal* (from Ng. *-tsotsa* 'dress in exaggerated style' and Afrik. *taal*). These vary in status from criminal argots to koines evolving in large cities as a result of long-term language and dialect contacts (Schuring 1985; Siegel 1985).

Native from an early date began to replace *Kaffir* in official and politer usage. The Tswana writer Plaatje (1916: 15) describes himself modestly as a 'South African native working man', and the African National Congress was founded in 1912 as the South African Native National Congress (Plaatje 1916: 16). Its present designation dates from 1925.

Bantu first appears in English in the sense reflected in *Bantu languages* in Bleek's note (1858: 35) on 'The languages of the Bantu family'. In this sense it is still an uncontroversial word. As a human noun, however, it has had a stormy history in South Africa.

In several Nguni languages, *Bantu* ('people') is the plural of *umuntu* ('person'). *Umuntu* is reflected in SAfrE *munt* [mʊnt], an offensive term for an African. The base form *-ntu* occurs in many African languages and in two words now moving into currency in South African English: *isiNtu* ('black tradition' or a 'black' language) and *(u)buntu* ('compassion, human-heartedness').

Olive Schreiner (1923), in an article dated 1901, regularly uses *the Bantu* of Africans, as did some other 'liberal' writers later in the century. It was felt perhaps that, unlike *native*, *Bantu* indicated, and indeed helped to establish, an identity for the people of whom it was used, and it became a favourite with Afrikaans writers on 'the native question'.

Thus *Bantu*, during the 1950s, became a key member of the vocabulary of 'separate development'. In legislation, it replaced *native* (as in the *Bantu Authorities Acts*, etc.). 'Native education' became *Bantu education* and there was a proliferation of such bodies as *Bantu Affairs Administration Boards* and *Urban Bantu Councils* (1961).

A further irritant was the use of *Bantu* as an English 'count' noun: as in 'a Bantu' or as in Fugard's 'You're one of the good Bantoes, hey' (cited in J. Branford 1987: 21). Not surprisingly, Africans came to hate *Bantu*. *African* had by now been long established in non-governmental and particularly in liberal usage. 'Please call us Africans' pleaded an editorial in *The World* (formerly *Bantu World*) in 1973. Bantu education was a major target of the Soweto uprising of 1976, and legislation passed early in 1978 replaced the word *Bantu* by *Black* in all previous Acts of Parliament. (See also section 9.5.2.)

Black was already strongly supported by 'resistance' forces such as the Black Consciousness movement led in South Africa by Steve Biko. *Black*, however, has both an 'exclusive' sense, that is 'African', and an inclusive sense, anybody not 'white'. For the 'African' sense, current usages vary. Thus *South Africa 1979*, an official yearbook, uses *Black* in the sense of 'African'. The independent *Race Relations Survey* (1987–8) uses *African* (as distinguished from, for example, 'coloured'). Archbishop Tutu remarked of the wording of an official document 'I think that there they mean the black blacks.'

9.4.3   Boor to Boer: 'Dutchman' to Afrikaner

The forebears at the Cape of *Afrikaners* of the present day appear under many designations in early English texts (1780–1838). They are called, for instance, (*the*) *Dutch*, *Dutch Boors*, (*Cape*) *Dutchmen*, *Cape Boors*, *African Boors* (occasionally) and, very often, simply *boors*, *Boors*, *boers* or *Boers*. Pringle (1835 [1966]: 48) pleasantly calls them 'Dutch-African colonists' perhaps by way of rendering the local designation *Afrikaander* (sometimes *Afrikaner* in English texts). There was thus a fairly complex situation of multiple naming.

But while *Dutch* or *Dutchmen* tends to be used for people both in the Cape Town area and for people up-country, *boor* on the whole is used only for the latter. This parallels the distinction noticed by Polson (1837: 80) between *Kaapenaars* 'Cape people' and *Afrikaanders* 'other native white inhabitants of the colony', seen as less sophisticated than the *Kaapenaars*. It is fair to add that Changuion's glossary of Cape Dutch (1848, cited in Van der Merwe 1971: 7) equates *Afrikaander* with *Kaapenaar* or *Kaapsche Kind* ('Child of the Cape').

Boor in the South African context is typically a rendering of Dutch *boer* 'farmer'. Ewart (1811) [1970]: 11) has 'The Cape Boors or Farmers'. But *boor* between 1795 and 1838 gains a new signification and changes its typical spelling to *Boer*. Alongside the 'occupational' sense of *Boor(s)*, in quite early texts, is the sense of 'nation'. This is anticipated in a despatch of 1799 (cited in Silva & Walker 1976: 126): 'the general Idea of Independence which undoubtedly prevails among the Boors'. The 'national' sense was strongly reinforced by the rise of the 'Boer' republics after the Great Trek; by 1846 Bowker is referring to 'the Boer government of Natal' (Silva & Walker 1976: 128) and the experience of the Anglo-Boer wars has made *Boer* to this day one of the 'words of power' to many South Africans, a symbol to many of threatened traditional values, and to others one of crudity, oppression or both.

Boer is now a complex word. J. Branford (1987) and Silva (1990), distinguish about seven established significations: (1) Dutch-speaking farmer; (2) Dutch-speaking inhabitant of a 'Trekker' republic; (3) militiaman of the Republican forces in the Anglo-Boer wars as in 'the Boers... kept up a heavy fire... all night' (1900); (4) Afrikaner; Afrikaans-speaking South African, often used pejoratively by blacks and affirmatively by contemporary right-wingers; (5) policeman or prison warder, as in *The boere threw the drunkard in the van*; (6) a South African soldier, as in a SWAPO instruction to *capture a boer prisoner* and (7) the South African government, as in a *Boer–Soviet pact*.

Boer, often in the 'combining form' *boere*, is a member of many high-frequency compounds, such as *boeremusiek* 'country-style dance music played usually by a *boereorkes*' (J. Branford 1987: 39), *boerestaat*, a traditional white republic envisaged for the future by right-wing politicians, and *boerewors* 'originally a country sausage, now commercially available everywhere' (J. Branford 1987: 40) and described elsewhere as 'the nearest thing we'll get to a national dish'.

Afrikaanders developed into *Afrikaners* and long ago replaced *the Dutch*. But in one of its early senses, *Afrikaander* denoted a person of mixed blood, as in the journal of Olof Bergh (1683: [1931]: 134) 'There we...sent out two of our whites with two Afrijkaanders' ('Daar wij...stierden 2 man van ons blancken uijt met twee Afrijkaanders'). This 'coloured' sense is fairly common in English texts of 1820–60: 'The Africander slave girl would consider herself disgraced by a connection with the Negro' (Bird 1823: 74), but seems to have died out slowly during the nineteenth century. .

The dominant sense in the early nineteenth century was, however, 'Dutch-speaking South African', as in 'All those who are born in the colony speak that language [*sc.* Dutch] and call themselves Afrikaanders...whether of Dutch, German or French origin' (Burchell 1822–4, I: 21). Later, *Afrikander* acquired for a time a new sense in English, namely that of 'anyone born in South Africa of European descent', as in 'There should be neither Boer nor Settler, but Afrikanders all' (J. Bailie, 10 April 1840, in Silva & Walker 1976: 20).

By the end of the century *Afrikander* had a well-established sense as 'any South African of European descent'. A narrower competing sense, and the reshaping of *Afrikander* as *Afrikaner*, are both related to the rise of Afrikaans.

The language known as *Cape Dutch, Colonial Dutch* (Pringle 1835 [1966]: 10) or more simply as the *Taal* (Du. 'language') had developed a distinct identity during the seventeenth and eighteenth centuries. The nineteenth century was a period of diglossia, with 'High Dutch' as the language of church and school and the *Taal* initially that of hearth and home, but later of serious writing too. In 1875 the *Genootskap van Regte Afrikaanders* ('Fellowship of True Afrikaners'), initially established in the Cape Colony, stated their aim as being 'To stand for our Language, our People and our Country' ('Om te staan vir ons Taal, vir ons Nasie en ons Land'), with a clear distinction between *Ons Taal* and the Dutch of Holland. It is about this time that the word *Afrikaans* first appears. The replacement of Dutch by Afrikaans has been sketched in section 9.1.2.

Afrikaner, similarly, replaced the often pejorative *Dutchman*; Sarah Gertrude Millin comments on this in 1926 (*OED*) and twenty years later the *Forum* (30 November 1946, 32) noted: 'Today only the prejudiced and unenlightened persist in calling Afrikaners Dutchmen' – though a fair number of the 'prejudiced and unenlightened' have survived into the 1990s. *Rooinek* (1896; 'red-neck') as a designation first for Englishmen and later for English-speaking South Africans was for long a kind of counterpart of *Dutchman* (though usually friendlier).

Afrikaner has in English far fewer compounds than *boer*, though *Afrikanerdom* has been an important political word ever since Lord Milner wrote in 1900 of 'Afrikanderdom and further discord'.

A number of jocular or offensive terms for *Afrikaner*, such as *hairyback* and *rock* (*spider*), seem to be relatively ephemeral. There has been a steady progression from the multiple naming of the early nineteenth century to *Afrikaner* and *Boer*, the dominant terms of the late twentieth century.

9.4.4   Hottentot to 'coloured'; other groups

Hottentot (1677) originated as a name devised by whites for a people who called themselves *Khoikhoi* (1801 'men of men', Kh.). *Hottentot* derives possibly from words of a Khoikhoi dance-song misheard by westerners (Nienaber 1963: 74). Lord Chesterfield considered Dr Samuel Johnson as 'a respectable Hottentot' (letter of 1751, cited in *OED*). Elphick (1977) suggests that *Hottentot* in the eighteenth century became a symbol of extreme human degradation, though Ewart (ca 1812) and others were to point out later that this reflected simply the miserable state of so many Khoikhoi under colonial rule.

Well before the Great Trek some bands of Khoikhoi or mixed descent, for example the *Griquas* (1815) and *Korannas* (1827), had established formidable communities well ahead of the fringe of white penetration. The *Grahamstown Journal* (Branford *et al.* 1984: 465) reported in 1845: 'The Griquas are found to be quite a match for the Boers, number to number – but both parties are alike in not venturing, if they can help it, within shot of one another.' The Griquas to this day are a people many of whom still desire 'nationhood'.

A common designation in English texts of 1795–1838 (and earlier Dutch ones) is *Bastaard* (*Hottentot*) denoting a person of mixed Khoikhoi/European descent, not necessarily with negative connotations. The Rhehoboth *Basters* of Namibia insist to this day on keeping their ancestral name. Many descendants of the Khoikhoi have now merged into the group now termed 'coloured'. *Hottentot* and *Hotnot* are now, however, terms of extreme insult (as in the stock collocation *hotnots, coolies and Kaffirs*), so that *Hottentot*, in contemporary standard usage, has been replaced by *Khoikhoi*.

A fairly large number of compounds, notably *Hottentot god* for a species of 'praying mantis', attest the formative role of *Hotnot*/*Hottentot* in South African naming, though most of these are now likely to go the way of those with *Kaffir*.

'*Coloured*' in the sense of 'South African of mixed descent' dates back to 1829 or earlier. Abrahams (1954: 44) has a pleasingly simplistic explanation of 'coloured' in an autobiographical fragment:

> 'You are Coloured. There are three kinds of people; white people, Coloured people and black people. The white people come first, then the coloured people, then the black people.'
> 'Why?'
> 'Because it is so.'

Coloured is typically defined in negative terms, as in Act no. 22 of 1928, in which *coloured person* means 'any person who is neither white nor a Turk; a member of an aboriginal race or tribe of Africa' (and much more). (*Statutes of the Union*, 1928: 394).

Wood (1987: 31–70) explores the concept 'coloured' in the South African context, focusing on the one hand on 'an identity based on shared experience' (31) and on the other (34) pointing out that 'People of every race and nationality can and do become members of the "coloured community"... while others manage to renounce their former membership: "Whites" are now legally entitled to marry into the group again... "coloured" people are regularly reclassified as "white', "black" as "coloured" and so on.' In recent writings *Coloured* has lost its capital letter and is frequently written with quotation marks as in *a store in the 'coloured' township* and often as *so-called 'coloured'*.

Brown people (translating Afrik. *bruinmense*) was occasionally used of 'coloureds', especially in the 1970s, but has now fallen into disuse.

Bushmen (1786 from Du. *Bosjesman*) originated as a designation for groups of Khoisan hunter–gatherers who used only clan names (e.g. *!Kung*), with no collective term for themselves as a people. *Bushman* once developed negative connotations, probably from its association with Afrik. *Boesman*, another abusive term for a 'coloured' person. It has thus sometimes been replaced by *San*, related to *Sonqua*, a Khoikhoi term for these people. *Bushman*, however, survives in everyday (and newspaper) usage. Few combinations with *Bushman* remain, except *Bushman paintings*, remarkable cave pictures which have survived their creators.

Indian indentured labourers first reached Natal in 1860 under the unhappy designation of *coolies*, now almost entirely replaced by *Indians*. With the first indentured labourers came smaller groups of 'passenger Indians' (mostly traders), who paid their own passages. Because many of these were Muslims, some came to be called *Arabs*: hence 'the humble petition of the undersigned Arab traders to the Volksraad of the Free State in May 1887' (cited in Bhana & Pachai 1984: 32).

Coolie has two main senses, occupational and racial. The occupational sense appears early at the Cape (Greig 1831: 19). The racial sense now came to the fore, as in *a coolie cook* (Boyle 1873: 285) or the following, from the *Eastern Province Herald* of 2 April 1897: 'All Coolie traders, being Indians, will be given three months to dispose of their stocks.'

Sammy for an Indian man and *Mary* for an Indian woman probably originated as names of convenience in the 1890s or earlier. Both are now felt as objectionable and are falling into disuse. Mesthrie (1986) suggests that *Sammy* is from Tamil *cami* 'god', a component of such personal names as *Ramasami*, while Natal *Mary* derived probably from Australian and New Zealand slang, 'possibly influenced by South Indian *Mari-amma*', a girls' name. Mesthrie can suggest no convincing origin for the *char* of *charra* and *char ou*, slang terms for an Indian and sometimes offensive, though *ou* ('chap') is a borrowing from Afrikaans.

9.4.5   Inclusive terms: South African

South African is the only well-established single term for designating *all* the peoples of southern Africa. *African* normally means a 'black African', though from quite early times it has been used in a wider sense, as in 'Farmer van der Spoei... an African born' (Sparrman 1786, I: 59).

European (1731) had a long history as an inclusive term for whites. Increasingly inappropriate for whites born in Africa, it seems now to be dying out. So is its counterpart *non-European* (?1925), with which it is frequently contrasted in signs reading EUROPEANS ONLY and (less frequently) NON-EUROPEANS ONLY.

Non-European was largely replaced by *non-White* (?1955) which drew much acid comment, such as 'If there were no Whites, then there wouldn't be Non-Whites' (*Drum*, 22 February 1972): hence, perhaps, its frequent replacement by *Black* in its inclusive sense. *Non-* would appear to be a dying prefix in designations of human groups. Schreiner (1923: 370) in a paper dated 1900 envisages 'the South African nation of the future' as made up of 'two great blended varieties, dark and light'. Years later *Drum* urged its readers: 'Keep on being proud of being Black. Keep on being proud of knowing we are South Africans.' The legal concept of 'South African' was severely damaged by the Black Homelands Citizenship Act of 1970 and related legislation, by which 'about eight million South Africans... lost... their South African citizenship' (Platsky & Walker 1985: 22). The Freedom Charter, the present government and the ANC seem now to agree on the principle of 'one citizenship for all South Africans' (*Race Relations Survey* 1987–8: 115).

One inclusive term competing with *South African* is *Azanian* (?1977). *Azania* (1976, perhaps from Arabic *Adzan* 'East Africa') is South Africa, present and future, in particular as envisaged by AZAPO, the Azanian People's Organisation, founded in 1978. 'One Azania! One nation!' was a common 'resistance' rallying cry in the 1970s, and *Azania/Azanian* are still (1990) important in the contemporary political vocabulary.

9.5 Other domains

9.5.1 *Human relationships and human types*

This section will briefly sample some key areas of the vocabularies of human relationships and human types. Since its focus is largely on loanwords, it must be stressed that South African speakers of English as L1 have typically at their disposal the full resources of 'general' English as well as those distinctively South African. The latter, furthermore, are not simply an *ad hoc* addition to a repertoire (see also 9.1); they meet important expressive needs. Thus the name *Ouma Smuts* in the 1940s related the wife of General Smuts, himself known as the *Oubaas*, to a world of values and loyalties which the 'translation' *Grandma Smuts* would simply not have reached.

South African English has an extensive repertoire of formulaic expressions: phatic, expressive, directive, and others hard to categorise. A common expressive is *Shame*! (1932) as in 'Oh shame, isn't she sweet with her baby' (cited in J. Branford 1987: 315, 'she' being Princess Diana). *Shame*! expresses 'sympathy or warmth towards something endearing or moving, attractive or small' (*ibid.*).

Most of these formulae are of Dutch–Afrikaans or Nguni origin, and several date back to the 'settler' period or earlier. Among directives are *Sa*! (1790) 'urging a dog to attack' (Pettman 1913: 516, probably from French via Dutch, used also in Xhosa or Zulu) and the abrupt dismissal *hamba*! (1827, Ng.): 'They say *hamba* for *get you gone*' (Thompson 1827, I, 376). Others are *Voetsak*! ('Scram!'), addressed typically to dogs but also sometimes to people (SAfrDu. *Voort seg ik*! 'Off, I say!', 1837) and *Pas op*! ('Look out!', 1837).

Phatic items of early date include the polite greeting *sakubona* ('we see you', Zu., 1837), perhaps primarily 'decorative' in English texts, the farewell *hamba kahle* ('go well', Zu., 1836), again decorative, but fully assimilated into English as *go well* (1948) and *thank you* as a polite refusal, translating Du. *dank u* in the same negative sense (1833).

There are many others of later date, such as *sies* (1868, expressing disgust), *eina!* (expressing pain, 1913) and *magtig!* (surprise or indignation, 1899, from *Allemagtig* 'almighty'). From recent army slang comes *Vasbyt!* (1970) 'Bite!' (on the bullet), now a general word of encouragement.

The adoption and survival of these suggests the following:

1   the influence of competent bilinguals, but also
2   the readiness of others to 'borrow' at the formulaic level from languages of which their knowledge may be only fragmentary; hence
3   perhaps, a measure of identification with other cultures and other tongues.

It must in fairness be added that most of the established English repertoire of swearwords, expletives and hesitation signals do heavy duty in South Africa.

The vocabularies of kinship and solidarity are closely related, and borrow heavily from Dutch–Afrikaans. Thus *boet* 'brother' and its diminutive *boetie* (1903), are used in English both for a relative and a friend. These are signals of affection or friendship, though they may also figure in contexts of reproof as in 'There's a lot of things you don't know, bootie' (1903, in Silva & Walker 1976: 142).

Other members of this set are *neef* ('nephew', 1838), *oom* ('uncle', 1822); *ouma* ('granny', 1910), *oupa* ('grandpa', 1920) and *tante* ('aunt', 1845). All of these may be used, often with overtones of affection, for either a relative or a friend. Thus *Oom* may be used in the following contexts:

1   to denote a speaker's real uncle (*We all love our Oom John*);
2   before a name, as a quasi-honorific, as in H. C. Bosman's 'Oom Schalk Lourens';
3   on its own as a term of respectful third-person address: 'What did Oom do in the Boer War?' (*Sunday Times*, 30 May 1982);
4   as an ordinary noun as in 'the ooms and oupas of the platteland' (*Outspan*, 20 July 1967: 37);

5 occasionally of a national figure as in *Oom Paul* for President Paul Kruger.

Thus, as in Afrikaans, *oom* has often an important 'levelling' signification, as in 'every one is oom or neef (uncle or nephew) to his neighbour' (Alexander 1838, [1967], I: 103–4).

The diminutives *oompie* and *oomie* may signal either affection or disrespect as in 'slack-eyed oomies leaning against the barn pillars' at a *mampoer* ('peach brandy') party (cited in J. Branford 1987: 250). Other members of this set may be used in similar ways, notably *tannie*, quasi-diminutive of *tante* as in 'every stiff-backed gloved and hatted tannie who ever sat in judgement' (*Grocott's Mail*, 1972, in J. Branford 1987: 362). The attitude depends, perhaps, on whether the speaker/writer's stance is within the ambience of the Afrikaner world and values or outside it. Interestingly, *pal*, in English contexts, is often Afrikanerised to *pellie* or *pellie blue* (see J. Branford 1987: 265).

Maat 'good buddy, mate', often in the phrase *ou maat* ('old friend'), occurs frequently in speech. South African English lacks, however, any equivalent to Australian *mate* in point of frequency and range of reference.

The African vocabulary of friendly or respectful address is widely reflected in English texts, though sometimes in a decorative role. One of its focal members is the honorific *Ma-* (in ST *Mme*, *Mma*) as in 'Ma Ngoyi, as she was affectionately known' (*Drum*, October 1983: 90). This precedes, as an honorific, the clan name of a woman's husband, and in Zulu a woman's own clan name, so that *Ma-Hadebe* is roughly 'daughter of the Hadebe clan'. It is also used, as in Livingstone's *Ma-Robert* ('Robert's mother'), with a child's name as 'mother-of'.

Among black men, and occasionally across the colour line, a frequent signal of affectionate solidarity is *Bra* (also *bla*), as in Motsisi (1978: 56) 'Bra Victor at the bottle store', or simply in *Heyta* ('hi there') *my bra*. *Bra* was possibly coined from US *brer* or Afrik. *broer* to match the long-established *Ma*.

Comrade in the 'resistance' vocabulary is used both as title, as in *Viva Comrade Blackburn* or as a signal of solidarity as in *Be strong comrades!* Its uses vary widely. *Comrades* in many press reports may simply render Xh. *amaquabane* 'comrades'. Some 'comrades' are committed Marxists; many are idealists, typically young, prepared to work and suffer for 'the people' and of varying political allegiance; others again are violent thugs. One type shades into another. Not surprisingly, the word is often between inverted commas – 'comrade' – in 'white' press reports. The basic concept seems to be that of commitment to 'the struggle' against apartheid (section 9.5.2). Hence *comrade* is typically a word of solidarity, though remote from *boet* and *oom*.

Among the pivotal words of the traditional vocabulary of master and servant are *baas*, *master* and *madam* vs *kaffir*, *girl* and *boy*. *Baas* appears early (1786) as 'the *baas*, an appellation given to all the christians here, particularly to bailiffs and farmers' (in J. Branford 1987: 16) and patterns syntactically as does *oom*. Its compounds include *kleinbaas* ('small master', 1896), *grootbaas* ('big master', 1812), *oubaas* ('old master', 1824) and *baasskap* ('domination', 1935).

Boyle (1882: 29) captures the 'ideal' notion of the master–servant relationship in 'Me your kaffir, baas, says he', but throughout South Africa, and for two centuries, white men were commonly addressed as *baas* or *master* by Africans and coloureds whether they were the employers of these people or not.

Boy for a 'native' servant has, of course, a long history outside South Africa. There are many kinds of 'boys': *delivery boy*, *garden boy*, *house boy*, *messenger boy*, *ricksha boy*, *tea boy*, though *boy* is now unlikely to last long; thus *boss boy* (1906 and probably earlier), typically in charge of a gang of miners, is now *team leader*. Also on the way out are names of convenience. Traditionally, African workers with unpronounceable names were often renamed by their employers (e.g. *Jim*, *Half-Bottle* or *Sixpence*); though the intention may have been friendly, the effect was denigrating. The common practice of addressing any African customer in a shop as *John* or *Jim* was drawing strong criticism by the 1970s.

Some of these practices relate, it seems, to the period 1870–1910, when the gathering in the mining and industrial centres of a large and in a sense 'anonymous' black labour force is likely to have had a dehumanising effect on urban labour relations generally. See also La Hausse (1988) on changing human relations on the larger farms.

9.5.2   Government, politics and ' the struggle'

The British in 1795 inherited at the Cape an adminstration which was modified only slowly and an administrative vocabulary some of which lasted well into the next century.

Near the centre, the Company's Honourable Independent Fiscal (*Edele Fiskaal Independent*) – public prosecutor, state auditor and collector of fines and taxes – became 'His Majesty's Fiscal', and is commemorated to this day in the name *fiscal shrike* for a bird also known as *butcher-bird, Jacky Hangman* or *Janfiskaal*.

The local dignitaries of a country district included the *Landdrost* (1731) a salaried civil magistrate, whose district and headquarters were both known as the *Drostdy* (1796), and the *predikant*, a licensed minister of religion (1821), also initially paid by government. The organisers of the burgher militia were the *veldwagtmeesters*, later (ca 1802) redesignated *Veld Cornets* ('field cornets'), who figure prominently in the records both of the Cape and of the Republics.

A much-hated word, namely *pass*, appears in a Proclamation of 1 November 1809: 'Lastly the Hottentots going about the country... must be provided with a pass... under penalty of being considered and treated as vagabonds' (Bird 1823: 248). Though repealed by Ordinance 50 of 1828, this early 'pass law' is one of a long chain of similar enactments stretching on to the Natives (Abolition of Passes) Act of 1952, which substituted for *passes* a *reference book*. Africans were quick to rename this *domboek, dompas* (from Afrik. *dom* 'stupid') and later *stinker* (*istinka* in township Zulu).

In 1833 the Slavery Abolition Act was passed by the British Parliament. The practice of 'apprenticeship' (*inboeking*), for instance of captured San or other women and children, preserved, however, a covert form of slavery under a conveniently different name for many years.

A major political event of the early nineteenth century was the exodus from the Cape Colony which came to be known as the Great Trek. Dutch has *trek* in the simple sense of *pull* (and many others), but its special sense of 'emigrate', particularly for the emigration of a community, appears to originate in South Africa. In South Africa, *trek* has become a word of many senses and derivatives (see J. Branford 1987: 377–80) and a powerful symbol of national endeavour. Both as noun and verb, it is one of the most widely used South African words in the English-speaking world.

Voortrekker as a title of honour for the Dutch pioneers was to become one of the names of power in Afrikanerdom. It hardly figures in the contemporary records. The Trekkers called themselves *boeren, trekboeren, emigrante, emigrante boeren* and, occasionally (in English), *Dutch South Africans*. In English texts of the period, the Trekkers appear also as *boers, Dutch (farmers), trek-boers* and *trekkers*. History has given us the simplifying terms *Voortrekker* (1873) and *Great Trek* (1882).

Burgher (1731) denoted a 'full' citizen with militia duties. Later the settler Goldswain (1838/58, in Silva & Walker 1976: 186) complains 'When we are caled one to do burger dutey we have to find our hone Horses and guns.' With the discovery of gold came an influx of *uitlanders* ('foreigners', 1884) into the Transvaal Republic. This led eventually to bitter disputes about 'the *burgher right*', Transvaal citizenship, a major cause of the second Anglo-Boer war.

It was the burghers of a Republic who elected its legislative assembly or *Volksraad* (SAfrDu., 1839). *Volksraad* is a South African creation of special interest. In Afrikaans it designates the existing parliament. Its translation 'Council of the People' – used by the Natal Volksraad – is eloquent of the Trekker spirit.

The complex vocabulary of white politics from 1910 to the present day can be only briefly sampled here.

The *South African National Party* formed the first 'Union' government in 1910 and soon became known as the *South African Party* (SAP) and its adherents as *Saps* (1920). The National Party, a basically Afrikaner party, familiarly 'the Nats' (1934), won the election of 1924 but 'fused' with the SAP in 1933–4 to form the *United South African Nationalist Party*, better known as the *United Party* (Davenport 1978: 217), which remained in power until 1948.

D. F. Malan, however, formed in 1934 the *Purified National Party* (*Gesuiwerde Nasionale Party*), reconstituted in 1939 as the *Reunited National Party* (*Herenigde Nasionale Party*), abbreviated *HNP*. Now simply the *National Party*, it has been since 1948 the majority party in Parliament.

The designations of the major parties ring the changes on just three terms: *South African*, *National* and *United*. The leadership seem to have hesitated to distinguish their parties, at any rate in name, too sharply from one another. There were other white parties, but from Union to 1948 the strongest contenders were clearly *Nat* and *Sap*.

The slogan of *apartheid* (later 'separate development') had a special aptness for the election of 1948. It reflected the *status quo* yet it promised a new order. It offered a seminal concept for the National Party regime. Its origins, moreover, were thoroughly respectable, going back to earnest politico-theological debate in Dutch Reformed Church circles since the 1930s. In 1944, the Leader of the National Party, D. F. Malan, was able to urge the electorate 'To ensure the safety of the white race and of Christian civilization by the honest maintenance of the principles of *apartheid* and guardianship' (as reported in the *Star*, 25 January 1944).

Apartheid in its new form generated a large and specialised vocabulary. Focal in this were (*race*) *classification*, *group area* and *homeland*. *Classification* involved a spate of *reclassifications*, for example in 1986 'African to Coloured, 387; African to Griqua, 16;...Coloured to Chinese 10; Coloured to White 314;...Malay to Indian 43' (*Race Relations Survey* 1987, 1:7).

In 1953 the first Group Areas Act put into currency the term *group area* (1950), an urban area reserved for a particular racial group and from which all members of other racial groups were moved in the process of *resettlement* (1954), if necessary by force or the threat of force. The result was a sizeable Gulag Archipelago of *resettlement camps* and *resettlement areas*, some notorious for appalling living conditions.

For Africans, the great theme of *separate development* (1955), brought a progression from *reserve* to *homeland* to *self-governing territory* to *national state* to '*independent*' *state*, all in the context of a *multinational commonwealth*. In 1976 the Transkei *homeland* became the first fully '*independent*' *state*, with its own state president. By this time *Bantustan* (1955), constructed on the analogy of *Pakistan* as an informal synonym for *homeland*, had already moved from semi-official into 'resistance' usage, in which it now appears typically with a lower-case initial as in *the bantustan policy*.

A similar fate has overtaken *apartheid*. Dropped long ago from official usage, it still provides a perfect one-word target for opponents of the regime. In 1990, *the apartheid society* was still a standard 'anti-South African' formula and *anti-apartheid* a long-established favourite both in the South African and the overseas press. *Bantu Education* (now *bantu education*) has undergone a similar change. Thus terms originating with the National Party regime are now mainly useful to its opponents.

Most of the vocabulary of traditional African political life has only a marginal status in South African English. One exception is *indaba* (Ng., 1827) 'conference or discussion', recently a favourite in the press, and current also in *That's your indaba* ('your problem'). But many key political terms, such as Ng. *amaphakati* 'councillors', discussed at 9.2.1, are marginal in South African English or outside it altogether. This reflects several factors, notably the variety and number of African social systems and languages, and the 'social distance' between most Africans and most whites.

From about 1894, a new 'resistance' vocabulary began to appear. Mahatma Gandhi founded the Natal Indian Congress in that year, responding to a wave of discriminatory measures against Indians, because 'Congress was the very life of India' (Gandhi 1927 [1983]: 146). *Congress* became one of the pivotal words of South African resistance politics. The South African Native National Congress was founded in 1912, renamed itself the African National Congress in 1923 (Davenport 1977: 197), and is now best known as the *ANC*. The ANC split in 1958 with a walk-out of *Africanists*, proponents of African leadership in African states, who eventually became the present *Pan-African Congress* (*PAC*).

For many decades, the Congress movement was dedicated to non-violence. Mahatma Gandhi's term *satyagraha* was coined about 1906 from suggestions offered by readers of *Indian Opinion*. 'Truth (*satya*) implies love, and firmness (*agraha*) engenders and therefore serves as a synonym for force' (Gandhi 1928: 109–15, cited in Bhana & Pachai 1984: 112). A practitioner of *satyagraha* is a *satyagrahi*; both terms have passed into the international political vocabulary.

Among the focal terms of the present 'resistance' or *alternative* political vocabulary are *the people*, *the system* and *the struggle*. None of these, of course, is South African in origin, but each, in the South African context, has taken on values of its own. They are tellingly collocated in 'She told them that we were agents of the system ... when her neighbours went ... to tell of the screams, the leaders said it was the work of the struggle' (Mathiane 1989: 7–8). The definite article ('*the* struggle') assumes the reader's familiarity with what is meant.

In 1989, a wide range of 'alternative structures' organised by 'comrades' (section 9.5.1) in the townships were controlled by 'the people' and outside the official 'system'. These included *street committees*, *area committees* and *people's courts* (1980). People's courts, in a number of cases, sentenced *sellouts* (1960, alleged supporters of 'the system') to death by *necklace* (1985, a petrol-filled tyre hung around the victim's neck and then ignited).

Black-on-black violence is regularly reported in the press in terms of battles between 'leftist' comrades and traditionalist 'vigilantes'. 'Vigilantes' in white press reports often renders a more traditional word, such as Zulu *amabutho*, members of a 'regiment' or age group.

9.5.3   Warfare

South Africa has a substantial vocabulary of warfare. Though much of this is of Dutch–Afrikaans origin, the names of many famous military units are still British, such as the Cape Town Highlanders, the Natal Carbineers, Prince Alfred's Guard and the Transvaal Scottish. An early appearance, indeed, of *Tommy Atkins* is in 'not like the trek-ox that "Tommy Atkins" had to put up with' (1881, cited in J. Branford 1987: 378).

Assegai (1677) spear or javelin, originally from Berber *al-zagayah*, 'the spear' is in South Africa a 'white' man's word for a black man's weapon. The Nguni word for 'spear' is *umKhonto*. *Assegai* appears to originate in the Portuguese-based lingua franca of the Indian Ocean. Assegais remain in regular use, both in action and in press reports. So do *knobkerries* (1832, Afrik. from Kh.). *Impi* (Zulu, 1838) a regiment or smaller body of warriors, is still used regularly by the press in reports of *faction fighting* (1897), typically clan or tribal conflict, 'carried over' into township or mine compounds.

Commando (1790, originally from Spanish *commando*) originated as a term for calling out the burgher militia *op comando* 'officially'. It soon took on the sense of 'an armed party of boors' (Burchell 1822–4, II: 119), though we read also of a 'Caffre commando' and 'a commando of Hottentots'. It became famous as a term for Republican units in the Anglo-Boer wars (still under *Field Cornets*) and passed into the international military vocabulary with the British *commando* assault troops of the Second World War, and later. It has since been widely revived in South Africa and elsewhere.

So has *commandeer* (SAfrDu., 1868) though now in the broad sense of 'take arbitrary possession of' as in *The revellers commandeered the owner's car*. Its earlier senses are 'to press men into military service' or 'requisition for military purposes'.

To the Boer commandos, the enemy were the *khakis* (Hindi, from the colour of their uniforms), some of whom, under orders, gathered the families of burghers whose farmhouses they had destroyed into *concentration camps* (1901). Thousands died in these camps, and *concentration camp*, now with even more tragic connotations, has since passed into the international political vocabulary.

The *laager* (1834) in the sense of 'a fortified encampment of waggons', after the defeat of a Zulu army by Boer forces 'in laager' in 1838 became one of the great symbols of Afrikanerdom. But it also became a hard-worked metaphor for a society on the defensive and a closed, isolationist outlook, as in *the laager mentality*.

Springbok has been discussed in section 9.3. National Service and the experience of war has generated a large unofficial military vocabulary since the 1970s. Of this the best-known word is probably *troepie* (also *troopie*, 1972), National Serviceman, seemingly from English *trooper*, with Afrikaans diminutive suffix *-ie*. There is a sketch of *troepie-talk* in Picard (1975).

9.5.4   *Lekker lewe; healing; countercultures*

An important theme of South African experience is captured in an advertising jingle of the 1970s: 'Braaivleis, rugby, sunny skies and Chevrolet', symbols of the contemporary (or just past?) *lekker lewe* ('sweet life'). The original *lekker lewe* (ca 1846) was 'the free and easy life of the frontier' (Silva & Walker 1976: 532). Its vocabulary will here be taken to be that of festivity, food and drink, past and present, sampled again only briefly.

A word which took the fancy of Lady Anne Barnard is *sopie* (1679, a small and usually sociable drink) as in 'a pipe, a soepie or whatever the Mynheers pleased' (1798 in Silva & Walker 1976: 742). She noticed also in 1797 the role of the *stoep* ('verandah or raised terrace') in social intercourse: 'the young Dutchmen ... prefer smoking their pipes on the stoep'. A third long-lived item is *lekker* as in 'Farmer Peck's' inn sign about 1840 (J. Branford 1987: 198)

> Lekker kost as much as you please
> Excellent beds without any fleas.

Lekker as 'nice' is now typically a children's word, but can also mean 'tipsy'. *Kost* (Du. 'food', Afrik. *kos*) suggests a pleasantly bilingual Farmer Peck.

The Cape vines about this time yielded both the select *Constantia* wine (1786) and the humbler brandy later called *Cape Smoke*, of which the settler Shone (1851) found that 'three or four glasses made me stupid'.

Another formidable liquor is *mampoer* (1934, distilled from peaches and other soft fruits; possibly named for a Sotho chief Mampuru), immortalised in the fiction of H. C. Bosman (1947 [1978]: 121): 'karee-mampoer is white and soft to look at.'

Braaivleis (1939) signifies both barbecued meat and a party of which it is the centre-piece. Its popular rival since 1984–5 has been *potjiekos*, a mixture cooked in a three-legged iron pot over a fire. Many cultures have contributed to the array of traditional foods; thus *bobotie* (1870) a savoury curried mince, is possibly from Malay or Javanese; the ragout *bredie* (1815) may take its name via Afrikaans from P *bredo* 'ragout'; *biriani* (?1961), a particularly festive curry, is from Urdu *biryani* (Mesthrie 1986: 5).

Except for *kost*, the items cited so far are (or were) 'common words' in the 'white' English of their time. This cannot be said of the large vocabularies of African beer and traditional *beer-drinks* (1895) as explained, for example, by McAllister (1989) or Schapera (1937). The many kinds of home-brewed 'beer', such as Ng. *utshwala* (1839) and *mahewu* (1913), tended in white usage to figure simply as *Kaffir beer* (1837).

With the large-scale movement of Africans to the cities, there began a sustained conflict between home-based sellers on the one hand – *shebeen queens* (?1959), more familiarly *Aunties* – and white authorities on the other determined to capture and divert the black liquor trade to *beerhalls* (1909) under municipal control – an important source of revenue (La Hausse 1988).

A substantial mythology, some of it true, grew up around the products of home brewers (e.g. *skokiaan*, 1926), and police raids on their premises. Casey Motsisi (1978) and others have built up a remarkable record of the vocabulary – such as *haja* or *half jack* ('half-bottle', 1953) – and culture of black Johannesburg's (drinking) *spots*, many of which are now legalised as *taverns*, whose controllers form the *Taverners' Association* (1982).

There is a sizeable traditional vocabulary, much of it still in common use, of medicine and healing. This includes *muti* (Zu., 1960), a common word among whites for medicine of any kind. White people as well as black may still consult a *witchdoctor* (1827) or other traditional healer, for example a *sangoma* (Zu., before 1894), 'a diviner' able to *smell out* (1836) witches or other sources of evil. A front-page item in the *Cape Times of* 29 June 1990 reports a sangoma's prediction that no. 7 would win the Durban July Handicap.

Dagga ('cannabis'), a staple of some contemporary counter-cultures, appears in 1670 as 'A powerful Root...Dacha...which causes Ebriety' (*OED Supplement*, 1972, I). The many and varied vocabularies of South African counter-cultures (e.g. prison gangs) cannot be explored in this chapter. A common term for a rascal is *skelm* (Du. *schelm*) with a long history in English but now 'archaic except in South Africa' (*OED*). Among many kinds of *skelm* are *brekers* ('breakers', 1975), usually white; *skollies* (1934, Afrik. from Du. *schoelje* 'scoundrel'), typically members of a 'coloured' street gang, and *tsotsis* (1949), African street thugs, often flashily dressed. *Tsotsi* (origin unknown) is possibly of *flytaal* origin (9.4.2). Among countless gang names are *Russians* (1959), allegedly Sotho groups 'with their blankets worn right up to their eyes' who terrorised the Johannesburg townships from the 1940s onwards.

There are many words for the homeless. A *bergie* is a vagrant living typically on the slopes of Table Mountain within easy distance of Cape Town. *Strollers* are children who have adopted a *bergie* lifestyle.

9.5.5 Miscellany

This section will briefly note some major areas and items of vocabulary not covered elsewhere.

South African technology has moved from the world of the *Cape cart* (1832, SAfrDu *kapkar* 'hooded cart') the oxwagon and the *roer* ('long flintlock musket', 1824) to that of the *National Road*, the *bakkie* and the armoured fighting vehicles noticed in section 9.3. The *bakkie* (1968, a light delivery truck, perhaps from Afrik. *bakkie* 'small container'), thanks partly to television commercials, has come to symbolise tough outdoor living, as did the oxwagon of the past.

The specialised vocabularies of finance and of farming and other technology are beyond this chapter's scope. A few words of the oxwagon vocabulary survive: *inspan* 'yoke or harness draft animals' (1815), now usually metaphorical, as in *Everyone is being inspanned for the Cathedral fete*. *Outspan* (1801, 'unyoke or unharness animals'), hence 'make a break in a journey') survived as a noun into the twentieth century as 'a place for grazing or encampment'.

The currency has undergone two major changes: from the *rixdollars* (1786), *schellings* (1731) and *stivers* (1697) of Company rule to British pounds, shillings and pence, and from these in 1961, to the *rands* and cents of the present day. *Rand* (1961) commemorates the gold-mining area of the Witwatersrand. A coin now much missed is the *tickey* ('threepenny piece', 1877, perhaps from Malay *tiga* 'three'), which gave its name to the *tickiedraai*, a fast twirling dance, and lived on in the phrase *two bricks and a tickey high*.

A useful commercial term is *voetstoots* (before 1934), as in *The property is sold* VOETSTOOTS *as it now stands*, that is 'with all defects latent and patent'. *Voetstoots* is a contraction of Du. *met de voet te stoten* 'to push with the foot', a pleasingly direct way of testing an article for sale.

9.6 Phonology

9.6.1 *Variation*

In contemporary mother-tongue South African English Pronunciation (hereafter SAEP) variation occurs along predictable lines. There are no single-style speakers; in many cases the accents of women differ significantly from those of men; the accents of more and less privileged groups are likely to differ.

There are traces, at any rate, of different societal/regional norms: for example for 'coloured' mother-tongue speakers in Cape Town and its environs; for white speakers of East Cape origin; for Indian speakers, mainly in Natal; for white speakers with a 'Natal' accent, and for white members of the Transvaal industrial working class. But variation tends to be more obviously a matter of class and upbringing than region (W. S. Mackie, lecture, 1950), modified by

1   formality of context;
2   the degree of accommodation (to the dialect of the hearer).

'Broad' or basilectal forms tend to be used by

1   dwellers in rural communities with regular contact with Afrikaans-speakers;
2   those (particularly in underprivileged urban groups) whose peers or schoolteachers (or both) have been largely Afrikaans-speaking.

'Conservative' or acrolectal forms are frequently associated with the so-called 'private schools' (British, 'public schools'), where 'privilege' and exposure to L1 teachers in all (or most) subjects are still part of the package, though less so than before 1948.

Though to a certain extent it makes sense to speak of 'varieties' of South African English, any study of individual speakers is likely to confirm the view of Le Page (1968: 197): 'The more one probes, the more the supposedly autonomous systems are seen to be constructs which each of us makes for himself, out of the data presented to us, and according to our needs.' Although there are a number of valuable studies of SAEP, ranging from Hopwood (1928) to the more recent work of Lanham, Lass, MacDonald and Wright, there are some unfortunate gaps. Those in the historical record will be discussed later. For contemporary SAEP, as Lass (personal communication) has pointed out, there is a lack of published phonetic profiles of individuals and small relatively homogeneous groups (cp. Lass & Wright 1985), though recent work by Lass and others is beginning to provide some of the small-scale detailed studies needed.

Studies of English as L1 outside the 'white' community are few and far between. (Wood 1987 is a valuable pioneer work.) We shall thus, regretfully, have to focus largely on the pronunciation of 'white' mother-tongue speakers of English. Lanham & MacDonald (1979) propose in some detail a contrast between three main varieties, which they term 'Conservative', 'Respectable' and 'Extreme'. In this sketch, however, we shall simply contrast 'Conservative' with 'Broad' or 'Extreme' renderings.

After a brief note on the concept of standard lexical sets, the rest of this section will offer an elementary 'panchronic' view of the sound system, with short vowels, long monophthongs, diphthongs and consonants each under separate headings. A final brief section, 'Whence South African English pronunciation?' will sum up these findings, which owe much, of course, to the earlier work of Hopwood, Casson, Jeffery, Lanham, Lass and Wright.

9.6.2   Standard lexical sets

It is difficult to avoid an apparent self-contradiction when describing the sound system of a dialect or dialect cluster which co-exists with an established prestige or 'standard' accent of which there are well-known detailed descriptions.

Any dialect – or idiolect – must be seen as an autonomous system, with its own particular units organised in its own particular way. Thus, ideally, its description is begun, as it were, *de novo*. It is convenient, however, to describe the new in terms of the known: hence such formulations as 'backed /ɑ/' or 'fronted, glide-weakened /aɪ/'. These, however, can be read as if they were part of a description of historical change, for example that in SAEP a variant rather like /ɔː/ in words like *cart* and *car* began as an /ɑ/-like vowel in the speech of earlier generations, and that 'backed' implies an actual backing of this vowel in the process of historical change.

This is hardly, however, what most originators of such formulations, well aware of the autonomy of language systems, can have intended. As long as we see 'backed /ɑ/' as a formulation of descriptive convenience only, without historical implications, there is little harm in using it. Lass (1988), however, makes the point that, for 'standard Capetonian

English', 'the use of RP-based symbolisations is both anachronistic and historically inept. It is not the case that any present-day ETE [Extraterritorial English] "descends" from RP proper ... It is rather the case that RP and say the SAE lectal complex are parallel developments.'

Wells (1982) provides a partial escape from an 'RP-based symbolisation' in an approach to vowels by way of *standard lexical sets*. Thus:

> The standard lexical set KIT is defined as comprising those words whose citation form in the two standard accents, RP and GenAm, has the stressed vowel /ɪ/ (deriving in most cases from the short /ɪ/ of Middle English). (Wells 1982: 127)

> The standard lexical set PRICE is defined as comprising those words whose citation form in RP and GenAm has the stressed vowel /aɪ/. (Wells 1982: 149)

'These' (and the like), adds Wells, 'enable one to refer concisely to large groups of words which tend to share the same vowel, and to the vowel which they share' (*ibid.*, xviii).

The role of RP in Wells' own formulation cited above makes it clear that this approach is not completely independent of RP. But contemporary SAEP, at any rate in its more conservative forms, and despite the existence, even in these, of a recognisable 'South African accent' is *approximately* isophonic with RP, with some divergences which we shall point out later.

9.6.3   Short vowels

The *short 'checked' vowels* of SAEP are as follows:

1   The TRAP vowel ranges from [æ] 'to a broad accent [ɛ], cardinal 3 or closer' (Wells 1982: 613), as in Jeremy Taylor's *Ag pleez Deddy*.

2   The vowel of DRESS ranges similarly from a conservative [ɛ] to a more typical [e], cardinal 2 or higher, and often highest in *yes* (occasionally [jis] in the extreme SAEP in which *bread* may be rendered as [briːd]. This is perhaps mainly of East Cape provenance. Before syllable-final /l/ this vowel tends to be lowered and retracted so that *help* for some speakers may have [æ].

3   The vowel of the set for which SAEP ranges through BIT and KIT to the Afrikaans loanword PIK ('little chap') undergoes some 'complex

allophonic variation' (Lass 1987: 304). Conservative speakers may have RP-like [ɪ]. Lass suggests that 'for most Respectable speakers the norm is a centralised [ï]; but particular realisations of this vowel will vary both with speakers and with phonetic context.

(a) In such contexts as *kiss*, *kit*, *gift*, *sing*, that is, in stressed syllables and when it adjoins a velar consonant, SAEP has typically 'a centralised front [ɪ]' (Lass, personal communication). And following a velar consonant in unstressed syllables, such as the second syllables of *ending*, *frantic* and *plastic*, many speakers of SAEP use likewise a relatively high [ɪ].

(b) In the complementary set of environments, such as '*bit, lip, tin, slim*, both syllables of *minutes* and all three of *limited*' (Wells 1982: 612) SAEP has a centralised or central vowel [ï], further back than [ɪ] 'but not fully central' (Lass & Wright 1986: 207).

(c) In broad accents, however, [ï] tends to be replaced by a more open variant, close to [ə], even in stressed syllables, so that *dinner* becomes ['dənə] and *limited* ['ləmətəd] (Wells 1982: 612) though versions like [dïnə] are probably commoner.

Australian English, incidentally, has [ə] in the final syllables of *boxes*, *banishes* and *pushes*, where RP has [ɪ], and New Zealand English a stressed [ə] in, for example, *ship*.

A vowel ranging typically from [ï] to [ə] is generally used in SAEP for DIK ('full to satiety'), PIK ('little chap') and SKRIK ('fright'). These are members of a sizeable set of loanwords from Afrikaans in which they are typically rendered with [ï] or a stressed schwa, as in [bət] 'to pray', spelt *bid* (Wissing 1982: 36; Lass, personal communication).

It is arguable that these words constitute a 'distinctive' set; thus DIK [dək] does not rhyme in SAEP with *Dick* [dɪk] in conservative speech, often [dɪk] elsewhere. Nor does it rhyme with *duck* in its conservative form [dʌk]. *Pik*, *pick* and *puck* are a similar trio.

4 The STRUT vowel is variable in SAEP. Conservative speakers use [ɐ] or [ʌ̈] in stressed syllables, reducing it to [ə] in unstressed contexts, as many British speakers do.

Lass (1987: 304) suggests [ɐ/ɜ] as the typical range of variation for this vowel and remarks (1988: 19) that this nucleus has 'an enormous phonetic range' in 'standard' Capetonian English. In rapid speech from many sources we find, however, [ɐ], for instance in *dustbin*, *but*, *coming* and *run*.

5 *Bakkie* ('light truck'), *bang* ('scared') and *pap* ('porridge') are members of a large class of loanwords, many of them from Afrikaans or South African Dutch, which we call the PAP set. These include also *Gammat* (Malay folk figure), *kak* ('shit!') and *lappie* ('cleaning rag').

Pap, for many speakers of SAEP, is phonemically distinct from *pip*, *pup* and *parp*. We shall represent its typical vowel as [ä]; compare Branford (1978: xxii), who notes that 'variants are between the extremes of the [ʌ] of *hut* on the one hand and the [ɒ] of *hot* on the other'.

Wissing (1982: 36) renders the corresponding Afrikaans vowel as [a] as in *bad* [bat], 'bath'. For some items in this class, conservative and other speakers may use [æ]. Thus one hears *lappie* ('cleaning rag, dishcloth') both as [lapi] and [læpi], and the commonest English pronunciation of *rand* (often [rant]), the principal South African currency unit, is probably /ræ:nd/.

6 The vowel of LOT is often less rounded and more central than in RP. A typical value for many speakers is [ö] (Lass 1988), though we have heard it as [o] in East Cape speech, and Lass reports [ä] from Natal. Thus the prestige *non-* in *non-Jewish* and *non-white* is often [nɐn] rather than [nɒn]. This is possibly a group feature typical of some Jewish and young white radical speakers.

In the initial syllables of words like *computer*, *confess*, and *condemn*, SAEP has often an [ɒ]-like vowel rather than [ə]. Wells (1982: 300) notes the same manifestation in 'Near-RP'. Here, then, we have either a residual northernism or a hypercorrection common in SAEP and other varieties.

7 The vowel of FOOT and PUT, typically [ʊ], may vary between this and a centralised [ö].

In summary, the short stressed vowels of SAEP relate to each other in such a pattern as this:

Short vowels

BIT, HIS /ɪ/ɪ/		FOOT /ʊ/ö/
	DIK /ï/ə/	
DRESS /ɛ/e/		
	CUT /ɐ/	
TRAP /æ/ɛ/		LOT /ɒ/
	(PAP [ä])	

All of these are invariably 'checked' vowels except [a], which may occur finally as in *gogga* [xɔ̃xa], 'insect', and loanwords of similar structure.

Points of interest here are:

the 'raising' of the front vowels compared with their reflexes in RP;
the 'borrowed' vowel represented in PAP; but otherwise
the isophonic relationship with the short vowels of other 'southern' dialects.

8 *Weak vowels: happy, letter, comma.* The final vowel of *happy* is usually not conservative [ɪ] but a vowel of [ʊ] quality, of varying lengths. Wells (1982: 166) remarks that this 'is now the most usual quality in...the southern hemisphere'. *Letter* and *comma* words are typically pronounced with final [ə], though this may be strengthened to [a] or [ɐ] by certain speakers.

Some brief historical notes on the short-vowel system are given below.

(a) TRAP. Afrikaans, Dutch and the southern Bantu languages all lack a vowel of [æ] quality, so that both African and Afrikaans speakers are likely to render English *bag* as [bɛg].

For the vowel of TRAP, a raised /æ⊥/ is reflected in the London usage of the early nineteenth century. Wyld (1920: 199) cites a warning against such pronunciations as *hed* for 'had', *led* for 'lad' and *men* for 'man' from Batchelor's *Orthoepical Analysis* (1809). Compare Bernard Shaw's ruffian Bill in *Major Barbara* (1906): 'Mike a menn o me! Aint Aw a menn?'

The TRAP vowel has similar manifestations in Broad Australian. Mitchell & Delbridge (1946) note Australian *man* heard as *men*. Turner (1965: 98) places the vowel of Australian *pat* as 'about cardinal [ɛ]' and cites the variant recorded by Baker of *old lags* as *old legs*. This is one of several parallels between Australian and South African English sound systems, suggesting either similar vowel shifts in both or the conservation in both of similar earlier forms.

(b) The DRESS vowel was similarly higher, at any rate for some speakers, in southern British lower-class speech in the 1830s. Thus in *The Pickwick Papers* (1837) Bob Sawyer's Betsey has (like Goldswain) 'the kittle', and in the same year we meet 'a young kipple' in Thackeray's *Yellowplush*

Papers. Wells (1982: 304) gives [e] (not [ɛ]) as the DRESS vowel for contemporary London English.

(c) BIT *and related vowels*. For some of the various manifestations of the BIT vowel in SAEP there are, again, British dialectal, Australian and Afrikaans analogues.

In Jane Austen's 'First act of a comedy' (*Minor Works*, ed. R. W. Chapman 1954: 173) the cook responds to an order with 'I wull, I wull.' This suggests a retracted and centralised /ï/, perhaps as in seventeenth-century English spellings of *bushop* for 'bishop', *dud* for 'did' and *wuth* for 'with'. Lass & Wright (1986: 210–11) cite from the *Survey of English Dialects* a number of English dialect manifestations of ME /i/ as a vowel ranging from [ï] to [ə].

Wells (1982: 404) notes that in Glasgow the KIT vowel 'ranges from [ɪ] to [ʌ]' and adds that 'there may indeed be a neutralization of the opposition /ɪ/ vs /ʌ/, so that *fin* may be identical to *fun* ([fʌn]) and *milk* rhyme with *bulk*' (as sometimes in South African English).

For the vowel of *pit* in Australian English the sound is often lowered and centralised to approach [ə] (Turner 1965: 97). In New Zealand this vowel is typically 'a lowered [ɨ]', not contrasted with [ə], so that *ship* in New Zealand English is regularly realised as [ʃəp] (Wells 1982: 606).

Such vowels, furthermore, are close to the [ï] which in SAEP we have noticed in loanwords from Afrikaans like *dik*. Hence, perhaps, the view of Lanham & MacDonald (1979: 46) that their 'low schwa' 'originates in Afrikaans which phonemically opposes /ɪ/:/ə/ in stressed syllables'. Jean Branford (similarly) takes 'the dropping and retraction of the /ɪ/ of the *sit*, *spin* set' as a 'phonetic manifestation of close contact with Afrikaans' (personal communication).

The Australian and New Zealand data suggest, however, that we may here have an established vowel in certain 'emigrant' dialects, which in South Africa was strongly reinforced, as it were, by contacts with Afrikaners, the experience of 'Afrikaans English' (and perhaps by Scottish schoolmasters?). Lanham here sees the competent English/ Afrikaans bilingual as the principal agent of change.

The spellings in the *Chronicle* (1819–58) of the settler Jeremiah Goldswain have provided an important source (though only one) for speculation about the origins of SAEP.

Lass & Wright (1985: 144) note a sprinkling of Goldswain's spellings which suggest a raised /æ/, such as *contrector* for 'contractor', *thenked* for 'thanked' and *thetch* for 'thatch'.

Goldswain, however, reverses this move when he spells, 'fresh' *frash*, 'hedge' *hadge*, 'escort' *ascort* and 'trekked' *tracked*. Orthographic ⟨a⟩ for ⟨e⟩ is in fact commoner in the manuscript than orthographic ⟨e⟩ for ⟨a⟩. Casson (1955: 11) suggests that the spellings may possibly reflect two distinct but rather similar vowels in Goldswain's personal dialect.

'Raised /e/' is likewise suggested in Goldswain's spellings of (for example) 'get' as *git*, 'kettle' as *kittle*, 'seldom' as *sildom* and 'wrenched' as *rinched*. Goldswain was from Buckinghamshire, and these reflect 'a well-known characteristic of the modern Bucks dialect' (Casson 1955: 12). Such spellings were condemned as vulgarisms in the late 17th century: the *Writing Scholar's Companion* (1695) stigmatises e.g. *git* for 'get' and *hild* for 'held'.

Again in Goldswain's spelling there is an 'apparently opposite movement: lowering of /ɪ/ to /ɛ/' (Lass & Wright 1985: 145). Casson (1955: 12) cites *begen* for 'begin', *Bretsh* for 'British' and *presner* for 'prisoner'. Wyld (1920: 227) shows in detail that the tendency to lower /ɪ/ to /e/ 'arose in the East Midlands... and gradually extended southwards'.

Jane Austen's Cook is echoed, incidentally, by Goldswain in such spellings as *buld* for 'build', *bult* for 'built', and *sturep* for 'stirrup', though this is by no means a firmly established pattern in Goldswain.

The chain-shift hypothesis. Lass & Wright (1985, 1986) hypothesise, with a wealth of supporting detail, a chain-shift for the front vowels corresponding roughly to their picture of SAEP vs RP and related dialects of '"one up" for the lower two heights and "one back" for the highest'. Adapting a diagram of theirs:

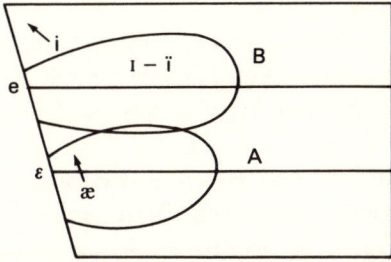

The shift originates, they suggest, in two areas of articulatory uncertainty or 'convergence zones' as reflected in Goldswain's alternating spellings ⟨a⟩ → ⟨e⟩, ⟨e⟩ → ⟨a⟩ (represented by zone A in the diagram) and ⟨e⟩ → ⟨i⟩, ⟨i⟩ → ⟨e⟩, represented by zone B. These convergences, they suggest, 'present the precondition for a chain shift along the front periphery of the vowel space' (Lass & Wright 1985: 147). Trudgill (1986: 133) presents a strikingly similar picture of 'innovation in Australian front vowels'.

Whether the SAE shift is explicable in terms of changes entirely 'within' the settler vowel systems and unaffected by Dutch–Afrikaans contacts is open to doubt. Lass & Wright, while arguing firmly for 'system integrity' and 'changes of L-internal origin' nevertheless point to the importance of 'the extensive English–Afrikaans contact that began in the Eastern Cape and continued on the Rand with the discovery of gold and diamonds in the 1870s'.

9.6.4   Long monophthongs

The *long monophthongs* of SAEP are variable and often 'replace' certain diphthongs of RP in more 'extreme' dialects or more informal styles.

9   The vowel of BATH, START, CAR, [ɑː] in conservative speech, has several variants elsewhere, tending to be 'very back and sometimes rounded' (Wells 1982: 615). A raised and rounded version, as in *park the car* as [pɔːk ðə kɔː], is a stereotype of working-class or rustic speech. It is a long-established item of SAEP, noted by Hopwood (1928: 12–13), who regards it as 'a Cockney English tendency', as in '*mawk* my words' for *mark my words* in *Punch*. (Cp. Wells (1982: 305) on the London variant.)

A similar raising is taking place in some contemporary Afrikaans, as when *die naam van die plaas* ('the name of the farm') is rendered with [ɑː → ɔː] in *naam* and *plaas*. Lanham (personal communication) suggests SAEP contacts as a possible cause.

In extreme SAEP the vowel of PRICE or TIME may take the form of a long, low fronted monophthong, for instance [ä] or [ɑː] in *I*, *I'll* and *I'm* and in the first vowel of *library*. (See also 16 in section 9.6.5.)

10   The THOUGHT vowel, 'a mid to open back rounded monophthong' (Wells 1982: 145) is [ɔː] in conservative speech. Both Lanham & Traill (1962: 201) and Lass (1988) agree in hearing a higher variant, [oː]; Turner (1965: 99) remarks: 'A slightly closer sound in Australian.'

11   The GOOSE vowel, high back and rounded [uː] in conservative speech, is often 'central [ü] rather than back', for example in *movies* and *use*.

Fronted [ʉ] occurs in several British dialect areas, including rural Devon (Wells 1982: 347), parts of Scotland (*ibid.*, 402; Gimson 1962: 114) and of East Anglia (Trudgill 1986: 114). Here a British or Scottish dialect origin seems highly probable, particularly in the light of Kidd's complaint about the Scottish accents of schoolmasters. Turner (1965: 100) notes that 'a monophthongal centralised [u] is common in New Zealand'.

12 The FLEECE vowel is typically stressed high front [ɪː] both in conservative and in broader SAEP. In more extreme accents it may be higher and more fronted than in RP. In such speech *his* and *he's* are regularly rendered with [ɪː]. In virtually all 'white' SAEP one will expect a phonemic contrast between *green* and *grin*.

13 The NURSE vowel, in RP 'a relatively long unrounded mid-central vocoid', [ɜː] (Wells 1982: 137), retains this value in 'the most RP-focussed conservative communities' but is otherwise characteristically rounded to [ø] (Lass, personal communication). Turner (1965: 100) describes this vowel as 'higher and more rounded in Australian English than in RP'.

14 The vowel of SQUARE is 'typically raised and glideless, even in open syllables': hence *fair hair* as [feː heː], with a vowel in the region of cardinal 2. (Lanham 1983: 339). See also 20 in section 9.6.5.

9.6.5   Diphthongs

The front-gliding diphthongs of SAEP are sketched below.

15 The vowel of FACE, PLAY and TAKE, in RP '/eɪ/...a front narrow closing diphthong' (Wells 1962: 141), has often a similar form in conservative SAEP. Lanham & MacDonald (1979: 46) describe this glide for broader SAE as 'backed, lowered, glide-weakened [aɪ]', with [Ä˙ə] as its most advanced variant.

This is interestingly close to the General Australian [ʌɪ] reported for the vowel by Mitchell & Delbridge (1965: 41) and Horvath (1985: 14).

16 The vowel of PRICE and TIME and the set which they represent varies between a diphthong [aɪ] in conservative speech through a 'considerably fronted and weakened' glide (Lanham & MacDonald

1979: 41) to a monophthong [ɑ:], so that *time* becomes, in extreme SAEP, [tɑːm]. This is the first of the 'eight salient variables' listed for SAEP by Lanham & MacDonald. Lass (1988: 22) finds that for about half of his Cape Town speakers [ä] is the only value.

Here the Broad Australian rendering is typically [ɒɪ]. Orton (1962) reports [ɑ:] as a British West Country variant, so that there is a just-possible input here from the speech of Cornish miners in the late nineteenth century. But monophthongisation of this vowel (e.g. to Yorkshire [ɑ:]) is widespread in Britain.

This vowel may vary within the same utterance, in SAEP: for example, in

> I tried to run after you into the street, but I couldn't find you.

with [aɪ] in *I* and *tried* and [ɑ:] in *find*, moving perhaps from a 'monitored' to a 'vernacular' rendering.

17　The vowel of CHOICE and BOY, in RP [ɔɪ], 'a wide diphthong with a starting-point which is back, rounded and approximately half-open' has sometimes in SAEP 'a higher onset than is usual in RP' (Lass 1988: 22).

Centre-gliding diphthongs are those of NEAR, CURE and occasionally the vowel of SQUARE.

18　In RP the NEAR vowel, /ɪə/, is 'a centring diphthong with a starting-point that is unrounded and fairly close and front' (Wells 1982: 153).

This glide can frequently be heard with a raised point of onset, resulting in an [ɪə] rather similar to the diphthong used by many mother-tongue speakers of Afrikaans in words like *geel* ('yellow').

19　For words of the CURE class in SAEP, as in RP, 'traditional /ʊə/ is now increasingly being replaced by /ɔ:/' (Wells 1982: 162: the CURE–FORCE merger). Some speakers have alternative versions, e.g. [kjʊə/kjɔ:] (Lass 1988: 23).

20　The vowel of SQUARE is one of the most typically South African sounds. Except among conservative speakers, it is regularly mon-ophthongised as a long [ɛː] or even [eː], so that *area*, for instance, becomes [eːrɪə]. The monophthong is quite often satirised on radio and television.

This vowel has glideless manifestations in British dialects, for example for some working-class speakers in Norwich (Wells 1982: 338). Significantly, it can be almost glideless for some Australians, for whom *fair* may be [fɛː] and *chair* [tʃɛː]. Mitchell & Delbridge (1965: 39) remark that 'In the pronunciation of some Australians, the glide in the centring diphthongs is very slight.'

The back-gliding diphthongs are the vowels of GOAT and MOUTH.

21   The GOAT vowel is a highly variable glide. Lanham (1967: 62) suggests typical values between [əʊ] and a monophthong [ʌː] in less conservative speech. Lass (1988: 23) hears the second element as unrounded, and the typical glide as /œö/.

Alan Paton, broadcasting in later life, had [ə̯ʊ] (perhaps [ʌʊ]?) in *no* and *those*. A student speaker from Johannesburg had [ə̯ʊ] in *Joburg* and in *home*. Another had [ɐ] in *only*. An East Cape student had [ɑː] in *foals* and [oʊ] in *old*, both in informal speech and within the same utterance. Not surprisingly, Lass remarks that 'phonetics students have more trouble deciding how to transcribe this than any other vowel in the system'.

Here again, there are British dialectal parallels, for example London [ʌʊ] as noted by Wells (1982: 312). But the South African values may simply represent a normal development of the diphthong, paralleled, for instance in Broad Australian, in *roller*, *rope* and *hoe* (Mitchell & Delbridge 1965: 43).

22   The MOUTH vowel is in RP typically a glide 'with a starting-point...about halfway between cardinals [a] and [ɑ]...in the direction of [ʊ], though so close and back a point is not always achieved' (Wells 1982: 151). Lanham & Traill (1962: 199) note 'a tendency towards fronting' and 'a much weaker, shorter glide' in broader accents. Lass (1988: 23) notes that 'this diphthong' has 'a strong tendency to monophthongise'. A more fronted sound than in RP is also characteristic of Australian English, though the resultant vowel is typically [æʊ].

9.6.6   Consonants

The consonants of SAEP, as might be expected, differ much less from those of southern British standard English than do the vowels. There is, however, at least one important 'loan consonant' and a number of characteristic consonantal articulations, particularly in the more 'extreme' varieties.

(a) A sizeable lexical class of loanwords from Afrikaans, such as the interjection *ga* [xa], expressing strong disgust, are pronounced with a 'borrowed' consonant, which has only marginal status in British English as the final sound of *loch*. This is an unvoiced fricative, velar [x], as in the first consonant of *gom* ('lout'). In SAEP, as in Afrikaans, this fricative is velar before high front vowels and palatal elsewhere (De Villiers 1962: 49).

This class includes some words of high frequency, such as *ga*, *Gammat*, the 'Malay' comic hero, the vulgar *gatvol* ('fed up'), the colloquial *nogal* ('what's more'), *gogga* (usually an insect), colloquial and ultimately of Khoisan origin, and many more. (Both consonants of *gogga* are likely to be voiced uvular fricatives [χ].) The level of bilingualism in 1990 is such that most mother-tongue speakers of SAEP use this consonant freely both in Afrikaans and in English loanwords of Afrikaans and other origins which require it. Here then is a clear case of borrowing from Afrikaans or South African Dutch, though this borrowing was possibly facilitated by the influence of Scottish speakers with good control of /x/.

(b) Much more marginal are the click consonants used or attempted by some speakers in loanwords from African languages, for instance the sound of the initial lateral click of *Xhosa*, which, in varying manifestations, is now quite frequent. Such items, however, involve far fewer speakers and smaller and more specialised lexical classes than does the widely distributed [x]. They are marginal to SAEP as [x] is not.

(c) Zulu [ɬ], similarly, is 'no more tractable in SAEP than in loanwords from Welsh'; hence the well-known game reserve *Hluhluwe*, Zulu [ɬuɬuːwɛ], is usually called something like [ʃluˈʃluːwəɪ] in SAEP (Wells 1982: 619).

(d) Though most varieties of South African English are non-rhotic, loanwords from Afrikaans or South African Dutch tend for many speakers to retain post-vocalic /r/. Examples of high frequency are the final syllable of *Afrikaner* and the second of *apartheid*.

(e) SAEP /r/ may, as in RP, materialise as a 'post-alveolar frictionless continuant' with a fricative allophone after /d/ (Gimson 1962: 201). Lanham & Traill (1962: 214) note in broader accents 'a tenser articulation with the tongue tip sufficiently close to the alveolar ridge to produce friction in all positions. In its extreme form /r/ is fully rolled. A half-way stage is 'one-tap [ɾ]'. Lanham (1978a: 151) suggests that the typical contexts for fricative /r/ are word-initial, as in East Cape renderings of *red-red roses*, or after /tr, dr/, as in *try* and *dry*. For the tap, the favoured contexts are the clusters /dr, kr, gr/.

Hopwood (1928: 29) notes in 'broader' SAEP a 'trilled or semi-rolled' /r/, which he traces to Scottish and Irish as well as Afrikaans English. Lanham, however, takes the view that 'obstruent' /r/ originates in the settler English of the Cape as a 'product of accommodation to trilled *r* of Afrikaans'. Hopwood is probably correct in tracing this sound to convergent influences – established tendencies in some settler dialects, especially those of Scots or Scottish parties, reinforced by accommodation to Afrikaans.

(f) *Voiced /h/*. In certain contexts [h] is manifested in its voiced form, [ɦ], giving the auditory impression of a 'dropped aitch', as in the proper name *Gledhill* as 'Gledill'. Hopwood (1928: 31) notes this in the speech of his time, and its occurrence in 'Afrikaans English'.

Lass & Wright (1985: 213) note that the Afrikaans norm for /h/ is [ɦ], adding that, as far as they know, 'There are no non-South African dialects of English that have [ɦ] ... and South African [ɦ] has precisely the sociolectal distribution that we could expect from an Afrikaans source.'

(g) *Unaspirated /p, t, k/*. Lanham & Traill (1962) report a 'tendency towards loss of aspiration' for /p, t, k/ 'even in strongly stressed syllables'. Lanham (1978a: 153) adds that this 'is ... regionally associated with the Cape (all social classes)' and elsewhere with extreme South African English.

Lanham (1978a: 153) suggests that unaspirated /p, t, k/ originate in the Cape 'through accommodation to Afrikaans'. Lass & Wright (1986: 212) suggest that this is 'perhaps the best candidate of the lot for Afrikaans origin'.

(h) *Devoicing*. Final voiced plosives may be devoiced, especially in polysyllabic words; thus *defeated* may end with [t] (Wells 1982: 619). For SAEP there is here a possible Afrikaans influence (see De Villiers 1962: 45), though all varieties of English devoice to some degree.

(i) *'Epenthetic schwa'*. A common rendering of *film* in broader South

African English can be heard as [ftləm]. This may be a case of 'epenthetic schwa' (Lanham 1978a: 154) or possibly simply of 'syllabification' of /m̩/. This occurs in some contemporary Irish accents (Wells 1982: 435) as well as in some British rural dialects as reflected in Kipling's 'Ellum she hateth mankind' from *Puck of Pook's Hill* (Kipling 1948: 497). It may thus have entered SAEP in settler dialects, but it is also common in Afrikaans (Le Roux & Pienaar 1927: 145) and in New York vernacular too. Hopwood (1928: 26) notes it in the SAEP of his time.

(j) *Word-initial /h/.* 'Dropped aitches' are infrequent even in broader SAEP, though Hopwood observed them in 1928, noting this as 'a common Provincial English trait, especially in the Midlands and the South'. Lanham notes [h > j] as in [kʌm jə] for *come here* as typically South African. The virtual disappearance of *h*-dropping in South Africa, as in Australia and New Zealand, suggests a combination of influences: for instance, Afrikaans, which never drops initial /h/; encouragement in schools of more prestigious forms; and possibly dialect mixture.

9.6.7   Origins: whence South African English pronunciation?

In the present state of knowledge about SAEP there can be little certainty about the exact processes by which its present-day systems or their constituent units came into being. It has, as Lass & Wright (1985: 137) have suggested, the characteristics of a post-eighteenth century southern English dialect or dialect cluster, 'aligning itself on the southern side of all the major isophones', for example:

1   vowels of [ʌ] type in the CUT class;
2   a contrast between the classes represented by CAT (typically with a vowel in the [æ] area) and PASS (with a vowel in the [ɑ:] area);
3   a contrast between the PULL class (typically with [ʊ]) and the POOL class (typically with [u:]);
4   a vowel of at least [æ] height in CAT.

As Trudgill (1986: 127–62) suggests in some detail, in accounting historically for the phonetics and phonology of a 'transplanted' mother-tongue variety of English we can follow one, or more, of several lines of explanation, for example:

1   conservation of earlier forms and patterns;
2   the 'internal dynamics' of the transplanted variety, which may involve processes which began before the transplantation;

3   dialect mixture;
4   language contact;
5   standardisation encouraged by formal education.

In the case of a variety or variety cluster with as complex a history as that of SAEP, we are unlikely to be able to construct a single monolithic explanation that will fit the observable facts. Lass & Wright (1986: 203) argue persuasively, without excluding the contact factor, that 'an endogenous account of an innovation is more parsimonious than, and preferable to, one based on movement of features from one system to another' on the grounds (*inter alia*) that 'the normal condition for a language system is to be a self-contained structural network'. 'Self-contained' seems a rather odd notion for South African English, for which the perspectives of Le Page (1968, cited in section 9.1) and Trudgill (1986) seem more helpful. In the evolution of SAEP each of the processes listed above has clearly taken some part. The most influential have probably been dialect mixture and language contact, in particular with Afrikaans and its predecessor South African Dutch, and the input from many competent bilinguals.

As indicated in section 9.1, we have taken as our focal hypothesis Trudgill's version of Giles' accommodation theory: 'If the sender in a dyadic situation wishes to gain the receiver's approval, then he may well adapt his accent patterns towards that of this person, i.e. reduce pronunciation dissimilarities' (Trudgill 1986: 2). This holds good, we suggest, both for dialect-contact and for language-contact situations, though both of these will be influenced also by the relative power and prestige of the participants.

Early SAEP, we must add, awaits a more thorough exploration than has yet been made. A wealth of writings by early settlers has been preserved, but most of those published to date are either by writers of the standard or, if not, have been silently regularised in the printed versions. A useful exception is the *Chronicle* (1819–58) of Jeremiah Goldswain, of which Una Long's edition (1946–9) preserves the original spelling. Casson (1955) is a valuable study of this text, but studies of the genesis of SAEP must remain conjectural until much more work of this kind has been done.

Hopwood (1928) provides a synchronic overview of the SAEP of his time, with many useful indications of the possible origins of particular features. Of special interest are the many salient features of contemporary SAEP recorded over sixty years ago. There was thus in

Hopwood's time a recognisable SAEP at many points similar to our own, though there have been significant changes since, like the restoration of 'dropped aitch'.

With reference to the rise of the front-vowel series explored by Lass & Wright, Jeffery, the originator of the hypothesis, has two valuable comments. First, 'One wants to see variables not wandering in a vacuum but moving within the constraints of phonological space' (Jeffery 1982: 257), that is, as a system. Lass & Wright have done much to build hypotheses for such a system, but Jeffery, postulating a push-chain movement, comes close to an integrated account in his second comment:

> glide-weakening of /aɪ/ and /aʊ/ made it expedient to move them out of the phonological space of /aː/ so that they came to be realised further forward (except apparently for /aɪ/ in Cape English, which was moved back and up ahead of them) ... in this chain-shift realisations of /ɪ/ were conditioned by an adjacent velar consonant, with the effect that allophones not so conditioned reached [ï] first and then moved down the non-peripheral path towards [ɪ̈] as the velar-conditioned allophones kept on coming up towards [ɪ̈]. Hence the apparently paradoxical conditioning. It seems likely that as these allophones drew apart they fell under the influence of Afrikaans /i/ and /ə/.

This short passage provides a very elegant synthesis of many phenomena. Though its main focus is on 'the internal dynamics of the transplanted variety', it makes reasonable allowance for the effect of language contact (witness also the phonetic 'borrowings' reflected in *pap* and *gat*) and it could easily be extended to the striking similarities between Australian, New Zealand and South African English which have been pointed out in this section.

9.7 Syntax

9.7.1 Presentation

The syntax of formal South African English approximates to that of formal standard British or international English. Colloquial varieties have a number of apparently distinctive syntactic items and structures, but it is difficult in the case of many of these to determine whether they are in fact indigenous to South African English, of English dialect origin, or merely characteristic of informal English generally. Many, furthermore, have reflexes in Afrikaans, though this does not rule out the possibility of an independent English origin for some.

The order of presentation for these characteristics will be according to whether they are manifested:

1   as sentence-initiators;
2   in the noun-phrase;
3   in the area of Chomsky's *Aux*;
4   in the verb phrase, including structures of complementation;
5   elsewhere, for example in prepositional usages;

that is, in an order which approximates very roughly to that of left to right in the simple sentence. Our presentation is necessarily summary and selective, and omits a large number of structures outlined by J. Branford (1987 and elsewhere).

9.7.2   *Sentence initiators*

These are a group of particles including non-negative *no* (of early date), *ag* (1894?), *aikona* (1882?), *shame* (1932; noticed in section 9.5.1) and *yes–no* (1900). These share a typical sentence-initial or clause-initial position, meanings sometimes indeterminate and a role as generalised attitudinal or continuity signals. The dates given are of earliest appearances recorded to date in written texts. In speech, many of these items are probably much older.

A very common response is phatic or affirmative *no*, as in *How's it?*, *No, I'm fine* or

> 'Can you deliver it?'
> 'No, sure, we'll send it this afternoon.'

This looks like a borrowing from Afrikaans. Its uses closely parallel those of Afrikaans *nee* as an affirmative sentence-initiator, as in

> 'Hoe gaan dit?'
> 'Nee, dit gaan goed.'
> (Literally: 'How goes it?' 'No, it goes well.')

Ag functions as a generalised attitude signal, long established in South African English before the famous song 'Ag pleez deddy, won't you take us to the drive-in?' made it one of the hallmarks of colloquial style in the popular mind. Again the probable source is Afrikaans.

Aikona (Ng., 1901) is an emphatic particle, signalling negation, as in 'Aikona-closed!' (Slapolepszy 1985: 14) or non-existence as in *Aikona tomatoes*. The origin is Nguni *hayi khona*, roughly 'not here'.

Ja–nee (literally 'yes–no') functions both as an emphatic confirmation – *Ja–nee, that's a fact* – apparently its original meaning in Afrikaans, and to signal hedging or hesitation, as in *Ja–nee. Well, it depends.* (Compare the comic formula *Ja well no fine.*)

9.7.3   Noun-phrase characteristics

Distinctive noun-phrase features are few and appear to relate mainly to the determiner system, for instance the omitted articles in *We went to bioscope* or *They're on honeymoon*, both of which have Afrikaans parallels. Another feature clearly paralleled in Afrikaans is the respectful third-person form of address, noted in 9.5.1: 'When does Tannie (Auntie) want me to bring it?' In this, third-person *does* is in concord with *Tannie*. This practice has parallels in Malay (Lewis 1947), once the language of substantial numbers of slaves and others at the Cape, which avoids second-person pronouns in respectful speech.

An interesting marker of quantification is the suffixed *and them*, as in *When are Bill and them coming?* in which *Bill and them* means roughly 'Bill and the other people'. This construction is normally restricted to references to people previously mentioned or known to both speakers. Cassidy & Le Page (1980: 11) record an identical construction in Jamaican English, *the cow and dem*; compare Bahamian *the ministers and them* (Holm & Shilling, 1982: 4). This points to a probable English dialect model for both the Caribbean and the South African usages, which also suggestively parallel the *you-all* plural of the southern states of the United States. But the South African English construction is also a reflex of Afrik. *Jan-hulle* 'John (and) them', so again an originally English dialect form is 'reinforced' by a contact language.

9.7.4   Auxiliary

Some of the most interesting syntactic developments of South African English are in the area mapped by Chomsky under the symbol *Aux*. One of the commonest of these is *busy* as a reinforcing marker of progressive aspect even with 'minus-action' predicates, as in

> He was busy lying in bed.
> We're busy waiting for him now. (Radio South Africa)

in both of which the normal 'activity' sense of *busy* has clearly fallen away.

Here again there is a Dutch–Afrikaans analogue, *besig om te*, which is also the regular marker of progressive aspect, reaching back to similar constructions in informal seventeenth-century Dutch, for example:

> Alsje besig zyt om wel gerust te leven.
> 'All are yet 'busy' in living quietly.'   (cited in Lass & Wright 1986: 215)

The English construction occurs in an early settler document, (Goldswain's *Chronicle*, written about 1860) as 'I was bisy talking.' Lass & Wright (1986: 217) relate this to a long-established English construction as in Jane Austen's letter to Cassandra, 25 October 1800: 'Our whole Neighbourhood is at present very *busy grieving* over poor Mrs Martin, who has virtually failed in her business.' The innovative move in South African English is not, therefore, the use of *busy* as a progressive marker, but the use with – ACTION predicates as in *I'm busy having new sunglasses made*. 'The L1 system (English)', as Lass & Wright (1986: 219) point out, 'does have a pattern which accommodates ... *busy* in constructions parallel to some of those with *besig* in Afrikaans and earlier in Dutch.'

Aux plays an important part in negation and propredicates in British and 'international' English. Two related developments in South African English are special usages of *never* and *is it? Never*, in children's and non-standard varieties, often functions as a simple marker of sentence-negation: thus *I never borrowed your tackies* ('tennis shoes') would regularly refer to one occasion of borrowing, not to many. This enables the child to by-pass the complexities of *do*-support in negative transformations. The above sentence, moreover, could be followed up in dialogue like this:

> 'I never borrowed your tackies.'
> 'You did'.
> 'I never.'

in which *I never* illustrates the common South African English use of *never* as negative propredicate (Palmer 1965) in informal speech. Both patterns occur in non-South African informal styles; their high frequency in South Africa relates possibly to that of Afrikaans *nooit* ('never') as an emphatic negative.

Another informal propredicate is *Is it?* in such exchanges as

(a)   'They got married on Friday.'
        'Is it?'
(b)   'He has to leave town.'
        'Is it?'

The usefulness of *Is it?* is illustrated by the fact that the 'standard' response to example (a) would be *Did they?* and to example (b) *Has he?* These involve the selection by the respondent of appropriate pronouns and auxiliary verbs. The selection problems fall away with *Is it?*, which is formulaic and thus invariant.

R. K. Tongue (1974) records an exactly parallel use of 'short-cut' *Is it?* in the English of Singapore and Malaysia. Here again there is a possible English source, as yet untraced, for both constructions. There is also a parallel in the *Is dit?* of standard Afrikaans, in exchanges like

> 'Ons gaan môre Kaap-toe.'
> 'Is dit?'
> ('We're going to the Cape tomorrow.' 'Is it?')

Here again it may simply be that the contact language reinforces (in this case rather strongly) an established English pattern.

A further possibility is that 'Quite often English is simplified, both here and in other parts of the world far removed from our own, by rather similar processes' (J. Branford 1987: x), without necessarily an earlier dialect input (Trudgill 1986).

Another auxiliary phenomenon is the 'neutral' use of *must*, particularly in such questions as *Must I seal the envelope?*, where standard English would normally use *shall* or *should*. Here SAfrE *must* does not signal 'Am I compelled to?' and there is again an Afrikaans parallel in the 'neutral' uses of model *moet*. But R. W. Burchfield (personal communication) has pointed out that there are British parallels.

Concord 'errors', incidentally, as in *The delegates is arriving tomorrow*, are very frequent in student writing and in SATV newscasts, though in the latter they typically reflect Afrikaans mother-tongue interference.

9.7.5   The verb phrase

Moving now, in Chomsky's terms, from Aux to VP, we find a number of non-British verbal structures, mainly formulaic, such as *drink pills, play sport* and *ride on water* ('convey water'). There are also characteristic patterns of complementation, for example such 'adjective with in-finitive' structures as *The tree is capable to withstand frost*, for which the British rendering would be *capable of withstanding*. Complementation is one of the most variable and idiosyncratic processes of English syntax. There is also, for instance, the well-established *Vivien explains me the assignment.* But while we could multiply examples of VP patterns which deviate from their British equivalents, our impression is that these tend to be more scattered, more sporadic and of lower frequency in South African English than the Aux phenomena sketched in 9.7.4. In terms of Fillmore's conception of a sentence as

Sentence → Modality + Proposition

it is possible that dialectal characteristics are more strongly marked in the area of 'modality' than in that of propositional form. This would be consistent with the view that dialect syntax is more likely to be reflected in the deictic and attitudinal constituents of a sentence rather than in fundamental predication. This, if it holds true, is incidentally reflected in the relatively high frequency in informal South African English of the Afrikaans 'modal adverbs' *darem*, *mos* and *sommer* as in *We were sommer standing around in the rain*, in which *sommer* ('just') is an example of other relaxation signals common in informal speech.

9.7.6   *Prepositional and other usages:*

Space forbids us to explore a very wide range of characteristic prepositional usages. Several have Afrikaans parallels, such as locative *by* as in *He's working by a chemist*; *under* in the sense of *among*, as in the settler Collett's diary for 1839, 'Frightful sickness under my flocks'; and *otherside* as in the early *They stopped the coach otherside the bridge*, for which Afrikaans would have *anderkant die brug*. The very common *She's on lunch* may relate to non-locative uses of Afrikaans *op* ('on'), though this is conjectural.

The patterns of *Mr de Klerk is verlig* vs *the verligte Mr de Klerk* show that English has in this case borrowed the distinctive predicative and attributive forms of the Afrikaans adjective: the same holds for *Dr Treurnicht is verkramp* vs *the verkrampte Dr Treurnicht*. The British as well as the South African English press regularly make borrowings from Afrikaans adjectival morphology.

9.8   Conclusions and prospects

This essay has presented evidence to support the main hypotheses of section 9.1, notably that South African English reflects a complex symbiosis of cultures and languages without sacrificing its basic Englishness. Of particular importance have been the contacts with a

Dutch–Afrikaans society and language long established before the first British occupation and with its own social dynamics and linguistic patterns. English contacts with Black and Khoisan peoples and languages began early. The twentieth century, and in particular its second half, has seen an increasing input from Black experience and Black languages.

This is not to minimise the English contribution. Most of South African English, setting aside the accent, is, in varying degrees, quite ordinary English. But at many points and in many systems there has been a convergence of factors, external and system-internal, which has helped to give South African English its own uniqueness. The detailed arguments of section 9.1 need not be recapitulated here.

South African English is both conservative and innovative: innovative in vocabulary, conservative in pronunciation, at any rate in formal styles. The importance, at least to the middle of this century, of British models for South African English may relate in the first place to the minority status of English-speaking South Africans and secondly to the rather conservative political outlook of most whites among these. It may also reflect the threat to their identity presented by both Afrikaner and African political movements. Kidd, Hopwood and Hooper all reflect in their strictures on SAEP a basic Anglocentrism. With them, we are a long way from the American Noah Webster in 1789: 'As an independent nation, our honour requires us to have a system of our own, in language as well as government. Great Britain...should no longer be *our* standard' (cited in Branford 1976b: 299).

Since the mid-century, there has been a striking change of attitude. At one level are the literary achievements of such major writers as Roy Campbell, Sydney Clouts, Athol Fugard and Alan Paton. At another, there is the obvious delight of the popular press in the expressive potential of South African English, so that an article on the foreign minister can be headlined POTJIEKOS POLITICIAN. South African English, if the world survives nuclear and other threats, can thus be expected to become more South African.

Informal South African English has been innovative ever since Lady Anne Barnard's adoption of *soepie, springer, stoep* and *vrouw*. A particularly innovative period seems to have been 1820–38, reflecting settler contacts with Afrikaner, Black and Khoisan peoples. Hopwood (1928) has demonstrated that many of the salient features of SAEP were conspicuous in colloquial styles over fifty years ago. Many 'common' words – *berg, dagga, oom* and *stoep* – have long records of use in English.

And contemporary urban and underworld subcultures are particularly innovative, reflecting the striving for distinct linguistic 'identities' as observed by Le Page (cited in 9.6.1). Witness *askari* for a 'turned' ANC cadre now serving with the police.

South Africa has a history of 'interesting times'. This perhaps partially explains its contributions to the international English vocabulary, for example in the nineteenth century of *Boer*, *trek*, *veld* and *Zulu*, and in the twentieth of *apartheid*, *concentration camp*, *satyagraha* and *springbok*.

Some of the themes and oppositions sketched in sections 9.3–9.5, for example that of the natural environment vs its desecration by man, are commonplaces of the present era. Others, in particular the distance between black and white experience, and the strategies of renaming, may be more specifically South African. But these too can be matched elsewhere; South Africa is interesting less as a unique society than as one in which so many conflicts of the present day are so clearly and often violently articulated. Substantial changes lie ahead. As Ndebele (1987: 2) has pointed out: 'the development of English in various parts of the world has taken forms that are beyond the control of the native speakers'. Alexander (1990: 134) sounds a similar warning: 'In a free South Africa/Azania it can be anticipated that the English which will become the spoken norm will be very different from the standard South African English which today in effect discriminates against the vast majority of the population.' Alexander, however, clearly sees English as the lingua franca of post-apartheid South Africa, and Ndebele might (reluctantly?) agree. All South Africans in most of the future dispensations imaginable in 1990 are likely to need some English. The minority status in South Africa of mother-tongue speakers of English makes it a more acceptable candidate for the status of a national language than are 'one-constituency' languages like Zulu. Alexander's proposals for a standardised Nguni and a standardised Sotho merit serious consideration. English, none the less, has a significant role in a future South Africa, but exactly what that role is to be is a matter both for explicit language planning and for the actual dynamics of a society which has yet to come into being.

FURTHER READING

Since the history of South Africa and of its languages is at present being rethought in many different quarters, suggestions for further reading are not easy. Lanham (1983) provides a well-informed overview and Lass (1987) a stimulating short one. On the sound system, Hopwood (1928) is still useful.

Lanham & Traill (1962) present a detailed analysis. Lanham & MacDonald (1979) explore the 'social meanings' of accent in the South African context. Lass & Wright (1985) and Lass (1980) present refreshingly new perspectives.

For the vocabulary Pettman (1913) remains insightful and informative, Jean Branford (1987) is an indispensable reference source, as are Silva & Walker (1976). A definitive treatment may be achieved by the *Dictionary of South African English on Historical Principles* in preparation at Rhodes University. An overview is given in Branford (1976b). Silva (1978) is useful on the settler contribution.

On syntax, there are useful pointers in Branford (1987) but no definitive treatment as yet.

For general history Walker (1928) is admirably clear and detailed as far as he goes. More recent are Davenport (1980 [1978]), Maylam (1986) and Peires (1981). Platsky & Walker (1985) provide a detailed history of 'resettlement' and its consequences. Malherbe (1925, 1966 and 1977) presents the educational system in critical detail, as does Young (1987).

On language policies and planning Alexander (1989 and 1990) is of special interest; also useful are Ndebele (1987), Prinsloo (1985) and Young (1987). Donaldson (1988) is useful for Afrikaans–English interactions.

Note (March 1994) *Bantu*, *Sintu* and *Springbok*

Sintu, from *isiNtu*, 'African values and language', has by 1994 replaced *Bantu* in many local writings about the 'Black' languages of Southern Africa. It has not been possible to reflect this change in the text.

Springboks has been abolished as a designation for international sports teams and their members. It was to have been replaced by the 'politically correct' *Proteas*, but newspapers, radio and television are using *South Africans* instead in March 1994.

10 ENGLISH IN SOUTH ASIA

Braj B. Kachru

10.1   Introduction

The history of English in South Asia is one of prolonged heated debates and controversies. The controversy about the legacy of English and desirability of its continued place in language policies and its cultural associations has still not abated. However, the political map of South Asia is completely altered now from the way it was when the English language was originally introduced to the subcontinent over two centuries ago. The profile of English in the subcontinent is also different from that in 1947 when the colonial period came to an end and the country was divided into India and Pakistan. One task of the two new governments was to determine the role of almost 560 sovereign states which were ruled by maharajas, nawabs and lesser luminaries depending on the status and revenue of each state. In 1972, an independent nation, Bangladesh, was carved out of Pakistan after considerable bloodshed. When we refer to contemporary South Asia, we are talking of the following seven sovereign states: India (pop. 1,042·5 million), Pakistan (pop. 162·46 million), Bangladesh (pop. 150·6 million), Sri Lanka (pop. 19·39 million), Nepal (pop. 24·0 million), Bhutan (1·9 million) and Maldives (pop. 0·272 million).[1]

The projected population of this region in the year 2000 is 1,401 million, which will be 22·4 per cent of the world's population. The largest percentage (74·4) of this population will be in India, and the smallest percentage (0·19) in Maldives. These political divisions, though meaningful at one level, are somewhat misleading at another level. This vast region gives an impression of immense diversity, linguistic and otherwise. However, there are many underlying shared linguistic, literary and sociolinguistic characteristics among the South Asian states.

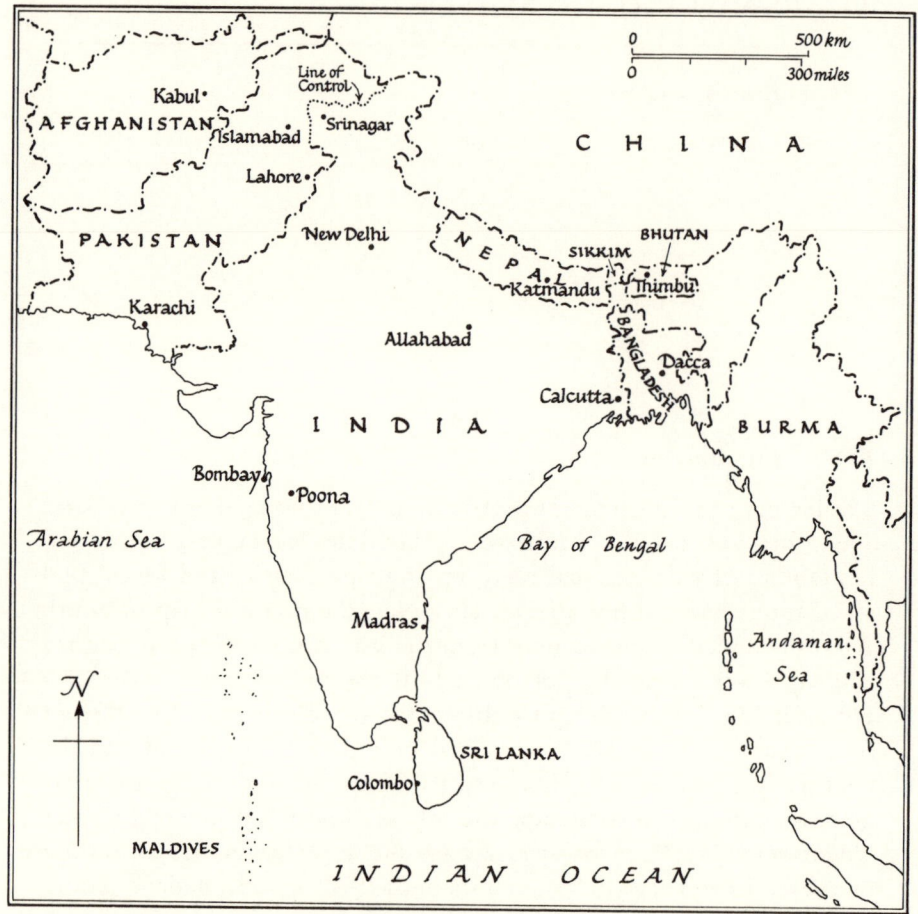

Map 10.1   South Asia

In linguistic terms there are four major language families: Indo-Aryan, used by the majority of the population, Dravidian, Tibeto-Burman, and Munda (see table 10.1).

It is not only that the language families are shared across the continent; there is also considerable linguistic convergence (*Sprachbund*) due to areal proximity and contact between typologically distinct languages, such as Dravidian and Indo-Aryan. This convergence is additionally the result of shared cultural and political history, shared literary and folk traditions, and all-pervasive substrata of Sanskrit, Persian and English, in that chronological order (Hock 1986: 494–512). All the major South Asian countries have a long tradition of societal

Table 10.1. *The main languages of South Asia*

Bangladesh	Bhutan	India					Maldives	Nepal		Pakistan			Sri Lanka	
Indo-Aryan	Tibeto-Burman	Dravidian	Indo-Aryan	Tibeto-Burman	Munda		Indo-Aryan	Indo-Aryan	Tibeto-Burman	Dravidian	Indo-Aryan	Indo-Iranian	Dravidian	Indo-Aryan
Bengali	Dzongkha	Tamil	Assamese	Bodo	Mundari	Divehi		Nepali	Newari	Brahui	Gujarati	Baluchi	Tamil	Sinhala
		Tulu	Bengali	Naga	Santhali						Punjabi	Pushto		
		Telugu	Gujarati								Sindhi			
		Malayalam	Hindi								Urdu			
		Kannada	Kashmiri											
			Marathi											
			Oriya											
			Punjabi											
			Sindhi											
			Urdu											

Braj B. Kachru

multilingualism, and several language areas include diglossic situations: using a learned variety of language in formal contexts and its colloquial variety in non-formal contexts (e.g. Tamil in Sri Lanka and India, Bengali in Bangladesh and India, Telugu in India, Nepali in Nepal and India). It is for these reasons that South Asia has been considered a linguistic area (Emeneau 1955, 1956; Masica 1976) and a sociolinguistic area (Pandit 1972; D'souza 1987). A number of these shared linguistic characteristics are transferred to South Asian English (hereafter SAE) and result in the *South Asianness* in this variety of English.

10.2   English in the South Asian linguistic repertoire

The formal introduction of English in South Asia has passed through several stages. What started as an educational debate in the seventeenth and early eighteenth centuries culminated in Lord Macaulay's much-maligned Minute of 2 February 1835, which initiated planned activity for introducing the English language into South Asian education.

Earlier, each Indian state had its own agenda for language in education and the political divisions did not foster a national language policy. In India, the largest country in the region, at least four languages had roles as languages of wider communication, or as bazaar languages: Hindi-Urdu (or varieties of Hindi and Hindustani), Sanskrit and Persian. The Hindus generally sent their children to *pāṭhśālās* (traditional Hindu school primarily for scriptural education) for the study of religious scriptures and for basic knowledge of the *śāstras* (Sanskrit instructional texts, and treatises). The Muslims sent their children to traditional *maktab* (schools for Koranic instruction). A number of denominational schools (*vidyālaya*) provided liberal arts curricula in Sanskrit, Persian, Hindi, Arabic or in the dominant language of the region. The policy for determining language in education, if there was one (see Kachru 1982: 60–85), was primarily an 'inward' policy; this education was secular only in a marginal sense. The Nālandā University (*viśvavidyālaya*, fifth century AD, in what is now the state of Bihar) was much closer to our present concept of a university; it was a Buddhist monastery established for scientific, theological and humanistic edu-cation and deliberation. Nālandā attracted students from neighbouring regions including Southeast Asia. Two other such universities were Vikramshila in Bihar and Takshashila in the North Western Frontier Province of Pakistan. There were also the *maṭha* (Hindu monasteries), which undertook the role of theological education, and this function of the *maṭha* continues even now. In Sri Lanka, this purpose was served by *pirivenas* (indigenous monastic institutes).

Only a small segment of the population could avail themselves of such opportunities. Thus there was no national language-in-education policy as we understand the term now. As Britain slowly gained administrative control of a large part of South Asia, attempts were made to develop a language-in-education policy. However, the new policy could not change the linguistic, cultural and religious diversity of the region. The educational Minute of 1835 did, however, provide for the first time a blueprint of a national language policy for the subcontinent, which sought to challenge tradition in initiating an 'outward-looking' policy.

And now, over 150 years later, it is clear that after the Minute was passed, the subcontinent was not the same, linguistically and educationally. And the diffusion of English has continued unabated in spite of sporadic efforts to arrest its spread. The roots of English are much deeper now than they were in 1947, when a new era of anti-English policies was expected to be introduced.

A detailed and cohesive history of the introduction and diffusion of bilingualism in English in South Asia has yet to be written. Whatever information is available is gleaned from the following types of studies: official reports concerning education, educational reforms and educational notifications (e.g. Sharp 1920), histories of education in South Asia (e.g. Law 1915; Nurullah & Naik 1951; Ruberu 1962), and from studies of histories of missionary activities, particularly those related to the introduction of literacy and education (e.g. Sherring 1884; Richter 1908; Neill 1984, 1985). The survey presented in this section is primarily based on the above sources.

The diffusion of English in South Asia is closely linked with the control of the region by the British, and its eventual colonisation for over two hundred years. The first South Asian contact with a speaker of English possibly dates to AD 882. It is claimed that the first English-speaking visitor to India may have been an emissary of Alfred the Great. According to the *Anglo-Saxon Chronicle*, Alfred's ambassador went to the subcontinent with gifts to be offered at the tomb of St Thomas. The next recorded attempts at contact started around the sixteenth century, and by the eighteenth and nineteenth centuries the political domination by the British was almost complete. As the British political power increased, so did the currency of the English language in various important functional domains. However, for understandable reasons, the earlier uses of English were restricted to a very small group of people: those who had to deal with the affairs of the British East India Company, and later those of the Raj.

In retrospect we see that the introduction of English into the language policies of the region has primarily gone through four stages. First, *exploration*; second, *implementation*; third, *diffusion*; and finally, *institutionalisation*. These four stages broadly capture the slow but goal-orientated efforts to bring to culmination the underlying policy of providing a secure place for English in South Asian education.

The foundation for the eventual introduction of English in the subcontinent was laid on 31 December 1600, when Queen Elizabeth granted a charter to a few merchants of the city of London, giving them the monopoly of trade with the east, primarily with the Dutch East Indies. The East India Company was essentially a small company of adventurous and enterprising merchants which had originally been conceived in 1599. A few trading 'factories' were established by the company in Surat (1612), Madras (1639–40), Bombay (1674) and Calcutta (1690). These 'factories' covered the major trade routes to the subcontinent. During the period of Charles II the Company became politically ambitious and consolidated its power as 'a state within the state'. It did not become a political power in the subcontinent until two favourable events took place: the victory of Lord Clive (1725–74) in the Battle of Plassey in 1757 and the land grant (diwānī) of three regions, Bengal, Bihar and Orissa by Emperor Shah Alam to the company in 1765. And, finally, when William Pitt's (1759–1806) India Act was passed in 1784, the Company gained joint responsibility for Indian affairs with the British Crown. However, the earlier attempts for the introduction of English cannot be attributed to one single group or agency, for the situation was much more complex than that. There were several groups working towards this goal, often with distinctly different motivations and interests.

During the phase of exploration, the role of the missionaries had been quite vital. At the beginning, the educational efforts of the Europeans

> had an ulterior purpose, viz. the propagation of the Gospel. Moreover, they were directed purely to religious education – the objects being the instillation of Christian doctrines into the minds of the people through their native language which the Europeans tried to master, as also the spread of Western education among the Indians in order to enable them to appreciate better the Christian doctrines.
>
> (Law 1915: 6–7)

Not all such schools used the native language for imparting education. There were several schools where English was used, for example, St Mary's Charity School, Madras (1715), the Charity Schools established at Bombay (1719) and Calcutta (1720–31), Lady Campbell's Female Orphan Asylum (1787) and the Male Asylum in Madras (1787), and the English Charity Schools in the South of India, Tanjore (1772), Ramnad (1785) and Sivaganga (1785).

The period of exploration is well documented in several studies (for India, Sherring 1884, Richter 1908, Law 1915; for Sri Lanka Ruberu 1962). The initial efforts of the missionaries started in 1614 and became more prominent after 1659. This was the time when the missionaries were permitted to use the ships of the East India Company. The 'missionary clause' was added to the charter of the East India Company at the time of the renewal in 1698 (see Sharp 1920: 3). This clause lasted for about sixty-seven years; in 1765, the policy changed, when support and encouragement of the missionary activities was abandoned.

The missionaries' reaction to this new policy was rather violent; the Clapham sect initiated agitation for continuation of missionary activities in the subcontinent. The efforts of Charles Grant (1746–1823) are particularly noteworthy in this context. Grant's concern was specifically about the 'morals, and the means of improving them' (Morris 1904). In Grant's view, the missionary activities were desirable for the moral uplift of the people, since it was the moral decay which was the main cause for the upheaval in the subcontinent. In his view, 'The true curse of darkness is the introduction of light. The Hindoos err, because they are ignorant and their errors have never fairly been laid before them. The communication of our light and knowledge to them, would prove the best remedy for their disorders' (Grant 1831–2: 60–1).

By 1813, the efforts of Charles Grant and his supporters, for example William Wilberforce, the Foreign Secretary, and Lord Castlereagh, bore fruit, and the House of Commons, in its thirteenth Resolution, resolved that:

> it is the opinion of this Committee that it is the duty of this country to promote the interest and happiness of the native inhabitants of the British dominations in India, and that measures ought to be introduced as may tend to the introduction among them of useful knowledge, and of religious and moral improvement. That in furtherance of the above objects sufficient facilities shall be afforded by law to persons desirous of going to, or remaining in, India.

It was in 1813 that William Wilberforce told Parliament to 'exchange its [India's] dark and bloody superstition for the genial influence of Christian light and truth'. The official sanction not only revitalised the missionary activities, but also gave a stimulus to the teaching of English, since initially English was one of the major languages used in the missionary schools (see for references, Kanungo 1962: 11–14).

The story of Ceylon, renamed Sri Lanka on 22 May 1972, is not much different: the island was declared a Crown Colony in 1802. However, before this declaration, in 1799, the Reverend James Cordiner went as a chaplain to the garrison in Colombo. He took over as principal of all schools in the settlement. The initial efforts to introduce English in Sri Lanka were again made by the missionaries; the government did not start imparting English education until 1831. By this time, Sri Lanka already had 235 protestant mission schools, and only ninety of them were under the direct control of the government.

By the time the government in Sri Lanka involved itself in imparting English education, the 'Christian Institution' was already there; its foundation was laid in 1827 by Sir Edward Barnes. The aim of the Institution was: 'to give a superior education to a number of young persons who from their ability, piety and good conduct were likely to prove fit persons in communicating a knowledge of Christianity to their countrymen' (Barnes 1932: 43; see also Ruberu 1962).

The Report of the Special Committee of Education (1943) in Sri Lanka makes it clear that in that country, until 1886, a large number of schools were Christian. The first British Governor, Frederick North, initiated far-reaching educational schemes and 'the Colebrooke–Cameron reforms of 1832 made explicit the position of English in Ceylon' (Fernando 1972: 73). It was in 1832 that English schools were established in five cities, Colombo, Galle, Kandy, Chilaw and Jaffna. Only sixteen years later, in 1848, the number of such schools had increased to sixty with 2,714 students (Mendis 1952: 76).

While the controversy concerning the role of English in India's education was going on, there was a small but influential group of Indians who were impressed by western thought and culture and its scientific and technological superiority. The English language was, therefore, preferable in their view to Sanskrit, Persian and Arabic, as it was a valuable linguistic tool for access to such knowledge. The most articulate spokesman of this group was Rammohan Roy (1772–1833). His letter, dated 11 December 1823, is often quoted as evidence for such local demand for English. The following excerpts from Roy's important letter are worth noting:

> Humbly reluctant as the natives of India are to obtrude upon the notice of Government the sentiments they entertain on any public measure, there are circumstances when silence would be carrying this respectful feeling to culpable excess. The present Rulers of India, coming from a distance of many thousand miles to govern a people whose language, literature, manners, customs and ideas are almost entirely new and strange to them, cannot easily become so intimately acquainted with their real circumstances as the natives of the country are themselves. We should therefore be guilty of ourselves, and afford our Rulers just ground of complaint at our apathy, did we omit on occasions of importance like the present to supply them with such accurate information as might enable them to devise and adopt measures calculated to be beneficial to the country, and thus second by our local knowledge and experience, their declared benevolent intentions for its improvement...
>
> When this Seminary of learning [a Sanskrit school in Calcutta] was proposed, we understand that the Government of England had ordered a considerable sum of money to be annually devoted to the instruction of its Indian subjects. We were filled with sanguine hopes that this sum would be laid out in employing European gentlemen of talents and education to instruct the natives of India in mathematics, natural philosophy, chemistry, anatomy, and other useful sciences, which the natives of Europe have carried to a degree of perfection that has raised them above the inhabitants of other parts of the world... We now find that the Government are establishing a Sanskrit school under Hindoo Pundits to impart such knowledge as is clearly current in India.

And, then, Roy adds arguments against spending government money on Sanskrit studies:

> If it had been intended to keep the English nation in ignorance of real knowledge the Baconian philosophy would not have been allowed to displace the system of the schoolmen, which was the best calculated to keep the country in darkness, if such had been the policy of the British legislature.   (see Roy 1823: 99–101; see also Wadia 1954: 1–13)

It is on the basis of pleas such as Roy's that Chaudhuri (1976: 89) ridicules the idea that English 'was imposed on a subject people by a set of foreign rulers for the sake of carrying on their alien government'. However, Chaudhuri is only partially right. The phase of implementation of English had to wait until the educational Minute of 1835 was passed. That Minute made English a constituent part of the language policy of South Asia.

The passing of this epoch-making Minute was not without extensive debate, which resulted in what has been labelled the Oriental and Occidental (Anglicist) controversy. The argument was about the indigenous system of education (the Oriental) as opposed to the western system of education (the Occidental), their merits and demerits, their relevance for the British interests and the interests and needs of the subcontinent. The debate began soon after 1765, when the East India Company was finally able to stabilise its authority in the subcontinent.

The main concern was to determine an official policy about the role and appropriateness of English in Indian education. The Orientalists proposed the *nativist theory* and the Occidentalists the *transplant theory*. Proponents for each side included administrators of the Empire, both in India and in Britain. The Orientalists included H. T. Prinsep (1792–1878), who acted as the spokesman of the group and who presented a dissenting view in a note dated 15 February 1835. Prinsep was supported by, among others, Houghton Hodgson, who worked for the Company, and John Wilson, a missionary scholar. The Occidentalists included Charles Grant (1746–1823), Lord Moira (1754–1826) and T. B. Macaulay (1800–59).

The Minute had the support of the powerful government lobby and was a classic example of using language as a vehicle for destabilising a subjugate culture with the aim of creating a subculture. As Macaulay says, this subculture in India would consist of 'a class who may be interpreters between us and the millions whom we govern, a class of persons Indian in blood and colour, but English in taste, in opinion, in morals and in intellect' (Sharp 1920: 116).

These words have frequently been quoted with various interpretations by researchers on Indian education and language policies. In Macaulay's view, this subculture could not be created using 'poor and rude' Indian vernaculars, and he believed that the learning of the East was 'a little hocus-pocus about the use of cusa-grass and the modes of absorption into the Deity' (Bryant 1932: 56–7). The answer to the debate, therefore, was to teach English. On 2 February 1835, he presented to the Supreme Council of India a Minute 'embodying his views and announcing his intention of resigning if they were not accepted' (Bryant 1932: 56).

The Minute finally received a Seal of Approval from Lord William

Bentick (1774–1839) on 7 March 1835 and an official declaration endorsing Macaulay's resolution was passed soon thereafter. This vital resolution for the introduction and diffusion of English in the subcontinent reads as follows:

> First. His Lordship in Council is of opinion that the great object of the British Government ought to be the promotion of European literature and science among the natives of India; and that all the funds appropriated for the purpose of education would be best employed on English education alone.
>
> Second. But it is not the intention of His Lordship to abolish any College or School of native learning; while the native population shall appear to be inclined to avail themselves of the advantages which it affords, and His Lordship in Council directs that all the existing professors and students at all the institutions under the superintendence of the Committee shall continue to receive their stipends. But His Lordship in Council decidedly objects to the practice which has hitherto prevailed of supporting the students during the period of education. He conceives that the only effect of such a system can be to give artificial encouragement to branches of learning which, in the natural course of things, would be superseded by more useful studies; and he directs that no stipend shall be given to any student that may hereafter enter at any of these institutions; and that when any Professor of Oriental learning shall vacate his situation, the Committee shall report to the Government the number and state of the class in order that the Government may be able to decide upon the expediency of appointing a successor.
>
> Third. It has come to the knowledge of the Governor-General-in-Council that a large sum has been expended by the Committee on the printing of Oriental works; His Lordship in Council directs that no portion of the funds shall hereafter be employed.
>
> Fourth. His Lordship in Council directs that all the funds which these reforms will leave at the disposal of the Committee be henceforth employed in imparting to the native population a knowledge of English literature and science through the medium of the English language; and His Lordship in Council requests the Committee to submit to Government, with all expedition, a plan for the accomplishment of this purpose. (Sharp 1920: 130–1)

With this declaration and approval of the Minute, yet another external language was added to the multilingual repertoire of South Asia. The implication of this imposition was that by 1882 over 60 per cent of primary schools were imparting education through the English medium. Macaulay's dream had, at last, been realised. In 1857, three metropolitan universities were founded by the government in Bombay, Calcutta and Madras which significantly contributed to imparting English education to enterprising Indians. There are, however, scholars who in retrospect feel that 'in the very conditions of their establishment and organization the seeds of the decline [of English] were present' (e.g. Nagarajan 1981: 663).

Was this the correct decision? The debate on this question, both among South Asian and western scholars, has continued since the Minute's final approval. Post-independence South Asian countries continue to argue about this issue from various perspectives (see e.g. Ram 1983).

The British linguist J. R. Firth (1890–1960) holds 'superficial Lord Macaulay' responsible for 'the superficiality characteristic of Indian education' (1930: 210–11). However, not all agree with the views represented by Firth. There are many, like Rammohan Roy, who were grateful to Macaulay and the British Empire for leaving the legacy of English to India. Macaulay stated twenty years later that he believed that the Minute 'made a great revolution' (Clive 1973: 426). There is no doubt that one has to grant him that (for detailed discussion see Banerjee 1878; Chatterjee 1976; Chaudhuri 1976; Sinha 1978).

The original role of English in South Asia was essentially that of a foreign language. However, with the diffusion of bilingualism in English, and its institutionalisation, English developed various South Asian varieties discussed in the following section.

10.3   Types of variation in South Asian English

The term SAE is used as a cover term for the educated variety of South Asian English. There are, however, several varieties within this variety. This situation, of course, is not different from the sociolinguistic context of any other institutionalised variety of English. The parameters determining variation include the following.

The first is the users' proficiency in English in terms of language acquisition and years of instruction in the language. The second is the region of South Asia to which the user belongs and the impact of the dominant language of that region on English. The dominant language may reflect characteristics of a single language (see e.g. Hindustani English, Pandey 1980; Kannada English, Murthy 1981; Maithili English, Chaudhary 1989 and Sadanandan 1981; Marathi English, Rubdy 1975 and Gokhale 1978; Pakistani English, Rahman 1990;

Punjabi English, Sethi 1976 and 1980; Rajasthani English, Dhamija 1976; Tamil English, Vijayakrishnan 1978 and Upendran 1980; Telugu English, Prabhakar Babu 1974; see also Ramunny 1976 for subjective reactions to regional and non-regional English accents in India) or shared characteristics of a language family (e.g. Dravidian English, Indo-Aryan English). The third variable is the ethnic background of the users. This variable has, for example, been used to describe Anglo-Indian English (Spencer 1966; Bayer 1986) and Burgher English in Sri Lanka. The term Burgher 'now indicates any persons who claim to be of partly European descent and is used in the same sense as "*half-caste*" and "*Eurasian*" in India proper' (Yule & Burnell 1886 [1903]: 130; see also Fernando 1972: particularly 73–5). Thus there is a *cline of proficiency* in English. The two ends of the spectrum are marked by educated South Asian English at one end and by Broken English at the other. There are other functionally determined varieties of South Asian English which have acquired various labels indicative of their function and the interlocutors involved in an interactional context. These are briefly discussed below.

10.3.1 *Babu (baboo) English* (Hindi-Urdu *bāp, bābā*)

Babu English was first used in reference to English-using clerks in the Bengali-speaking parts of undivided India. This regional restriction does not apply any more to the use of the term, and it is now used in most of north India, in Nepal and in some circles in south India. This term originally referred to the style of administrative English, but that register restriction is no longer applicable. This style is marked by excessive stylistic ornamentation, politeness and indirectness. The discourse organisation is typically that of a South Asian language. This variety has drawn the attention of scholars for over a century, and has provided linguistic entertainment in various forms. This style is used in T. A. Guthrie's *Baboo Jabberjee, B.A.* (1897); Cecil Hunt's *Honoured Sir from Babujee* (1931) and *Babuji Writes Home: being a new edition of 'Honoured sir' with many additional letters* (1935). The following examples are from '*Baboo English*' or *Our Mother-tongue as our Aryan brethren understand it: Amusing specimens of composition and style or, English as written by some of Her Majesty's Indian subjects*. This volume was collected and edited by T. W. J. (H. P. Kent & Co., Calcutta, n.d.)

Braj B. Kachru

Application for a post
Sir,

Being in much need and suffering many privations I have after long time come to the determination to trouble your bounteous goodness. To my sorrow I have not the good friendships with many people hence my slow rate of progression and destitute state.

Here on earth who have I but thee, and there is Our Father in heaven, needless to say that unless your milk of human kindness is showered on my sad state no other hope is left in this world.

Be not angry my Lord at this importunity for my case is in the very worst state. If your honour kindly smile on my efforts for success and bestows on me a small birth (berth) of rupees thirty or more per mensem then I can subsist myself and my families without the hunger of keen poverty, with assurance that I am ever praying for your goodness and liberality.

> I remain
> Yours obedient
> S. C. (p. 9)

Application for a situation
HON'D SIR,

In the holy bible of your honours religion it is said that knock and it shall open to you therefore I am humbly knocking at the door of your honour, hoping that by special grace of Heavenly Father your honour may cast the pitying glance on my object state.

Although not of Christian religion I enjoy much respect for it. It is true I am only a poor Hindoo but of highest caste which was also the religion of forefathers and mothers since the time memorial ('immemorial') many of my ancestors and posterities are now dependent on me for daily bread.

> Your Obedient servant,
> N. C. B. (p. 11)

Letter received by a magistrate who was about to retire from the Civil service
HONOURED AND BELOVED SIR,

I have heard with deepest emotion, and never ending regret, that my honoured master is shortly to proceed to Europe where his last days may be spent in bosom of family, and in contemplation of his good works, which have been done in such exalted manner and in which fear of friend or foe has never been allowed to appear, since I have been allowed to shelter under the wing of your kindness, my lot has been envy of many, and I have prospered so far the world's good is concerned, still I am dependent upon you, and therefore humbly beg to your honour some mark of respect or good feeling before you are 'lost to my sight and memory dear.' You can no doubt interest your successor in my welfare and advice him to cast the shadows of his favour also on me, that I may sustain my life with honour. For which mark of your kindness I shall evermore be thankful, and pray, notwithstanding, that you never have the less shadows.

Lastly, I implore your generosity in increase my pay before it is too late.

Man wants by little when alone, but I am in deepest dread for the prosperity of my family, whose wants are many as the sand of sea shores.

'Think of me

When this you see,'

and do the needful in my behalf more and for ever

I remain

Sir

for ever your attached servant

J. C. A.

(pp. 158–9)

10.3.2   *Butler English* (also called *Kitchen English* and *Bearer English*)

This variety is a result of language simplification in functionally restricted interactional contexts. It also shows limited control of the language. Butler English, though first described with reference to its use in the Madras Presidency (Yule & Burnell 1886 [1903]: 133–4), was used and continues to be used in major metropolitan cities in South Asia where English-speaking foreigners live.

It was primarily used by butlers, the head servants of English households, in communicating with their masters. An interesting aspect of this variety was that the native speakers of English used the same variety to communicate with their servants. In its structure, Butler English is like a 'minimal' pidgin and its formal features reflect the characteristics of the local languages, though it has simple SVO word order. One major characteristic of this variety is in the use of tense. The tendency is (Yule & Burnell, 1886 [1903]: 133–4) to use the present participle for the future indicative, *I telling* ('I will tell'), and the preterite indicative formed by *done*, *I done tell* ('I have told'), *done come* ('actually arrived'). There is, thus, deletion of auxiliaries and a high frequency of *-ing* forms. Additionally Butler English has a highly restricted lexical stock. Some lexical items have acquired specific meanings (e.g. *family* used for 'wife'). The characteristics noted in the nineteenth-century Butler English (Schuchardt 1891) are present in twentieth-century Butler English too (Hosali 1982). These include, in addition to the features and examples given just above, the Dravidian influence on the pronunciation of [je] for [e] and [wo] for [o]; *yexit* for 'exit' and *wonly* for 'only' and use of *got* to mean 'have'. The following examples are illustrative (Hosali & Aitchison 1986: 57).

(1)   Tea, I making water. Is boiled water. Want anybody want mixed tea, boil the water, then I put tea leaves, then I pour the milk and put sugar. [description of how to make tea]

(2)   One master call for come India … eh England. I say not coming. That master very liking me. I not come. That is like for India – that hot and cold. That England for very cold. [report of an invitation to England by a butler]

Butler English shows several underlying characteristics which are associated with pidginisation, for example deletion of verb inflections and prepositions, and indirect speech reported directly (Hosali 1982).

10.3.3   Boxwāllā(*h*) English (*-wālāh* or *vālā*; Hindi-Urdu suffix denoting 'owner, possessor')

This is a pidgin variety of broken English and is used by door-to-door sellers of wares (e.g. *papier-mâché*, jewelry and shawls). The itinerant pedlars, with boxes or bundles of wares, are found in the affluent neighbourhoods of metropolitan cities in South Asia, or in hotels. Such pedlars primarily visit locations where foreigners or the well-to-do local population lives. Boxwāllā(h) English has considerable code-mixing from one or more languages and a very simplified syntax.

> *I come go*: I am going away, but I'll be back.
> *One man no chop*: Eating is not the privilege of only one person.
> *This good, fresh ten rupee*: This is good and fresh; it is only ten rupees.
> *He thief me*: He robs, robbed, etc. me.
> *sāb, best, čiz, price good*: Sāb (sāhib) (mode of address generally used for a European) the price is good.

In some studies variation in South Asian English has been described in terms of a lectal range: acrolect, mesolect, basilect (e.g. for Sri Lankan English, Fernando 1989). However, in these studies the data for analysis are so limited that no meaningful generalisations are possible.

The recognition of varieties within South Asian English is a clear indicator of the institutionalisation of the language, its range in terms of functional allocation, and its depth in terms of societal penetration. The educated variety has pan-regional intelligibility. Additionally, it has a large number of shared contexts for comprehensibility of meaning (locutionary force), and interpretability of underlying sociocultural patterns (illocutionary force). This point is important here, since shared comprehensibility and interpretability are markers of the acculturation of English in South Asia (see Smith & Nelson 1985). There is thus a cline of intelligibility on which the educated variety of South Asian English ranks high. This is the variety discussed in this chapter.

10.4   The South Asianness of South Asian English

The major features which contribute to the distinctiveness of South Asian English are varied and complex. First, English is an additional language in South Asia; this means that in the total linguistic repertoire of the users of English, English may be a second, third, or *n*-th language. Only a small number of the total English-using population claim it as their first or only language. Such a claim, for example, has been made by some members of the Anglo-Indian community in India (Spencer 1966; Bayer 1986) and the Burgher English users in Sri Lanka (Fernando 1972). Second, English is acquired in typical sociolinguistic, educational and pragmatic contexts of South Asia. These contexts differ from one major region to another and from one South Asian country to another. Naturally, such contexts determine the way English has been taught, and the functional domains in which the language is used. Third, in the South Asian educational system, English has traditionally been taught as if it were a classical language, that is, as a written language and not as a spoken language. The result is that spelling or orthographic pronunciation plays an important part in the acquisition of English: at the beginning, orthography is the only serious access to the phonetic/phonological component of the language. One notices it in, for example, the use of double consonants in words such as *innate*, *illegal*, and *oppressive* and in the pronunciation of unaccented prefixes. Later, varieties of South Asian English provide an aural input for the language learner (see e.g. Appa Rao 1978; Gupta 1980; Premalatha 1978; Krishnamurti 1978).

The *South Asianness* of English, then, has to be characterised both in terms of its linguistic characteristics and in terms of its contextual and pragmatic functions. In a pragmatic sense, this variety has now deviated significantly from the mother-tongue varieties. Also there is hardly any serious input from the native speakers in terms of providing a pedagogical model, in the classroom or in other interactional contexts. The South Asian users of English have marginal interaction with the native speakers of the language. English in South Asia is essentially used as an intranational language.

The following sections present a brief outline of some linguistic characteristics of educated South Asian English.

10.4.1 *Phonology*

In its phonetic and phonological features, educated South Asian English has several shared characteristics. Though this variety has intranational and international intelligibility, it is used by only a small segment of the English-using population of the region. What has been presented (e.g. Nihalani, Tongue & Hosali 1979) as a surprisingly large range of variation, is actually not much different from that of any other native or institutionalised non-native variety. The shared identificational features of educated South Asian English are the following.

Consonants. There are some differences between RP and SAE consonant systems, but 'as a system, the consonant system of Indian English is often identical with that of RP and other accents of English' (Wells 1982: 627). The major differences are as follows. The alveolar series of consonants (t, d) are replaced by a retroflex series which are pronounced with the tongue-tip curled up towards the hard palate, for example [ṭiː] 'tea', [ḍɑːrk) 'dark'. The retroflexion increases considerably in Dravidian English (Tamil speakers in India and Sri Lanka, Malayalam, Telugu and Kannada speakers in India, and Brahui speakers in Pakistan); the fricatives [θ] and [ð] are replaced by plosives [th], [d] or [dh]; no distinction is made between the 'dark' and 'clear' varieties of *l*; /f/ is generally pronounced as aspirated /p/ (e.g. [phan] for 'fun'); no distinction is made between the voiceless palato-alveolar [ʃ] and its voiced counterpart [ʒ]; /r/ is generally retained after a vowel. A small group of radio and television announcers and some teachers use a non-rhotic variety but the speakers of this variety are an insignificant minority (Khan 1974; Bansal 1990).

The initial voiceless plosives are not aspirated, since aspiration of plosive consonants is distinctive in many South Asian languages (cf. in Hindi, Urdu, *pal* 'moment' vs *phal* 'fruit'). In English, aspiration of initial voiceless plosives is automatic, and it contrasts with the delayed onset of voicing in the voiced plosives; [pin] as pronounced by some South Asian English speakers is often heard as [bin] by the native speakers of English; /v/ and /w/, /n/ and /ŋ/ are not distinguished in the speech of some South Asian English speakers.

The distribution of consonant clusters is different in several sub-varieties: for instance, sk-, sl-, st- do not occur in initial position in several languages of north India (e.g. Hindi) and Pakistan (e.g. Urdu). In such varieties of English, *school, station, student, store* and *speech* are pronounced with an epenthetic vowel as in [isku:l], [isteʃan], isṭuḍant], [isṭo:r], and [ispi:tʃ] respectively. It is true that in Sanskrit borrowing in educated or High Hindi such clusters are present, for example, in *skandh* 'shoulder', *spardhā* 'competition', *sthāpit* 'established', *spaṣṭ* 'clear', etc. However, in colloquial (less well-educated) Hindi these are pronounced as *askandh, aspardhā, asthāpit* and *aspaṣṭ*. The Kashmiri speakers pronounce these words as [səku:l], [səte:ʃan], [sətu:ḍənt], [səto:r] and [səpi:tʃ]. In some varieties [ʒ] as in *pleasure* is replaced by [z]. Marathi speakers replace it by [dʒ] or [ɲɦ], and Punjabis and Kashmiris use [j]. Marathi speakers tend to replace friction at the place of articulation by glottal friction (Rubdy 1975).

Vowels. In the use of vowels, there is considerable regional variation. A majority of South Asian English speakers, however, use monophthongs where English uses diphthongs. Those speakers with a Dravidian language background use glides [j] and [w] with word-initial high vowels (e.g. *yem, ye, yel, yel, bi* for 'M.A.L.L.B.' and *wopen* for 'open'). There is no vowel reduction, and no distinction is made between the strong and weak forms of vowels. A large number of South Asian English speakers, termed speakers of General Indian English (GIE) have a seventeen-vowel system. It consists of eleven pure vowels and six diphthongs (Bansal 1990: 222–3).

The pure vowels: /i:/ as in *lead*; /ɪ/ as in *this*; /e:/ as in *game*; /ɛ/ as in *send*; /æ/ as in *mat*; /a:/ as in *charge*; /ɔ/ as in *shot*; /o:/ as in *no*; /ʊ/ as in *book*; /u:/ as in *tool*; /ə/ as in *bus*. The vowel glides are as follows: /aɪ/ as in *five*; /ɔɪ/ as in *boy*; /aʊ/ as in *cow*; /iə/ as in *here*; /eə/ as in *there* and /ʊə/ as in *poor*. In General Indian English vowels in diphthongs are not consistently long, and vowel length is not reduced before voiceless consonants. As mentioned earlier, a majority of speakers use ortho-graphic pronunciation: thus weak vowels (ə, ɪ, ʊ) in unaccented syllables are generally pronounced according to their spelling. This also applies to the pronunciation of unaccented prefixes and suffixes.

In Andhra Pradesh, the Telugu speakers do not use the diphthongs [eə] as in *there*, and [ʊə] as in *poor*; instead they use [e:r] and [u:r] in *fair* and *poor* (Prabhakar Babu 1974). In Punjabi English generally the distinction between [ɛ] and [æ], and between [ɑ:] and [ɒ] is not maintained (Sethi 1978).

Syllabification. There is variation between the use of syllabic /n/ and /l/. These are generally replaced by /ən/ and /əl/ (e.g. *button* ['bətən], *apples* ['æpəls]). In inflectional suffixes many speakers use [d] in place of [t] (e.g. [a:skd] *asked*).

Stress, rhythm and intelligibility. Differences in stress and rhythm are two good clues which mark a speaker in South Asian English. The differences in rhythm are noted in the division of 'sense groups' and 'tone groups', pauses in speech and in the 'intonation nucleus' (see Bansal 1969: 171 and 1990: 227–8 for Indian English). A broad characterisation of South Asian English stress is that the stressless vowels are not pronounced as [ə] 'losing both their quantity and quality whereas in IE [Indian English] stressless vowels appear to lose only their quantity but retain their quality' (Chaudhary 1989: 85). Masica and others (see e.g. Masica 1972: 7) have suggested that the difference in South Asian English and other varieties is one of syllable prominence.

The notion of stress and rhythm in South Asian English has also been discussed in terms of regional phonological characteristics; that of South Asian languages being syllable-timed as opposed to English which is a stress-timed language (see e.g. Chatterji 1926 [1970]; Nelson 1982). In a stress-timed language the stressed syllables occur at regular intervals of time, while the number of intervening unstressed syllables is not vital. This characteristic is termed 'isochronism'. On the other hand, in syllable-timed languages, all syllables in an utterance receive equal prominence and a length of time relative to the numbers of segments each contains. This characteristic has been termed 'isosyllabism'. Nelson's investigation involving American and Indian English (1982: 69–70) shows 'that the perception set for isochronicity in American English is created largely on the basis of the contrast of inter-stress intervals having zero and one unstressed syllable... The findings suggested that, in general, Indian English speakers do not shorten the stressed syllables before an unstressed to the extent that American speakers do.'

In several studies on Indian English stress, attempts have been made to show that there is a regular predictable pattern in Indian English stress (see e.g. Vijayakrishnan 1978; Pandey 1980, 1985; Sadanandan 1981; Chaudhary 1989). Chaudhary (1989: iii) claims that there is 'a very great deal of similarity and systematicity in the English spoken by educated speakers from nine different parts of India... Differences witnessed between different varieties are limited to the surface and can be predicted like differences between different dialects of any natural language.' He provides a set of rules with which 'one can predict the lengthening, reduction and elision of vowels, gemination of consonants and word stress in all these varieties' (1989: iii)

The non-segmental features of Sri Lankan English are discussed in Passé (1947). The main points are that stress (or force) accent is comparatively weak in Sinhalese and Tamil and that is reflected in Sri Lankan English too; there is no vowel reduction; and no distinction is maintained between strong and weak forms. Gopalakrishnan's observations on Tamil English of south India (1960) also apply to the Tamilians of Sri Lanka: He claims that there is an unawareness of patterns of primary as well as secondary stress, such as [mæk'beθ] for [mek'beθ], ['tjuːʃʌn] for ['tjuiʃʌn]; there is non-differentiation of stress patterns of nouns and adjectives on the one hand and verbs on the other hand, and there is an unawareness of the shift in stress formed in different parts of speech derived from the same Latin or Greek root.

The following tendencies have also been noticed: (a) placing of stress on the suffix itself; (b) according weak–strong stress to nouns as well as verbs in the group of two-syllable words showing grammatical contrast through stress; (c) giving full value to auxiliary verb forms written as contractions, and assigning them relatively strong stress as well; and (d) breaking up grammatical units arbitrarily within sentences, thus violating the confines of 'sense groups' and placing a strong stress on words other than those normally formed to have 'sense stress'.

Spencer (1966: 66–7) discussing the Anglo-Indian speech observes that

> It is, however, in certain prosodic features that the most distinctive deviation from R.P. is to be observed, in particular the relationship between stress, pitch and syllable length. The tendency in Anglo-Indian is for stressed syllables to be accompanied by a fall in pitch; indeed for a fall or low–rise to replace stress, since Anglo-Indian pronunciation does not show such marked variation in syllable intensity as R.P. The fall in pitch on the 'stressed' syllable is normally followed by a rise on the succeeding syllable, even on final unstressed

> syllables in statements. The tonic 'accent' is accompanied by a lengthening of the syllable in question; but this lengthening usually takes the form of doubling of the final consonant(s) before the transition to the following 'unstressed syllable'.

Elision of syllables also contributes to international unintelligibility, for example *government* ['gɒrmɛent], *university* [jʊ'nəstiː].

The differences in intonation are mainly in division of 'sentences into intonation groups' and in locating 'the intonation nucleus' (Bansal 1990: 228). Three studies on regional varieties of South Asian English further attest to the differences, Prabhakar Babu (1974) and Dhamija (1976) for Telugu English, Gokhale (1978) for Marathi, Latha (1978) for Malayalam, Sethi (1976) for Punjabi English, and Rahman (1991a) for the varieties of Pakistani English.

A comparative study of stress, rhythm and intonation of twenty Indian speakers representing five Indo-Aryan languages and three Dravidian languages, and five native speakers of English (Prabhakar Babu 1971) showed interesting results: Indian English had 70 per cent agreement with RP in word accent. The greatest divergence with RP in stress assignment was in words beginning with *re-*, *de-*, *dis-*, *com-* and words ending in *-self*, *-ity*, *-ic*, *-ical*; and the rhythm of Indian English speech was not exactly syllable-timed or stress-timed.

The range of variation in South Asian English, as seen in the preceding discussion, is wide, but the subvarieties, regional, ethnic and others, share a common core which makes them mutually intelligible and functionally effective.

10.4.2 Grammar

When we come to the grammatical characteristics of South Asian English, we are on rather difficult terrain. There is as yet no large-scale study of spoken or written South Asian English. Nor has any serious attempt been made to distinguish the features in terms of the proficiency scale, the register-specificity of the features and the distribution of grammatical features with reference to the regions.

The available studies are either impressionistic or based on analyses of restricted texts, from which some generalisations have been made. These studies, useful as they are, leave much scope for further research. A number of these studies date back to the 1930s (e.g. Kindersley 1938).[2] During the post-1960s, several register-specific empirical studies and contrastive studies have been undertaken using various theoretical approaches. These contrastive studies focus on selected aspects of structural comparisons between English and a particular South Asian language.[3] I shall summarise below some selected grammatical features of educated South Asian English.

Sentence structure. There is a tendency to use complex (over-embedded) sentences as opposed to simple sentences. One reason for this tendency may be traced to the diglossic nature of several major South Asian languages. In these languages, there are two styles, colloquial and formal (śiṣṭa). The formal style is a 'learned' style, and displays excessive lexical ornamentation and grammatical complexity. An example of such sentence complexity may make this clearer:

> In fact, schemes for the compilation of technical terminology, setting up of units of the Department of official language and Hindi type-writing and Hindi stenography training centres at division level and granting cash awards for commendable work done in Hindi both at the Secretariat and non-Secretariat level [*sic*] etc. have already been finalized and a sum of Rs. 10 lacs [Rs. 1 million] has been sanctioned for the purpose of meeting expenditures on these during the current year.
>
> (S. Dwivedi. 1981. *Hindi on Trial*. New Delhi: p. 243)

Function items. The typical South Asian use of the article (definite, indefinite and zero) has been discussed extensively in the literature for several decades. Dustoor (1954, 1955) classifies the Indian use of the article as 'missing', 'intrusive', 'wrong', 'usurping' and 'dispossessed'.

Is there a systematic use of the articles in South Asian English? The present research does not provide a definitive answer. It can be argued that if South Asian English is compared to British English, the types of difference indicated by Dustoor account for all the varieties of South Asian English. There are differences in frequency of the use of the article, and a number of differences are related to the acquisitional level of the user (see e.g. Agnihotri, Khanna & Mukherjee 1984 for the use of articles in English by Hindi/Punjabi-speaking undergraduates at Delhi University).

Tag questions. The structure of tag questions in South Asian English is identical to that of many other non-native institutionalised varieties of English (e.g. West African, Southeast Asian). In the native varieties of English, the tag question is attached to a statement. There is a contrasting polarity in such structures: a positive main clause is followed by a negative tag and vice versa. The parallel structure, such as in Hindi-

Urdu, consists of a single clause with a postposed particle *na*. In British English the tag questions form a set, out of which an appropriate choice has to be made according to the context. In South Asian English generally, that choice is restricted to *isn't it?*: *You are going tomorrow, isn't it?, He isn't going there, isn't it?*

Question formation. There is a tendency to form information questions without changing the position of the subject and auxiliary items: *What you would like to eat?, When you would like to go?*

Selection restrictions. In English, certain verbs govern certain forms of complements, for example *want* takes only an infinitive complement (e.g., *want to read*), *enjoy* only a gerund (*enjoy reading*), and *like* both. In South Asian English, these restrictions are not adhered to: for example, *The Baluchistan Clerks Association has **announced to take out** a procession; He doesn't **hesitate from using** four-letter words; She said that her party wanted **that we should not intervene** in internal affairs of Afghanistan* (Baumgardner 1987).

Reduplication. This is used both in spoken and written educated varieties of South Asian English and includes various word classes, such as *hot, hot coffee* ('very hot coffee'), *small, small things* ('many small things'), *to give crying crying* ('incessantly crying'), *who and who came to the party* ('who came to the party'). The use of reduplication is found in all the educated varieties of South Asian English and is used for various stylistic and other effects (Fernando 1989).

There are regional characteristics in the use of grammar too, which have been noted, for example earlier by Kindersley (1938) and recently by Sridhar (forthcoming). Sridhar's study was conducted in Bangalore, South India, and involved thirty undergraduate students. Sridhar notes the following features: the use of reflexives for emphasis (e.g. *Each of her word [sic] was respected as though it was God's orders **itself**; If you falter in the first few steps **itself***); the use of a quotative marker (*Indian woman was considered **as** a machine [as 'to be']*); the use of a limiter/qualifier as a clitic (*[They were] built up to live like that **only***); the use of discourse adverbs (**Like this** *the position of women has been changed* (this shows the transfer of Kannada *hīge*)); lack of agreement between antecedent and pronoun (**Women** *should take initiative to do any work **she** wants to do*). A number of examples are about tense and aspect (e.g. progressive for simple; present or past perfect for simple past). Sridhar also notices the tendency of 'idiom transfer' from Kannada (*In olden days women just worked **like a bullock*** (cf. Kannada *ettinante*); *Since her birth, she has been **under the hands of men*** (cf. Kannada *kay kelage*)).

In grammar, British English continues to provide a yardstick for standardisation of South Asian English. The above examples are merely indicative of the tendencies which mark the differences. An extensive grammar of South Asian English and its varieties is as yet an unexplored research area.[4]

10.4.3   Lexical Resources

The earliest South Asian lexical compilation is *Indian Vocabulary, to which is prefixed the form of Impeachment* (1788, Stockdale). Lexical studies such as these have resulted in a genre with several shared ethnographic, sociopolitical, administrative and descriptive characteristics. The glossaries of Robarts (1800) and of Sir Charles Wilkins (1813, see Yule & Burnell 1886: xxiv) are the earliest, though understandably amateurish, attempts at lexical listing. The main motivation for the Raj lexicography, as these studies may be characterised, was pragmatic: to provide lexical manuals or handbooks for the large network of administrators in a linguistically complex and culturally pluralistic subcontinent.

One such register-orientated study is *A Glossary of Judicial and Revenue Terms* compiled by H. H. Wilson (1855). The second part of the title clearly brings out the registral focus of the compilation: *and of useful words occurring in official documents, relating to the Administration of the Government of British India, from the Arabic, Persian, Hindústání, Sanskrit, Hindi, Bengálí, Uriyá [Oriya], Maráthi, Guzaráthí [Gujarati], Telugu, Karnáta [Kannada], Tamil, Mayalálam [Malayalam], and other languages.* In their compilation, published in 1886, Yule & Burnell concur that Wilson's work 'leaves far behind every other attempt in that kind' (p. xv). In Sri Lanka, a compilation of the 'native words' was published fifteen years after Wilson's work with the title *Ceylonese Vocabulary: Lists of Native Words Commonly Occurring in Official Correspondence and other Documents* (Colombo 1869).

A detailed review of such works is given in Kachru (1980). Out of a long list, one work certainly stands out with an esoteric title: *Hobson-Jobson: a Glossary of Colloquial Anglo-Indian Words and Phrases, and of Kindred terms, Etymological, Historical, Geographical and Discursive.* The title *Hobson-Jobson* is from the British soldiers' rendering of the Shia Muslim wailing cry '*Ya: Hasan! Ya: Hosain!*' at the time of the

Moharam ceremony – the mourning period observed by the Shia Muslims in commemoration of the death of Hassan and of his brother Husain (AD 669 and 680). In 1903, William Crook edited a new edition of this monumental book. In recent years, it has been reprinted both in England and India. Yule & Burnell were well aware of the register-specificity of lexical compilations that preceded their work: 'Of modern Glossaries, such as have been the result of serious labour, all, or nearly all, have been of a kind purely technical, intended to facilitate the comprehension of official documents by the explanation of terms used in the Revenue department, or in other branches of Indian administration' (1886: xv). In their work, Yule & Burnell deal with

> a *selection* of those administrative terms, which are in such familiar and quotidian use as to form part of the common Anglo-Indian stock, and to trace all (so far as possible) to their true origin – a matter on which, in regard to many of the words, those who hourly use them are profoundly ignorant – and to follow them down by quotation from their earliest occurrence in literature.
>
> (1886: xvi)

Almost all the studies discussed above were compiled by the British administrators of the Raj, or by other Europeans interested in South Asia. The first serious book-length study by a native South Asian scholar is by Rao (1954), who undertook his study within the context of 'Indo-British cultural and linguistic relations'. In his book, the South Asian lexical stock in the English language is discussed in linguistic (phonetic, grammatical and semantic), sociocultural and historical contexts.

South Asian lexical stock in English

There have been primarily two sources for entry of South Asian lexical stock into English: a small number of lexical items came through travel literature, including words related to flora, fauna, local customs, festivals and rituals, and a number of words related to the legal system, revenue and administration came from various other sources.

In Wilson (1855 [1940]: i) the pragmatic need for such South Asian borrowing is discussed with illustrations. Wilson suggests that the use of *ryot* and *ryotwār* is better than 'cultivator' or 'peasant', for the local terms 'suggest more precise and positive notions in connection with the subject of land revenue in South India'.

A period of major lexical intrusion came after the 1930s and this intrusion has not abated as yet. By 1783, the earlier trickle of lexical borrowing had increased considerably, and Edmund Burke was provoked to comment:

> This language is indeed of necessary use in the executive department of the company's affairs; but it is not necessary to Parliament. A language so foreign from all the ideas and habits of the far greater part of the members of the House, has a tendency to disgust them with all sorts of inquiry concerning this subject. They are fatigued into such a despair of ever obtaining a competent knowledge of the transactions in India, that they are easily persuaded to remand them ... to obscurity.
>
> (quoted in Rao 1954: 5)[5]

During the seventeenth and eighteenth centuries, in the register of administration and agriculture the following lexical items were adopted, not many of which have survived: *batta* 'travelling allowance' (1632, Urdu/Hindi); *bigha* 'measure of land areas, 3035 sq. yds (1763, Hindi-Urdu); *cadi* 'civil judge' (1608, Urdu from Arabic); *chit* 'a note or a letter' (1608, Hindi); *crore* 'ten million' (1623, Hindi/Urdu); *dawk* 'mail' (1623, Hindi/Urdu); *firman* 'imperial order' (1614, Urdu from Persian); *hashish* or *hasheesh* 'narcotic drug' (1598–1613, Urdu/Hindi from Arabic); *jumma* 'assessment for land revenue' (1781, Urdu/Hindi); *jowār* 'tall millet' (1636, Hindi/Urdu); *kotwal* 'police officer' (1623, Urdu/Hindi); *rahdaree* 'transit-duty, toll' (1623, Urdu/Hindi); *sunnud* 'deed of grant' (1759 Urdu/Hindi from Arabic); *zamindari* 'system of land tenure, jurisdiction of zemindar' (1757, Urdu/Hindi from Persian).

Types of lexical intrusion and range

The South Asian lexical intrusion into the English language is primarily of two types. The first class consists of those lexical items which have been assimilated across varieties of language, specifically in British English and American English (e.g. *pundit*, *mantra*). However, it is true that, for reasons of past close historical and political connections and sociocultural interaction, British English has assimilated a larger percentage of such lexical items. This is evident in the recent edition of the *Oxford English Dictionary* (*OED*2). The second type comprises those items which have not necessarily crossed the proverbial Seven Seas. Such items occur frequently in various registers of the South Asian varieties of English. Thus, a large majority of this second class of words are not included in the dictionaries of English. However, these do form an integral part of the glossaries or dictionaries focusing on South Asia. Hawkins' work is a step in this direction, particularly the supplement (1976: 685–717) which is 'intended for those who, because they live in the region or are interested in it, read current books and periodicals and older literature about India, Pakistan, Bangladesh and Sri Lanka' (685).

Thus words such as *gherao* 'surrounding and detaining a person to extract a concession'; *idli* 'steamed cake of rice and black grain'; *janta* 'the people, the masses'; *naxalite* 'violent agrarian revolutionary'; *razakar* 'volunteer'; *satyagraha*, 'friendly passive resistance' are included in the supplement.

The South Asian lexical stock may be divided into three major classes: those items which are borrowed from South Asian languages as *single* items and which may undergo various types of semantic shift once borrowed into English; those hybrid items which comprise elements of two or more languages in which, at least, one item is from a South Asian language, and the other from English; and those English lexical items which have undergone semantic extension or restriction in South Asian English.

The first class of words, single lexical items, are to be separated from the hybridised items or neologisms. A vast number of such single items have actually not been assimilated into the native varieties of English, though a small percentage have been assimilated and are included in the major dictionaries of English. The following are illustrative of the range of such items: *ahimsa* 'non-violence', *almirah* 'cupboard', *bangle* 'ring bracelet or anklet', *bindi* 'dot marked on forehead by Hindu women', *bungalow* 'one-storeyed house', *catamaran* 'boat or raft with two hulls side by side', *cheetah* 'large leopard-like animal with black spots', *cheroot* 'cigar with both ends open', *chota* 'small, junior', *coolie* 'native hired labourer', *cowrie* 'small sea-shell of Indian Ocean, used as money in some parts of Asia', *cummerbund* 'waist-sash', *curry* 'dish cooked with mixed spices and eaten with rice', *dinghy* 'small boat', *dungaree* 'coarse Indian calico, overalls', *gunny* 'coarse sack of jute fibre', *guru* 'Hindu spiritual or religious teacher', *jungle* 'land overgrown with vegetation', *jute* 'fibre from bark, used for sacking', *kurta* 'loose fitting tunic usually made of cotton', *myna* 'a bird', *pan* 'betel leaf', *pariah* 'social outcast', *pukka* 'real, genuine', *sarvodaya* 'uplift of all', *veranda* 'open pillared gallery around a house'.

The second class involves hybridised lexical items which consist of two or more elements from at least two distinct languages. A distinction is made between a hybridised form which has no grammatical constraint on the selection of items, and an item which has such a constraint. Examples of the first type are *lathi charge* 'baton charge', and *bindi mark* 'a dot-like mark put on the forehead by Hindu women'. The second type includes items such as *police walla* 'a policeman' or *brahmanic*. The productive suffixes *-wallah* and *-ic* have selection constraints in the sense that these can only be preceded by a fixed set of lexical items. Other such examples are *chowkidared* and *challaned*, where the *-ed* suffix has been added to *chowkidar* 'a watchman' and *challan* 'citation', and *cooliedom* and *goondaism*, where suffixes *-dom* and *-ism* have been added to *coolie* 'a labourer' and *goonda* 'a thug, rowdy'.

Hybrid innovations include the following major types. (a) *Hybrid collocations*: these are generally restricted to one register in South Asian English, although the register restriction does not apply to their South Asian elements in a South Asian language. The following hybrid collocations, for example, occur in the political register in Indian English: *Sarvodaya leader* ('a leader belonging to the Sarvodaya organisation'), *Sarvodaya Party* ('name of a party'), *satyagraha movement* ('insistence on the truth movement' associated with the Indian leader M. K. Gandhi), *Swatantra Party* ('Swatantra (independent) Party), *Janata Party* (Janata (masses) party). (b) *Hybrid lexical sets*: this is a functionally restricted semantic set, and operates in one register of a variety of South Asian English. An example of such a set is *purdah woman* ('a woman in a veil'), *-system*, *-lady*, which is frequently used in India, Pakistan, Bangladesh and in Nepal. In South Asian English this set is used only with reference to sociocultural contexts associated with Islam. However, in Hindi and Urdu, the word *purdah* ('veil') has no such semantic or register restriction. (c) *Hybrid reduplication*: this class is comprised of two elements from two languages in which the individual elements have the same connotative meaning, for instance in *lathi stick, cotton kapas, court kachari* and *curved kukri* the South Asian duplicated items have the same meaning as the English word which constitutes a part of the hybrid reduplication (Kachru 1983; 156–63).

The third class includes English lexical items used with extended or restricted semantic connotations and involves several productive processes:

1   neologisms transferred from underlying South Asian languages into South Asian English, such as *bull work, caste-mark, cousin-brother, cousin-sister, cow-worship, to break rest*;

2   innovations formed on the analogy of British English or in some cases American English, for instance *caste-proud* formed on the analogy of *house-proud*;

3   innovations which are the result of institutionalisation of English in South Asian sociocultural contexts, such as *eating-leaves* 'leaves on which food is eaten, mainly banana leaves', *military hotel* 'a non-vegetarian restaurant'.

In formal terms there are regular underlying processes involved in such formations. A number of these have been discussed in detail in Kachru (1983). Some of these innovations are area-specific; for example, *to break rest* and *bull work* are primarily used in Sri Lanka, and *coconut paysam* 'a dish made of coconut' (*paysam* 'pudding') is restricted to South India.

These processes have been discussed with illustrations in Kachru (1983, 1986a; see also Baumgardner 1990, 1993 for Pakistani English; Fernando 1989 for Sri Lankan English).

10.5   Models of English in South Asia

In South Asia, as in other parts of the world, there is a difference between linguistic behaviour and an idealised linguistic norm. Traditionally, for historical reasons, southern British English has been the norm presented to the South Asians through the BBC, a small percentage of the English administrators and some teachers. In the written mode the exocentric norm came in the form of British literature and newspapers. In reality there is a wide gap between the perceived norm and the performance of users. Educated South Asian English was the variety actually used in South Asia in the past and it continues to be used now (see Kachru 1985b: especially 214–16).

However, attitudinally it is a post-1960s phenomenon that identificational modifiers such as 'Indian', 'Sri Lankan' and 'Pakistani' are used with a localised variety without necessarily implying a derogatory connotation. A speaker of South Asian English approximating RP has always been marked as socially and educationally separate, and such speakers form a very small minority, which includes some radio and television announcers and selected teachers (Bansal 1990: 222). In Sri Lanka even in the 1940s, users of 'standard English' were considered 'apes of their betters' (Passé 1947: 33). The reasons for this attitude are sociological. However, during the past three decades, as the studies of Kachru (1985) and Shaw (1981) show, a different picture emerges. The attitudes towards exocentric models (e.g. British and American), and endocentric models (e.g. Indian) are changing. Tables 10.2–10.4 illustrate these trends. Kandiah (1981) clearly indicates that in the 1980s an RP-sounding Sri Lankan was less acceptable to fellow Sri Lankans than was a speaker of recognised 'Lankan English'.

The recent situation, then, is that there is a realistic attitude towards the issue of a model; there is recognition, and increasing acceptance, of the endocentric educated varieties, and there is also a significant impact

Table 10.2. *Indian faculty preference for models of English for instruction*

Model	Preference		
	I	II	III
American English	3·07	14·35	25·64
British English	66·66	13·33	1·53
Indian English	26·66	25·64	11·79
Don't know		5·12	

Table 10.3. *Indian graduate students' attitude towards various models of English and ranking of models according to preferences*

Model	Preference		
	I	II	III
American English	5·17	13·19	21·08
British English	67·6	9·65	1·08
Indian English	22·72	17·85	10·74
Don't know		5·03	
'Good English'		1·08	

Table 10.4. *Indian graduate students' self-labelling of the variety of their English*

Identity-marker	%
American English	2·58
British English	29·11
Indian English	55·64
'Mixture' of all three	2·99
Don't know	8·97
'Good English'	0·27

Source: Kachru 1976

of American English through films, television programmes, the Voice of America, newspapers and literature. The earlier British linguistic connection has become much more fragile, and 'RP and the British Standard have increasingly gone out of use while remaining an academic reference' (Hashmi 1989: 17). Hashmi's reference is to Pakistan, but it is true of the whole of South Asia. The discussion of the question of a model, whether it should be exocentric or endocentric, still continues, as is evident from the number of studies on the topic (see Aggarwal 1982; Ramaiah 1988).

10.6 Bilinguals' creativity in South Asian English

The term 'bilinguals' creativity' is used here to refer to creative uses of English in South Asia by those who are bilingual or multilingual, and who use English as one of the languages in their linguistic repertoire. South Asia has a long tradition of creative uses of English in journalism, broadcasting, literary genres and advertising.

India, to take one example from the region, is the third largest English book-producing country after the United States and the United Kingdom, and in book publishing it ranks eighth in the world. Among the languages in which books are published in India, the largest number of titles are in English. The average number of English titles per million of population published each year is 360, which is higher than the world average.

In three major English-using countries in South Asia – India, Pakistan and Sri Lanka – creative writing in English is being considered an integral part of the pluralistic literary traditions, in spite of opposition in some circles (see below).

In many important intra- and inter-regional domains of use, English, often mixed with local languages, continues to have currency. One can travel in any part of the region and find that even in an average-sized city, there is a newspaper in English, and the local radio and/or television station (if there is one) allocates some time to English. This is particularly true of India and Pakistan.

The English press in South Asia has a long history dating back to 29 January 1780, when the first English (newspaper) weekly, the *Bengal Gazette* or *Calcutta General Advertiser*, was published by an Englishman, James Augustus Hicky, who was its owner and editor. In India, the English press has immense influence, disproportionate to its circulation. This influence is not decreasing; rather it continues to increase. This trend has been particularly noticeable since 1947.

In South Asia, the English press has been instrumental in introducing various genres of journalism. In India, for example, there are seven daily papers which have been in existence for over one hundred years and out of these, four are in English: the *Times of India* (Bombay, 1850); the *Pioneer* (Lucknow, 1865); the *Mail* (Madras, 1867), and *Amrita Bazar Patrika* (Calcutta, 1868). In 1984, according to the twenty-ninth annual report of the Registrar of Newspapers for India, there were 21,784 newspapers and periodicals in India, out of which 16·9 per cent (3,691) were English publications and 29·2 per cent (6,370) were in Hindi. The Hindi newspapers had the highest circulation, followed by the English newspapers. The government of India publishes the highest number of periodicals in English, followed by Hindi. The pan-regional nature of English newspapers deserves emphasis here. Out of thirty-one states and Union Territories (areas directly administered by the central government) in India, English newspapers and periodicals appear in twenty-eight. In Pakistan there are eighteen English-language daily newspapers, thirty-five weeklies, thirty-three fortnightlies, 152 monthlies and 111 quarterlies (Baumgardner 1990). In 1985 Nepal had a total of thirty-two English language publications, and English was second only to Nepali (Verma 1988: 3). Sri Lanka has over half a dozen dailies and weeklies in English. In Bhutan and Maldives there are bilingual or trilingual papers and periodicals which include English.

It is, however, in South Asian English literature that the stylistic innovations and experimentation have been most creative. At present there is actually no pan-South Asian literature other than that written in English; it is the only writing which has a market in all the South Asian nations (however meagre), and has also created a market for itself internationally.

In South Asia, India has the largest, most vibrant, productive and articulate group of writers in English. There are both historical and educational reasons for this. True, the Indian writers in English have been controversial, and various issues concerning their identity and loyalty have been raised (Lal 1969: i–xliv; Jussawalla 1985). This controversy is somewhat muted now, and in the 1980s there was a slow reversal of the controversy. There seems to be an acceptance of Indian English literature as 'one of the voices in which India speaks', as the venerable Indian critic Iyengar said three decades ago (1962: 3). He does recognise that 'it is a new voice, no doubt, but it is as much Indian as the others'. Hashmi (1989: 2) considers English in Pakistan 'equally (if not more than equally) a Pakistani language'. In Sri Lanka English has become 'a means of self-expression divorced from the self-consciousness that had accompanied it before' (Wijesinha 1988: i).

Actually, South Asian English literature is not a very new voice.

Attempts at creativity in English go back to the 1830s; Kashiprasad Ghosh's *Shair and Other Poems* (1830) is considered the earliest South Asian attempt at writing poetry in English. Sochee Chunder Dutt, another Bengali, was the first writer of fiction. He also consciously initiated the process of Indianisation of English by translating Indian expressions into English. It is believed that Cavelly Venkata Boviah (1776–1803) was 'the first great [Indian] master of English prose' (Ramaiah 1988: xiii).

However, in the beginning, understandably, it was the deeply nationalistic political writing in English which dominated: this tradition can be traced back to Rammohan Roy (1772–1833). In such writing English was used as a linguistic tool in the freedom struggle; it was the language of an elite culture which cut across linguistic, cultural and religious boundaries. And now in the 1980s and 1990s, the same tradition continues and English is still the language of Indian (or, as Indians prefer to call it, 'All-Indian') and pan-South Asian dialogue (see Iyenger 1985).

South Asian novelists not only nativised the language by extensive stylistic experimentation, but also acculturated English in terms of the South Asian context. The processes of nativisation vary in their subtlety from one writer to another (see Mukherjee 1971; Kachru 1986a).

Indian English poetry dates back to the nineteenth century. The earlier poets include Aurobindo Ghosh (1872–1950), Henry Louis Vivian Derozio (1809–31), Manmohan Ghose (1869–1924), Toru Dutt (1857–77) and Sarojini Naidu (1879–1949). The modern period began in the 1950s and shows considerable influence from T. S. Eliot (1888–1965), W. H. Auden (1907–73) and other western poets. However, it has also initiated a period of considerable stylistic innovation and Indian identity. (See, for a detailed discussion and references, King 1987.)

The tradition of English writing in Pakistan dates back to the pre-partition days. However, this writing is recently being studied as national writing in English. Hashmi believes that in spite of the shifts in official language policy 'the creative writing in English has flourished' (1989: 8). He adds that 'Pakistani literature in English has been responsive, increasingly and almost inevitably as a national literature, to the society in which it is created, and to the sensitivities that the society engenders' (*ibid.*). Hashmi has anthologised Pakistani poets in his *Pakistani Literature: the Contemporary English Writers* (1987; see also Hashmi 1989 and Rahman 1991b; for Sri Lanka, see Wijesinha 1988).

Why write in English? This question has been seriously asked in India, in Sri Lanka, and in recent years in Pakistan. After the independence of India in 1947, and of Sri Lanka in 1948, this question naturally acquired new undertones. The creative writers in English are attacked on many counts: their commitment to the nation is considered suspect for abandoning the national or regional language and writing in a western 'foreign' language, their 'alien' medium is considered inappropriate for expressing culturally and socially determined sensibilities, and they are accused of catering to a foreign readership, and thus focusing on the exotic to satisfy the taste of such readership. The list of accusations and counter-arguments is long, as is the body of literature representing such points of view. A number of these points are discussed, for example, in Lal 1969 and Jussawalla 1985 (for Sri Lanka, see Kandiah 1971, 1981).

There is, of course, no one answer to the question, 'Why write in English?' One linguistically meaningful answer is that in multilingual and multicultural societies, which all the major countries of South Asia are, English has become, and is used as, yet another linguistic and literary resource. In the case of India, just to give one example, Indian English literature is one of the twenty-two national literatures recognised by the National Academy of Letters (Sahitya Academi). The creative and critical writing in all these languages, including English, is annually considered for national awards for excellence. In Pakistan, the Pakistan Academy of Letters recognises English works for its national literature prizes.

South Asian English literatures are part of the worldwide contact literatures in English. Contact literatures are essentially the result of the diffusion of English in its second diaspora in multilingual and multicultural contexts across the world (see Dissanayake 1985; Thumboo 1985; B. Kachru 1992).

At one level such literatures in English have national identities – Indian, Pakistani and Sri Lankan; and, at another level, contact literatures are components of world literatures in English, and they share the medium with the varieties of language in the 'Inner Circle of English' (e.g. the United States, Britain, Canada, Australia and New Zealand). The traditional canonical points of reference are not necessarily shared by these varieties. This, indeed, is an important point of divergence.

The bilingual writers in South Asia use several devices which contribute to the acculturation of South Asian English, and result in their 'national identity'. In these literatures a new historical and cultural backdrop is introduced to English literature. In many cases, as with Raja Rao, the discoursal strategies and the processes of lexicalisation do not necessarily belong to the traditional norms. The interpretation of such texts has to be in tune with South Asian cultural assumptions and linguistic innovations.

An analysis and description of the language design of such texts, therefore, demands going beyond the conventional conceptualisation and descriptive apparatus of the monolinguals' structural resources. Such resources include all the linguistic levels from lexicalisation to discourse and style. Within this view, creativity has to be interpreted in a broader context: the sociolinguistic context of 'verbal repertoire' or 'code repertoire'. The interactional characteristics of code repertoire and the convergence of such repertoires from two or more languages result in a distinct configuration, a marked language design. The identity features of the texts are not merely structural. In fact, the structural features provide only one aspect of such creativity. Equally important is the contextualisation of the text within the new context of situation. Linguistic innovations and contextual extension are two primary components of South Asian English literature.

What we see, then, is that the national literature of, for example, Britain or North America is only one of the identities of English literature. The other national identities of English (e.g. Indian, Pakistani or Sri Lankan) make up the total picture. The recognition of multiple identities of English, its linguistic and literary pluricentricity, does not simplify matters; the multi-identity of English unfolds a host of questions concerning textual interpretability.

I must revert here to the question of the distinctiveness of South Asian English literatures, and the characterisation of this body of writing in linguistic terms. In recent years this aspect of non-native varieties of English has been the focus of many investigations. I shall summarise the major points here.

First, such creativity entails the contextual nativisation of a text, embedding the text within its South Asian sociocultural and historical contexts. There is thus a shift from the traditional presuppositions of English, a crossover from one underlying canon to another (Kachru 1986a: 159–73). In linguistic terms, grammatically, lexically or collocationally, the texts may not be very South Asianised. The nativisation may be rather in the historical and cultural presuppositions in the text. It is in this sense that the cultural milieu of English has been expanded. It is this type of cultural and linguistic identity that gives validity to the claim that English has acquired pluricentricity in its underlying cultural presuppositions and in its linguistic norms.

Second, there is an altered concept of textual cohesiveness and cohesion. The organisation of textual structure may not necessarily be the preferred structure associated with English. It may be, and often is, a transfer from another underlying dominant language, and may involve a lexical shift: direct lexical transfer, hybridisation, code-switching, etc.

Third, the rhetorical strategies are not consistent with those used in the native varieties of English. The devices used for nativising rhetorical strategies include similes and metaphors from local languages which may result in 'unusual' collocations, combinations of lexical items, for the native speakers. The speech acts and culture-specific interactional markers are translated from South Asian languages. This device is clearly seen, for example, in the Pakistani novelists Ahmad Ali and Bapsi Sidhwa, the Indian novelists Mulk Raj Anand, Raja Rao and Khushwant Singh, and Sri Lankan novelists James Goonewardene and Punyakante Wijenaike. The bilingual writer chooses styles not only appropriate to the 'high culture' and 'popular culture' but also appropriate to the specific cultural and linguistic group of South Asia. This linguistic device, for example, is skilfully exploited by Raja Rao in his *The Serpent and the Rope* (1960) and *The Chessmaster and his Moves* (1987). The bilinguals' creativity also shows in the 'mixing' and 'switching' of languages.

The above discussion naturally leads to a more complex question concerning cross-cultural discourse: to what extent does the bilinguals' creativity in English represent the underlying thought patterns of South Asian languages? An answer to this provocative question is not easy, since very little research has been done in this area. I have briefly discussed this with appropriate references elsewhere (Kachru 1986a: 168–71; see also Kachru 1986b, Y. Kachru 1992 and Fernando 1976, 1989, particularly the section on 'styles for narrative, descriptive and serious discourse').

10.7   Contact and impact: Englishisation

Englishisation, the impact of the English language and English literature on South Asian languages and literatures, is one of the more lasting legacies of the British period. The prolonged contact of English with South Asian languages has resulted in a deep and subtle influence on the languages of the region, both major and minor.

In the preceding sections I have outlined various processes which have resulted in the South Asianisation of the English language. There is another, equally important facet to this contact, that of the Englishisation of South Asian languages. In the past, the South Asian languages have undergone three main linguistic influences: one major and all-pervasive influence has been that of Sanskrit, not only on the Indo-Aryan languages but also on the linguistically unrelated family of Dravidian languages. Sanskrit has, in fact, functioned as a rich repository for centuries and has provided models for literary forms and themes to most of the South Asian languages. Then came, much later, the impact of Persian. However, the Persian influence was restricted to those regions which came under the rule of the Muslims. In a series of major linguistic contacts, the contact with English is the latest and is in some sense multidimensional. It began with the introduction of bilingualism in English as discussed in section 1 of this chapter, and continues unabated even now.

Englishisation was responsible for changes in the outlook of English-educated people, and conceptualisation of things within entirely different sociocultural, political and philosophical frameworks. It opened up a new way of looking at social order, and the concepts of liberalism, secularisation and the fundamentals of humanistic culture as understood in the Judaeo-Christian tradition. One therefore agrees with George's observation, specifically made about Malayalam, a Dravidian language spoken in south India, that 'Apart from Sanskrit, no other language has *touched* Malayalam as deeply and as effectively as English' (his emphasis, 1972: 244). This observation applies to all South Asian languages and literatures. Chatterji, the noted linguist (1963: 135), sees this impact in a larger context; he says, 'contact with the European spirit through English literature brought in a real Indian renaissance, and gave a new course to literature in modern Indian languages'. The politician and visionary Nehru concurred with this view when he wrote, 'through the impact of English and of ideas through English our regional languages developed new forms of expression' (1963: 5).

A word of caution is appropriate here: one has to differentiate between those South Asian languages which had a well-established and rich literary tradition when they came in contact with English (e.g. Bengali, Marathi, Sinhala, Tamil, Telugu) and those languages which had essentially an oral tradition (e.g. Santhali, Munda). I believe that Singer's distinction between the 'Great Tradition' and the 'Little Tradition' (1972: 55–65) is useful here. English provided yet another model to the Great Tradition for developing literary genres. This is what Sanskrit has been doing for centuries as well as Persian to a lesser degree for some languages.

The impact of Englishisation has several facets. The first facet is related to the extent of the impact this language has had on all the major and minor languages of the subcontinent. By 'major languages', I mean those recognised as state languages by the governments in the region (e.g. Bengali in Bangladesh; Hindi and seventeen other languages recognised as the Scheduled languages in India's constitution; Nepali in Nepal; Urdu in Pakistan; and Sinhala and Tamil in Sri Lanka). A minor language is minor in the sense that it has no constitutional status. A minor language, however, may have a regional status within a country, or a government may recognise it in some other form. In India, for example, the National Academy of Letters (Sahitya Academi) does not restrict its support to the languages listed in India's constitution; it also supports additional languages (e.g. Rajasthani, Maithili, Dogri). This practice is followed by private or official organisations for support and encouragement of local literatures in other countries in South Asia.

The second facet is related to the new direction which English provided to the literatures and languages of the region. English contributed to conceptualisation of literature and literary theory within new sociological, literary and linguistic paradigms. It made models available for the development of literary genres traditionally not associated with South Asian literatures, for example, Walter Scott's (1771–1832) historical novels inspired prose writers to look at the past with a sense of historical curiosity, particularly in fiction. In Assamese, for example, Rajanikanta Bardoloi (1867–1939) was the first to attempt historical novels such as *Mirijīyarī* (1894), *Monomoti* (1900), *Nirmal Bhakat* (1926) and *Radhai Ligirī* (1930). In Gujarati, to take another literature from central India, Scott's influence is found in Nandshankar's (1835–1905) treatment of the historical theme in *Karan Ghelo* (1866). The same is true of Hindi, Sinhala and Nepali. These are not isolated examples; they are indicative of a major trend of the period.

The third facet concerns the contribution English made towards the extension of the thematic range of literatures and a new way of treating themes, particularly in literatures of the Great Tradition (e.g. Bengali, Hindi, Kannada, Marathi, Sinhala). This happened in many ways: by the expansion of genres which were already present and by the introduction of social realism, secularism and concepts of a social order different from the ones known to the subcontinent. A period of self-awareness was initiated. In India and Sri Lanka, for example, European modernism, introduced through English, provided dynamic paradigms of literary creativity. As a response to European modernism, new literary schools were established and innovative uses of diction were made to suit contemporary sociocultural and political themes.

The fourth facet is the function of English as a resource for formal innovation within a genre, such as blank verse, the sonnet and short expository essays. Additionally, English became a resource for the transmission of literary controversies, innovations and trends from major European (and some non-European) languages and literatures. A good example of this is the paradigm of 'progressive' writing introduced by the Progressive Writers' Movement in the 1930s. The impact of this movement has been immense in changing the direction of South Asian literatures in terms of both their thematic focus and stylistic innovations. The call of the progressive movement was to break away from the well-enthroned Great Tradition and accepted norms of literary creativity. The norms of Sanskritisation and Persianisation were seriously questioned (for further discussion and case studies see Coppola 1988). Such innovation was not restricted to the progressive movement. The influence of the Romantic movement has been substantial in initiating stylistic shifts, new metaphors and new literary movements. In Hindi, as in other South Asian literatures, the literary movement termed *rahasyavād* ('mysticism') was the result of the impact of the Romantic movement. A number of post-Romantic movements had their influence too, as had T. S. Eliot (1888–1965) and others.

There is general agreement that English has functioned as the main agent for releasing the South Asian languages from the rigorous constraints of the classical literary traditions. With the influence of English literature came new experimentation, and resultant controversies. The issues were seen in new theoretical and methodological frameworks. Some of the major languages, particularly those used in the metropolitan cities like Calcutta (Bengali) and Bombay (Marathi and Gujarati), became the vehicles for channelling the impact of English into other languages. What is called 'the Bengal Renaissance' did not influence only the neighbouring languages, Assamese and Oriya, but the gains of the renaissance were transmitted to Hindi and Urdu, among other languages. In turn, these literatures transmitted the literary and linguistic impact of Englishisation to Punjabi, Dogri, Kashmiri and so forth. It is in this way that Englishisation became a pan-South Asian phenomenon.

The processes of Englishisation further increased as the diffusion of English expanded in its societal depth and functional range. Englishisation became a symbol of modernisation both for the people and for their languages (see D'souza 1986).

And now, turning from the broad contours of the impact of English to specific formal exponents of Englishisation, I shall discuss the major features of this influence at various linguistic levels (for a detailed discussion see Kachru 1994, originally presented at Cambridge, UK, in 1987).

10.7.1   Lexicalisation

The lexis of a language is open to the greatest intrusion from a language in contact. I shall identify below some productive processes used in such lexicalisation, and their functional import.

> *Loanwords* (nativised in phonology). The intrusion of lexical items is found in practically every domain. However, the registers of science, technology, fashion, television, cinema and advertising have a particularly high frequency of such items (see e.g. Bhatia 1987; Meraj 1993).
>
> *Loan shifts* (internal creation). These are of two types: extension of a lexical item from English (e.g. *transport* is translated into Tamil as *pokkuvaraṭṭu* 'going and coming'), and lexis-bound translation in which the aim is to establish lexical equivalence (e.g. *illegal licence* is translated as *donga laysensū* and *common man* is translated as *sri samanya* 'Mr Common' in Telugu and Kannada respectively).
>
> *Hybridisation*. In hybridisation, as explained in section 10.4.3, at least one component is from English (e.g. *riṭ arjī* in Kannada and *riṭ darkhāsti* in Telugu, for 'writ petition', and Marathi *ṭikiṭ ghar* for 'ticket office').
>
> *Parallel lexical sets*: The use of parallel lexical sets which have roughly the same denotative meaning is an interesting example of the structure of the multilinguals' verbal repertoire. Consider, for example, the following sets from the Sanskritised, Persianised and Englishised verb formations in selected South Asian languages with the structure V + auxiliary.

Sanskritisation	Persianisation	Englishisation	Gloss
dayā karnā	raham karnā	piṭi karnā	'to pity'
ghriṇā karnā	naphrat karnā	haṭe karnā	'to hate'
pratikshā karnā	intizar karnā	waiṭ karnā	'to wait'
pyār karnā	muhabat karnā	love karnā	'to love'

One can multiply examples from other languages of the region.

A note of caution concerning two points is warranted here. First, it is not claimed here that one cannot discuss topics related to administration, agriculture or politics without lexicalisation from English. At one level, one can do without English. In agriculture, for example, farmers in South Asia have been successfully farming for centuries without the use of English. On the other hand, at another level within each domain of language use there is an Englishised communicative strategy. Second, it is true that in some domains of use English lexical items fall under the traditional definition of 'borrowing', that is the adoption of lexical items from one language into another to fill 'lexical gaps'. In this case, then, English is a 'giver' language, and it is performing the same function towards a South Asian 'receiver' language as Latin, Greek, German, French, Italian or Spanish performed in the earlier linguistic history of English. However, borrowing from English does not necessarily result in filling the lexical gaps. In fact, in most cases, English provides an additional lexical item for which there already is a native lexical item.

In many South Asian languages, the borrowed word from English is perceived as 'neutral' in many interactional contexts, or its use implies a certain status, class or level of education. This may not be true, in the same sense, of a word from Sanskrit, Persian or from a local source. That explains why in Tamil, for example, common words like *wife* and *rice* from English are sometimes preferred to the native words. In Kashmiri, English *widow*, *cancer*, *bathroom*, *sex* are preferred by educated natives to the Kashmiri words. The native words – in Tamil or Kashmiri – have caste, class or regional connotations. This is not true of an English word, and in that sense, then, English has 'neutrality'. One therefore sees that 'using English words or phrases where correct translation equivalents are available in an Indian language is common in educated informal speech' (Krishnamurti & Mukherjee 1984: 109). In Pakistan, as in other parts of South Asia 'the use of an English word is believed to add a note of refinement and elegance to conversation in the 'lower' languages (Hands 1983: iii).

10.7.2 Grammar

Englishisation at the grammatical level is mode-dependent and register-dependent. By 'mode-dependent' is meant restricted in terms of spoken or written mode. This distinction is not necessarily in absolute terms, and may primarily be in terms of frequency. The 'register-dependent' features have high frequency in a specific register. The impersonal and the passive constructions are two good examples. It has been observed that 'the use of passives and impersonal constructions in Dravidian languages is an innovation normalized in the newspaper style under the influence of [English]' (Krishnamurti & Mukherjee 1984: 110).

One important reason for such mode-restriction and register-dependence is related to the technology used in the media, especially telex, the teleprinter and telegraphic transmission of the news. Until very recently, these technological aids were used exclusively in English newspapers. The South Asian language newspapers and broadcasts to a large extent depended on translations from English. The features originally introduced by translation gradually initiated a language change, and eventually became institutionalised (for a discussion of translation and syntactic change see Danchev 1984).

The following are illustrative of the Englishisation at the grammatical level.

> *Impersonal construction.* The impersonal construction has become an areal feature of South Asian languages. This construction is no longer register-specific, and is now used in the colloquial style in Hindi-Urdu, for example *kahā gayā hai* 'it is said'; *zāhir hai* 'it is evident', and in other languages, too, such as Kashmiri *bōzān čhi* 'it is heard'.
>
> *Passive construction.* In the case of South Asian languages, some modifications in the passive are attributed to English, particularly the passives with the NP agent. In Hindi-Urdu a construction with overt manifestations of the agent has a high frequency in formal registers (e.g. *hemleṭ shekspiar ke dwārā likhā gayā thā* 'Hamlet was written by Shakespeare') *Word order.* The SVO construction in Hindi-Urdu is used for stylistic effect, as opposed to the traditional SOV construction. In the case of Indo-Aryan languages, particularly Hindi-Urdu, the following constructions are also attributed to the influence of English.

Indirect speech. In such constructions there is a back-shifting of a pronoun as in

bil ne kahā ki vo khā rahā hai.

'Bill said that he is eating.' (here *maĩ* (I) shifts to *vo* (he))

Post-head modifier 'jo' ('who') as in

voh laṛka jo āyā thā čalā gayā.

'That boy who came has left.'

Parenthetical clause. This construction has been attributed to contact with Persian and English. The use of such a construction has pragmatic implications which indicate reaction to a situation as in the following Hindi sentence.

Anita kal sakul mẽ thī, aur jahān tak maĩ samajhtī hũ, voh akelī sakul āyi thī.
'Anita was in school yesterday, and so far as I understand, she came alone to the school.'

10.7.3 The 'mixers' and 'mixing'

In the specific context of this chapter, the 'mixers' are South Asian bilinguals who 'mix' a South Asian language and English. Mixing implies the use of two or more languages in a cohesive way within a stream of discourse.[6]

The use of mixing with English is found in both spoken and written modes of South Asian languages. Code-mixed texts have a wide range of use, such as interactional contexts from personal to formal discourse, literary texts, newspaper stories and captions, and advertising. The motivations for the use of code-mixing with English include the following:

(a) *Register-identification*, particularly the registers of science and technology. In the case of South Asian languages, this is particularly true since the registers of local languages are as yet not quite stable and institutionalised.

(b) *Style-identification*. Both in interpersonal interaction and literary creativity, attitudinally speaking, the Englishisation of style is a marker of education, modernity and westernisation.

(c) *Elucidation and interpretation*. In using specialised vocabulary or technical concepts after using the term in the local language, a close equivalent in English is used to elucidate the term. It is like providing a 'translation equivalent'.

More important than these pragmatic motivations seems to be the social value attached to the knowledge of English and resultant

Englishisation. Social value represents the interlocutor's attitude towards a person who has linguistic flexibility in English, since the use of English is considered an indicator of status, modernisation, mobility and 'outward-looking' attitude.

Mixing South Asian languages with English is all-pervasive. In some registers, for example that of newspapers, the bilingual competence of readers is taken for granted. This explains the use of mixing in the following newspaper captions:

Panchayat system upholds ideals of human rights.

(*The Rising Nepal*, Kathmandu, 7 May 1977)

Pan masala 'causes rare disease'.

(*The Hindustan Times*, New Delhi, 5 May 1981)

Krishibank branch needed. (*The Bangladesh Observer*, Dacca, 21 June 1979)

Women to oppose Shariah bill. (*The Muslim*, Islamabad, 1 August 1990)

Advani begins rathyatra to 'promote nationalism'.

(*The Hindustani Times*, 28 September 1990)

The glosses of the local lexical items are as follows: *panchayat system* 'village council', *pan masala* 'betelnut mix', *krishibank* 'agricultural bank', *Shariah* 'Islamic religious laws', *rathyatra* 'chariot procession'. As is evident for most of these items, there are appropriate English equivalents but the local lexical items are preferred.

Englishisation goes beyond the units such as words, clauses, and sentences. It has contributed to the development of several stylistic and discoursal strategies which are approximations of the strategies used in the native languages and English. On the one hand, we have nativised English discourse, and on the other hand we have Englishised discourse in South Asian languages. In nativised English the speech acts, strategies of persuasion, request, apology and command, are South Asian, while the lexicalisation is English; it is in this sense that English has a local cultural identity (see e.g. K. Sridhar 1989a for use of such strategies in requesting in Indian English; see also Kachru 1965). South Asian languages have adopted certain strategies, for example of thanking, introducing, etc., which show the clear influence of English speech patterns.

The written mode of South Asian languages has also been Englishised; the whole system of punctuation marks has been adopted from the English writing system. In most South Asian languages (e.g. Hindi, Punjabi, Bengali) the punctuation marks were traditionally restricted to two vertical lines '‖' termed *virām*, for marking the end of a paragraph, or a 'thought unit', and one vertical line '|' termed *ardha virām*, for a full stop. This traditional system has now been completely replaced by a full set of English punctuation marks. The practice of breaking a text into paragraphs has also been introduced.

10.8   English in post-1947 language policies

The end of the British Raj in the subcontinent during the 1940s was supposed to initiate the slow but sure demise of the English language in South Asia. That actually did not happen. It is true that during the past half-century we have seen a wide range of attitudes towards the continued use of English in various official and public documents. However, the reality of use is different. The actual picture is one of ever-greater social penetration of English. The functional domains in which English is used have actually expanded rather than shrunk.

In linguistically explosive regions of South Asia – and most of South Asia is full of linguistic mines – a more or less *laissez-faire* policy has been adopted. In general, the trend is to leave the linguistic hornet's nest untouched, particularly when it comes to English. In India that policy has calmed down a situation that used to result in frequent language riots. In Bangladesh, Pakistan and Sri Lanka there have been several policy switches, but they have not drastically reduced the enthusiasm for English in the general public. In all the countries of South Asia, it has been realised that issues relating to English, and attitudes towards the language, are much more complex than the nationalists, educationists and language policy designers had made us believe.

What we see in India, which at present includes almost 78 per cent of the population of the region, is to a large extent true of other countries in South Asia. The central government seems to have a deliberate policy of 'wait and watch', while the state governments have generally oscillated on this issue from one position to another. There are, therefore, regional differences in policy making and its implementation in the twenty-two states and the centrally administered Union Territories of the Republic of India.

There is already an abundance of studies on English in South Asia's language planning, and this body of literature is ever increasing. The debate on this topic primarily centres around the pros and cons of the inclusion of English in the language policies (for detailed bibliographical references see Aggarwal 1982 and Ramaiah 1988).

The controversy is basically about three issues. What should be the function of the English language at various stages of education? What should be the role of regional language, national language and English? And in some selected circles there is even discussion of what model of English should form part of the curriculum (see Kachru 1982).

The first two questions have been raised in one form or another in Bangladesh, Pakistan, India and Sri Lanka, and the issues get more politicised at certain specific times, particularly at the time of elections. What makes matters more difficult is that attempts are generally made to seek political solutions to language problems which, naturally, leave educationists frustrated (see e.g. Tambiah 1967; Shah 1968; Annamalai 1979). As Nehru, the first Prime Minister of India, observed, the language question does not 'have anything to do with politics as such, but, unfortunately, the whole language question has got entangled in political issues' (1963: 1).

A retrospective look at the continued debate on English in South Asia confirms that the Orientalist/Occidentalist controversy of almost two hundred years ago has actually not concluded; the issues that confronted the proponents of the two sides of that controversy continue to surface in various forms in each South Asian country. However, there is one serious difference: the articulation of various positions takes a much more violent form now than when the debate first came up.

In the post-independence period, several attempts have been made to take a serious look at the issue of language-in-education, and particularly at the role of English. A brief summary of such attempts is given below.

In India, to take the largest country first, the President appointed the Official Language Commission on 7 June 1955 under the chairmanship of B. G. Kher (1888–1957). The commission was charged with the duty to make recommendations to the President of the Republic concerning the following points: (1) the progressive use of the Hindi language for the official purposes of the Union; (2) restrictions on the English language for all or any of the official purposes of the Union; (3) the language to be used for all or any purposes mentioned in Article 343 of the Constitution; (4) the form of numerals to be used for any one or more specific purposes of the Union; (5) the preparation of the time schedule according to which Hindi may gradually replace English as the official language of the Union, and as a language for communication between the Union and the State government; and so on (see *Report of the Official Language Commission* [*ROLC*] *1956*).

This Report is a vital document for understanding the post-independence position of English in India; it presents, among other matters, two rather opposing views about the functions of English in free India, one represented by the dean of South Asian linguistics, Suniti Kumar Chatterji (see his note of Dissent appended to the Report, 1957: 217–314) and P. Subbarayan. These two were less enthusiastic about an immediate switch-over to Hindi. The other view, the majority view, was held by those members of the Commission who supported an immediate change-over to Hindi and other Indian languages.

In the debate on the role of English in India, it is important to mention Article 343(2) of the Indian Constitution; the Article specified that the English language was to be used for all official purposes of the Union until 26 January 1965, and, according to Article 343(1), after that date Hindi was to be the official language of the Republic. This recommendation, however, could not be implemented, since the language controversy took a violent turn. In Tamil Nadu, in particular, anti-Hindi riots erupted in May 1963, and West Bengal also expressed its resentment towards the 'imposition' of Hindi in many ways, and not always in a non-violent form. This resulted in the Indian Parliament enacting an Official Language Act (1967). The Act extended English's lease on life as an additional language with Hindi to be used for purposes of the Union and in Parliament.

The Official Language (Amendment) Act was enacted to reassure the non-Hindi speakers that their interests would not suffer. This Amendment, however, did not allay the fears of those groups who felt that there was a conflict between their language and Hindi, or the groups supporting continued use of English. More importantly, no specific language policy was proposed. That job was taken up by a series of commissions which looked into the functions of English in the overall language policy, and the restructuring of the curriculum at various stages of education. I will just mention some of the more important commissions here: S. Radhakrishan (1888–1975), educationist and philosopher, and President of the Republic of India (1962–7), headed the University Education Commission. The Report submitted by this commission (*The Report of the Education Commission* 1950/1) was a thorough evaluation and provided a blueprint for Indian education. The Report naturally discusses the role of English in India (see especially 316–26). The past role of English is aptly summarised in the following words:

> it is true that the English language has been one of the potent factors in the development of unity in the country. In fact, concept of nationality and the sentiment of nationalism are largely the gifts of the English

language and literature to India ... English has become so much a part of our national habit that a plunge into an altogether different system seems attended with unusual risks.   (p. 316)

There could be no better refutation of Macaulay's original design for the introduction of English in the subcontinent. Macaulay's aim was, as quoted in section 10.2, to create a class of Indians 'English in taste, in opinion, in morals, and in intellect'. That did not happen; on the contrary, English became a vehicle for national unity, and for initiating a pan-Indian cultural and political awakening. The Report feels that 'the plunge is inevitable', and states that 'English cannot continue to occupy the place of state language as in the past. Use of English as such divides that people into two nations, the few who govern and the many who are governed. The one unable to talk the language of the other, and mutually uncomprehending. This is negation of democracy.' However, the Report does not negate the use of English in India's language policies; it adopts a pragmatic position, for 'we must take into account our *Yugadharma* [duty according to the needs of time]'. And the need of the time suggests, as the Report says, 'that English be studied in high schools and in the universities in order that we keep in touch with the living stream of ever-growing knowledge'.

This commission was to be followed by an appointment of a committee by the University Grants Commission in 1955, under the chairmanship of H. N. Kunzru (1887–1978). The Committee was formed specifically to review the status of English. The Kunzru Commission Report was published in 1965 (see *Report of the English Review Commission*). The Commission's major recommendations were the following:

A.   that the change from English to an Indian language as the medium of instruction at the state universities should not be hastened;

B.   that even when a change in the medium of instruction is made, English should continue to be studied by all university students;

C.   that it would be necessary to have textbooks prepared on scientific principles and that the Government of India or the Council of Secondary Education should take up this question for consideration;

D.   that in relation to the Three-Year Degree course, which is now proposed to be introduced in our universities, the teaching of English be given special attention in the pre-university class;

E.   that the teaching of English literature should be related to the study of Indian literatures so that, apart from its value for linguistic purposes, it could be an effective means of stimulating critical thinking and writing in the Indian languages;

F.   that it is desirable to have the question of courses of study in English and methods of teaching English at the state universities examined by an expert body and the recommendations of that body adopted by all the universities;

G.   that where English is not the medium of instruction at any university it is necessary to adopt special methods to secure an adequate knowledge of English as a second language;

H.   that far greater attention should be given to linguistics in our universities and in our teacher training colleges; and

I.   that it is in our educational interest that English should be retained as a properly studied second language in our universities even when an Indian language is used as the ordinary medium of teaching.   (p. 39)

In 1958, the Central Institute of English and Foreign Languages at Hyderabad organised a forum to deliberate upon the recommendations of the Kunzru Commission. Yet another Committee was appointed by the University Grants Commission under the chairmanship of G. C. Banerjee. The charge to the Committee was to examine the issues involved in the teaching of English.

What is the present situation? In the 1960s, after great debate, the Three Language Formula was proposed as a solution to language-in-education policy. It was endorsed by almost all the states and Union Territories, by some with excitement and by others with cynicism. Tamil Nadu and Manipur did not endorse it. The formula proposes studying at least three languages in the school years: the regional language, Hindi and English. In the so-called Hindi belt, which includes the Uttar Pradesh, Bihar, Rajasthan and Madhya Pradesh, it entailed teaching a Dravidian language (Kannada, Malayalam, Tamil or Telugu), the idea being that in the states comprising the Hindi belt, Hindi would function as the regional language. The underlying motive for teaching a Dravidian language was to balance in an even manner the language load of all the schoolchildren throughout the nation. However, during the last three decades holes in the formula have begun to appear. On paper, the proposal seemed to make sense, but in its implementation more problems surfaced than were envisaged. The main problem in implementation was that not all the states of the Union accepted the formula with enthusiasm; it was interpreted as bringing Hindi through the back door. In the Madhya-deśa (central India, core of the Hindi belt), the teaching of a Dravidian language was done in a superficial way, to pay lip service to the formula.

In the early 1980s, the government of India adopted a 'New

Educational Policy'. In its essential provisions it is not very different from the 1966 policy; it reiterates its support of the Three Language Formula and recommends its enthusiastic implementation in the states.

The controversies and agony which India shows in relation to the role of English as a language-in-education is shared by other South Asian countries. In all South Asian countries there are language conflicts, the differences being in degree and in the number of languages involved. In Pakistan, the tension is among the speakers of Urdu, Sindhi, Punjabi and Pushtu; in Sri Lanka, between Sinhala and Tamil; and in Nepal, among Nepali, Newari and Bhojpuri. All the countries have to assign a role to English and to a language of religious and ritualistic identity – Sanskrit in the case of Hindus, Arabic for the Muslims, and Pali for the Buddhists.

I have discussed the post-1947 deliberations concerning English in India in detail. In other South Asian countries, the issues about English in education and its international and intranational roles have been identical. I shall briefly present these below.

The Pakistan Constitution of 1956, and amendments of 1968, 1972 and 1985, recognise Urdu as the official language of the country: 'the English language may be used for official purposes until arrangements are made for its replacement by Urdu'. This position is reflected in various reports of the government of Pakistan. In 1981, the President of Pakistan set up a Study Group on the Teaching of Languages, the convenor of the group being Anjum Riyazul Haque. The report

> recommends that Urdu should continue to be the only medium of instruction at the school level, with no exception, overt or covert in any school, and that a federal agency should ensure the implementation of this policy. English and Arabic should be introduced from class six onwards, though Arabic will be taught as part of Islamiyat curriculum all through school.
>
> (*Report Study Group on the Teaching of Languages*, Islamabad, 1982. p. vi)

The report adds that students will have a choice 'to choose Urdu or English as the medium of examination, and institutions the option to offer instruction in either language' (p. vi).

Bangladesh was part of Pakistan until 1971. Urdu was the national language of both the wings of Pakistan (East and West). English was the official second language and the link language. The Bengali majority resented the imposition of Urdu which resulted in violent language riots; 21 February is commemorated as Language Martyrs Day. Since its formation as an independent state, Bangladesh has not adopted a consistent policy towards the role of English; it falls between an ESL and an EFL country. In 1987 the Bangla Procolon Ain 1987 (Bangla Implementation Act 1987) was passed, giving Bengali the status of an official language. However, the declaration does not stipulate the future role of English. On 19 January 1989, English was introduced as a compulsory language from classes I to XII. Students must qualify in English and Bengali in the Secondary Certificate Examinations. At the university level English is taught as a much sought-after optional subject (see Islam 1975).

In the Kingdom of Nepal, English has been used as a primary foreign language; Nepali (also known as Gorkhali, Khas-Kura, Parbatiya), an Indo-Aryan language, is the national language recognised by the Constitution, and over 58·4 per cent of the population speak it as their mother tongue. In one respect Nepal is unique among the South Asian nations discussed in this chapter: it was never politically colonised by a western power, nor has it been open to the influence of Christian missionaries for proselytisation. The tradition of English education and methods for curriculum design came from neighbouring India. Until Tribhuvan University was established in 1960, all teachers, administrators and the cultural elite were trained in Indian universities. The Tri-Chandra College, established in 1918, was earlier affiliated with Calcutta University and later with Patna University, both in India. In 1951, when the king's authority was established, as opposed to that of the hereditary prime ministers from the Rana family, a process of democratisation was initiated. English-language teaching, journalism and broadcasting have now relatively more support. The National Education System Plan, introduced in 1971, includes English as one of the important languages.

Nepal's economy essentially depends on tourism; therefore, in Kathmandu (the capital) and other tourist spots English is used for advertising, and for interaction with tourists. Mixing of English with local languages is as common in Nepal as in other parts of South Asia. There are several English 'coaching shops' in Kathmandu where English instruction is available. These tutorial shops are in great demand, though of questionable quality. In Bhutan a department of education was set up in 1961. The teaching staff is primarily from India, and the teaching materials are developed by Indian specialists.

Maldives has no university, and students go to other countries for education. Basic English instruction is locally available so that Maldivian students can benefit from instruction abroad.

10.9   Attitudes and schizophrenia about English

The controversies that Macaulay's Minute and its implementation initiated in the 1830s actually never ended. Right from Macaulay's period, there have continued to be three distinct attitudes toward the role of English in South Asian language policies. One attitude is that English has played an important mathetic role in South Asia, and that its continuation and diffusion contribute to keeping South Asian countries abreast of the scientific, technological and humanistic developments of the world. This position may be labelled the 'Rammohan Roy Syndrome'. Roy, as noted in section 10.2, pleaded for the introduction of western knowledge in India.

This position with reference to India is articulated in several earlier studies and in more recent ones. One such representative study, appropriately named *The Great Debate* (Wadia 1954) brings several perspectives together.

In 1988 Girilal Jain, an Indian political commentator, reiterated this position with reference to India:

> I for one doubt whether we could have managed our political order as well as we have (even if we accept Prof. Galbraith's description of it as a functioning anarchy) if we had not retained the English language as the medium of higher education and inter-regional communication. This, in my view has not only helped us maintain a measure of continuity with the Raj, the first properly founded and durable state in India capable of rising above social divisions and conflicts, but also to sustain and expand a class of people capable of thinking and acting in all India terms. We can call them neo-Brahmins because the Brahmins constituted the first historically known pan-Indian group.
>
> (*The Times of India*, November–December 1988, Special sesquicentennial Concept 5: 127–8)

There is another attitude concerning the role of English in South Asia. The words of Macaulay's Minute continue to reverberate in the mind of those who have this attitude, particularly Macaulay's use of words such as 'poor and rude' for the vernacular languages, and his vision of using English to create 'brown *sahibs*' in South Asia. In this view, English has no role in the language policies of South Asian countries.

The third view rejects the enthusiasm of these two positions and has adopted a somewhat neutral position – neutral in the sense that its proponents would like to see English as one of the languages in the linguistic repertoire, as one of the foreign languages, but not in competition with local languages.

The past has thus resulted in several types of prejudices about the uses of English in South Asia, both in the minds of native speakers and in South Asians who have articulated their positions on this vital issue. I have discussed these positions in Kachru (1982). It is not, as is generally believed, the international uses of English which contributed to the change in the attitude towards English in post-1947 South Asia. Immediately after the political independence what Wijesinha (1988: i) says about Sri Lanka was true of other South Asian countries too: 'English symbolized the continued domination of the nation by a Western elite. It was this that understandably prompted the Swabhasha or Indigenous Languages policies of almost all political parties.' The implementation of such policies resulted in a multitude of other problems. In the case of Sri Lanka, the monolingual Sinhalese and Tamil had 'no means of communication with members of the other communities' (Wijesinha 1988: i). This happened in other parts of the region too, and the result was quiet re-evaluation of the role of English within new pragmatic intranational realities (see also Musa 1981).

Reactions and attitudes towards English are also determined by the functional power and status which this language has acquired during the last fifty years (see Kachru & Smith 1986). A number of symbols are used to convey the status and power of English. In Sri Lanka, for example, the power of English is symbolised by the word *kaduwa* 'sword', and to speak in English is *kadden kapanava* 'to cut (down) with the sword', 'and by implication, intimidate the listener by doing so' (Kandiah 1984: 117). By extension, the meaning *kadu panti* is used for 'English classes'; again representing the power of the language.

10.10 Current issues

The current issues related to South Asian English in a way reflect the concerns of all non-native institutionalised varieties of English (e.g. West African, Singaporean). The main points of the debate, specifically in South Asia, are as follows: attitudes towards the ontological status of South Asian English; teaching and acquisition of English in a multilingual and multicultural context; pragmatics of the uses and users of English; cultural identity of the varieties of English and its implications with respect to intelligibility, comprehensibility and interpretability (see Smith & Nelson 1985; Kachru 1986a); hypotheses concerning communicative competence in English, their validity across varieties and manifestations of the bilinguals' creativity in each variety; and the development of non-native literatures in English.

In recent years it has been shown that the 'deficit' and 'deviational' approaches to South Asian English are not very meaningful, since these two discount the contextual and pragmatic variables (Kachru 1986a). There is a paradigm shift in another sense, too; the exocentric 'monomodel' position is less favoured, and the 'functional polymodel' approach has proved more insightful. The nativist position, in its extreme form, is presented in Prator (1968), and Quirk (1988, 1989). The functional polymodel approach emphasises issues of identity, and sociocultural and interactional contexts (see e.g. Kachru 1983, 1986a; Kandiah 1991).

The South Asian varieties of English raise interesting theoretical questions concerning second-language acquisition and creativity. These questions have been raised with reference to some dominant paradigms in, for example, Lowenberg & Sridhar (1986). Some of these questions relate to concepts such as 'interlanguage' and 'fossilisation' (see Sridhar & Sridhar 1986).

There is concern with broader issues too, such as the pluricentricity of English and the manifestation of its multicultural identities, English as a vehicle of ideological change, and the study of institutionalised varieties of English within the framework of contact linguistics.

It is not only in theoretical aspects that South Asian English has proved to be a fruitful area of research. In the areas of applied theory, a number of potential areas of research have been identified, for example lexicographical research on the varieties of non-native Englishes (e.g. Kachru 1980), curriculum design and the parameters for communicative competence in English (Kachru 1988), to mention just three such areas. There is another area in which research on South Asian English has been instrumental in dispelling several unverified or partially verified hypotheses concerning the Outer Circle of English (e.g. South Asia, West Africa, Southeast Asia; see Kachru 1985a). These hypotheses have naturally resulted in the emergence of several fallacies of which the following six may be mentioned as representative:

1   that in the Outer Circle, English is essentially learnt in order to communicate with the native speakers of English;

2   that English is learnt to understand and teach British and American cultural values;

3   that the goals for acquisition of English are to adopt the exonormative models of English; that the varieties of English used in the Outer Circle are 'interlanguages' and the goal of acquisition is to acquire 'native-like' competence;

4   that native speakers of English, as teacher trainers, curriculum developers and academic administrators, provide serious input in the operation of teaching English in the Outer Circle;

5   that diversity, innovation and variation are necessarily indicators of the 'decay' of English;

6   that English is learnt with an 'integrative' motivation rather than an 'instrumental' motivation, and the 'integrative' motivation is more conducive to successful language learning.

In several recent studies it has been shown that these hypotheses are empirically and sociolinguistically flawed (see Kachru 1986a).

10.11   Conclusion

The case study of South Asian English discussed in this chapter clearly demonstrates the complexity of describing an institutionalised (non-native) variety of English. There are several dimensions to South Asian English: historical, linguistic, sociolinguistic, attitudinal, ideological, educational and cultural. It is only recently that these issues are being raised, and the limitations of the earlier 'paradigm trap' are being discussed. However, in terms of the research potential – historical, linguistic and sociolinguistic – what we have seen so far is merely the proverbial 'tip of the iceberg'.

FURTHER READING

Excellent sources of bibliographical resources for the history, functions and innovations of English in South Asia are Aggarwal (1982), Ramaiah (1988) and Singh, Verma & Joshi (1981). Aggarwal lists 1,182 items, divided into nineteen sections, and Ramiah includes 1,015 items, divided into ten sections. Singh, Verma & Joshi (1981) focus primarily on Indian literature in English (1827–1979). Rahman (1991a and b) are useful guides for Pakistan. There are extensive bibliographies in Cheshire (1991) and Kachru (1983, 1986a [1990]).

There is no single volume that provides a detailed and well-researched introduction to the history of English in South Asia: Ram (1983), gives a rather one-sided view of 'trading in language'. However, it contains a useful bibliography on this topic, as does Kachru (1983).

An overview of the formal and functional characteristics of varieties of South

Asian English is presented in Baumgardner (1992, forthcoming); Bansal (1969), Kachru (1983, 1986a [1990]), Masica (1976) and Parasher (1991).

Major book-length studies on the development of South Asian English literature are Iyengar (1985), Lal (1969) and Naik (1982) for India; and Rahman (1991c) for Pakistan.

Nihalani, Tongue & Hosali (1979) is 'a handbook of usage and pronunciation' for 'Indian and British English'. Yule & Burnell (1886, fortunately reprinted in 1968) continues to be an insightful and entertaining major resource for lexical innovations in South Asia. A recent addition to this genre of lexical studies is Lewis (1991). The topic of discoursal and stylistic nativisation is treated at length in Kachru (1986a [reprinted 1990]: chs. 2, 4, 9, 10; 1992: chs. 14, 16, 17, 18).

The papers in Y. Kachru (1991) are specially on speech acts in South Asian English. These papers raise various theoretical and methodological questions related to nativised speech acts, providing a framework for research and a bibliography.

NOTES

1 These estimated population figures for the year 2000 are based on *World Population Prospects 1988* (Population Studies no. 106, New York: United Nations, 1989).

2 For references see Aggarwal (1982) and Ramaiah (1988).

3 Most of these studies are in the form of dissertations and theses submitted to various universities in South Asia, particularly the Central Institute of English and Foreign Languages, Hyderabad, Shivaji University, Kolhapur, Delhi University, Delhi, Jawaharlal Nehru University, New Delhi, University of Poona, Pune, Tribhuvan University, Kathmandu, Osmania University, Hyderabad, to name the major centres of such research (for specific references, see two useful bibliographical resources, Aggarwal 1982 and Ramaiah 1988).

4 I believe that this task will be made easier by recent attempts for large-scale corpus collection and analysis of South Asian English and its varieties (see e.g., Shastri 1988 for Indian English). Baumgardner is planning to initiate a similar project for Pakistani English.

5 There were two attitudes towards lexicalisation from South Asian languages: one of disapproval of such borrowing, and the other of considering such borrowing vital for the administration of the Raj. Regardless of these diametrically opposite views, the South Asian lexicalisation of English continued to increase.

6 There is now a considerable body of literature across languages exploring the sociolinguistic, psycholinguistic, literary and other motivations for such mixing, specifically with English and South Asian languages (see Kachru 1983: 193–207; Bhatia & Ritchie 1989).

GLOSSARY OF LINGUISTIC TERMS

This glossary aims only to provide brief working definitions of the more important linguistic terms that are used in the essays in this volume, omitting such terms as phonetic classifications, for which the reader in difficulty should consult a standard textbook on the subject, such A. C. Gimson's *An Introduction to the Pronunciation of English*, 3rd edn (Edward Arnold, 1980), or the introduction to J. C. Wells' *Longman Pronunciation Dictionary* (Longman, 1990). It is not a comprehensive glossary of linguistic terms, and the explanations are only intended to be sufficient to allow the reader who is unacquainted with such terminology to gain more easily a full understanding of what is being read. For a fuller treatment of linguistic terms readers may wish to consult David Crystal's *A Dictionary of Linguistics and Phonetics*, 2nd edn (Basil Blackwell, 1985).

Terms that are defined *in situ* and are used only there are normally excluded from the glossary. The illustrative examples are drawn as far as possible from the essays themselves.

acrolect The variety of speech associated with the highest social stratum of a community; in a creole continuum, the variety of speech closest to the standard. **acrolectal** *a*. Cf. **basilect, mesolect**.

adstrate language Any language in contact with a creole which is neither its **superstrate** nor its **substrate**.

Aitken's Law A widespread sound change affecting the duration of vowels in Scots in the medieval period, resulting in the virtual elimination of phonemic length distinctions.

allomorph A conditioned realisation of the same morpheme: e.g. /z/ in *dogs* and /s/ in *cats* are allomorphs of the modern plural marker.

allophone An individual speech sound which is accepted by the listener as being part of an identifiable and seemingly indivisible **phoneme**, e.g. the initial consonants in the words *keep*, *cap* and *cool* are allophones of the phoneme /k/. **allophonic** *a*.

anterior The time prior to the time under discussion, usually equivalent to either the English past tense (prior to the present) or the past perfect (prior to the past).

aphetic Of or relating to aphesis, the loss of a short unaccented vowel at the beginning of a word, as in *squire* for *esquire*.

apocope The cutting off or omission of the last letter or syllable of a word. **apocopated** *a*.

aspect A verbal category referring not to time (tense) but rather to the duration, frequency or manner of an action, e.g. **completive, habitual, progressive**.

assibilation The process by which a stop consonant (like *d*, *t*) becomes a sibilant one by assimilation with a following /j/, e.g. pronouncing *duke* as /dʒuːk/ instead of /djuːk/.

assimilation A process by which a sound is replaced by one which in its articulation more closely resembles a neighbouring sound in the same or a contiguous word. **assimilated** *a*.

auxiliary verb One of a group of common verbs (*be, do, have, may*, etc.) used to form the tenses, moods and voices of other verbs.

back-spelling A spelling which suggests a pronunciation used prior to a sound change, adopted by false analogy for words in which that sound change did not in fact occur.

basilect The variety of speech associated with the lowest social stratum of a community; in a creole continuum, the variety of speech farthest from the standard. **basilectal** *a*. Cf. **acrolect, mesolect**.

bilingual *a*. Able to speak two languages.

bilingualism Ability to speak two languages; also, the habitual use of two languages.

bound morpheme A morpheme which cannot occur on its own as a separate word, e.g. the affixes *de-, dis-, -ment, -tion*. See **free morpheme**.

breaking The diphthongisation of a vowel resulting from the development of an off-glide towards the articulatory position for the following consonant.

calque A word-for-word or morpheme-for-morpheme translation of a word or idiomatic phrase, e.g. *foreword* from German *Vorwort*. **calquing** *vbl.n*.

case The relation of a word to other words in a sentence; also, a form of a noun, adjective or pronoun expressing this.

citation form A careful pronunciation of a word in isolation.

cleft sentence A two-clause sentence derived from a single clause in order to highlight or focus attention on a particular element of the clause, the resultant sentence starting with *it is* or another part of the verb *to be*: (not highlighted) *You need a good rest most*; (cleft construction) *It is a good rest that you need most*. **clefting** *vbl n*. See **pseudo-cleft sentence**.

clitic *n*. A word pronounced with so little emphasis that it is taken in as part of an adjacent word, e.g. *-na* in Scots *canna* 'cannot', *isna* 'is not'. **cliticised** *a*. See **enclitic** and **proclitic**.

coarticulation The simultaneous pronunciation of two consonantal sounds, such as /kp/ or /gb/ in some West African and creole languages. **coarticulated** *a*.

code-mixing Combining features of more than one language or dialect as in some varieties of South Asian English.

code-switching The practice of alternating between one language or dialect and another in the speech of an individual or speech community.

collective noun A noun that is grammatically singular and denotes a collection or number of individuals, e.g. *audience*, *choir*, *flock*.

combinative change A sound change affecting a given phoneme under certain circumstances only. Contrast **isolative change**.

comment See **topicalisation**.

complement One or more words added to the subject or subject and verb to complete the sense of a clause or sentence, e.g. *partially irrelevant* in *The question became partially irrelevant*.

complementiser A word that signals that a complement follows, e.g. *that* in *that he must go*, or *to* before an infinitive (*to go*).

completive aspect A verbal category indicating that an action has already been completed.

count noun A noun that can form a plural or be used with the indefinite article, e.g. *illustration*, *leg*.

creole A language which develops out of a **pidgin** that has come to be used as the first language of an entire speech community.

creole continuum In countries where creole languages coexist with their European lexical source language as the official medium, a spectrum of speech varieties ranging from those farthest from the standard to those closest.

Creole English Restructured varieties of English in the Caribbean, West Africa and elsewhere arising out of a specific kind of contact with other languages that led to **creolisation**.

creolisation The reorganisation of a language's structure when it becomes a creole. **creolised** *a.*

decreolisation The process in a creole continuum caused by the influence of the acrolect, in which overt creole features are progressively avoided in favour of those of the standard variety. **decreolise** *v.*

deictic Applied to pronouns and adverbs which are capable of a temporal or locational contrast: *this/that, now/then, here/there* are deictic words.

dentalisation The process of changing a non-dental consonantal sound into a dental one, a feature of Irish English.

determiner Any of a class of words, e.g. articles (*a, the*), demonstratives (*this, that*), numerals, quantifiers (*all, few, more*), etc., that determine the kind of reference a noun has.

diachronic Concerned with the study of the historical development of a language, opp. **synchronic**.

diagloss A line on a linguistic map separating dialectally distinct linguistic features.

dialect-mixing The merging of linguistic features in adjacent dialects.

dialect mixture A merging of dialects that occurs when dialect speakers from different areas are intermingled by emigration to a new country.

diglossia The state where two radically different varieties of a language coexist in a single speech community: e.g. *High Dutch* as the language of Church and school in nineteenth-century South Africa and the *Taal* as that used at home. **diglossic** *a.*

digraph A group of two letters representing a single sound, as in *ph* and *th*.

diminutive *a.* Of a word or affix, implying smallness, either actual or imputed in token of affection, disdain, etc. (*-kin, -let, -ling*).

diphthong A vowel sound within a syllable in which the articulation begins as for one sound and moves as for another (as in *loin, crown* and *find*). **diphthongal** *a.*

diphthongisation The process of converting a simple vowel into a diphthong. **diphthongise** *v.*

do-support The introduction of *do* as a 'dummy' auxiliary, e.g. in the interrogative and negative sentences in the following pairs: *They often go to Paris/Do they often go to Paris?*; *We received your parcel/We did not receive your parcel.*

dual In some languages (e.g. Maori) a distinctive pronoun denoting two persons or things (additional to singular and plural).

dynamic *a.*   See **stative**.

embedding   A process of sentence construction in which a subordinate clause or phrase is built into (i.e. embedded in) the structure of another. In *The car that is kept in the garage is not mine* the clause *that is kept in the garage* is embedded in the sentence *The car is not mine.* **embedded** *a.*

enclitic   A **clitic** that follows another word. Also as *adj.*

encliticisation   The process of merging a reduced form of an unstressed word with a preceding stressed word, e.g. Northern English *it* reduced to *'t*, and *-na* 'not' in Scots *canna* 'cannot'.

endocentric model   An internal model (e.g. the form of Indian English used for instruction in India) as opposed to an **exocentric model**, an external model (e.g. British or American English used for instruction in India, Pakistan, etc.).

epenthesis   The insertion of an unetymological sound within a word, e.g. *film* pronounced as /ˈfɪləm/. **epenthetic** *a.*

ergative case   In certain languages, e.g. Eskimo, Basque and some Aboriginal languages in Australia, the name of a grammatical case where there is a formal parallel between the object of a transitive verb and the subject of an intransitive one, i.e. they display the same case.

ethnolinguistic *a.*   Of a group: associated with a distinct ethnicity and language.

etymon   The primary word that gives rise to a derivative, e.g. OE *stān* is the etymon of modern *stone*.

euphonic *r*   See **intrusive** *r*.

exclusive   See **inclusive, exclusive** *adjs.*

exocentric model   See **endocentric model**.

free morpheme   A morpheme which can occur as a separate form, e.g. *chair* and *man* in *chairman*, *self* in *unselfish*. See **bound morpheme**.

fronting   The placing of a syntactic element in initial position instead of in the middle or end of a sentence or clause, e.g. WE *Coal they're getting out, mostly.*

function word   A word not carrying a full lexical meaning, but having an essential grammatical (or functional) significance, e.g. *a/an* (indefinite article), *do* (auxiliary verb), *to* (infinitive marker), etc. Cf. **marker**.

g-dropping   In StE the loss of /g/ in the combination /ŋg/ at some point in the early seventeenth century in words ending in *-ing*.

g-fulness   The retention of /g/, i.e. /ŋg/ instead of just /ŋ/ in some English dialects in words like *ring, singing, thing*.

glottalisation Articulation involving a simultaneous glottal constriction, esp. a glottal stop, as in the substitution of /ʔ/ for final /t/ in *what*.

glottal stop A sound produced by the audible release of a complete closure of the glottis. It is transcribed as /ʔ/; e.g. Cockney /bɒʔl/ for RP /bɒt(ə)l/.

grapheme A distinctive unit of orthography; a letter as a representative of a sound. **graphemic** *a*.

Great Vowel Shift A series of sound changes in the fifteenth and sixteenth centuries affecting nearly all the long vowels in standard English: fully described in volume II.

habitual aspect A verbal category indicating that an action recurs over an extended period of time.

h-dropping The absence of /h/ in the pronunciation of words like *hat* (rendered as /æt/) in some regional forms of English.

head The dominant element in a phrase or group: e.g. in *a brown hat*, *hat* is the head, *a* a determiner and *brown* an adjectival modifier.

high rise terminal A distinctive rise in intonation at the end of declarative statements, a characteristic feature of Australian and New Zealand English. Also called **high rising tone** (or **HRT**).

homonym A word of the same spelling or sound as another but of different meaning: e.g. *calf* (young bovine animal), derived from OE *cælf*; and *calf* (fleshy hind part of the human leg), derived from ON *kálfi*.

homophone A word having the same sound as another but of different meaning or origin: e.g. *air/heir*, *aloud/allowed*. **homophonous** *a*. **homophony** *n*.

homorganic *a*. Of or relating to sounds which are produced at the same place of articulation, e.g. /p/, /b/ and /m/.

hypercorrection A spelling, pronunciation or construction falsely used in a conscious effort to move in the direction of an acrolect: e.g. pronouncing *classic* as /ˈklɑːsɪk/ instead of as RP /ˈklæsɪk/.

hyper-rhoticity The addition of /r/ after a final schwa, e.g. *window* RP /ˈwɪndəʊ/ pronounced as /ˈwɪndər/ in some West Country dialects in England.

hyperurbanism Another word for **hypercorrection**.

hypocorism A pet name or diminutive, e.g. *mossie* 'mosquito'. The use of hypocorisms is a marked feature of Australian and New Zealand English.

hyponym A specific term in relation to a more inclusive term: e.g. *wallaby* and *pademelon* are hyponyms of *kangaroo*; *daffodil*, *rose*, *tulip* are hyponyms of *flower*.

iconic *a.* Used of a structure in which the form reflects the meaning without simply being imitative: a structure is constructionally iconic if the form reflects the meaning by being more complex the more complex the meaning is.

idiolect The form of language used by an individual person within the total structure of a language.

inclusive, exclusive *adjs.* Of pronouns, **inclusive** is used (in contrast with **exclusive**) to refer to a first-person role where the speaker and the addressee are both included, e.g. *we* = 'me and you'.

intrusive *r* An unetymological /r/ introduced as a bridge between the final vowel sound of one word or syllable and a vowel sound at the beginning of the next, e.g. *China-r-office, draw-r-ing* 'drawing'. Also occas. called **euphonic** *r* in early studies.

irrealis A verbal category indicating that an action is not (yet) a part of reality, corresponding to the English future, conditional or perfect conditional.

isogloss A line on a linguistic map separating regionally distinct linguistic features.

isolative change A sound change affecting a given phoneme throughout its distribution. Contrast **combinative change**.

isophone An isogloss on a linguistic map drawn round an area of a particular feature of pronunciation. **isophonic** *a.*

koine A speech variety that has developed out of the contact of several dialects of the same language which have undergone levelling, or the elimination of features not shared, e.g. the merging of UK and Irish dialects of English in Australia and New Zealand.

lect A speech variety, as in **dialect, idiolect, sociolect**.

lenition In Celtic languages, the process or result of articulating a consonant 'softly', that is, with muscular tension relaxed: in Irish English the use of the alveolar fricatives /ţ/ and /d/ as allophones of /t/ and /d/. **lenited** *a.*

lexeme A basic lexical unit capable of generating inflected forms, as *ride* (vb) yielding *rides, riding, rode, ridden*; *large* yielding *larger, largest*. By convention a lexeme is the form used as a headword in dictionaries.

lexicon The vocabulary of a language; all the lexical items in a language.

lexicosemantic *a.* Of or relating to both lexical and semantic aspects of a word, phrase, etc., esp. one adopted from one language into another. **lexicosemantics** *n.pl.* const. as *sg.*

lexis   The vocabulary of a language; the lexicon of a language.

linking *r*   A letter ⟨r⟩ in word-final position that is normally pronounced before a following vowel but is silent before a final consonant, as in *far, far away*.

loanword   A word adopted by one language from another, e.g. PDE *cappuccino* (frothy milky coffee) from Italian.

locative   Used as a preposition, as *na* in the Surinamese creoles, expressing location.

***l*-vocalisation**   The transformation of /l/ in certain positions into a vowel, for example as an important historical change in Scots (thus accounting, for example, for the silent ⟨l⟩ in the place-names *Kirkcaldy, Culross*); and as a feature in some types of non-standard or regional speech, e.g. *milk* pronounced as /mɪʊk/.

macro-level *attrib. n.*   Concerned with all (linguistic) aspects of a language or dialect.

marker   A word, affix, etc., which distinguishes or determines the class or function of the form, construction, etc., with which it is used; e.g. a final ⟨s⟩ is the most common marker of plurality in English. **marking** *vbl n.*

merger   The coming together or convergence of linguistic units which were originally distinguished; e.g. the variable convergence of /ɪə/ and /eə/ in NZE *fear* and *square*, chiefly as /ɪə/.

mesolect   The variety of speech associated with the middle social stratum of a community; in a creole continuum, the intermediate varieties between the **basilect** and the **acrolect**.

metathesis   The transposition of sounds or letters in a word, e.g. /'pætrən/ for *pattern* in some forms of Irish and Scottish English.

minimal pair   A pair of words distinguished only by a single sound, e.g. *bill/mill, amble/ample*.

modal verb   One of a group of auxiliary verbs, e.g. *shall, will, can, may, must*, used to express the mood of another verb. **modality** the expression of obligation, necessity, time, etc., by means of **modal verbs.**

modifier   A word, esp. an adjective or a noun used attributively, that qualifies the sense of another word, e.g. *wooden* and *garden* in *a wooden garden fence*.

monoglot *a.*   Able to use or speak only one language.

monolingual *a.*   Able to speak or use only one language. **monolingualism** *n.*

monomorphemic *a.*   Consisting of a single morpheme, e.g. the word *move* as opposed to *movement, brood* as opposed to *brewed* (= *brew + ed*).

monophthong   A single vowel sound within a syllable, as distinct from a **diphthong**. **monophthongal** *a*.

monophthongisation   The process by which a diphthong is reduced to a monophthong. **monophthongise** *v*.

mood   A distinct form or set of forms of a verb serving to indicate whether it is to express fact (the indicative mood; e.g. *He writes a note each time*), command (imperative; e.g. *Please write me a note!*), a wish, etc. (subjunctive; e.g. *They insisted he write a note*).

mora   A unit of timing (or rhythm) equal to the length of a consonant and a short vowel.

morpheme   A minimum distinctive unit of grammar that cannot be further divided, e.g. *com-*, *part* and *-ment* forming *compartment*; *come*, *-ing* forming *coming*. Cf. **bound morpheme, free morpheme, monomorphemic**.

morphology   The (study of the) structure and form of words. **morpho-logical** *a*.

morphophonemic *a*.   Of or relating to a **morphophoneme**. For example, the ⟨i⟩ in *crime* represents /aɪ/, but in *criminal* in the same morpheme the ⟨i⟩ represents /ɪ/. The alternation between these two phonemes within the same morpheme indicates the presence of a morphophoneme.

morphosyntactic *a*.   Of or relating to both morphology and syntax, e.g. number which affects both morphology (as in the plural inflexion) and syntax (as in subject–verb agreement).

multilingual *a*.   Able to speak more than two languages.

multilingualism   Ability to speak more than two languages; also, the habitual use of more than two languages by an individual or by a community.

mutation plural   A noun plural formed by a change in the stem vowel instead of a suffix, e.g. *men*, *mice*.

nativisation   The process by which a pidgin acquires native speakers; also, the adaptation a language undergoes in its phonology, grammar, vocabulary and discourse strategies when used in a different linguistic, cultural and social context, e.g. English in Singapore, India, Nigeria.

neutralisation   In phonology, the levelling out of the distinction between two phonemes in a particular environment; e.g. in German /p/ and /b/ are distinguished at the beginning of words (*Paar* /pɑːr/ 'pair' but *Bar* /bɑːr/ 'bar'), but only /p/ occurs at the end of words (*gelb* /gelp/ 'yellow'. **neutralise** *v*.

non-rhotic *a*.   The opposite of **rhotic**. Of or relating to a language or dialect in which medial *r* before a consonant other than *r* (*pearl*, *sort*) or *r* in final position (*after*) is not pronounced.

non-stative *a*   See **stative**.

noun possessor   A noun signifying the possessor of something material (e.g. *the rich*) or of some quality (e.g. *the brave*).

noun possessum   A noun signifying what is possessed by a **noun possessor**.

off-glide   An articulatory movement which occurs as the vocal organs leave the position needed for one speech sound and move towards the position required for the next sound or towards a position of rest.

on-glide   An articulatory movement which occurs as the vocal organs approach the position for the articulation of a speech sound either from the position of a sound just produced or from a position of rest.

orthoepist   One of a number of sixteenth- and seventeenth-century scholars whose aim was to describe a 'correct' pronunciation of English, and to reform the spelling system to make it reflect such a pronunciation more accurately.

palaeotype   The name of a system of writing devised by the nineteenth-century scholar A. J. Ellis in which existing Roman letters and other characters were used to form a universal phonetic alphabet.

palatal   A consonant articulated with the tongue touching or approaching the hard palate.

palatalisation   Articulation of a consonant resulting from the raising of the tongue towards the hard palate as in the initial sound of *dew* /djuː/ as opposed to *do* /duː/. **palatalised** *a*. pronounced with some degree of palatalisation.

paragogic *a*.   Of a vowel: required at the end of a word by a language's phonotactic rules, e.g. the final -*o* in Srinan creole *mofo* from English *mouth*.

particle   A minor part of speech, esp. one that is short and indeclinable, a relation-word, e.g. *to* before an infinitive; also the subordinate unit(s) in a phrasal verb (*up* and *with* in *meet up with*). *Not* is often called a negative particle.

patronymic   A name derived from the name of a father or ancestor, e.g. *Johnson, O'Brien, MacDonald*. The Welsh markers *ap* (male) and *ach* (female) illustrate the same phenomenon (*Dafydd ap Llywelin, Elizabeth ach Morgan*).

periphrastic *a*.   (In grammar specifically) of or relating to uses of the auxiliary verb *do* with a finite verb, as in *did go* instead of *went*. Also, more generally of a phrase (e.g. *of the people*) used instead of the normal inflected form (*the people's*).

phatic *a.* (Of greetings, etc.) used to establish a social contact or as a formulaic farewell rather than to convey a specific message, e.g. *How do you do!*, *Nice day, isn't it?* (SAfr) *Go well!*

phonaesthetic *a.* Of or relating to the association of a particular group of sounds with a particular meaning, as *sl-* suggesting 'unpleasantness' in *sleazy*, *slime*, *slum*, etc.

phoneme Any of the units of sound in a specified language that distinguish one word from another, as the initial /b/, /k/, /d/, /f/ of *bad, cad, Dad, fad*. Hence **phonemic** *a.* Cf. **allophone**.

phonotactic *a.* Of or relating to the permissible sequences of phonemes in a given language, e.g. the presence of a homorganic *d* in PDE *thunder* (OE *ðunor*) but not in Scots; and the absence of initial /ŋ/ in Present-Day English but its presence in Maori (e.g. *ngaio* name of a tree, pronounced /'naɪəʊ/ in New Zealand English but /ŋaɪɔ/ in Maori).

pidgin A contact language used between groups which have no language in common, especially a simplified variety of one group's language which has become somewhat stabilised for a special purpose such as trade. A pidgin is not the first language of any of its speakers; contrast **creole**. **pidginisation** the process by which such a contact language emerges.

polysemy The existence of many meanings (of a given word, phrase, etc.); e.g. *balloon* 'inflatable decorative rubber pouch; an aerial vehicle capable of carrying passengers, meteorological equipment, etc.; a large globular brandy glass'. Cf. **homonym**.

pre-nasalised stop A stop consonant preceded by a homorganic nasal, e.g. /mb/, /nd/, /ŋk/ functioning as a single phoneme: characteristic of many African languages and Atlantic creoles.

pre-verbal *a.* (Of a tense or aspect marker) placed in front of the stem of a verb.

proclitic A word pronounced with so little emphasis that it becomes merged with the stressed word that follows it, e.g. in some forms of regional British English down to the first half of the nineteenth century, *chill* from *ich* 'I' + *will*.

progressive aspect A verb marker indicating that an action is in progress, e.g. Jamaican creole *im de sing* 'he is singing'.

pronoun exchange A characteristic feature of some west midland south-west dialects in England in which standard English subject and object pronouns appear in reverse use, e.g. the type *Her told I* 'She told me'.

propredicate A word-sequence echoing a statement just made while repeating only part of it, e.g. '*They got married on Friday.*' '*Did they?*' (= 'Did they get married on Friday?').

prosody A term used in phonetics to refer collectively to variations in pitch, stress (loudness), tempo and rhythm. (These features are also called **suprasegmentals**.) **prosodic** *a*.

pseudo-cleft sentence One which, like the **cleft sentence**, makes explicit the division between given and new parts of a statement. The pseudo-cleft equivalent of *You need a good rest most* is ***What you need most*** *is a good rest*.

quantifier A word indicating quantity that is used to modify another word or words, e.g. numbers (*one*, *two*, etc.), or words like *all, every, few, some* and *several*.

r-coloured *a*. See **retroflexion**.

r-dropping The absence of rhoticity in the pronunciation of words containing medial pre-consonantal ⟨r⟩ (*born, heart*) or final ⟨r⟩ (*after, sever*).

Received Standard See RP.

reduplication The repetition of some part of the root of a word, esp. in the case of verbal forms (chiefly the perfect tense) in Greek and Latin, e.g. λύω 'unfasten', (perfect) λέλυκα 'I have unfastened'; *cadō* 'I fall', (perfect) *cecidī* 'I have fallen'; also, as shown in the English types *helter-skelter, mumbo-jumbo*.

referent The idea or thing that a word symbolises. Thus the object describable as 'the natural satellite of the earth, illuminated by the sun and reflecting some light to the earth' is the referent of English *moon*.

reflex An item in the sound system of a language which is directly related, by regular phonological change, to a specific item in the language at an earlier stage of its history.

relexification A language's one-for-one exchange of words while retaining much of its original structure; the proposed explanation for the transformation of pidgin Portuguese into pidgin English, French etc. in seventeenth-century West Africa. **relexify** *v*.

retroflexion The articulation of a speech sound with the tip of the tongue curling towards the hard palate, esp. that occurring in words containing ⟨r⟩ (*bird, earth*, etc.): a marked feature of American English. In such circumstances the vowel preceding a retroflex ⟨r⟩ is said to be ***r-coloured*** or **rhotacised**.

rhotic *a*. Of or relating to a form of English, esp. Modern Scots and American English, that retains historical /r/ in most circumstances (*river, Arthur, far from*, etc.). The state or condition of being rhotic is **rhoticity** or **rhotacism**. RP is notable for its **non-rhoticity**.

rounding   A term used in phonetics in the classification of lip position: the lips are said to be rounded for the pronunciation of certain speech sounds (e.g. regional English /ʊ/ in *some*), and unrounded for others (e.g. /ʌ/ in RP *some*).

RP   Received Pronunciation (also called **Received Standard**), the form of spoken English based on educated speech in southern England.

schwa   The name of the indistinct vowel sound /ə/, often found in unstressed syllables in English, as in *another* /ə'nʌðə/.

serial verb   In a variety of African, South Asian and East Asian languages and Atlantic creoles, a construction consisting of a series of verbs with the same subject and no intervening conjunctions or complementisers, e.g. Jamaican CE *Mi ron guo lef im* (lit. 'I run go leave him'), 'I ran away from him'.

sociolect   A linguistic variety or **lect** of a language defined on social, as opposed to regional, grounds; a social dialect.

sociolinguistic *a.*   Relating to or concerned with language in its social aspects.

spelling pronunciation   The pronunciation of a word according to its written form, e.g. pronouncing *forehead* as /'fɔː,hɛd/ instead of /'fɒrɪd/.

stative *a.*   Applied to verbs which express a state or condition, e.g. *be, know, mean*, etc., as opposed to dynamic or non-stative verbs, e.g. *change, grow, run* (*I am running*), etc.

stress-timed *a.*   Designating a language, e.g. English, in which primary stresses occur at approximately equal intervals, irrespective of the number of unstressed syllables in between. Opposed to **syllable-timed** *a.*

substratum (or **substrate language**)   A linguistic variety or set of forms which has influenced the structure or use of a more dominant variety or language within a community; *specif.*, in the language contact leading to a pidgin or creole, the language(s) spoken by the group(s) with less power. Contrast **superstrate (language)**.

superstrate (language)   (Applied to) a linguistic variety or set of forms which has influenced the structure or use of a less dominant variety or language within a community; *specif.*, in the language contact leading to a pidgin or creole, the language spoken by the group with more power, which becomes the source of the new language's lexicon. Contrast **substrate (language)**.

suprasegmentals   In phonology, a term used to describe phonetic features of a sound or sequence of sounds other than those constituting the consonantal and vocalic segments, esp. stress, pitch and intonation. See **prosody**.

suspended (*t*ꞌ)   A. J. Ellis' term for a reduced form of the definite article used in some (esp. northern) English dialects, often a glottalised /t/ or a glottal stop.

syllable-timed *a.*   Designating a language, e.g. French, in which the syllables occur at roughly regular time intervals. Opposed to **stress-timed** *a.*

synchronic *a.*   Designating a method of linguistic study concerned with the state of a language at one time, past or present, as opposed to an historical or **diachronic** method.

tag question   A short interrogative formula placed at the end of a declarative statement, e.g. *aren't you?* in *You are going to London tomorrow, aren't you?* Sometimes in abbreviated form as **tag**.

tap   The name given to a speech sound produced by a single momentary contact between the tongue and the roof of the mouth. In many words a Maori tapped /r/ is rendered in New Zealand English as /d/, e.g. Maori *piripiri* → NZE *biddy-biddy*.

tense   A verbal category indicating the time of an action, e.g. *walks* (present) vs *walked* (past).

***t*-glottaling**   The replacement of /t/ by a glottalised *t* or a **glottal stop**.

Thurstone tests   Tests devised by Louis Leon Thurstone (1887–1955) for the measurement of mental abilities and attitudes.

topic   The part of a sentence (often the subject) which is marked as that on which the rest of the sentence makes a comment, asks a question, etc.

topicalisation   The process by which an element or elements in a sentence are given prominence, making it or them the 'topic' on which a 'comment' is made.

unrounded, unrounding   See **rounding**.

vocalisation   See ***l*-vocalisation**.

vowel harmony   A phonological pattern in some languages in which all the vowels in a word share certain features, e.g. Suriname creole *ala* 'all', *bigi* 'big', *brudu* 'blood'.

yod   The semi-vowel sound /j/ as in *yes* /jɛs/.

yod-dropping   The absence of yod /j/ after certain consonants in the pronunciation of such words as *assume, new* and *enthusiasm* as /əˈsuːm/, /nuː/, /ɪnˈθuːzɪˌæz(ə)m/ instead of /əˈsjuːm/, etc.

yod-formation   In some northern English dialects, the prefixing of an unetymological yod in words like *yance* 'once', *yane* 'one'.

y-tensing   The pronunciation of the final syllable of words like *coffee* and *folly* as /iː/ instead of as RP /ɪ/.

BIBLIOGRAPHY

1 Introduction

Burchfield, R. (1985). *The English Language*. Oxford: Oxford University Press.
  (1992). *Points of View*. Oxford: Oxford University Press.
Görlach, M. (1992). Englishes. A selective bibliography 1984–1991 (excluding Britain, Ireland and USA/Canada). *English World-wide* 13, 1: 59–109.
Greenbaum, S. (1990). Whose English? In Ricks & Michaels (eds.), 15–23.
Quirk, R. (1988). The question of standards in the international use of English. In P. H. Lowenburg (ed.) *Language Spread and Language Policy*. Washington, DC: Georgetown University Press, 229–41.
  (1990). Language varieties and standard language. *English Today* 21: 3–10.
Quirk, R. & H. G. Widdowson (eds.) (1985). *English in the World*. Cambridge: Cambridge University Press.
Ricks, C. & L. Michaels (eds.) (1990). *The State of the Language*. Berkeley and Los Angeles: University of California Press.
Strevens, P. (1985). Standards and the standard language. *English Today* 2: 6.
Sweet, H. (1908). *The Sounds of English*. Oxford: Clarendon Press.
Wakelin, M. (1988). *The Archaeology of English*. London: B. T. Batsford.

2 English in Scotland

Abercrombie, D. (1954). A Scottish vowel. *Le Maître phonétique* 68: 23–4.
  (1979). The accents of standard English in Scotland. In Aitken & McArthur (eds.), 68–84.
Agutter, A. (1988a). Standardisation in Middle Scots. *Scottish Language* 7: 1–8.
  (1988b). The Not-so-Scottish Vowel-length Rule. In Anderson & MacLeod (eds.), 120–32.
Agutter, A. & L. N. Cowan (1981). Changes in the vocabulary of Lowland Scots dialects. *Scottish Literary Journal* suppl. 14: 49–62.

Aitken, A. J. (1971). Variation and variety in written Middle Scots. In Aitken, McIntosh & Palsson (eds.), 167–209.

(1977). How to pronounce Older Scots. In Aitken, McDiarmid & Thomson (eds.), 1–21.

(1979). Scottish speech: a historical view. In Aitken & McArthur (eds.), 85–119.

(1981a). The good old Scots tongue: does Scots have an identity? In Haugen, McClure & Thomson (eds.), 72–90.

(1981b). The Scottish Vowel-length Rule. In Benskin & Samuels (eds.), 131–57.

(1982). Bad Scots: some superstitions about Scots speech. *Scottish Language* 1: 30–44.

(1983). The Language of Older Scots poetry. In McClure (ed.), 1983b: 18–49.

Aitken, A. J. & T. McArthur (eds.) (1979). *Languages of Scotland*. Edinburgh: Chambers.

Aitken, A. J., M. P. McDiarmid & D. S. Thomson (eds.) (1977). *Bards and Makars*. Glasgow: Glasgow University Press.

Aitken, A. J., A. McIntosh & H. Palsson (eds.) (1971). *Edinburgh Studies in English and Scots*. London: Longman.

Anderson, A. O. (1948). Ninian and the Southern Picts. *Scottish Historical Review* 27: 25–47.

Anderson, J. M. & C. Jones (eds.) (1974). *Historical Linguistics* (North Holland Linguistic Series 12b). Amsterdam: North-Holland.

Anderson, J. M. & N. MacLeod (eds.) (1988). *Edinburgh Studies in the English Language*. Edinburgh: John Donald.

Bald, M. A. (1926). The Anglicisation of Scottish printing. *Scottish Historical Review* 23: 107–15.

(1927). The pioneers of Anglicised speech in Scotland. *Scottish Historical Review* 24: 179–93.

Bannerman, J. (1990). The Scots language and the kin-based society. In Thomson (ed.), 1–19.

Barrow, G. W. S. (ed.) (1974). *The Scottish Tradition: Essays in Honour of Ronald Gordon Cant*. Edinburgh: Scottish Academic Press.

Benskin, M. & M. L. Samuels (1981). *So Meny People Longages and Tonges: Philological Essays in Scots and Mediaeval English presented to Angus McIntosh*. Edinburgh: Edinburgh University Press.

Bitterling, K. A. (1970). *Der Wortschatz von Barbours Bruce*. Berlin: Freie Universität.

Bonner, S. J. (ed.) (1992). *Creativity and Tradition in Folklore: New Directions. Essays in Honor of W. F. H. Nicolaisen*. Utah: Utah State University Press.

Brown, E. K. & M. Millar (1980). Auxiliary verbs in Edinburgh speech. *Transactions of the Philological Society*, 81–135.

Caldwell, S. (1974). *The Relative Pronoun in Early Scots*. Helsinki: Société Néophilologique.

Carter, J. & J. Pittock (eds.) (1987). *Aberdeen and the Enlightenment*. Aberdeen: Aberdeen University Press.

Chambers, R. W., E. C. Batho and H. W. Husbands (eds.) (1938–41). *The Chronicles of Scotland* (Scottish Text Society Third Series 10, 15). Edinburgh: Blackwood.

Coldwell, D. C. (ed.) (1951–6). *Virgil's Aeneid translated into Scots verse by Gavin Douglas* (Scottish Text Society Third Series 25, 27, 28, 30). Edinburgh: Blackwood.

Craigie, J. (ed.) (1944–50). *The Basilikon Doron of King James VI* (Scottish Text Society Third Series 16, 18). Edinburgh: Blackwood.

Craigie, W. (1924). The earliest records of the Scots tongue. *Scottish Historical Review* 22: 61–80.

Devitt, A. J. (1989). *Standardizing Written English: Diffusion in the Case of Scotland 1520–1659*. Cambridge: Cambridge University Press.

Dickinson, W. C. & A. A. M. Duncan (1977). *Scotland from Earliest Times to 1603*. Oxford: Clarendon.

Dieth, E. (1932). *A Grammar of the Buchan Dialect*, vol. I: *Phonology – Accidence*. Cambridge: Heffer.

Ellenberger, B. (1977). *The Latin Element in the Vocabulary of the Earlier Makars Henryson and Dunbar* (Lund Studies in English 51). Lund: CWK Gleerup.

Fenton, A. (1987). A North-East farmer's working vocabulary. In Macafee & McLeod (eds.), 135–65.

Gburek, H. (1986). Changes in the structure of the English verb system: evidence from Scots. In Strauss & Drescher (eds.), 115–24.

Glauser, B. (1970). *The Scottish-English Linguistic Border: Lexical Aspects*. Berne: Francke.

Görlach, M. (ed.) (1985). *Focus on Scotland* (Varieties of English Around the World General Series 5). Amsterdam: Benjamins.

(1987). Lexical loss and lexical survival: the case of Scots and English. *Scottish Language* 6: 1–20.

Graham, J. J. (1979). *The Shetland Dictionary*. Stornoway: Thule Press.

Gregor, W. (1866). *The Dialect of Banffshire*. London: Asher.

Guiter, H. (1968). La langue des Pictes. *Boletin de la Real Sociedad Vascongada de los Amigos del Pais* 24: 281–321.

Haugen, E., J. D. McClure & D. S. Thomson (eds.) (1981). *Minority Languages Today*. Edinburgh: Edinburgh University Press.

Henderson, T. F. (1898). *Scottish Vernacular Literature*. London: Nutt.

Hettinga, J. (1981). Standard and dialect in Anstruther and Cellardyke. *Scottish Literary Journal* Supplement 14: 37–48.

Hewitt, D. S. (1987). James Beattie and the languages of Scotland. In Carter & Pittock (eds.), 251–60.

Hughes, J. & W. S. Ramson (1982). *Poetry of the Stewart Court*. Canberra: Australian National University Press.

Jackson, K. H. (1955). The Pictish language. In Wainwright (ed.), 129–66.

(1969). *The Gododdin: the Oldest Scottish Poem*. Edinburgh: Edinburgh University Press.

Johnston, P. (1985). The rise and fall of the Kelvinside/Morningside accent. In Görlach (ed.), 37–56.

Kinsley, J. (ed.) (1979). *The Poems of William Dunbar*. Oxford: Clarendon.

Kniesza, V. (1986). What happened to Old French /ai/ in Britain? In Strauss & Drescher (eds.), 103–14.

(1990). The sources of the ⟨I⟩-digraphs: the place-name evidence. In McClure & Spiller (eds.), 442–50.

Kohler, K. J. (1967). Aspects of MSc phonemics and graphemics. *Transactions of the Philological Society* 32–61.

Lamb, G. (1988). *Orkney Wordbook*. Birsay: Byrgisey.

Lass, R. (1974). Linguistic orthogenesis? Scots vowel quantity and the English length conspiracy. In Anderson & Jones (eds.), vol. II, 311–43.

Letley, E. (1988). *From Galt to Douglas Brown: Nineteenth-century Fiction and Scots Language*. Edinburgh: Scottish Academic Press.

Lorimer, W. L. (1983). *The New Testament in Scots*. Edinburgh: Southside.

Low, T. G. (ed.) (1901–5). *The New Testament in Scots* (Scottish Text Society First Series 46, 49, 52). Edinburgh: Blackwood.

Lyall, R. J. & F. Riddy (eds.) (1981). *Proceedings of the Third International Conference on Scottish Language and Literature, Mediaeval and Renaissance, Stirling 1981*. Stirling and Glasgow: Universities of Stirling and Glasgow.

Macafee, C. (1981). Nationalism and the Scots Renaissance now. *English World-wide* 2, 1: 29–38.

(1983). *Varieties of English Around the World: Glasgow*. Amsterdam: Benjamins.

(1990). Middle Scots dialects: extrapolating backwards. In McClure & Spiller (eds.), 429–41.

Macafee, C. & I. Macleod (eds.) (1987). *The Nuttis Schell: Essays on the Scots Language Presented to A. J. Aitken*. Aberdeen: Aberdeen University Press.

MacAulay, R. K. (1977). *Language, Social Class and Education: a Glasgow Study*. Edinburgh: Edinburgh University Press.

McClure, J. D. (1970). Some features of standard English as spoken in South-West Scotland. Edinburgh University, unpublished M.Litt. dissertation.

(ed.) (1975). *The Scots Language in Education*. Aberdeen: Waverley Press.

(1977). Vowel duration in a Scottish accent. *Journal of the International Phonetic Association* 7, 1: 10–16.

(1981a). Scottis, Inglis, Sudroun: language labels and language attitudes. In Lyall & Riddy (eds.), 52–69.

(1981b). The language of *The Entail*. *Scottish Literary Journal* 8, 1: 30–51.

(1981c). The synthesisers of Scots. In Haugen, McClure & Thomson (eds.), 91–9.

(1983a). Scots in dialogue: some uses and implications. In McClure (ed.), 1983b: 129–48.

(1983b). *Scotland and the Lowland Tongue: Studies in the Language and Literature of Lowland Scotland in honour of David Murison*. Aberdeen: Aberdeen University Press.

(1986). What Scots owes to Gaelic. *Scottish Language* 6: 85–98.

(1987). Language and genre in the 1721 Poems of Allan Ramsay. In Carter & Pittock (eds.), 261–9.

(1988). *Why Scots Matters*. Edinburgh: Saltire Society.

(1992). What, if anything, is a Scotticism? In Bonner (ed.), 205–21.

McClure, J. D. & M. R. G. Spiller (eds.) (1990). *Bryght Lanternis: Essays on the Language and Literature of Medieval Scotland*. Aberdeen: Aberdeen University Press.

McDiarmid, M. P. (ed.) (1968–9). *Hary's Wallace* (Scottish Text Society Fourth Series, 4–5). Edinburgh: Scottish Text Society.

(1983). The *Gododdin* and other heroic poems of Scotland. In McClure (ed.), 1–17.

McIntosh, A. (1978). The dialectology of Middle Scots: some possible approaches to its study. *Scottish Literary Journal* Supplement 6: 38–43.

MacKinnon, K. (1990). A century on the Census: Gaelic in twentieth-century focus. In Thomson (ed.), 163–83.

Macleod, I. (ed.) (1990). *The Scots Thesaurus*. Aberdeen: Aberdeen University Press.

McPhee, W. H. (1983). Mining terms in Fife. *Scottish Language* 2: 33–41.

MacQueen, L. (1957). The last stages of the older literary language of Scotland. Edinburgh University, unpublished Ph.D thesis.

Mather, J. Y. (1966). Aspects of the linguistic geography of Scotland II: East coast fishing. *Scottish Studies* 10: 129–53.

(1969). Aspects of the linguistic geography of Scotland III: fishing communities of the East coast (Part 1). *Scottish Studies* 13: 1–16.

(1975). Social variation in present-day Scots speech. In McClure (ed.), 44–53.

Mather, J. Y. & H. H. Speitel (1975, 1977, 1986). *The Linguistic Atlas of Scotland*, vols. I, II, III. London: Croom Helm.

Melchers, G. (1985). Language attitudes in the Shetland Isles. In Görlach (ed.), 87–100.

Millar, M. & E. K. Brown (1979). Tag-questions in Edinburgh speech. *Linguistische Berichte* 60: 24–45.

Miller, J. & E. K. Brown (1982). Aspects of Scottish English syntax. *English World-wide* 3, 1: 3–17.

Morgan, E. (1983). Glasgow speech in recent Scottish literature. In McClure (ed.), 195–208.

Munro, M. (1985). *The Patter: a Guide to Current Glasgow Usage*. Glasgow: Glasgow District Libraries.

Murison, D. D. (1971). The Dutch element in the vocabulary of Scots. In Aitken, McIntosh & Palsson (eds.), 159–76.

(1974). Linguistic relationships in mediaeval Scotland. In Barrow (ed.), 71–83.

Murray, J. (1872a). The dialect of the Southern counties of Scotland. *Transactions of the Philological Society*. 1–251.

(ed.) (1872b). *The Complaynt of Scotlande*. Early English Text Society. London: EETS Extra Series 17 and 18.

Nicolaisen, W. F. H. (1976). *Scottish Place-Names: their Study and Significance*. London: Batsford.

Omand, D. (ed.) (1972). *The Caithness Book*. Inverness: Highland Printers.

Padel, O. J. (1972). Inscriptions of Pictland. Edinburgh University, unpublished M.Litt. dissertation.

Pollner, C. (1985). Old words in a young town. *Scottish Language* 4: 5–15.

Price, G. (1984). *The Languages of Britain*. London: Arnold.

Pride, G. (1987). Scottish building terms. *Scottish Language* 6: 33–41.

Renwick, R. (ed.) (1887–9). *Extracts from the Records of the Royal Burgh of Stirling*, 2 vols. Glasgow: Scottish Burgh Records Society.

Riach, W. A. D. (1988). *A Galloway Glossary* (ASLS Occasional Papers 7). Aberdeen: Association for Scottish Literary Studies.

Robinson, M. (1983). Language choice in the Reformation: the Scots Confession of 1560. In McClure (ed.), 54–69.

(ed.) (1985). *The Concise Scots Dictionary*. Aberdeen: Aberdeen University Press.

Romaine, S. (1978). Post-vocalic /r/ in Scottish English: sound-change in progress? In Trudgill (ed.), 59–78.

(1980a). The relative clause marker in Scots English: diffusion, complexity and style as dimensions of syntactic change. *Language in Society* 9: 221–47.

(1980b). Stylistic variation and evaluative reactions to speech: problems in the investigation of linguistic attitudes in Scotland. *Language and Speech* 23: 213–32.

(1981a). Contributions from Middle Scots syntax to a theory of syntactic change. In Lyall & Riddy (eds.), 70–84.

(1981b). Syntactic complexity, relativisation and stylistic levels in Middle Scots. *Folia Linguistica Historica* 2, 1: 71–97.

Ross, J. (1972). A selection of Caithness dialect words. In Omand (ed.), 241–60.

Rutherford, S. (1885). *Quaint Sermons of Samuel Rutherford Hitherto Unpublished*. London: Hodder and Stoughton.

Sandred, K. I. (1983). *Good or Bad Scots? Attitudes to Optional Lexical and Grammatical Usages in Edinburgh*. Uppsala: Almqvist and Wiksell.

Scur, G. S. (1968). On the non-finite forms of the verb *can* in Scottish. *Acta Linguistica Hafniensia* 11, 2: 211–18.

Simpson, K. (1988). *The Protean Scot: the Crisis of Identity in Eighteenth-Century Scotland*. Aberdeen: Aberdeen University Press.

Sprotte, A. C. (1906). *Zum Sprachgebrauch bei John Knox*. Berlin: Mayer and Müller.

Stewart, A. (ed.) (1979). *The Complaynt of Scotland* (Scottish Text Society Fourth Series 11). Edinburgh: Scottish Text Society.

Strauss, D. & H. W. Drescher (eds.) (1986). *Scottish Language and Literature, Mediaeval and Renaissance*. Frankfurt-on-Main: Lang.

Swanton, M. (ed.) (1970). *The Dream of the Rood*. Manchester: Manchester University Press.

Taylor, M. V. (1974). The great Southern Scots conspiracy: pattern in the development of Northern English. In Anderson & Jones (eds.), 403–26.

Thomson, D. S. (ed.) (1990). *Gaelic and Scots in Harmony: Proceedings of the Second International Conference on the Languages of Scotland*. Glasgow: Glasgow University Press.

Trudgill, P. (ed.) (1978). *Sociolinguistic Patterns in British English*. London: Arnold.

Wainwright, F. T. (ed.) (1955). *The Problem of the Picts*. Edinburgh: Nelson.

Watson, G. (1923). *The Roxburghshire Wordbook*. Cambridge: Cambridge University Press.

Wells, J. C. (1982). *Accents of English*, vol. II. Cambridge: Cambridge University Press.

Williamson, A. H. (1979). *Scottish National Consciousness in the Age of James VI*. Edinburgh: John Donald.

Williamson, I. K. (1982, 1983). Lowland Scots in education: a historical survey. *Scottish Language* 1: 54–77, and 2: 52–87.

Wilson, J. (1926). *The Dialects of Central Scotland*. Oxford: Oxford University Press.

Withers, C. W. J. (1984). *Gaelic in Scotland 1698–1981*. Edinburgh: John Donald.

Wölck, W. (1965). *Phonematische Analyse der Sprache von Buchan*. Heidelberg: Winter.

Wood, H. H. (ed.) (1977). *James Watson's Choice Collection of Comic and Serious Scots Poems* (Scottish Text Society Fourth Series 10). Edinburgh: Scottish Texts Society.

Zai, R. (1942). *The Phonology of the Morebattle Dialect, East Roxburghshire*. Lucerne: Raeber.

3   English in Wales

Aitchison, J. & H. Carter (1985). *The Welsh Language, 1961–1981; an Interpretive Atlas*. Cardiff: University of Wales Press.

Awbery, G. M. (1976). *The Syntax of Welsh: a Transformational Study of the Passive*. Cambridge: Cambridge University Press.

Bailey, R. W. (1985). The conquests of English. In Greenbaum (ed.), 9–19.

Bailey, R. W. & M. Görlach (eds.) (1982). *English as a World Language*. Ann Arbor: University of Michigan Press.

Bellin, W. (1984). Welsh and English in Wales. In Trudgill (ed.), 449–79.

Blake, N. F. (1981). *Non-standard Language in English Literature*. London: André Deutsch.

Census 1981: Welsh Language in Wales. London: HMSO, 1983.

Coupland, N. (1985). Sociolinguistic aspects of place-names: ethnic affiliation and the pronunciation of Welsh in the Welsh capital. In Viereck (ed.), 29–43.

(1988). *Dialect in Use: Sociolinguistic Variation in Cardiff English*. Cardiff: University of Wales Press.

(1989). 'Standard Welsh English': a variable semiotic. In Coupland & Thomas (eds.), 232–57.

Coupland, N. & A. Thomas (eds.) (1990). *English in Wales: Diversity, Conflict and Change*. Multilingual Matters.

Crystal, D. (1982). *Linguistic Controversies: Essays in Linguistic Theory and Practice in Honour of F. R. Palmer*. London: Arnold.

De Quincey, T. (1856). *Confessions of an English Opium Eater*. London: Bell.

Edwards, J. (1985). *Talk Tidy: the Art of Speaking Wenglish*. Cowbridge: D. Brown.

Fishman, J. (ed.) (1978). *Advances in the Study of Societal Multilingualism*. New York: Mouton.

Fodor, I. & C. Hagége (eds.) (1983/4). *Language Reform: History and Future*, vol. III. Hamburg: Buske.

Giles, H. (1973). Accent mobility: a model and some data. *Anthropological Linguistics* 15: 87–105.

Giles, H. & P. F. Powesland. (1975). *Speech Style and Social Evaluation*. London: Academic Press.

Gimson, A. C. (1965). *An Introduction to the Pronunciation of English*. London: Edward Arnold.

Greenbaum, S. (ed.) (1985). *The English Language Today*. Oxford: Pergamon.

Griffiths, D. (1969). *Talk of my Town*. Buckley: Young People's Cultural Association.

Hughes, J. (1822). *An Essay on the Ancient and Present State of the Welsh Language with Particular Reference to its Dialect*. London.

Hughes, J. A. (1924). *Wales and the Welsh in English Literature from Shakespeare to Scott*. Wrexham: Hughes.

Hüllen, W. (ed.) (1980). Understanding bilingualism. *Forum Linguisticum* 27. Frankfurt-on-Main: Peter Lang.

Jones, I. G. (1980). Language and community in nineteenth century Wales. In David Smith (ed.), 47–71.

Jones, M. & A. R. Thomas (1977). *The Welsh Language: Studies in its Syntax and Semantics*. Cardiff: University of Wales Press for the Schools Council.

Kirk, J. M., S. Sanderson & J. D. A. Widdowson (eds.) (1985). *Studies in Linguistic Geography*. London: Croom Helm.

Leith, D. (1983). *A Social History of English*. London: Routledge and Kegan Paul.

Lewis, E. G. (1978). Migration and the decline of the Welsh language. In Fishman (ed.), 263–352.

Mathias, R. (1973). The Welsh language and the English language. In Stephens (ed.), 32–63.

Matsumura, Y. (ed.) (1983). *The English Language around the World*. (In Japanese.) Tokyo: Kenkyusha.

Parry, D. (1964). Studies in the linguistic geography of Radnorshire, Breconshire, Monmouthshire and Glamorganshire. MA thesis, University of Leeds.

(1972). Anglo-Welsh dialects in south-east Wales. In Wakelin (ed.), 140–63.

(1977, 1979). *The Survey of Anglo-Welsh dialects*, vol. I: *The South-east*; vol. II: *The South-west*. Swansea: University College.

(1985). On producing a linguistic atlas: the Survey of Anglo-Welsh dialects. In Kirk, Sanderson & Widdowson (eds.), 51–66.

Penhallurick, R. J. (1991). *The Anglo-Welsh Dialects of North Wales* (University of Bamberg Studies in English Linguistics 27). Frankfurt-on-Main: Peter Lang.

Pilch, H. (1983/4). The structure of Welsh tonality. *Studia Celtica* 18/19: 234–52.

Pryce, W. T. R. (1990). Language shift in Gwent, c. 1770–1981. In Coupland & Thomas (eds.), 48–83.

Rees, Alwyn D. (1950). *Life in a Welsh Countryside: a Social Study of Llanfihangel yng Ngwynfa*. Cardiff: University of Wales Press.

Roberts, E. G. (ed.) (1976). *Anglesey Family Letters 1840–1935*. Published by the editor.

Russ, Charles V. J. (1982). The geographical and social variation of English in England and Wales. In Bailey & Görlach (eds.), 11–55.

Sharp, D., B. Thomas, E. Price, G. Francis & I. Davies (1973). *Attitudes to Welsh and English in the Schools of Wales*. Cardiff: Macmillan/University of Wales Press.

Smith, D. (ed.) (1980). *A People and a Proletariat: Essays on the History of Wales 1780–1980*. London: Pluto Press in association with Llafur, the Society for the Study of Welsh Labour History.

Smith, Ll. B. (1987). The grammar and commonplace books of John Edwards of Chirk. *Bulletin of the Board of Celtic Studies* 34: 174–84.

Stephens, M. (ed.) (1973). *The Welsh Language Today*. Llandysul: Gomer Press.

Thomas, A. R. (1973). *The Linguistic Geography of Wales*. Cardiff: University of Wales Press.

(1980). Some aspects of the bilingual situation in Wales. In Hüllen (ed.), 147–63.

(1982). Change and decay in language. In Crystal (ed.) 209–19.

(1983). The English language in Wales. In Matsumura (ed.), 137–93.

(1984). Welsh English. In Trudgill (ed.), 178–94.

(1985). Welsh English: a grammatical conspectus. In Viereck (ed.), 213–22.

Trudgill, P. (1984). *Language in the British Isles*. Cambridge: Cambridge University Press.

(1986). *Dialects in Contact*. Oxford: Blackwell.

Viereck, W. (ed.) (1985). *Focus on: England and Wales* (Varieties of English around the World, 4). Amsterdam: John Benjamins.

Wakelin, M. F. (ed.) (1972). *Patterns in the Folk Speech of the British Isles*. London: Athlone Press.

Wells, J. C. (1970). Local accents in England and Wales. *Journal of Linguistics* 6: 231–52.

(1982). *Accents of English*, 3 vols. Cambridge: Cambridge University Press.

Wells, S., G. Taylor, J. Jowett & W. Montgomery (eds.) (1986). *Shakespeare: the Complete Works*. Oxford: Clarendon.

West, J. (1983/4). An historical survey of the language planning movement in Wales. In Fodor and Hagége (eds.), 382–95.

Williams, D. (1950). *Modern Wales*. London: John Murray.

Williams, G. (ed.) (1978). *Social and Cultural Change in Rural Wales*. London: Routledge and Kegan Paul.

Williams, G., E. Roberts & R. Isaac (1978). Language and aspirations for upward social mobility. In Williams (ed.), 193–206.

Williams, S. J. (1980). *A Welsh Grammar*, Cardiff: University of Wales Press.

4 English in Ireland

Adams, G. B. (1958). The emergence of Ulster as a distinct dialect area. *Ulster Folklife* 4: 61–73.

(1964a). The last language census in Northern Ireland. In Adams 1964c: 111–45.

(1964b). A register of phonological research on Ulster dialects. In Adams 1964c: 193–201.

(ed.) (1964c). *Ulster Dialects: an Introductory Symposium*. Cultra Manor: Ulster Folk Museum.

(1973). Language in Ulster, 1820–1850. *Ulster Folklife* 19: 50–5.

(1976). Aspects of monoglottism in Ulster. *Ulster Folklife* 22: 76–87.

(1977). The dialects of Ulster. In Ó Muirithe 1977b: 56–69.

(1986). *The English Dialects of Ulster*, ed. M. Barry & P. Tilling. Cultra Manor: Ulster Folk and Transport Museum.

Adams, J. R. R. (1989). A preliminary checklist of works containing Ulster dialect 1700–1900. *Linen Hall Review* 6, 3: 10–12.

Aitken, A. J. (1981). The Scottish vowel-length rule. In M. Benskin & M. L. Samuels (eds.), *So Meny People Longages and Tonges: Philological Essays in Scots and Mediaeval English Presented to Angus McIntosh*. Edinburgh: Edinburgh University Press, 131–57.

Aldus, J. B. (1976). Anglo-Irish dialects: a bibliography. *Regional Language Studies... Newfoundland* 7: 7–28.

Allsopp, R. (1980). How does the creole lexicon expand? In A. Valdman & A. Highfield (eds.) *Theoretical Orientations in Creole Language Studies*. London: Academic Press, 89–107.

Athbheochan (1965). *Athbheochan na Gaeilge: the Restoration of the Irish Language*. Dublin: Stationery Office.

Barnes, W. (ed.) (1867). *A Glossary, with some Pieces of Verse, of the Old Dialect of the English colony in the Baronies of Forth and Bargy, County of Wexford, Ireland, by J. Poole*. London.

Barry, M. V. (ed.) (1981a). *Aspects of English Dialects in Ireland*, vol. I. Belfast: Queen's University of Belfast.

(1981b). The methodology of the Tape-recorded Survey of Hiberno-English Speech. In Barry (ed.) 1981a: 18–46.

(1981c). The southern boundaries of Northern Hiberno-English speech. In Barry (ed.) 1981a: 52–93.

(1982). The English language in Ireland. In R. W. Bailey & M. Görlach (eds.) *English as a World Language*. Ann Arbor: University of Michigan Press, 84–133.

Bartley, J. O. (1942). The development of a stock character. *The Modern Language Review* 37: 438–47.

(1947). Bulls and bog witticisms. *The Irish Book Lover* November: 59–62.

(1954). *Teague, Shenkin and Sawney*. Cork: Cork University Press.

Benskin, M. (1988). Irish adoptions in the English of Tipperary, ca. 1432. In E. G. Stanley & T. F. Hoad (eds.) *Words: for Robert Burchfield's Sixty-fifth Birthday*. Cambridge: Brewer, 37–67.

(1989). The style and authorship of the Kildare poems: (I) *Pers of Bermingham*. In J. L. MacKenzie & R. Todd (eds.) *In Other Words: Transcultural Studies in Philology, Translation and Lexicography presented to Hans Heinrich Meier on the Occasion of his Sixty-fifth Birthday*. Dordrecht: Foris, 57–75.

(1990). The hands of the Kildare poems manuscript. *Irish University Review* 20 (1): 163–93.

Benskin, M. & A. McIntosh (1972). A mediaeval English manuscript of Irish provenance. *Medium Aevum* 41: 128–31.

Berry, H. F. (ed.) (1907). *Statutes and Ordinances, and Acts of the Parliament of Ireland. King John to Henry V*. Dublin: Stationery Office.

Bertz, S. (1987). Variation in Dublin English. *Teanga* 7: 35–53.

Bigger, F. J. (1923). *Montiaghisms*. Rept. Belfast: Linen Hall Library, 1976.

Blake, M. J. (1902). *Blake Family Records 1300 to 1600*. 1st ser. London: Elliot Stack.

Bliss, A. J. (1965). The inscribed slates at Smarmore. *Proceedings of the Royal Irish Academy* 64, section C: 33–60.

   (1972a). Languages in contact. *Proceedings of the Royal Irish Academy* 72, section C: 63–82.

   (1972b). A Synge glossary. In S. B. Bushrui (ed.) *Sunshine and the Moon's Delight: a Centenary Tribute to John Millington Synge*. Gerrards Cross: Colin Smythe, 297–316.

   (1976). *The English Language in Ireland*. Dublin: Clódhanna Teoranta.

   (ed.) (1977a). *A Dialogue in Hybernian Stile*, by J. Swift. Dublin: Cadenus Press.

   (1977b). The emergence of modern English dialects in Ireland. In Ó Muirithe 1977b: 7–19.

   (1979). *Spoken English in Ireland: 1600–1740*. Dublin: Dolmen Press.

   (1984a). English in the south of Ireland. In Trudgill (ed.), 135–51.

   (1984b). Language and literature. In J. Lydon (ed.) *The English in Medieval Ireland*. Dublin: Royal Irish Academy, 27–45.

Bliss, A. & J. Long (1987). Literature in Norman French and English. In Cosgrove (ed.), 708–36.

Bradshaw, B. (1979). *The Irish constitutional revolution of the sixteenth century*. Cambridge: Cambridge University Press.

Braidwood, J. (1964). Ulster and Elizabethan English. In Adams (ed.) 1964c: 5–109.

Breatnach, R. B. (1967–8). Review of S. Ó hAnnracháin, *Caint an Bhaile Dhuibh*. *Éigse* 12: 237–8.

Brewer, J. S. & W. Bullen (1867). *Calendar of the Carew Manuscripts. 1515–74*. London: Longmans, Green, Reader and Dyer.

   (eds.) (1871). *Calendar of the Carew Manuscripts. Book of Howth, Miscellaneous*. London: Longman.

British and Irish Communist Organisation (1973). *'Hidden Ulster' Explored: a Reply to Pádraig Ó Snodaigh's 'Hidden Ulster'*. Belfast: British and Irish Communist Organisation.

Britton, D. & A. J. Fletcher (1990). Medieval Hiberno-English inscriptions on the inscribed slates of Smarmore: some reconsiderations and additions. *Irish University Review* 20, 1: 55–72.

Burke, W. (1896). The Anglo-Irish dialect. *Irish Ecclesiastical Record* 3rd ser. 17: 694–704, 777–89.

Bush, J. (1769). *Hibernia curiosa*. London.

Cahill, E. (1938). Norman French and English languages in Ireland. *Irish Ecclesiastical Record* 5th ser. 51: 159–73.

Canny, N. (1980). Review of A. Bliss, *Spoken English in Ireland. Studia Hibernica* 20: 167–72.

Chart, D. A. (1935). *The Register of John Swayne*. Belfast: Stationery Office.

Clarke, S. (1986). Sociolinguistic patterning in a New World dialect of Hiberno-English. In Harris, Little & Singleton (eds.), 67–81.

Clery, A. E. (1921). Accents: Dublin and otherwise. *Studies* 10: 545–52.

Commins, P. (1988). Socioeconomic development and language maintenance in the Gaeltacht. *International Journal of the Sociology of Language* 70: 11–28.

Comórtas (1922–3). *An Sguab* 1: 203, 242–3; (1923–5) 2: 17–8, 59.

Conrick, M. (1981). Error analysis of Irish students learning French. *Teanga* 2: 70–5.

Corrigan, K. P. (1990). Northern Hiberno-English: the state of the art. *Irish University Review* 20, 1: 91–119.

Cosgrove, A. (ed.) (1987). *A New History of Ireland II: Medieval Ireland 1169–1534*. Oxford: Clarendon Press.

Croghan, M. (1986). The brogue: language as political culture. In Harris, Little & Singleton (eds.), 259–69.

(1988). A bibliography of English in Ireland: problems with names and boundaries. In B. Bramsbäck and M. Croghan (eds.) *Anglo-Irish and Irish Literature: Aspects of Language and Culture*, vol. I. Stockholm: Almqvist and Wiksell, 103–15.

Croker, T. C. (ed.) (1841). *Narratives Illustrative of the Contests in Ireland in 1641 and 1690*. London: Camden Society.

Curtis, E. (1919). The spoken languages of medieval Ireland. *Studies* 8: 234–54.

(ed.) (1932). *Calendar of Ormond deeds. 1172–1350*. vol. I. Dublin: Stationery Office.

Dahl, Ö. (1985). *Tense and Aspect Systems*. Oxford: Basil Blackwell.

Daonáireamh (1985). *Daonáireamh na hÉireann: Census of population 1981*, vol. VI. Dublin: Stationery Office.

[Davies, J.] (1613). *A discoverie of the state of Ireland*. [Place of publication unknown.]

Dolan, T. P. & D. Ó Muirithe (eds.) (1979). *Poole's Glossary with some Pieces of Verse, of the Old Dialect of the English Colony in the Baronies of Forth and Bargy*. *The Past*: Organ of the Uí Ceansealaigh Historical Society, no. 13.

Douglas-Cowie, E. (1978). Linguistic code-switching in a Northern Irish village. In Trudgill (ed.), 37–51.

Eachard, L. (1691). *An Exact Description of Ireland*. London.

Edgeworth, M. (1848 [1801]). Essay on Irish bulls. In M. Edgeworth, *Tales and Novels*, vol. IV. London, 81–192.

Filppula, M. (1986). *Some Aspects of Hiberno-English in a Functional Sentence Perspective*. Joensuu: University of Joensuu.

(1990). Substratum, superstratum, and universals in the genesis of Hiberno-English. *Irish University Review* 20, 1: 41–54.

(1991). Subordinating *and* in Hiberno-English syntax: Irish or English origin? In P. S. Ureland & G. Broderick (eds.). *Language Contact in the British Isles*. Tübingen: Max Niemeyer, 617–31.

Finlay, C. & M. McTear (1986). Syntactic variation in the speech of Belfast schoolchildren. In Harris, Little & Singleton (eds.), 175–86.

Fitzgerald, G. (1984). Estimates for baronies of minimal levels of Irish-speaking amongst successive decennial cohorts. *Proceedings of the Royal Irish Academy* 84, section C: 117–55.

Fraser, R. (1807). *Statistical Survey of the County of Wexford*. Dublin.

Furnivall, F. J. (ed.) (1896). *The English Conquest of Ireland* (EETS Original ser. 107). London: Kegan Paul.

Garvin, J. (1977). The Anglo-Irish idiom in the works of major Irish writers. In Ó Muirithe (ed.) 1977b: 100–14.

Gilbert, J. T. (1879). *A Contemporary History of Affairs in Ireland from 1641 to 1652*. Dublin: Irish Archaeological and Celtic Society.

(1885a). Archives of the municipal corporation of Waterford. *Historical Manuscripts Commission, Tenth Report*, appendix, part V. London: Stationery Office, 265–339.

(1885b). Archives of the town of Galway: Queen's College, Galway. *Historical Manuscripts Commission, Tenth Report*, appendix, part V. London: Stationery Office, 380–520.

(ed.) (1889). *Calendar of Ancient Records of Dublin*, vol. I. Dublin: Municipal Corporation.

Goeke, D. & J. Kornelius (1976). On measuring Irishisms. *Fu Jen Studies* 9: 45–60.

Greene, D. (1979). Perfects and perfectives in modern Irish. *Ériu* 30: 122–41.

Gregg, R. J. (1972). The Scotch–Irish dialect boundaries in Ulster. In M. F. Wakelin (ed.), *Patterns in the Folk Speech of the British Isles*. London: Athlone Press, 109–39.

Guilfoyle, E. (1983). Habitual aspect in Hiberno-English. *McGill Working Papers in Linguistics* 1, 1: 22–32.

(1986). Hiberno-English: a parametric approach. In Harris, Little & Singleton (eds.), 121–32.

Hamill, F. (1986). Belfast: the Irish language. *Éire-Ireland* 21, 4: 146–50.

Hamilton, H. C. (ed.) (1860). *Calendar of the State Papers Relating to Ireland, Henry VIII, Edward VI, Mary, and Elizabeth*. London.

(1867). *Calendar of the State Papers Relating to Ireland, Elizabeth 1574–1585*. London.

Hardiman, J. (ed.) (1846). *A Chorographical Description of West or H-Iar Connaught*, by R. O'Flaherty. Dublin: Irish Archaeological Society.

Harris, J. (1983). The Hiberno-English 'I've it eaten' construction: what is it and where does it come from? *Teanga* 3: 30–43.

(1984a). English in the north of Ireland. In Trudgill (ed.), 115–34.

(1984b). Syntactic variation and dialect divergence. *Journal of Linguistics* 20: 303–27.

(1985a). *Phonological Variation and Change: Studies in Hiberno-English*. Cambridge: Cambridge University Press.

(1985b). *The Polylectal Grammar Stops Here*. Trinity College Dublin, Centre for Language and Communication Studies, Occasional Paper no. 13.

(1986). Expanding the superstrate. *English World-wide* 7: 171–99.

(1987). On doing comparative reconstruction with genetically unrelated languages. In A. G. Ramat, O. Carruba & G. Bernini (eds.), *Papers from the 7th International Conference on Historical Linguistics*. Amsterdam: Benjamins, 267–82.

(1990). More on brogues and creoles: what's been happening to English short u? *Irish University Review* 20, 1: 73–90.

Harris, J., D. Little & D. Singleton (eds.) (1986). *Perspectives on the English language in Ireland*. Dublin: Trinity College Dublin, Centre for Language and Communication Studies.

Hayden, M. & M. Hartog (1909). The Irish dialect of English. *Fortnightly Review* new ser. 85: 775–85, 933–47.

Henry, P. L. (1957). *An Anglo-Irish dialect of North Roscommon*. Dublin: University College Dublin, Department of English.

(1958). A linguistic survey of Ireland: preliminary report. *Lochlann* 1: 49–208.

(1960–1). The Irish substantival system and its reflexes in Anglo-Irish and English. *Zeitschrift für Celtische Philologie* 28: 19–50.

(1972). The Land of Cokaygne. *Studia Hibernica* 12: 120–41.

(1974). *Language, Culture, and the Nation*. Dublin: Comhdhail Náisiúnta na Gaeilge.

(1977). Anglo-Irish and its Irish background. In Ó Muirithe (ed.) 1977b: 20–36.

(1981). Review of A. Bliss, *Spoken English in Ireland*. *Éigse* 18: 319–26.

(1986). Anglo-Irish verse in translation from Irish. In Harris, Little & Singleton (eds.), 11–29.

Heuser, W. (1904). *Die Kildare-Gedichte* (Bonner Beiträge zur Anglistik, 14). Bonn: P. Hanstein.

Hickey, R. (1982). Syntactic ambiguity in Hiberno-English. *Studia Anglica Posnaniensia* 15: 39–45.

(1984). Coronal segments in Irish English. *Journal of Linguistics* 20: 233–50.

(1986). Possible phonological parallels between Irish and Irish English. *English World-wide* 7: 1–21.

Hill, A. (1962). A conjectural restructuring of a dialect of Ireland. *Lochlann* 2: 23–37.

Hogan, J. (1927). *The English Language in Ireland*. Dublin: The Educational Company of Ireland.

Hughes, C. (ed.) (1903). *Shakespeare's Europe: Unpublished Chapters of Fynes Moryson's Itinerary*. London: Sherrat and Hughes.

Hume, A. (1878). *Remarks on the Irish Dialect of the English Language*. Rept. from the *Transactions of the Historic Society of Lancashire and Cheshire*, vol. 30. Liverpool.

Ihalainen, O. (1976). Periphrastic *do* in affirmative sentences in the dialect of East Somerset. *Neuphilologische Mitteilungen* 77: 608–22.

Irish words (1900–01). Irish words in the spoken English of Leinster. *Irisleabhar Na Gaedhilge* 11: 92–4, 108–10, 123–5, 140–3, 153–5, 174–5, 187–90; 12 (1902): 14–15.

Irwin, P. J. (1933). Ireland's contribution to the English language. *Studies* 22: 637–52.

(1934). Some emendations in the chronology of the N.E.D. *Journal of English and Germanic Philology* 33: 502–5.

(1935). A study of the English dialects of Ireland, 1172–1800. Unpublished Ph.D. thesis, University of London.

Joyce, P. W. (1910). *English as we Speak it in Ireland*. Dublin: Gill. Rept. Dublin: Wolfhound Press (1979, 1988).

Kallen, J. L. (1981). A global view of the English language in Ireland. *Teanga* 2: 32–43.

(1985). The study of Hiberno-English. In Ó Baoill (ed.), 1–15.

(1986). The co-occurrence of *do* and *be* in Hiberno-English. In Harris, Little & Singleton (eds.), 133–47.

(1987). Review of R. Wall, *An Anglo-Irish dialect Glossary for Joyce's Works*. *Hermathena* 142: 75–7.

(1988). The English language in Ireland. *International Journal of the Sociology of Language* 70: 127–42.

(1989). Tense and aspect categories in Irish English. *English World-wide* 10: 1–39.

(1990). The Hiberno-English perfect: grammaticalisation revisited. *Irish University Review* 20, 1: 120–36.

(1991). Sociolinguistic variation and methodology: *after* as a Dublin variable. In J. Cheshire (ed.) *English around the World: Sociolinguistic Perspectives*. Cambridge: Cambridge University Press, 61–74.

Kelly, P. (1989). Afterthoughts on AFTER + DOING. Paper presented to joint meeting, Linguistics Association of Great Britain/Irish Association for Applied Linguistics, Belfast.

Kelly, R. J. (1897). An old school in Galway. *Journal of the Royal Society of Antiquaries of Ireland*. 5th ser. 7: 191–2.

Kiely, B. (1977). Dialect and literature. In Ó Muirithe (ed.) 1977b: 88–99.

Krause, D. (1960). *Sean O'Casey: the Man and his Work*. London: Macgibbon and Kee.

Lass, R. (1986). 'Irish influence': reflections on 'standard' English and its opposites, and the identification of calques. *Studia Anglica Posnaniensia* 18: 81–7.

(1987). *The Shape of English: Structure and History*. London: J. M. Dent.

(1990). Early mainland residues in southern Hiberno-English. *Irish University Review* 20, 1: 137–48.

Legge, M. D. (1968). The significance of Anglo-Norman. University of Edinburgh Inaugural Lecture no. 38.

Lunny, A. (1981). Linguistic interaction: English and Irish in Ballyvourney, West Cork. In Barry (ed.) 1981a: 118–41.

Lysaght, E. E. (1915). Irish words and English speakers. *New Ireland* 2 October: 333–4; 9 October: 349–50.

Mac Aodha, B. S. (1985–6). Aspects of the linguistic geography of Ireland in the early nineteenth century. *Studia Celtica* 20/1: 205–20.

McCawley, J. (1971). Tense and time reference in English. Rept. in J. McCawley (ed.) (1976), *Grammar and Meaning: Papers on Syntactic and Semantic Topics*, corrected edn. London: Academic Press, 257–72.

McIntosh, A. & M. L. Samuels (1968). Prolegomena to a study of mediaeval Anglo-Irish. *Medium Aevum* 37: 1–11.

McIntosh, A., M. L. Samuels & M. Benskin (1986). *A Linguistic Atlas of Late Mediaeval English*, 4 vols. Aberdeen: Aberdeen University Press.

MacLysaght, E. (1944). Report on documents relating to the wardenship of Galway. *Analecta Hibernica* 14: 3–249.

(1979). *Irish Life in the Seventeenth Century*. 4th rev. edn (1st edn 1939). Dublin: Irish Academic Press.

McNeill, C. (ed.) (1930). Reports on the Rawlinson collection of manuscripts preserved in the Bodleian Library, Oxford. *Analecta Hibernica* 1: 12–178.

Martin, F. X. (1987a). Allies and an overlord. In Cosgrove (ed.), 67–97.

(1987b). Diarmait MacMurchada and the coming of the Anglo-Normans. In Cosgrove (ed.), 43–66.

(1987c). Overlord becomes feudal lord, 1172–85. In Cosgrove (ed.), 98–126.

Mason, W. S. (1814–19). *A Statistical Account, or Parochial Survey of Ireland*, 3 vols. Dublin.

Millar, S. (1987). The question of ethno-linguistic differences in Northern Ireland. *English World-wide* 8: 201–13.

Mills, J. (ed.) (1905). *Calendar of the Justiciary Rolls or Proceedings in the Court of Justiciar of Ireland. 23 to 31 Edward I*. Dublin: Stationery Office.

Milroy, J. (1976). Length and height variations in the vowels of Belfast vernacular. *Belfast Working Papers in Language and Linguistics* 1: 69–110.

(1981). *Regional Accents of English: Belfast*. Belfast: Blackstaff Press.

(1986). The methodology of urban language studies: the example of Belfast. In Harris, Little & Singleton (eds.), 31–48.

Milroy, J. & J. Harris (1980). When is a merger not a merger? *English World-wide* 1: 199–210.

Milroy, J. & L. Milroy (1978). Belfast: change and variation in an urban vernacular. In Trudgill (ed.), 19–36.

(1985). Linguistic change, social network and speaker innovation. *Journal of Linguistics* 21: 339–84.

Milroy, L. (1980). *Language and Social Networks*. (2nd edn 1987.) Oxford: Basil Blackwell.

(1984). Comprehension and context: successful communication and communicative breakdown. In P. Trudgill (ed.) *Applied Sociolinguistics*. London: Academic Press, 7–31.

(1987). *Observing and Analysing Natural Language*. Oxford: Basil Blackwell.

Montgomery, M. (1989). Exploring the roots of Appalachian English. *English World-wide* 10: 227–78.

Morrissey, J. F. (ed.) (1939). *Statute Rolls of the Parliament of Ireland. 12/13 to 21/22 Edward IV*. Dublin: Stationery Office.

Murphy, D. (ed.) (1896). *The Annals of Clonmacnoise*, trans. Conell Mageoghagan. Dublin: University Press.

Murray, L. P. (1912–15). Poets and poetry of the parish of Kilkerly, Haggardstown. *Journal of the County Louth Archaeological Society* 3: 369–84.

Nally, E. V. (1971). Notes on a Westmeath dialect. *Journal of the International Phonetic Association* 1: 33–8.

Ní Ghallchóir, C. (1981). Aspects of bilingualism in NW Donegal. In Barry (ed.) 1981a: 142–70.

Ó Baoill, D. (ed.) (1985). *Papers on Irish English*. Dublin: Irish Association for Applied Linguistics.

O Casaide, S. (1930). *The Irish Language in Belfast and County Down: A.D. 1601–1850*. Dublin: Gill.

Ó Coileáin, A. (ed.) (n.d.). *The Irish Language in a Changing Society*. Dublin: Bord Na Gaeilge.

Ó Cuív, B. (1951). *Irish Dialects and Irish-speaking Districts*. Dublin: Dublin Institute for Advanced Studies.

Ó Dochartaigh, C. (1987). *Dialects of Ulster Irish*. Belfast: Queen's University of Belfast.

Ó Glaisne, R. (1981). Irish and the protestant tradition. Rept. in M. P. Hederman & R. Kearney (eds.) (1982), *The Crane Bag Book of Irish Studies*. Dublin: Blackwater, 864–75.

Ó Háinle, C. G. (1986). Neighbours in eighteenth century Dublin: Jonathan Swift and Seán Ó Neachtain. *Éire – Ireland* 21, 4: 106–21.

Ó hAnnracháin, S. (1964). *Caint an Bhaile Dhuibh*. Dublin: An Clóchomhar Tta.

Ó Muirithe, D. (1977a). The Anglo-Normans and their English dialect of south-east Wexford. In Ó Muirithe (ed.) 1977b: 37–55.

(ed.) (1977b). *The English Language in Ireland*. Dublin: The Mercier Press.

(1990). A modern glossary of the dialect of Forth and Bargy. *Irish University Review* 20, 1: 149–62.

Ó Murchú, M. (1970). *Urlabhra agus Pobal/Language and Community*. (Comhairle Na Gaeilge, Occasional Paper no. 1.) Dublin: Stationery Office.

(1985). *The Irish language*. Dublin: Dept of Foreign Affairs and Bord na Gaeilge.

Ó Neachtain, E. (ed.) (1918). *Stair Éamuinn Uí Chléire*, by Seán Uí Neachtain. Dublin: M. H. Mac an Ghuill.

O'Neill, D. (1987). Ethnolinguistic differences within a Northern Irish community. Unpublished MPhil. dissertation, Trinity College Dublin.

O'Neill, P. (1947). A North-County Dublin glossary. *Béaloideas* 17: 262–83.

O'Rahilly, T. F. (1932). *Irish Dialects Past and Present*. Dublin: Browne and Nolan.

Ó Riagáin, P. (1988a). Bilingualism in Ireland 1973–1983. *International Journal of the Sociology of Language* 70: 29–51.

(1988b). Introduction. *International Journal of the Sociology of Language* 70: 5–9.

Ó Snodaigh, P. (1973). *Hidden Ulster*. Dublin: Clódhanna Teo.

Patterson, D. (1860). *The Provincialisms of Belfast and the Surrounding Districts Pointed out and Corrected*. Belfast: Mayne.

Patterson, W. H. (1880). *A Glossary of Words in Use in the counties of Antrim and Down*. London: English Dialect Society.

Pender, S. (ed.) (1939). *A Census of Ireland, circa 1659*. Dublin: The Stationery Office.

Pitts, A. H. (1985). Urban influence on phonological variation in a Northern Irish speech community. *English World-wide* 6: 59–85.

(1986). Differing prestige values for the (ky) variable in Lurgan. In Harris, Little & Singleton (eds.), 209–21.

Pritchard, R. M. O. (1990). Language policy in Northern Ireland. *Teangeolas* 27: 26–35.

Quin, E. G. (1977). The collectors of Irish dialect material. In Ó Muirithe (ed.) 1977b: 115–26.

Rickford, J. R. (1986). Social contact and linguistic diffusion. *Language* 62: 245–89.

Robinson, P. S. (1984). *The Plantation of Ulster*. Dublin: Gill and Macmillan.

Russell, C. W. (1858). On the inhabitants and dialect of the Barony of Forth, in the County of Wexford. *The Atlantis* 1: 235–44.

Salmon, V. (1965). Sentence structure in colloquial Shakespearian English. *Transactions of the Philological Society*, 105–40.

Scott, A. B. & F. X. Martin (eds.) (1978). *Expugnatio Hibernica: the Conquest of Ireland*, by Giraldus Cambrensis. Dublin: Royal Irish Academy.

Seymour, St. J. (1929). *Anglo-Irish Literature 1200–1582*. Cambridge: Cambridge University Press.

(1932–4). Three medieval poems from Kilkenny. *Proceedings of the Royal Irish Academy* 41, section C: 205–9.

Shee, G. (1882). The Irish 'brogue' in fiction: a protest. *The Month* 45: 363–75.

Sheridan, T. (1780). *A General Dictionary of the English Language*. London.

(1781). *A Rhetorical Grammar of the English Language*. Dublin.

Shields, H. (1975–6). The Walling of New Ross: a thirteenth-century poem in French. *Long Room* 12/13: 24–33.

Shirley, E. P. (ed.) (1856–7). Extracts from the journal of Thomas Dineley. *The Journal of the Kilkenny and South-East of Ireland Archaeological Society* New ser. 1: 143–6, 170–88; 2 (1858–9), 22–32, 55–6.

Short, I. (1980). On bilingualism in Anglo-Norman England. *Romance Philology* 33: 467–79.

Sommerfelt, A. (1958). Review of M. Traynor, *The English Dialect of Donegal*. *Norsk Tidsskrift for Sprogvidenskap* 18: 415–16.

Stanyhurst, R. (1577). A treatise contayning a playne and perfect description of Irelande. In R. Holinshed *The historie of Irelande from the first inhabitation thereof, unto the yeare 1509*. London.

State Papers (1834). *State Papers Published under the Authority of his Majesty's Commission*, vol. II, pt iii; vol. III, pt iii. London.

Statutes (1786). *The Statutes at Large, Passed in the Parliaments Held in Ireland, 3 Edward II to 26 George III*, vol. I. Dublin.

Steele, R. R. (ed.) (1898). *Secreta Secretorum* (EETS Extra ser. 74). London.

Stemmler, T. (1977). The vernacular snatches in the *Red Book of Ossory*: a textual case-history. *Anglia* 95: 122–9.

Stockley, W. F. P. (1927). Not bad English, but older English. *The Catholic Bulletin* 17: 511–18.

Sullivan, J. P. (1980). The validity of literary dialect: evidence from the theatrical portrayal of Hiberno-English forms. *Language in Society* 9: 195–219.

Taniguchi, J. (1956). *A Grammatical Analysis of Artistic Representation of Irish English*. Tokyo: Shinozaki Shorin.

Tilling, P. M. (1985). A Tape-recorded Survey of Hiberno-English in its context. In Ó Baoill (ed.), 16–26.

Todd, L. (1984). By their tongue divided: towards an analysis of speech communities in Northern Ireland. *English World-wide* 5: 159–80.

(1989a). Cultures in conflict: varieties of English in Northern Ireland. In O. García & R. Otheguy (eds.) *English across Cultures/Cultures across English*. Berlin: Mouton de Gruyter, 335–55.

(1989b). *The Language of Irish Literature*. London: Macmillan.

Tovey, H. (1988). The state and the Irish language: the role of Bord na Gaeilge. *International Journal of the Sociology of Language* 70: 53–68.

Traynor, M. (1953). *The English Dialect of Donegal*. Dublin: Royal Irish Academy.

Trudgill, P. (1974). Linguistic change and diffusion: description and explanation in sociolinguistic dialect geography. *Language in Society* 3: 213–46.

(ed.) (1978). *Sociolinguistic Patterns in British English*. London: Edward Arnold.

(ed.) (1984). *Language in the British Isles*. Cambridge: Cambridge University Press.

Ua Broin, L. (1944). A south-west Dublin glossary. *Béaloideas* 14: 162–86.

Vallancey, C. (1788). Memoir of the language, manners and customs of an Anglo-Saxon colony settled in the baronies of Forth and Bargie in the county of Wexford, Ireland in 1167, 1168 and 1169. *Transactions of the Royal Irish Academy* (2), Antiquities: 19–41.

van Hamel, A. G. (1912). On Anglo-Irish syntax. *Englische Studien* 45: 272–92.

Vendryes, J. (1937). Chronique. *Études Celtiques* 2: 178–216.

Visser, F. Th. (1969–73). *An Historical Syntax of the English Language*, 3 pts in 4 vols. Leiden: Brill.

Walker, J. (1802). *A Critical Pronouncing Dictionary, and Expositor of the English Language*, 3rd edn (1st edn 1791). London.

Wall, R. (1986). *An Anglo-Irish Dialect Glossary for Joyce's Works*. Gerrards Cross: Colin Smythe.

(1990). Dialect in Irish literature: the hermetic core. *Irish University Review* 20, 1: 8–18.

Wells, J. C. (1982). *Accents of English*, 3 vols. Cambridge: Cambridge University Press.

Williams, J. P. (1986). Hiberno-English and white West Indian English: the historical link. In Harris, Little & Singleton (eds.), 83–94.

Williams, N. (1986). *I bprionta i leabhar: na protastúin agus prós na Gaeilge 1567–1724*. Dublin: An Clóchomhar Tta.

Williams, N. J. A. (ed.) (1981). *Pairlement Chloinne Tomáis*. Dublin: Dublin Institute for Advanced Studies.

Wright, T. & J. O. Halliwell (eds.) (1841–3). *Reliquiae antiquae*, 2 vols. London.

Young, A. (1780). *A Tour in Ireland*, 2 vols. Dublin.

Younge, K. E. (1923–4). Irish idioms in English speech. *The Gaelic Churchman* 5: 167.

5   The dialects of England since 1776

Barnes, W. (1886). *A Glossary of the Dorset Dialect with a Grammar*. Dorchester: M. & E. Case, County Printers. (Reprinted St Peter Port, Guernsey via Britain: The Toucan Press, 1970.)

Barry, M. (1972). The morphemic distribution of the definite article in contemporary regional English. In M. Wakelin (ed.) *Patterns in the Folk*

Speech of the British Isles. London: Athlone Press of the University of London, 164–81.

Beale, J. (1987). The grammar of Tyneside and Northumbrian English. In J. Milroy & L. Milroy (eds.) *Regional Variation in British English Syntax*. London: Economic and Social Research Council, 1–21.

Blake, N. F. (1981). *Non-standard Language in English Literature*. London: André Deutsch.

Bonaparte, L. L. (1875–6). On the dialects of Monmouthshire, Herefordshire, Worcestershire, Gloucestershire, Berkshire, Oxfordshire, South Warwickshire, South Northamptonshire, Buckinghamshire, Hertfordshire, Middlesex, and Surrey, with a new classification of the English dialects. *Transactions of the Philological Society*, 570–81.

Brokesby, F. (1691). Some observations made and communicated by Mr. Francis Brokesby, concerning the dialect and various pronunciation of words in the East Riding of Yorkshire (attached to the 1691 edition of Ray 1674).

Bronstein, A. J. (1990). The development of pronunciation in English language dictionaries. In Ramsaran (ed.) 1990a: 137–52.

Brook, G. L. (1963). *English Dialects*. London: André Deutsch.

Brown, G. N. (1833). The York Minster Screen. In the dialect of the North Riding of Yorkshire. In Skeat (ed.) (1896), 1–13.

Campion, G. E. (1976). *Lincolnshire Dialects*. Boston: R. Kay.

CCDE (*A Corpus of Contemporary Dialects of England*). A machine-readable collection of transcriptions of tape-recorded dialectal English from the 1970s. University of Helsinki. (See Ihalainen 1988a, 1988b, 1990b.)

Chambers, J. K. & P. Trudgill (1980). *Dialectology*. Cambridge: Cambridge University Press.

Cheshire, J. (1982). *Variation in an English Dialect: a Sociolinguistic Study*. Cambridge: Cambridge University Press.

Chope, R. P. (1891). *The Dialect of Hartland, Devonshire* (English Dialect Society 65). London: K. Paul, Trench, Trübner. (Reprinted Vaduz: Kraus, 1965.)

Coote, C. (1788). *Elements of the Grammar of the English Language*. London.

Cullum, Sir J. (1813). *Words in Use at Hawsted, Suffolk* (English Dialect Society 23). London: Trübner. (Reprinted Vaduz: Kraus, 1965.)

Darlington, T. (1887). *The Folk-Speech of South Cheshire* (English Dialect Society 53). London: Trübner. (Reprinted Vaduz: Kraus, 1965.)

Defoe, D. (1724–6). *A Tour Thro' the Whole Island of Great Britain*. With an Introduction by G. D. H. Cole. London: Peter Davies, 1927.

Dobson, E. J. (1968). *English Pronunciation 1500–1700*, vols. I and II. Oxford: Clarendon Press.

Eaton, R., O. Fischer, W. Koopman & F. Van den Leek, (eds.) (1985). *Papers from the Fourth International Conference on English Historical Linguistics*. Amsterdam & Philadelphia: John Benjamins.

Edwards, V. & B. Weltens (1985). Research on non-standard dialects of British English: progress and prospects. In Viereck (ed.) 1985b: 97–139.

Ellis, A. J. (1889). *On Early English Pronunciation, Part V, The Existing Phonology of English Dialects Compared with That of West Saxon* (Early English Text Society, Extra Series 56). Reprinted New York: Greenwood Press, 1968.

Elworthy, T. (1875). *The Dialect of West Somerset.* (From *Transactions of the Philological Society* (1875–6), 197–272.) (Reprinted Vaduz: Kraus, 1965.)

(1877/9). *An Outline of the Grammar of the Dialect of the West Somerset.* (From *Transactions of the Philological Society* (1877–9), 143–257.) (Reprinted Vaduz: Kraus, 1965.)

(1886). *The West Somerset Word-Book: a Glossary of Dialectal and Archaic Words and Phrases Used in the West of Somerset and East Devon* (English Dialect Society 50). London: Trübner. (Reprinted Vaduz: Kraus, 1965.)

Eustace, S. (1969). The meaning of the palaeotype in A. J. Ellis's *On Early English Pronunciation*, 1869–89. *Transactions of the Philological Society*, 31–79.

Fischer, A. (1976). *Dialects in the South-West of England: a Lexical Investigation* (The Cooper Monographs. English Dialect Series 25). Bern: Francke.

(ed.) (1989). *The History and the Dialects of English. Festschrift for Eduard Kolb* (Anglistische Forschung 203). Heidelberg: Carl Winter Universitäts-verlag.

Forby, R. (1830). *The Vocabulary of East Anglia*, vols. I and II. London: J. B. Nichols.

Frogley, R. (1983). A descriptive account of the living dialect of Harrow in North-West London. Unpublished BA thesis, University of Leeds.

Gachelin, J. M. (1991). Gender and deixis in Southwestern dialects. *Neuphilologische Mitteilungen*, 92, 1: 83–93.

Gibson, P. H. (1955). Studies in the linguistic geography of Staffordshire. Unpublished MA thesis, University of Leeds.

Gil, A. (1619). *Alexander Gill's Logonomia Anglica (1619).* Part II. Biographical and Bibliographical Introductions, notes by B. Danielsson & A. Gabrielson, translation by R. C. Alston (Acta Universitatis Stockholmiensis/Stockholm Studies in English 27). Stockholm: Almqvist and Wiksell, 1972.

Giles, H. & P. Powesland (eds.) (1975). *Speech Style and Social Evaluation.* London, New York and San Francisco: Academic Press.

Giles, H., N. Coupland, K. Henwood, J. Harriman & J. Coupland (1990). The social meaning of RP: an intergenerational perspective. In Ramsaran (ed.) 1990a: 191–211.

Gimson, A. C. (1989). *An Introduction to the Pronunciation of English*, 4th edn revised by S. Ramsaran. London, New York, Melbourne, Auckland: Edward Arnold.

Glauser, B. (1974). *The Scottish–English Linguistic Border. Lexical Aspects* (The Cooper Monographs. English Dialect Series 20). Bern: Francke.

(1991). Transition areas versus focal areas in English dialectology. *English World-wide* 12, 1: 1–24.

Grose, F. (1787). *A Provincial Glossary, with a Collection of Local Proverbs, and Popular Superstitions.* London: printed for S. Hooper. (Corrected edition 1790.)

Halliwell, J. O. (1881). *A Dictionary of Archaic and Provincial Words, Obsolete Phrases, Proverbs, and Ancient Customs, from the Fourteenth Century*, vols. I and II, 10th edn (first published 1847). London: John Russell Smith.

Harris, M. (1967). The phonology and grammar of the dialect of South Zeal, Devonshire. Unpublished PhD dissertation, University of London.

(1969). Demonstrative adjectives and pronouns in a Devonshire dialect. *Transactions of the Philological Society*, 1–11.

Hedevind, B. (1967). *The Dialect of Dentdale in the West Riding of Yorkshire* (Acta Universitatis Upsaliensis/Studia Anglica Upsaliensia 5). Uppsala: Appelbergs Boktryckeri AB.

Heslop, O. (1892). *Northumberland Words: a Glossary of Words Used in the County of Northumberland and on the Tyneside*, vol. I (English Dialect Society 66, 68, 71). London: Kegan Paul, Trench, Trübner. (Reprinted Vaduz: Kraus, 1965.)

Hewett, S. (1892). *The Peasant Speech of Devon*. London: Elliott Stock.

Hole, W. (1746 [1778]). *An Exmoor Scolding and Courtship* (English Dialect Society 25), ed. F. T. Elworthy. London: Trübner, 1879. (Reprinted Vaduz: Kraus, 1965.)

Holmberg, B. (1964). *On the Concept of Standard English and the History of Modern English Pronunciation* (Lund Universitets Årsskkrift. N.F. Avd. 1. vol. 56, no. 3). Lund: CWK Gleerup.

Honey, J. (1988). Talking proper: schooling and the establishment of English 'Received Pronunciation'. In Nixon & Honey (eds.), 209–27.

Hughes, A. & P. Trudgill (1979). *English Accents and Dialects: an Introduction to Social and Regional Varieties of British English* (accompanied by a recording). London: Edward Arnold.

Hurford, J. (1967). The speech of one family: a phonetic comparison of the speech of three generations in a family of East Londoners. Unpublished PhD dissertation, University of London.

Ihalainen, O. (1976). Periphrastic 'do' in affirmative sentences in the dialect of East Somerset. *Neuphilologische Mitteilungen* 77: 608–22.

(1980). Relative clauses in the dialect of Somerset. *Neuphilologische Mitteilungen* 81: 187–96.

(1986). An inquiry into the nature of mixed grammars: two cases of grammatical variation in dialectal British English. In Kastovsky & Szwedek (eds.), 371–9.

(1987). Towards a grammar of the Somerset dialect: a case study of the language of J. M. *Neophilologica Fennica: Modern Language Society 100 Years*

(Mémoires de la Société Néophilologique 45), ed. L. Kahlas-Tarkka. Helsinki: Société Néophilologique, 71–86.

(1988a). Creating linguistic databases from machine-readable dialect texts. In Thomas (ed.) 569–84.

(1988b). Working with dialectal material stored in a dBase file. In M. Kytö, O. Ihalainen & M. Rissanen (eds.) *Corpus Linguistics: Hard and Soft*. Amsterdam: Rodopi, 137–44.

(1990a). Methodological preliminaries to the study of linguistic change in dialectal English: evaluating the grammars of Barnes and Elworthy as sources of linguistic evidence. In S. Adamson, V. Law, N. Vincent & S. Wright (eds.) *Papers from the 5th International Conference on English Historical Linguistics, Cambridge, 6–9 April, 1987*. Amsterdam: John Benjamins, 189–203.

(1990b). A source of data for the study of English dialectal syntax: the Helsinki Corpus. In J. Aarts & W. Meijs (eds.) *Theory and Practice in Corpus Linguistics*. Amsterdam: Rodopi, 83–103.

(1991). The grammatical subject in educated and dialectal English: comparing the London–Lund Corpus and the Helsinki Corpus of Modern English Dialects'. In S. Johansson & A.-B. Stenström (eds.) *English Computer Corpora. Selected Papers and Research Guide*. Berlin and New York: Mouton de Gruyter, 201–14.

(forthcoming a). Continuity and change in Northern English. To appear in *Neuphilologische Mitteilungen*.

(forthcoming b). Verb agreement as a dialect marker in contemporary dialects of England. To appear in *Neuphilologische Mitteilungen*.

Jennings, J. (1825). *Observations on Some of the Dialects in the West of England, Particularly Somersetshire*. London: Baldwin, Cradock and Joy.

Johnson, S. (1755). *A Dictionary of the English Language*. London. Reprinted Hildesheim: Olms, 1968.

Jones, D. (1909). *The Pronunciation of English*. Cambridge: Cambridge University Press.

(1917). *An English Pronouncing Dictionary*, 1st edn. London: J. M. Dent.

Jones, V. (1985). Tyneside syntax: a presentation of some data from the Tyneside Linguistic Survey. In Viereck (ed.) 1985b: 163–77.

Jones, W. E. (1952). The definite article in living Yorkshire dialect. *Leeds Studies in English and Kindred Languages* 7–8: 81–91.

Jones-Sargent, V. (1983). *Tyne Bytes: a Computerised Sociolinguistic Study of Tyneside* (Bamberger Beiträge zur englischen Sprachwissenschaft 11). Frankfurt: Peter Lang.

Jonson, B. (1640). The English Grammar. Made by Ben. Iohnson. For the benefit of all strangers, out of his observation of the English Language now spoken, and in use. [Publisher's name and place not given.]

Kastovsky, D. & A. Szwedek, eds. (1986). *Linguistics across Historical and*

Geographical Boundaries. In Honour of Jacek Fisiak on the Occasion of His Fiftieth Birthday, vol. I: *Linguistic Theory and Historical Linguistics* (Trends in Linguistics, Studies and Monographs 32). Berlin: Mouton de Gruyter.

Kerman, R. (1991). Lancashire and Essex English: a comparison. Unpublished MA thesis, University of Helsinki.

Klemola, J. (forthcoming a). Dialect areas in the south-west of England: an exercise in cluster analysis. To appear in W. Viereck (ed.) *ZDL-Beiheft 74: Verhandlungen des internationalen Dialektologenkongresses. Bamberg 1990*, vol. III. Stuttgart: Franz Stein, 1994.

(forthcoming b). Periphrastic 'do' in south-western dialects of British English: a reassessment. To appear in *Dialectogia et Geolinguistica* 2 (1994).

Knowles, G. (1987). *Patterns of Spoken English: an Introduction to English Phonetics*. London and New York: Longman.

Kökeritz, H. (1932). *The Phonology of the Suffolk Dialect. Descriptive and Historical* (Uppsala Universitets Årsskrift 1932). Uppsala: A.-B. Lundequistska Bokhandeln.

(1938/9). Alexander Gill (1621) on the dialects of South and East England. *Studia Neophilologica* 11: 277–88.

Kolb, E. (1965). Skandinavisches in den nordenglischen Dialekten. *Anglia* 83: 127–53.

(1966). *Phonological Atlas of the Northern Region*. Berne: Francke.

Larwood, J. (1800). A Norfolk dialogue. In Skeat (ed.) (1896), 117–22.

Lass, R. (1987). *The Shape of English: Structure and History*. London and Melbourne: J. M. Dent.

Lodge, K. R. (1984). *Studies in the Phonology of Colloquial English*. London and Sydney: Croom Helm.

Lowth, R. (1762). *A Short Introduction to English Grammar*. Delmar, New York: Scholars' Facsimiles and Reprints, 1979.

Marshall, W. (1787). Provincialisms of East Norfolk. (English Dialect Society 1, 1873). London: Trübner, 44–54. (Reprinted Vaduz: Kraus, 1965.)

(1788). Provincialisms of East Yorkshire (English Dialect Society 1, 1873). London: Trübner, 15–43. (Reprinted Vaduz: Kraus, 1965.)

(1789). Provincialisms of the Vale of Glocester (English Dialect Society 1, 1873). London: Trübner, 55–60. (Reprinted Vaduz: Kraus, 1965.)

(1790). Provincialisms of the Midland Counties (English Dialect Society 1, 1873). London: Trübner, 61–8. (Reprinted Vaduz: Kraus, 1965.)

(1796). Provincialisms of West Devonshire (English Dialect Society 1, 1873). London: Trübner, 69–75. (Reprinted Vaduz: Kraus, 1965.)

Matthews, W. (1938/72). *Cockney Past and Present: a Short History of the Dialect of London*. Reprinted 1972 with additional preface. London and Boston: Routledge and Kegan Paul.

Melchers, G. (1972). *Studies in Yorkshire Dialects Based on Recordings of 13 Dialect*

Speakers in the West Riding, Parts I and II (Stockholm Theses in English 9). Stockholm.

Meriton, G. (1684). A Yorkshire Dialogue in its pure natural dialect as it is now commonly spoken in the North parts of Yorkshire. In Skeat (ed.) (1896), 149–76.

Milroy, J. & L. Milroy (1985). *Authority in Language. Investigating Language Prescription and Standardisation.* London, Boston and Henley: Routledge and Kegan Paul.

(eds.) (1987). *Regional Variation in English Syntax.* Swindon: The Economic and Social Research Council.

Moore, S. (1964). *Historical Outlines of English Sounds and Inflections*, revised by A. H. Marckwardt. Ann Arbor, MI: George Wahr.

Nixon, G. & J. Honey (eds.) (1988). *An Historic Tongue: Studies in English Linguistics in Memory of Barbara Strang.* London and New York: Routledge.

North, D. (1979). Two West Kent dialects: a comparative phonological study of the dialects of Hever and Chiddingstone, Kent. Unpublished MA thesis, University of Leeds.

Orton, H. (1933). *The Phonology of a South Durham Dialect.* London: K. Paul, T. Trübner.

Orton, H. & N. Wright (1974). *A Word Geography of England.* London, New York and San Francisco: Seminar Press.

Page, N. (1973). *Speech in the English Novel* (English Language Series 8). London: Longman.

Påhlsson, C. (1972). *The Northumbrian Burr: a Sociolinguistic Study* (Lund Studies in English 41). Lund: CWK Gleerup.

Peacock, E. (1889). *A Glossary of Words used in the Wapentakes of Manley and Corringham, Lincolnshire*, 2nd edn (English Dialect Society 58, 59). London: Trübner. (Reprinted Vaduz: Kraus, 1965.)

Petyt, M. (1980). *The Study of Dialect: an Introduction to Dialectology* (The Language Library). London: André Deutsch.

(1985). *Dialect and Accent in Industrial West Yorkshire* (Varieties of English Around the World G 6). Amsterdam and Philadelphia: John Benjamins.

Preston, D. (1988). Methods in the study of dialect perceptions. In Thomas (ed.), 373–95.

(1990). *Perceptual Dialectology: Non-linguists' Views of Areal Linguistics.* Dordrecht: Foris.

Puttenham, G. (1589). *The Arte of English Poesie*, ed. E. Arber. London: Murray, 1869.

Ramsaran, S. (ed.) (1990a). *Studies in the Pronunciation of English. A Commemorative Volume in Honour of A. C. Gimson.* London and New York: Routledge.

(1990b). RP: fact and fiction. In Ramsaran (ed.) 1990a: 178–90.

Ray, J. (1674). *A Collection of English Words Not Generally Used, With Their*

Significations and Original: in Two Alphabetical Catalogues: The One of Such as Are Proper to the Northern, the Other to the Southern Counties (English Dialect Society 6, Series B: Reprinted Glossaries XV–XVII), ed. W. Skeat. London: Trübner, 1874. (Reprinted Vaduz: Kraus, 1965.)

Rock, W. F. (1867). Jim an' Nell. In Skeat (ed.) (1896), 19–50.

Rohrer, F. (1950). The border between the Northern and North-Midland dialects. *Transactions of the Yorkshire Dialect Society*, vol. 8, Part L, 29–37.

Rydland, K. (1982). *Vowel Systems and Lexical–Phonemic Patterns in South-East Cumbria.* Bergen: Department of English, University of Bergen.

Samuels, M. (1985). The great Scandinavian belt. In Eaton *et al.* (eds.), 269–81.

Seward, W. (1801). A Lonsdale dialogue: in the dialect of Burton-in-Lonsdale'. In Skeat (ed.) (1896), 125–31.

Sheridan, T. (1762). *A Course of Lectures on Elocution.* Reprinted Menston, Yorks.: The Scolar Press, 1974.

  (1780). *A General Dictionary of the English Language.* Reprinted Menston, Yorks.: The Scolar Press, 1967.

Shorrocks, G. (1980). A grammar of the dialect of Farnworth and district (Greater Manchester County, formerly Lancashire). Unpublished PhD dissertation, University of Sheffield.

Sivertsen, E. (1960). *Cockney Phonology* (Oslo Studies in English 8). Oslo: Oslo University Press.

Skeat, W. W. (ed.) (1873). *Reprinted Glossaries.* Series B. (English Dialect Society 1). London: Trübner. (Reprinted Vaduz: Kraus, 1965.)

  (ed.) (1896). *Nine Specimens of English Dialects Edited from Various Sources* (English Dialect Society 76). London: Henry Frowde. (Reprinted Vaduz: Kraus, 1965.)

  (1911). *English Dialects from the Eighth Century to the Present Day.* Cambridge: Cambridge University Press.

Skeat, W. W. & J. H. Nodal (comps.) (1877). *A Bibliographical List* (English Dialect Society 2, 8, 18). London: Trübner. (Reprinted Vaduz: Kraus, 1965.)

Spurdens, W. T. (1840). Supplement to Forby's 'Vocabulary of East Anglia'. (English Dialect Society 23). London: Trübner. (Reprinted Vaduz: Kraus, 1965.)

Sykes, D. R. (1956). The linguistic geography of Shropshire and Worcestershire. A phonological survey. Unpublished MA thesis, University of Leeds.

Thomas, A. R. (ed.) (1988). *Methods in Dialectology. Proceedings of the Sixth International Conference Held at the University College of North Wales, 3rd–7th August 1987* (Multilingual Matters 48). Clevedon and Philadelphia: Multilingual Matters.

Tidholm, H. (1979). *The Dialect of Egton in North Yorkshire.* Göteborg: Bokmaskinen.

Trudgill, P. (1974). *The Social Differentiation of English in Norwich* (Cambridge Studies in Linguistics 13). Cambridge: Cambridge University Press.

(ed.) (1978). *Sociolinguistic Patterns in British English.* London: Edward Arnold.

(1983). *On Dialect. Social and Geographical Perspectives.* New York and London: New York University Press.

(ed.) (1984). *Language in the British Isles.* Cambridge: Cambridge University Press.

(1986). *Dialects in Contact.* Oxford: Basil Blackwell.

(1990). *The Dialects of England.* Oxford: Basil Blackwell.

Trudgill, P. & T. Foxcroft (1978). On the sociolinguistics of vocalic mergers: transfer and approximation in East Anglia. In Trudgill (ed.) 69–79.

Viereck, W. (1966). *Phonematische Analyse des Dialekts von Gateshead-upon-Tyne/Co. Durham* (Britannica et Americana 14). Hamburg: Cram, de Gruyter.

(1975). *Regionale und soziale Erscheinungsformen des britischen und amerikanischen Englisch* (Anglistische Arbeitshefte 4). Tübingen: Max Niemeyer.

(1980). The dialectal structure of British English: Lowman's evidence. *English World-wide* 1, 1: 25–44.

(ed.) (1985). *Focus on: England and Wales* (Varieties of English Around the World G 4). Amsterdam and Philadelphia: John Benjamins.

(1986). Dialectal speech areas in England: Orton's lexical evidence. In Kastovsky & Szwedek (eds.), 725–40.

Viereck, W. in collaboration with H. Ramisch (1991). *The Computer Developed Linguistic Atlas of England,* vol. I. Tübingen: Max Niemeyer.

Viereck, W., E. Schneider & M. Görlach (comps.) (1984). *A Bibliography of Writings on Varieties of English, 1965–1983.* Amsterdam and Philadelphia: John Benjamins.

Wakelin, M. (1975). *Language and History in Cornwall.* Leicester: Leicester University Press.

(1977). *English Dialects: an Introduction,* 2nd, rev. edn. London: The Athlone Press of the University of London.

(1983). The stability of English dialect boundaries. *English World-wide* 4, 1: 1–15.

(1984). Rural dialects in England. In Trudgill (ed.) 70–93.

(1986a). *The Southwest of England* (Varieties of English Around the World, Text Series 5). Amsterdam and Philadelphia: John Benjamins.

(1986b). The 'Exmoor Courtship' and 'Exmoor Scolding': an evaluation of two eighteenth-century dialect texts. In Kastovsky & Szwedek (eds.) 741–51.

(1988a). The phonology of South-Western English 1500–1700. In J. Fisiak (ed.) *Historical Dialectology: Regional and Social*. Berlin, New York and Amsterdam: Mouton de Gruyter, 609–44.

(1988b). *The Archaeology of English*. London: B. T. Batsford.

Walker, J. (1791). *A Critical Pronouncing Dictionary and Expositor of the English Language: to which are prefixed Principles of English Pronunciation; the whole interspersed with Observations, Philological, Critical, and Grammatical.* London.

Wells, J. (1982). *Accents of English*. 3 vols. Cambridge: Cambridge University Press.

Weltens, B. (1983). Non-standard periphrastic *do* in the dialects of south west Britain. *Lore and Language* 3, 8: 56–64.

Widén, B. (1949). *Studies on the Dorset Dialect* (Lund Studies in English 16). Lund: C. W. K. Gleerup.

Wilson, J. (1913). *The Dialect of the New Forest in Hampshire (as Spoken in the Village of Burley)*. London: Oxford University Press for the Philological Society.

Wright, J. (1892). *A Grammar of the District of Windhill, in the West Riding of Yorkshire*. London: Kegan Paul, Trübner.

Wright, P. (1989). The dialect of English secondary schoolchildren. In Fischer (ed.), 231–43.

Wyld, H. C. (1956). *A History of Modern Colloquial English*. Re-issue of enlarged edn of 1936. Oxford: Basil Blackwell.

6   English in Australia

Adams, C. M. (1969). A survey of Australian English intonation. *Phonetica* 20: 81–130.

Allan, K. (1984). The component functions of the high rise terminal contour in Australian declarative sentences. *Australian Journal of Linguistics* 4: 19–32.

The Australian Encyclopaedia, 4th edn, 12 vols. Sydney: Grolier Society, 1983.

The Australian National Dictionary: Australian Words and their Origins (AND) ed. W. S. Ramson. Melbourne: Oxford University Press.

Baker, S. J. (1966). *The Australian Language*. Sydney: Currawong.

Baugh, A. C. (1951). *A History of the English Language*. London: Routledge and Kegan Paul.

Bennett, G. (1834). *Wanderings in New South Wales, Batavia, Pedir Coast, Singapore, and China, being the journal of a naturalist in those countries, during 1832, 1833, and 1834*. London.

Bernard, J. R. L. (1963). An extra phoneme of Australian English. *AUMLA* 20: 346–52.

(1969). On the uniformity of Australian English. *Orbis* 18, 1: 62–73.

(1975). A note on two minor prosodic effects in Australian English. Macquarie University, Speech and Language Research Centre. *Working Papers* 1, 2: 29–35.

Blainey, G. (1966). *The Tyranny of Distance*. Melbourne: Sun Books.

Blair, D. (1975). On the origins of Australian pronunciation. Macquarie University, Speech and Language Research Centre. *Working Papers* 1, 2: 17–27.

Blake, B. J. (1981). *Australian Aboriginal Languages*. Sydney: Angus and Robertson.

Bloomfield, L. (1935). *Language*. London: Allen and Unwin.

Boldrewood, R. (1890). *The Miner's Right: a Tale of the Australian Goldfields*. London: Macmillan.

Bradley, D. (1979). A study of Australian English vowels by phonetics/phonology students. *Talanya* 6: 67–75.

(1986). Review of Horvath 1985. *Australian Journal of Linguistics* 6, 2: 278–86.

(1989). Regional dialects in Australian English phonology. In Collins & Blair (eds.), 260–70.

Bradley, D. & M. Bradley (1979). Melbourne vowels. University of Melbourne. *Working Papers in Linguistics* 5: 64–84.

Brumby, E. & E. Vaszolyi (1977). *Language Problems and Aboriginal Education*. Mount Lawley: Mount Lawley College of Advanced Education.

Bryant, P. (1989). Regional variation in the Australian English lexicon. In Collins & Blair (eds.) 301–14.

Bull, J. W. (1884). *Early Experiences of Life in South Australia*. Adelaide: E. S. Wigg; London: Sampson Low.

Burgess, O. N. (1968). Extra phonemes in Australian English: a further contribution. *AUMLA* 30: 180–7.

Bynon, T. (1977). *Historical Linguistics*. Cambridge: Cambridge University Press.

Clacy, C. (1963). *A Lady's Visit to the Gold Diggings of Australia in 1852–3 Written on the Spot*. Melbourne: Lansdowne Press.

Clark, M. (1957). *Sources of Australian History* (The World's Classics). London: Oxford University Press.

Collins, H, E. (1975). The sources of Australian pronunciation. Macquarie University, Speech and Language Research Centre. *Working Papers* 1, 1: 115–28.

Collins, P. & D. Blair (eds.) (1989). *Australian English: the Language of a New Society*. St Lucia: University of Queensland Press.

Cook, J. (1968). *The Journals of Captain Cook on his Voyages of Discovery: the Voyage of the Endeavour 1768–1771*, ed. J. Beaglehole. Cambridge: Cambridge University Press.

Corbett, G. & K. Ahmad (1986). A computer corpus of Australian English. *Australian Journal of Linguistics* 6: 251–6.

Crowley, F. (1980). *A Documentary History of Australia*. Melbourne: Nelson.

Cunningham, P. M. (1827). *Two Years in New South Wales; a Series of Letters, comprising sketches of the actual state of society in that colony, of its peculiar*

advantages to emigrants, of its topography, natural history, etc., etc. London:
Henry Colburn.

Delbridge, A. (1970). The recent study of spoken Australian English. In
Ramson (ed.), 15–31.

Dixon, J. (1822). *Narrative of a Voyage to New South Wales and Van Diemans Land
in the Ship 'Skelton' during the Year 1820.* Edinburgh: printed for J.
Anderson.

Dixon, R. M. W. (1980). *The Languages of Australia* (Cambridge Language
Surveys). Cambridge: Cambridge University Press.

Donaldson, I. & T. Donaldson (eds.) (1985). *Seeing the First Australians.*
London: Allen and Unwin.

Douglas, W. H. (1976). *The Aboriginal Languages of the South-west of Australia,*
2nd edn (Australian Aboriginal Studies. Research and Regional Studies
no. 9), Canberra: Australian Institute of Aboriginal Studies.

(1977). *Illustrated Topical Dictionary of the Western Desert language.* Canberra:
Australian Institute of Aboriginal Studies.

Dunderdale, G. (n.d., *c.* 1870). *The Book of the Bush containing many truthful
sketches of the early life of squatters, whalers, convicts, diggers, and others who left
their native land and never returned.* London: Ward and Lock (Penguin
Facsimile, 1973).

Eagleson, R. D. (1989). Popular and professional attitudes to prestige dialects.
In Collins & Blair (eds.), 150–7.

Eagleson, R. D. & I. McKie (1968–9). *The Terminology of Australian National
Football,* Parts I–III (Occasional papers nos. 12–14). University of Sydney,
Australian Language Research Centre.

Eisikovits, E. (1987). Variation in the lexical verb in Inner-Sydney English.
Australian Journal of Linguistics 7: 1–24.

Elliott, I. (1977). Sex differences in the Mitchell & Delbridge study of
Australian adolescents. University of Melbourne *Working Papers in
Linguistics* 3: 57–67.

Ellis, A. J. (1889). *On Early English Pronunciation,* vol. V (Early English Text
Society ES 56). Oxford: Oxford University Press.

Facey, A. B. (1981). *A Fortunate Life.* Ringwood: Penguin.

Flinders, M. (1814). *A Voyage to Terra Australis; undertaken for the purpose of
completing the discovery of that vast country, and prosecuted in the years 1801, 1802,
and 1803 in His Majesty's Ship the Investigator,* 2 vols. London: G. and W.
Nicol.

Flint, E. H. (1964). The survey of Queensland speech. Linguistic Circle of
Canberra *Bulletin* 1: 6.

Froude, J. A. (1886). *Oceana or England and her Colonies.* London: Longmans
Green.

Furphy, J. (1903). *Such is Life.* Sydney: The Bulletin Newspaper Company.
(1948). *The Buln-buln and the Brolga.* Sydney: Angus and Robertson.

Gardiner, J. (1977). Teaching standard English as a second dialect to speakers of Aboriginal English. In Brumby & Vaszolyi (eds.), 165–99.

Giles, E. (1889). *Australia Twice Traversed: the Romance of Exploration being a Narrative compiled from the journals of Five Exploring Expeditions into and through Central South Australia and Western Australia from 1872 to 1876.* London: Sampson Low, Marston, Searle and Rivington.

Gimson, A. C. (1962). *An Introduction to the Pronunciation of English.* London: Arnold.

Gunn, J. S. (1965). *The Terminology of the Shearing Industry* (Occasional Papers nos. 5–6). University of Sydney, Australian Language Research Centre.

 (1971). *Distribution of Shearing Terms in New South Wales* (Occasional Paper no. 16). University of Sydney, Australian Language Research Centre.

Guy, G. R. & J. Vonwiller (1984). The meaning of an intonation in Australian English. *Australian Journal of Linguistics* 4: 1–17.

Halliday, M. A. K. (1976). Anti-languages. *UEA Papers in Linguistics* 1: 15–43.

Hammarström, G. (1980). *Australian English: its Origin and Status* (Forum Phoneticum 19). Hamburg: Buske.

Harris, A. (1953). *Settlers and convicts or recollections of sixteen years' labour in the Australian backwoods by an emigrant mechanic,* ed. C. M. H. Clark. Melbourne: Melbourne University Press.

Hill, R. (1968). Assembling evidence for early Australian pronunciation. *English in Australia* 8: 21–7.

Holm, J. (1989). *Pidgins and Creoles,* vol. II. Cambridge: Cambridge University Press.

Horne, D. (1975). *The Education of Young Donald.* Harmondsworth: Penguin.

Horvath, B. M. (1985). *Variation in Australian English: the Sociolects of Sydney* (Cambridge Studies in Linguistics 45). Cambridge University Press.

Hotten, J. C. (1872). *The Slang Dictionary or, the Vulgar Words, Street Phrases, and 'Fast' Expressions of High and Low Society, many with their Etymology and a few with their History Traced.* London: Hotten.

Hughes, R. (1988). *The Fatal Shore.* London: Pan Books.

Jernudd, B. H. (1973). A listener experiment; variants of Australian English. Monash University: *Linguistic Communications* 10: 26–40.

Jespersen, O. (1922). *Language: its Nature, Development, and Origin.* London: Allen and Unwin.

Jolley, E. (1983). *Mr Scobie's Riddle.* Ringwood: Penguin.

Keesing, N. (1967). *Gold Fever.* Sydney: Angus and Robertson.

Knight, A. (1988). South Australian Aboriginal words surviving in Australian English. In T. Burton & J. Burton (eds.) *Lexicographical and Linguistic Studies.* Cambridge: D. S. Brewer, 151–62.

Labov, W. (1966). *The Social Stratification of English in New York City.* Washington DC: Center for Applied Linguistics.

 (1978). *Sociolinguistic Patterns.* Oxford: Blackwell.

Lake, J. A. (1898). *A Dictionary of Australian Words*. Springfield: Merriam. (A supplement to *Webster's International Dictionary*.)

Leitner, G. (1984). Australian English or English in Australia – linguistic identity or dependence in broadcast language. *English World-wide* 5: 55–85.

McBurney, S. (1887). Colonial pronunciation. *Press* (Christchurch) 5 October 1887. (Reprinted in Turner 1967.)

(1889). Australasian South Eastern – a comparative table of Australasian pronunciation. In Ellis, 236–48.

McGregor, R. L. (1980). The social distribution of an Australian English intonation contour. Macquarie University, Speech and Language Research Centre. *Working Papers* 2, 6: 1–26.

Mackiewicz-Krassowska, H. (1976). Nasality in Australian English. Macquarie University, Speech and Language Research Centre. *Working Papers* 1, 3: 27–40.

Martino, J. (1982). The phoneme /θ/ and its alternative realization as /f/: a study of variation in Australian English among primary school boys according to socioeconomic background. University of Melbourne *Working Papers in Linguistics* 8: 35–42.

Matsuda, Y. (1982). *Out of* vs *out* in four varieties of English. (*Ronkō* 51: 245–57.) Nishinomiya: Kwansei Gakuin University.

Mencken, H. L. (1980). *The American Language*, 4th edn. New York: Knopf.

Mitchell, A. G. (1946). *The Pronunciation of English in Australia*. Sydney: Angus and Robertson.

Mitchell, A. G. & A. Delbridge (1965a). *The Pronunciation of English in Australia* (revision of Mitchell 1946). Sydney: Angus and Robertson.

(1965b). *The Speech of Australian Adolescents: a Survey*. Sydney: Angus and Robertson.

Morris, E. E. (1898). *Austral English: a Dictionary of Australasian Words, Phrases, and Usages*. London: Macmillan.

Mudie, J. (1964). *The Felonry of New South Wales*. Melbourne: Lansdowne Press.

Mühlhäusler, P. (1991). Overview of the pidgin and creole languages of Australia. In S. Romaine (ed.) *Language in Australia*. Cambridge: Cambridge University Press, 159–73.

(forthcoming). Pidgins, creoles and post-contact Aboriginal languages in Western Australia. *Anthropological Forum*. Perth: University of Western Australia.

Mundy, G. C. (1852). *Our Antipodes: or, residence and rambles in the Australian colonies with a glimpse of the gold fields*, 3 vols. London: Bentley.

Phillip, A. (1789). *The Voyage of Governor Phillip to Botany Bay; with an Account of the Establishment of the Colonies of Port Jackson and Norfolk Island; compiled from Authentic Papers, which have been obtained from the several Departments, to which are added The Journals of Lieuts Shortland, Watts, Ball, and Capt. Marshall with an Account of their New Discoveries*. London: Stockdale.

Pilch, H. (1971). Some phonemic peculiarities of Australian English. In L. L. Hammerich, R. Jakobson, E. Zwirne (eds.), *Form and substance. Phonetic and linguistic papers presented to Eli Fischer-Jorgensen*. Copenhagen: Akademisk Forlag, 269–75.

Platt, J. T. (1972). *An Outline Grammar of the Gugada Dialect: South Australia* (Australian Aboriginal Studies no. 48, Linguistic Series no. 20). Canberra: Australian Institute of Aboriginal Studies.

Poynton, C. (1989). The linguistic realisation of social relations: terms of address in Australian English. In Collins & Blair (eds.), 55–69.

Ramson, W. S. (1964). *The Currency of Aboriginal Words in Australian English* (Occasional Paper no. 3). University of Sydney, Australian Language Research Centre.

(1966). *Australian English: an Historical Study of the Vocabulary 1788–1898*, Canberra: Australian National University Press.

(ed.) (1970). *English Transported: Essays on Australasian English*. Canberra: Australian National University Press.

(1987). *The Australian National Dictionary: a foretaste*. In R. Burchfield (ed.) *Studies in Lexicography*. Oxford: Clarendon Press, 136–55.

Reynolds, H. (1982). *The Other Side of the Frontier: Aboriginal Resistance to the European Invasion of Australia*. Ringwood: Penguin.

Ridge, B. (1984). Of theories, selves, and conflicts. In C. E. Nicholson & R. Chatterjee (eds.) *Tropical Crucible: Self and Theory in Language and Literature*. Singapore: University of Singapore Press, 317–45.

Ross, A. S. C. & A. W. Moverley (1964). *The Pitcairnese Language* (The Language Library). London: André Deutsch.

Samuels, M. L. (1972). *Linguistic Evolution, with Special Reference to English* (Cambridge Studies in Linguistics 5). Cambridge: Cambridge University Press.

Sandefur, J. R. (1979). *An Australian Creole in the Northern Territory: a Description of Ngukurr-Bamyili Dialects* (Workpapers of SIL-AAB series B: 3). Darwin, Summer Institute of Linguistics, Australian Aborigines Branch.

Sapir, E. (1921). *Language: an Introduction to the Study of Speech*. New York: Harcourt Brace.

Shnukal, A. (1982). You're gettin' somethink for nothing: two phonological variables of Australian English. *Australian Journal of Linguistics* 2: 197–212.

Shopen, T. (1978). Research on the variable (ING) in Canberra, Australia. *Talanya* 5: 42–52.

Sivertsen, E. (1960). *Cockney Phonology* (Oslo Studies in English no. 8). Oslo: Oslo University Press.

Spence, C. H. (1971). *Clara Morison*. Adelaide: Rigby.

Sussex, R. (1989). North American English as a prestige model in the Australian media. In Collins & Blair (ed.), 158–68.

Teichelmann, C. G. & C. W. Schürmann (1840). *Outlines of a Grammar, Vocabulary and Phraseology of the Aboriginal Language of South Australia.* Adelaide: privately published.

Tench, W. (1961). *Sydney's first four years: being a reprint of A narrative of the expedition to Botany Bay and a complete account of the settlement at Port Jackson,* with an introduction and annotations by L. F. Fitzhardinge. Sydney: Angus and Robertson.

Thackeray, W. M. (1959). *Pendennis* (Everyman's Library). London: Dent.

Thuan, E. A. (1973). The codification of Australian English. Monash University: *Linguistic Communications* 10: 108–16.

  (1976). Agencies of language standardisation in Australia. In M. Clyne (ed.) *Australia Talks: Essays on the Sociology of Australian Immigrant and Aboriginal languages* (Pacific Linguistics Series D no. 23). Canberra: Australia National University, 79–88.

Trudgill, P. (1972). Sex, covert prestige, and linguistic change in the urban British English of Norwich. *Language in Society* 1: 179–95. (Revised reprint in Trudgill 1984: 169–85.)

  (1984). *On Dialect: Social and Geographical Perspectives.* New York: New York University Press.

  (1986). *Dialects in Contact.* Oxford: Blackwell.

Trudgill, P. & J. Hannah (1982). *International English: a Guide to Varieties of Standard English.* London: Arnold.

Turner, G. W. (1960). On the origin of Australian vowel sounds. *AUMLA* 13: 33–45.

  (1966). *The English Language in Australia and New Zealand.* London: Longman (rev. edn 1972).

  (1967). Samuel McBurney's newspaper article on colonial pronunciation. *AUMLA* 27: 81–5.

  (1976). A landscape known as home. *The Round Table* 261: 52–7.

Twopeny, R. E. N. (1883). *Town Life in Australia.* London: Elliot Stock.

Vaux, J. H. (1964). *The Memoirs of James Hardy Vaux including his Vocabulary of the Flash Language,* ed. Noel McLachlan. London: Heinemann.

Walker, J. (1791). *A Critical Pronouncing Dictionary and Expositor of the English Language.* London.

Warburton, P. E. (1875). *Journey across the Western Interior of Australia,* ed. H. W. Bates. London: Sampson Low, Marston, Low and Searle.

Wells, J. C. (1982). *Accents of English.* Cambridge: Cambridge University Press.

Wentworth, H. & S. B. Flexner (1960). *Dictionary of American Slang.* New York: Crowell.

White P. (1973). *The Vivisector.* Ringwood: Penguin.

Wilkes G. A. (1981). *The Stockyard and the Croquet Lawn.* Melbourne: Arnold.

  (1985). *A Dictionary of Australian Colloquialisms* rev. edn. Sydney: Sydney University Press.

Williams, R. (1961). *Culture and Society 1780–1950*. Harmondsworth: Penguin.
Wood, T. (1953). *Cobbers*, 3rd edn. London: Oxford University Press.

7 English in the Caribbean

Albury, P. (1975). *The Story of the Bahamas*. London: Macmillan Caribbean.
Alleyne, M. C. (1980). *Comparative Afro-American*. Ann Arbor: Karoma.
Assadi, B. (1983). Rama Cay Creole English. In Holm (ed.) 1983b: 115–22.
Bailey, B. L. (1966). *Jamaican Creole Syntax: a Transformational Approach*. Cambridge: Cambridge University Press.
Barry, M. V. (1982). The English language in Ireland. In R. Bailey & M. Görlach (eds.) *English as a World Language*. Ann Arbor: University of Michigan Press, 84–133.
Bickerton, D. (1975). *Dynamics of a Creole System*. Cambridge: Cambridge University Press.
  (1981). *Roots of Language*. Ann Arbor: Karoma.
Boretzky, N. (1983). *Kreolsprachen, Substrate und Sprachwandel*. Wiesbaden: Harrassowitz.
Boswell, T. (1980). Puerto Rico. *Academic American Encyclopedia*, vol. XV. Princeton: Arete, 614–16.
Byrne, F. (1984). *Fi* and *fu*: origins and functions in some Caribbean English-based creoles. *Lingua* 62: 97–120.
Carrington, L. (1981). *Literacy in the English-speaking Caribbean*. Paris: UNESCO.
Carter, H. (1979). Evidence for the survival of African prosodies in West Indian creoles. Society for Caribbean Linguistics, occasional paper 13.
  (1982). The tonal system of Jamaican English. Paper presented to the Society for Caribbean Linguistics, Suriname.
  (1987). Suprasegmentals in Jamaican: some African comparisons. In Gilbert (ed.), 213–63.
Cassidy, F. G. (1961). *Jamaica Talk: Three Hundred Years of the English Language in Jamaica*. London: Macmillan.
  (1964). Toward the recovery of early English–African Pidgin. In *Symposium on Multilingualism (Brazzaville)*. London: Conseil Scientifique pour Afrique; Commission de Coopération Technique en Afrique, publication 87.
  (1980). The place of Gullah. *American Speech* 55: 3–15.
Cassidy, F. G. & R. B. Le Page (1980). *Dictionary of Jamaican English*. Cambridge: Cambridge University Press (1st edn 1967).
Christie, P. (1980). In search of the boundaries of Caribbean creoles. Paper presented to the Society for Caribbean Linguistics, Aruba.
Cooper, V. O. (1982). Historical and social dimensions of the St. Kitts-Nevis vernacular. Paper presented to the Society for Caribbean Linguistics, Suriname.

(1983). A sociolinguistic profile of the Virgin Islands. In V. Clark & V. Cooper (eds.) *Educational Issues in the Virgin Islands.* St Thomas: College of the Virgin Islands.

Crowley, D. (1966). *I Could Talk Old-Story Good: Creativity in Bahamian Folklore.* Berkeley: University of California Press.

DeBose, C. E. (1983). Samaná English: a dialect that time forgot. *Proceedings of the Ninth Annual Meeting of the Berkeley Linguistics Society*, 47–53.

Edwards, W. F. (1983). A community-based approach to the provenance of urban Guyanese Creole. Paper presented at York Creole Conference: Urban Pidgins and Creoles.

Eersel, C. H. (1976). A few remarks on some sound patterns in Sranan. Paper presented to the Society of Caribbean Linguistics, Guyana.

Escure, G. (1983). Belizean Creole. In Holm (ed.) 1983b: 29–70.

Gilbert, G. (ed.) (1987). *Pidgin and Creole Languages: Essays in Memory of John E. Reinecke.* Honolulu: University Press of Hawaii.

Goodman, M. (1985). Review of Bickerton (1981). *International Journal of American Linguistics* 51, 1: 109–37.

(1987). The Portuguese element in the American creoles. In Gilbert (ed.), 361–405.

Görlach, M. & J. Holm (eds.) (1986). *Focus on the Caribbean* (Varieties of English around the World, G8). Amsterdam/Philadelphia: John Benjamins.

Hancock, I. F. (1980a). Gullah and Barbadian: origins and relationships. *American Speech* 55: 17–35.

(1980b). Lexical expansion in creole languages. In A. Valdman & A. Highfield (eds.) *Theoretical Orientations in Creole Studies.* New York: Academic Press, 63–88.

Herskovits, M. J. (1930–1). On the provenience of the Portuguese in Saramacca Tongo. *De West Indische Gids* 12: 545–57.

Herzfeld, A. (1983). The creoles of Costa Rica and Panama. In Holm (ed.) 1983b: 131–56.

Holm, J. A. (1978). The Creole English of Nicaragua's Miskito Coast: its sociolinguistic history and a comparative study of its lexicon and syntax. Ph.D thesis, University of London. Ann Arbor: University Microfilms.

(1980a). African features in White Bahamian English. *English World-wide* 1, 1: 45–65.

(1980b). The creole 'copula' that highlighted the world. In J. L. Dillard (ed.) *Perspectives on American English.* The Hague: Mouton, 367–75.

(1983a). On the relationship of Gullah and Bahamian. *American Speech* 58, 4: 303–18.

(ed.) (1983b). *Central American English.* Heidelberg: Groos.

(1988). *Pidgins and Creoles*, 2 vols. Cambridge: Cambridge University Press.

Holm, J. A. with A. Shilling (1982). *Dictionary of Bahamian English*. Cold Spring, NY: Lexik House.

Huttar, G. L. (1981). Some Kwa-like features of Djuka syntax. *Studies in African Linguistics* 12, 3: 291–323.

Hymes, D. (ed.) (1971). *Pidginization and creolization of Languages*. Cambridge: Cambridge University Press.

Joyner, C. (1984). *Down by the Riverside: a South Carolina Slave Community*. Urbana and Chicago: University of Illinois Press.

Koelle, S. (1854). *Polyglotta Africana*. (1963 reprint. Fourah Bay College, Sierra Leone.)

Lalla, B. (1986). Tracing elusive phonological features of early Jamaican Creole. In Görlach & Holm (eds.), 117–32.

Lalla, B. & J. D'Costa (1990). *Language in Exile: Three Hundred Years of Jamaican Creole*. Tuscaloosa and London: University of Alabama Press.

Larsen, J. (1950). *Virgin Islands Story*. Philadelphia: Muhlenberg Press.

Le Page, R. B. (1977). Decreolization and recreolization: a preliminary report on the Sociolinguistic Survey of Multilingual Communities. Stage II: St Lucia. *York Papers in Linguistics* 7: 107–28.

Le Page, R. B. & D. DeCamp (1960). *Jamaican Creole: Creole Studies I*. London: Macmillan.

Le Page, R. B. & A. Tabouret-Keller. (1985). *Acts of Identity: Creole-based Approaches to Language and Ethnicity*. Cambridge: Cambridge University Press.

Matthews, W. (1935). Sailors' pronunciation in the second half of the 17th century. *Anglia* 59: 192–251.

Parry, J. H. & P. Sherlock. (1974). *A Short History of the West Indies*. London: Macmillan.

Parsons, J. J. (1954). English-speaking settlement of the Western Caribbean. *Yearbook of the Association of the Pacific Coast Geographers* 16: 2–16.

Poplack, S. & D. Sankoff (1987). The Philadelphia story in the Spanish Caribbean. *American Speech* 62, 4: 291–314.

Powles, L. D. (1888). *The land of the pink pearl*. London.

Price, R. (1975). Kikoongo and Saramaccan: a reappraisal. *Bijdragen tot de Taal-, Land- en Volkenkunde* 131, 4: 461–78.

Reinecke, J. E. (1937). Marginal languages: a sociological survey of the creole languages and trade jargons. Ph.D dissertation, Yale University. Ann Arbor: University Microfilms.

Rickford, J. (1974). The insights of the mesolect. In D. DeCamp and I. Hancock (eds.) *Pidgins and Creoles: Current Trends and Prospects*. Washington, DC: Georgetown University Press, 92–117.

(1977). The question of prior creolization in Black English. In A. Valdman (ed.) *Pidgin and Creole Linguistics*. Bloomington: Indiana University Press, 190–221.

(1980). How does *doz* disappear? In R. Day (ed.) *Issues in English Creoles: Papers from the 1975 Hawaii Conference* (Varieties of English around the World, G2). Heidelberg: Groos.

(1986). Social contact and linguistic diffusion: Hiberno English and New World Black English. *Language* 62, 2: 245–89.

(1987). *Dimensions of a Creole Continuum*. Stanford: Stanford University Press.

Rountree, C. (1972). The phonological structure of stems in Saramaccan. In J. Grimes (ed.) *Languages of the Guianas*. Summer Institute of Linguistics, University of Oklahoma.

Saunders, D. G. (1978). The slave population of the Bahamas, 1783–1834. Unpub. MA thesis, University of the West Indies, Mona.

Smith, N. (1987). The genesis of the creole languages of Surinam. Ph.D dissertation, University of Amsterdam.

Thomason, S. G. & T. Kaufman (1988). *Language Contact, Creolization, and Genetic Linguistics*. Berkeley and Los Angeles: University of California Press.

Todd, L. (1973). To be or not to be? What would Hamlet have said in Cameroon Pidgin? An analysis of Cameroon Pidgin's 'be' verb. *Archivum Linguisticum* 4: 1–15.

Turner, L. D. (1949). *Africanisms in the Gullah Dialect*. (1974 reprint. Ann Arbor: University of Michigan Press.)

Verdi, B. (1984). Preliminary research to a field study of Bermudian English. New York University, 32-p. mimeo.

Vigo, J. (ms.) Language maintenance and ethnicity: a sociolinguistic study of Samaná, Dominican Republic. Ph.D dissertation, Yale University.

Voorhoeve, J. (1957). The verbal system of Sranan. *Lingua* 6: 374–96.

(1961). Le ton et la grammaire dans le saramaccan. *Word* 17: 146–63.

(1964). Creole languages and communication. *Symposium on Multilingualism*. London: Conseil Scientifique pour Afrique/Commission de Coopération Technique en Afrique, 233–42.

(1973). Historical and linguistic evidence in favor of the relexification theory in the formation of creoles. *Language in Society* 2: 133–45.

Warantz, E. (1983). The Bay Islands English of Honduras. In Holm (ed.) 1983b: 71–94.

Washabaugh, W. (1983). The off-shore island creoles: Providence, San Andrés, and the Caymans. In Holm (ed.) 1983b: 157–79.

Williams, J. (1983). Dutch and English Creole on the Windward Netherlands Antilles: an historical perspective. *Amsterdam Creole Studies* V. 91–112.

Winer, L. (1984). Early Trinidadian Creole: the *Spectator* texts. *English World-wide* 5, 2: 181–210.

(forthcoming). Dictionary of Trinidadian English.

Wood, D. (1968). *Trinidad in Transition: the Years after Slavery*. Oxford: Oxford University Press.

Wood, P. (1974). *Black majority: Negroes in Colonial South Carolina from 1670 through the Stono Rebellion*. New York: Knopf.

Wullschlägel, H. R. (1856). *Deutsch–Negerenglisches Wörterbuch*. Amsterdam: Emering (1965 reprint).

Zentella, A. C. (1981). Language variety among Puerto Ricans. In C. Ferguson & S. Heath (eds.) *Language in the USA*. Cambridge: Cambridge University Press, 218–38.

8   English in New Zealand

Allan, S. (1990). The rise of New Zealand intonation. In Bell & Holmes (eds.), 115–28.

anon. (1944). *A Short Guide to New Zealand*. Washington: War and Navy Departments.

Arnold, R. (1981). *The Farthest Promised Land*. Wellington: Victoria University Press and Price Milburn.

Baker, S. J. (1941). *New Zealand Slang: a Dictionary of Colloquialisms*. Christchurch: Whitcombe and Tombs.

Bartlett, C. (1990). Research in progress on the Southland variety of NZ English. Paper presented at the Seminar on Language and Society, Wellington, May.

Bauer, L. (1986). Notes on New Zealand phonetics and phonology. *English World-wide* 7: 225–58.

(1987a). New Zealand English morphology: some experimental evidence. *Te Reo* 30: 37–53.

(1987b). Approaching the grammar of New Zealand English. *New Zealand English Newsletter* 1: 12–15.

(1988). Number agreement with collective nouns in New Zealand English. *Australian Journal of Linguistics* 8: 247–59.

(1989a). The verb *have* in New Zealand English. *English World-wide* 10: 69–83.

(1989b). Marginal modals in New Zealand English. *Te Reo* 32: 3–16.

(1989c). Irregularity in past non-finite verb forms. *New Zealand English Newsletter* 3: 13–15.

(1989d). A note on the New Zealand weekend. *New Zealand English Newsletter* 3; 15–16.

Bauer, W. (1981). Hae.re vs ha.e.re: a note. *Te Reo* 24: 31–6.

Bayard, D. (1987). Class and change in New Zealand English: a summary report. *Te Reo* 30: 3–36.

(1989). 'Me say that? No way!' the social correlates of American lexical diffusion in New Zealand English. *Te Reo* 32: 17–60.

(1990a). 'God help us if we all sound like this': attitudes to New Zealand and other English accents. In Bell & Holmes (eds.), 67–96.

(1990b). Minder, Mork and Mindy? (-t) glottalisation and post-vocalic (-r) in younger New Zealand English speakers. In Bell & Holmes (eds.), 149–64.

Bell, A. & J. Holmes (eds.) (1990). *New Zealand Ways of Speaking English.* Clevedon, Avon: Multilingual Matters, and Wellington: Victoria University Press.

Bennett, J. A. W. (1943). English as it is spoken in New Zealand. *American Speech* 18: 81–95.

Benton, R. A. (n.d. [1966]). *Research into the English Language Difficulties of Maori School Children 1963–64.* Wellington: Maori Education Foundation.

(1991) Maori English: a New Zealand myth? In J. Cheshire (ed.), *English around the World.* Cambridge: Cambridge University Press, 187–99.

Bernard, J. (1969). On the uniformity of spoken Australian English. *Orbis* 18: 62–73.

Biggs, B. (1989). Towards a study of Maori dialects. In R. Harlow & R. Hooper (eds.), *VICAL 1: Oceanic Languages.* Auckland: Linguistic Society of New Zealand, 61–75.

Bradley, D. (1989). Regional dialects in Australian English phonology. In Collins & Blair (eds.), 260–70.

Bryant, P. (1989). Regional variation in the Australian English lexicon. In Collins & Blair (eds.), 301–14.

Burchfield, R. W. (1986). *The New Zealand Pocket Oxford Dictionary.* Corrected reprint 1990. Auckland: Oxford University Press.

(1988). Some unedited New Zealand words. In Burton & Burton (eds.), 185–97.

Burton, T. L. & J. Burton (eds.) (1988). *Lexicographical and Linguistic Studies. Essays in Honour of G. W. Turner.* Cambridge: Brewer.

Cochrane, G. R. (1989). Origins and development of the Australian accent. In Collins & Blair (eds.), 176–86.

Collins, P. (1981). Investigating acceptability in Australian English. *Word* 32: 15–33.

Collins, P. & D. Blair (eds.) (1989). *Australian English: the Language of a New Society.* St Lucia: University of Queensland Press.

Deverson, T. (1988). A bibliography of writings on New Zealand English. *New Zealand English Newsletter* 2: 17–25.

Durkin, M. E. (1972). A study of the pronunciation, oral grammar and vocabulary of West Coast schoolchildren. Unpublished MA thesis, University of Canterbury, NZ.

Ellis, A. J. (1889). *On Early English Pronunciation with Especial Reference to Shakspere and Chaucer*, Part V (EETS, Extra Serres 56). Reprinted by Haskell House, New York, 1969.

Gibson, C. J. (1971). Demographic history of New Zealand. Unpublished Ph.D dissertation, University of California, Berkeley.

Gordon, E. (1983). 'The flood of impure vocalisation' – a study of attitudes towards New Zealand speech. *NZ Speech Therapists' Journal* 31, 8: 16–29.

Gordon, E. & T. Deverson (1985). *New Zealand English*. Auckland: Heinemann.

(1989). *Finding a New Zealand Voice*. Auckland: New House.

Gordon, E. & M. A. Maclagan (1989). *Beer* and *bear*, *cheer* and *chair*: a longitudinal study of the *ear/air* contrast in New Zealand English. *Australian Journal of Linguistics* 9: 203–20.

Gordon, I. A. (1982). *The New Collins Concise Dictionary of the English Language*, New Zealand edn. Auckland: Collins.

(1988). 'British regional survivals in New Zealand English'. In Burton & Burton, (eds.), 179–84.

Grace, P. (1986). *Potiki*. Auckland: Penguin.

Hammarström, G. (1980). *Australian English: its Origin and Status*. Hamburg: Helmut Buske.

Holmes, J. & A. Bell (1990). Attitudes, varieties, discourse: an introduction to the sociolinguistics of New Zealand English. In Bell & Holmes (eds.), 1–28.

Ihimaera, W. (1986). *The Matriarch*. Auckland: Heinemann.

Jacob, J. (1990). A grammatical comparison of the spoken English of Maori and Pakeha women in Levin. Unpublished MA thesis, Victoria University of Wellington.

Kuiper, K. (1990). Some more areas for research in New Zealand English syntax. *New Zealand English Newsletter* 4: 31–4.

Lass, R. (1987). *The Shape of English*. London and Melbourne: Dent.

(1990). Where do extraterritorial Englishes come from? Dialect input and recodification in transported Englishes. In S. Adamson, V. Law, N. Vincent and S. Wright (eds.), *Papers from the Fifth International Conference on English Historical Linguistics*. Amsterdam: John Benjamins, 245–80.

Legge, C. A. (1989). A transcription of Dumont D'Urville's manuscript Les Zélandais histoire australienne and the accompanying notes, followed by a study of some literary and historical aspects of the text. Unpublished Ph.D thesis, Victoria University of Wellington.

Lloyd Prichard, M. F. (1970). *An Economic History of New Zealand to 1939*. Auckland and London: Collins.

McBurney, S. (1887). Article in *The Press*, Christchurch, 5 October, p. 4.

McCallum, J. (1978). In search of a dialect: an exploratory study of the formal speech of some Maori and Pakeha children. *New Zealand Journal of Educational Studies* 13: 133–43.

McGeorge, C. (1984). Hear our voices we entreat. *The New Zealand Journal of History*, 18: 3–18.

McGill, D. (1988). *Up the Boohai Shooting Pukakas. A Dictionary of Kiwi Slang*. Lower Hutt: Mills.

(1989). *Up the Boohai Shooting Pipis with a Hayrake. The Dinkum Kiwi Dictionary.* Lower Hutt: Mills.

Meyerhoff, M. (1990). Sounds real ethnic eh? – a pragmatic particle in Porirua speech. Paper presented at the Seminar on Language and Society, Wellington, May.

Oliver, W. H. (ed.) (1981). *The Oxford History of New Zealand.* Oxford and Wellington: Oxford University Press.

Orsman, H. W. (1966). The Southland dialect. In A. H. McLintock (ed.), *An Encyclopedia of New Zealand*, vol. II. Wellington: Government Printer, 680–1.

(1979). *The Heinemann New Zealand Dictionary*, 2nd edn, 1989. Auckland: Heinemann.

(1980). Early New Zealand English vocabulary and the Australian connection (some data and notes). In D. Norton & R. Robinson, (eds.), *Views of English*, vol. II. Wellington: Victoria University of Wellington, Department of English, 29–54.

Sinclair, K. (1959). *A History of New Zealand*, revised and enlarged edition, 1980. London: Allen Lane.

Trudgill, P. (1986). *Dialects in Contact.* Oxford: Blackwell.

Turner, G. W. (1972). *The English Language in Australia and New Zealand.* 2nd edn. London: Longman.

Wall, A. (1938). *New Zealand English: a Guide to the Correct Pronunciation of English*, 2nd edn. Christchurch: Whitcombe and Tombs.

Wells, J. C. (1982). *Accents of English*, 3 vols. Cambridge: Cambridge University Press.

9   English in South Africa

Abrahams, P. (1954). *Tell Freedom.* London: Faber.

Alexander, J. (1838). *Narrative of a Voyage of Observation ... and of a Campaign in Kaffir-land.* London: Henry Colburn.

(1837). *An Expedition of Discovery into the Interior of Africa*, 2 vols. London: Henry Colburn. (Struik Facsimile reprint 1967).

Alexander, N. (1989). *Language Policy and National Unity in Azania/South Africa.* Cape Town: Buchu Books.

(1990). The language question. In R. Schrire (ed.) *Critical Choices for South Africa.* Cape Town: Oxford University Press, 127–45.

Appleyard, J. (1850). *The Kafir Language, comprising a Sketch of its history; which includes a general classification of South African dialects, ethnological and geographical; Remarks upon its Nature and a Grammar.* King William's Town: Wesleyan Missionary Press.

Austen, J. (1953). *Minor Works*, ed. R. W. Chapman. London: Oxford University Press.

Baker, S. J. (1966). *The Australian Language*. Sidney: Currawong.

Barnard, Lady A. (1973). *Letters of Lady Anne Barnard to Henry Dundas, 1793–1803*, ed. Lewin Robinson. Cape Town. A. A. Balkema.

Bergh, O. (1683). *Journal of Olof Bergh, 1683*. Cape Town: Van Riebeeck Society.

Bernstein, B. (1973). *Class, Codes and Control*. St Albans: Granada.

Bhana, S. & B. Pachai (ed.) (1984). *A Documentary History of South African Indians*. Cape Town: David Philip.

Bird, W. (1823). *State of the Cape of Good Hope in 1822*. London: John Murray.

Birkby, C. (1941). *Springbok Victory*. Johannesburg: Libertas.

Bleek, W. H. (1858). *The Library of his Excellency Sir George Grey, K.C.B., Philology I.i.* London: Trubner.

Bosman, H. (1947 [1978]). *Mafeking Road*. Cape Town: Human and Rousseau.

Boyle, F. (1873). *To the Cape for Diamonds*. London: Chapman and Hall.

 (1882). *Savage Life. A New Edition*. London: Chatto and Windus.

Bradlow, F. & E. Bradlow (eds.) (1979). *William Somerville's Narrative 1799–1802*. Cape Town: Van Riebeeck Society.

Branford, J. (1976). Some problems of dialect lexicography with particular reference to the preparation of an experientially categorized draft Dictionary of South African English. Grahamstown, unpublished Ph.D thesis, Rhodes University.

 (1987 [1978]). *A Dictionary of South African English*, 3rd edn. Cape Town: Oxford University Press (1st edn 1978).

 (1988). Adam's dilemma: a note on the early naming of kinds at the Cape. In E. Stanley and T. Hoad (eds.) *Words for Robert Burchfield's Sixty-Fifth Birthday*. Bury St Edmunds: D. S. Brewer, 69–80.

Branford, J., W. Branford, M. Britz & J. Pargiter (1984). Agterryer: an interim presentation of materials for a Dictionary of South African English. Unpublished report, Rhodes University, Dictionary Unit.

Branford, W. (1976a). Introduction to *Voorloper*: an interim presentation of materials for a dictionary of South African English. Unpublished report, Rhodes University.

 (1976b). A dictionary of South African English as a reflex of the English-speaking cultures of South Africa. In A. De Villiers (ed.), 297–316.

 (1984). Introduction to *Agterryer*: an interim presentation of materials for a dictionary of South African English on historical principles. Unpublished report, Rhodes University.

 (1987). *The South African Pocket Oxford Dictionary*. Cape Town: Oxford University Press.

Burchell, W. (1822–4). *Travels in the Interior of Southern Africa*, 2 vols. London: Longman.

Bureau of Census and Statistics (1960). *Union Statistics for Fifty Years: 1910–1960*. Pretoria: Bureau of Census and Statistics.

Cassidy, F. G. and R. B. Le Page (1980). *Dictionary of Jamaican English*. Cambridge: Cambridge University Press.

Casson, L. (1955). *The Dialect of Jeremiah Goldswain, Albany Settler*. (Inaugural Lecture, University of Cape Town). Cape Town: Oxford University Press.

Cole, D. T. (1964). Fanagalo and the Bantu languages in South Africa. In D. Hymes (ed.) *Language in Culture and Society*. New York: Harper and Row, 547–54.

Davenport, T. R. H. (1980). *South Africa: a Modern History*, 3rd edn. London: MacMillan. (1st edn 1977, 2nd edn 1978.)

De Villiers, A. (ed.) (1976). *English-Speaking South Africa Today*. Cape Town: Oxford University Press.

De Villiers, M. (1962). *Die Afrikaanse Klankleer*. Cape Town: Balkema.

Donaldson, B. (1988). *The Influence of English on Afrikaans*. Pretoria: Serva.

Downes, W. (1984). *Language and Society*. London: Fontana.

Elphick, R. (1977). *Kraal and Castle*. New Haven: Yale University Press.

Ewart, J. (1811–14 [1970]). *James Ewart's Journal, 1811–1814*, ed. A. Gordon-Brown. Cape Town: C. Struik.

Eybers, G. W. (1918). *Select Constitutional Documents illustrating South African History, 1795–1910*. London: Routledge.

Fanaroff, D. (1972). *South African English Dialect: a Literature Survey*. Pretoria: Human Sciences Research Council.

Fishman, J. A. (1972). *The Sociology of Language*. Rowley, MA: Newbury House.

Fitzpatrick, J. (1907). *Jock of the Bushveld*. London: Longmans Green.

Gandhi, M. (1927 [1983]). *An Autobiography*, trans. M. K. Desai. Harmondsworth: Penguin.

Gandhi, M. K. (1928). *Satyagraha in South Africa*. Ahmedabad: Navajiran.

Gimson, A. (1962). *An Introduction to the Pronunciation of English*. London: Edward Arnold.

Goldswain, J. (1946, 1949), *The Chronicle of Jeremiah Goldswain, 1819–1858*, ed. Una Long, 2 vols. Cape Town: Van Riebeeck Society.

Goold-Adams, R. (1936). *South Africa Today and Tomorrow*. London: John Murray.

Greig, G. (1831). *The South African Almanac and Directory for 1831*. Cape Town: George Greig.

Holden, W. (1855). *History of the Colony of Natal*. London: Alexander Haylin.

Holm, J. & A. Shilling (1982). *Dictionary of Bahamian English*. New York: Lexik.

Hooper, A. G. (1945). A preliminary report of an investigation of spoken English in South Africa. *South African Journal of Science* 41: 476–84.

Hopwood, D. (1928). *South African English Pronunciation*. Cape Town: Juta.

Horvath, B. M. (1985). *Variation in Australian English*. London: Cambridge University Press.

Hudson, R. (1980). *Sociolinguistics*. Cambridge: Cambridge University Press.

Jacobson, D. (1956). *A Dance in the Sun*. London: Weidenfeld and Nicholson.

Jeffery, C. (1982). Review of Lanham & MacDonald, 1979. *Folia Linguistica Historica* 3: 251–63.

Jeffreys, M. (1971). Some usages of the words Afrikaner: Afrikander. *Africana Notes and News* 19: 1.

Kidd, A. G. (1910). *The English Language and Literature in South Africa*. Cape Town: SA Association for the Advancement of Science.

Kipling, R. (1948). *Rudyard Kipling's Verse, Definitive Edition*. London: Hodder and Stoughton.

Kuiper, H., A. Opprel, & P. Van Mallsen. (1904). *Van Dale's Groot Woordeboek der Nederlandsche Taal*, 4th edn. The Hague and Leiden: Nijhoff en Sijthoff.

Labov, W. (1969). The social motivation of a sound-change. *Word* 19: 273–309.

La Hausse, P. (1988). *Brewers, Beerhalls and Boycotts*. Johannesburg: Ravan Press.

Lanham, L. W. (1967). *The Pronunciation of South African English*. Cape Town: Balkema.

 (1978a). South African English. In Lanham & Prinsloo (eds.), 138–65.

 (1978b). An outline history of the languages of southern Africa. In Lanham and Prinsloo (eds.), 13–28.

 (1983). English in South Africa. In R. Bailey & M. Görlach (eds.) *English as a World Language*. Ann Arbor: University of Michigan Press, 324–52.

Lanham, L. W. & C. MacDonald (1979). *The Standard in South African English and its Social History*. Heidelberg: Julius Gros.

Lanham, L. W. & K. Prinsloo (eds.) (1978). *Language and Communication Studies in South Africa*. Cape Town: Oxford University Press.

Lanham, L. W. & A. Traill. (1962). *South African English Pronunciation*. Johannesburg: Witwatersrand University Press.

Lass, R. (1980). *On Explaining Language Change*. Cambridge: Cambridge University Press.

 (1987). *The Shape of English*. London: J. M. Dent.

 (1988). The vowel phonology of Cape Town Standard English. Unpublished typescript.

Lass, R. & S. Wright (1985). The South African Chain Shift: Order out of Chaos? In R. Eaton, O. Fischer, W. Koopman & F. van der Leek (eds.) *Papers from the 4th International Conference on English Historical Linguistics, Amsterdam, 10–13 April 1985*. Amsterdam, John Benjamins, 137–61.

 (1986). Endogeny versus contact: 'Afrikaans influence' on South African English. *English World-wide*, 7, 2: 201–23.

Le Page, R. B. (1968). Problems of description in multilingual communities. *Transactions of the Philological Society*, 190–211.

Le Roux, T. H. & P. de V. Pienaar (1927). *Afrikaanse Fonetiek*. Cape Town: Juta.

Lewis, M. B. (1947). *Teach yourself Malay*. London: English Universities Press.

Lichtenstein, H. (1812–15). *Travels in Southern Africa 1803–1806*, trans. A. Plumptre, 2 vols. Edinburgh: Goldie; Dublin: Cumming.

McAllister, P. A. (1989). Hamba bhekile: notes on Xhosa drinking terms. Unpublished typescript, Grahamstown, Rhodes University Anthropology Department.

Malherbe, E. G. (1925). *Education in South Africa*, vol. I: *1652–1922*. Cape Town: Juta.

  (1966). *Demographic and Socio-Political Forces Determining the Position of English in the South African Republic*. Johannesburg: English Academy of Southern Africa.

  (1977). *Education in South Africa*, vol. II: *1925–1977*. Cape Town: Juta.

Malherbe, V. C. (ed.) (1971): *What They Said...a Selection of Documents from South African History*. Cape Town: Maskew Miller.

Mathiane, N. (1989). The Mandela Affair. *Frontline* 8, 7: 7–8.

Matshoba, M. (1979). *Call me not a Man*. Johannesburg: Ravan Press.

Maylam, P. (1986). *A History of the African Peoples of South Africa*. London and Cape Town: Croom Helm and David Philip.

Medley, G. (1731, translation of P. Kolb). *The Present State of the Cape of Good Hope*. London: W. Inngs.

Mendelssohn, S. (1910). *Mendelssohn's South African Bibliography*. London: Kegan Paul, Trench, Trubner.

Mesthrie, R. (1986). Lexicon of South African Indian English. Unpublished typescript.

Mfusi, H. (1990). Soweto Zulu slang. BA Honours mini-thesis, Pretoria, University of South Africa.

Milroy, J. and L. Milroy (1978). Belfast: change and variation in an urban vernacular in P. Trudgill (ed.) *Sociolinguistic Patterns in British English*. London: Edward Arnold, 19–36.

Mitchell, A. G. & A. Delbridge (1965). *The Pronunciation of English in Australia*. Sydney: Angus and Robertson.

Morse Jones, E. (1969). *Roll of the British Settlers in South Africa*, Part I: *Up to 1826*. Cape Town: A. A. Balkema (2nd edn 1971).

Motsisi, C. (1978). *Casey and Co.*, ed. M. Mutloatse. Johannesburg: Ravan Press.

Ndebele, N. (1987). The English language and social change in South Africa, *English Academy Review* 4: 1–16.

Ngugu wa Thiongo (1986). *Decolonizing the Mind: the Politics of Language in African Literature*. London: James Curry.

Nienaber, G. S. (1963). *Hottentots*. Cape Town: Van Schaik.

Norton, B. D. (1983). An exploratory study of linguistic change in South African English. Unpublished MA dissertation, Reading University.

Orton, H. (1962–71). *Survey of English Dialects*. Leeds: Arnold.

Palmer, F. R. (1965). *A Linguistic Study of the English Verb*. London: Longman.

Paton, A. (1948 [1983]). *Cry, the Beloved Country*. Harmondsworth: Penguin.

Peires, J. (1981). *The House of Phalo: a History of the Xhosa People*. Cape Town: Ravan Press.

Pettman, C. (1913). *Africanderisms: a Glossary of South African Colloquial Words and Phrases*. London: Longmans Green.

Picard, J. H. (1975). Roofies and Oumanne. Military English in South Africa. *English Usage in South Africa*, 6, 1: 36–40.

Plaatje, S. (1916 [1982]): *Native Life in South Africa*. Johannesburg: Ravan Press.

Platsky, L. & C. Walker (1985). *The Surplus People*. Johannesburg: Ravan Press.

Polson, N. (1837). *A Subaltern's Sick Leave*. Calcutta: S. H. Hultmann.

Pringle, T. (1835 [1966]). *Narrative of a Residence in South Africa*. London: Moxon. Facsimile reprint, Cape Town: C. Struik, 1966.

Prinsloo, K. (1985). The status and future of Afrikaans in multilingual South Africa. *SA Journal of Linguistics* 3, 4: 67–80.

Race Relations Survey 1986, vols. I and II. Johannesburg: South African Institute of Race Relations.

Race Relations Survey 1987–8, Johannesburg: South African Institute of Race Relations.

Ramson, W. (1988). *The Australian National Dictionary*. Melbourne: Oxford University Press.

Romaine, S. (1982). *Socio-Historical Linguistics*. Cambridge: Cambridge University Press.

Ross, L. (1870 [1963]). *Life at the Cape, by a Lady*. Cape Town: C. Struik.

Schapera, I. (ed.) (1937). *The Bantu-Speaking Tribes of South Africa*. London: Routledge.

Schlemmer, L. (1976). English-speaking South Africans today: identity and integration into the broader national community. In de Villiers (ed.), 91–135.

Schreiner, O. (1883 [1975]). *The Story of an African Farm*. Johannesburg: Ad Donker.

(1923). *Thoughts on South Africa*. London: Fisher Unwin.

Schuring, S. K. (1985). *Kosmopolitiese Omgangstale*. Pretoria: Human Sciences Research Council.

Shone, T. (1838–). *Diaries 1838–1867*, typed transcript and ms. Cory Library, Rhodes University, Grahamstown.

Shuring, G. K. & C. F. Ellis (1987). Shared languages and 'language gaps' in South Africa: an analysis of census data. *South African Journal of Labour Relations* 11, 3: 37–45.

Siegel, J. (1985). Koines and koineization. *Language in Society* 14: 357–78.

Silva, P. (1978). The 1820 settlement – some aspects of its influence on the vocabulary of South African English. *English in Africa* 5, 1: 61–70.

(1990). Unpublished drafts for *A Dictionary of South African English on Historical Principles*. Grahamstown, Rhodes University, Dictionary Unit.

Silva, P. & J. Walker (1976). *Voorloper: an Interim Presentation of Materials for a Dictionary of South African English*. Grahamstown: Institute for the Study of English in Africa, Rhodes University.

Slapolepszy (1985). *Saturday Night at the Palace*. Craighall: Ad Donker.

Smith, C. A. (1966). *Common Names of South African Plants*, ed. E. Phillips & E. van Hoepen. Pretoria: Government Printer.

South Africa 1979: Official Yearbook of the Republic of South Africa (1979). Johannesburg: Chris van Rensburg.

Sparrman, A. (1786). *A Voyage to the Cape of Good Hope*, trans. G. Forster, 2nd edn. London: G. and J. Forster.

Steedman, A. (1835). *Wanderings and Adventures in the Interior of Southern Africa*. London: Longman.

Thompson, G. (1827). *Travels and Adventures in Southern Africa*. London: Henry Colburn. (Reprint 1967.)

Tongue, R. (1974). *The English of Singapore and Malaysia*. Singapore: Eastern Universities Press.

Trudgill, P. (1983). *On Dialect*. Oxford: Blackwell.

(1986). *Dialects in Contact*. Oxford: Blackwell.

Trudgill, P. & J. Hannah (1985). *International English: a Guide to Varieties of Standard English*, 2nd edn. London: Edward Arnold.

Turner, G. W. (1965). *The English Language in Australia and New Zealand*. London: Longman.

Until we have our liberty... Thirty Years of the Freedom Charter, 1985. Johannesburg: Community Resource and Information Centre.

Van Dale. (1904). See H. Kuiper *et al*.

Van der Merwe, H. J. J. M. (ed.) (1971): *Vroeë Afrikaanse Woordelyste*. Pretoria: Van Schaik.

Walker, E. (1928). *A History of South Africa*. London: Longmans Green.

Watts, H. (1976). A social and demographic portrait of English-speaking White South Africans. In de Villiers (ed.), 41–89.

Weinreich, U. (1953). *Languages in Contact*. New York: Linguistic Circle of New York.

Wells, J. C. (1982). *Accents of English*. Cambridge: Cambridge University Press.

Wierzbicka, A. (1986). Does language reflect thought? Evidence from Australian English. *Language in Society* 15: 349–74.

Wissing, D. P. (1982). *Algemene en Afrikaanse Generatiewe Fonologie*. Johannesburg: Macmillan South Africa.

Wood, T. (1987). Perceptions of, and attitudes towards, varieties of English in the Cape Peninsula, with particular reference to the 'Coloured Community'. Unpublished MA thesis, Rhodes University.

Wyld, H. (1920). *A History of Modern Colloquial English*. London: Fisher Unwin.

Young, Douglas (ed.) (1987). *Language Planning and Medium in Education*. Cape Town: Language Education Unit, University of Cape Town.

10   English in South Asia

Aggarwal, N. K. (1982). *English in South Asia: a Bibliographical Survey of Resources*. Gurgaon and New Delhi: Indian Documentation Service.

Agnihotri, R. K., A. L. Khanna & A. Mukherjee (1984). The use of articles in Indian English. *IRAL* 22, 2: 115–29.

Annamalai, E. (ed.) (1979). *Language Movement in India*. Mysore: Central Institute of Indian Languages.

Appa Rao, S. R. (1978). Orthography as underlying representation: a study of the vocalic phonology of RP and Telugu English within the framework of generative phonology. Unpublished MLitt. dissertation, Central Institute of English and Foreign Languages, Hyderabad.

Banerjee, S. (1878). *Lord Macaulay and Higher Education in India*. Calcutta: I. C. Bose.

Bansal, R. K. (1969). *Intelligibility of Indian English*. Hyderabad: Central Institute of English and Foreign Languages.

    (1990). The pronunciation of English in India. In S. Ramsaran (ed.) *Studies in the Pronunciation of English: a Commemorative Volume in Honour of A. C. Gimson*. London: Routledge, 219–30.

Barnes, Sir E. (1932). *The History of Royal College*. Colombo.

Baumgardner, R. J. (1987). Utilizing Pakistani newspaper English to teach grammar. *World Englishes* 6, 3: 241–52.

    (1990). The indigenization of English in Pakistan. *English Today* 21, 6.1: 59–65.

    (ed.) (1993). *The English Language in Pakistan*. Karachi: Oxford University Press.

    (ed.) (forthcoming). *South Asian English: Structure, Use and Users*. Urbana, IL: University of Illinois Press.

Bayer, J. M. (1986). *A Sociolinguistic Investigation of the English Spoken by the Anglo-Indians in Mysore City*. Mysore: Central Institute of Indian Languages.

Bhatia, T. K. (1987). English in advertising: multiple mixing and media. *World Englishes* 6, 1: 33–48.

Bhatia, T. K. & W. Ritchie. (eds.) (1989). *Code-Mixing: English Across Languages*. Special Issue of *World Englishes* 8.3: 261–4.

Bryant, A. (1932). *Macaulay*. Edinburgh: Edinburgh University Press.

Chatterjee, K. K. (1976). *English Education in India: Issues and Opinions*. Delhi: Macmillan.

Chatterji, S. K. (1926 [1970]). *The Origin and Development of the Bengali Language*, 2 vols. London: George Allen and Unwin.

(1963). *The Literary Unity of India*. In S. Mukherji (ed.) *Towards a Literary History of India*. Mysore: Central Institute of Indian Languages, 118–36.

Chaudhary S. C. (1989). *Some Aspects of the Phonology of Indian English*. Ranchi: Jayaswal Press.

Chaudhuri, N. C. (1976). The English language in India – past, present and future. In A. Niven (ed.) *The Commonwealth Writer Overseas: Themes of Exile and Expatriation*. Brunells: Librairie Marcel Didier SA, 89–105.

Cheshire, J. (ed.) (1991). *Sociolinguistic Perspectives of English as a World Language*. Cambridge: Cambridge University Press.

Clive, J. (1973). *Macaulay: the Shaping of the Historian*. New York: Knopf.

Coppola, C. (1988). *Marxist Influences and South Asian Literature*. Delhi: Chanakya.

Danchev, A. (1984). Translation and syntactic change. In J. Fisiak (ed.) *Historical Syntax* (Trends in Linguistics, Studies and Monographs 23). The Hague: Mouton, 47–60.

Dhamija, P. V. (1976). A phonological analysis of Rajasthani English. Unpublished MLitt. dissertation, Central Institute of English and Foreign Languages, Hyderabad.

Dissanayake, W. (1985). Towards a decolonized English: South Asian creativity in fiction. *World Englishes* 4, 2: 233–42.

D'souza, J. (1986). Language modernization in a sociolinguistic area. *Anthropological Linguistics* 28, 4: 455–71.

(1987). South Asia as a sociolinguistic area. Unpublished Ph.D. dissertation. University of Illinois at Urbana-Champaign.

Dustoor, P. E. (1954). Missing and intrusive articles in Indian English. *Allahabad University Studies* 31: 1–70.

(1955). Wrong, usurping and dispossessed articles in Indian English. *Allahabad University Studies* 32: 1–17.

Emeneau, M. B. (1955). India and linguistics. *Journal of the American Oriental Society* 75: 145–215.

(1956). India as a linguistic area. *Language* 32: 3–16.

Fernando, C. (1976). English and Sinhala bilingualism in Sri Lanka. *Language in Society* 6: 341–60.

Fernando, S. (1989). Style range in Sri Lankan English fiction: an analysis of four texts. *World Englishes* 8, 2: 119–31.

Fernando, T. (1972). The Burghers of Ceylon. In N. P. Gist & A. G. Dworkin (eds.) *The Blending of Races: Marginality and Identity in World Perspective*. New York: John Wiley, 61–78.

Firth, J. R. (1930). *Speech*. London: Benn's Sixpenny Library, no. 121; reprinted, London: Oxford University Press, 1966.

George, K. M. (1972). *Western Influence on Malayalam Language and Literature*. New Delhi: Sahitya Academi.

Gokhale, S. B. (1978). A study of intonation patterns in Marathi and Marathi

English. Unpublished MLitt. dissertation, Central Institute of English and Foreign Languages, Hyderabad.

Gopalakrishnan, G. S. (1960). Some observations on the South Indian pronunciation of English. *Teaching English* 6, 2: 62–7.

Grant, C. (1831–2). Observations on the state of society among the Asiatic subjects of Great Britain, particularly with respect to morals, and the means of improving it. In *General Appendix to Parliamentary Papers 1831–32*. London.

Gupta, S. M. (1980). Vowel reduction in U.P. English: an instrumental study. *CIEFL Bulletin* 16, 1: 31–40.

Guthrie, T. A. (1897). *Baboo Jabberjee B.A.* London: J. M. Dent.

Hands, S. (1983). *Pakistan: a Country Study*, 4th edn (Foreign Area Studies, The American University). Washington DC: US Government.

Hashmi, A. (1978 [1987]). *Pakistani Literature: the Contemporary English*. Islamabad: Gulmohar.

(1989). Prolegomena to the study of Pakistani English and Pakistani literature in English. Paper presented at the International Conference on English in South Asia, Islamabad, 4–9 January.

Hawkins, R. E. (1976). Supplement of words from India, Pakistan, Bangladesh, and Sri Lanka. In G. Ostler (comp.) *The Little Oxford Dictionary of Current English*. Delhi: Oxford University Press.

Hock, H. H. (1986). *Principles of Historical Linguistics*. The Hague: Mouton de Guyter.

Hosali, P. (1982). Butler English: form and function. Unpublished Ph.D dissertation, Central Institute of English and Foreign Languages, Hyderabad.

Hosali, P. & J. Aitchison (1986). Butler English: a minimal pidgin? *Journal of Pidgin and Creole Linguistics* 1,1: 51–79.

Hunt, C. (1931). *Honoured Sir from Babujee*. London: P. Allen.

(1935). *Babuji Writes Home: being a new edition of 'Honoured sir' with many additional letters*. London: P. Allen.

Islam, R. (1975). Language planning in Bangladesh. *Indian Linguistics* 36, 3: 186–90.

Iyengar, K. R. S. (1962). *Indian Writing in English*. Bombay: Asia Publishing House.

(1985). *Indian Writing in English*, revised and updated edition. New Delhi: Sterling.

Jussawalla, F. F. (1985). *Family Quarrels: Towards a Criticism of Indian Writing in English*. New York: Peter Lang.

Kachru, B. B. (1965). The *Indianness* in Indian English. *Word* 21, 3: 391–410.

(1976). Models of English for the third world, white man's linguistic burden or language pragmatics. *TESOL Quarterly* 10, 2: 221–39.

(1978). Code-mixing as a verbal strategy in India. In J. E. Alatis (ed.)

International Dimensions of Bilingual Education (Georgetown Monographs on Languages and Linguistics). Washington, DC: Georgetown University Press, 107–24.

(1980). The new Englishes and old dictionaries: directions in lexicographical research on non-native varieties of English. In L. Zgusta (ed.) *Theory and Method in Lexicography: a Western and Non-Western Perspective*. Chapel Hill, NC: Hornbeam Press, 71–101.

(1982). Language policy in South Asia. *Annual Review of Applied Linguistics 1981* 2: 60–85.

(1983). *The Indianization of English: the English language in India*. Delhi: Oxford University Press.

(1985a). Standards, codification and sociolinguistic realism: the English language in the outer circle. In R. Quirk & H. G. Widdowson (eds.) *English in the World: Teaching and Learning the Language and Literatures*. Cambridge: Cambridge University Press, 11–30.

(1985b). Institutional second language varieties. In S. Greenbaum (ed.) *The English Language Today*. Oxford: Pergamon Press, 211–26.

(1986a). *The Alchemy of English: the Spread, Functions and Models of Non-native Englishes*. London: Prentice-Hall. (Reprinted Urbana: University of Illinois Press, 1990).

(1986b). The power and politics of English. *World Englishes* 5, 2–3: 121–40.

(1987). The bilingual's creativity: discoursal and stylistic strategies in contact literatures. In L. E. Smith (ed.) *Discourse across Cultures: Strategies in World Englishes*. London: Prentice Hall, 125–40.

(ed.) (1992a). *The Other Tongue: English Across Cultures*, 2nd edn. Urbana, IL: University of Illinois Press.

(1992b). The second diaspora of English. In T. W. Machan and C. T. Scott (eds.) *English in its Social Contexts: Essays in Historical Sociolinguistics*. New York: Oxford University Press, 230–52.

(1994). Englishization and contact linguistics. *World Englishes* 13, 2.

Kachru, B. B. & L. Smith (1986). *The Power of English: Cross-cultural Dimensions in Literature and Media*. Special issue of *World Englishes* 5, 2–3.

Kachru, Y. (1985). Discourse analysis, non-native Englishes and second language acquisition research. *World Englishes* 4, 2: 223–32.

(1987). Cross-cultural texts, discourse strategies and discourse interpretation. In L. E. Smith (ed.), *Discourse Across Cultures: Strategies in World Englishes*. London: Prentice Hall, 87–100.

(ed.) (1991). Symposium on speech acts in World Englishes. *World Englishes* 10, 3: 295–340.

(1992). Culture, style and discourse: expanding noetics of English. In B. Kachru (ed.), 340–52.

Kandiah, T. (1971). New Ceylon English (Review Article). *New Ceylon Writing*, 90–4.

(1981). Lankan English schizolossia. *English World-wide* 2, 1: 63–81.

(1984). 'Kaduva': power and the English language weapon in Sri Lanka. In P. Colin-Thomé and A. Halpé (eds.) *Honouring E. F. C. Ludowyk: Felicitation Essays*. Dehiwela: Tisara Prakasakayo, 117–54.

(1991). Sociolinguistic perspectives in English in South Asia. In Cheshire (ed.), 271–87.

Kanungo, G. B. (1962). *The Language Controversy in Indian Education: Historical Study*. Chicago: Comparative Education Center, University of Chicago.

Khan, N. (1974). A phonological analysis of English spoken by All-India Radio newsreaders. Unpublished Research Diploma dissertation, Central Institute of English and Foreign Languages, Hyderabad,

Kindersley, A. F. (1938). Notes on the Indian idiom of English: style, syntax and vocabulary. *Transactions of the Philological Society*. 25–34.

King, B. (1987). *Modern Indian Poetry in English*. Delhi: Oxford University Press.

Krishnamurti, Bh. (1978). Spelling pronunciation in Indian English. In R. Mohan (ed.), *Indian Writing in English*. Madras: Orient Longman, 129–39.

Krishnamurti, Bh. & A. Mukherjee (eds.) (1984). *Modernization of Indian Languages in News Media*. Hyderabad: Osmania University.

Lal, P. (1969). *Modern Indian Poetry in English: An anthology and a Credo*. Calcutta: Writers Workshop.

Latha, P. (1978). Intonation of Malayalam and Malayalee English: a study in comparison and contrast. Unpublished MLitt. dissertation, Central Institute of English and Foreign Languages, Hyderabad.

Law, N. N. (1915). *Promotion of Learning in India by Early European Settlers*. London: Longman.

Lewis, I. (1991). *Sahibs, Nawabs and Boxwalahs; a Dictionary of the Words of Anglo-India*. Bombay: Oxford University Press.

Lowenberg, P. & S. N. Sridhar (eds.) (1986). *World Englishes and Second Language Acquisition Research*. Special issue of *World Englishes*, 5.1.

Malla, K. P. (1977). *English in Nepalese Education*. Kathmandu: Ratna Pustak Bhandar.

Masica, C. P. (1972). *The Sound System of General Indian English* (Monograph no. 7). Hyderabad: Central Institute of English and Foreign Languages.

(1976). *Defining a Linguistic Area: South Asia*. Chicago: University of Chicago Press.

Mendis, G. C. (1952). *Ceylon under the British*. Colombo: the Colombo Apothecarien.

Meraj, S. (1993). The use of English in Urdu advertising in Pakistan. In Baumgardner (ed.) (1993), 221–52.

Morris, H. (1904). *The Life of Charles Grant*. London: J. Murray.

Mukherjee, M. (1971). *The Twice-born Fiction: Themes and Techniques of the Indian novel in English*. New Delhi: Arnold Heinemann.

Murthy, S. (1981). A study of the attitudinal function of intonation in Kannada

English. Unpublished MLitt. dissertation, Central Institute of English and Foreign Languages, Hyderabad.

Musa, M. (1981). *Language Planning in Sri Lanka*. Dacca: Bani Mudron.

Nagarajan, S. (1981). The decline of English in India: some historical notes. *College English* 43, 7: 663–70.

Naik, M. K. (1982). *A History of Indian English Literature*. Delhi: Sahitya Akademi.

Nehru, J. L. (1963). The language problem in India. *Bulletin of the Central Institute of English and Foreign Languages* 3: 1–6.

Neill, S. (1984). *History of Christianity in India: the Beginnings to 1707*. Cambridge: Cambridge University Press.

(1985). *History of Christianity in India: 1707–1858*. Cambridge: Cambridge University Press.

Nelson, C. (1982). Intelligibility and non-native varieties of English. In B. Kachru (ed.) *The Other Tongue: English Across Cultures*, 1st edn. Urbana, IL: University of Illinois Press, 58–73.

Nihalani, P., R. K. Tongue & P. Hosali (1979). *Indian and British English: a Handbook of Usage and Pronunciation*. Delhi: Oxford University Press.

Nurullah, S. & J. P. Naik (1951). *A History of Education in India*. Bombay: Macmillan.

Pandey, P. K. (1980). Stress in Hindustani English: a generative phonological study. Unpublished MLitt. dissertation, Central Institute of English and Foreign Languages, Hyderabad.

(1985). Word accentuation in Hindustani English in relation to word accents in English and Hindustani. Unpublished Ph.D dissertation. Deccan College, University of Poona.

Pandit, P. B. (1972). *India as a sociolinguistic area*. Poona: University of Poona.

Parasher, S. V. (1991). *Indian English: Functions and Form*. New Delhi: Bahri.

Passé, H. A. (1947). *The English language in Ceylon*. Unpublished Ph.D thesis, University of London.

Prabhakar Babu, B. A. (1971). Prosodic features in Indian English: stress, rhythm and intonation. Unpublished Research Diploma dissertation, Central Institute of English and Foreign Languages, Hyderabad.

(1974). A phonological study of English spoken by Telugu speakers in Andhra Pradesh. Unpublished Ph.D thesis, Osmania University, Hyderabad.

Prator, C. H. (1968). The British heresy in TESOL. In J. Fishman, C. A. Ferguson & J. Das Gupta (eds.) *Language Problems of Developing Nations*. New York: Wiley, 459–76.

Premalatha, M. (1978). The vowels of Malayalee English: a generative phonological study. Unpublished MLitt. dissertation, Central Institute of English and Foreign Languages, Hyderabad.

Quirk, R. (1988). The question of standards in the international use of English.

In P. H. Lowenberg (ed.) *Language Spread and Language Policy: Issues, Implications, and Case Studies*. Washington DC: Georgetown University Press, 229–241.

(1989). Language varieties and standard language. *JALT Journal* 11, 1: 14–25.

Rahman, T. (1991a). Pakistani English: some phonological and phonetic features. *World Englishes* 10, 1: 83–95.

(1991b). *Pakistani English*. Islamabad: National Institute of Pakistan Studies; Qaid-i-Azam University.

(1991c). *A History of Pakistani Literature in English*. Lahore: Vanguard.

Rajagopalachari(ar), C. (1962). *The Question of English*. Madras: Bharathan.

Ram, T. (1983). *Trading in Language: the Story of English in India*. Delhi: GDK.

Ramaiah, L. S. (1988). *Indian English: a Bibliographical Guide to Resources*. Delhi: Gian.

Ramunny, K. (1976). Subjective reactions to regional and non-regional English accents in India. Unpublished MLitt. dissertation, Central Institute of English and Foreign Languages, Hyderabad.

Rao, G. S. (1954). *Indian Words in English: a Study in Indo-British Cultural and Linguistic Relations*. London: Oxford University Press.

Report of the Official Language Commission. 1956 (1957). New Delhi: Government of India Press.

Report of the Special Committee on Education, Ceylon (1943). *Sessional papers, XXIV*. Colombo: Sri Lanka.

Richter, J. (1908). *A History of Missions in India*, trans. S. H. Moore. New York: F. H. Revell.

Robarts, T. T. (1800). *An Indian glossary consisting of some thousand words and forms commonly used in the East Indies ... extremely serviceable in assisting strangers to acquire with ease and quickness the language of that country*. London: Murray and Highley.

Roy, R. (1823). Letter to Lord Amherst, 11 December. In *Selections from Educational Records, Part I (1781–1838)*. Calcutta: Bureau of Education, Government of India, 99–101.

Rubdy, R. (1975). A phonological analysis of English spoken by ten Marathi speakers from Maharashtra. Unpublished MLitt. dissertation, Central Institute of English and Foreign Languages, Hyderabad.

Ruberu, R. (1962). *Education in Colonial Ceylon: Being a Research Study on the History of Education in Ceylon for the Period 1796 to 1834*. Kandy: Kendy.

Sadanandan, S. (1981). Stress in Malayalee English: a generative phonological approach. Unpublished MLitt. dissertation, Central Institute of English and Foreign Languages, Hyderabad.

Schuchardt, H. (1891). Indo-English. In *Pidgins and Creole Languages: Selected Essays*, ed. and trans. G. G. Gilbert, 1980. London: Cambridge University Press.

Sethi, J. (1976). English spoken by educated Punjabi speakers in India: a phonological study. Unpublished Ph.D thesis, Punjabi University, Chandigarh.

    (1978). The vowel system in educated Punjabi speakers' English. *Bulletin of the Central Institute of English* 14.2: 35–48.

    (1980). Word accent in educated Punjabi speakers' English. *Bulletin of the Central Institute of English* 16.2: 31–55.

Shah, A. B. (ed.) (1968). *The Great Debate: Language Controversy and Higher Education*. Bombay: Asia Publishing House.

Sharp, H. (ed.) (1920). *Selections from Educational Records*. Calcutta; Bureau of Education, Government of India.

Shastri, S. V. (1988). The Kolhapur corpus of Indian English and work done on its basis so far. *ICAME Journal* 12: 15–26.

Shaw, W. D. (1981). Asian student attitudes towards English. In L. Smith (ed.) *English for Cross Cultural Communication*, London, Macmillan, 108–22.

Sherring, M. A. (1884). *The History of Protestant Missions in India from their Commencement in 1706 to 1871*. London and Edinburgh: Religious Tract Society.

Singer, M. (1972). *When a Great Tradition Modernizes*. New York: Praeger.

Singh, A., R. Verma & I. M. Joshi (eds.) (1981). *Indian Literature in English, 1827–1979: a Guide to Information Sources*. Detroit, MI: Gale.

Sinha, S. P. (1978). *English in India: a Historical Study with Particular Reference to English Education in India*. Patna: Janaki Prakashan.

Smith, L. & C. Nelson (1985). International intelligibility of English: directions and resources. *World Englishes* 4, 3: 333–42.

Spencer, J. (1966). The Anglo-Indians and their speech: a sociolinguistic essay. *Lingua* 16: 57–70.

Sridhar, K. K. (1989a). Pragmatic differences between native and indigenized varieties: requesting in Indian English. In T. J. Walsh (ed.) *Synchronic and Diachronic Approaches to Linguistic Variation and Change*. Washington, DC: Georgetown University Press, 326–41.

    (1989b). *English in Indian Bilingualism*. New Delhi: Manohar.

Sridhar, K. K. & S. N. Sridhar (1986). Bridging the paradigm gap: second language acquisition theory and indigenized varieties of English. *World Englishes* 5, 1: 3–14.

Sridhar, S. N. (forthcoming). Toward a grammar of South Asian English. In Baumgardner (ed.), forthcoming.

Sridhar, S. N. & P. H. Lowenberg (eds.) (1986). *World Englishes and Second Language Acquisition Research*. Special issue of *World Englishes* 5, 2–3.

Tambiah, S. J. (1967). The politics of language in India and Ceylon. *University of Ceylon Review* 8, 2: 131–73.

Thumboo, E. (1985). Twin perspectives and multi-ecosystems: tradition for a commonwealth writer. *World Englishes* 4, 2: 213–21.

Upendran, S. (1980). The intelligibility of English spoken by Tamilians. Unpublished MLitt. dissertation, Central Institute of English and Foreign Languages, Hyderabad.

Verma, Y. P. (1988). *The Press in Nepal: an Appraisal*. Kathmandu: Pratibha.

Vijayakrishnan, K. G. (1978). Stress in Tamilian English: a study within the framework of generative phonology. Unpublished MLitt. dissertation, Central Institute of English and Foreign Languages, Hyderabad.

Wadia, A. R. (1954). *The Future of English in India*. Bombay: Asia Publishing House.

Wells, J. C. (1982). *Accents of English*, 3 vols. Cambridge: Cambridge University Press.

Wijesinha, R. (ed.) (1988). *An Anthology of Contemporary Sri Lankan Poetry in English*. Colombo: The British Council, Sri Lanka.

Wilson, H. H. (1855). *A glossary of judicial and revenue terms and of useful words occurring in official documents, relating to the administration of the government of British India*. London: W. H. Allen. (Reprint 1940.)

Yule, H. & A. C. Burnell (1886). *Hobson-Jobson: a glossary of colloquial Anglo-Indian words and phrases, and of kindred terms, etymological, historical, geographical and discursive*. New edn by W. Crooke, 1903. London: J. Murray.

INDEX

THE CAMBRIDGE HISTORY
OF THE ENGLISH LANGUAGE

GENERAL EDITOR Richard M. Hogg

VOLUME I   *The Beginnings to 1066*
EDITED BY Richard M. Hogg

THE CAMBRIDGE HISTORY
OF THE ENGLISH LANGUAGE

GENERAL EDITOR Richard M. Hogg

VOLUME II *1066–1476*

EDITED BY Norman Blake

VOLUME VI *English in North America*

EDITED BY John Algeo
(in alphabetical order by contributor)

Introduction
JOHN ALGEO

Social dialects
GUY BAILEY

American influences on other varieties
RICHARD W. BAILEY

Language engineering and language policy
DENNIS BARON

Grammar
RONALD R. BUTTERS

Americanisms
FREDERIC G. CASSIDY AND JOAN HALL

British antecedents
JOHN H. FISHER AND MICHAEL B. MONTGOMERY

Onomastics
KELSIE HARDER

Mainland Canadian English
MURRAY A. KINLOCH

Newfoundland English
WILLIAM J. KIRWIN

Slang and special vocabularies
JONATHAN E. LIGHTER

Black English and Gullah
SALIKOKO MUFWENE

Pronunciation
LEE PEDERSON

Regional dialects
LEE PEDERSON

Contact with other languages
SUZANNE ROMAINE

Spelling
RICHARD L. VENEZKY